FEDERALISM AND THE TUG OF WAR WITHIN

Federalism and the

Tug of War Within

Erin Ryan

OXFORD
UNIVERSITY PRESS

OXFORD
UNIVERSITY PRESS

*Oxford University Press, Inc., publishes works that further Oxford University's objective of excellence
in research, scholarship, and education.*

Oxford   New York
Auckland   Cape Town   Dar es Salaam   Hong Kong   Karachi   Kuala Lumpur   Madrid   Melbourne
Mexico City   Nairobi   New Delhi   Shanghai   Taipei   Toronto

With offices in
Argentina   Austria   Brazil   Chile   Czech Republic   France   Greece   Guatemala   Hungary   Italy
Japan   Poland   Portugal   Singapore   South Korea   Switzerland   Thailand   Turkey   Ukraine
Vietnam

Library of Congress Cataloging-in-Publication Data
Ryan, Erin.
    Federalism and the tug of war within / Erin Ryan.
        p. cm.
    Includes bibliographical references and index.
    ISBN 978-0-19-973798-7 ((hardback) : alk. paper)
1. Federal government—United States. I. Title.
    KF4600.R93 2012
    342.73'042—dc23

                                      2011022606

1 2 3 4 5 6 7 8 9

Printed in the United States of America on acid-free paper

To my family,
and especially my father.

Contents

Acknowledgments

A project of this scope has left me indebted to many knowledgeable and generous colleagues. For their invaluable commentary during my various phases of writing, I am endlessly grateful to David Adelman, Bill Buzbee, Lan Cao, Erwin Chemerinsky, Amy Cohen, Robin Craig, Barry Cushman, Nestor Davidson, Holly Doremus, Dave Douglas, Bob Ellickson, Kirsten Engel, Lee Fennell, Michael Gerhardt, Heather Gerken, Robert Glicksman, Vicki Jackson, Michael Klarman, Allison LaCroix, Richard Lazarus, John Leshy, Gillian Metzger, Michael Moffit, John Nagle, Hari Osofksy, Bob Percival, Ed Purcell, J.B. Ruhl, Ned Ryan, Robert Schapiro, Larry Susskind, and Bill Van Alstyne.

For critical guidance at various stages of my research, I thank Tony Arnold, Angela Banks, David Barron, Bob Bordone, Lynda Butler, Scott Dodson, Dan Farber, Brian Galle, Laura Heymann, Rick Hills, Eric Kades, Howard Latin, Linda Malone, Paul Marcus, John Nolon, Dave Owen, Larry Palmer, Judith Resnik, Paula Ryan, Cathy Sharkey, Jonathan Siegel, Joe Singer, Michael Stein, Lisa Sun, Rick Su, Mark Tushnet, Wendy Wagner, Laura Underkuffler, John Vile, and Ernie Young. I am also grateful to the many state and federal officials who shared their experiences with me, including Melanie Davenport, Roscoe Howard, Mike Murphy, Jeff Reynolds, Laurie Ristino, Melissa Savage, Rick Weeks, and many others who requested anonymity so that their comments would not be mistaken for official administrative pronouncements. This project would not have been possible without the outstanding research assistance I have received over the years from Brianna Coakley, Jessica Deering, Tal Kedem, Syed Masood, Janet McCrae, Katy Mikols, Catherine Rylyk, Tara St. Angelo, Ryan Stephens, Matthew Whipple, Jim Zadick, and most especially Jessie Coulter and Perry Cooper.

Parts of the book have been published previously in article form. The first six chapters stem from a set of ideas originally published in "Federalism and the Tug of War Within: Seeking Checks and Balance in the Interjurisdictional Gray Area," 66 *Maryland Law Review* 503 (2007). (Some of these ideas were also published as "How the New Federalism Failed Katrina Victims" in *Law and Recovery from Disaster: Hurricane Katrina* (Robin Malloy & John Lovett, eds, 2009), a book chapter drawing on the original "Tug of War" article.) Chapter Seven is based on "Federalism at the Cathedral: Property Rules, Liability Rules, and Inalienability Rules in Tenth Amendment Infrastructure," 81 *University of Colorado Law Review* 1 (2010). Substantial portions of Chapters Eight, Nine, and Ten originally appeared in "Negotiating Federalism," 52 *Boston College Law Review* 1 (2011). I am grateful to the editors of these publications for their assistance in honing my ideas and for their permission to republish them here.

Finally, I dedicate this book to my miraculous family, who has shared me with the project for too many years now. I thank my husband for his infinite patience and unfailing support. My new son provides daily inspiration to make the world a better place, through academic scholarship and otherwise. My mother remains my bedrock and my sister my muse, together with my wonderful and multiple extended families. Most of all, I thank my father, for beginning this intellectual journey with me and accompanying me every step of the way since then.

Introduction

This book probes the tensions that lie at the very heart of American federalism, and the issues with which the architects, scholars, and practitioners of American governance have been struggling for over two centuries: How should we understand the constitutional design? In which realms of regulatory decision making should the national government trump, and in which should state or local decision makers lead? How should governance operate in regulatory realms that straddle the two? Which branches of government should we entrust with making these calls? What theoretical tools should help us interpret vague federalism directives? What are these directives designed to accomplish? The introduction outlines the questions I hope to address, charts the course of the discussion, and introduces my theoretical approach.

Written both for audiences new to these questions and those long familiar with them, the book begins a philosophical conversation about the meaning of federalism through the lenses of the competing values that undergird it and through the theoretical models for interpreting federalism that animate policy making and adjudication. I argue that federalism is best understood not just in terms of the conflict between states' rights and federal power, or the debate over judicial constraints and political process, or even the dueling claims over original intent—but instead through the inevitable conflicts that play out among federalism's core principles. In regulatory realms where these tensions are most heightened—such as environmental law, land use law, and public health and safety regulation—the "tug of war" among underlying federalism values has resulted in fluctuating Supreme Court interpretations and controversial decisions. Heightened jurisdictional overlap in environmental law has especially pushed the Court's federalism decisions to extremes, helpfully exposing the fault lines between competing values. But unfolding federalism conflicts over health law, consumer protection, and gay marriage are close on the heels of the controversies that environmental federalism has helped expose.

Providing a new conceptual vocabulary for wrestling with these old dilemmas, the book traces federalism's internal tug of war through history and into the present, proposing a series of innovations to bring judicial, legislative, and executive efforts to manage it into more fully theorized focus. I outline a theory of Balanced Federalism that mediates the tensions within federalism on three separate planes: (1) fostering balance among the competing federalism values, (2) leveraging the functional capacities of the three branches of government in interpreting federalism, and (3) maximizing the wisdom of both state and federal actors in so doing. After critiquing the Court's recent embrace of greater jurisdictional separation and stronger judicial constraints, the book imagines three successive means of coping with the values tug of war within federalism, each experimenting with different degrees of judicial and political leadership at different levels of government. Along the way, the analysis provides clearer theoretical justification for the ways in which the tug of war is already legitimately mediated through various forms of balancing, compromise, and negotiation.

A. Federalism and the Quandaries Within

Through federalism directives both express and implied, the Constitution mandates a federal system of dual sovereignty, establishing new authority in a national government while preserving distinct authority within the more local state governments. Nevertheless, federalism has taken different forms in countless nations worldwide and over the course of history. What exactly does the Constitution require in allocating unique authority to the separate state and federal governments? Are these allocations meant to be mutually exclusive? If not, what should happen in areas of legitimate overlap?

In practical terms, the question really comes down to *who gets to decide*—the state or federal government? In allocating authority this way, the Constitution essentially tells us who should determine what regulatory policy looks like in various public spheres. To be sure, some realms of governance are uncontroversially committed to one side or the other—for example, the powers to coin money, wage war, and regulate interstate commerce are delegated to the national government,[1] while the states administer elections, local zoning, and police services.[2] But between the easy extremes are realms in which it is much harder to know what the Constitution says about who calls the shots. Locally regulated land uses become entangled with the protection of navigable waterways that implicate interstate commerce. State and local police remain bound by federal proscriptions against unreasonable search and self-incrimination.[3] And to what extent should national regulations apply to the integral operations of state government?

In fact, American governance is so characterized by overlapping state and federal jurisdiction that it has been compared not only to a layer cake but to a marble cake, with entangled swirls of interlocking local and national law.[4] Even so, when policy-making conflicts erupt within these contexts of jurisdictional overlap, the "who gets to decide" question looms large. Is this a realm in which federal power legitimately preempts contrary state law under the Supremacy Clause, or a policy-making realm beyond the federally enumerated powers that

---

[1] U.S. CONST. art. I, § 8.

[2] U.S. CONST. art. I, §§ 1–2, amend. XVII, art. II § 1, and amend. XII (describing state role in congressional and presidential elections). *See* Young v. American Mini Theaters, 427 U.S. 50, 80 (1976) (J. Powell, concurring) (identifying zoning as one of the essential functions of local government).

[3] Miranda v. Arizona, 384 U.S. 436, 444 (1966).

[4] MORTON GRODZINS, THE AMERICAN SYSTEM 8, 60–153 (Daniel J. Elazar, ed., 2d ed. 1984).

has been purposefully reserved to the states?[5] And even if federal law *could* legally trump local initiative, does that necessarily mean that it should? How should we decide?

For that matter, when the looming question is "who gets to decide—the state or federal government," then the critical corollary becomes "who gets to decide *that*?" When either the regulatory context or the federalism directive itself is unclear, which branch of government should determine what the Constitution is actually trying to say about who decides regulatory policy? Are these decisions appropriately committed to the discretion of Congress, where federalism concerns will be safeguarded by the political process in which state-elected representatives make national laws?[6] Or should the Supreme Court be the final arbiter of these issues, by creating judicially enforceable federalism constraints?[7] We generally entrust the Supreme Court to interpret the constitutional meaning of anti-majoritarian individual rights, but is structural federalism different? What is the proper role of the executive branch, especially in an age of increasing executive agency power?[8] Is there a role for state governmental actors in interpreting these questions?

In other words, interpreting federalism not only requires that we figure out what the Constitution tells us about *who gets to decide*—who calls the shots in which regulatory context—but also what it says about *who decides whether* it will be the state or federal government. The Constitution allocates authority not only vertically between local and national actors, but horizontally among the three separate branches of government.[9] The legislative, executive, and judicial branches each bring different interpretive resources to the constitutional project based on their distinct features of institutional design. How should each branch participate in the interpretation and implementation of American federalism? At times, political and judicial federalism rhetoric draws heavily on a model of "zero-sum" federalism, suggesting winner-takes-all jurisdictional competition between state and federal policy makers and either/or oversight by legislative or judicial arbiters.[10] But how well does this model reflect what actually happens in practice, deep within the intertwining folds of federalism-sensitive governance? How well should it?

The constitutional ambiguity that makes answering these questions so difficult leads to the next question, often overlooked in the federalism discourse: *which federalism?*—or,

---

[5] U.S. Const. art. VI (federal supremacy); amend. X (reserving non-enumerated powers to the states).

[6] *E.g.,* Herbert Wechsler, *The Political Safeguards of Federalism: The Role of the States in the Composition and Selection of the National Government,* 54 Colum. L. Rev. 543, 588 (1954); Jesse H. Choper, Judicial Review and the National Political Process 175–76 (1980).

[7] *E.g.,* Lynn A. Baker & Ernest A. Young, *Federalism and the Double Standard of Judicial Review,* 51 Duke L.J. 75, 128 (2001); William Van Alstyne, *Federalism, Congress, the States and the Tenth Amendment: Adrift in the Cellophane Sea,* 1987 Duke L.J. 769, 782–83, 797–98 (1987).

[8] *E.g.,* Gillian E. Metzger, *Administrative Law as the New Federalism,* 57 Duke L.J. 2023 (2008); Bradford R. Clark, *Separation of Powers as a Safeguard of Federalism,* 79 Tex. L. Rev. 1321 (2001).

[9] Horizontal federalism, which describes the interrelationships among the states, is another important dimension of constitutional federalism. *See* Allan Erbsen, *Horizontal Federalism,* 93 Minn. L. Rev. 493 (2008).

[10] *See, e.g.,* Ed Hornick, *"Tenther" Movement Aims To Put Power Back in States' Hands,* CNN, Feb. 10, 2010, http://www.cnn.com/2010/POLITICS/02/10/tenth.amendment.movement/index.html (describing sovereign antagonism in the political sphere); United States v. Morrison, 529 U.S. 598, 617–18 (2000) ("The Constitution requires a distinction between what is truly national and what is truly local.").

which theoretical model of federalism should we use in interpreting this textual ambiguity? The Constitution mandates but incompletely describes American dual sovereignty, leaving certain matters open for interpretation by unspecified decision makers who must employ some kind of theory—a philosophy about how federalism should operate—in order to fill in these gaps. Yet constitutional interpreters can choose from more than one theoretical model of federalism in doing so, just as the Supreme Court has done over the centuries in which its jurisprudence has swung back and forth in answering similar questions differently at various times. The "dual federalism" model, dividing state and federal jurisdiction largely along lines of subject matter, has predominated federalism theory at various points in American history, especially during the nineteenth century.[11] A model of tolerating greater jurisdictional overlap, often referred to as "cooperative federalism," has predominated federalism practice since at least the New Deal.[12] And there are other alternatives. Are these different approaches to understanding federalism—each sharing basic contours but diverging on the details—all valid? If more than one are valid, how should we choose among them?

The "which federalism" dilemma leads back to the ultimate issue, the most important of all: *why federalism?* Why did the architects of the Constitution choose a federal system? What is our federal system of government meant to accomplish? If we can understand what American federalism is for, then we are in a better position to choose which model of federalism to follow in answering the perennial questions about who decides what in which context. However, this last question proves more difficult than at first it may seem, because American federalism is really *for* a number of different things—a collection of goals that are not always themselves in agreement. Here is where federalism theory gets especially interesting, and where this book makes its most important contribution.

As the Court regularly reaffirms, structural federalism is not an end in itself; it is crafted in service of the Constitution's more substantive commitments.[13] Exploring the *why* of federalism yields a number of good governance values that undergird it, each representing an ideal in governance that federalism helps accomplish: checks and balances between opposing centers of power that protect individuals, governmental accountability and transparency that enhance democratic participation, local autonomy that enables interjurisdictional innovation and competition, and the regulatory synergy that federalism enables between the unique capacities of local and national government for coping with interjurisdictional problems that neither could resolve alone. Each of these principles advances the ideal system of government that the framers of the Constitution sought to build, and they have since gone on to take root in international good governance norms. Nevertheless—and as demonstrated

---

[11] *E.g.*, Robert A. Schapiro, Polyphonic Federalism 33–36 (2009); Edward A. Purcell, Jr., Originalism, Federalism, and the American Constitutional Enterprise: A Historical Inquiry 177–79 (2007).

[12] *Cf.* Erwin Chemerinsky, Enhancing Government: Federalism for the 21st Century, 16–25, 31–47 (2008); Schapiro, *supra* note 11, at 40–47.

[13] *E.g.*, Bond v. United States, No. 09-1227, 564 U.S. __, *9 (slip opinion) (2011), 2011 Westlaw 2369334 (U.S.) ("Federalism is more than an exercise in setting the boundary between different institutions of government for their own integrity. State sovereignty is not just an end in itself: Rather, federalism secures to citizens the liberties that derive from the diffusion of sovereign power."); New York v. United States, 505 U.S. 144, 181 (1992).

by the Supreme Court's vacillating federalism jurisprudence—these values exist in tension with one another, setting federalism interpretation up as a site of contest between honorable but occasionally competing principles.

The tug of war between competing federalism principles is built into American dual sovereignty by design. For example, the strong checks and balances enabled by parallel state and federal governments compromise the value of governmental transparency to some extent, making it necessarily harder for average Americans to understand which elected representatives are responsible for which policies simply by virtue of there being two choices. Similarly, if local autonomy and innovation were all that mattered, there would be no need for a national government at all; its existence reflects a purposeful choice to prioritize the individual-rights' protective features of a system of checks and balances and the pragmatic problem-solving value of a national federation for coping with shared interests and border-crossing problems. Meanwhile, powerful tension can exist between the goal of preserving offsetting centers of state and federal power while also harnessing problem-solving synergy between them in collaborative contexts. Some regulatory contexts exacerbate these tensions more than others, but they are implicated in all federalism controversies to varying degrees.

As noted, the fields of environmental law, land use law, and public health and safety regulation especially showcase federalism's internal tug of war.[14] Sometimes, these fields involve regulatory attempts to grapple with relatively newly identified problems—that is, problems without a historically settled answer to the question of who should decide, such as climate change. Other times, evidence increasingly reveals that a previously presumed "local" problem—such as water pollution, disease control, marriage legitimacy, waste disposal, disaster response, or even land use planning—also has important national implications. Meanwhile, such presumably national problems as telecommunications, counterterrorism, and even international relations are increasingly bound up with exercises of state and local authority. The "proper" level of regulatory authority in these areas is often contested, underscoring conflicts between federalism values that have resulted in judicial and political controversy.

With this tug of war lurking within all federalism quandaries, each resolution requires the decision maker to choose, consciously or otherwise, how to prioritize among competing values when they conflict. In the political sphere, the tug of war within is often obscured by the heat and light generated by the substantive policy debates that spur actual federalism controversies—for example, the respective roles of state and federal government in

---

[14] *Cf.* Holly Doremus, *Shaping the Future: The Dialectic of Law and Environmental Values*, 37 U.C. Davis L. Rev. 233 (2003).

regulating minimum wages,[15] radioactive waste,[16] gun rights,[17] violence against women,[18] criminal law enforcement,[19] health-care policy,[20] immigration,[21] and marriage rights.[22] Public debate often focuses on the first-order policy question rather than second-order structural issues about who should get to decide, and interest groups have often strategically deployed federalism rhetoric to advance a substantive agenda, only to abandon regard for federalism when it no longer serves that interest.[23] Theoretical shifts in the Supreme Court's famous "New Federalism" cases further obfuscate these tensions, implying that the only value of consequence is the preservation of checks and balances between the separate reservoirs of local and national authority.[24]

Yet the tug of war continues, overtly or covertly, in each judicial, legislative, and administrative decision that confronts these federalism controversies. This book proposes an alternative model that finally accounts for this perpetual tug of war within federalism—one that seeks balance between competing values and interpretive roles, rooting its analysis in the Tenth Amendment of the Constitution.

---

[15] Nat'l League of Cities v. Usery, 426 U.S. 833, 838–40 (1976) (overruling prior precedent to hold that the Tenth Amendment exempts state employment from federal requirements); Garcia v. San Antonio Metro. Transit Auth., 469 U.S. 528 (1985) (overruling *Nat'l League of Cities*).

[16] New York v. United States, 505 U.S. 144, 174–75 (1992) (invalidating on Tenth Amendment grounds a federal law requiring states to create waste disposal facilities or assume liability for harm).

[17] United States v. Lopez, 514 U.S. 549, 551 (1995) (overturning the Gun-Free School Zones Act of 1990 for exceeding federal commerce authority); Printz v. United States, 521 U.S. 898, 935 (1997) (invalidating under the Tenth Amendment parts of the Brady Handgun Control Act of 1993 for compelling state law enforcement).

[18] United States v. Morrison, 529 U.S. 598, 613 (2000) (invalidating portions of the Violence Against Women Act of 1994 (VAWA) for exceeding Congress's commerce power).

[19] Bond v. United States, No. 09-1227, 564 U.S. __ (2011), 2011 Westlaw 2369334 (U.S.) (holding that a criminal defendant had standing to challenge on Tenth Amendment grounds her conviction under a federal statute implementing an international treaty).

[20] Complaint for Declaratory and Injunctive Relief, Virginia v. Sebelius, No. 3:10-CV-188 (E.D. Va. Mar. 23, 2010) (arguing that the Patient Protection and Affordable Care Act, H.R. 3590 of March 2010, exceeds federal power under the Commerce and General Welfare Clauses and conflicts with state law); Complaint, Florida v. Dep't of Health & Human Servs., No. 3:10-cv-91 (N.D. Fla. Mar. 23, 2010) (similar challenge in a suit joined by more than a dozen other states); Complaint, Shreeve v. Obama, No. 1:10-cv-71 (E.D. Tenn. Apr. 8, 2010) (similar suit).

[21] United States v. Arizona, 2010 U.S. Dist. LEXIS 75558 (D. Ariz. July 28, 2010).

[22] *E.g.*, Massachusetts v. U.S. Dept. Health & Human Servs., No. 1:09-cv-11156-JLT, 21-36 (D. Mass. July 7, 2010) (holding that the federal Defense of Marriage Act violates the Tenth Amendment).

[23] *See infra* Chapter Two, notes 7–16 and accompanying text.

[24] Beginning in the 1990s, the Supreme Court issued a series of decisions known as its "New Federalism" cases that articulated a more forceful judicial role in policing federalism. *See infra* Chapter Three, notes 216–49 and accompanying text.

B. The Tug of War and the Tenth Amendment

Over most of the last century, the primary federalism debates among jurists and scholars have focused on the extent of the Constitution's grant of federal authority to regulate commerce[25] and to enforce the provisions of the post Civil-War amendments that eliminated slavery, protected African-American voting rights, and guaranteed due process and equal protection of the law.[26] The extent of state sovereign immunity from lawsuits under the Eleventh Amendment has also generated controversy,[27] as have isolated attempts to revive debate about congressional reach under the federal Spending Power,[28] and more recently, the Necessary and Proper Clause.[29]

Although it is the structural lodestar of constitutional federalism—affirming the default rule that powers not delegated to federal government are reserved to the states[30]—only a handful of twentieth-century federalism cases hinged on the Tenth Amendment. By one view of the Constitution, interpreters might have relied heavily on its explicit text—"[t]he powers not delegated to the United States by the Constitution, nor prohibited by it to the States, are reserved to the States respectively, or to the people"—to limit federal authority to strictly interpreted enumerated powers. (Indeed, this is the view Thomas Jefferson took in protesting the early Alien and Sedition Acts of 1789.[31]) Instead, most modern judicial federalism analyses sideline the Tenth Amendment as surplusage, and the Supreme Court's directly interpretive decisions mostly address the narrow question of when federal law may

---

[25] U.S. CONST. art. I, § 8 (empowering Congress to regulate commerce with foreign nations, among the states, and with Indian tribes); *e.g.*, United States v. Morrison, 529 U.S. 598, 613 (2000); United States v. Lopez, 514 U.S. 549, 551 (1995); Gonzales v. Raich, 545 U.S. 1, 32–33 (2005) (affirming federal authority to proscribe intrastate production and use of medical marijuana).

[26] U.S. CONST. amends. XIII (proscribing slavery), XIV (guaranteeing equal protection and due process), and XV (protecting African-American voting rights); *e.g.*, Bd. of Trustees v. Garrett, 531 U.S. 356, 374 (2001) (invalidating remedies under the Americans with Disabilities Act of 1990 for exceeding congressional power under Section Five of the Fourteenth Amendment); Kimel v. Fla. Bd. of Regents, 528 U.S. 62, 82–83 (2000) (invalidating the Age Discrimination in Employment Act of 1967 for the same reason); City of Boerne v. Flores, 521 U.S. 507, 536 (1997) (invalidating the Religious Freedom Restoration Act of 1993 for the same reason); *Morrison*, 529 U.S. at 627 (declining to sustain the challenged portions of the VAWA under Section Five).

[27] U.S. CONST. amend. XI (protecting states from certain citizen suits); *e.g.*, Alden v. Maine, 527 U.S. 706, 712 (1999) (limiting Congress's power to authorize suits against states in state courts); Seminole Tribe v. Florida, 517 U.S. 44, 47 (1996) (limiting Congress's power to authorize suits against states in federal courts).

[28] U.S. CONST. art. I, § 8 (empowering Congress to tax and spend for the public welfare); *e.g.*, South Dakota v. Dole, 483 U.S. 203, 206 (1987) (upholding federal power to condition federal highway funds on state adoption of a minimum drinking age); Sabri v. United States, 541 U.S. 600, 602 (2004) (affirming a federal statute prohibiting bribery involving federal funds under the spending power); Pierce County v. Guillen, 537 U.S. 129, 147–48 (2003) (affirming under the doctrine a federal law restricting certain publicly collected data from use as trial evidence).

[29] In Gonzales v. Raich, 545 U.S. 1, 33 (2005), Justice Scalia emphasized his concurrence on the basis of the Necessary and Proper Clause. Challenges to federal health reform have also been raised on these grounds. *See* Kevin Sack, *Terrain Shifts in Challenges to the Health Care Law*, NY TIMES, Dec. 29, 2010, at A10.

[30] U.S. CONST. amend. X.

[31] *See infra* Chapter Three, notes 25–29 and accompanying text.

not conscript state agents.[32] Nevertheless, these cases provide an uncluttered window into the Court's evolving efforts to cope with federalism's internal tug of war—setting new benchmarks for jurisprudential instability.

Instability, of course, breeds opportunity. As the twenty-first century begins, an invigorated federalism discourse has emerged in the political sphere that centers specifically and passionately on the Tenth Amendment. About half the states are challenging the 2010 health reform legislation on Tenth Amendment grounds in litigation certain to reach the Supreme Court.[33] Thirty-eight states have introduced nonbinding resolutions or state constitutional amendments reaffirming Tenth Amendment principles of state sovereignty in opposition to the new law, and seven such bills have passed at least one state legislative house.[34] Nullification bills based on the Tenth Amendment have also been introduced in various state legislatures to repudiate federal gun laws,[35] tax collection,[36] driver's license requirements[37] and the deployment of National Guard troops abroad.[38] One bill declared state authority to take federal lands through eminent domain.[39] In 2011, the Supreme Court permitted a woman convicted of harassing her neighbor under a chemical weapons treaty to challenge her conviction on Tenth Amendment grounds—raising controversial questions about the scope of federal authority to implement international obligations at the local level.[40] The Tenth

---

[32] *See supra* note 15 (discussing *National League of Cities* and *Garcia*); New York v. United States, 505 U.S. 144, 174–75 (1992) (holding that federal law compelling legislative participation violates the Tenth Amendment); Printz v. United States, 521 U.S. 898, 935 (1997) (holding that compelling state executive participation does the same); Reno v. Condon, 528 U.S. 141, 151 (2000) (holding that federal law regulating state use of driver's license applicants' personal information does not violate the Tenth Amendment).

[33] Patient Protection and Affordable Care Act, Pub. L. No. 111-148 (2010); *supra* note 20 (describing multiple state-filed suits challenging the constitutionality of the Act).

[34] PBS Newshour, *States Challenge Health Care Reform* (April 16, 2010), http://www.pbs.org/newshour/interactive/static/tables/health-states/.

[35] Montana Firearms Freedom Act, MONT. CODE ANN. § 30-20-101 (2009).

[36] *E.g.*, State Authority and Tax Fund Act, H.B. 877, 2010 Sess. (Ga. 2010), State Sovereignty Act, H.B. 2810, 2010 Sess. (Okla. 2010); Washington State Sovereignty and Federal Tax Escrow Account of 2010, H.B. 2712, 2010 Sess. (Wash. 2010).

[37] ACLU, *Anti-REAL ID Legislation in the States*, http://www.realnightmare.org/news/105/ (noting that no state met the December 2009 deadline contemplated by the statute, and over half enacted or considered legislation prohibiting compliance with the Act, defunding its implementation, or calling for its repeal). *See also* Anthony D. Romero, Editorial, *Opposing View: Repeal Real ID*, USA TODAY, Mar. 5, 2007, http://www.usatoday.com/news/opinion/2007-03-05-opposing-view_N.htm (arguing that REAL ID violates the Tenth Amendment, destroys dual sovereignty, and makes Americans vulnerable to identity theft).

[38] *See* Kirk Johnson, *States' Rights Is Rallying Cry for Lawmakers*, N.Y. TIMES, Mar. 16, 2010, http://www.nytimes.com/2010/03/17/us/17states.html (reporting on a Utah bill).

[39] *Id.* (reporting on bills considered in Rhode Island, Vermont, and Wisconsin); Jim Carlton, *Federal Land Seizures Urged by Utah Governor*, WALL ST. J., Mar. 30, 2010, http://online.wsj.com/article/SB10001424052702304370304575151693915722022.html (reporting on a Utah law).

[40] Bond v. United States, No. 09-1227, 564 U.S. __ (2011), 2011 Westlaw 2369334 (U.S.). Although the Court's decision was limited to the question of standing, Bond's substantive claim addresses the limits of federal authority in implementing international treaties that displace state authority. *See* Missouri v. Holland, 252 U.S. 416 (1920).

Amendment has become a rallying cry among advocates for state right-to-die legislation,[41] home schooling,[42] and sectarian education,[43] and among opponents of Medicaid and Medicare,[44] federal financial reform[45] and national climate regulation.[46] For all their differences, these efforts all share a basic premise that the relationship between state and federal power implied by the Tenth Amendment has somehow gone astray.

Invocations of the Tenth Amendment have come primarily from the right and are often associated with the Tea Party,[47] but they come increasingly from the left as well—in support of gay rights, right-to-die statutes, and local climate initiatives, and in opposition to national security policies alleged to threaten privacy and civil rights.[48] In one notable example from 2010, a Massachusetts federal district court invalidated on Tenth Amendment grounds portions of the federal Defense of Marriage Act that impose certain federal proscriptions on gay marriage even in states that have legalized it.[49] Some members of the right and left have found common ground in opposing the federal government's unprecedented levels of deployment of state National Guard troops in the Iraq and Afghanistan wars.[50] A new political movement known as "the Tenthers" has coalesced around the ideals its adherents locate in the

---

[41] *See, e.g.*, Craig Peyton Gaumer & Paul R. Griffith, *Whose Life Is It Anyway?: An Analysis and Commentary on the Emerging Law of Physician-Assisted Suicide*, 42 S.D. L. REV. 357, 372 (1997) (arguing that if the Tenth Amendment requires greater federal deference to states rights, it should also require greater federal deference to certain individual rights); Emily J. Sovell, *Elderly, Be Alert: The Battle Continues over Deathbed Rights*, 45 S.D. L. REV. 670, 675 (2000) (discussing how right-to-die proponents rely on the Tenth Amendment). *Cf.* Gonzales v. Oregon, 546 U.S. 243 (2006) (upholding the Oregon Death with Dignity Act without directly invoking the Tenth Amendment but broadly addressing the relationship between state and federal power).

[42] *See, e.g.*, Lynn M. Stuter, *Are Public Schools Constitutional?*, Jan. 20, 2003, http://www.newswithviews.com/Stuter/stuter9.htm (arguing that the Tenth Amendment prevents the federal government from interfering in education).

[43] *See, e.g.*, EDWARD KEYNES & RANDALL K. MILLER, THE COURT VS. CONGRESS: PRAYER, BUSING AND ABORTION 176 (1989) (arguing that the Tenth Amendment reserves state authority to assist sectarian schools and encourage religious activities in public schools).

[44] *See supra* notes 20 and 33–34.

[45] Brian Roberts, *Welcome to the Constitutional Crisis*, TENTH AMENDMENT CENTER, Apr. 27, 2010, http://www.tenthamendmentcenter.com/2010/04/27/welcome-to-the-constitutional-crisis/ (reporting on states' rights challenges to federal authority for proposed climate and financial reform legislation, among other bills).

[46] *Id.*

[47] *E.g.*, Johnson, *supra* note 38. For a more scholarly discussion of the Tea Party, see Ilya Somin, *The Tea Party Movement and Popular Constitutionalism*, 105 NW. U. L. REV. COLLOQUY 300 (2011).

[48] *Id.*; Robert A. Schapiro, *Not Old or Borrowed: The Truly New Blue Federalism*, 3 HARV. L. & POL'Y REV. 33 (2009) (discussing state leadership in progressive policymaking and interactive state-federal governance).

[49] Massachusetts v. U.S. Dept. Health & Human Servs., No. 1:09-cv-11156-JLT, 21-36 (D. Mass. July 7, 2010) (ruling that the federal Defense of Marriage Act violates the Tenth Amendment).

[50] TENTH AMENDMENT CENTER, *Bring the Guard Home Legislation* (2010), http://www.tenthamendmentcenter.com/nullification/bring-the-guard-home/ (listing state campaigns to reassert governors' control over state national guard troops); Benson Scotch, *Legal Memo on Wisconsin Safeguard the Guard Act*, BRING THE GUARD HOME!, Mar. 13, 2010, http://www.bringtheguardhome.org/publications/scotch_legal_memo_wisconsin_safeguard_guard (legal memo to state veterans' committee defending proposed legislation to impose state review of U.S. presidential requests to federalize state national guard troops).

language of the Tenth Amendment.[51] Given the near void of legal precedential hooks for many of these Tenth Amendment arguments, they do not necessarily reflect a practical strategy for litigation. Instead, this popular recourse to Tenth Amendment principles seems to reflect an openly philosophical movement about the meaning of dual sovereignty within the American federal system.

Most previous federalism scholarship has understandably focused on interpreting the constitutional provisions that have held the most practical power in answering questions about who gets to decide: the Commerce Clause, Section V of the Fourteenth Amendment, the Eleventh Amendment, and the Spending Power. These parts of the Constitution have attracted controversial judicial attention in recent decades, and they remain important, complex, and potentially unstable areas of law. However, like the emerging contemporary discourse, this book centers around the Tenth Amendment—the Constitution's most explicit (if Delphic federalism directive—because it provides the best constitutional locus for a philosophical conversation about the critical opening questions: *How should we understand American federalism? What is federalism for? Who gets to decide?*

In contrast to the constitutional implications of the Supremacy Clause and the federally enumerated powers, the Tenth Amendment directly acknowledges dual sovereignty in specifically juxtaposing distinct sets of state and federal authority. Its open-ended commitment to dual sovereignty conveys both the ambition and indeterminacy that complicate American federalism, inviting both the philosophical invocations we are currently seeing in the political sphere and the rich, reflective decisions we see from the judiciary in adjudicating Tenth Amendment claims. To be sure, fewer cases have been litigated under the Tenth Amendment than the Commerce Clause, the primary practical arbiter of federal regulatory reach. Nevertheless, Tenth Amendment cases deal most directly with the theoretical issues of dual sovereignty that undergird all other areas of federalism doctrine. Unpacking federalism theory through Tenth Amendment jurisprudence sheds light on the total package. After all, there is no separate theory of federalism for Tenth Amendment and Commerce Clause cases; answers to the questions raised in both doctrinal realms stem from a single understanding about how to allocate power in a federal system.[52]

The Tenth Amendment presents not only the best textual hook for our discussion, but also the best scientific laboratory for its theoretical inquiry—precisely because the limited number of cases allow clearer analysis of developments in the Supreme Court's theoretical models of federalism over time. Because only a few Tenth Amendment cases have been

---

[51] Rick Montes, *What is a Tenther?*, NEW YORK TENTH AMENDMENT CENTER (2010), http://www. tenthamendmentcenter.com/2010/05/06/what-is-a-tenther/ (defining the movement); Radley Balko, *The "Tenther" Smear*, REASON.COM, Sept, 21, 2009, http://reason.com/blog/2009/09/21/the-tenther-smear (defending the movement).

[52] *See, e.g.,* United States v. Morrison, 529 U.S. 598, 617–18 (2000), as quoted *supra* note 10 (demonstrating that the theory of federalism underlying the new Commerce Clause economic activity test reflects the same as that underlying the new Tenth Amendment anti-commandeering rule). *See also* Bond v. United States, No. 09-1227, 564 U.S. __, *13 (slip opinion) (2011), 2011 Westlaw 2369334 (U.S.) ("The principles of limited national powers and state sovereignty are intertwined. While neither originates in the Tenth Amendment, both are expressed by it."). This book could not cover the ground it does had it engaged every line of federalism doctrine at the same level of detail, but neither is it necessary for this theoretical analysis.

decided in each generation, each one imposed special responsibility on the Court to think through its approach without the weight of much controlling precedent. Each case also conferred a powerful opportunity to reshape the doctrine according to the Court's then-operative theory. Analysis of this smaller but complete set accordingly showcases evolving federalism theories in use by policy makers and adjudicators.

In contrast, the overall body of Commerce Clause jurisprudence is vast and amalgamated, representing the undifferentiated accumulation of theoretical approaches by many judicial interpreters over time. With dramatic exceptions at the margin, federalism practice under the Commerce Clause largely continues to reflect New Deal era assumptions of vast (but not unlimited) federal authority.[53] The buffering effect of incrementally developed Commerce and Spending Clause jurisprudence is important in its own right, explaining how overall federalism practice remains relatively stable despite the shifts in prevailing judicial federalism theory more evident in such areas as the Tenth, Eleventh, and Fourteenth Amendments and certain areas of the Courts' preemption jurisprudence.[54]

However, in exploring the different approaches available to federalism interpreters, the cases that push the doctrine in new directions are the clearest revelations of new operative theory, and the Tenth Amendment cases provide the best laboratory for this analysis. The environmental federalism cases that significantly fracture federalism values play an important role in this analysis for the same reason. These cases occasionally test the margins of constitutional doctrine in comparison to more mainstream economic regulation, but the fact that they push Tenth Amendment, commerce, and spending doctrines to their logical limits forces us to think carefully about the foundations of federalism doctrine and the purpose of the federal system.[55] Engaging the starkest realms of the Court's federalism jurisprudence allows the clearest analysis of its motivating theory, as well as the best opportunity for our own reflective evaluation.

The Tenth Amendment is thus where the Constitution most directly tells us that federalism is important, and its jurisprudence offers a fitting laboratory for analysis of the overarching issues in all corners of federalism doctrine. All that said, however, what exactly *does* the Tenth Amendment tell us about federalism values and how to vindicate them? As a purely textual matter, surprisingly little.

Famously critiqued as circular,[56] the Tenth Amendment affirms simultaneous, separate, sovereign authority in both the federal and state governments: "[t]he powers not delegated to the United States by the Constitution, nor prohibited by it to the States, are reserved to the States respectively." The federal powers enumerated in Article I establish more about

---

[53] *E.g., Morrison*, and United States v. Lopez, 514 U.S. 549, 551 (1995) (articulating the economic activity test).

[54] Although this book focuses on the Tenth Amendment, recent cases under the Eleventh Amendment, Section V of the Fourteenth Amendment, and the foreign affairs preemption power reflect similar theoretical trajectories. *See* CHEMERINSKY, *supra* note 12, at 68–90, 234–40; *infra* Chapter Four.

[55] *Cf.* ROBIN KUNDIS CRAIG, THE CLEAN WATER ACT AND THE CONSTITUTION (2d ed. 2009) (discussing the occasionally awkward fit in applying the economic model of Commerce Clause regulation to environmental law).

[56] United States v. Darby, 312 U.S. 100, 124 (1941).

what authority, exactly, is delegated to the United States,[57] while other constitutional provisions (such as those requiring a republican form of government[58] and full faith and credit[59]) tell us more about what is prohibited to the states. The Supremacy Clause tells us something about what happens when state and federal law conflict,[60] and the Eleventh Amendment says something about when states can be sued in federal court.[61] Some believe that the (even-more-Delphic) Ninth Amendment tells us something important about federalism as well.[62] But all of these constitutional texts leave plenty of room for interpretation in marginal cases—those where it is not entirely clear whether the regulatory power at issue is one that has been delegated to the federal government, prohibited to the states, or reserved to the states without federal interference. If nothing else, the federalism dilemmas that arise in each generation affirm that there has been no shortage of marginal cases.

For that reason, it is up to us, and perhaps each generation anew, to revisit the foundational questions about what American federalism means, what it is for, and what we ask it to accomplish for us. We call the architects of the Constitution *framers* because they have given us a framework powerful enough to survive the forces of economic upheaval and cultural change—but implementation remains our duty, and interpretation is the first task of implementation. Interpreting federalism is more complicated than some have given it credit, for it is not simply a matter of following allegedly simple constitutional instructions.[63] The instructions are not very simple, and the generations of ongoing federalism controversy prove the point. Instead, interpreting federalism requires coping with the underlying tug of war between the fundamental federalism values, developing a theoretical model for interpretive guidance, and allocating responsibility among the branches and levels of government for doing the critical interpretive work that will ultimately decide—well, who gets to decide.

The era in which the Tenth Amendment was dismissed as sheer textual surplusage may be coming to a close . . . or not.[64] Either way, its passionate invocation in the political sphere, its revolving interpretation by the Supreme Court, even its suggestively poetic language all beckon us to consider—through its very ambition and indeterminacy—what American federalism is all about. Today's Tenth Amendment revival has intensified in the wake of broad regulatory responses to the Great Recession of 2008, just as federalism concerns ignited a previous generation over New Deal regulatory responses to the Great Depression of 1929. In the New Deal era, the need for powerful federal responses to a nationwide economic crisis

---

[57] U.S. Const. art. I, § 8.

[58] U.S. Const. art. IV, § 4.

[59] U.S. Const. art. IV, § 1.

[60] U.S. Const. art. VI.

[61] U.S. Const. amend. XI. What it actually says, however, departs markedly from how it is currently interpreted. *See* William A. Fletcher, *A Historical Interpretation of the Eleventh Amendment*, 35 Stan. L. Rev. 1033 (1983).

[62] *E.g.*, Kurt T. Lash, *The Inescapable Federalism of the Ninth Amendment*, 93 Iowa L. Rev. 801 (2008); Randy E. Barnett, *The Ninth Amendment: It Means What It Says*, 85 Tex. L. Rev. 1, 80 (2006).

[63] *Cf.* Purcell, *supra* note 11.

[64] *See* Bond v. United States, No. 09-1227, 564 U.S. __, *14 (slip opinion) (2011), 2011 Westlaw 2369334 (U.S.) (acknowledging the question "[w]hether the Tenth Amendment is regarded as simply a 'truism,' or whether it has independent force of its own"); Mark R. Killenbeck (ed.), The Tenth Amendment and State Sovereignty (2002) (further discussing the issue).

that had exceeded state grasp led the prevailing federalism interpreters to choose a model prioritizing interjurisdictional problem solving over all other considerations.[65] The contemporary discourse arises from an era in which the prevailing judicial and political federalism rhetoric has privileged checks and balances over competing values.[66]

It is impossible to know how the unstable jurisprudence will next turn. Yet it *is* possible to ground the debate in a more nuanced model for understanding federalism—one that can account for the twists and turns of history while stabilizing the tug of war within a framework that allows for the values dialectic without requiring a theoretical paradigm shift in each instance. Though it is no modest task, it is my hope that this book will help channel the federalism debate into this more fruitful territory.

C. Charting the Course

The book sets out to accomplish four things, in four parts. Part I argues that the key to understanding federalism is not through the political competition between advocates of states' rights and centralized power, but in the theoretical tensions among its constituent values—revealing the tug of war that so complicates federalism interpretation. Chapter One frames the inquiry, highlighting the nature of federalism interpretation as a choice among competing theoretical models. It explores the constitutional basis for federalism interpretive uncertainty, and it illustrates the stakes of the choice by analyzing the role of federalism-related conflicts in the failed response to Hurricane Katrina. Chapter Two probes the principles of good government on which federalism is premised, exploring their basis in history and contemporary jurisprudence, and the tensions that flare among them. Chapter Three reveals how this tug of war has surfaced in the Supreme Court's evolving approach to federalism over the twentieth century. It traces how the Court's decisions showcase a series of theoretical federalism models that variously privilege one value over another without ever recognizing the source of instability.

Part II discusses the challenges of administering federalism in contexts of concurrent regulatory jurisdiction, and analyzes how theoretical elements in the Court's status quo approach fall short. Bringing the analysis to the present day, it explores how the tug of war within federalism is heightened in contexts of overlap where both the federal and state governments have legitimate regulatory interests or obligations. Chapter Four describes the philosophical nostalgia for the old dual federalism model that surfaces in many of the Supreme Court's New Federalism cases, critiquing the failure of this model to contend with the problems of accelerating jurisdictional overlap. It follows the logical trajectory of the Tenth Amendment and contemporaneous preemption cases toward greater separation between state and federal authority notwithstanding the predominance of jurisdictional overlap in American governance.

Chapter Five introduces the interjurisdictional gray area that pervades cooperative federalism and confounds dual federalism—a rich soil of regulatory uncertainty from which the

---

[65] *See infra* Chapter Three, notes 115–57 and accompanying text.
[66] *See infra* Chapter Four.

most pressing federalism controversies emerge. It illustrates gray area regulatory challenges with examples from environmental, public health, financial, and national security law, with special attention to the challenges of water pollution, climate change, and disaster response that most exacerbate the tensions of federalism. These are the examples that push federalism doctrine to its extremes, demonstrating the fault lines created in regulatory realms where interests in local autonomy and national uniformity most directly collide.

In consideration of the unresolved tug of war, Part III introduces the Balanced Federalism alternative at the heart of the book: a theoretical model that focuses on the equipoise between competing federalism values and between the distinct interpretive contributions of the branches of government at both the state and federal levels. Balanced Federalism explicitly accounts for the tug of war within, offers better tools for coping with jurisdictional overlap, and identifies opportunities for all branches of all levels of government to participate in safeguarding federalism values. It provides the means for a theorized exit from the cycle of jurisprudential instability, in which federalism theory is continually haunted by the formalist ghost of nineteenth-century dualism despite the functional demands of jurisdictional overlap.

In the first of a three-stage proposal, Chapter Six imagines judicial Balanced Federalism constraints that could operate in lieu of the judicial constraints established by the New Federalism Tenth Amendment cases. Its jurisprudential standard would assess the real problem in Tenth Amendment contexts—the risk that challenged activity in the gray area undermines federalism principles, taken as a whole. The chapter details the factors such a balancing test might consider, considers the advantages and disadvantages of judicial balancing in these contexts, and illustrates its application in federalism controversies ranging from climate governance to health insurance reform. The balancing test most forthrightly illustrates the values-balancing principle of the model, although the strong role it articulates for judicial review is progressively moderated by the successive proposals.

Chapter Seven explores a more modest proposal emphasizing greater judicial deference to legislative intergovernmental bargaining. It considers how the Constitution confers jurisdictional entitlements to state and federal actors, and explores the extent to which federalism doctrine allows their consensual exchange.[67] Taking the example of ongoing conflict over radioactive waste siting as a case study of jurisdictional overlap, it argues that in *New York v. United States*,[68] the Court unwisely withdrew the potential for state-led bargaining over Tenth Amendment entitlements. The chapter shows why facilitating legislative bargaining of the sort outlawed in *New York* is ultimately more faithful to the underlying values of federalism than current doctrine, and more consistent with the rest of the Court's federalism jurisprudence. The judicial deference this proposal calls for would trump the judicial balancing test in application to consensual bargaining over Tenth Amendment entitlements, and it lays the conceptual groundwork for even broader deference to intergovernmental bargaining proposed in Part IV.

---

[67] *Cf.* Guido Calabresi & A. Douglas Melamed, *Property Rules, Liability Rules and Inalienability: One View of the Cathedral*, 85 HARV. L. REV. 1089 (1972) (analyzing legal entitlements through the conceptual vocabulary adopted in Chapter Seven).

[68] 505 U.S. 144 (1992).

Drawing on the theoretical tools established in Part III, Part IV more fully explores the undertheorized role of the political branches in protecting federalism at both the state and federal levels. The final chapters explore the extent to which federalism-sensitive governance is already the product of widespread intergovernmental bargaining, and the extent to which values-balancing in negotiated federalism is a legitimate means of interpreting constitutional directives. Chapter Eight situates the importance of state-federal bargaining within the historic federalism safeguards debate, which has previously considered only which branch of the federal government best protects federalism. It then maps the existing landscape of federalism bargaining, surveying constitutional and statutory forums in which legislative, executive, and even judicial actors negotiate with counterparts across state-federal lines. Chapter Nine incorporates primary and secondary research to extrapolate the negotiating norms and media of exchange that define the structural safeguards of federalism bargaining. By merging state and federal interests in policy making and enforcement decisions, bilaterally negotiated governance honors federalism concerns at a structural level independent from competing first-order policy concerns.

Finally, Chapter Ten proposes criteria for recognizing interpretive partnerships among the three branches on both sides, identifying the procedural constraints that confer legitimacy on the results of state-federal legislative and executive bargaining. It provides justification for judicial deference to federalism bargaining after establishing that these baseline criteria are met, along with a fully theorized basis to account for the legitimately negotiated governance that is already widespread under cooperative federalism. In the final stage of the Balanced Federalism proposal, I argue that state-federal negotiation is a legitimately constitutional way of interpreting federalism—that is to say, of deciding *who gets to decide*—when the bargaining process is consistent with the principles of fair bargaining and the core federalism values introduced in Part I.

After all, the federalism values are themselves procedural aspirations of good governance: shepherding us toward public process that checks power to protect individuals, ensures accountability to enable democratic participation, fosters localism to cultivate autonomy and innovation, and affords opportunities for interjurisdictional synergy. When the bargaining process is faithful to these values, the political consensus yields constitutionally valid results that warrant judicial deference—even when substantive consensus on the federalism question cannot be won. Moreover, bilateral bargaining structurally reinforces protection for federalism values that transcends the subjective concerns of the negotiators and surpasses the political safeguards available at the purely unilateral level. In this way, federalism bargaining supplements other means of interpreting federalism, filling inevitable substantive gaps by utilizing the unique interpretive capacity that all branches of government bring to the table.

This final stage of the proposal advances all three goals of Balanced Federalism, enabling more conscientious balancing among the competing federalism values, the interpretive capacity of each branch of government, and the wisdom of both state and federal perspectives in locating appropriate results in each circumstance. Procedural deference to qualifying bargaining trumps the Chapter Six balancing test and all other judicial federalism constraints while subsuming the more limited deference proposed in Chapter Seven. Judicial balancing remains available to test unilateral and extreme gray area governance against federalism concerns, but it is appropriately moderated by the procedural deference that Balanced Federalism seeks for governance that meets the criteria set forth in Chapter Ten.

D. The Balanced Federalism Alternative

Before the journey begins, I offer a final note about the relationship between Balanced Federalism theory and its predecessors. The federalism debates have long raged between advocates of greater state autonomy and greater national power (reviewed more fully in Part II), as well as between champions of judicially enforceable federalism constraints and believers in the procedural safeguards built into the constitutional design (reviewed more fully in Part IV). To grossly oversimplify the discourse, many advocates for state autonomy urge judicial doctrine that enforces a zone of state sovereignty free of federal incursion, while process federalists maintain that the balance of state and federal power is sufficiently protected by the political process itself.[69] And of course, there are countless examples of outlying decisions and creative federalism theory that defy these caricatures entirely, proposing more nuanced and entirely different ways of understanding American federalism.[70]

The values-based theory of Balanced Federalism proposed in this book is also positioned somewhere between these rough poles, providing theoretical justification for the functional account embraced by the process school while preserving a limited role for the judicial review advocated by the sovereignty school (and thus with the potential to jar those fully committed to either one or the other view).[71] In contrast to recent scholarship focusing primarily on the judicial role, my approach fully embraces the federalism of policy-making authority, balancing its theory of judicial review with a more theorized account of the interpretive role that state and federal political branches also play in federalism implementation. Contextualizing abstract ideas with rich factual examples, the book explores the application of Balanced Federalism ideals within case studies of disaster response, stormwater management, nuclear waste siting, and climate governance.

Importantly, however, the theory of federalism I advance here is not committed to locating dominant political power at either the state or national level. Like other scholarship in the emerging literature of dynamic federalism, this book emphasizes the value of fluidity and

---

[69] *See* Heather Gerken, *Federalism All the Way Down*, 124 HARV. L. REV. 4, 11–21 (2010) (providing a contemporary intellectual history of the federalism debates).

[70] *E.g., id.*; Edward L. Rubin & Malcolm Feeley, *Federalism: Some Notes on a National Neurosis*, 41 UCLA L. REV. 908–14 (1994); Ernest A. Young, *Two Cheers for Process Federalism*, 46 VILL. L. REV. 1349 (2001).

[71] Outstanding contrary work from within each school will alternatively take issue with my reading of New Federalism's debt to dual federalism, my embrace of constitutional balancing, and my faith in some role for judicial discretion and political bargaining. The discourse is too vast for me to respond where we part company while making the contribution I hope to add, but footnotes throughout the book provide a road map to various viewpoints that have paved the way. For a small sample of this compelling literature, see JENNA BEDNAR, THE ROBUST FEDERATION (2009); CHEMERINSKY, *supra* note 12; JOHN HART ELY, DEMOCRACY AND DISTRUST (1980); ROBERT A. GOLDWIN (ED.), A NATION OF STATES: ESSAYS ON THE AMERICAN FEDERAL SYSTEM (1974); MICHAEL S. GREVE, REAL FEDERALISM: WHY IT MATTERS, HOW IT COULD HAPPEN (1999); GRODZINS, *supra* note 4; MALCOLM M. FEELEY AND EDWARD RUBIN, FEDERALISM: POLITICAL IDENTITY AND TRAGIC COMPROMISE (2008); ALISON L. LACROIX, THE IDEOLOGICAL ORIGINS OF AMERICAN FEDERALISM (2010); ROBERT F. NAGLE, THE IMPLOSION OF AMERICAN FEDERALISM (2001); JOHN NUGENT, SAFEGUARDING FEDERALISM: HOW STATES PROTECT THEIR INTERESTS IN NATIONAL POLICYMAKING (2009); PURCELL, *supra* note 11; SCHAPIRO, *supra* note 11; DAVID L. SHAPIRO, FEDERALISM: A DIALOGUE (1995).

overlap between state and federal authority when that is consistent with basic constitutional premises.[72] Sometimes ideal governance in federalism-sensitive realms takes place municipally, sometimes through the state, and sometimes at the national level. And sometimes, as the climate dilemma in Chapter Five portends, regulatory challenges require collaboration at all points along the spectrum of political scale, given the unique sources of authority, expertise, and regulatory capacity for response at each. One critique of dynamic federalism is that enabling regulatory overlap may effectively preempt one level's decision *not* to regulate in a given sphere.[73] However, when demands for governance are reasonably within the consensus of government obligation, then the dialectic of regulatory backstop created by this fluidity is a desirable feature of multilevel governance.[74] Time and again, history offers testimony to the value of overlapping state and federal regulatory authority in protecting individual rights, stewarding public goods, and inspiring regulatory innovation.[75]

As source material in the book suggests, my own interest in federalism was inspired by environmental law, which provides an excellent example of dual sovereignty at its best. Historical events match a recent era of state regulatory dominance with a preceding era of federal regulatory dominance in which each took up slack left by the other. In the 1970s, the federal government enacted comprehensive environmental statutes to fill the state regulatory void that had allowed air and water quality to degrade beyond public tolerance.[76] The availability of redundant regulatory authority at the federal level helped forestall even greater public health and natural resource crises, though federal efforts were themselves modeled after successful state innovators.[77] Then, beginning in the 2000s, state and local governments stepped into the federal void to explore how best to mitigate and adapt to the anticipated harms of climate change.[78] State and local experimentation has yielded critical developments

---

[72] *E.g.*, CHEMERINSKY, supra note 12; SCHAPIRO, *supra* note 11; William W. Buzbee, *Interaction's Promise: Preemption Policy Shifts, Risk Regulation, and Experimentalism Lessons*, 57 EMORY L. J. 145 (2007); Kirsten H. Engel, *Harnessing the Benefits of Dynamic Federalism in Environmental Law*, 56 EMORY L.J. 159 (2006); Gerken, *supra* note 69; Hari M. Osofsky, *Diagonal Federalism and Climate Change: Implications for the Obama Administration*, 62 ALA. L. REV. 237 (2011); Judith Resnik et al., *Ratifying Kyoto at the Local Level: Sovereigntism, Federalism, and Translocal Organizations of Government Actors (TOGAs)*, 50 ARIZ. L. REV. 709 (2008). *See also* LACROIX, *supra* note 71, (charting the legal history of jurisdictional multiplicity); PURCELL, *supra* note 11 (arguing that the Constitution's dynamic balance of power does not mandate a specific normative theory of federalism).

[73] *See* Gillian Metzger, *Federalism Under Obama*, 53 WM. & MARY L. REV. __ (forthcoming, 2011) (assessing this critique).

[74] *See infra* Part I Introduction, notes 19–22 and accompanying text; Chapter Two, notes 41–56 and accompanying text.

[75] *Cf.* Douglas Laycock, *Protecting Liberty in a Federal System: The U.S. Experience, in* PATTERNS OF REGIONALISM AND FEDERALISM: LESSONS FOR THE UK 119 (Jörg Fedtke & Basil S. Markesinis eds., 2006).

[76] Clean Air Act, 42 U.S.C. § 7401 *et seq.* (2006); Clean Water Act, 33 U.S.C. § 1251 *et seq.* (2006).

[77] For example, California's pioneering air pollution regulation became a model for the federal Clean Air Act. *See* Ann E. Carlson, *Shaping the Future: What Our Decisions Today Mean for Tomorrow*, 37 U.C. DAVIS L. REV. 281, 286 (2003).

[78] *E.g.*, Kirsten Engel, *State and Local Climate Change Initiatives: What Is Motivating State and Local Governments To Address a Global Problem and What Does This Say About Federalism and Environmental Law?*, 38 URB. LAW. 1015 (2006).

in green building laws, transportation and land use planning, renewable resource portfolio standards, emissions controls, and even carbon markets—all of which have since become the subject of congressional interest in proposed federal climate legislation.[79] But for the availability of redundant regulatory authority at the state level, the people of the United States would enjoy far reduced environmental security.

The history of state-federal turn-taking on civil rights and even property rights tells a similar tale. The federal government intervened before and during the Jim Crow era to more fully protect the rights of black Americans,[80] and many states are now stepping into the void of federal law to protect the rights of gay and lesbian Americans.[81] No federal law bars discrimination against sexual orientation in employment,[82] while many states now do.[83] But again, roles are occasionally reversed even within a period of state or federal dominance. For example, California voters amended the state constitution in 2008 to recognize only marriages between a man and a woman,[84] but in 2010, a federal judge invalidated the provision for transgressing the U.S. Constitution's promise of equal protection.[85] Although the decision may yet be overturned on appeal,[86] it was the first in the nation to uphold gay marriage rights on federal constitutional grounds.[87] Meanwhile, federal law innovated due process protection

---

[79] Kirsten H. Engel, *Whither Subnational Climate Change Initiatives in the Wake of Federal Climate Legislation?*, 39 PUBLIUS 432 (2009).

[80] *E.g.*, Marilyn K. Howard, *Discrimination*, *in* 1 THE JIM CROW ENCYCLOPEDIA 222, 226–27 (Nikki L.M. Brown & Barry M. Stentiford eds., 2008).

[81] *See, e.g.*, VT. STAT. ANN. tit. 15, § 8 (2009) (amending marriage definition from union between a man and woman to a union between two people); COLO. REV. STAT. §§ 24-34-401 and 24-34-402 (2007) (barring discrimination in hiring based on sexual orientation); Goodridge v. Dep't of Pub. Health, 798 N.E.2d 941 (Mass. 2003) (in invalidating a state statutory ban on same-sex marriages, asserting that the Massachusetts constitution is more protective of civil rights than the federal Constitution). *Cf.* Heather Gerken, *Dissenting by Deciding*, 57 STAN. L. REV. 1745 (2005) (discussing San Francisco's decision to issue gay marriage licenses despite contrary state law).

[82] The Human Rights Campaign, *Employment Non-Discrimination Laws on Sexual Orientation and Gender Identity* (2010), http://www.hrc.org/issues/4844.htm ("Although Title VII of the Civil Rights Act of 1964 prohibits workplace sex discrimination, federal courts of appeal have uniformly held that Congress did not intend that the term 'sex' include sexual orientation").

[83] For example, Illinois's Human Rights Act bars discrimination based on sexual orientation and gender identity regarding employment, real estate transactions, public accommodations, and access to financial credit. 775 ILL. CODE 5/1-102 (2010). Minnesota bans discrimination against sexual orientation and gender identity in employment, education, housing, public accommodation, and public services. MINN. STAT. §§ 363A.02 (2009). However, the governor of Virginia recently declined to reissue an executive order barring state employment discrimination on the basis of sexual orientation. *See* Rosalind Helderman, *State Employee Argues to Va. Supreme Court That He Was Fired for Being Gay*, WASH. POST, Apr. 2, 2010, http://voices.washingtonpost.com/virginiapolitics/2010/04/whenever_gov_bob_mcdonnell_dis.html.

[84] CAL. CONST. art. I, § 7.5 (amended 2008).

[85] Perry v. Schwarzenegger, 2010 U.S. Dist. LEXIS 78817 (N.D. Cal. Aug. 4, 2010).

[86] Jesse McKinley, *Both Sides in California's Gay Marriage Fight See a Long Court Battle Ahead*, N.Y. TIMES, June 26, 2010, http://www.nytimes.com/2010/06/27/us/27prop8.html?_r=1.

[87] Maura Dolan & Carol J. Williams, *Ruling Against Prop. 8 Could Lead to Federal Precedent on Gay Marriage*, L.A. TIMES, Aug. 4, 2010, http://www.latimes.com/news/local/la-me-gay-marriage-california-20100805,0,2696248.story.

for previously unrecognized property interests in *Goldberg v. Kelly*,[88] while many states invented new protections for real property against eminent domain after *Kelo v. City of New London*.[89]

Not every aspect of American federalism can be generalized from the wrenching conflicts posed by these areas of law, but the most difficult cases provide insight into the governing norms, and the extremes often suggest something valuable about what normal should look like. Moreover, the political landscape is increasingly strewn with equally difficult cases in other regulatory arenas, such as state laws governing medical marijuana and assisted suicide, and federal health care and financial reform. Difficult cases, it would seem, are again the federalism norm.

The history of our federalism is one of both gradual adjustment and dynamic change, as Americans continue to grapple with the societal issues of the day, the purposes of government, and the implications of multiple sources of authority within a federal system. This book offers a theoretical tour of some of these issues, and an alternative concept of federalism that allows flexibility for the ongoing dialectic between those periods in history when local innovation is most needed and those when national uniformity must prevail. Hopefully clear by now, it is more a work of federalism theory than an exegesis of federalism doctrine. Understanding federalism as that sum total of doctrinal rules within which cases are decided is critical for the practice of law, but this treatment analyzes federalism through the theoretical lens interpreters use to consider these issues in the first instance. It focuses on the cases and dilemmas that define shifts in the underlying theoretical terrain, and its proposals engage purposefully and provocatively in theory-building from the ground up, leaving open questions in their wake.

Ultimately, my aim is to clarify the goals of federalism, the tensions within, and the promise that a more balanced model dual sovereignty offers for coping with the most pressing issues of our time. Values balancing and intergovernmental bargaining reframe the obligations of conscience and deference that operate among all three branches in both state and federal realms, demonstrating the interpretive role each plays in implementing our federal system. Balanced Federalism theory defuses some of the more hegemonic assumptions that resurfaced in the New Federalism revival and begins a more honest conversation about the genuine interpretive choices and trade-offs that federalism requires. A more balanced approach to understanding state-federal relations offers hope for moving beyond the paralyzing features of the federalism discourse that have stymied it for so long. In the end, the proposals in the book may raise as many questions as they answer, but the questions are surely worth our time.

---

[88] 397 U.S. 254 (1970) (holding that government entitlements are property interests protected by due process).

[89] 545 U.S. 469 (2005) (holding that the Fifth Amendment does not necessarily prohibit the use of eminent domain that transfers property from one private party to another for economic development purposes); Tim Hoover, *Eminent Domain Reform Signed*, KAN. CITY STAR, July 14, 2006, at B2 (reporting on new state law property rights).

Federalism and the Tug of War Within

THIS PART LOCATES the constitutional indeterminacy that enables alternative theoretical models of federalism, reveals the competing values at the heart of American federalism, and explores the tug of war between them in the case law, literature, and over history. It begins with a brief introduction to the theoretical conflict between the dual and cooperative federalism models, both of which are reflected in different aspects of current federalism doctrine and practice.

In the most famous rhetorical gesture of the federalism jurisprudence for which he would become known, the late Chief Justice Rehnquist opined that "*[t]he Constitution requires a distinction between what is truly national and what is truly local.*"[1] But even conceding the merits of the federalism principles implied, a question hangs well after the rhetorical satiety dissipates: *What about everything in between?* Where does climate regulation fit on that continuum? Counterterrorism efforts? What does the Constitution require in these instances? The question makes a simple point about a complex body of jurisprudence—the Supreme Court's controversial "New Federalism" decisions of 1992–2000[2]—in essence, that the New Federalism breeds controversy

---

[1] United States v. Morrison, 529 U.S. 598, 617–18 (2000) (emphasis added).

[2] In the standard litany of the New Federalism decisions, the Court addressed: (1) the extent of the federal commerce power, *see, e.g.*, Morrison, 529 U.S. at 627 (invalidating a section of the Violence Against Women Act of 1994 (VAWA)); United States v. Lopez, 514 U.S. 549, 551

precisely because it imposes an overly simple theoretical model on some very complex areas of law.

Indeed, just as the bellwether fields of environmental, public health, and national security law began to embrace the need for greater interconnectivity in managing multi-jurisdictional regulatory problems, this small set of powerful judicial decisions charted a course toward greater jurisdictional separation—setting the stage for conflict between judicial federalism theory and governing federalism practice. The decade since Chief Justice Rehnquist's words suggest that the divide remains alive and well, as jurisdictional overlap remains the dominant feature of American governance and New Federalism precedents remain intact. The resulting tension is most palpable in the most interjurisdictional fields of law, but in all fields, federalism thinkers should question the apparent disconnect between the ideas motivating the newest judicial federalism doctrine and those propelling actual governance. If there is really a gap, who has it right? How can we tell? Who should decide?

American federalism will weather the latest storm, as it has all previous theory-driven transitions. But they have come at such regular intervals, and over such important issues— civil rights, public health and safety, commercial regulation, environmental protection—that we might do well to approach the task this time with more powerful conceptual tools. At a minimum, we should start by acknowledging the tension between the underlying federalism values that fuel the storm cycle (the subject of Part I), and the interjurisdictional challenges that so exacerbate this tension (the subject of Part II). With these tools in hand, we can undertake the project of imagining ways to better mediate the tug of war within federalism (the subjects of Parts III and IV) so as to best realize the objectives of our constitutional design.

We begin here by searching for the objectives of the Constitution's structural federalism directives, in consultation with the various normative models of state-federal relations

---

(1995) (overturning the Gun-Free School Zones Act of 1990 as beyond the scope of commerce power); *but see* Gonzales v. Raich, 545 U.S. 1, 32–33 (2005) (affirming federal authority to proscribe intrastate production and use of medical marijuana despite contrary state law); (2) the extent of Congress's power under the post-Civil War Amendments, *see, e.g.*, Bd. of Trs. v. Garrett, 531 U.S. 356, 374 (2001) (finding that the pecuniary remedy in the Americans with Disabilities Act of 1990 (ADA) did not satisfy the requirements of congruence and proportionality, which are needed to establish a valid exercise of congressional power under the Fourteenth Amendment), *Morrison*, 529 U.S. at 627 (refusing to sustain a section of the VAWA under Section Five of the Fourteenth Amendment), Kimel v. Fla. Bd. of Regents, 528 U.S. 62, 82–83 (2000) (concluding that the Age Discrimination in Employment Act of 1967 (ADEA) is "not 'appropriate legislation' under Section Five of the Fourteenth Amendment"), City of Boerne v. Flores, 521 U.S. 507, 536 (1997) (finding that the Religious Freedom Restoration Act of 1993 (RFRA) exceeded Congress's authority under Section Five of the Fourteenth Amendment); (3) the extent of Congress's ability to command state executive branch and legislative activity, *see, e.g.*, Printz v. United States, 521 U.S. 898, 935 (1997) (holding that Congress may not compel state and local law enforcement to implement a federal regulatory program), New York v. United States, 505 U.S. 144, 161 (1992) (holding that the Tenth Amendment forbids Congress from "commandeering" state legislative action under a federal regulatory program); *but see* Reno v. Condon, 528 U.S. 141, 151 (2000) (finding that a federal law regulating state action did not commandeer state legislative and administrative process); and (4) the extent of state sovereign immunity, *see, e.g.*, Alden v. Maine, 527 U.S. 706, 712 (1999) (limiting Congress's power to authorize suits against state governments in state courts); Seminole Tribe v. Florida, 517 U.S. 44, 47 (1996) (limiting Congress's power to authorize suits against state governments in federal courts).

available to help us interpret them. The New Federalism cases point to a compelling alternative: the dual federalism model that has predominated at various points in American history, especially during the first half.[3] (What I will periodically refer to as "classical dual federalism" reached its theoretical apex during the later nineteenth century, though historians suggest that it possesses no more claim to original constitutional meaning than other models.[4]) Extrapolating from the constitutional premise of dual sovereignty, dual federalism emphasizes not only separate sources of state and federal authority but separate zones in which to wield that authority, idealizing the state and federal governments as operating in mutually exclusive jurisdictional spheres.[5] In its purest terms, the model understands different regulatory targets as properly local or national and then segregates jurisdiction accordingly (by preempting improper local activity and enforcing the limits of the federally enumerated powers). Implicitly, the Tenth Amendment polices an idealized bright-line boundary in between.

In the New Federalism revival of classical dualism explored more fully in Chapter Four, the Rehnquist Court articulated a series of formalistic, judicially enforceable constraints on federal assertions of power that the majority believed transgressed that boundary, while simultaneously preempting state laws that did the same.[6] Professor Robert Schapiro has recently published an especially compelling analysis of the Court's recent revival of dualism in its federalism and preemption jurisprudence,[7] and Dean Erwin Chemerinsky has also explored the combined force of separation between the Rehnquist Court's federalism and preemption cases.[8]

Even if chapters of early American history harmonized with this ideal, it stands in bold contrast to the existing map of American government—so characterized by areas of concurrent jurisdiction that its dual sovereignty has been likened to marble cake.[9] But as both history and scholarship affirm, the dual federalism model is not the only normative choice for

---

[3] *E.g.*, SCHAPIRO, *supra* Introduction, note 11, at 33–36; Edward S. Corwin, *The Passing of Dual Federalism*, 36 VA. L. REV. 1 (1950). Note that some scholars see more nuance in the Rehnquist Court's federalism jurisprudence, critiquing scholarship like this for oversimplifying the New Federalism's theoretical underpinnings. *E.g.*, Ernest A. Young, *The Rehnquist Court's Two Federalisms*, 83 TEX. L. REV. 1, 4–5, 13–49 (2004) (describing its competing themes); Allison H. Eid, *Federalism and Formalism*, 11 WM. & MARY BILL OF RTS. J., 1191, 1221–29 (2003) (refuting the standard critique of New Federalism as overly formalistic). I discuss the history and competing views on the New Federalism era more fully in Chapter Four.

[4] *See generally* PURCELL, *supra* Introduction, note 11 (arguing that dual federalism, *inter alia*, reflects neither original intent nor original practice); *id.* at 17–37 (describing structural ambiguity and historical dissensus among the Framers), 177–78 (describing the rise of the dual federalism model in the late nineteenth century). *Cf.* LACROIX, *supra* note Introduction, note 71, at 188–89 (discussing the debates as early as 1789 over concurrent jurisdiction and overlapping authority).

[5] *Cf.* Roderick M. Hills, Jr., *The Political Economy of Cooperative Federalism: Why State Autonomy Makes Sense and "Dual Sovereignty" Doesn't*, 96 MICH. L. REV. 813, 850–51 (1998).

[6] *Infra* Chapter Four & note 153. *See also* SCHAPIRO, *supra* Introduction, note 11, at 45–81; CHEMERINSKY, *supra* Introduction, note 12, at 57–85, 225–37.

[7] *See* SCHAPIRO, *supra* Introduction, note 11.

[8] CHEMERINSKY, *supra* Introduction, note 12, 57–97, 225–45.

[9] GRODZINS, *supra* Introduction, note 4, at 8.

making sense of our federalism. Political scientists have identified scores of competing theoretical models in the discourse, and the Supreme Court has experimented with several over time.[10] Indeed, the New Federalism decisions drew controversy precisely because they parted so dramatically from the cooperative federalism model that had animated Supreme Court jurisprudence for the previous six decades.[11]

Cooperative federalism anticipates concurrent state and federal jurisdiction both informally and through purposeful intergovernmental partnerships, rejecting the jurisdictional separation idealized in dual federalism and the need for judicial constraints to enforce it.[12] However, as discussed more fully in Chapter Three, the cooperative federalism model is critiqued for offering more of a descriptive vocabulary (explaining what state-federal relations *do* look like) than an underlying normative theory that would explain what state-federal relations *should* look like, and why.[13] As Professor Schapiro explains, "[w]hile an essential corrective to dual federalism, cooperative federalism gives an incomplete specification of federal-state relations," blessing voluntary state-federal interaction while doing little to sort out the conflicts that arise.[14]

Boasting a clearer normative account, the New Federalism revival has powerfully altered the modern discourse, challenging how we think about the allocation of state and federal power in modern regulatory endeavors. For better or worse, the movement would alter not only the role of the judiciary, but the way that Congress approaches lawmaking and the executive branch approaches administration. The New Federalism ethos has thus far survived the transition from the Rehnquist to the Roberts Court intact,[15] although differences are emerging in the new Court's treatment of preemption and dormant Commerce Clause issues.[16] However, its legacy of dual federalism idealism has moved beyond judicial and academic preoccupation and into popular political consciousness, as demonstrated by contemporary movements such as the Tenthers and the Tea Party.[17]

Nevertheless, the rhetoric of the New Federalism, Tenther, and Tea Party movements lay too proprietary a claim to the essence of American federalism itself—implying that

---

[10] *See* PURCELL, *supra* Introduction, note 11, at 24 (discussing surveys of federalism in political science); *infra* Chapter Three (discussing transitions in the Court's federalism theory).

[11] *Cf.* SCHAPIRO, *supra* Introduction, note 11, at 40–47; CHEMERINSKY, *supra* Introduction, note 12, at 16–25, 31–47.

[12] *Infra* Chapter Three, notes 158–215 and accompanying text (more fully discussing cooperative federalism).

[13] *Id.*

[14] SCHAPIRO, *supra* Introduction, note 11, at 90–91.

[15] *See infra* Chapter Three, notes 239–40 and accompanying text.

[16] *E.g.*, Wyeth v. Levine, 129 S. Ct. 1187 (2009) (declining to preempt state tort claim under federal pharmaceutical labeling regulations); Altria Group v. Good, 555 U.S. 70 (2008) (declining to preempt state law prohibiting deceptive advertising by federal regulation of cigarette advertising); United Haulers Ass'n v. Oneida–Herkimer Solid Waste Mgmt. Auth., 550 U.S. 330 (2007) (declining to preempt restrictive waste processing rules favoring state facilities under the dormant Commerce Clause). *See also* United States v. Comstock, 130 S. Ct. 1949 (2010) (affirming broad federal authority under the Necessary and Property Clause to civilly commit mentally ill federal inmates beyond their prison sentences).

[17] *See supra* Introduction, notes 33–51 and accompanying text.

faithfulness to the Constitution requires their approach and *only* that approach,[18] when federalism is really a more variegated institution. This part explores how different models of American federalism have variously prioritized different concerns over time, revealing dual federalism as merely one alternative among many, each true to constitutional design in its unique vindication of the fundamental federalism values. Like so many other constitutional concepts, federalism ultimately invites interpretive choices. Just as New Federalism privileges its favorite values, so have other models privileged theirs. Recognizing this, we should invest in the jurisprudential development of federalism theory that more explicitly acknowledges the competition among values than have the various federalism models guiding Supreme Court jurisprudence over the last century. Only then will we be able to realize the structure of governance that best meets the demands we make upon our political institutions.

There is, of course, a wide range of views about what those demands should rightly be. Some advocate for ambitious regulatory problem solving, others for a government that interferes with private activity as little as possible.[19] Some, perhaps chafing against the collateral damage of federalism's tug of war, have suggested that American federalism is itself an anachronism that may as well fade into the same obscurity to which the distinction between law and equity has retired.[20] But the real issue is not *whether* federalism but *what kind* of federalism best serves the hopes and needs that Americans hang on the continued vitality of our system of government.[21] My first proposition is thus positivist but value-neutral: regardless of our competing views on what constitutes good government, we should recognize that the interpretive model of federalism we embrace is linked with this determination, understanding that different blends of the foundational federalism values will foster distinctive characteristics in governance.

Acknowledging that reasonable minds will disagree on the characteristics of ideal government, I nevertheless take a normative stance in my criticism of the nineteenth-century dualism that haunts federalism theory, making my second proposition less value-neutral. In critiquing its failure to account for interjurisdictionality, I proceed from the assumption that good government should address those market failures, negative externalities, and other collective action problems that individuals are ill-equipped to resolve on their own (and that so threaten public welfare as to warrant a regulatory response despite the libertarian-highlighted risks that inherently attend the exercise of governmental authority).[22] As we face interjurisdictional problems that meet these criteria—such as the Hurricane Katrina emergency

---

[18] *E.g.*, Andrew Romano, *America's Holy Writ: Tea Party Evangelists Claim the Constitution as Their Sacred Text*, NEWSWEEK, October 25 (2010), at 34–37; *infra* Chapter Four.

[19] *Compare* RICHARD J. LAZARUS, THE MAKING OF ENVIRONMENTAL LAW (2004) (endorsing a regulatory approach) *with* MURRAY N. ROTHBARD, FOR A NEW LIBERTY: THE LIBERTARIAN MANIFESTO (rev. ed. 1978).

[20] *E.g.*, Edward L. Rubin, *The Fundamentality and Irrelevance of Federalism*, 13 GA. ST. U.L. REV. 1009, 1010 (1997).

[21] *Cf.* Vicki C. Jackson, *Federalism and the Uses and Limits of Law: Printz and Principle?*, 111 HARV. L. REV. 2180, 2213–23 (1998) (praising federalism's continued vitality while critiquing the New Federalism approach).

[22] *See infra* Chapter Five, text between notes 15–16 (discussing my approach); ROTHBARD, *supra* note 19, at 45–69 (making the libertarian critique).

reviewed in Chapter One—we deserve a model of federalism that accounts for the gray area and the federalism values competition that is heightened there.

Part I begins that quest by asking what it is, exactly, that American federalism is for. It takes on the brute introductory question: *Why federalism?* Why does this idea permeate the Constitution, and without a more satisfying internal definition? What is American federalism designed to accomplish? *Which federalism?* Which theoretical model best shepherds our interpretation of ambiguous federalism directives toward these goals? Chapter One reviews the textual basis for uncertainty in interpreting constitutional federalism directives, framing the inquiry as one of choice between competing constitutional values and the need for a theoretical model in support of the task. Then, demonstrating the flesh-and-blood dimension of a discourse that so often seems academic and removed, the chapter turns to the stakes of the choice—exploring the role of federalism theory in the failed response to the devastating 2005 Hurricane Katrina in New Orleans.

The Katrina aftermath provides an excruciating example of how an operative model of federalism can affect interjurisdictional governance, in this case by sowing confusion about the permissible scope of jurisdictional overlap. By many accounts, dual federalism idealism on the part of political actors contributed to confusion on the ground and delay in federal assistance. First responders were hampered by dual federalism directives in the National Response Plan, and news reports indicated that even as public pressure mounted on the White House to assume responsibility for the failing local response, senior advisors were paralyzed in debate over the federalism implications of doing so. Katrina is a particularly mediagenic example of federalism breakdown in interjurisdictional governance, but similar confusion has arisen in contexts from environmental to national security law, resulting in litigation, uncertain policy making, and chilled intergovernmental partnerships.[23] Still, the competing views of what federalism should accomplish that were broadcast to the world during the Katrina disaster accentuate the question of exactly *which federalism* our system of government should be aiming for.

In search of answers, Chapter Two explores why the U.S. Constitution establishes a federal system at all, probing the individual principles of good government on which federalism is premised. In addition to discussing the checks and balances, governmental accountability, and protection for local autonomy on which federalism is premised, Chapter Two identifies federalism's implicit pragmatism, including the problem-solving value embedded within the subsidiarity principle that governance take place as locally as possible.

Chapter Three then examines how the tug of war among these values has encouraged the evolution of successive approaches to federalism interpretation over the course of the twentieth century—each model responding to failures of the past by anointing new favorites among the values. With a nod to historical trends from the founding of the republic to the present, it focuses on movement in the Court's approach to federalism from the post-industrial Progressive/Lochnerian era into the Great Depression and the New Deal, then from the post-World War II era through the Civil Rights Movement and the Great Society, culminating in the modern New Federalism period.

---

[23] *Infra* Chapter Five.

1

WHICH FEDERALISM?: THE CHOICE AND THE STAKES

THIS CHAPTER ESTABLISHES foundations for the provocative suggestion that neither New Federalism nor cooperative federalism nor any other theoretical model holds a monopoly on the truth of what American federalism really means. Reviewing the sources of textual ambiguity in the Constitution's federalism directives, it explores the imperative that interpreters appeal to some theoretical model for guidance. It also reflects on the interpretive dilemma of choosing between competing constitutional values in circumstances where each holds independent virtue. Finally, given the availability of different interpretive models to cope with constitutional indeterminacy, the chapter considers the stakes of the choice, examining the role of federalism theory in the aftermath of Hurricane Katrina in New Orleans.

A. Which Federalism?

Roughly defined, federalism refers to a system of government in which power is divided between a central authority and regional political subunits, each with authority to directly regulate its citizens. Federal governments worldwide display a variety of structural choices by which this design is accomplished, but domestic federalism is well-defined in the concurrent sovereign authority of the central U.S. government and the fifty states, commonly referred to as "dual sovereignty."[1] Americans are citizens of both the United States and the individual

---

[1] For example, the United States, European Union, Canada, India, and Switzerland are all federalism-based polities whose federations exhibit unique characteristics. *See, e.g.,* Laycock, *supra* Introduction, note 75, at 119 ("Every federalism responds to a unique history, and thus every federalism is different from every other.").

states in which they reside, and subject to the respective laws of each. The Constitution enumerates those powers under which the federal government is authorized to make law (e.g., the commerce, spending, and war powers), and the states may regulate in any area not preempted by legitimate federal law.[2]

Yet the fact that Americans are citizens of two separate sovereigns does not resolve the precise contours of the relationship between the two.[3] Constitutional analysis reveals pockets of textual ambiguity that must be resolved by application of some interpretive federalism theory—a model that describes how the given federal system should work. Accordingly, there is more to federalism variety than the specific array of regional subunits around a centrality. Even within a single structural polity, conceptual variation may exist in how to (and who may) construe the details of the relationship between sovereigns and the framework of federalism designed to protect it. This is amply demonstrated in the United States by the Supreme Court's ongoing experimentation with federalism constraints, in pursuit of its evolving vision of the dual sovereignty that is mandated but incompletely described by the Constitution.

I. PARSING THE TENTH AMENDMENT IN CONTEXT

American dual sovereignty is implied in various constitutional provisions that refer to the separate states, such as Article I's acknowledgment of commerce "among the several states,"[4] Article IV's promise to protect them from invasion,[5] and Article VI's admonition that state judges are bound by federal law.[6] However, the distinct sources of state and federal power are most encapsulated as a constitutional directive in the Tenth Amendment's affirmation that "[t]he powers not delegated to the United States by the Constitution, nor prohibited by it to the States, are reserved to the States respectively, or to the people."[7] These powers and prohibitions are detailed in other provisions of the Constitution. For a superficial review:

The Constitution confers federal authority in the various provisions of Article I that delegate specific powers to Congress (inter alia, to provide for the common defense, regulate interstate commerce, naturalize citizens, coin money, collect taxes, spend for the general welfare, and make laws necessary and proper for carrying federal powers into execution);[8] those in Article II that empower the president (inter alia, to command the military, make international treaties with the consent of the Senate, and oversee the enforcement and implementation of the laws);[9] and those in Article III that empower the federal judiciary to

---

[2] U.S. CONST. art. I, § 8 (establishing federal powers); amend. X (reserving state power).

[3] *See generally* PURCELL, *supra* Introduction, note 11; MICHAEL GREVE, CONSTITUTIONAL DISORDER: THE PROMISE AND PATHOLOGY OF AMERICAN FEDERALISM, text accompanying notes 26–34 (2011).

[4] U.S. CONST. art. I, § 8.

[5] U.S. CONST. art. IV, § 4.

[6] U.S. CONST. art. VI, cl. 2.

[7] U.S. CONST. amend. X.

[8] U.S. CONST. art. I, § 8.

[9] U.S. CONST. art. II, § 2.

decide federal cases and controversies;[10] as well as in other freestanding provisions such as the Article IV power to regulate federal territory and property.[11] Provisions in constitutional amendments that were ratified after the Civil War, most notably Section Five of the Fourteenth Amendment, further empower Congress to enforce against the states the nationwide prohibition on slavery,[12] the universal guarantees of due process of law and equal protection under the law,[13] and new protections for voting rights.[14]

The Constitution confers responsibilities on the states to elect federal representatives,[15] recognize the official acts of other states,[16] submit to federal judicial resolution of interstate disputes,[17] and participate in ratifying and amending the Constitution.[18] Among other things, it prohibits states from entering into alliances, interfering with contract obligations, recognizing alternative currencies, granting titles of nobility, or passing bills of attainder or ex post facto laws.[19] It also guarantees to them a republican form of government[20] and that their citizens will enjoy the privileges and immunities of federal citizenship.[21]

The sovereign authority of both the federal and state governments has also been limited by the individual rights described in the main text of the Constitution, the Bill of Rights, the post-Civil War amendments, and other amendments that have followed.[22] These limitations on governmental power include personal rights to religious freedom, free speech, press, and assembly,[23] and to jury trials, witness confrontation, and habeas corpus.[24] They also include personal rights against unreasonable search and seizure,[25] double jeopardy and self-incrimination,[26] cruel and unusual punishment,[27] the taking of private property for public

---

[10] U.S. CONST. art. III, § 2.

[11] U.S. CONST. art. IV, § 2.

[12] U.S. CONST. amend. XIII.

[13] U.S. CONST. amend. XIV, § 1.

[14] U.S. CONST. amend. XV (on the basis of race), amend. XIX (sex), amend. XXVI (or age); amend. XXIV (prohibiting poll taxes on federal elections).

[15] U.S. CONST. art. I, § 4; amend. XII, amend. XVII.

[16] U.S. CONST. art. IV, § 1.

[17] U.S. CONST. art. III, § 2.

[18] U.S. CONST. art. VII, V.

[19] U.S. CONST. art. I, § 10.

[20] U.S. CONST. art. VI, § 4.

[21] U.S. CONST. art. VI, § 2; amend. XIV, § 1.

[22] For fuller discussion of how the constitutional rights specifically named against either the federal or state governments are interpretively incorporated against the other, *see, e.g.*, Akhil Reed Amar, *The Bill of Rights and the Fourteenth Amendment*, 101 YALE L.J. 1193 (1992); Louis Henkin, *"Selective Incorporation" in the Fourteenth Amendment*, 73 YALE L.J. 74 (1963).

[23] U.S. CONST. amend. I.

[24] U.S. CONST. amend. VI (criminal jury trial and confrontation); amend. VII (civil jury trial); art. I, § 9 (habeas corpus).

[25] U.S. CONST. amend. IV.

[26] U.S. CONST. amend. V.

[27] U.S. CONST. amend. VIII.

use without just compensation,[28] and other deprivations of life, liberty, or property without due process of law.[29] The Ninth Amendment further specifies that the enumeration of these rights should not be construed to disparage others retained by the people,[30] and again, the Tenth Amendment adds that those powers that are neither delegated to the federal government nor prohibited to the states "are reserved to the States respectively, or to the people."[31]

The Tenth Amendment establishes that the Constitution (1) delegates some powers to the federal government, (2) prohibits some to the states, and (3) reserves powers that fit in neither of these two sets to the states (or perhaps the people). Standing alone, the Tenth Amendment's only unique contribution is to suggest that there are at least some unspecified powers that may belong wholly to the states. But it does not specify what these are; we can only parse them out by negative inference to other constitutional provisions that specifically delegate federal authority or proscribe state action. The Tenth Amendment further (and unremarkably) affirms that the Constitution delegates some authority to the federal government, and, read together with the inherently vague Supremacy Clause,[32] suggests that at least some of this authority may be wielded exclusively at the federal level, preempting contrary state law.

However, neither the Tenth Amendment nor the Supremacy Clause nor any other provision in the Constitution decisively resolves whether there may also be regulatory spaces in which *both* the states and the federal government may operate (if they have not been withdrawn from either's commission by express constitutional limitation or unambiguous congressional preemption). This is the realm of jurisdictional overlap that engenders so much federalism controversy and uncertainty. How far into the realm of traditional state authority can Congress reach under its enumerated powers? Even if the federal government may preempt, when should it nevertheless leave room for state autonomy? Should states be able to legislate on matters that could indirectly affect foreign affairs or national markets? Or does the Constitution require a clearer line between state and federal prerogative?

Drawing the conclusion that the Constitution allows for overlapping regulatory space requires an interpretive leap, but so does the extrapolation of mutually exclusive spheres of authority.[33] Either conclusion demands application of some exogenous theory about what American federalism means, or what, in essence, federalism is *for*. The fact that we have relied on one theory or another to resolve the matter—in ways that may eventually come to seem obvious if only by virtue of their repetition—does not negate the role of federalism theory in

---

[28] U.S. CONST. amend. V. *See also id.* at amend. III (limiting the quartering of troops on private property).

[29] U.S. CONST. amend. V.

[30] U.S. CONST. amend. IX.

[31] U.S. CONST. amend. X.

[32] U.S. CONST. art. VI, cl. 2 ("This Constitution, and the Laws of the United States which shall be made in Pursuance thereof; and all Treaties made, or which shall be made, under the Authority of the United States shall be the supreme Law of the Land; and the Judges in every State shall be bound thereby, any Thing in the Constitution or Laws of any State to the Contrary notwithstanding."). The Supremacy Clause tells us that federal law is "supreme," but from there to field preemption nevertheless requires an interpretive leap.

[33] *E.g.*, PURCELL, *supra* Introduction, note 11, at 6–9; Jackson, *supra* Part I Introduction, note 21, at 2191.

getting us to that interpretive point. And when the Constitution leaves open multiple possibilities, interpretive choices are inevitable.

These choices become particularly difficult when they pit competing constitutional values against one another, each one an independently desirable feature of governance in its own right. An interpretation preferring mutually exclusive jurisdictional spheres may maximize checks and balances between state and federal authority, facilitating local autonomy and diversity. But an interpretation allowing for greater jurisdictional overlap fosters a different kind of checks and balances that may better safeguard rights and preferences, as well as intergovernmental partnerships that harness problem-solving synergy between local and national regulatory capacity. Constitutional checks on sovereign authority to protect against government overreaching are a critical innovation of the American system, just as its multiple sources of sovereign authority heralds the pragmatic innovation of interjurisdictional governance (for example, to regulate interstate commerce). The values of local autonomy compete with the privileges of national citizenship. In making sense of the dual sovereignty directive's empty space, constitutional interpretation must mediate this clash of values (among others).

2. INTERPRETATION AND CONSTITUTIONAL VALUES

Other empty spaces in the Bill of Rights further illustrate the role of normative theory in navigating the uncertainty between clashing constitutional values. In the summer of 2010, shortly after stepping down from the bench, Justice David Souter gave a commencement address at Harvard Law School in which he explained what he had learned about constitutional judging over his eighteen years as a member of the U.S. Supreme Court.[34] Constitutional judging, he said, requires a level of interpretation that goes beyond the simple application of absolute text to clear facts (because the most important text in the Constitution is rarely clear, and facts rarely absolute).[35] Responding to the criticism that the justices "make up the law" rather than read it, he told the new graduates why constitutional judging requires more than reading text:

> The Constitution has a good share of deliberately open-ended guarantees, like rights to due process of law, equal protection of the law, and freedom from unreasonable searches. These provisions cannot be applied like the requirement for 30-year-old senators; they call for more elaborate reasoning to show why very general language applies in some specific cases but not in others, and over time the various examples turn into rules that the Constitution does not mention.
>
> But this explanation hardly scratches the surface. The reasons that constitutional judging is not a mere combination of fair reading and simple facts extend way beyond the recognition that constitutions have to have a lot of general language in order to be

---

[34] *Text of Justice David Souter's Speech* (Harvard Commencement remarks, as delivered), HARVARD GAZETTE, May 27, 2010, http://news.harvard.edu/gazette/story/2010/05/text-of-justice-david-souters-speech/ [hereinafter *Souter Speech*].

[35] *Id.*

useful over long stretches of time. *Another reason is that the Constitution contains values that may well exist in tension with each other, not in harmony...* [T]he Constitution is no simple contract, not because it uses a certain amount of open-ended language that a contract draftsman would try to avoid, but because *its language grants and guarantees many good things, and good things that compete with each other and can never all be realized, all together, all at once.*[36]

To illustrate the point, he told the graduates about how the Court had come to grips with the seeming paradox in the First Amendment's admonition that "Congress shall make no law . . . abridging the freedom of speech, or of the press."[37] In the end, he explained, the Justices were forced to understand that the clarion words "no law" could not really mean *no* law—allowing cries of fire in a public theater and prepublication of military strategy in wartime—because "the First Amendment was not the whole Constitution."[38] After all, the same Constitution "also granted authority to the government to provide for the security of the nation, and authority to the president to manage foreign policy and command the military."[39] Neither was the First Amendment of small order, however, and so in such cases as the famous Pentagon Papers suit, the Court found that the government had failed its heavy burden to justify a prior restraint.[40] But this was not because "no law" meant *no law.* As Justice Souter summarized,

> Even the First Amendment, then, expressing the value of speech and publication in the terms of a right as paramount as any fundamental right can be, does not quite get to the point of an absolute guarantee. It fails because the Constitution has to be read as a whole, and when it is, other values crop up in potential conflict with an unfettered right to publish, the value of security for the nation and the value of the president's authority in matters foreign and military. *The explicit terms of the Constitution, in other words, can create a conflict of approved values, and the explicit terms of the Constitution do not resolve that conflict when it arises.* The guarantee of the right to publish is unconditional in its terms, and in its terms the power of the government to govern is plenary. A choice may have to be made, not because language is vague but because the Constitution embodies the desire of the American people, like most people, to have things both ways. We want order and security, and we want liberty. And we want not only liberty but equality as well. These paired desires of ours can clash, and when they do a court is forced to choose between them, between one constitutional good and another one.[41]

---

[36] *Id.* (emphasis added).

[37] U.S. CONST. amend. I.

[38] *Souter Speech, supra* note 34.

[39] *Id.*

[40] New York Times Co. v. United States, 403 U.S. 713 (1971) (upholding the rights of newspapers to publish classified documents, but contemplating circumstances in which serious public harm could justify a prior restraint).

[41] *Souter Speech, supra* note 34 (emphasis added).

Americans do want it both ways, and federalism is no exception. We want local autonomy, *and* we want centralized power to protect rights and solve collective action problems. We want protective checks and balances between independent sovereigns, *and* for them to collaborate as needed to cope with interjurisdictional problems. Justice Souter's speech provides naked insight into the role of all interpreters asked to make sense of the competing principles that the Constitution simultaneously endorses without clarification. At the level of first inquiry, there is no instruction manual for managing conflicts and omissions.[42] Americans want security and liberty, order and equality, and indeed, the Constitution promises all in relative degrees of absolute. The task of the interpreter is to identify the competing claims, evaluate their merits, and ascertain how to prioritize among them in each factual context.

But nobody does this in a theoretical vacuum—nobody can. Justice Souter's account makes the consummate case for the inevitability of interpretive choices among competing constitutional values, but it stops short of delving into the theoretical models that enable these choices (no doubt because the matter becomes much murkier from there). Yet each interpretive choice requires some theoretical model of what the Constitution requires in cases of unspecified conflict, such as that between free press and imminent public harm, or between state and federal authority in contexts of jurisdictional overlap. It requires a model of how the Constitution is supposed to work.[43] More difficult still, it requires a model of how constitutional interpretation is supposed to work.

3. FEDERALISM AND INDETERMINACY

In coping with this inherent constitutional indeterminacy, interpreters must thus draw on normative models of constitutional meaning and methods of interpretation, but the diversity of alternatives only furthers the array of potential interpretations. As Justice Souter's speech acknowledges, some have argued that the only valid interpretation is that of the original architects of the Constitution, and that anything else reflects "judicial activism" or inappropriate judicial aggrandizement.[44] Originalists avoid interpretive indeterminacy by searching for the intentions of the Constitution's original drafters when deciphering constitutional meaning.[45] For many originalists, when textual directives prove problematic over time, the appropriate response is not to engage in "interpretive subterfuge" but to correct the

---

[42] Although legal history provides nonbinding interpretive resources, it also reveals divided views even among the original drafters of the Constitution. *See* PURCELL, *supra* Introduction, note 11.

[43] For compelling models of how the Constitution works beyond the standard civics-class account, see BRUCE ACKERMAN, WE THE PEOPLE: FOUNDATIONS (1991); Ernest A. Young, *The Constitution Outside the Constitution*, 117 YALE L.J. 408 (2007).

[44] *See, e.g.*, RAOUL BERGER, GOVERNMENT BY JUDICIARY 403–29 (2d ed. 1997); ANTONIN SCALIA, A MATTER OF INTERPRETATION: FEDERAL COURTS AND THE LAW 46 (1997); Robert H. Bork, *The Constitution, Original Intent, and Economic Rights*, 23 SAN DIEGO L. REV. 823, 824–25 (1986); Edwin Meese III, *Toward a Jurisprudence of Original Intent*, 11 HARV. J.L. & PUB. POL'Y 5, 7 (1988); William H. Rehnquist, *The Notion of a Living Constitution*, 54 TEX. L. REV. 693, 698 (1976); Antonin Scalia, *Originalism: The Lesser Evil*, 57 U. CIN. L. REV. 849 (1989).

[45] PURCELL, *supra* Introduction, note 11, at 3.

defect by formal amendment.[46] For example, the original Constitution's tacit approval of slavery and dated plans for federal taxation were corrected respectively by the Thirteenth and Sixteenth Amendments.[47]

Others argue that all constitutional interpretive choices—including "originalist" interpretations—are equally subject to the hermeneutic biases of the interpreter by virtue of the pockets of ambiguity that are inherently embedded within written texts.[48] Proponents of the Living Constitution argue that the document was purposefully and ingeniously framed in broad terms so that each generation can interpret these subtle conflicts anew.[49] Although few would dispute the proper recourse to amendment for correcting clearly defective textual provisions, they argue—as does Justice Souter—that some degree of interpretive lawmaking is a necessary part of the judicial function in applying vague constitutional commands to new controversies.[50]

Especially in the context of federalism, Professor Edward Purcell convincingly argues that originalist interpretations are of limited value because there *was* no consensus among the original drafters about how to interpret the federal structure on which they ultimately compromised.[51] Quoting first Benjamin Franklin and then James Madison on the process, he writes:

> "The players of our game are so many, their ideas so different, their prejudices so strong and various, and their particular interests independent of the general, seeming so opposite," [Franklin] explained, that the delegates were compelled to resort to compromise and avoidance. "[N]ot a move can be made that is not contested; the numerous objections confound the understanding; [and] the wisest must agree to some unreasonable things, that reasonable ones of more consequence can be obtained." The Constitution's final draft was as much the result of accident and circumstance as of reason and deliberation. Thus, "chance has its share in many of the determinations," he concluded, "so that the play is more like *tric-trac* with a box of dice."

---

[46] William Van Alstyne, *Interpreting This Constitution: The Unhelpful Contributions of Special Theories of Judicial Review*, 35 U. Fla. L. Rev. 209 (1983).

[47] U.S. Const. amend. XIII, amend. XVI.

[48] *See, e.g.*, Reva B. Siegel, *She the People: The Nineteenth Amendment, Sex Equality, Federalism, and the Family*, 115 Harv. L. Rev. 947, 1032–34 (2002) (asserting that incorporation of historical understanding into modern constitutional interpretation is an "irreducibly normative" endeavor); Peter J. Smith, *Sources of Federalism: An Empirical Analysis of the Court's Quest for Original Meaning*, 52 UCLA L. Rev. 217, 287 (2004) (reviewing the "vast body of primary historical materials . . . that support a spectrum of constitutional meaning" and the accordingly futile project of originalist interpretive constraints); Stephen R. Munzer & James W. Nickel, *Does the Constitution Mean What It Always Meant?*, 77 Colum. L. Rev. 1029 (1977); Robert Post, *Theories of Constitutional Interpretation*, 30 Representations 13 (1990).

[49] *See* Ronald M. Dworkin, Law's Empire (1986).

[50] *See, e.g.*, Laurence H. Tribe, Comment, *in* Scalia, A Matter of Interpretation, *supra* note 44, at 68–72 (discussing the problem of choosing the correct "level of abstraction" at which constitutional clauses should be construed).

[51] Purcell, *supra* Introduction, note 11.

Madison agreed. The Constitution's final form "shows that the convention must have been compelled to sacrifice theoretical propriety to the forces of extraneous considerations." Many disagreements among the delegates "could be terminated only by compromise." It was "not pretended that every insertion of ormission in the Constitution is the effect of systematic attention," he admitted in 1791. "This is not the character of any human work, particularly the work of a body of men." Indeed, as [historian] Lance Banning has shown Madison's own thinking about the proper structure of the Union and the nature of its new Constitution evolved throughout the 1780s, shifted during the convention itself, changed again as he wrote his *Federalist* essays, and continued to evolve thereafter."[52]

Purcell's historically grounded conclusion is that "the Constitution did create a governmental structure with an essential and unalterable core [but] that the core lay not in any 'assigned' or 'carefully crafted' balance but rather in a dynamic combination of [] interrelated elements that allow a range of acceptable permutations."[53]

To front my own interpretive approach, my analysis proceeds from the Living Constitution assumption in finding deliberate interpretive space in the Constitution generally, and from Purcell's historical account in finding it specifically in the model of federalism that its directives imply. Like Professor Purcell, I find them both inevitable. In the specific context at issue, the Tenth Amendment confirms dual sovereignty in its elliptical affirmation that the establishment of the federal government did not disestablish the states and its acknowledgement that their sovereign authority derives from separate sources. But it leaves much beyond that for interpretation that neither the Commerce Clause, the Necessary and Proper Clause, nor the Supremacy Clause resolves. Deciphering state-federal relations inevitably forces interpreters to draw upon underlying theories about what American federalism is meant to do. As Justice Souter's speech foreshadows, understanding federalism opens yet another interpretive forum for coping with conflicts between competing constitutional goods—here, constitutional goods that are even less directly specified in the text.

As elaborated in Chapter Two, polities turn to federalism to promote a set of governance values that they hope federalism will help yield. Foremost among them are the preservation of individual liberties through checks and balances on accountable sovereign power and the promotion of diversity and competition associated with local autonomy, both tempered with a healthy regard for the role of government as the superintendent of local and national collective action problems.[54] But as with the competing goods of security and liberty, the core federalism values are suspended in a network of tension with one another. Preserving local autonomy can conflict with the protection of individual liberty. Centralized resolution of collective action problems can undermine checks and balances. In protecting its preferred vision of dual sovereignty, each interpretive approach advances the fundamental federalism values in some way, but the tension among them means that emphasizing one value may result in the de-emphasis of another. In deciding which values take precedence under what

---

[52] *Id.* at 25–26.

[53] *Id.* at 8.

[54] *See infra* Chapter Two.

circumstances, we choose, consciously or not, among different models of federalism that then inform lawmaking and adjudication.

In the United States, political discourse has tended more and more to treat the ideals of the diffusion of sovereign power and the pragmatic concerns of problem solving as a federalism thesis and antithesis—principles in opposition to one another, rather than complementary elements of the overall federalism project. For example, the New Federalism, Tenther, and Tea Party revivals of dual federalism theory tend to subordinate pragmatic concerns to the maintenance of formalist boundaries between distinct reservoirs of state and federal power.[55] Judicially enforceable constraints police regulatory activity to discourage trespass by either side—even in contexts where the boundary is difficult to locate, or where both sides hold simultaneously legitimate regulatory interests. For these reasons, as I argue in Part II, the dualist model can lead to regulatory confusion in contexts of genuine jurisdictional overlap that defy its theoretical premise, and in the worst cases, chill needed interjurisdictional problem solving.

A model that makes this trade-off is clearly a legitimate political choice. Yet despite the rhetoric attending the New Federalism and its modern political counterparts, it is not the *only* interpretive possibility, nor the only model true to the principles enshrined in the Constitution. The same principles support a variety of other models, many of which have been experimented with over the course of our nation's history (and sometimes simultaneously by different members of the Court).[56] Each serves a slightly different understanding of the dual sovereignty relationship and promises a slightly different construction of governmental priorities, thereby leading to slightly different substantive ends.

For interpreters of the American Constitution, then, the relevant choice is not one between federalism and nonfederalism, but of *which federalism*—which model of federalism best promotes the kind of governance that we seek. These are, of course, the real stakes at hand. And so it could certainly be that, in the end, most Americans want exactly the kind of government promoted by dual federalism (although as discussed below, popular reaction to the Katrina disaster casts doubt on that suggestion).[57] Ultimately, I argue that it is not the best available choice, given its weak ability to contend with the interjurisdictional problems that confront all levels of government. Either way, however, we should at least recognize the true nature of the choice as one among alternatives—and make that choice with attention to the stakes involved. Indeed, this is not merely the stuff of political grandstanding and academic navel-gazing; the costs of our choices about federalism are very much extracted at the level of everyday lives (in the most tragic of cases, many at a time).

---

[55] *See* CHEMERINSKY, *supra* Introduction, note 12, at 68–85; Romano, *supra* Part I Introduction, note 18; *infra* Chapter Four.

[56] *See* David J. Barron, *Fighting Federalism with Federalism: If It's Not Just a Battle Between Federalists and Nationalists, What Is It?*, 74 FORDHAM L. REV. 2081 (2006) (discussing how different Supreme Court justices have implicitly invoked different models of federalism in justifying their analyses).

[57] *See, e.g., NBC Nightly News: FEMA Director Michael Brown Discusses Relief Efforts in Hurricane Zone* (NBC television broadcast Sept. 1, 2005) [hereinafter *NBC Nightly News*] (news anchor publicly criticizing FEMA's response to leadership; quoted *infra* at text accompanying note 152); *infra* notes 68, 125, and accompanying text.

For this reason, our discussion begins with a brief consideration of the stakes of the federalism debate, illustrating the kinds of governmental decision making that take place in the shadow of the philosophy of federalism we embrace. The catastrophic aftermath of Hurricane Katrina in New Orleans provides such a scenario, one that called for governmental response from the most local to the most national level, requiring regulatory decision makers to contend with questions about how federalism principles should dictate their interaction.[58] Surely, the spectacularly failed response owes much to the unprecedented demands of the circumstances (and perhaps to more ordinary problems of incompetence) that have nothing to do with federalism. And yet, the additional overlay of federalism issues helped further derail what might otherwise have been a more effective response, thanks to uncertainty among state and federal actors about their respective roles.

To be clear, no judicial decision by the Rehnquist Court or any other mandated this particular response, which was the combined product of decisions by local, state, and federal political actors interpreting legislative and executive mandates. But the hesitating response stemmed in part from an apparent set of beliefs about state-federal relations that coincides with classical dual federalism,[59] demonstrating how federalism theory operates in governance independently from judicial decisions. Public outrage over the failed response indicated diverging views of state-federal relations.

B. Federalism and Katrina

Of all that was striking during the national tragedy of the 2005 Hurricane Katrina aftermath, a few things stood out: the shameful images of abject poverty within the United States,[60] the inspiring heroism of individuals who rose to the occasion, the staggering force of nature's fury, and the stunning failure of the most powerful nation on earth to respond effectively to the foreseeable effects of a predicted storm.[61] But if we should not have been surprised by the poverty, heroism, or storm surge, the latter failure was hard to fathom—and by many accounts, proceeded from unprecedented confusion among federal, state, and

---

[58] For reflections on the topic by a Tulane law professor from New Orleans, see Stephen M. Griffin, *Stop Federalism Before It Kills Again: Reflections on Hurricane Katrina*, 21 ST. JOHN'S J. LEGAL COMMENT. 527 (2007).

[59] *See supra* Part I Introduction, note 4 and accompanying text (describing nineteenth-century classical dualism).

[60] Equally shameful were the lingering dynamics of racial unfairness suggested by these images of abject poverty. *E.g.*, Representative John Lewis, "*This Is a National Disgrace,*" NEWSWEEK, Sept. 12, 2005, at 52.

[61] *See* U.S. HOUSE OF REPRESENTATIVES, A FAILURE OF INITIATIVE, FINAL REPORT OF THE SELECT BIPARTISAN COMMITTEE TO INVESTIGATE THE PREPARATION FOR AND RESPONSE TO HURRICANE KATRINA 133–34 (2006) [hereinafter HOUSE KATRINA REPORT], http://www.gpoaccess.gov/serialset/creports/pdf/hr109-377/framework.pdf ("The consequences of a major hurricane, defined as a category 4 or greater storm, striking New Orleans were well-known within Louisiana, the emergency management community, and DHS.").

local responders regarding the allocation of their roles and responsibilities and how to proceed in the face of this uncertainty.[62]

I. "OPERATING SYSTEM CRASH" BY THE NATIONAL RESPONSE PLAN

According to eyewitness accounts and primary documents cataloging the relevant events,[63] the response to Katrina was characterized by failures in coordinated command and communications among local, state, federal, and volunteer responders as authorities struggled to determine what the federalism directives in applicable federal laws mandated regarding who should be responsible for which parts of the response. Revised after the 9/11 attacks, the Department of Homeland Security's 2004 National Response Plan (NRP) recognized saving lives and protecting public health as top priorities of incident management.[64] However, the NRP also demarcated that, in emergency situations, states would be responsible for the implementation of police powers traditionally within their purview (such as local law enforcement, fire protection, and delivery of food and shelter), and the federal government would act in a supportive capacity, responding only to specific requests by state authorities for assistance.[65]

Although the Federal Emergency Management Agency's (FEMA) seeming paralysis in the face of the post-Katrina crisis may suggest incompetent leadership,[66] it is also attributable to a federalism-related "operating system crash" under the NRP, which faltered just as software does when unable to parse unanticipated inputs. According to the NRP's federalism directive, federal authorities could not act preemptively lest they tread in the protected realm of state sovereign authority.[67] However, state authorities were unable to make the specific requests for assistance anticipated under the NRP. Local infrastructure was so damaged by the storm that communications were down,[68] and state and local authorities were apparently

---

[62] *E.g.*, Joe Whitley et al., *Homeland Security After Hurricane Katrina: Where Do We Go from Here?*, 20 NAT. RESOURCES & ENV'T 3, 3 (2006) (describing failures of state and federal coordination).

[63] For a compilation of documents collected by congressional investigators, including a conference call transcript between state and federal authorities before Katrina struck New Orleans, see Eric Lipton, *Key Documents Regarding the Government Response to Katrina*, http://www.nytimes.com/ref/national/nationalspecial/10katrina-docs.html (last visited Mar. 15, 2007).

[64] U.S. DEP'T OF HOMELAND SEC., NATIONAL RESPONSE PLAN 6 (2004), http://www.iir.com/global/FusionCenter/NRPbaseplan.pdf [hereinafter NRP]. For an excellent review of the federal statutory framework dictating federal involvement in disaster response, see DANIEL A. FARBER & JIM CHEN, DISASTERS AND THE LAW: KATRINA AND BEYOND 24–56 (2006).

[65] NRP, *supra* note 64, at 8, 15.

[66] HOUSE KATRINA REPORT, *supra* note 61, at 132–35 (finding faulty performance by DHS Secretary Michael Chertoff and other high-ranking federal officials). In particular, former FEMA Director Michael Brown did not fare well in media accounts of his performance. *E.g.*, Paul Krugman, Op-Ed., *The Effectiveness Thing*, N.Y. TIMES, Feb. 6, 2006, at A23 (characterizing Brown's performance as "ludicrous"); Evan Thomas et al., *How Bush Blew It*, NEWSWEEK, Sept. 19, 2005, at 30, 38 (questioning Brown's credentials for appointment as head of FEMA).

[67] *See* NRP, *supra* note 64, at 9.

[68] The *New York Times* described the crippling effect on the National Guard: "The morning Hurricane Katrina thundered ashore, Louisiana National Guard commanders thought they were prepared to save their state.

so overwhelmed themselves that they did not know what to ask for.[69] It may also be that state authorities were simply unprepared or incompetent to play the role that the NRP anticipated of them.[70] But as former FEMA Director Michael Brown would later testify before Congress in defense of his agency's decision making: "The role of the federal government in emergency management is generally that of coordinator and supporter. . . . [a role] fully supported by the basic concept of federalism, recognizing that the sovereign states have primary responsibility for emergency preparedness and response in their jurisdictions."[71] Thus, as Katrina bore down on the Gulf Coast, these departures from the NRP's script left regulatory responders struggling to decipher, in essence, which parts of the response effort were the proper purview of the state and which were that of the federal government.[72]

Global security specialist Joseph Whitley, former general counsel at the U.S. Department of Homeland Security, made the following observations following the response to Katrina:

> During the first few hours and days after landfall, we saw breakdowns in communication within and among every level of government: between federal, state and local officials; and, perhaps most critically, between government and the citizens of the

---

But when 15-foot floodwaters swept into their headquarters, cut their communications and disabled their high-water trucks, they had their hands full just saving themselves. For a crucial 24 hours after landfall on Aug. 29, Guard officers said, they were preoccupied with protecting their nerve center from the waves topping the windows at Jackson Barracks and rescuing soldiers who could not swim. The next morning, they had to evacuate their entire headquarters force of 375 guardsmen by boat and helicopter to the Superdome. It was an inauspicious start to the National Guard's hurricane response, which fell so short that it has set off a national debate about whether in the future the Pentagon should take charge immediately after catastrophes." Scott Shane & Thom Shanker, *When Storm Hit, National Guard Was Deluged Too*, N.Y. TIMES, Sept. 28, 2005, at A1.

[69] WHITE HOUSE, THE FEDERAL RESPONSE TO HURRICANE KATRINA: LESSONS LEARNED 42 (2006), http://www.globalsecurity.org/security/library/report/2006/katrina-lessons_wh_060223_ch4.htm. [hereinafter WHITE HOUSE KATRINA REPORT] According to the White House's own report: "An important limiting factor of the Federal response . . . is that the Federal response is predicated on an incident being handled at the lowest jurisdictional level possible. A base assumption to this approach is that, even in cases where State and local governments are overwhelmed, they would maintain the necessary incident command structure to direct Federal assets to where they are most needed. In the case of Katrina, the local government had been destroyed and the State government was incapacitated, and thus the Federal government had to take on the additional roles of performing incident command and other functions it would normally rely upon the State and local governments to provide." *Id.*

[70] Michael Brown told Congress that his "biggest mistake was not recognizing, by Saturday [August 27, 2005], that Louisiana was dysfunctional." *Hurricane Katrina: The Role of the Federal Emergency Management Agency: Hearing Before the H. Select Bipartisan Comm. to Investigate the Preparation for and Response to Hurricane Katrina*, 109th Cong. 12 (2005) (testimony of Michael Brown) [hereinafter *September 27 Katrina Hearing*].

[71] *Id.* at 3–4.

[72] *See* Eric Lipton et al., *Storm and Crisis: Breakdowns Marked Path from Hurricane to Anarchy*, N.Y. TIMES, Sept. 11, 2005, § 1 [hereinafter Lipton et al., *Breakdowns*] (noting that dozens of interviews with officials showed that "the crisis in New Orleans deepened because of a virtual standoff between hesitant federal officials and besieged authorities in Louisiana"); Eric Lipton et al., *Storm and Crisis: Political Issues Snarled Plans for Troop Aid*, N.Y. TIMES, Sept. 9, 2005, at A1 [hereinafter Lipton et al., *Political Issues*] ("Interviews with officials in Washington and Louisiana show that as the situation grew worse, they were wrangling with questions of federal/state authority."); Thomas et al., *supra* note 66, at 40 (reporting that as of September 2, "[a] debate over 'federalizing' the National Guard had been rattling in Washington for the previous three days").

affected areas. We saw an inability to establish with any certainty what was actually happening and to deploy the appropriate resources to deal with each situation. Many citizens in the Gulf Coast region and elsewhere in the United States may have lost confidence in the government's ability to respond to a catastrophic event.[73]

By Whitley's evaluation, later echoed by a bipartisan congressional report on the Katrina response,[74] coordination failures stemmed partly from inconsistencies between the two primary sources of procedural guidance for state and federal cooperation during emergencies— the Robert T. Stafford Disaster Relief and Emergency Assistance Act (the Stafford Act)[75] and the NRP—and partly from the tensions inherent in catastrophic disaster management, due to the respect given by federal and state actors to the principles of federalism.[76]

In his account of the disaster response, Whitley explained that the historic relationship among the federal, state, and local governments is best described as a "pull" approach, in which the federal government presumes that states and localities can cope independently with a disaster unless they specifically request (or pull) resources from the federal government.[77] This view of federalism in disaster response—that state officials are directly responsible for the health and safety of their citizens and that federal assistance is supplementary only—defers to the dual federalism ideal and has long been the general rule.[78] Yet greater expectations of federal assistance have evolved in circumstances where federal response capacity exceeds what is available locally. Although the pull approach still works in the majority of instances, Whitley and others have argued that disasters of Katrina's magnitude show that federal policy must enable a "push" approach where needed, in which the federal government intervenes to provide assistance even without a direct request by the state or local government.[79] As he wrote, "[t]he 'pull' approach simply cannot work when the state and local governments are, as they were after Katrina, without communication, without the ability to assess the extent of damages or needs, and without even adequate personnel to make requests for everything needed."[80]

---

[73] Whitley et al., *supra* note 62, at 3. Whitley, writing as a member of Alston & Bird LLP's Global Security & Enforcement Practice Team, further observed: "From top to bottom, Katrina exposed some of our vulnerabilities as a nation.... Critically, DHS must immediately address areas of potential ambiguity or perceived confusion—who declares an emergency, who leads the response and recovery efforts, how are resources managed—and we must create an expedited, transparent, and effective contracting and contract oversight process." *Id.*

[74] HOUSE KATRINA REPORT, *supra* note 61, at 136–38 (finding that "[a] proactive federal response, or push system, is not a new concept, but it is rarely utilized," and that it should have been utilized in the Katrina response).

[75] 42 U.S.C. §§ 5121–5205 (2000).

[76] Whitley et al., *supra* note 62, at 4–6; HOUSE KATRINA REPORT, *supra* note 61, at 136–38 (describing the "push" and "pull" alternatives).

[77] Whitley et al., *supra* note 62, at 4.

[78] *Id.*

[79] *Id.*

[80] *Id.*

Although Whitley assigned a fair share of blame to state and local governments for their inadequate response, he held the federal government especially accountable for failing to "promptly trigger[] the necessary federal legal authorities to begin the process of implementing federal assistance in the immediate aftermath of the storms" when the state and local authorities were so incapacitated that they could not possibly have followed the rituals anticipated by the Stafford Act or the NRP.[81] "Under such a catastrophic scenario," Whitley concluded, "the federal government, without being asked, must intervene more promptly in the immediate aftermath of an event."[82] The push approach he advocated would effectively enable the demands of an extreme emergency to trump the classical dual federalism premise of traditional disaster response.

Even before Hurricane Katrina struck the Gulf Coast, NRP drafters were growing sympathetic to this concern, aware that state and local governments might become overwhelmed during a catastrophic event.[83] In fact, when Katrina hit, they had just finalized a "Catastrophic Incident Annex" to the NRP that would enable a push approach for exactly these reasons.[84] However, it was a politically complicated innovation because it contradicted relevant language in the Stafford Act—the congressional statute that authorizes federal disaster assistance to the states, sets forth the primary role of state and local responders, and affirms the supplementary nature of federal support.[85] As the bipartisan House Committee that later investigated the Katrina response reported, "operational procedures for a push are not well exercised, practiced, or utilized" because of the way they depart from the traditional pull model.[86] The Catastrophic Incident Annex was not invoked to trigger a purposeful push response,[87] but the House Committee found that "federal officials in the field began, in an ad hoc fashion, to switch from a pull response to a push system because of the operational demands of the situation."[88]

The investigating House Committee ultimately verified the account Whitley provided after the storm,[89] in which he suggested the need to reconcile the Stafford Act with the new NRP Catastrophic Incident Annex to enable a clearer push approach in catastrophic circumstances.[90] Congress responded in 2009, amending the Act to permit accelerated

---

[81] *Id.* at 7.

[82] *Id.*

[83] *Id.* at 4.

[84] *Id.*; HOUSE KATRINA REPORT, *supra* note 61, at 137.

[85] Whitley et al., *supra* note 62, at 4.

[86] HOUSE KATRINA REPORT, *supra* note 61, at 137 (noting that the NRP Catastrophic Incident Annex has never been exercised, that federal personnel are inexperienced and uncomfortable instituting a proactive response, and that "if the Homeland Security Secretary does not invoke the [index], federal personnel have no clear instruction to switch from a reactive approach to a proactive approach").

[87] *Id.*

[88] *Id.* at 138.

[89] *Id.* at 136–38.

[90] Whitley et al., *supra* note 62, at 4. Reflecting similar anxiety, in the immediate aftermath of Katrina, Congress enabled the U.S. president to deploy the military in response to natural disasters and other major domestic emergencies without consent of the states involved. John Warner National Defense Authorization Act for Fiscal Year 2007, Pub. L. No. 109–364, § 1076, 120 Stat. 2083 (2006) [hereinafter Warner Act]. However, the law was repealed the very next year. National Defense Authorization Act for Fiscal Year 2008, Pub. L. No. 110–181, § 1068, 122 Stat. 3 (2008).

federal assistance without state invitation during a declared "major disaster" as needed to save lives, prevent suffering, and mitigate severe damage.[91] Allowing this kind of accelerated, unrequested federal assistance moves toward the push response needed in a catastrophe of Katrina's magnitude. However, and consistent with the traditional pull model, the declaration of a "major disaster" requires state consent—thereby maintaining some of the same contradictory policy signals that confused responders during Katrina.[92]

In addition, various government bodies reported on flaws revealed in the NRP in the wake of the Katrina response,[93] and Congress mandated that the plan be revisited in the Post-Katrina Emergency Management Reform Act of 2006.[94] Acknowledging that the NRP was less a plan than a "framework for coordinated national incident management,"[95] the Department of Homeland Security revised it in 2008, streamlining the document and renaming it the National Response Framework (NRF).[96] The NRF maintains the same basic structure as the NRP, but incorporates post-Katrina lessons and suggestions.[97] It clarifies the principles underlying national emergency response and incorporates the Catastrophic Incident Annex, which identifies conditions enabling proactive federal response.[98] It sets forth familiar roles for responding entities, but includes new partner guidelines that better describe how local, tribal, state, federal, and private-sector responders may contribute, and removes the requirement that an "incident of national significance" must be declared before federal involvement.[99] Nevertheless, a GAO report criticized the NRF drafting process for failing to incorporate input from nonfederal stakeholders to the extent intended by the Post-Katrina Act,[100] while others castigated it for failing to restore

---

[91]   42 U.S.C. §5170(a)(5).

[92]   See FARBER & CHEN, supra note 64, at 33 (noting the requirement of state consent).

[93]   These included reports from the bipartisan House Committee to Investigate the Preparation for and Response to Hurricane Katrina, the Senate Homeland Security and Governmental Affairs Committee, the White House Homeland Security Council, the Department of Homeland Security Inspector General, and FEMA itself. U.S. GOVERNMENT ACCOUNTABILITY OFFICE, NATIONAL RESPONSE FRAMEWORK: FEMA NEEDS POLICIES AND PROCEDURES TO BETTER INTEGRATE NON-FEDERAL STAKEHOLDERS IN THE REVISION PROCESS 7 (2008), http://www.gao.gov/new.items/do8768.pdf [hereinafter GAO REPORT ON FEMA & STAKEHOLDER INPUT].

[94]   Pub. L. No. 109–295 §509(b)(1), 120 Stat. 1355, 1405 (2006).

[95]   U.S. Dep't of Homeland Security, National Response Framework: Frequently Asked Questions, http://www.fema.gov/pdf/emergency/nrf/NRF_FAQ.pdf (last visited Sept. 27, 2010) [hereinafter NRF FAQ].

[96]   U.S. DEP'T OF HOMELAND SECURITY, NATIONAL RESPONSE FRAMEWORK (2008), http://www.fema.gov/pdf/emergency/nrf/nrf-core.pdf [hereinafter NATIONAL RESPONSE FRAMEWORK].

[97]   NRF FAQ, supra note 95.

[98]   Id. at 1; FEMA, CATASTROPHIC INCIDENT ANNEX TO NRP (2008), http://www.fema.gov/pdf/emergency/nrf/nrf_CatastrophicIncidentAnnex.pdf.

[99]   NATIONAL RESPONSE FRAMEWORK, supra note 96, at 4, 8. See also Suburban Energy Management Project, What Is the New National Response Framework?, Oct. 21, 2007, http://www.semp.us/publications/biot_reader.php?BiotID=472 (discussing removal of the declaration requirement).

[100]   GAO REPORT ON FEMA & STAKEHOLDER INPUT, supra note 93, at 24.

centralized response leadership in FEMA.[101] Disaster law continues to grapple with the daunting federalism issues raised during catastrophes of this magnitude.[102]

Although Whitley's blow-by-blow account of the post-Katrina failures is chilling, it also praises the great acts of generosity and self-sacrifice by those involved in the relief effort, commending members of the U.S. Coast Guard, FEMA, the National Guard, and local first responders and law enforcement officers for their particularly heroic efforts to save lives and offer comfort to victims.[103] His seasoned evaluation of the Katrina response indicates that failures were not the result of callous or careless behavior by individuals but were institutional ones based on confusion over who—in the end—should decide. In particular, failures stemmed from the rules or perceived rules of law that persuaded political actors not to proceed with the "push" response that was clearly necessary out of fear that doing so would, in essence, violate the Constitution.

2. THE PRESIDENT, THE GOVERNOR, THE MAYOR, AND THE STAFFORD ACT

Federalism concerns were not limited to managerial choices in the field but pervaded the response effort up to the highest levels. News reports indicated that "[f]or days, Bush's top advisers argued over legal niceties about who was in charge,"[104] that "[i]nterviews with officials in Washington and Louisiana show that as the situation grew worse, they were wrangling with questions of federal/state authority,"[105] and that "the crisis in New Orleans deepened because of a virtual standoff between hesitant federal officials and besieged authorities in Louisiana."[106] Most snarling the response was uncertainty about the point at which the federal government should stop waiting for state instruction and deploy its superior command capacity through military or federalized National Guard troops,[107] and after that, confusion about who would then be in charge.

Even as it became clear that federal assistance was necessary, uncertainty plagued all three levels of government about who should control the troops to be deployed.[108] Apparently desperate for results, New Orleans Mayor Ray Nagin supported federalizing the response, while Louisiana Governor Kathleen Babineaux Blanco balked, and President

---

[101] Editorial, *Department of Brazen Bureaucracy*, N.Y. TIMES, Sept. 13, 2007, http://www.nytimes.com/2007/09/13/opinion/13thu3.html?_r=1&pagewanted=all&oref=slogin (criticizing the draft Framework for failing to restore the independent powers FEMA possessed under the Clinton administration); Spencer S. Hsu, *Proposed Disaster-Response Plan Faulted: Details Insufficient, Chain of Command Unclear, State and Local Officials Say*, WASH. POST, Sept. 12, 2007, http://www.washingtonpost.com/wp-dyn/content/article/2007/09/11/AR2007091102080.html?nav=rss_politics (reporting on calls to make FEMA a stand-alone, cabinet-level agency).

[102] *See, e.g.*, FARBER & CHEN, *supra* note 64, at 68–78.

[103] Whitley et al., *supra* note 62, at 3.

[104] Evan Thomas et al., *The Lost City*, NEWSWEEK, Sept. 12, 2005, at 41, 48. [hereinafter *The Lost City*]

[105] Lipton et al., *Political Issues, supra* note 72, at A1.

[106] Lipton et al., *Breakdowns, supra* note 72, at § 1 (supporting this contention by "interviews with dozens of officials").

[107] *The Lost City supra* note 104, at 48–49.

[108] *Id.* at 40.

George W. Bush, hesitant to offend the dual federalism principles of the traditional pull model, waited for clarity.[109]

In one infamous exchange four days into the crisis at a strategy session aboard Air Force One, the distraught mayor reportedly slammed the conference table with his hand and asked the president "to cut through this and do what it takes to have a more-controlled command structure. If that means federalizing it, let's do it."[110] Mayor Nagin recommended the Pentagon's "on-scene commander," Lieutenant General Russel Honoré, to lead the flailing relief effort on behalf of the federal government.[111] According to another meeting participant, President Bush turned to Governor Blanco and asked, "well, what do you think of that, Governor?"[112] But Governor Blanco declined to discuss the matter except in a private meeting with the president, which apparently followed the strategy session.[113] However, there was still no agreement over one week later,[114] leaving idle the assistance of an estimated hundred thousand National Guard troops accessible on short notice in neighboring states.[115] News accounts suggest that Governor Blanco did ask the president for forty thousand federal troops, but did not agree to surrender oversight of the relief effort to the federal government.[116]

Had Governor Blanco surrendered her claim to control over the relief effort, President Bush would have been able to reconcile the urgency of providing needed federal assistance with the federalism principles that he apparently believed foreclosed such authorization in the interim.[117] Nevertheless, contemporaneous news accounts indicate that the Justice

---

[109] *Id.* The troops of each state's National Guard report to their governor unless they are "federalized" by presidential order in accordance with the terms of the Stafford Act. 42 U.S.C. §§ 5191–5192 (2000). At a minimum, the president may federalize emergency response at the request of a state's governor.

[110] Thomas et al., *supra* note 66, at 40.

[111] *Id.* Nagin later detailed his own experience of these negotiations in a self-published book. C. RAY NAGIN, KATRINA'S SECRETS: STORMS AFTER THE STORM (VOL. I) (2011).

[112] Thomas et al., *supra* note 66, at 40.

[113] *Id.*

[114] *Id.*

[115] John M. Broder, *Guard Units' New Mission: From Combat to Flood Duty*, N.Y. TIMES, Aug. 30, 2005, at A13.

[116] *See* Karen Tumulty et al., *4 Places Where the System Broke Down: The Governor*, TIME, Sept. 19, 2005, at 34, § 2. *Time* reported: "Further tangling the post-Katrina disaster effort was a struggle for power. On the Friday after the hurricane, as the Governor met with Bush aboard Air Force One on the tarmac of the New Orleans airport, the President broached a sensitive question: Would Blanco relinquish control of local law enforcement and the 13,268 National Guard troops from 29 states that fall under her command?... [S]he thought the request had a political motive. It would allow Washington to come in and claim credit for a relief operation that was finally beginning to show progress. . . . Blanco asked for 24 hours to consider it, but as she was meeting at midnight that Friday night with advisers, [Chief of Staff Andrew] Card called and told her to look for a fax. It was a letter and memorandum of understanding under which she would turn over control of her troops. Blanco refused to sign it." *Id.*; *see also Katrina Aftermath, Louisiana: Don't Want You On My Dance Card*, AMERICAN POLITICAL NETWORK, THE HOTLINE, Sept. 8, 2005, at 7 (discussing the governor's rejection of federal control of troops in Louisiana).

[117] It remains unclear why Governor Blanco did not, given that the state resources at her disposal had proved insufficient to manage the relief effort independently. Viewed most generously, it may be that she was reluctant to turn control over to a federal government that had so far shown nothing but incompetence in its own

Department's Office of Legal Counsel researched the matter and "concluded that the federal government had authority to move in even over the objection of local officials."[118] Many commentators—including some close to the Bush administration, such as former Deputy Assistant Attorney General John Yoo—argued vigorously that the president did not need the governor's consent to federalize the response in light of available jurisdictional hooks in the Stafford Act, including state incapacity and federal obligation.[119]

In addition to the president's authority to unilaterally federalize a state's National Guard in time of insurrection or war,[120] the Act authorizes the president to coordinate *all* disaster relief, including the use of federal and state assets, in a time of crisis whenever "primary responsibility for response rests with the United States because the emergency involves a subject area for which, under the Constitution or laws of the United States, the United States exercises exclusive or preeminent responsibility and authority."[121] But to be fair, what exactly does that mean? What counts as "a subject area for which, under the Constitution or laws of the United States, the United States exercises exclusive or *preeminent responsibility and authority*"?[122]

No court has interpreted this provision of the Stafford Act, because it has never arisen in a justiciable controversy.[123] But it goes to the heart of the federalism quandary: what does the

---

handling of the disaster. Viewed less generously, her decision to refuse federal aid in the face of state incapacity tyrannically exacerbated the suffering of her own citizens by contributing to the delay. If she refused to relinquish control on federalism grounds while being unable to provide the needed resources independently, then her view of federalism warrants just as much criticism as that of the federal government. *See supra* note 70 and accompanying text (discussing Michael Brown's testimony on the role of federalism considerations during the response effort).

[118] Michael Greenberger, *Yes, Virginia: The President Can Deploy Federal Troops to Prevent the Loss of a Major American City from a Devastating Natural Catastrophe*, 26 Miss. C.L. Rev. 107, 115 (2006) (internal quotation marks omitted).

[119] John Yoo, Editorial, *Trigger Power*, L.A. Times, Oct. 2, 2005, at M5; *see also* Greenberger, *supra* note 118, at 108 (arguing that the president had clear authority to intervene); Candidus Dougherty, *While the Government Fiddled Around, The Big Easy Drowned: How the Posse Comitatus Act Became the Government's Alibi for the Hurricane Katrina Disaster*, 29 N. Ill. U.L. Rev. 117 (2008) (arguing that the Posse Comitatus Act did not bar the deployment of federal troops because it does not prohibit the military from providing humanitarian aid).

[120] Insurrection Act, 10 U.S.C. §§ 331–335 (2000).

[121] 42 U.S.C. § 5191(b) (2000). Unlike 42 U.S.C. § 5170, this section does not require the consent of a given state's governor, though it does require as much consultation with the governor as is practicable. The Stafford Act leaves the determination of when the United States exercises preeminent responsibility or authority up for interpretation, though such commentators as John Yoo have suggested that the particular circumstances after Katrina would have qualified as a national emergency warranting unilateral presidential action. Yoo, *supra* note 119, at M5.

[122] 42 U.S.C. § 5191(b) (emphasis added). The BP oil spill off the Louisiana Coast during the summer of 2010 presents a compelling example of a crisis that probably meets the definition without controversy, given the Oil Pollution Act's requirement that the president direct the response to a spill of that magnitude. Pub. L. 101–380, 104 Stat. 484 (1990). But absent such clear statutory jurisdiction, it is hard to know where the margins of that preeminent responsibility lie.

[123] Immediately after Katrina, Congress affirmed that the president *could* unilaterally deploy federal troops, including National Guard troops in federal service, to respond to a major domestic emergency such as a

Constitution tell us about when the United States exercises "preeminent responsibility and authority"? Although Yoo was convinced that the text authorizes at least some measure of federal disaster response without gubernatorial request, the question is unsettled. Yet this uncertainty makes President Bush's decision *not* to invoke his potential authority at that time—especially in the face of such hideous suffering and news-cycle pressure to act[124]—all the more significant.

Indeed, President Bush's reluctance to respond more proactively was not well received by the public, prompting his subsequent request that Congress study proposals for guidance on federal initiative in future scenarios.[125] However, most significant about the president's decision is *why* he declined to exercise the potential Stafford Act authority in the first place, given the overwhelming political pressure to do so and his confidence asserting untested federal executive authority in other realms.[126] One patent explanation for the president's hesitancy to explore all avenues of potential authority during the most devastating natural disaster in U.S. history—and the one eventually offered to Congress by the director he appointed to FEMA—is the pure intellectual gravity of the classical dual federalism model.[127] Federalizing the Louisiana National Guard and subjecting state and city police to federal command would have blurred the lines of authority that model so earnestly endeavors to preserve.

The best alternative explanation—and one equally troubling—is that the White House relied on New Federalism rhetoric for political cover while avoiding involvement with the unfolding mess. By this hypothesis, administration officials invoked the rhetoric of vertical checks and balances to account for federal restraint, even if it was not the real reason for failing to intervene more effectively in the crisis. Either way suggests a serious problem. That dual federalism theory could either stall effective governance at such a key moment or provide reliable cover to such a monumental abdication casts doubt on the merits of the model.

---

natural disaster—but the new law did not provide additional bases of authority to federalize a state's National Guard in the first place, leaving the Stafford Act issue unresolved. *See* Warner Act, Pub. L. No. 109–364, § 1076, 120 Stat. 2083, 2404 (2006) (briefly codified at 10 U.S.C. § 333). Nevertheless, that law was repealed the very next year, returning us to the Katrina baseline of legal guidance. National Defense Authorization Act for Fiscal Year 2008, Pub. L. No. 110–181, § 1068, 122 Stat. 3, 325. For more on the issue, see Greenberger, *supra* note 118, at 107–08.

[124] *E.g., NBC Nightly News*; *supra* note 57 (quoting a news anchor demanding better response from FEMA). Mayor Nagin later complained that the President eventually asserted this authority anyway. *See* NAGIN, *supra* note 111.

[125] *See* Shane & Shanker, *supra* note 68, at A1.

[126] President Bush is often noted (both with praise and criticism) for expanding federal executive authority beyond that exercised by any previous administration. *See, e.g.,* Jeffrey Rosen, *Bush's Leviathan State: Power of One*, THE NEW REPUBLIC, July 24, 2006, at 8 (noting that a "defining principle[] of the Bush administration has been a belief in unfettered executive power," and that the conservative ideology devoted to limited government "has been transformed into the largest expansion of executive power since FDR"); Press Release, Senator Patrick Leahy, *Statement on Presidential Signing Statements* (July 25, 2006), http://leahy.senate.gov/press/200607/072506a.html (criticizing Congress for enabling "the questionable actions of this Administration" in expanding federal power "regardless of the consequences to our Constitution or civil liberties").

[127] *See infra* note 160 and accompanying text.

Reasonable people may disagree on how best to apportion blame among the amply culpable local, state, and federal authorities for the failed response, subsequently heralded as "a national disgrace."[128] That said, it remains difficult to digest the confirmed reports that after fifteen-foot floodwaters swept through the Jackson Barracks headquarters of the Louisiana National Guard Headquarters—severing communication lines, flooding high-water trucks, and converting the entire nerve center force into 375 more New Orleans refugees in need of a water rescue[129]—White House officials stalled in Washington, debating how the finer principles of federalism dictated the scope of national intervention.[130] In their defense, the debate was at least warranted by a faithful interpretation of the federalism theory advanced by the majority of the sitting Supreme Court. But it does raise the fair question, in light of the results that would flow from that model—is this really the federalism we intend?

3. THE PRICE OF FAILURE

While the president's senior advisers fiddled with federalism, New Orleans drowned. Five years later, the details of the debacle are now painfully well-known to most Americans, but they bear repeating to highlight the scope of the failed response. Over a thousand residents perished in their homes and neighborhoods,[131] and up to thirty-four died in the makeshift mass shelters at the New Orleans Superdome and Morial Convention Center,[132] where some thirty-nine thousand evacuees were encamped without adequate food, water, power, or sanitary facilities for as many as seven days.[133] Two-thirds of the occupants were women, children, or elderly, many of them infirm, and they huddled in darkness and 100-degree temperatures amid the unbearable stench of human waste covering the floors and the ceiling debris fallen from holes torn from the roof by the storm.[134]

Reports of unchecked lawless behavior terrorized citizens and local law enforcement alike, both within the emergency shelters and on the flooded city streets.[135] The near total collapse of landline, satellite, and cell phone communications hindered the ability of local law

---

128 *E.g.*, Lewis, *supra* note 60, at 52.

129 Shane & Shanker, *supra* note 68, at A1.

130 *Supra* note 72 (listing reporting on policy makers' federalism debates).

131 *Katrina's Official Death Toll Tops 1,000*, CNN.COM, Sept. 21, 2005, http://www.cnn.com/2005/US/09/21/ katrina.impact; Louisiana Department of Health and Hospitals, *Reports of Missing and Deceased* (Aug. 2, 2006), http://www.dhh.louisiana.gov/offices/page.asp?ID=192&Detail=5248.

132 Lipton et al., *Breakdowns, supra* note 72, at A1 (quoting official reports of ten deaths at the Superdome and twenty-four at the convention center).

133 *Id.* Food and water supplies stashed at the planned emergency shelter of the Superdome ran out within the first few days after Katrina made landfall. *Id.* After the Superdome had filled far beyond capacity, an additional fifteen thousand refugees were directed to the convention center, where there were no food or water supplies. *Id.; see also* John Riley & Craig Gordon, *Katrina—What Went Wrong*, NEWSDAY, Sept. 3, 2005, at A4 (describing the deplorable conditions in the convention center).

134 Lipton et al., *Breakdowns, supra* note 72, at A1 (citing Chief Lonnie C. Swain, an assistant police superintendent who oversaw ninety police officers on patrol at the Superdome).

135 *See id.* (quoting Captain Jeffrey Winn, head of the convention center's police SWAT team: "The only way I can describe it is as a completely lawless situation.").

enforcement and the Louisiana National Guard to coordinate a response; even available radio channels were so jammed with traffic that they became useless.[136]

The chaotic rescue and evacuation efforts impacted families as well, with the National Center for Missing and Exploited Children indicating that 1,831 children from Louisiana, Alabama, and Mississippi were reported as missing in the aftermath of the storm, and that even weeks later, only 360 of these cases had been resolved.[137] At least a million evacuees took shelter in other cities and states,[138] and by March 2006 the federal government had committed $6.9 billion in shelter and direct financial assistance to Gulf Coast residents affected by the hurricane.[139] Countless thousands of starving and injured companion animals continued to roam the streets or languish trapped within the homes of evacuated owners for weeks following the storm, most perishing before rescue but not before ghastly suffering.[140]

Damage to oil infrastructure was the worst ever experienced by the industry.[141] More than nine million gallons were reported spilled,[142] and gas prices skyrocketed to as high as $6 per gallon in the following weeks.[143] Chemical spills, rotting remains, and flooding resulted in environmental hazards ranging from land-based toxic sludge to poisoned water supplies that will continue to threaten human health and safety into the foreseeable future.[144] Congress allocated approximately $88 billion in federal aid toward relief, recovery, and rebuilding in 2005,[145] and another $26 billion in 2007 for victims of Katrina and the subsequent

---

[136] Shane & Shanker, *supra* note 68, at A1.

[137] Barbara Kantrowitz & Karen Breslau, *Some Are Found, All Are Lost*, NEWSWEEK, Sept. 19, 2005, at 51. Young children were often separated from parents during chaotic boat rescues and bus evacuations. *Id.* at 52.

[138] Refugees fled to forty-nine different states and the District of Columbia. Press Release, White House, Fact Sheet: Gulf Coast Update: Hurricane Relief, Recovery, and Rebuilding Continues (Mar. 8, 2006), http://georgewbush-whitehouse.archives.gov/news/releases/2006/03/20060308-8.html [hereinafter Gulf Coast Fact Sheet]. *See also* Lester R. Brown, *Global Warming Forcing U.S. Coastal Population to Move Inland*, EARTH POL'Y INST., Aug. 16, 2006, http://www.earth-policy.org/Updates/2006/Update57.htm (noting that Katrina forced one million people to move inland from the afflicted coastal cities); Eric Lipton, *Storm and Crisis: Hurricane Evacuees Face Eviction Threats at Both Their Old Homes and New*, N.Y. TIMES, Nov. 4, 2005, at A20 (discussing the influx of refugees to Texas).

[139] Gulf Coast Fact Sheet, *supra* note 138.

[140] *E.g.*, Karlyn Barker & Nia-Malika Henderson, *Plight of Stranded Animals Worsening Daily*, WASH. POST, Sept. 8, 2005, at B4 (estimating that thousands of starving animals abandoned by their owners after Katrina were in peril); Norma Mendoza, *Task Force Members Describe Devastation in New Orleans*, EDWARDSVILLE INTELLIGENCER, Oct. 11, 2005, at 1, 3 ("Another sad sight was the dogs that were everywhere, strays and abandoned pets that rescue workers wouldn't allow people to bring with them. Some died, trapped in the houses where they were left. Others were starving and the officers had nothing to give them.").

[141] *See* Pam Radtke Russell, *Gulf Platform Damage Still Being Assessed*, NEWHOUSE NEWS SERV., Mar. 23, 2006 (on file with author).

[142] Mike Taibbi, *Oil Coats Homes, Water After Katrina*, MSNBC.COM, Nov. 8, 2005, http://www.msnbc.msn.com/id/9972220.

[143] Robert J. Samuelson, *Hitting the Economy*, NEWSWEEK, Sept. 12, 2005, at 54.

[144] *See* Thomas et al., *supra* note 66, at 34–35.

[145] Gulf Coast Fact Sheet, *supra* note 138.

Hurricane Rita.[146] Moneys were earmarked for programs including unemployment assistance,[147] community disaster loans to local governments,[148] housing assistance,[149] and public assistance projects.[150] Separate grants were also awarded, including a $1.6 billion special congressional appropriation to the Department of Education for public and private schools where relocated students enrolled.[151]

Americans watched their televisions in disbelief (and increasingly agitated journalists watched on the scene) as day after day passed before anything resembling an organized disaster response was assembled in the devastated city of New Orleans. Even journalists of ordinarily studied neutrality found themselves challenging official accounts of the relief effort. For example, in an interview with FEMA Director Michael Brown three days into the crisis, NBC Nightly News anchor Brian Williams incredulously demanded to know why federal helicopters circling the area could not be used to deliver food and medical supplies to the encamped evacuees:

> Why can't some of the Chinook helicopters and Black Hawks that we have heard flying over for days and days and days simply lower pallets of water, meals ready to eat, medical supplies, right into downtown New Orleans? "Where is the aid?" It's the question [] people keep asking us on camera![152]

Public outrage brimmed over in the days and weeks following the crisis, exemplified by the observation in one news story that "[t]he descent of the Superdome from haven to a fetid, crime-infested hellhole by the time mass evacuations began Thursday was emblematic of what appeared to many to be a government failure of epic proportions last week, leaving experts and ordinary citizens alike puzzled and infuriated."[153]

To be sure, much of the devastation that Gulf Coast residents suffered from the winds and rain of Katrina cannot be blamed on bad disaster management. Setting aside the degree to

---

[146] Pam Fessler, *Much Long-Term Katrina Recovery Aid Unspent*, Aug. 29, 2007, NPR, http://www.npr.org/templates/story/story.php?storyId=14009346; However, not all appropriated moneys were actually spent, and experts had predicted that $150 billion would be needed for full recovery efforts. Nina J. Easton, *Katrina Aid Falls Short of Promises*, Boston Globe, Nov. 27, 2005, at A1.

[147] FEMA, *Frequently Requested National Statistics Hurricane Katrina–One Year Later* (last modified Aug. 11, 2010) http://www.fema.gov/hazard/hurricane/2005katrina/anniversary_factsheet.shtm [hereinafter *FEMA Katrina Statistics*] (allocating $410 million for disaster unemployment assistance).

[148] FEMA Press Release, *By the Numbers: FEMA Recovery Update in Louisiana* (Mar. 24, 2006), http://www.fema.gov/news/newsrelease.fema?id=24505 (allocating $700 million in loans to local governments in need of assistance).

[149] *FEMA Katrina Statistics*, *supra* note 147 (noting that FEMA provided victims nearly $6 billion for housing and other assistance through the Individuals and Households Assistance Program).

[150] Over $4.8 billion was set aside for debris removal and restoration of roads, bridges, public utilities, etc. *Id.*

[151] *Gulf Coast Fact Sheet*, *supra* note 138.

[152] *See NBC Nightly News*, *supra* note 57. In response, Brown indicated that the federal government had only just become aware that day of the thousands of desperate refugees. *Id.*

[153] Riley & Gordon, *supra* note 133, at A4.

which anthropogenic climate change contributes to the intensity of storms like Katrina,[154] hurricanes are a force of nature that we have long learned to fear. River and wetland management choices along the Mississippi Delta exacerbated the flooding that proved the worst of New Orleans's battles,[155] and Americans are right to ask for better long-term planning from the local, state, and federal authorities responsible for these activities.[156] But it was the bungled humanitarian relief effort—the disorganized response that stranded the sick and injured, separated young children from their parents, and left the most vulnerable members of society struggling to survive amid prolonged *Lord of the Flies* conditions[157]—that triggered public outrage.

Most of this public outrage betrayed a different vision of how state-federal relations should work, one involving less hesitation by the governor to accept federal help and by the president to intervene. Although some critics would later praise federal restraint for principled reasons,[158] the wholesale castigation the federal government earned after Katrina mostly suggested wide public tolerance for a degree of jurisdictional overlap inconsistent with the dual federalism model protected by the National Response Plan and the White House debates. Whether or not its participants realized it, public outcry was largely an open conversation about which federalism model should apply.

4. CODA: WHICH FEDERALISM?

Given the proven ability of the United States to respond quickly and effectively in the face of natural disaster (for example, our immediate and ambitious relief effort in response to

---

[154] *Compare* Stefan Rahmstorf et al., *Hurricanes and Global Warming—Is There a Connection?*, REAL CLIMATE, Sept. 2, 2005, http://www.realclimate.org/index.php?p=181 (suggesting that anthropogenic increases in greenhouse gases have contributed to rising ocean temperatures, tending toward more destructive hurricanes such as Katrina) *with* James K. Glassman, *Katrina and Disgusting Exploitation*, TCS DAILY, Aug. 31, 2005, http://www.tcsdaily.com/article.aspx?id=083105JKG (refuting the nexus between global warming and the severity of Hurricane Katrina).

[155] *See* Erin Ryan, *New Orleans, the Chesapeake, and the Future of Environmental Assessment: Overcoming the Natural Resources Law of Unintended Consequences*, 40 U. RICH. L. REV. 981, 990–97 (2006) (describing the natural resource management choices made along the Mississippi River that made New Orleans particularly vulnerable to Hurricane Katrina's storm surge).

[156] *Cf.* John Schwartz, *Army Builders Accept Blame over Flooding*, N.Y. TIMES, June 2, 2006, at A1 (reporting that an Army Corps of Engineers' study concluded that the design of the New Orleans levees was flawed and incapable of handling a storm the strength of Katrina).

[157] *E.g., The Lost City supra* note 104, at 44–45 (comparing the images of helpless families and children begging for food and water to third-world conditions in Mogadishu or Port-au-Prince).

[158] *Cf.* Robert J. Spratlin, Editorial, *Bash Mayor, Governor for Katrina Response, Not Bush*, BURLINGTON COUNTY TIMES, Sept. 19, 2005, at 6A (arguing that the federal government properly abstained from interfering absent invitation); Ed McClure, Letter to the Editor, *In Times of Catastrophe, Responsibility Starts at Local Level*, ST. PETERSBURG TIMES, Sept. 6, 2005, http://www.sptimes.com/2005/09/06/Opinion/In_times_of_catastrop.shtml (arguing that state and local governments should have been able to handle the crisis); Douglas L. Marriott, *Keep Out Federal Bureaucracy in Katrina Recovery*, USA Today Opinion Blog, http://blogs.usatoday.com/oped/2007/09/keep-out-federa.html (arguing against further federal involvement).

the South Asian tsunami just nine months earlier[159]), what could possibly account for this spectacular failure of governance? In the face of such unimaginable domestic despair, which prompted ordinary Americans from the four corners of the nation to arrive at New Orleans's doorstep with whatever they had to offer, why couldn't the U.S. government properly protect, feed, and evacuate its own?

In his post-storm congressional testimony, then-FEMA director Michael Brown provided a straightforward answer, and in so doing invoked several of the important federalism issues with which we began Part I. In defending his agency's performance on federalism grounds, he explained:

> Princip[les] of federalism should not be lost in a short-term desire to react to a natural disaster of catastrophic proportions, for if that concept is lost, the advantages of having a robust state and local emergency management system will lead not only to waste of taxpayer dollars at the federal level, but will inherently drive decision-making best left to the local and state level, to a centralized federal government, which inherently cannot understand the unique needs of each community across this nation.[160]

Brown's testimony shows how the dual federalism idea can compromise regulatory response in contexts of jurisdictional overlap, whether it is operating at the level of the judiciary, the executive, or popular consciousness. Whether self-serving or sincere, his statement is important for three reasons.

First, he correctly articulates a central problem of federalism: structural constraints are only meaningful if they are followed in difficult times as well as easy times. By his account, allowing the federal government to cross federalism's proverbial line in the sand to satisfy a short-term desire would undermine the very principles of constitutional government. But this brings us to the second important point in Brown's statement, which is his invocation of the fallacy (perpetuated by much of the New Federalism's rhetoric) that the classical dual

---

[159] *See* Bureau of Int'l Info. Programs, U.S. Dep't of State, Going the Distance: The U.S. Tsunami Relief Effort 2005, at 1 (2005), http://usinfo.state.gov/products/pubs/tsunami/tsunami.pdf (reporting that more than fifteen thousand U.S. military personnel were involved in providing relief support in the affected region, that twenty-five ships and ninety-four aircraft were participating in the effort, and that the U.S. military delivered 2.2 million pounds of relief supplies to affected nations); Brigadier General John Allen, Principal Director of Asia and Pacific Affairs, Office of the Secretary of Defense, "Update—U.S. Government Relief Efforts in Asia," Foreign Press Center Briefing, Washington, D.C. (Jan. 3, 2005), http://www.pacom.mil/speeches/sst2005/050103-wh-presstranscript.shtml (explaining that "[w]ithin minutes of our notification of this disaster, we began military planning to assist in the U.S. Governmental response to this crisis... Within hours, U.S. forces began to move to the affected area"). The tsunami relief effort also demonstrated the superior federal capacity for command and coordination that was so devastatingly missing from the Katrina response. *See* Ralph A. Cossa, President of the Pacific Forum Center for Strategic and International Studies, *South Asian Tsunami: U.S. Military Provides "Logistical Backbone" for Relief Operation*, eJournal USA: Foreign Policy Agenda (Nov. 2004), http://usinfo.state.gov/journals/itps/1104/ijpe/cossa.htm (noting that "the most invaluable U.S. contribution focused around another Defense Department unique capability: command, control, communications, and coordination. These attributes, critical in wartime, proved equally critical in ensuring an effective, coordinated response").

[160] *See September 27 Katrina Hearing, supra* note 70, at 3 (statement of Michael Brown).

federalism model is *itself* federalism, as opposed to one vision among alternatives. Although earlier federal intervention might have violated the tenets of the strict dual federalism ideal, it might have been an acceptable move within an alternative conception that anticipates jurisdictional overlap.

This brings us to the third important reference point in Brown's statement—and as it happens, back to the core question raised in this part—namely that of *which federalism*? If there is a legitimate interpretive choice among alternatives, we should choose the model that best enables the kind of governance that serves the values we ascribe to government. In Brown's account, the regulatory impulse "to react to a natural disaster of catastrophic proportions" is little more than a "short-term desire,"[161] a crassly self-satisfying move in the foreground of a much greater drama about the grand diffusion of separately sovereign power. But to what end is power so divided if neither one nor the other level of government can intervene to prevent the most galling episode of domestic human suffering in a generation? Is Michael Brown's the vision of governance that we want? Or does it suggest the value of a different model of federalism, one that can afford meaningful constraints without requiring such sacrifice?

Importantly, Brown's testimony impugns the dual federalism model even if his appeal to its principles were a mere self-serving effort to absolve his own failures. Either the model really does justify Brown's halting regulatory approach, or it is dangerously vulnerable to abuse by regulators who seek shelter for abdication in its fundamentalist premise of strict separation. If dual federalism really does require federal emergency management to hold back under such circumstances, then this is good evidence that it is a bad model of federalism. Alternatively, a model that gives political cover to incompetent administration is also deeply flawed. The overwhelming public sentiment for a different kind of response—for better coordination up front and faster federal initiative to protect public safety—was a call for a different model of state-federal relations, or a different model of federalism.

In the end, it is important to remember that clear errors were made by federal, state, and local authorities that had nothing to do with federalism. For example, New Orleans failed to consider the plight of many citizens without the means or strength to evacuate themselves,[162] and the Army Corps of Engineers later acknowledged that levees protecting the city had not been designed to withstand the combination of known soil subsidence patterns[163] and projected levee-top overflow during a storm of Katrina's magnitude.[164] Indeed, it is possible

---

[161] *Id.*

[162] Joe Whitley observes that "[w]hile more than 1.2 million people were successfully evacuated from coastal areas before Katrina hit, tens of thousands of people were not, including citizens from two of Louisiana's most populous localities, New Orleans and Jefferson Parishes. Despite the eventual declaration of a mandatory evacuation on Sunday before landfall, New Orleans officials were unable to provide adequate transportation to evacuate the population." Whitley et al., *supra* note 62, at 6.

[163] *See* Ryan, *supra* note 155, at 990–97 (noting how channelization of the Mississippi River has led to soil subsidence in the Delta and explaining its implications for New Orleans during Hurricane Katrina).

[164] Schwartz, *supra* note 156, at A1. The Corps' 6,113-page report was remarkably candid about the failed levee system, observing that "[t]he region's network of levees, floodwalls, pumps and gates lacked any built-in resilience that would have allowed the system to remain standing and provide protection even if water flowed over the tops of levees and floodwalls. . . . Flaws in the levee design that allowed breaches in the city's drainage

to imagine a successful response even within the dual federalism framework if state and federal officials had only reached quicker consensus (although perfect worlds make for poor stress tests).

Nevertheless, we should be troubled by accounts from Brown and others who suggest that the most devastating post-storm errors—those crystallized in the delayed and uncoordinated relief effort—flowed from the well-intended but ill-fated vehemence with which political actors hewed to a principled reading of the constitutional balance of state and federal power. While this may have surprised the average outraged American at the time, it would have come as less of a surprise to those following transitions in federalism theory in the political sphere and on the Supreme Court in preceding years. Before we review the relevant jurisprudence more fully in Chapter Four, however, let us explore where all models of federalism begin: as good-faith attempts to grapple with the tug of war within.

---

canals were not foreseen, and those floodwalls failed even though the storm waters did not rise above the level that the walls were designed to hold." *Id.*

2

FEDERALISM AND THE TUG OF WAR WITHIN

THIS CHAPTER TAKES on the critical question of why the Constitution establishes a federal system at all. After considering the political origins of federalism, the fraught relationship between structural federalism and first-order policy concerns, and the distinction between federalism and decentralization, it explores the individual principles of good government on which federalism is premised: checks and balances, participatory and accountable government, local autonomy, and problem-solving synergy.

A. Why Federalism?

In choosing the federalism we intend and building a workable theoretical model, we must start by understanding the reasons for creating a federal system. What are the underlying values promoted by federalism that make us willing to struggle with these problems in the first place?

With unsurprising uniformity, federal systems have historically arisen through the union of separately functioning polities or distinctive cultural groups, such as the original thirteen American colonies, the provinces of Canada, or the nation-states of the European Union.[1] A federal system makes intuitive sense in such cases, drawing efficiently on the competencies

---

[1] *See* Sanford Levinson, *Is Secession the Achilles Heel of "Strong" Federalism?*, *in* PATTERNS OF REGIONALISM AND FEDERALISM, *supra* Introduction, note 75, at 207, 211 (comparing the transformation of sovereign nation-states into the European Union to the original thirteen American colonies); Allen M. Linden, *Flexible*

of preexisting authorities while protecting the interests of political subunits, which often organize around distinct language, ethnic, religious, and/or cultural groups.

Enthusiasm for federalism among the early Americans is understandable on these grounds alone, given eighteenth-century uncertainties about whether the new union they would form would really be any "more perfect" than the status quo. But two centuries of success later, the value of American federalism must rest on different grounds from those that support other systems continuing to negotiate more divided subpolities.[2] Red and blue state politics notwithstanding, the modern United States is characterized by remarkable homogeneity.[3] With some exceptions, we share a dominant language and a common heritage of immigrant origins, and most of the rich diversity that exists within the nation is relatively similarly dispersed within the fifty states.[4] As such, our continued commitment to structurally distinct local and national authority must stem from a conviction that it confers architectural advantages beyond the historical accident of our aggregative origins. Even at that time, many of these values were championed by the early federalism theorists among the Framers, most famously chronicled in the exchanges among James Madison, Alexander Hamilton, and John Jay in the Federalist Papers.[5] In the United States, then, federalism's diffusion of power was never crafted for its own sake; it has always existed to promote more substantive Constitutional goals.[6]

Still, we are well advised not to take our assumptions about the importance Americans place on constitutional federalism too far. As a structural feature of government, federalism is inherently content-neutral with regard to specific political issues.[7] As a result, some suggest that for most Americans, federalism is a secondary political preference that has always received less consideration than first-order substantive issues such as civil rights, gun control, abortion, or the environment.[8] For example, some advocate judicial federalism constraints based on evidence that political constraints may fail, not because voters lack the knowledge or impetus to check the behavior of their representatives, but because "[t]he problem is more

---

Federalism: The Canadian Way, in PATTERNS OF REGIONALISM AND FEDERALISM, *supra* Introduction, note 75, at 17, 21–22.

[2] *Cf.* Rubin & Feeley, *supra* Introduction, note 70 at 908–14 (arguing that the colonial benefits of American federalism no longer apply).

[3] *E.g.,* SCHAPIRO, *supra* Introduction, note 11, at 16–30 (discussing nationalizing trends in politics and culture).

[4] *Id.; see also* Rubin & Feeley, *supra* Introduction, note 70 at 922–23, 944–49 (arguing that the "nation-wide dispersion of ethnic and cultural identities, paralleling the dispersion of economic or ideological identities" indicates that the truly meaningful political community within the United States *is* the United States); John O. McGinnis & Ilya Somin, *Federalism vs. States' Rights: A Defense of Judicial Review in a Federal System,* 99 Nw. U.L. REV. 89, 96 (2004) (explaining why citizens increasingly "lack the attachments to their states that may have motivated them to pay attention to issues of federal structure in the past").

[5] *See, e.g.,* THE FEDERALIST PAPERS, NO. 46, at 294–300 (James Madison) (Clinton Rossiter ed., 1961) [hereinafter, THE FEDERALIST].

[6] *E.g.,* Bond v. United States, No. 09-1227, 564 U.S. __, *9–10 (slip opinion) (2011), 2011 Westlaw 2369334 (U.S.).

[7] *See* Paul D. Moreno, *"So Long as Our System Shall Exist": Myth, History, and the New Federalism,* 14 WM. & MARY BILL RTS. J. 711, 721 (2005); *see also* Lynn A. Baker, *Should Liberals Fear Federalism?,* 70 U. CIN. L. REV. 433, 454 (2002).

[8] Neal Devins, *The Judicial Safeguards of Federalism,* 99 Nw. U.L. REV. 131, 133 (2004).

pervasive: No one really cares about federalism."[9] Tracing opportunistic invocation of federalism ideals from the Louisiana Purchase to the modern day, Professor Neal Devins argues that:

> [T]he willingness of lawmakers and interest groups to manipulate federalism in order to secure preferred substantive policies is the rule. Indeed, the historical record is so overwhelming that it is hard to believe that a majority of informed voters would suspend their personal policy preferences in order to reap the benefits of structural federalism.
>
> The propensity of the American people to pay more attention to desired results than to which level of government is acting on their behalf dates back to the Framers. . . Rather than adhere to a consistent position on federalism, Americans have always let their views on first order policy priorities dictate their views on federalism.[10]

Among the more famous examples of such federalism opportunism is the role reversal between pro-slavery and abolitionist interests before and after the Civil War.[11] Beforehand, abolitionists decried fugitive slave laws as constitutionally inappropriate federal intrusions into the proper realm of state law (while pro-slavery interests approved of this exercise of national authority).[12] But their views on federalism reversed after the war, when abolitionists favored the use of national law and policy to forbid slaveholding, and pro-slavery interests championed their cause under the banner of states' rights.[13]

Professors Edward Rubin and Malcolm Feeley make a similar argument in support of their contrary proposition that judicial constraints are not necessary.[14] Despite their opposing view on judicial federalism enforcement (stemming from skepticism that federalism offers much value in the modern United States at all),[15] their analysis of Americans' opportunistic use of federalism parallels Devins's:

> During the Kennedy-Johnson era and the heyday of the Warren Court, states' rights became a rallying cry of those who opposed desegregation, social welfare, and controls on law enforcement agents. During the years of the Reagan and Bush administrations and the Rehnquist Court, proponents of abortion, gay rights, and abolition of the

---

[9] *Id.* at 131, 137. If it were really true that no one cared about federalism, of course, we might also ask why judicially enforceable constraints are preferable to political safeguards that effectuate the people's will.

[10] *Id.* at 134.

[11] *Id.* at 134–35; *see also* Moreno, *supra* note 7, at 725–27 (noting, with irony, that "during the 1850s, many southerners became Marshallian judicial nationalists, while many northerners became Jeffersonian-Jacksonian states-rights advocates.").

[12] Devins, *supra* note 8, at 134.

[13] *Id.* at 134–35.

[14] *See* Rubin & Feeley, *supra* Introduction, note 70, at 910–14. For the iconic argument that federalism values are better protected by the political process than by judicial intervention, *see* Wechsler, *supra* Introduction, note 6.

[15] *See* Rubin & Feeley, *supra* Introduction, note 70, at 907.

death penalty became enamored of federalism for equivalent reasons. This is perfectly good political strategy, but it is hardly a convincing argument for federalism. In fact, it demonstrates the weakness of federalism as a normative principle; because federalism's force is symbolic and not truly normative, it quickly becomes a proxy for more compelling substantive views that it happens to support.[16]

Professors Rubin and Feeley level an additional challenge to the notion that Americans care deeply about federalism, asserting that even when Americans do tout the benefits of federalism, they are really praising something other than federalism. Instead, they are celebrating *decentralization*, a managerial concept that refers to the instrumental "delegation of centralized authority to subordinate units of either a geographic or a functional character" without reference to any kind of dual sovereignty.[17] In other words, American federalism proponents often point to advantages yielded by the protection of local autonomy and diversity, but these localism values are more appropriately attributed to an architectural choice of decentralized authority that may or may not have any relationship to federalism. A government can arguably preserve the benefits of decentralized localism without a federal system of dual sovereignty,[18] and a system of dual sovereignty will not necessarily protect genuine local autonomy.[19] The argument for a federal system over a unitary system must contend with this critical point, and a model of federalism that will live up to its billing must take account of the fact that simply protecting an exclusive realm of state authority does nothing for the values associated with local autonomy so often claimed in support of federalism.

Accordingly, some have argued that the Rehnquist Court's embrace of dual federalism either fails to meaningfully protect the values it claims to champion[20] or reflects an opportunistic political ploy to achieve substantive objectives under the unrelated guise of preserving federalism.[21] The criticism became more poignant when, as discussed in Chapter Four, the same Court that so often invalidated federal authority in the name of states' rights simultaneously preempted several high-profile state laws that appeared to offend competing first-order policy preferences.

Gonzalez v. Raich remains the most famous example of this (though it split the usual New Federalism coalition), holding that Congress's Commerce Clause authority includes the

---

[16] *Id.* at 935.

[17] *Id.* at 910.

[18] *Id.* at 914–26 (arguing that the principal justifications for federalism are really for decentralization, cloaked in the "flag-waving-in-the-breeze rhetoric that characterizes the entire subject"). As Rubin and Feeley explain, "[o]f the standard arguments for federalism, four are really arguments that specific national policies are best implemented by decentralized decision-making; these are public participation, effectuating citizen choice through competition among jurisdictions, achieving economic efficiency through competition among jurisdictions, and encouraging experimentation." *Id.* at 914–15.

[19] *See* David J. Barron, *A Localist Critique of the New Federalism*, 51 DUKE L.J. 377, 378–79 (2001) (arguing that limiting central power may not preserve local autonomy because the two spheres are intertwined).

[20] *See, e.g.*, CHEMERINSKY, *supra* Introduction, note 12, at 98.

[21] *Cf.* Neal Devins, *The Majoritarian Rehnquist Court?*, 67 LAW & CONTEMP. PROBS. 63, 63–65 (2004); Albert C. Lin, *Erosive Interpretation of Environmental Law in the Supreme Court's 2003–04 Term*, 42 HOUS. L. REV. 565, 626 (2005).

power to prosecute purely local cultivation of marijuana for medical use, despite a statewide referendum legalizing intrastate use and production of marijuana for approved medical purposes.[22] Dissenting in *Lorillard Tobacco Co. v. Reilly*, Justice Stevens suggested that the New Federalism cases harbor a partisan antiregulatory agenda, comparing (1) *Lorillard Tobacco*'s holding that the Federal Cigarette Labeling and Advertising Act preempted local efforts to protect children by banning billboard cigarette advertising near schools with (2) the same court's holding in *United States v. Lopez* that the federal government lacked authority to protect children by banning the sale of guns near schools.[23]

Despite these criticisms, there may be more principled explanations for these departures than that of the gored ox. I take the words of the Rehnquist Court majority and the arguments of proponents seriously and at face value, in order to join the conversation they have so powerfully engaged since the New Federalism revival. Indeed, that conversation demonstrates that the most commonly cited rationales for American federalism have remained remarkably consistent since publication of the Federalist Papers (notwithstanding provocative challenges by such theorists as Rubin and Feeley).[24]

Then and now, favorable (and content-neutral) answers to the question "*why federalism?*" tend to reference three sets of structural good governance values, stated in various permutations: (1) the maintenance of checks and balances that safeguard individuals against tyranny; (2) the promotion of accountable and participatory democratic government; and (3) the socially valuable benefits associated with local autonomy, especially diversity, innovation, and interjurisdictional competition.[25] The following discussion reviews these and surfaces an additional, less obvious value that is neither stronger nor weaker than the others: (4) the pragmatic problem-solving premise of federalism, by which the federal system enables the development and exchange of unique regulatory capacity to cope with interjurisdictional problems.[26] Although none of these values is mentioned by name in the Constitution, they

---

[22] 545 U.S. 1, 32–33 (2005); *see also id.* at 34–35 (Scalia, J., concurring in the judgment and emphasizing the Necessary and Proper Clause in his analysis). Justice Kennedy joined the majority opinion, and Justice Scalia concurred separately, while Chief Justice Rehnquist and Justices O'Connor and Thomas dissented. *Id.* at 3.

[23] 533 U.S. 525, 590, 598 & n.8 (2001) (Stevens, J., concurring in part and dissenting in part).

[24] *See supra* notes 14–19 and accompanying text. For a thoughtful rebuttal of their claims, see Jackson, *supra* Part I Introduction, note 21, at 2217–20.

[25] *See, e.g.,* Gregory v. Ashcroft, 501 U.S. 452, 458 (1991) (explaining that the federalist structure assures sensitivity to diverse societal needs, increases democratic involvement, allows for governmental experimentation, and makes government responsive by fostering competition); Deborah Jones Merritt, *The Guarantee Clause and State Autonomy: Federalism for a Third Century*, 88 COLUM. L. REV. 1, 3–10 (1988) (identifying four positive features of federalism: (1) limitation on power of federal government, (2) citizen participation in the political process, (3) political and cultural diversity, and (4) state experimentation); *see also* Richard W. Garnett, *The New Federalism, the Spending Power, and Federal Criminal Law*, 89 CORNELL L. REV. 1, 22 (2003) (adding that federalism also protects the contribution of nongovernment "associations and mediating institutions" to the preservation of political liberty against centralized authority); Jackson, *supra* Part I Introduction, note 21, at 2214 (adding to the federalism list: "enhancing personal and group liberty or empowerment, by providing multiple layers of government to which citizens may appeal").

[26] For excellent dynamic federalism accounts of the full array of these values, see CHEMERINSKY, *supra* Introduction, note 12, at 98–144, and SCHAPIRO, *supra* Introduction, note 11, at 98–108.

are variously touted throughout the federalism discourse by scholars, policy makers, and judges.

The challenge for federalism is that good governance cannot always vindicate all of these values simultaneously, because they operate in tension with one another. The previous literature has done little to account for this tension, let alone provide guidance for those wrestling with it in practice. But as discussion of Justice Souter's speech foreshadowed, the Constitution forces choices between "good things that compete with each other and can never all be realized, all together, all at once."[27] Ultimately, a viable model of federalism must deliver on the advantages claimed by its proponents, but alternative models of federalism deliver on these values in differing ratios. Therefore, the choice among models of federalism is really one about the best balance of protection afforded these underlying values when tensions arise—which values will cede to which others under what circumstances. Dual federalism offers one such choice, cooperative federalism another, and Parts III and IV introduce yet another. But in honor of the Supreme Court's most recent interpretive struggles with the task, the discussion below focuses on how these values find expression within the New Federalism cases and the cooperative federalism baseline from which they depart.

B. Checks on Sovereign Authority to Safeguard Individuals

A primary value associated with American federalism—and the one least vulnerable to confusion with the values of nonfederal decentralization—is its architectural promise of checks and balances.[28] Indeed, the erection of checks and balances is a core feature of American constitutional design in general, protecting individual rights against government overreach not only through the state-federal competition of vertical federalism, but also in the horizontal division of labor among the three branches of government. In the vertical federalism context, the division of authority between national and local government is designed to curb ambition on both sides of the divide, such that neither accumulates power beyond the counterbalancing forces of the other. As Alexander Hamilton described in the Federalist Papers, this serves as a bulwark against tyranny, safeguarding individual liberties against assault by an unchecked, overly powerful sovereign:

> [In the constitutional system] the people, without exaggeration, may be said to be entirely the masters of their own fate. Power being almost always the rival of power, the general government will at all times stand ready to check the usurpations of the state governments, and these will have the same disposition towards the general government. The people, by throwing themselves into either scale, will infallibly make

---

[27] *Souter Speech, supra* Chapter One, note 34.

[28] *E.g.,* Ilya Somin, *Closing the Pandora's Box of Federalism: The Case for Judicial Restriction of Federal Subsidies to State Governments,* 90 GEO. L.J. 461, 471 (2002) (discussing "the role of the states as a bulwark against federal tyranny"); Michael W. McConnell, *Federalism: Evaluating the Founders' Design,* 54 U. CHI. L. REV. 1484, 1504 (1987) (noting that "[t]he diffusion of power, in and of itself, is protective of liberty"); Andrzej Rapaczynski, *From Sovereignty to Process: The Jurisprudence of Federalism after Garcia,* 1985 SUP. CT. REV. 341, 380 (observing this as the most frequently cited rationale for federalism).

it preponderate. If their rights are invaded by either, they can make use of the other as the instrument of redress.[29]

Emphasizing the goals of liberal political theory, Hamilton assured his readers that the balance of power in the new federal system would successfully check any attempt by either side "to establish a tyranny."[30] Indeed, anxiety among the Framers about unchecked governmental authority was also evident in their adoption of such structural features as the bicameral legislature,[31] the shared executive and legislative role in making treaties and appointing federal judges,[32] and provisions protecting individuals directly from the excesses of state power (e.g., the protection of habeas corpus, the proscription of ex post facto laws, and the additional protections for individuals defined in the Bill of Rights).[33]

Heeding the adage that "absolute power corrupts absolutely," the check-and-balance value furthers a vision of good government in which sovereign authority is never stored all in one reservoir, and no governmental actor or agency becomes so powerful that it can act capriciously or beyond the law.[34] It was the value of paramount importance to the early pioneers of American federalism, who were understandably concerned that the new national government not recapitulate the tyrannical exercise of unchecked authority that the colonists had rejected in separating from the British monarchy.[35] Yet American history has since shown that assaults on individual liberties are as likely to come from either side of the divide. Just as the states harbored entrenched racial and gender oppression (via slavery, Jim Crow laws, and legalized race and sex discrimination in employment until late in the twentieth century), the federal government has given us McCarthyism, the World War II era anti-sedition laws, and alleged excesses under the Patriot Act (such as the warrantless federal wiretapping of private citizens held to violate the Foreign Intelligence Surveillance Act).[36]

---

[29] THE FEDERALIST, No. 28, at 180–81 (Alexander Hamilton), *supra* note 5. James Madison further described the value of this arrangement: "In a single republic, all the power surrendered by the people is submitted to the administration of a single government; and the usurpations are guarded against by a division of the government into distinct and separate departments. In the compound republic of America, the power surrendered by the people is first divided between two distinct governments, and then the portion allotted to each subdivided among distinct and separate departments. Hence a double security arises to the rights of the people. The different governments will control each other, at the same time that each will be controlled by itself." *Id.*, No. 51, at 323.

[30] *Id.*, No. 28, at 180–81 (Alexander Hamilton).

[31] U.S. CONST. art. I, § 1.

[32] U.S. CONST. art. II, § 2.

[33] U.S. CONST. art. I, § 9, amends. I–X.

[34] *Cf.* ALEXIS DE TOCQUEVILLE, DEMOCRACY IN AMERICA 263, ed. J. P. Mayer, trans. George Lawrence trans. (1835; repr. Garden City, N.Y.: Anchor Books 1969) ("Municipal bodies and county administrations are like so many hidden reefs retarding or dividing the flood of the popular will.").

[35] Somin, *supra* note 28, at 471.

[36] In re Nat'l Sec. Agency Telecomm. Records Litig., 700 F. Supp. 2d 1182 (N.D. Cal. 2010) (holding the FBI and other federal actors civilly liable under the Foreign Intelligence Surveillance Act for illegally eavesdropping on private communications without a warrant). *See* Charlie Savage & James Risen, *Federal Judge Finds N.S.A. Wiretaps Were Illegal*, N.Y. TIMES, Mar. 31, 2010, http://www.nytimes.com/2010/04/01/us/01nsa.html.

The dual federalism ideal of strictly separated state and federal authority serves this value, and it is thus featured prominently in the New Federalism cases that embrace that model. For example, in *Gregory v. Ashcroft*, the Rehnquist Court invoked Hamilton's words in a preamble to the New Federalism cases,[37] upholding as the "prerogative [of] citizens of a sovereign State" the mandatory retirement provision in the Missouri Constitution that had been challenged by state judges as age-based discrimination.[38] The majority opinion observed:

> The constitutionally mandated balance of power between the States and the Federal Government was adopted by the Framers to ensure the protection of our fundamental liberties. Just as the separation and independence of the coordinate branches of the Federal Government serve to prevent the accumulation of excessive power in any one branch, a healthy balance of power between the States and the Federal Government will reduce the risk of tyranny and abuse from either front. . . . One fairly can dispute whether our federalist system has been quite as successful in checking government abuse as Hamilton promised, but there is no doubt about the design.[39]

The decision warned that the design is of no value if the states' ability to check the power of the federal government loses credibility: "If this 'double security' is to be effective, there must be a proper balance between the States and the Federal Government. These twin powers will act as mutual restraints only if both are credible. In the tension between federal and state power lies the promise of liberty."[40]

Gregory v. Ashcroft thus identifies the check-and-balance value as the principle protector of the individual rights the Constitution elsewhere establishes, explaining the importance dual federalism places on fortifying strong boundaries between state and federal jurisdiction. If a healthy balance of state and federal power ensures liberty, then it is wise indeed to protect it against erosion. Nevertheless, it is not at all clear that these checks and balances are best served by the dual federalism ideal of jurisdictional separation. By contrast, consider how the opposite approach—an interpretive model emphasizing greater jurisdictional overlap—would also add force to the system of checks and balances by enabling citizens to wield authority at one level when they are unsatisfied with governmental performance at the other level.[41]

Indeed, the cooperative federalism era showcases an array of circumstances in which the federal and states governments have alternatively championed individual rights and regulatory obligations against neglect by the other side. These range from the federal assertion of

---

[37] 501 U.S. 452, 458–59 (1991) (citing THE FEDERALIST, No. 28, at 180–81 (Alexander Hamilton), *supra* note 5).

[38] *Id.* at 473. Although the Court decided the case by interpreting petitioners' claims under the ADEA and Equal Protection Clause, it grounded this analysis in a detailed disposition of the proper balance of state and federal power within the American system of federalism. *Id.* at 457–64.

[39] *Id.* at 458–59 (citations and internal quotation marks omitted).

[40] *Id.* at 459.

[41] *Cf.* SCHAPIRO, *supra* Introduction, note 11 and CHEMERINSKY, *supra* Introduction, note 12 (both proposing models of federalism that emphasize the benefits of broad overlap).

rights for African Americans and women during the civil rights movement to state protection for rights beyond those afforded at the federal level, from gay rights to property rights.[42] State and local innovations in climate governance in the face of federal inaction provide the most recent example.[43] In other words, like the innovation of the bicameral legislature, a little redundancy may strengthen, rather than weaken, the check-and-balance value.

By this view, jurisdictional overlap allows healthy competition between sovereigns in a way that jurisdictional separation does not, along with the promise of a regulatory backstop by either side against abdication or gridlock by the other. Writing for the Court in its most recent Tenth Amendment decision, *Bond v. United States*, Justice Kennedy nodded to the backstop function of federalism in explaining that "[b]y denying any one government complete jurisdiction over all the concerns of public life, federalism protects the liberty of the individual from arbitrary power."[44] Surrounding context suggests that Justice Kennedy was primarily interested in protecting state power,[45] but the principle itself applies in both directions. As Professor Kirsten Engel has observed, "one benefit of the compound nature of our federal system of government is that it is self-policing; by enabling policymaking on either level of government, it contains a built-in antidote to interest group capture."[46] Moving beyond the descriptive account of cooperative federalism, Dean Erwin Chemerinsky urges us to theorize federalism as empowerment rather than limitation, by which he means the potential for broadly overlapping multiple sources of authority to backstop failures by the other.[47]

Dean Chemerinsky also critiques the Rehnquist Court's invocation of separationist checks and balances as a means of protecting liberty, given the majority's use of jurisdictional separation in its Fourteenth Amendment (Section Five) and Commerce Clause cases to limit the scope of individual rights conferred by such statutes as the Religious Freedom Restoration Act,[48] the Age Discrimination in Employment Act,[49] the Americans with Disabilities Act,[50] and the Violence Against Women Act.[51] Under its Eleventh Amendment

---

[42] *Supra* Introduction notes 75–89 and accompanying text.

[43] *Infra* Chapter Five notes 144–189 and accompanying text.

[44] Bond v. United States, No. 09-1227, 564 U.S. __, *10 (slip opinion) (2011), 2011 Westlaw 2369334 (U.S.).

[45] Bond v. United States, No. 09-1227, 564 U.S. __, *9 (slip opinion) (2011), 2011 Westlaw 2369334 (U.S.) (noting that federalism "allows States to respond, through the enactment of positive law, to the initiative of those who seek a voice in shaping the destiny of their own times without having to rely solely upon the political processes that control a remote central power").

[46] Engel, *supra* Introduction note 72, at 181. James Madison also discussed the threat of such "factions" in the Federalist Papers. THE FEDERALIST, No. 10, at 80 (James Madison), *supra* note 5.

[47] CHEMERINSKY, *supra* Introduction note 12, at 146–47.

[48] City of Boerne v. Flores, 521 U.S. 507, 536 (1997) (invalidating the Act for exceeding Congress's authority under Section Five of the Fourteenth Amendment).

[49] Kimel v. Fla. Bd. of Regents, 528 U.S. 62, 82–83 (2000) (invalidating the Act for exceeding federal power under the Fourteenth Amendment and violating state sovereign immunity).

[50] Bd. of Trs. v. Garrett, 531 U.S. 356, 374 (2001) (invalidating certain remedies under the Act for exceeding federal power under the Fourteenth Amendment and violating state sovereign immunity).

[51] United States v. Morrison, 529 U.S. 598, 627 (2000) (declining to sustain the challenged portions of the Act under the Commerce Clause or Section Five of the Fourteenth Amendment).

sovereign immunity cases, the Rehnquist Court further reduced opportunities for individuals to vindicate rights against state governments.[52] Each of these New Federalism cases invalidated individual statutory rights in the service of preserving checks and balances between state and federal power. Dual federalism boundaries were clearly affirmed, but Chemerinsky questions whether individual liberties were truly protected as a result.[53]

Consistent with the classical dualism of earlier American history,[54] the New Federalism decisions cite the check-and-balance value as the "principle benefit" of federalism, promising liberty and good governance.[55] However, the foregoing discussion reveals that even the meaning of checks and balances is contested, between the classical vision of counterbalanced but separate authority and the overlap vision of checking sovereign authority through regulatory backstop. Indeed, by either measure, the healthy balance of state and federal authority has the potential to check both tyrannical assertions and irresponsible abdications of governmental authority. Structural tension between state and federal power has yielded benefits claimed on both sides of the political divide, and any model true to the intentions of a federal system (and not simply a decentralized system) must contend with threats to this fundamental federalism value.

That said, it is not the only value undergirding American federalism. After all, if the only purpose of federalism were the preservation of tension between the authority of two independent sovereigns, then we might best be served by a system of dual sovereignty between true "equals"—in other words, one without the Supremacy Clause, departing from the constitutional model described in *McCulloch v. Maryland*.[56] Yet it is difficult to imagine the success of such an approach, which seems doomed to the sort of political gridlock that forced early America's reconsideration of the Articles of Confederation.[57] Though a dual sovereignty between equals might perfect checks and balances, it would overly compromise the very regulatory problem-solving that the framers hoped the new Union would enable. Moreover, the separationist vision of checks and balances did little to cope with the demands of interjurisdictional problem solving made manifest during Hurricane Katrina, confusing rather than clarifying regulatory roles at a time when problem-solving needs were paramount.

As discussed further below, the maintenance of structural tension between two independent sovereigns also confounds governmental accountability to the voters, and does not

---

[52] Alden v. Maine, 527 U.S. 706, 712 (1999) (limiting Congress's power to authorize suits against state governments in state courts); Seminole Tribe v. Florida, 517 U.S. 44, 47 (1996) (limiting Congress's power to authorize suits against state governments in federal courts). These decisions held that Congress may authorize suits against state governments only under Section Five of the Fourteenth Amendment, leading to the decisions overturning rights and remedies exceeding that authority in *Kimel*, *Garrett*, and others.

[53] CHEMERINSKY, *supra* Introduction note 12, at 107–13. Indeed, Chemerinsky's ultimate argument goes even farther, questioning whether any of the Supreme Court's decisions since 1937 hold a defensible relationship with the underlying values of federalism. *Id.* at 116–17.

[54] *See supra* Part I Introduction, note 4 and accompanying text (describing nineteenth-century classical dualism).

[55] *See* Gregory v. Ashcroft, 501 U.S. 452, 458 (1991) ("Perhaps the principal benefit of the federalist system is a check on abuses of government power.").

[56] 17 U.S. (4 Wheat.) 316, 425–36 (1819); *see infra* Chapter Four, notes 30–33 and accompanying text.

[57] *Cf.* SCHAPIRO, *supra* Introduction, note 11, at 31–32; *infra* Chapter Three, notes 5–10 and accompanying text.

necessarily promote any of the values of localism and decentralization that are so often championed as advantages of federalism.[58] Checks and balances are thus foundational to our system, but they can operate in different ways—and they are not the only issue of concern.

C. Accountability and Democratic Participation

Governmental accountability is another good governance value that we ask federalism to help us realize, but the two have an especially complicated relationship.[59] Accountability and transparency in government enables meaningful participation by informed voters who advance policy preferences through elected representatives at all levels of the jurisdictional spectrum.[60] A healthy federal system, with strong states and localities in addition to national government, enhances the democratic process by affording citizens multiple avenues of participation along the spectrum of political scale. States are said to be "closer to the people," offering the best forums for local constituencies and individual citizens to address their concerns.[61] As Justice Kennedy wrote in *Bond*, federalism "allows States to respond, through the enactment of positive law, to the initiative of those who seek a voice in shaping the destiny of their own times without having to rely solely upon the political processes that control a remote central power."[62] Foreshadowing the localism values of federalism, locating the decisions of governance as locally as possible may also afford the best opportunity for direct participation and oversight.[63]

As the New Federalism Tenth Amendment decisions suggest, the dual federalism model may offer additional protection for governmental accountability by mitigating the voter confusion that jurisdictional overlap may invite.[64] Justice Scalia grounded his opinion in *Printz v. United States*, holding that federal law may not conscript the performance of state agencies, in the affirmation that the Constitution "contemplates that a State's government will represent and remain accountable to its own citizens."[65] To accomplish this, citizens must be able to recognize which elected officials are responsible for which policies, and to reward or punish policy choices accordingly. If you can always tell the difference between state and federal regulatory realms, goes the logic, then you always know which bums to throw out

---

[58] For example, tension between the independent sovereigns of the United States and the Soviet Union yielded few decentralizing benefits to the citizens of either nation during the Cold War.

[59] *See* D. Bruce La Pierre, *Political Accountability in the National Political Process: The Alternative to Judicial Review of Federalism Issues*, 80 NW. L. REV. 577 (1985); *cf.* CHEMERINSKY, *supra* Introduction, note 12, at 121–22.

[60] *E.g., Gregory*, 501 U.S. at 458.

[61] *E.g.*, SHAPIRO, *supra* Introduction, note 71, at 92.

[62] Bond v. United States, No. 09-1227, 564 U.S. __, *9 (slip opinion) (2011), 2011 Westlaw 2369334 (U.S.).

[63] SHAPIRO, *supra* Introduction, note 71, at 92.

[64] *See, e.g.*, Merritt, *supra* note 25, at 61–62 (describing how federal officials can escape accountability by compelling state governments to take action).

[65] 521 U.S. 898, 920 (1997) (overturning the Brady Handgun Violence Prevention Act's "commandeering" of state law enforcement databases to help enforce interstate background checks before gun purchases (Pub.L. 103-159, 107 Stat. 1536)).

when you don't like how things are going in a particular regulatory context. The more blurred the line between them becomes, the more accountability is compromised. As *Printz* emphasized, when the federal government requires the states to enact or enforce federal law, the lines of accountable governance is blurred beyond justification.

The New Federalism accountability argument made its dramatic debut in *New York v. United States*, another Tenth Amendment case in which the Court overturned portions of the Low-Level Radioactive Waste Policy Act that were held to "commandeer" state legislative authority.[66] Writing for the Court, Justice O'Connor warned that "where the Federal Government compels States to regulate, the accountability of both state and federal officials is diminished" by frustrating citizens' ability to keep track of which sovereign is responsible for what regulation of hazardous waste disposal.[67] She clarified:

> If the citizens of New York, for example, do not consider that making provision for the disposal of radioactive waste is in their best interest, they may elect state officials who share their view. That view can always be pre-empted under the Supremacy Clause if it is contrary to the national view, but in such a case it is the Federal Government that makes the decision in full view of the public, and it will be federal officials that suffer the consequences if the decision turns out to be detrimental or unpopular. But where the Federal Government directs the States to regulate, it may be state officials who will bear the brunt of public disapproval, while the federal officials who devised the regulatory program may remain insulated from the electoral ramifications of their decision.[68]

The decision thus worries that blurring the lines of regulatory accountability this way will mislead voters, who may hold state actors accountable for policy choices forced upon them by federal actors who then escape criticism by the same confused voters. Assuming this level of voter confusion, the federal commandeering of state authority as part of a federal regulatory regime would directly assault these critical lines of governmental accountability, explaining the rigor of the accountability rationale in the anti-commandeering line of New Federalism decisions.[69] For similar reasons, the accountability problem doubtlessly influenced the federal officials who were hesitant to assume control of the Katrina response effort without Governor Blanco's blessing. More recently, legal scholars have identified federalism's accountability value as a driving force behind the Tea Party movement.[70]

However, the same concerns over blurring lines of accountability could apply even in less dramatic instances of regulatory overlap. Almost all programs of cooperative federalism run the same risk, even those that do not involve outright commandeering. With these in mind, Professor Bruce La Pierre articulates a theory of political accountability that justifies jurisdictional overlap in most programs of cooperative federalism, on grounds that the national

---

[66] 505 U.S. 144, 180 (1992). For fuller discussion of the case, see *infra* Chapter Seven.

[67] 505 U.S. at 168.

[68] *Id.* at 168–69.

[69] *E.g.*, Jackson, *supra* Part I Introduction, note 21, at 2205.

[70] *E.g.*, Somin, *supra* Introduction, note 47, at 301.

political process effectively internalizes its costs politically and fiscally in the vast majority of cases.[71] Yet regulatory overlap is often criticized when Congress attempts to avoid accountability for policy choices that unreasonably impose costs on the states via "unfunded mandates." The problem of unfunded federal mandates to the states has received considerable and warranted attention. Even if voters were not confused about how a federal program imposed costs on their state, they might be unable to evaluate the degree to which this cost shifting undermined other state policies.[72]

Interestingly, though, the vigorous political response to unfunded mandates undermines the force of the blurred-line concern—showcasing the successful vindication of federalism concerns through apparently accountable governance notwithstanding the peril these efforts sought to correct. Beginning in the Reagan administration and continuing through the Clinton administration, the unfunded mandates problem received sustained federal attention, beginning with executive orders and culminating in the Unfunded Mandates Reform Act of 1995 that requires both Congress and federal agencies to carefully and publicly consider cost-shifting measures, and to limit those that would displace state and local priorities.[73] These examples demonstrate that voters concerned about cost imposition on their states were able to successfully identify the problem and voice their dissatisfaction through federal representatives, who responded affirmatively to their concerns.

The unfunded mandates example belies a weakness in the voter-confusion transparency rationale for dual federalism. Justice O'Connor's argument in *New York* rests on the unsupported empirical premises that voters will be unable to determine whether the state or federal government is responsible for a given outcome, and that state officials will be unable to inform their constituents when Congress is really to blame.[74] The rationale assumes that voters either cannot understand the interplay between federal and state policy making or that they cannot effectively voice their political preferences to federal representatives if they object to federal policies that impact the states. However, at least in the case of unfunded mandates, they were apparently able to do both. The executive and legislative versions of

---

[71] *E.g.*, La Pierre, *supra* note 59, at 665 (suggesting that Congress may employ the states as agents in a cooperative federalism program so long as his criteria are met, and that the rare cases in which they are not justify judicial intervention).

[72] *E.g.*, Lewis B. Kaden, *Politics, Money, and State Sovereignty: The Judicial Role*, 79 COLUM. L. REV. 847, 890 (1979) (discussing how unfunded federal mandates can force states to choose a federal agenda over their own).

[73] President Reagan and President Clinton both required agencies to conduct a pre-promulgation cost analysis. Exec. Order No. 1,229,146 Fed. Reg. 13,193 (Feb. 17, 1981); Exec. Order No. 12,866, 58 Fed. Reg. 51,735 (Sept. 30, 1993). The Unfunded Mandates Reform Act of 1995, Pub. L. No. 104-4, 109 Stat. 48 (codified in scattered sections of 2 U.S.C.) is designed "to end the imposition, in the absence of full consideration by Congress, of Federal mandates on State, local, and tribal governments without adequate Federal funding, in a manner that may displace other essential State, local, and tribal governmental priorities." 2 U.S.C. § 1501(2) (2000). Congress also required agencies to consider the costs of proposed regulations on state, local, and private entities. *Id.* at § 1501(7)(B); Regulatory Flexibility Act of 1980, 5 U.S.C. §§ 601–612 (2000) (requiring agencies to prepare regulatory flexibility analysis for any regulation that have will have a significant economic impact on small entities).

[74] H. Geoffrey Moulton, Jr., *The Quixotic Search for a Judicially Enforceable Federalism*, 83 MINN. L. REV. 849, 877 (1999).

unfunded mandates reform exemplify federally enacted political constraints on federal power, reflecting voter preferences that overrode conflicting self-interest in unfettered (or at least unmonitored) discretion.

The accountability case for dual federalism has also been critiqued for its assumptions of what limiting federal power will actually accomplish, given how far the regulatory playing field is already blurred by jurisdictional overlap coming from both directions. For example, state-based regulation and litigation wields nationwide impact in the fields of consumer protection, environmental regulation, and securities regulation.[75] Scholars have also critiqued the accountability justification for the anti-commandeering rule specifically, calling into question "the empirical accuracy of the Court's assumptions about how state and federal institutions interact with each other to promote democratic and constitutional values."[76] Moreover, although *New York* and its New Federalism brethren highlight the importance of protecting governmental accountability, whether they have actually succeeded in doing so remains a matter of debate. (For example, as detailed in Chapter Seven, *New York* helped created a "hot potato" political morass for which both sides appear to have abdicated regulatory responsibility and escaped accountability.[77])

Without denigrating the critical goals of transparent and accountable governance, the rationale cannot support the weight it is given in such decisions as *New York* and *Printz.*[78] There may be other reasons to limit federal commandeering, but voter confusion seems the weakest. Sophisticated voters and their representatives appear to communicate effectively about the sources of state and federal policy and how to respond at the ballot box, especially in the age of the twenty-four hour news cycle. Jurisdictional overlap is already so entrenched that the effort to preserve undiluted lines of policy authority is not only of questionable wisdom but futile. Meanwhile, a host of other constitutional features are even more clearly designed to preserve transparent, noncorrupt federal government, including the requirement of regular elections at fixed intervals, limits on forms of corruption and self-dealing by elected officials, and public availability of representatives' voting records.[79] Stringent First Amendment protections for core political speech are another constitutional tool for ensuring accountable governance.[80]

By contrast—and further highlighting the tug of war among competing federalism values—federalism as an architectural choice muddies the dualist understanding of accountability by design. The maintenance of simultaneous state and federal authority renders American citizens the subjects of two sovereigns in ways that confuse the legally uninitiated

---

[75] Comment, Timothy Meyer, *Federalism and Accountability: State Attorneys General, Regulatory Litigation, and the New Federalism*, 95 CAL. L. REV. 885 (2007) (showing how states' attorneys general coordinate to affect national policy).

[76] *Id.* at 886; Jackson, *supra* Part I Introduction, note 21, at 2205; *cf.* Jessica Bulman-Pozen & Heather K. Gerken, *Un-cooperative Federalism*, 118 YALE L.J. 1256 (2009).

[77] *See infra* Chapter Five, notes 116–31, and Chapter Seven, notes 59–81 and accompanying text.

[78] *E.g.*, Jackson, *supra* Part I Introduction, note 21, at 2205 ("Political accountability may be relevant but does not of itself justify the broad rule adopted by the Court.").

[79] *Id.* at 2201 & nn.96–99.

[80] *See* CHEMERINSKY, *supra* Introduction, note 12, at 121.

even without reference to the uncertain scope of Congress's commerce authority.[81] If infallible lines of governmental accountability were the most important feature of good governance, then a unitary or even a confederate system might be preferable.[82] Nobody would confuse which level was responsible for policy successes and failures if citizens only had to keep track of one level of government. And yet we tolerate dual sovereignty's assault on this particular strain of governmental accountability because the unitary and confederate alternatives would undermine (inter alia) the check-and-balance advantages discussed above and the problem-solving advantages discussed below. The point is not that accountability doesn't matter, only that it is not the only federalism value in the mix.

Moreover, there is no reason the underlying purposes of the accountability value cannot be advanced—enabling voters to participate meaningfully in their respective circles of democratic process—in a model of federalism that welcomes jurisdictional overlap. Federalism enhances voters' opportunities to participate in the democratic process by giving them multiple levels at which to participate, even though multiplicity is inherently more complex. The *New York* and *Printz* cases focus on segregating the two to avoid voter confusion, but those concerns are better satisfied by more direct means of ensuring transparency in government and accurate information among voters.

For example, the Obama administration has not shied away from jurisdictional overlap in its embrace of such controversial cooperative federalism initiatives as health care and financial services reform. Yet on his first day in office, President Obama issued a presidential memorandum committing his administration to a set of good governance practices that aim at the very values of accountability and democratic participation that we ask of federalism.[83] The "Open Government Initiative" commits to "an unprecedented level of openness in Government . . . to ensure the public trust and establish a system of transparency, public participation, and collaboration [in order to] strengthen our democracy."[84] Reading like a textbook account of the importance of accountable and participatory democracy, the Initiative pledges that:

> **Government should be transparent.** Transparency promotes accountability and provides information for citizens about what their Government is doing. Information maintained by the Federal Government is a national asset. My Administration will take appropriate action, consistent with law and policy, to disclose information rapidly in forms that the public can readily find and use. Executive departments and agencies should harness new technologies to put information about their operations

---

[81] Nonlawyers are often surprised to discover that different states maintain different statutory and common law treatments of such basic legal institutions as marriage, tort, and contract law.

[82] *E.g.*, Hills, *supra* Part I Introduction, note 5, at 828.

[83] Barack Obama, *Transparency and Open Government*, Presidential Memorandum for the Heads of Executive Department and Agencies, Jan. 21, 2009, http://www.whitehouse.gov/the_press_office/ TransparencyandOpenGovernment/ (directing the Chief Technology Officer, Director of the Office of Management and Budget, and Administrator of General Services to coordinate on instructions to executive agencies "to take specific actions implementing the principles set forth").

[84] *Id.*

and decisions online and readily available to the public. Executive departments and agencies should also solicit public feedback to identify information of greatest use to the public.

Government should be participatory. Public engagement enhances the Government's effectiveness and improves the quality of its decisions. Knowledge is widely dispersed in society, and public officials benefit from having access to that dispersed knowledge. Executive departments and agencies should offer Americans increased opportunities to participate in policymaking and to provide their Government with the benefits of their collective expertise and information. Executive departments and agencies should also solicit public input on how we can increase and improve opportunities for public participation in Government.

Government should be collaborative. Collaboration actively engages Americans in the work of their Government. Executive departments and agencies should use innovative tools, methods, and systems to cooperate among themselves, across all levels of Government, and with nonprofit organizations, businesses, and individuals in the private sector. Executive departments and agencies should solicit public feedback to assess and improve their level of collaboration and to identify new opportunities for cooperation.[85]

On December 8, 2009, the Director of the Office of Management and Budget issued the Open Government Directive, a memorandum to the heads of executive agencies and departments directing specific actions to implement the policies in the president's memorandum.[86] Among the many directives in the memo, the first requires that agencies err on the side of openness in making government information as available as possible to the public online.[87]

Similarly, on the opening day of the 112th Congress in 2011, the new Republican majority in the House of Representatives introduced new rules that Speaker John Boehner pledged would enhance "real transparency [and] greater accountability" in lawmaking, including additional time for members and the public to scrutinize proposed bills before they come to a vote.[88] It remains to be seen whether the president's and speaker's aspirations succeed, but they take solid aim at achieving accountable and accessible governance of the sort champions of federalism praise. At the very least, they should afford a corrective to concerns about voter confusion—especially regarding relevant information that is made quickly available to voters and the press over the Internet.

Finally, naked claims that federalism increases public participation bear additional scrutiny, as they stray perilously close to transgressing the distinction Professors Rubin and Feeley

---

[85] *Id.*

[86] Peter R. Orszag, *Open Government Directive*, Memorandum for the Heads of Executive Department and Agencies, Dec. 8, 2009, http://www.whitehouse.gov/open/documents/open-government-directive.

[87] *Id.* ("With respect to information, the presumption shall be in favor of openness (to the extent permitted by law and subject to valid privacy, confidentiality, security, or other restrictions).").

[88] *Boehner's First Remarks as House Speaker*, N.Y. TIMES, Jan. 5, 2001, http://www.nytimes.com/2011/01/06/us/politics/06cong-text.html?ref=politics.

warn of between federalism and decentralization.[89] It may be that a federal system increases citizen involvement in the democratic process, perhaps by enticing greater participation with the promise of more meaningful localized influence than might be true in a unitary system. However, to support true federalism rather than mere decentralization, the distinction must be less about the quantity of participatory opportunity and more about the qualitative value of participating in decision making independent from centralized authority. After all, even a fully centralized polity may still rely heavily on localized participation, even if the outer bounds of local decision making are constrained within a centralized plan. For example, the French government operates as a unitary semi-presidential system with a bicameral legislature, but it is divided into more than two dozen regions (subdivided into some one hundred departments that are further subdivided into some 350 *arrondissements* for administrative purposes).[90]

For these reasons, the accountability value of federalism is also multifaceted. The voter-confusion account preferred by the Rehnquist Court seems the weakest component and the easiest to mitigate. Yet the Court's underlying rationale—the importance of enabling meaningful democratic participation through transparent and accountable government at all levels of political scale—holds substantial constitutional gravity. When independent sources of sovereign authority strengthen the ability of citizens to participate in democratic governance, federalism advances the accountability value.

D. The Benefits of Local Autonomy: Innovation, Diversity, and Competition

The Federalist Papers emphasize the value of federalism's checks and balances, and the New Federalism Tenth Amendment cases emphasize federalism's role in preserving accountable government. However, the federalism values most celebrated by academic federalism theorists are those associated with the benefits of local autonomy, especially the potential for self-determined diversity and innovation. Economic federalism theorists emphasize the benefits of interjurisdictional competition among autonomous state governments, which—like competing firms in a marketplace—create greater social welfare through more efficient regulatory policies that are more responsive to citizen preferences. Enhancing self-determination through accessible and responsive local governance also advances the ideals of republican political theory.[91]

The preference for localized over centralized decision making proceeds from the conviction that "[t]here is a value in ensuring that local jurisdictions have the discretion to make the decisions that their residents wish them to make."[92] The Supreme Court has praised federalism because "it increases opportunity for citizen involvement in democratic processes; it allows for more innovation and experimentation in government; and it makes government

---

[89] Rubin & Feeley, *supra* Introduction, note 70, at 915.

[90] Nicolas Marie Kublicki, *An Overview of the French Legal System from an American Perspective*, 12 B.U. INT'L L.J. 57, 59–60 (1994).

[91] *See* SCHAPIRO, *supra* Introduction, note 11, at 78–79.

[92] Barron, *supra* note 19, at 382.

more responsive by putting the States in competition for a mobile citizenry."[93] But academic accounts of federalism's localism value tend to omit the strained claim about increased participation (reviewed above as potentially confusing federalism and decentralization), centering instead on the promotion of localized diversity and the encouragement of innovation and efficiency through interjurisdictional competition.[94]

As an initial caveat, there are important differences between the protection of state authority against federal incursion and the promotion of true local autonomy, which many treatments of federalism—including this one—threaten to conflate.[95] By and large, federalism protects the autonomy of states, and not the countless municipal entities within them where the governance most implicating these values takes place. To paraphrase the wry observation of Professor David Shapiro, enhancing the agency of individuals in governance may not be significantly improved by reducing the size of the polity from three hundred million Americans to thirty million Californians (or for that matter, nine million Los Angelinos).[96] Most federalism and preemption doctrines are insensitive to the difference between states and their municipalities (with the exception of Eleventh Amendment sovereign immunity doctrine that protects states but not their municipalities from most unauthorized suits).[97]

For the sake of simplification, my discussion frequently lumps municipal, state, and regional governance (everything more localized than the national government) together under the heading of *local*, to best contrast the federal and state-based authority that most federalism doctrine differentiates. However, important scholarship has shown the significance of intra- and interjurisdictional governance that takes place between localities independently of their states (and occasionally their nation-states) and between municipal and federal collaborators—exposing not only the horizontal but the diagonal dimensions of interjurisdictional governance.[98] Greater sensitivity to localism values throughout the spectrum of political scale is a fitting element for consideration by normative federalism theory, as the closing section of this discussion attests.

I. DIVERSITY

In protecting a sphere of local autonomy, federalism is frequently viewed as a refuge for regional diversity and multiculturalism. As the Supreme Court opined in *Gregory v. Ashcroft*,

---

[93] *Id.*

[94] *See, e.g.,* Steven G. Calabresi, "*A Government of Limited and Enumerated Powers*": In Defense of United States v. Lopez, 94 MICH. L. REV. 752, 775–77 (1995) (arguing that responsiveness to diverse local preferences and interstate competition are principal arguments in favor of federalism); McConnell, *supra* note 28, at 1493–94, 1498–1500 (same); Somin, *supra* note 28, at 464–65, 468–69 (same).

[95] For a full exposition of the difference between empowering states and supporting localism (and the importance of this difference to federalism), see Barron, *supra* note 19; Nestor M. Davidson, *Cooperative Localism: Federal-Local Collaboration in an Era of State Sovereignty*, 93 VA. L. REV. 959 (2007).

[96] SHAPIRO, *supra* Introduction, note 71, at 93.

[97] Jinks v. Richland County, 538 U.S. 456 (2003).

[98] E.g., Davidson, *supra* note 95; Resnik et al., *supra* Introduction, note 72; Osofsky, *supra* Introduction, note 72; Barron, *supra* note 19; Judith Resnik, *Foreign as Domestic Affairs: Rethinking Horizontal Federalism and Foreign Affairs Preemption in Light of Translocal Internationalism*, 57 EMORY L.J. 31 (2007).

federalism ensures that government "will be more sensitive to the diverse needs of a hetero-geneous society."[99] By enabling local majorities to pursue distinctive policy-making prefer-ences, federalism should produce greater citizen satisfaction than can be accomplished by a unitary, "one-size-fits-all" government. Professor Ilya Somin describes the premise:

> If, for example, some state-level majorities prefer a policy of high taxes and high levels of government services while others prefer low taxes and low service levels, they can each be accommodated by their respective state governments. A unitary government with a one-size-fits-all policy will, by contrast, likely leave a larger proportion of the population dissatisfied with the resulting package of policies.[100]

Moreover, at least in contexts more regionally heterogeneous than the United States (for example, in Switzerland, where four national languages and distinctive regional cultures coexist among twenty-six states),[101] federalism can "ease racial, ethnic, and ideological conflicts by allowing each of the opposing groups to control policy in its own region."[102]

Of course, diversity in the United States is less regionalized than it is in other federal soci-eties more markedly divided by language, religion, race, or ethnicity.[103] Moreover, many of the political issues that most divide contemporary Americans—such as abortion, affirmative action, or gay marriage—involve contentions about individual rights that could trump struc-tural federalism if an individual right protected against federal or state incursion is shown. In this respect, diversity-based claims for federalism that are poignantly real in other federalist nations may be overstated in the United States. As Professor Robert Schapiro has shown, the political differences Americans share tend to be distributed within states rather than clus-tered among different ones, reflected by the purple of the more granulated presidential elec-toral maps that are obscured by the red and blue of the electoral college system.[104] The proliferation of Starbucks, Gaps, McDonalds, and other identical franchises on Main Streets across the United States testifies to nationalizing forces at the level of consumer culture as well.[105] (Yet one would not mistake the politics of San Francisco, California for Houston, Texas or Nashua, New Hampshire—suggesting that the greatest bastions of local diversity remain at the municipal level.)

Confronting the disappearing distinctiveness of the states, Professor Donald Regan argues, "[o]ur national culture is already too homogenized to expect great differences between the states, but what cultural differences still remain should not be further eroded

---

[99] Gregory v. Ashcroft, 501 U.S. 452, 458 (1991).

[100] Somin, *supra* note 28, at 464–65.

[101] Swiss Fed. Statistical Office, Statistical Data on Switzerland 2006, at 4–5 (2006), http://www.bfs.admin.ch/bfs/portal/en/index/themen/die_schweiz_in_ueberblick/ts.Document.76607.pdf.

[102] Somin, *supra* note 28, at 465; *see also* Schapiro, *supra* Introduction, note 11, at 10–30.

[103] *See supra* note 3–4 and accompanying text (discussing national homogeneity in the United States).

[104] *See* Schapiro, *supra* Introduction, note 11, at 28–29 (noting that not only states but "people are purple").

[105] *Id.* at 16–30.

by central legislation without good reason."[106] Federalism enables the localized expression of regional preferences that have not been foreclosed by centralized requirements of uniformity—such as the preference of most Oregonians that citizens be entitled to choose euthanasia in certain circumstances,[107] that of most Californians that local property taxes be assessed on the basis of acquisition value instead of market value,[108] or that of most Missourians that their judges not exceed a certain age.[109] Localized diversity at the municipal level impacts decisions about some of the most compelling matters of public policy, including crime control, education, and land use planning.[110] The diversity value of federalism becomes even more powerful when coupled with the possibility of interjurisdictional competition and innovation.

2. COMPETITION AND INNOVATION

By enabling local policy-making autonomy, federalism encourages interjurisdictional competition between separate state and local governments (horizontally) and among local, state, and national government (vertically) toward innovative strategies less likely to be discovered through centralized planning alone. Through interjurisdictional competition and innovation, federalism promotes both the market-based efficiency championed by economic federalism theorists and the "laboratory of ideas"[111] championed by Justice Brandeis that are so often touted among federalism's chief assets.

According to the interjurisdictional competition ideal, mobile citizens pursue their regulatory preferences by establishing roots in desirably governed localities while maintaining the option of leaving (or the potential of "exit") if prospects appear better elsewhere. If they become disillusioned with their chosen locality, or another adopts preferable policies, citizens can "vote with their feet" by relocating to the preferred jurisdiction.[112] Ideally, interstate competition, like ordinary market competition, encourages states "to provide citizens with the most attractive possible package of public services at the lowest possible cost in taxes and

---

[106] Donald H. Regan, *How to Think About the Federal Commerce Power and Incidentally Rewrite* United States v. Lopez, 94 MICH. L. REV. 554, 558 (1995).

[107] *See* Gonzales v. Oregon, 126 S. Ct. 904, 911 (2006) (discussing the ballot measure-approved Oregon Death with Dignity Act).

[108] This is the policy behind California's famous Proposition 13. *See, e.g.*, CAL. TAXPAYERS ASS'N, PROPOSITION 13: LOVE IT OR HATE IT, ITS ROOTS GO DEEP (1993), http://www.caltax.org/research/prop13/prop13.htm (discussing background of Proposition 13).

[109] *See* Gregory v. Ashcroft, 501 U.S. 452, 471 (1991) (noting that the challenged provision of the Missouri Constitution, which established a mandatory retirement age of seventy for judges, was "approved by the people of Missouri as a whole"). For critics, this case represented a scenario in which individual rights should trump federalism concerns. Nevertheless, the Supreme Court has not applied the same level of scrutiny in reviewing claims of age discrimination that it has for claims of race or gender discrimination. *Id.* at 470.

[110] Barron, *supra* note 19, at 381.

[111] *See* New State Ice Co. v. Liebmann, 285 U.S. 262, 311 (1932) (Brandeis, J., dissenting) (comparing the states to laboratories in which to "try novel social and economic experiments").

[112] Richard A. Epstein, *Exit Rights under Federalism*, 55 LAW & CONTEMP. PROBS. 147, 150 (1992).

regulatory burdens."[113] Professor Somin distinguishes the force of this competition value from the more passive mechanism of the diversity value:

> Whereas the theory of interstate diversity assumes merely that states are responsive to the preferences of citizen-voters already residing within their boundaries, the theory of interstate competition asserts that states actively compete with each other to attract new citizens, who can improve their lot through the power of "exit" rights. Conversely, states also strive to ensure that current residents will not depart for greener pastures offered by competitors. Citizens dissatisfied with state policy have the option not only of lobbying for changes but also of moving to another state that deliberately seeks to attract them with more favorable policies. To the benefits of political voice provided by interstate diversity, the possibility of interstate competition adds those of exit.[114]

The hope is that market-like competition between localities will improve governance and keep it closely tethered to citizens' dynamic preferences. The model is sometimes known as "competitive federalism."

This theory of interstate competition draws its insight from Professor Albert Hirschman's classic theory of how the recovery mechanisms of "exit" and "voice" enable organizations to effectively adapt and survive amid changing consumer, investor, and employee preferences.[115] However, the proposition that citizens will (or should) leave their homes in dissatisfaction over any particular local policy choices is less convincing than Professor Hirschman's original thesis, which applied to the behavior of firms in the marketplace. As some have argued, the cultural and family ties that bind individuals to their communities operate with more force than product, brand, or even employee loyalty.[116] Others question whether those who suffer under the policy preferences of a local majority should bear the burden of exit, especially majoritarian policies that unfairly target minority interests.[117]

In addition, most localities simultaneously pursue so many different policies that it would be difficult to tie a given citizen's decision to relocate to a particular failed policy choice, at least for all but the most motivated single-issue advocates.[118] For example, there has been no apparent influx into Massachusetts by gay couples seeking to take advantage of laws enabling gay marriage by state citizens, nor a marked exodus of citizens from Massachusetts who

---

[113] Somin, *supra* note 28, at 469.

[114] *Id.* at 468 (citation omitted).

[115] ALBERT O. HIRSCHMAN, EXIT, VOICE, AND LOYALTY (1970). *See also* Gerken, *supra* Introduction, note 69 (exploring how the voice element in the Hirschman model should inform federalism theory).

[116] *See* Patrick C. Jobes et al., *A Paradigm Shift in Migration Explanation, in* COMMUNITY, SOCIETY AND MIGRATION 1, 23 (Patrick C. Jobes et al. eds., 1992) (demonstrating that, contrary to the economic model, migration patterns "indicate that noneconomic factors continue to help determine why, when, where and who moves"); Shauhin A. Talesh, Note, *Welfare Migration to Capture Higher Benefits: Fact or Fiction?*, 32 CONN. L. REV. 675, 712 (2000) (reminding migration analysts not to overlook the importance of human relationships).

[117] *Cf.* SCHAPIRO, *supra* Introduction, note 11, at 77.

[118] *See, e.g.*, Barry Friedman, *Valuing Federalism*, 82 MINN. L. REV. 317, 387–88 (1997) ("Even when moves occur, they tend to be for reasons largely unrelated to government policy decisions.").

oppose that policy.[119] Moreover, citizens are statistically more likely to move within their home states than between states,[120] but federalism does not prevent states themselves from adopting centralized policies that frustrate local diversity and competition under the Hirschman model.

Nevertheless, if the conventional wisdom is true that most relocations take place for economic reasons (when the need to follow job or educational opportunities overcomes the roots of place), then the effects of interjurisdictional competition may be most observable through state policies that encourage or discourage economic opportunities. For related reasons, state tax policies may motivate exit and loyalty choices among particularly sensitive classes of citizens, such as retirees and young people. For example, Florida's decision to collect neither personal income taxes nor estate taxes may have contributed to the in-migration of many retirees in recent decades[121] (although it raised counter-concerns about falling state investment in public schools[122]). Similarly, California's 1978 voter referendum to tax real estate on acquisition value rather than conventional market value appears to have led to retention of long-time homeowners reluctant to lose their favorable tax status (although at the expense of new families more likely to leave the state in search of affordable homes).[123] Some argue that the most significant results of interjurisdictional competition are experienced not by citizens but by businesses. For example, firms flock to incorporate under Delaware's business-friendly state laws, and perhaps to states with forgiving business tax policies such as Florida or Nevada.[124]

Whether or not citizens invoke their exit rights, interjurisdictional innovation and competition also enable states to function as the "laboratories of ideas" that Justice Brandeis famously invoked in 1932 in support of federalism, praising how "a single courageous State

---

[119] *But see* Bill Zajac, *Gay Marriage War Heats Up*, REPUBLICAN, Jan. 13, 2004, at A1 (reporting that anti-gay partisan groups expanded into Massachusetts in the wake of the ruling).

[120] Abraham Bell & Gideon Parchomovsky, *Of Property and Federalism*, 115 YALE L.J. 72, 77 (2005) (reporting U.S. Census statistics indicating that of the 43.4 million Americans who moved between March 1999 and March 2000, only 19.4 million moved to new states).

[121] *See* StateofFlorida.com, Florida Tax Guide, http://www.stateofflorida.com/flortaxguid.html (last visited Mar. 15, 2007) (boasting the lack of income tax). Another possible explanation, however, is the weather. Federalism scholars have debated whether the recent in-migrations to southern states are better attributed to innovative tax incentives and other local policy choices or technological innovations in inexpensive air conditioning.

[122] *Cf.* Matthew J. Meyer, *The Hidden Benefits of Property Tax Relief for the Elderly*, 12 ELDER L.J. 417, 419–20 (2004) (reporting that cuts in state aid have forced municipalities to either reduce school budgets or raise taxes).

[123] *Cf.* Les Picker, *The Lock-in Effect of California's Proposition 13*, NBER DIG., Apr. 2005, at 4 (study confirming that residents are less likely to move as they wish in order to reap the tax advantages of longer-owned homes).

[124] *See, e.g.*, CURTIS S. DUBAY & CHRIS ATKINS, TAX FOUND., 2007 STATE BUSINESS TAX CLIMATE INDEX 2 fig. 1 (2006), http://www.taxfoundation.org/files/bp52.pdf (finding Florida and Nevada as the fourth and fifth most-friendly states in terms of business taxes). However, while the Tax Foundation rated Wyoming above all other states for the business desirability of its tax laws and New York forty-seventh, there is much more business conducted in New York than in Wyoming (revealing the limits of such conjecture).

may, if its citizens choose, serve as a laboratory; and try novel social and economic experiments without risk to the rest of the country."[125] Under the dual federalism model, the laboratory model gives states like Florida and California full independence to experiment with novel tax policies. Even under the jurisdictional overlap afforded by cooperative federalism, the laboratory model enables states to pursue independent approaches to solving interjurisdictional problems for which the federal government could otherwise mandate uniform national solutions. Many programs of cooperative federalism addressing national collective action problems, such as the Clean Air and Water Acts, offer states a choice between accepting national regulation or designing their own laws to curtail their own externalities.[126] Setting aside legitimate questions about the extent to which citizens are appropriate subjects for all such experimentation,[127] state autonomy in the laboratory model enables policy makers to experiment with potentially beneficial regulatory strategies that may fortuitously benefit sister states and ultimately the nation as a whole.

The laboratory metaphor demonstrates how the innovation/competition value simultaneously serves competing federalism models that emphasize alternatively more localist or nationalist ends. From the localist perspective, the laboratory is valuable because competing states pursuing different policies afford citizens greater choice in a marketplace of regulatory alternatives. From the nationalist perspective, the laboratory is valuable because it produces better regulatory solutions than centralized planning, enabling proven solutions to be adopted nationally with fewer risks. As Professors Samuel Issacharoff and Catherine Sharkey have observed, Justice Brandeis was sympathetic to the latter perspective in the oft-ignored second half of his famous quote, in which he praised the possibility that "novel social and economic experiments" would be undertaken "without risk to the rest of the country."[128] (Dovetailing with discussion of the next federalism value, it bears mention that the "laboratory of ideas" feature of federalism is as much about regulatory problem solving as it is about local autonomy.)

The laboratory/competition value of federalism has indeed produced important regulatory innovations, many of which have later been adopted by other states or the nation as a whole. Environmental law offers many examples of state-based policy innovations.[129] For example, California pioneered the regulation of automobile emissions, leading to the adoption of a federal vehicle emissions standard.[130] New York was the first to offer tax incentives

---

[125] New State Ice Co. v. Liebmann, 285 U.S. 262, 311 (1932) (Brandeis, J., dissenting).

[126] See 33 U.S.C. §§ 1251–1387 (2000) ("Clean Water Act"); 42 U.S.C. §§ 7401–7671 (2000) ("Clean Air Act").

[127] See G. Alan Tarr, Laboratories of Democracy? Brandeis, Federalism, and Scientific Management, PUBLIUS, Winter 2001, at 37, 40–41 (discussing appropriate limits on state experimentation in the federalism laboratory).

[128] Id. (emphasis added); see also Samuel Issacharoff & Catherine M. Sharkey, Backdoor Federalization, 53 UCLA L. REV. 1353, 1355 (2006).

[129] E.g., John Pendergrass, States Heating Up as Feds Cool Off, 23 ENVTL. FORUM 8, 8 (May/June 2006) (describing new state environmental initiatives in Washington, Maine, Maryland, Michigan, and Pennsylvania).

[130] Jonathan H. Adler, The Fable of Federal Environmental Regulation: Reconsidering the Federal Role in Environmental Protection, 55 CASE W. RES. L. REV. 93, 103 (2004).

to the builders and developers of environmentally friendly buildings,[131] a lead now followed by forty-seven other states that offer tax incentives for energy efficiency and use of renewable energy sources in buildings.[132] Similarly, a coalition of Northeastern and Mid-Atlantic states formed the Regional Greenhouse Gas Initiative in 2005, the first regulatory cap-and-trade partnership in the United States.[133] California again presaged federal regulation through its early attempts to regulate greenhouse gas emissions from motor vehicles.[134]

The socially valuable benefits of localism are thus powerful rationales for federalism—or, at least, for a particular kind of federalism. The choice of a federal system more generally does not necessarily ensure that these values will be advanced, especially at the municipal level. As noted above, dual sovereignty divides authority between the national and state governments, but most states are far too big to function as local communities; many are on par in size with the nation-states of Europe, and some even rank among the world's largest economies.[135] Nothing in the Constitution prevents state governments from becoming the very central planners, scorned by economic theory federalists, that would suppress local autonomy, diversity, and competition. As the champions of state autonomy-driven theories of federalism may forget (but the victims of Jim Crow laws would not), the states are equally vulnerable to tyrannical assertions of power.[136] Normative federalism models that balance the importance of municipal localism with other federalism values are possible, but require intentional and nuanced design.

Cooperative federalism generally lacks intentional design, and dual federalism, generally prioritizing checks and balances over competing considerations, lacks the necessary nuance. Cooperative federalism mostly trusts the protection of local interests to the fact that many of the federal agents empowered to allocate contested authority are elected locally. Meanwhile, although New Federalism proponents claim localism in support of the revival, the cases' support for uncritical dual federalism move them in a potentially anti-municipal direction (especially when considered in tandem with preemption cases that reverse the presumption

---

131 *See* National Resources Defense Council, New York's Green Building Tax Credit, http://www.nrdc.org/cities/building/nnytax.asp (last visited Mar. 15, 2007).

132 *See* Database of State Incentives for Renewables & Efficiency, Financial Incentives for Renewable Energy, http://www.dsireusa.org/summarytables/finre.cfm (last visited Sept. 27, 2010); Database of State Incentives for Renewables & Efficiency, Financial Incentives for Energy Efficiency, http://www.dsireusa.org/summarytables/finee.cfm (last visited Sept. 27, 2010).

133 Participating states are Connecticut, Delaware, Maine, Maryland, New Hampshire, New Jersey, New York, Rhode Island, and Vermont. Regional Greenhouse Gas Initiative: An Initiative of Northeast and Mid-Atlantic States of the U.S., http://www.rggi.org/about/history (last visited Sept. 27, 2010).

134 Cent. Valley Chrysler-Jeep, Inc. v. Goldstene, 529 F. Supp. 2d 1151, 1189 (E.D. Cal. 2007) (upholding the regulations in part on the basis of the Supreme Court's decision in Massachusetts v. EPA, 549 U.S. 497 (2007)).

135 For example, in 2001 the State of California beat out the nation of France to become the world's fifth largest economy. *California Now World's Fifth-Largest Economy*, SILICON VALLEY/SAN JOSE BUS. J., June 15, 2001, http://sanjose.bizjournals.com/sanjose/stories/2001/06/11/daily58.html. In 2004, the Texas state economy ranked as the eighth largest in the world. Bus. & Indus. Data Ctr., Overview of the Texas Economy, http://www.bidc.state.tx.us/overview/2-2te.htm (last visited Mar. 15, 2007).

136 *See supra* text between notes 35–36. *See also* Justice O'Connor's admonition in *Gregory v. Ashcroft* of the need for the "double-security" of federalism's checks and balances, *supra* notes 39–40.

against preemption in traditional police power realms).[137] Professor David Barron argues that the New Federalism movement has not demonstrated great regard for localism values, and critiques the federalism discourse generally for failing to submit localism claims to meaningful scrutiny against a coherent baseline.[138]

As Barron has explained, strengthening a zone of state authority to compete with national authority can actually enable it to override contrary municipal preferences, potentially undermining localism values at the level from which many of their benefits most organically stem.[139] For him, the New Federalism decisions ignore the complexity of local autonomy, which cannot be promoted by simply and uncritically reducing national power.[140] The disjuncture between what New Orleans Mayor Nagin and Louisiana Governor Blanco separately wanted from the Katrina response effort evidences the critical difference between empowering local and state autonomy.[141] Barron's work demonstrates that strong state authority (and/or weak national authority) may actually compromise localism values by suppressing municipal autonomy or otherwise frustrating a local community's ability to pursue its desired ends in partnerships with others or without outside interference.[142]

Barron's insights into the interdependence of local and national authority go to the heart of the interjurisdictional gray area, in which disparate entities discover interlinked interests in what may at first seem an overtly local or national problem. These are the land use decisions that impact the quality of navigable waters and the national security programs that affect local law enforcement, forcing local communities out of isolation and exposing the tension between localism and other federalism values. After all, if local autonomy were all that mattered, we could always disintegrate the Union—but the history of the Constitution's embrace of a federation in the first place exposes the problem. As the original thirteen states once learned, the ability of local communities to pursue their desired ends relies on coordinated activity with other communities. Indeed, these states' recognition that central coordination was necessary for efficient commerce, common defense, and interstate dispute resolution led to their rejection of the Articles of Confederation in favor of constitutional federalism.[143]

A confederal system that subjugates national authority to state sovereignty also lacks the benefits of checks and balances, and it has a potentially ambiguous relationship with accountability values. From the perspective of participatory democracy, the advantages of decentralized local government appear self-evident: it is easier to become involved, easier to remain informed, and easier to oversee the activity of a smaller polity in which each individual plays a proportionately larger role. From the perspective of accountable governance, however,

---

[137] See CHEMERINSKY, *supra* Introduction, note 12, at 225–37; S. Candice Hoke, *Preemption Pathologies and Civic Republican Values*, 71 B.U.L. REV. 685, 750–52 (1991) (discussing the Supreme Court's extension of the preemption doctrine to state laws that achieve an "improper state purpose"); *infra* Chapter Four, note 153.

[138] See Barron, *supra* note 19, at 377–81.

[139] *Id.* at 382–90.

[140] *Id.* at 377–81.

[141] See *supra* Chapter One, notes 108–116 and accompanying text.

[142] Barron, *supra* note 19, at 382–90.

[143] *Infra* Chapter Three, notes 5–10 and accompanying text.

political science tells another story—showing how the local government is often most subject to capture by special interests, notwithstanding the ease with which other citizens seem enabled to monitor and prevent it.[144] Even James Madison in the Federalist Papers recognized the threat of special-interest capture at the local level relative to the national level, advocating the larger federal republic so as to overcome the dangers in smaller polities posed by "factions."[145] In other words, the localist values of federalism are suspended in the overall web of tension just like all the others.

For many academic treatments of federalism values, this might well prove the end of the discussion. However, Professor Barron's recognition of the limitations of state autonomy in vindicating municipal interests leads nicely to final federalism value in this treatment. Federalism can promote good governance, in various degrees, by forestalling tyranny, encouraging accountability and public participation, and fostering local innovation and competition. Yet there is an additional, often overlooked value further embedded in the way in which we generally conceive of the relationship between federalism and localism.

E. Subsidiarity and State-Federal Problem-Solving Synergy

The final value in the mix represents another means by which federalism promotes good government and a separate benefit yielded by the choice of a federal system. As Madison's admonitions and the failed Articles of Confederation attest, one of the purposes of the Constitution was to enable the federation to cope effectively with interjurisdictional problems that the states could not manage on their own.[146] One of the proven benefits of the federal arrangement has been the development of interjurisdictional synergy between the unique sources of regulatory capacity that have subsequently evolved at the local, state, and federal levels. But these functional accounts of federalism's problem-solving benefits are related to a normative premise of federalism itself. Federalism's implicit problem-solving value is inconspicuously partnered with the preference for localism in the familiar federalism premise that extols localized over centralized decision making as much possible. As explained below, the magic words are "as much as possible," and the unfamiliar name of the familiar concept is "subsidiarity."

Whether emphasizing checks, accountability, or localism, most accounts of American federalism proceed from a presumption that government action should be taken at the most local level possible—or conversely, that higher levels of government should never take action that could be accomplished as well or better at a more local level.[147] (An extreme localist position might argue that *all* public action should take place locally, but this more confederate position ultimately collides with federalist dual sovereignty.) The premise that governance

---

[144] *See* CHEMERINSKY, *supra* Introduction, note 12, at 102–03; Helen Hershkoff, *Welfare Devolution and State Constitutions*, 67 FORDHAM L. REV. 1403, 1430–31 (1999); Ashira Pelman Ostrow, *Minority Interests, Majority Politics*, 86 DENV. U.L. REV. 1459, 1466–67 (2009).

[145] THE FEDERALIST, NO. 10, at 80 (James Madison), *supra* note 5.

[146] *Infra* Chapter Three, notes 5–10 and accompanying text.

[147] *E.g.*, Alexander Tabarrok, Presentation at University of California Hastings College of the Law: Arguments for Federalism (Sept. 20, 2001), http://www.independent.org/issues/article.asp?id=485.

should take place at the most local level possible is "subsidiarity," which literally means "to 'seat' ('sid') a service down ('sub') as close to the need for that service as is feasible."[148] Subsidiarity implies that local governance is best, but affords space for higher levels of government to cope with the spillover effects and externalities that cannot be governed at the most local level.[149]

The subsidiarity principle has a rich intellectual history in both the United States and Europe, drawing its origins from early Greek and Catholic philosophy. Some scholarly accounts trace it to Aristotle, though it surfaced as a modern sociopolitical doctrine through the writings of Thomas Aquinas.[150] As a first principle from which to structure government, subsidiarity is most formalized in the European Union's governing structure, as set forth in the Maastricht Treaty:

> In areas which do not fall within its exclusive competence, the [European] Community shall take action, in accordance with the principle of subsidiarity, only if and insofar as the objectives of the proposed action cannot be sufficiently achieved by the Member States and can therefore, by reason of the scale or effects of the proposed action, be better achieved by the Community.[151]

Just as the nationalists and the federalists negotiated the relationship between the federal and state governments during the American Constitutional Convention, the Maastricht subsidiarity rule establishes a relationship between the European Community and its member states that prevents "an overcentralization of power at the EU level and . . . thereby ensure[s] the acceptance of the EU among the citizens."[152]

---

[148] Robert K. Vischer, *Subsidiarity as a Principle of Governance: Beyond Devolution*, 35 IND. L. REV. 103, 103 (2001). For various accounts of the subsidiary principle, see David P. Currie, *Subsidiarity*, 1 GREEN BAG 2D 359 (1998); James L. Huffman, *Making Environmental Regulation More Adaptive through Decentralization: The Case for Subsidiarity*, 52 U. KAN. L. REV. 1377 (2004); John F. Stinneford, *Subsidiarity, Federalism, and Federal Prosecution of Street Crime*, 2 J. CATH. SOC. THOUGHT 495 (2005); W. Gary Vause, *The Subsidiarity Principle in European Union Law—American Federalism Compared*, 27 CASE W. RES. J. INT'L L. 61 (1995); Jared Bayer, Comment, *Re-Balancing State and Federal Power: Toward a Political Principle of Subsidiarity in the United States*, 53 AM. U. L. REV. 1421 (2004).

[149] *Cf.* CHEMERINSKY, *supra* Introduction, note 12, at 118–19 (discussing federalism as a means of policing spillovers and externalities).

[150] Nicholas Aroney, *Subsidiarity, Federalism and the Best Constitution: Thomas Aquinas on City, Province and Empire*, 26 LAW & PHIL. 161, 165–66 (2007). In an attempt to find a balance between laissez-faire capitalism and state-controlled socialism, Pope Pius XI suggested subsidiarity as the most effective methodology for carrying out the Catholic Church's task of Christian charity. Pope Pius XI, *Quadragesimo Anno*, VATICAN. VA, May 15, 1931, at paras. 79–80, http://www.vatican.va/holy_father/pius_xi/encyclicals/documents/ hf_p-xi_enc_19310515_quadragesimo-anno_en.html. *But see* Reimer von Borries & Malte Hauschild, *Implementing the Subsidiarity Principle*, 5 COLUM. J. EUR. L. 369, 369 (1999) (contrasting the "subsidiary function" tenet of the Catholic Church with the constitutional law principle of "subsidiarity").

[151] Treaty of Amsterdam Amending the Treaty on European Union, the Treaties Establishing the European Communities and Certain Related Acts, art. 5, Oct. 2, 1997, 1997 O.J. (C 340) 1, 182–83 (modifying 1992 Treaty on European Union, art. 3b).

[152] Von Borries & Hauschild, *supra* note 150, at 369.

Although the term *subsidiarity* is best known for its prominence in the Maastricht Treaty, appearances of subsidiarity in the American federalism discourse have long predated its role in the formation of the European Union (though often by other names).[153] The principle itself was in clear circulation at the time of the Constitutional Convention, implicitly prompting the movement to retire the failed Articles of Confederation.[154] In the Federalist Papers, James Madison gave it indirect expression in his impassioned plea to the adversaries of the Constitution who fretted that the national government would intrude on the existing powers of the states. Urging that the federalist distribution of power contemplated by the Constitution was necessary to accomplish the very goals for which Americans looked to governance, he argued:

> [I]f. . . the Union be essential to the happiness of the people of America, is it not pre-posterous to urge as an objection to a government, without which the objects of the Union cannot be attained, that such a government may derogate from the importance of the governments of the individual States? Was, then, the American Revolution effected, . . . not that the people of America should enjoy peace, liberty, and safety, but that the governments of the individual States, that particular municipal establishments, might enjoy a certain extent of power and be arrayed with certain dignities and attributes of sovereignty? . . . It is too early for politicians to presume on our forgetting that the public good, the real welfare of the great body of the people, is the supreme object to be pursued; and that no form of government whatever has any other value than as it may be fitted for the attainment of this object.[155]

Thus, even to Madison—for whom anti-tyranny concerns were central—classical checks and balances should yield before they threaten the federal system's ability to accomplish the ends for which it was created. Checks and balances are critical, but must be weighed against the need that government be enabled to solve the very problems that motivated the Union.[156] Madison's admonition demonstrates that pragmatism is more than something exogenous to federalism, a separate goal with which federalism values must compete in the operation of government. Rather, it is built into federalism itself, a value in tension with others, as part of the allocation of powers between the national and the local level. Some have even credited the premise of subsidiarity as the primary means of reading content into the otherwise tautological text of the Tenth Amendment.[157]

---

[153] In contrast to the European Union, subsidiarity does not expressly appear in the text of the Constitution—but for that matter, neither do the terms "checks and balances," "accountability," or "local innovation and competition."

[154] *Infra* notes Chapter Three, notes 5–10 and accompanying text.

[155] THE FEDERALIST, NO. 45, at 288–89 (James Madison), *supra* note 5.

[156] *Cf.* CHEMERINSKY, *supra* Introduction, note 12, at 118–19.

[157] *See* David T. Koyzis, *Subsidiarity and Federalism*, COMMENT, Jan. 2004, at 3, http://www.cardus.ca/comment/article/230 (noting that the Tenth Amendment is the constitutional embodiment of the subsidiarity principle).

The subsidiarity principle was also introduced to contemporary federalism theory by Russell Kirk, who propounded a model of federalism in the early 1960s that would inspire the proponents of the New Federalism revival decades later.[158] Kirk's model adopted the principle of subsidiarity as a primary consideration in his theory of "territorial democracy," which takes as definitional that "federalism is an order in which the smaller circles and communities are granted the *maximum possible* power to direct their own affairs."[159] Although his model of territorial democracy never refers to subsidiarity by that name, it is an unmistakable element. In contrast to European Union federalism, American statements of federalism theory such as Kirk's generally situate subsidiarity as one part of a broader rubric; still it is usually stated as a primary component.[160]

Subsidiarity has received increasing scholarly and political attention in the United States in recent years.[161] It was incorporated as a federalism premise of the Department of Homeland Security's original National Response Plan, which emphasized that "[a] basic premise of the NRP is that incidents are generally handled *at the lowest jurisdictional level possible*."[162] The 2008 National Response Framework similarly adopts the principle of subsidiarity as an underlying architectural premise.[163]

Of note, subsidiarity has been most enthusiastically embraced—even by name—by conservative commentators in support of the New Federalism.[164] The principle is also embraced by libertarians, who take as a natural corollary that when any government is necessary, it should be imbued with as limited power as possible.[165] The core libertarian position is thus consonant with subsidiarity's directive that higher government actors never be given tasks that could be accomplished as effectively by a more local actor. Professor Donald Regan invokes a core insight of the subsidiarity principle in his proposal of a simple alternative for constraining federal authority under the Commerce Clause:

> The kernel of my positive suggestion is so obvious that I would be embarrassed to offer it, if it did not seem necessary that someone should: when we are trying to decide whether some federal law or program can be justified under the commerce power, we should ask ourselves the question, "Is there some reason the federal government must

---

[158] Russell Kirk, *The Prospects for Territorial Democracy in America, in* A NATION OF STATES: ESSAYS ON THE AMERICAN FEDERAL SYSTEM 42 (Robert A. Goldwin ed., 1963).

[159] *Id.* at 45 (emphasis added).

[160] *See, e.g.,* George A. Bermann, *Taking Subsidiarity Seriously: Federalism in the European Community and the United States,* 94 COLUM. L. REV. 331, 451–52 (1994).

[161] *E.g.,* Vischer, *supra* note 148; Stinneford, *supra* note 148.

[162] NRP, *supra* Chapter One, note 64, at 6.

[163] NATIONAL RESPONSE FRAMEWORK, *supra* Chapter One, note 96, at 8.

[164] *E.g.,* Tabarrok, *supra* note 147 (listing subsidiarity as one of four principal arguments for federalism).

[165] Walter Block, *Decentralization, Subsidiary, Rodney King and State Deification: A Libertarian Analysis,* 16 EUR. J.L. & ECON. 139, 140 (2003) (noting that for libertarians "subsidiarity is the goal," and thus a libertarian "tends to favor city government over state, and the latter vis a vis the federales").

be able to do this, some reason why we cannot leave the matter to the states?" Federal power exists where and only where there is special justification for it.[166]

Even former president George W. Bush appealed to subsidiarity in his philosophy of compassionate conservativism, which prefers social programs by local community groups over state and local services, and state and local services over federal programs.[167] He has justified compassionate conservativism on grounds that the "philosophy trusts individuals to make the right decisions for their families and communities, and that is far more compassionate than a philosophy that seeks solutions from distant bureaucracies."[168]

Subsidiarity is thus a clear and present element in American federalism consciousness. But what does this add to our discussion? Is it really any different from the preference for localism already addressed? Quite so. Examined closely, the subsidiarity principle really embodies two sets of underlying values—one familiar, one new. In directing that governance take place at the most local level possible, subsidiarity fosters the very localism values discussed above: the promotion of localized autonomy, diversity, and interjurisdictional innovation. But subsidiarity implies another principle of good government as well—the implied corollary of the first, but one so easily missed that it usually is.

In directing that public decisions be taken as locally as possible—in other words, by the most local level of government competent to the task—subsidiarity couples the preference for localized decision making with a pragmatic element, the requirement of competence, or *capacity*. In other words, the principle directs that decision making take place at the most local level that can get the job done. Thus, at least to the extent that citizens may rightly look to regulatory assistance in solving a given problem,[169] subsidiarity directs that if the most local level of government lacks the capacity to address it, citizens should be entitled to expect that the next level up with capacity should at least be authorized to try. This is the *problem-solving* principle of federalism—the flip side of subsidiarity's preference for localism.

It was the problem-solving value that James Madison invoked in *Federalist No. 45* when he chided the opponents of the Constitution to recall that "the public good, the real welfare of the great body of the people, is the supreme object to be pursued; and that no form of government whatever has any other value than as it may be fitted for the attainment of this object."[170] He clarified the problem solving of what Justice Black would later call "Our Federalism"[171] in explaining that our federal system was created so that "the people of America

---

166 Regan, *supra* note 106, at 555.

167 Franklin Foer, *Spin Doctrine: The Catholic Teachings of George W.*, THE NEW REPUBLIC, June 5, 2000, at 18 (explaining compassionate conservativism, and reporting President Bush's acknowledgement of its "debt to subsidiarity" in a discussion with Catholic leaders).

168 RONALD KESSLER, A MATTER OF CHARACTER: INSIDE THE WHITE HOUSE OF GEORGE W. BUSH 58 (2004); *see also* Vischer, *supra* note 148, at 103 (noting the connection between subsidiarity and compassionate conservativism).

169 Identifying with precision which problems are susceptible regulatory solutions is a separate problem. *See infra* Chapter Five, text between notes 15 and 16 (discussing my approach).

170 THE FEDERALIST, NO. 45, at 289 (James Madison), *supra* note 5.

171 Younger v. Harris, 401 U.S. 37, 44 (1971).

should enjoy peace, liberty, and safety" and pointedly *not* so that "the governments of the individual States, that particular municipal establishments, might enjoy a certain extent of power and be arrayed with certain dignities and attributes of sovereignty."[172]

Similarly, it was the problem-solving value of federalism that the Department of Homeland Security incorporated into the NRP when it included the statement of subsidiarity in its preamble, and even the White House invoked it in explaining the ultimate federal response to Katrina. According to the White House's own report, *The Federal Response to Hurricane Katrina: Lessons Learned*:

> An important limiting factor of the Federal response . . . is that the Federal response is predicated on an incident being handled *at the lowest jurisdictional level possible*. . . . In the case of Katrina, the local government had been destroyed and the State government was incapacitated, and thus the Federal government had to take on the additional roles of performing incident command and other functions it would normally rely upon the State and local governments to provide.[173]

Although it appears the White House did not learn this lesson in time to prevent the failures discussed in Chapter One, hindsight made the importance of the problem-solving principle crystalline clear. As the sad events of the Katrina emergency unfolded, downed state communication and command infrastructure made it abundantly clear that the most local level of government with the needed response capacity was actually the national government. While respecting the check-and-balance principle may mean that federal actors should take a very "hard look" before stepping into such a situation, the White House report is at least a post-hoc acknowledgement that checks and balances should not come between the federal government and its highest responsibility to protect the lives and safety of its citizens.[174]

Pragmatic problem-solving values are ever-present in the sleeves-rolled-up world of regulatory decision making under cooperative federalism, but it has been mostly absent from consideration by the New Federalism decisions and the dualist model they reflect. The Supreme Court has never decided a case on the basis of subsidiarity, although Justice Breyer invoked the principle in dissenting from *United States v. Morrison*'s invalidation of the Violence Against Women Act, pointing to the European Union's subsidiarity principle as an alternative approach to protecting the federalism values that were the subject of the case.[175] Suggesting that the majority's separationist approach to protecting federalism values would prove unworkable, Justice Breyer proposed that these values might be better protected by the procedural approach Congress had taken before passing the Act, in which it carefully established that victims of gender violence were chronically underprotected at the state level—an approach that he expressly analogized to subsidiarity.[176] Under this approach, Congress

---

[172] THE FEDERALIST, No. 45, at 289 (James Madison), *supra* note 5.

[173] WHITE HOUSE KATRINA REPORT *supra* Chapter One, note 69, at 42 (emphasis added).

[174] *See* NRP, *supra* Chapter One, note 64, at 4.

[175] 529 U.S. 598, 633 (2000) (Breyer, J., dissenting) (citing to Bermann, *supra* note 160, at 378–403).

[176] *Id.* at 663–64.

would take a "hard look" at whether the federal regulatory intervention is truly warranted in an area in which the states have traditionally regulated, and legislation would proceed only if Congress could demonstrate that additional response is needed at the federal level.[177]

As Justice Breyer's cautious endorsement indicates, allowing the problem-solving value alone to determine federal involvement would endanger other features of federalism. If broad sources of federal legal and fiscal capacity lead to exaggerated demands for federal involvement, problem-solving claims could collide with the preservation of a healthy balance of state and federal power. Pragmatism competes with the check-and-balance value, which is pointedly served by other structural features of American governance that also purposely sacrifice efficiency (such as the bicameral legislature). In other words, the problem-solving value may not care whether resolution occurs by local or national authority, but the check-and-balance value cares very deeply, lest *every* problem become the subject of national attention and state authority wane accordingly. It is this concern that Professor William Van Alstyne invoked in his admonition that we would soon find federalism adrift in a "cellophane sea" if Congress were permitted to legislate on any topic it could encase in the "cellophane wrapper" of a putative connection to interstate commerce.[178]

However, a framework of federalism that accounts for all component values need not be so at risk. First, the subsidiarity framework pairs the problem-solving value with the preference for localism, moderating problem solving in the local direction and supporting the antityranny goal of checks and balances. Just as important, the preference for localism is moderated by the requirement for problem-solving capacity—and the federal government will lack competence in many regulatory arenas that demand local expertise, authority, or boots-on-the-ground enforcement capability. This bidirectional moderating influence prevents the problem-solving principle from overwhelming the anti-tyranny principle, just as the problem-solving principle keeps the anti-tyranny principle in service of the ultimately pragmatic purposes of government acclaimed by Madison.[179]

The careful maintenance of structural tension between these underlying principles promotes healthy federalism in the same way that the careful maintenance of tension between state and federal power promotes the health of the overall system. The problem-solving value does not endorse any one particular vision of dual sovereignty or another, so long as structural tension is maintained without overly compromising pragmatic response. It implies the importance of a model that protects true localism values, but its capacity requirement

---

[177] *Id.* As Justice Breyer explained, "[o]f course, any judicial insistence that Congress follow particular procedures might itself intrude upon congressional prerogatives and embody difficult definitional problems. But the intrusion, problems, and consequences all would seem less serious than those embodied in the majority's approach. . . . I recognize that the law in this area is unstable and that time and experience may demonstrate both the unworkability of the majority's rules and the superiority of Congress' own procedural approach—in which case the law may evolve toward a rule that, in certain difficult Commerce Clause cases, takes account of the thoroughness with which Congress has considered the federalism issue." *Id.*

[178] *See* Van Alstyne, *supra* Introduction, note 7, at 782–83 (noting that "[a]ll laws affect commerce in one way or another"); *see also* Eric R. Claeys, *The Living Commerce Clause: Federalism in Progressive Political Theory and the Commerce Clause after Lopez and Morrison*, 11 Wm. & Mary Bill Rts. J. 403, 404–05 (2002).

[179] *See* The Federalist, No. 45, at 289 (James Madison), *supra* note 5; *see also* Moreno, *supra* note 7, at 715 ("By 'constitutional' government, the framers meant *effective* but limited government.") (emphasis added).

demands room for negotiation up the chain if neither the local nor state level, acting alone, possesses the needed jurisdiction or expertise.

In the end, the problem-solving value is not the most important federalism value, and subsidiarity is not the defining federalism principle. And though the former derives some provenance from the latter, the problem-solving value and subsidiarity are not interchangeable. Subsidiarity has been criticized for encouraging too much bifurcation in localized and centralized regulatory response, even when more integrative solutions to interjurisdictional problems are needed.[180] This reading understands subsidiarity as assigning responsibility for problem solving to one governmental actor at a time, when interjurisdictional problem solving often demands a collaborative approach—as in the Katrina response discussed above, or the management of radioactive waste discussed in Chapter Seven.

However, the problem-solving value that helps undergird federalism goes beyond simple subsidiarity. Federalism's problem-solving value encapsulates the insights of subsidiarity, the pragmatic advantages of the constitutional federation over the previous confederation, and the synergy federalism enables between unique state and federal capacity that makes so many examples of collaborative state-federal governance effective.[181] We can unpack the constituent components of the problem-solving value in the same way we can unpack the constituent components of the localism value—and in the same way we have just unpacked the constituent components of American federalism itself.

F. Values and Federalism Theory

The forgoing discussion reviews the four fundamental good governance values that undergird American federalism—checks and balances, accountability and participation, local innovation and competition, and state-federal problem-solving synergy—as well as the tensions that inhere between them. In revealing these tensions, it demonstrates that a normative approach to federalism interpretation will not promote federalism values indiscriminately. Rather, it will promote a specific constellation of support for some federalism values at the expense of others—a distinct model of federal-state relations that is one of many possible variations.

For example, the dual federalism model embraced by the New Federalism prevents tyranny by emphasizing the checks and balances of jurisdictional separation, and may reduce voter confusion in service of the accountability value. It serves localism values only superficially (at the state level), and compromises the problem-solving value by inhibiting jurisdictional

---

[180] Cf. John R. Nolon, *Champions of Change: Reinventing Democracy through Land Law Reform*, 30 Harv. Envtl. L. Rev. 1, 18–20 (2006) (advancing a model of integrated federalism that relies on greater cooperation based on each governmental actor's capacity for problem solving in a given context); telephone Interview with John Nolon, Professor, Pace Law School, in White Plains, N.Y. (Feb. 24, 2006) ("Subsidiarity's problem is that it tends to lead toward dual sovereignty and bifurcation, disallowing the different levels of government to cooperate in the more integrated fashion often necessary to solve problems."). Indeed, some American proponents of subsidiarity have mistaken it to stand for the model of classical dual federalism itself. Cf. Foer, *supra* note 167.

[181] See *infra* Chapter Eight (describing examples of state-federal collaborative governance).

overlap even when needed. Cooperative federalism offers a different recipe, forestalling tyranny through the checks and balances of jurisdictional overlap, which can also serve the problem-solving value. However, it has an uncertain relationship with accountability and an undertheorized relationship with localism values.

Despite rhetorical claims to the contrary, however, neither holds a monopoly on the true essence of American federalism; they are just two interpretive possibilities among others. In fact, the history of federalism in the United States reveals their role in the development of a variety of conceptual models of federalism, each faithful to the federalism values in different configurations. These different models of American federalism, especially those that evolved over the twentieth century, reflect repeated attempts to find the right balance between them. The next chapter reviews this evolution.

3

AMERICAN FEDERALISMS: FROM NEW FOUNDATIONS

TO NEW FEDERALISM

LIKE ALL GOOD tales of legal history, the story of American federalism is largely one of competition between compelling principles in tension with one another, stretching the legal framework in one direction and then overcorrecting in another. Visualizing operative federalism theory as a four-dimensional pendulum, we can see it swinging freely over time among the independent federalism values, pointing to a favorite at one period in history and another in a different era. Ongoing uncertainty about how judicial doctrine should resolve these issues is reflected by the Supreme Court's vacillating case law over time. If New Federalism pushed the pendulum toward classical checks and balances, it was surely in response to a previous swing toward the pragmatic side, when federal jurisdiction expanded after the Great Depression and vitiated the capacity of states and localities to respond to the overwhelming economic collapse.[1] The swing of the pendulum is not necessarily graceful; powerful historical events such as the Civil War and Great Depression can wrench it in sudden and extreme directions. Its arc reflects the combined forces of gradual ideological oscillation and occasionally violent tug of war as social events impact the evolution of interpretive federalism theory.

We might therefore understand the theoretical contrast between the Court's New Federalism cases and the predominant cooperative federalism baseline as one of many iterations in this episodic tug of war between competing federalism values. American federalisms'

---

[1] Martin S. Flaherty, *Byron White, Federalism, and the "Greatest Generation(s)," 74 U. COLO. L. REV. 1573, 1596–97 (2003) (describing the pragmatic expansion of federal power and rejection of judicial constraints during the New Deal).

progression across the twentieth century especially reveals this dialectic, through the various models embraced during the Progressive/*Lochner* era and into the New Deal, later moderated by cooperative federalism until the New Federalism challenge. Ultimately, New Federalism's exaltation of the check-and-balance value above all others was a response to the New Deal's like exaltation of the problem-solving value above all else, which was itself a reaction to the preceding circumstances. Shifts in theoretical emphasis between one model and another reflect continuing efforts by judicial and political actors to order the values clash under the demands of new circumstances, even when their choice of model is made unaware.

Accordingly, this chapter traces the swing of the pendulum through the latter part of American history, understanding its multidimensional arc in terms of shifting theories about how best to balance competing federalism values. The full story of American federalism has been told by better tellers in more hallowed volumes,[2] and the legal history of the Court's Tenth Amendment jurisprudence is addressed more fully in Chapter Four. However, this chapter's summary of a few periods in American history explores how important societal events and legal ideas correspond to the different constellations of values used in political and judicial federalism interpretation of the time. The dialectic emphasizes both continuity and change—continuity in the recurring quest to balance the same basic tensions within federalism, and change in the unique social facts that bring different values to the fore at various times. Within this narrative, federalism interpreters explicitly and implicitly appeal to different theoretical models to make sense of their task, through ideological transitions marked by the cyclical refrain of the values clash of the intrusion of unique historical circumstance.

The first section introduces important events in early American history that showcase the difficulties American federalism pioneers faced in deciphering what their new concept of dual sovereignty meant in practice. Dual federalism emerged as the theoretical touchstone of nineteenth century federalism, establishing the classical idealism for which later dualist models would yearn. Even so, the challenges of jurisdictional overlap grew steadily over time, beginning as early as the Constitutional Convention's replacement of the Articles of Confederation. This brief summary of the first century of federalism provides context for the more detailed discussion of twentieth century federalisms that follows. The second part of the chapter explores how policy makers and judges variously managed the tug of war during the Progressive and *Lochner* eras, the Great Depression and the New Deal, the Civil Rights

---

[2] For excellent historical accounts of American law generally and federalism particularly, see PURCELL, *supra* Introduction, note 11; LaCROIX, *supra* Introduction, note 71; DAVID P. CURRIE, THE CONSTITUTION IN CONGRESS: DEMOCRATS AND WHIGS: 1829–1861 (2005); DAVID P. CURRIE, THE CONSTITUTION OF THE UNITED STATES: A PRIMER FOR THE PEOPLE (1988); BARRY CUSHMAN, RETHINKING THE NEW DEAL COURT (1998); LAWRENCE M. FRIEDMAN, LAW IN AMERICA: A SHORT HISTORY (2002); LAWRENCE M. FRIEDMAN, A HISTORY OF AMERICAN LAW (1985); KERMIT L. HALL & PETER KARSTEN, THE MAGIC MIRROR: LAW IN AMERICAN HISTORY (2009); SAMUEL ELIOT MORISON, THE OXFORD HISTORY OF THE AMERICAN PEOPLE (1965); JACK N. RAKOVE, THE BEGINNINGS OF NATIONAL POLITICS: AN INTERPRETIVE HISTORY OF THE CONTINENTAL CONGRESS; ROBERT V. REMINI, A SHORT HISTORY OF THE UNITED STATES (2008).

Movement and the Great Society era that led to the entrenchment of cooperative federalism, and finally, the New Federalism challenge under the Rehnquist Court.

A. The First Century

The federalism quandaries that would unfold over American history began well before the Constitution was ratified. As Professor Allison LaCroix describes, the idea of jurisdictional multiplicity that would ultimately take root in American federalism owed a debt to prior sources both ideological and pragmatic, from the continental political philosophy of Pufendorf and Grotius to experiments with confederal unions between the prerevolutionary colonies.[3] Informed by these ideas and experiences, the early architects of the Constitution arrived at the paradigm-shifting proposal that, in LaCroix's words, "multiple independent levels of government could legitimately exist within a single polity, and that such an arrangement was not a defect to be lamented but a virtue to be celebrated."[4]

Before and after the war for independence, the colonists were dubious about repeating their experience with distant, centralized power, and their first attempt at self-government reflected this anxiety. The Articles of Confederation created a simple legislative alliance between the original thirteen states, purposely without an executive or judicial system.[5] In a precursor to the Tenth Amendment, the Articles gave the new legislature specific substantive authority over such areas of government as foreign affairs, postage, and currency, but meticulously reserved to the states "every power, jurisdiction, and right, which is not by this Confederation expressly delegated" to the new legislative body.[6] Each state's single delegate enjoyed a single vote, and legislative action often required unanimity or supermajority support.[7]

Reluctant to cede their newly won sovereignty (and authority that some had wielded for more than a century), the states created a purposefully weak confederal partnership, operating more like a treaty governing the relations among sovereign states than a unifying institution.[8] The legislature had no authority over commercial issues, and the emerging national economy was plagued by problems of parochialism and collective action. State legislatures erected trade barriers that stunted the potential for overall economic growth, and state judiciaries often favored local interests over out-of-state creditors, inhibiting the development of interstate credit markets.[9] In addition, the Articles conferred only limited central authority to raise revenue, preventing adequate funding of the military force needed to cope with ongoing conflicts among the European powers.[10]

---

[3] LaCroix, *supra* Introduction, note 71, at 11–29.

[4] *Id.* at 6.

[5] *Id.* at 126–31.

[6] *Id.* at 127.

[7] Schapiro, *supra* Introduction, note 11, at 31–32.

[8] *Id.*

[9] *Id.* at 32.

[10] *Id.*

In conceding the failure of the decentralizing Articles of Confederation, the Constitution's architects explored different ways of balancing centralized authority with local autonomy. Virginia's early proposal for the federation emphasized stronger national power and proportional representation in a bicameral legislature (effectively favoring the interests of the larger states), while New Jersey and the smaller states countered with a plan maintaining equal state representation in a unicameral legislature.[11] James Madison's proposal that the national legislature be empowered to veto unconstitutional state law was incorporated into the Virginia Plan, but ultimately rejected by Constitutional Convention delegates in favor of judicial review.[12] Grounding the dual federalism model that would take hold in the years to come, the delegates labored to determine the distinct subject-matter boundaries within which each level of government would operate (although as Professor LaCroix notes, their adoption of the Supremacy Clause reveals early ideological acknowledgement of the inevitability of jurisdictional overlap).[13]

Responding to editorials attacking the new constitutional plan, Alexander Hamilton, James Madison, and John Jay advocated for the federal arrangement in a series of newspaper articles published between 1787 and 1788 that later became known as the Federalist Papers.[14] The federalist/antifederalist debate continued during President Washington's administration in the interpretive combat between Hamilton's respective emphasis on strong central power and Jefferson's regard for states' rights.[15] Even after the Constitution was ratified, among the many important questions left unsettled was "the locus of authority in construing the Constitution and resolving conflicts between the central government and the states."[16]

After serving in both the federal legislative and executive branches before becoming chief justice of the new Supreme Court, John Marshall would reflect on the problem in one of his most important decisions, *McCulloch v. Maryland*:

> This government is acknowledged by all, to be one of enumerated powers. The principle, that it can exercise only the powers granted to it . . . is now universally admitted. But the question respecting the extent of the powers actually granted, is perpetually arising, and will probably continue to arise, as long as our system shall exist.[17]

As legal historian Edward Purcell succinctly explains, "[t]he matter had not been settled for an obvious reason. The founders harbored too many vague, incomplete, and conflicting ideas on the subject to underwrite any clear consensus."[18] Without consensus among the architects

---

[11] MORISON, *supra* note 2, at 307; Virginia Plan, http://www.usconstitution.net/plan_va.html.

[12] LaCROIX, *supra* Introduction, note 71, at 135–39 (the federal "negative"), 147–48 (incorporation into the Virginia Plan); 158–66 (judicial review).

[13] *Id.* at 175.

[14] *Supra* Chapter Two, note 5.

[15] JOHN FERLING, THE ASCENT OF GEORGE WASHINGTON 289–307 (2009); MORISON, *supra* note 2, at 323–31.

[16] PURCELL, *supra* Introduction, note 11, at 140.

[17] McCulloch v. Maryland, 17 U.S. 316, 405 (1819).

[18] PURCELL, *supra* Introduction, note 11, at 140.

or clear guidance in the document, versions of the same debate—*who should decide?*—would continue to play out over and over in new contexts, just as the debate continues today.

Even after ratification of the Constitution in 1789, federalism controversy erupted immediately when Congress established a national bank in 1791.[19] Federalist proponents, including then-Secretary of the Treasury Alexander Hamilton, made the (subsidiarity-premised) argument that a central bank was necessary to unify the multiple currencies then in use, enable meaningful national credit, and generally establish financial order in the new federation.[20] Antifederalist opponents, many of them southern agriculturalists, were less dependent on a centralized currency and deeply suspicious of this assertion of national power. Thomas Jefferson in President Washington's cabinet and James Madison in the House of Representatives both objected that the bank was unconstitutional, paving the way toward the defeat of its renewal when its charter expired in 1811.[21]

However, in a move that exposed the instability of federalism theory even among its originators, Madison later reinstituted the bank as president in 1816 having decided that it was a legitimate exercise of federal power after all. Capitulating to federalism's pragmatic values, he presumably conceded that a national bank was proper because it was necessary—just as the Constitution anticipated some exercises of federal power would be in order to effectuate other enumerated powers.[22] Indeed, in 1819, the Necessary and Proper Clause would ultimately vindicate the bank against constitutional challenge in *McCulloch v. Maryland.*[23] Nevertheless, the controversial institution did not survive the later administration of President Andrew Jackson.[24]

Federalism controversy continued in 1798 when the Federalist Party-controlled Congress passed a set of laws in the midst of military conflict with France that became known as the Alien and Sedition Acts. These laws dubiously eased the detention and deportation of non-citizens deemed a threat to public order and effectively criminalized the criticism of government policy and officials.[25] Thomas Jefferson and James Madison strongly denounced these laws and urged states to nullify them as unconstitutional exercises of federal power. The assaults on liberty and free speech are most patent today, but the constitutional violation Jefferson most passionately decried was that of the Tenth Amendment.[26]

In a resolution adopted by the Kentucky state legislature, he argued that the powers to create and punish such crimes, having never been enumerated to Congress, were reserved to the states, and that states should reject the Alien and Sedition Acts as inconsistent with

---

[19] *See* Michael J. Klarman, *How Great Were the "Great" Marshall Court Decisions?*, 87 VA. L. REV. 1111, 1128–29 (2001) (discussing controversy over the new central bank).

[20] *See* Jerry W. Markham, *Banking Regulation: Its History and Future*, 4 N.C. BANKING INST. 221, 223 (2000).

[21] *See* Klarman, *supra* note 19, at 1128–29.

[22] U.S. CONST. art. I, § 8.

[23] 17 U.S. 316 (1819).

[24] FRIEDMAN, A HISTORY OF AMERICAN LAW, *supra* note 2, at 179 (discussing its demise).

[25] REMINI, *supra* note 2, at 63–64. *See also* HALL & KARSTEN, *supra* note 2, at 81–82 (calling the Sedition Act "the first national experiment in using legal authority to reap political benefit").

[26] The Kentucky resolution that Jefferson authored, adopted by the state legislature on Nov. 10, 1798, is available at http://www.constitution.org/cons/kent1798.htm.

various constitutional promises.[27] Madison authored another resolution adopted by the Virginia legislature equally asserting the importance of the states as a check on federal power. Both resolutions declared that the states held the ultimate authority to interpret the Constitution and were "duty bound" to take action against unconstitutional congressional acts.[28] At this early juncture in American history, opposition to the laws was staged in the political sphere. Judicial redress for unconstitutional laws had yet to be confirmed in the landmark 1803 case of *Marbury v. Madison*, by which time the offending laws had mostly expired.[29]

Federal judicial power was also challenged in the earliest days of the republic, when states resisted the Supreme Court's 1793 holding in *Chisholm v. Georgia* that a state could be held responsible for out-of-state revolutionary war debt.[30] States had been extremely concerned about suits by such creditors after the war, and Hamilton had used the Federalist Papers to reassure the antifederalists that the Constitution would not allow states to be sued this way without their consent.[31] The Court's contrary holding in its first significant ruling rekindled fears that federal courts would undermine state autonomy under the federal system. Outcompeting the values of governmental accountability and checks on sovereign authority implied by judicial redress in such cases, strong localist sentiment led to the ratification of formal Eleventh Amendment protections for state sovereign immunity against suit by citizens of another state.[32]

Nevertheless, federal power was discovered and asserted in a variety of new contexts during the state-building period from the nation's founding though the Civil War. The Supreme Court established federal supremacy over state court interpretation of constitutional questions in 1816 in *Martin v. Hunter's Lessee*, rejecting Virginia's attempt to prevent the Court from overruling its own interpretation of federal law.[33] Controversy that began over the National Bank in 1791 culminated in *McCulloch v. Maryland*'s 1819 recognition that the Necessary and Proper Clause implied federal power to create such an institution, dramatically invalidating Maryland's attempts to impede the Bank's operation by taxing it.[34] In 1824, *Gibbons v. Ogden* recognized federal legislative power to regulate interstate transportation under the Commerce Clause, further confirming federal supremacy over conflicting state law.[35] Decisions such as these shaped an emerging Madisonian recognition by the

---

[27] *Id.* In the alternative, Jefferson also argued that the Acts were void because the First Amendment prevented Congress from passing laws that interfered with free speech—but this was subsidiary to the Resolution's overarching claim that the power required to pass such laws had been reserved to the states. *Id.* at paragraph 3.

[28] PURCELL, *supra* Introduction, note 11, at 44, 143–44.

[29] 5 U.S. 137 (1803).

[30] 2 U.S. (2 Dall.) 419 (1793); MORISON, *supra* note 2, at 340–41.

[31] THE FEDERALIST, NO. 81, at 455–56 (Alexander Hamilton), *supra* Chapter Two, note 5.

[32] U.S. CONST. amend XI; HALL & KARSTEN, *supra* note 2, at 80.

[33] 14 U.S. 304 (1816).

[34] 17 U.S. 316 (1819).

[35] 22 U.S. 1 (1824). *See* Norman R. Williams, *Gibbons*, 79 N.Y.U. L. REV. 1398 (2004) (discussing the decision's flirtation with the dormant commerce clause established in later years).

Supreme Court that federalism did not simply refer to the protection of states' rights, but also to the articulation of the nation's powers.[36]

Yet recognizing greater federal power was not inconsistent with the dual federalism ideal of jurisdictional separation that reached its apex during the nineteenth century.[37] The Supreme Court's jurisprudence highlights the growing predominance of dual federalism ideology, as in Chief Justice Roger Taney's mid-century admonition that "[t]he powers of the General Government, and of the State, although both exist and are exercised within the same territorial limits, are yet separate and distinct sovereignties, acting separately and independently of each other within their respective spheres."[38] Even as Congress took on a more active (and occasionally controversial) role in encouraging public works projects such as roads and railways,[39] the commitment to protecting large spheres of local autonomy from central regulatory intrusion retained ideological gravity—especially regarding the institution of slavery. Indeed, as Professor Schapiro observes, "the imperative to avoid federal regulation of slavery lent considerable support to the idea of limiting federal power" and dividing state and federal subject matter jurisdiction.[40] Still, as the new republic gradually found its institutional legs, conflicts continued to emerge between state and federal authority where overlap was inevitable, especially in matters relating to commerce.[41]

Such a political crisis arose in 1832 when South Carolina claimed sovereign authority to nullify federal law, declaring the federal Tariff Acts of 1828 and 1832 unconstitutional and void within state boundaries.[42] The tariffs had been enacted as price supports for northern goods competing with cheap imports, but they weakened the economic position of southern interests forced to pay higher prices for out-of-state goods.[43] After both South Carolina and President Jackson threatened force to resolve the conflict—and South Carolina threatened secession—the standoff was ended through passage of the compromise Tariff Act of 1833.[44] However, the crisis renewed the simmering debate about the appropriate relationship between state sovereignty and federal power. It also furthered antagonism between the northern and southern states, which gathered steam as further political events propelled the states toward the Civil War.

In fact, the drafters of the Constitution had carefully avoided a crisp stance on slavery, one of the primary sources of conflict during the Constitutional Convention between those

---

[36] PURCELL, *supra* Introduction, note 11, at 22.

[37] *See generally* Corwin, *supra* Part I Introduction, note 3; PURCELL, *supra* Introduction, note 11, at 177–79. Professor Purcell's work shows that even "classical" nineteenth-century dualism was not uniform, as it was shaded differently at times for different purposes.

[38] Abelman v. Booth, 62 U.S. (21 How.) 506, 516 (1859). *See also* Kentucky v. Dennison, 65 U.S. (24 How.) 66 (1861).

[39] FRIEDMAN, LAW IN AMERICA, *supra* note 2, at 39–40.

[40] SCHAPIRO, *supra* Introduction, note 11, at 35.

[41] *E.g.*, Cooley v. Bd. of Wardens, 53 U.S. (12 How.) 299 (1851) (distinguishing between commercial subjects subject to federal regulation and those reserved to the states).

[42] *Cf.* PURCELL, *supra* Introduction, note 11, at 59.

[43] REMINI, *supra* note 2, at 93, 102–03.

[44] CURRIE, THE CONSTITUTION IN CONGRESS, *supra* note 2, at 99–117.

favoring more and less federal power.[45] The détente between factions lasted so long as coalitions among the states were able to exploit national power for shared ends without triggering this underlying divide.[46] But as federal power was called upon to adjudicate questions of slavery, both judicially and legislatively, the simmering conflict boiled over.[47] Federal enforcement of the Fugitive Slave Acts, which required the return of runaway slaves to their masters, provoked further crisis when the Supreme Court invalidated conflicting northern laws protecting escaped slaves and those who assisted them, as in *Prigg v. Pennsylvania*.[48] The 1857 case of *Dred Scott v. Sandford*, in which the Court affirmed the institution of slavery by narrowly interpreting federal power to regulate slavery in the territories, proved the judicial culmination of this unresolved tension.[49]

The resulting Civil War posed the greatest political challenge to federalism in American history, dramatically confirming the supremacy of federal power over state autonomy within the dual sovereignty framework. The history of the Civil War reflects the force of social and ideological factors that lie beyond the scope of this treatment, but the federalism implications are especially profound. To the Confederates, the outcome of the war portended a failure of the checks and balances that federalism had promised between state and federal power. But more specifically, the outcome suggests the success of one model of federalism over another, especially regarding competing visions of the check-and-balance value.

If the check-and-balance value serves only the neutral goal of counterbalancing state and federal power in a consensual union, then military confirmation that state sovereignty does not include the power to secede represents a serious blow to this conception of states' rights. However, if the normative purpose of dividing state and federal power is to protect *individuals* against tyranny, then the war's termination of slavery—the greatest assault on individual rights in our nation's history—represents the ultimate triumph of checks and balances. Here, federal authority was used as needed to help forge a union in which sovereign authority would be more accountable to all citizens, though at the expense of local autonomy. The example demonstrates that normative federalism theory must not only resolve tension among the federalism values, but in some instances, it must also assign meaning to the contested values themselves.

The Civil War punctured the nineteenth-century ideal of jurisdictional separation in conceding the subsidiarity-based need for federal intervention in a traditional state law institution (slavery) that unacceptably burdened fundamental human rights.[50] The protections for

---

[45] HALL & KARSTEN, *supra* note 2, at 143.

[46] MORISON, *supra* note 2, at 400.

[47] HALL & KARSTEN, *supra* note 2, at 157–58.

[48] 41 U.S. 539 (1842); *see also* Ableman v. Booth, 62 U.S. 506 (1859).

[49] 60 U.S. 393 (1857).

[50] The suspension was situational, however, and the Court continued to invoke dual federalism ideals in other cases. *See, e.g.*, Collector v. Day, 78 U.S. (11 Wall.) 113, 124 (1870) ("The general government, and the States, although both exist within the same territorial limits, are separate and distinct sovereignties, acting separately and independently of each other, within their respective spheres. The former in its appropriate sphere is supreme; but the States within the limits of their powers not granted, or, in the language of the tenth amendment, 'reserved,' are as independent of the general government as that government within its sphere is independent of the States.").

individual liberties in the Bill of Rights were originally designed to constrain only federal authority and did not apply to state law. However, the constitutional amendments that followed the Civil War would begin the long process of enforcing individual rights against the states—and they would forever change the relationship between state and federal power.

The Thirteenth Amendment banned slavery in the United States,[51] and the Fifteenth Amendment attempted to enfranchise slaves and their descendants by prohibiting abridgment of the right to vote on the basis of race or former condition of servitude.[52] The Fourteenth Amendment established that all persons born in the United States were American citizens entitled to the privileges or immunities thereof, and it prohibited the states from depriving any person of due process or equal protection under the law.[53] Each amendment conferred specific, new authority on Congress to enforce these provisions by appropriate legislation, establishing new sources of federal authority that would become increasingly important in the subsequent century. Section Five of the Fourteenth Amendment, conferring federal authority to enforce new constitutional promises of due process and equal protection, would become especially important.

The post-Civil War amendments would spawn great federalism controversies in the following century, when the Fourteenth Amendment's promise of equal protection and due process was interpreted to incorporate other individual rights in the Bill of Rights against the states as well.[54] After the war, however, Congress attempted to use its new authority with more mixed results, enacting a series of civil rights laws that conflicted with discriminatory state laws. For example, in the Civil Rights Act of 1866, Congress declared that slaves and their descendants were citizens with the same rights as white citizens to enforce contracts, hold property, and access the courts.[55] Yet federal law notwithstanding, Jim Crow laws would operate to the contrary in many states for decades to come.

In the Civil Rights Act of 1871, Congress provided a federal civil remedy for African-Americans whose constitutional rights had been violated under color of state law, a civil rights remedy that remains among the most critical in force today.[56] In the Civil Rights Act of 1875, Congress tried to prohibit racial discrimination in places of public accommodation (as the Civil Rights Act of 1964 eventually would under the commerce power[57]). Nevertheless, the Supreme Court invalidated the 1875 Act as exceeding federal authority under the Fourteenth Amendment.[58] It later affirmed the constitutionality of state segregation laws in

---

[51] U.S. CONST. amend. XIII.

[52] U.S. CONST. amend. XV.

[53] U.S. CONST. amend. XIV.

[54] HALL & KARSTEN, *supra* note 2, at 160–61.

[55] The content is now codified at 42 U.S.C. § 1981.

[56] The content is now codified at 42 U.S.C. § 1983 (declaring that anyone who acts "under cover of any statute, ordinance, regulation, custom, or usage, of any State or Territory" to deprive another of "any rights, privileges, or immunities secured by the Constitution and laws" will be "liable to the party injured in an action at law, Suit in equity, or other proper proceeding for redress").

[57] 42 U.S.C. § 2000 *et seq.* (1964).

[58] The Civil Rights Cases, 109 U.S. 3 (1883).

1896 in *Plessy v. Ferguson*,[59] reinforcing the failure of the 1875 Act. The surviving Acts of 1866 and 1871 had little effect until the 1960s, when courts finally began using them (especially the latter) as a check on Jim Crow laws.

After the Civil War, two forces converged to accelerate the expansion of federal judicial and legislative power, further challenging the antebellum dualist balance. The first was morally based. As Professors Kermit Hall and Peter Karsten explain, the Civil War transformed the Constitution from a system of negative power to a system of positive potential, one that could proactively safeguard the philosophy of individual rights that had helped inspire the federal design in the first place:

> The antislavery bar's stress on the positive responsibility of the national government to advance individual rights converged with the nationalism of Marshall, Story, and Abraham Lincoln. The resulting new view of the Constitution held that it imposed duties on the national government "to act positively, as an instrument, to realize purposes that had inspired the creation of the nation."[60]

This view of federal responsibility coincided with the postbellum realization of checks and balances as the defender of individual rights rather than state rights, or state autonomy for its own sake.

The second force accelerating federal power was economic. In the nineteenth century, states jealously guarded their regulatory privileges until the rise of the national economy created problems beyond the jurisdiction of any single state. In this respect, the rise of federal power reflected some of the same expectations Americans have of the national government since the rejection of the Articles of Confederation. As Professor Lawrence Friedman explains:

> What changed the situation, and created a stronger central government, was the rise of a *national* economy. A national economy meant national problems—Congress passed the Interstate Commerce Commission Act in 1887, in response to demands for control over the giant railroad nets. Farmers and small merchants felt they were at the mercy of the big, bad railroads; state regulation was a pitiful failure, because railroads were beyond the control of any particular state. Only a federal agency had any chance to be effective.[61]

This view of federal responsibility coincided with the subsidiarity-tempered problem-solving value, recognizing the need for central oversight of economic collective action problems that exceeded state regulatory capacity.

Growing expectations about the role of the national government were also reflected in the increasing demand for federal court adjudication. The Judiciary Act of 1869 established nine new circuit court judgeships, and Congress nationalized the organization and jurisdiction of

---

[59] 163 U.S. 537 (1896).

[60] HALL & KARSTEN, *supra* note 2, at 160 (citation omitted).

[61] FRIEDMAN, LAW IN AMERICA, *supra* note 2, at 126.

the lower federal courts.[62] Most lower federal courts had not been busy before the Civil War, but caseloads exploded as the population and economy grew.[63] *Swift v. Tyson* in 1842 had established the federal common law of commerce,[64] and the lower courts now became forums in which interstate businesses could bring claims without fear of parochial bias.[65] The Removal Act of 1875 further encouraged use of the federal courts by the interstate business community, allowing litigants to remove a case from state to federal court if the parties were from different states, or if the case raised a question of federal law.[66]

Struggles over who would decide (and how) continued to preoccupy constitutional interpreters during postbellum Reconstruction and into the new century, when federalism's tug of war was modified by the new constitutional norms of the post-Civil War amendments and the economic and social consequences of rapid industrialization. The Fourteenth Amendment provided an enormously important source of federal authority to protect individual rights against contrary state law. But it was the harnessing of electrical power and new manufacturing technology in the late stages of the industrial revolution that set a new stage for federalism controversies at the turn of the twentieth century. During the early years of the new century, Congress was just beginning to test the scope of its affirmative commerce authority, and the Supreme Court was using the Fourteenth Amendment not to invalidate racially discriminatory state laws but progressive state labor laws.

B. Postbellum Expansion, the Progressive Movement, and the *Lochner* Era

Together with the new sources of post-Civil War federal authority, regulatory responses to the social and economic consequences of the second industrial revolution initiated the parade of federalism models with which Americans experimented over the following century. We begin our review with the Progressive movement and the Supreme Court's notorious *Lochner* era.

Rapid industrialization at the turn of the twentieth century multiplied links across interstate markets while spawning working and living conditions that triggered outrage among the burgeoning Progressive movement.[67] Interstate commerce flourished as industrialization began to transform the United States from a rural agrarian nation to one of rapidly developing port and manufacturing centers. Congress began experimenting more with use of its affirmative commerce authority, displacing state laws regulating such vulnerable matters as railroads and other common carriers. The Interstate Commerce Act of 1887 was enacted to assert federal authority over the all-powerful national railroads as channels of

---

[62] HALL & KARSTEN, *supra* note 2, at 250.

[63] *Id.* at 249–50.

[64] 41 U.S. 1 (1842).

[65] HALL & KARSTEN, *supra* note 2, at 250, 258. *See also* TONY A. FREYER, FORUMS OF ORDER: THE FEDERAL COURTS AND BUSINESS IN AMERICAN HISTORY (1979) (exploring the evolving influence of the federal courts).

[66] *Id.* at 251.

[67] *See* RICHARD HOFSTADTER, THE AGE OF REFORM 174–214 (1955).

interstate commerce,[68] and the Sherman Antitrust Act of 1890 was enacted to protect interstate commerce from price-fixing, monopolies, and other anticompetitive market activity.[69] When the Supreme Court upheld the Lottery Act of 1895, by which Congress prohibited the sale of lottery tickets across state lines, it marked an important step toward judicial recognition of a plenary federal commerce power.[70]

In the early decades of the new century, Congress continued to experiment with its authority to regulate interstate commerce, taxing items in interstate commerce,[71] prohibiting interstate human trafficking under the Mann Act of 1910,[72] and supporting state efforts at Prohibition by regulating the interstate transport of alcohol under the Webb-Kenyon Act of 1913.[73] In 1906, Congress enacted the Pure Food and Drug Act in response to public outcry over state law impotence in dealing with poor quality foods and mislabeled drugs that were shipped beyond state lines.[74] In 1916, the Sixteenth Amendment was ratified, legalizing direct federal income taxes and paving the way for expanded use of the federal spending power in the following decades.[75] In the same year, Congress established the Federal Reserve to administer a national banking system and the Federal Trade Commission in 1914 to police unfair interstate trade practices.[76] Progressive President Theodore Roosevelt also expanded national power at the executive level through his own establishment of eighteen national monuments and his support for the legislative establishment of five national parks.[77]

At the same time that Congress was beginning to flex its affirmative commerce authority, the Supreme Court was expanding its limitation of state laws under the dormant Commerce Clause, the negative inference of Congress's grant of federal power to regulate commerce.[78] A dualist premise reinforcing the negative commerce power is that the Constitution delegates

---

[68] Interstate Commerce Act of 1887, 24 Stat. 379 (codified as amended in scattered sections of 49 U.S.C.).

[69] Sherman Act, ch. 647, 26 Stat. 209, 15 U.S.C. §1 *et seq.* (1890); *see also* Moreno, *supra* Chapter Two, note 7, at 736–38 (describing some successes in Congress's early attempts at Progressive legislation).

[70] *See* Champion v. Ames, 188 U.S. 321 (1903).

[71] *E.g.,* Oleomargarine Act of 1902, Pub. L. No. 57–110, 32 Stat. 194 (raising the federal excise tax on interstate sales of margarine); *see* Barry Cushman, *The Structure of Classical Public Law,* 75 U. CHI. L. REV. 1917 (2008) (reporting on the federalism debate over the Act in the political sphere).

[72] Still in effect, the modern statute specifically prohibits the interstate transport of persons relating to prostitution and other sex crimes. 18 U.S.C. § 2421 (1998).

[73] *See* Seaboard Air Line Ry. v. North Carolina, 245 U.S. 298 (1917) (upholding the Act).

[74] Pub. L. 59–384, 34 Stat. 768 (1906).

[75] U.S. CONST. amend. XVI; art. I, § 8. Federal grants to state aid programs began to emerge during the 1920s.

[76] 12 U.S.C. § 221 *et seq.* (2010) (establishing the Federal Reserve); 15 U.S.C. § 41–58 (2010) (establishing the Federal Trade Commission).

[77] JAMES RASBAND ET AL., NATURAL RESOURCES LAW & POLICY 130 (2d ed. 2009).

[78] In 1842, a fractured Supreme Court in Prigg v. Pennsylvania, 41 U.S. 539 (1842), found a state law regulating the return of fugitive slaves to be preempted by the federal Fugitive Slave Law of 1793—one of the first uses of "dormant" federal power to preempt state law on matters committed to national jurisdiction even when Congress had not yet acted. Judith V. Royster, *Federalism, in* THE ENCYCLOPEDIA OF AMERICAN POLITICAL HISTORY 142 (2001). After the Civil War, the Court used the dormant Commerce Clause to invalidate a series of state regulatory regimes that discriminated against interstate commerce. *E.g.,* Welton v. Missouri, 91 U.S. 275 (1875) (invalidating under Congress's dormant power to regulate interstate commerce a state sales tax that penalized out of state-produced goods).

the regulation of interstate commerce to the federal government, effectively prohibiting the states from regulating in ways that burden interstate commerce even if Congress has not explicitly spoken on the issue. Federal courts had been invalidating state statutes under the dormant Commerce Clause for half a century,[79] but the practice accelerated between 1890 and 1936 to enable greater economic freedom in an unfettered national economy.[80] For example, in *Leisy v. Hardin*, the Supreme Court invalidated a progressivist Iowa statute banning the sale of alcohol on grounds that interstate commerce required rules of national uniformity.[81] At the same time, the Court developed an aggressive doctrine of field preemption, holding in such cases as *Southern Railway Co. v. Reid* that federal legislation could preempt all state legislation in the same field, even without an actual conflict or statement of congressional intent.[82]

Nor did the Court widely tolerate congressional initiatives at the margin of federal authority, rejecting several important legislative forays into new regulatory territory. For example, Congress had enacted the Sherman Act in an attempt to rein in market abuses by interstate manufacturing monopolies operating beyond the reach of single-state regulators. But in 1895, the Court weakened the Act even while upholding its constitutionality by narrowly construing the scope of federal commerce power.[83] In *United States v. E.C. Knight*, the government had charged that American Sugar Refining Corp., with control over 90 percent of the nation's sugar refining capacity, had illegally secured its monopoly by agreements that restrained trade and imposed higher prices on consumers.[84] The Court conceded that possibility, but took a limited view of Congress's authority in distinguishing between interstate commerce and manufacturing, holding that federal law could not extend to the manufacturing operations at issue.[85] (It did, however, leave open the possibility that other forms of anti-competitive behavior, such as predatory pricing, might fall within reach of the commerce power.[86]) Recentering from the Civil War apex of central dominance, these doctrines effectively reaffirmed commitment to the mutually exclusive spheres of dual federalism—though as the combined force of affirmative and negative commerce doctrine show, not always in support of local autonomy.[87]

Meanwhile, the emerging Progressive movement acted in relentless pursuit of reform—addressing a panoply of issues ranging from voting rights to labor practices to Prohibition—but mostly through the passage of uniform legislation at the state level.[88] In 1913, the

---

[79] *E.g.*, Prigg v. Pennsylvania, 41 U.S. 539 (1842).

[80] *E.g.*, SCHAPIRO, *supra* Introduction, note 11, at 37–40.

[81] 135 U.S. 100 (1890).

[82] 222 U.S. 424 (1912); *see* Stephen Gardbaum, *New Deal Constitutionalism and the Unshackling of the States*, 64 U. CHI. L. REV. 483, 511 (1997).

[83] United States v. E.C. Knight Co., 156 U.S. 1 (1895).

[84] *Id.* at 10–11.

[85] *Id.*

[86] *See* Charles McCurdy, *The Knight Sugar Decision of 1895 and the Modernization of American Corporation Law*, 53 BUS. HISTORY REV. 304 (1979) (refuting the standard claim that the Sherman Act eviscerated *Knight*).

[87] *Cf.* SCHAPIRO, *supra* Introduction, note 11, at 37–40.

[88] *See, e.g.*, Moreno, *supra* Chapter Two, note 7, at 732.

Progressives also championed ratification of the Seventeenth Amendment, which provided for the direct election of U.S. senators by popular state referendum rather than state legislatures.[89] Despite a platform of widely diverse priorities, most Progressives were champions of localism, embracing national legislation "only as a last resort, in cases where the states had failed."[90] However, large numbers of Progressive state laws were invalidated by the Supreme Court under its emerging theory of Fourteenth Amendment "economic substantive due process," or economic liberty to contract free from undue state law constraints.[91]

This confusing era of American federalism was thus characterized by the Progressives' emphatic appeal to state and local authorities to take on the perceived regulatory problems of the day,[92] coupled with a Supreme Court jurisprudence that deferred neither to state legislative fact-finding nor to the states' police power obligations to protect the public welfare. In the most famous of these cases, *Lochner v. New York*, the Court used the Fourteenth Amendment's due process clause to invalidate a state labor law setting maximum working hours for bakery employees, finding it an "unreasonable, unnecessary and arbitrary interference with the right and liberty of the individual to contract."[93] In *Hammer v. Dagenhart* (more fully reviewed in Chapter Four), the Court infamously struck down a prohibition on the interstate shipment of goods produced by children under the age of fourteen.[94] Though the law suffered for a number of reasons, Justice Day reminded Congress that "[i]n interpreting the Constitution it must never be forgotten that the Nation is made up of States to which are entrusted the powers of local government. And to them and to the people the powers not expressly delegated to the National Government are reserved."[95]

The *Lochner* line of cases became known for partnering Fourteenth Amendment protection for freedom of contract against state law interference with a limited view of Congress's commerce authority to accomplish similar objectives.[96] Other scholarship takes on the received wisdom that this judicial era was driven exclusively by contract liberty ideals, suggesting that the cases also contain important themes of judicial concern for governmental

---

[89] U.S. CONST. amend. XVII.

[90] *Id.*

[91] Between 1900 and 1937, the "*Lochner* era" that is discussed next, the Court struck down between fifty to two hundred laws under the Due Process Clause (sometimes coupled with another constitutional provision), depending on who is counting. *Compare* GEOFFREY R. STONE ET AL., CONSTITUTIONAL LAW 755–56 (5th ed. 2005) (citing the number at two hundred) *with* Michael J. Phillips, *How Many Times Was Lochner-Era Substantive Due Process Effective?*, 48 MERCER L. REV. 1049 (2007) (arguing the number is 160 at best, and closer to fifty).

[92] The progressives saw almost all social problems as proper targets of government regulation, reflecting a widespread nineteenth-century view that the state had a duty to help individuals control their negative impulses, even alcohol consumption. Moreno, *supra* Chapter Two, note 7, at 733.

[93] 198 U.S. 45 (1905).

[94] 247 U.S. 251 (1918); *see also* Bailey v. Drexel Furniture Co., 259 U.S. 20 (1922).

[95] Hammer, 247 U.S. at 275; *id.* at 271–72 (distinguishing between Congress's authority to regulate commerce and its lack of authority to regulate manufacturing, and between products that are inherently harmful and those that harm by means of their production).

[96] *E.g.*, David E. Bernstein, *Lochner Era Revisionism, Revised:* Lochner *and the Origins of Fundamental Rights Constitutionalism*, 92 GEO. L.J. 1, 1–4 nn.2–7 (2003) (cataloguing literature about the era).

neutrality, other fundamental rights, and even means-end reasonableness.[97] As Professor Barry Cushman has argued, "Lochnerism was a phenomenon with more than one face"— describing an overall jurisprudential complexity that is frequently lost in its invocation as a cautionary tale against judicial overreaching.[98] Similarly, even as it rejected these legislative expansions of national power, the Supreme Court was also serving as a powerful agent of nationalization in other doctrinal areas, asserting muscular judicial power over state legislatures and courts.[99] Just as the New Federalism decisions were about more than just classical dualism, it is important to recall that the *Lochner* era decisions cannot be reduced merely to economic due process and federal restraint.

Nevertheless, the *Lochner* era is most often characterized as a period of rampant antiregulatory activism, and by whatever metric, the Court subjected economic regulation to much more scrutiny during this time than it has since.[100] After a series of legislative efforts to curb child labor and food safety abuses were rejected, President Roosevelt declared his frustration with the era as "[a] riot of individualistic materialism, under which complete freedom for the individual . . . turned out in practice to mean perfect freedom for the strong to wrong the weak."[101] Criticizing the failure of any legal constraints, he complained that the "power of mighty industrial overlords" had increased dramatically, but the methods of controlling them through government "remained archaic and therefore practically impotent."[102]

In using federal judicial power to invalidate far more state than federal statutes, the *Lochner* cases broadly participate in the federalism discourse by definitely answering the question of *who decides* (specifically, against state autonomy and in favor of judicial safeguards).[103] Still, the fact that the cases also target federal law suggests the Court's understanding of its role as a neutral defender of liberty against all threats, not just a faithful arm of the federal government.[104] In addition, legal historians remind us that the Court also upheld many state and federal laws regulating working conditions and other economic concerns by both the state and federal government during this time.[105]

This narrative demonstrates several competing theories of federalism that appear to have been operating during this period. Although generalizing about the Progressives is difficult,

---

[97] *Id.*; Barry Cushman, *Some Varieties and Vicissitudes of Lochnerism*, 85 B.U. L. Rev. 881, 998–99 (2005).

[98] *Id.* at 998. *See also* MICHAEL J. PHILLIPS, THE LOCHNER COURT, MYTH AND REALITY 58, 86–97 (2001).

[99] *See* Edward A. Purcell, Jr., Ex Parte *Young and the Transformation of American Courts, 1890–1917*, 40 U. TOLEDO L. REV. 931 (2009) (discussing the doctrinal consolidation of federal judicial power during this era).

[100] Barry Cushman, *Lost Fidelities*, 41 WM. & MARY L. REV. 95, 102 (1999); *see also supra* note 91.

[101] MORISON, *supra* note 2, at 764.

[102] *Id.*

[103] A potential objection to reading federalism into Lochnerism this way is that it implies that *every* federal court decision identifying federal constitutional rights is somehow discussing a federalism issue. Yet in identifying realms in which federal law trumps contrary state law, these are exactly the issues with which federalism theory should be concerned.

[104] *E.g.*, Robert Post, *Federalism in the Taft Court Era: Can It Be Revived?*, 51 DUKE L.J. 1513, 1580–1605 (2002).

[105] For example, Professor Cushman rejects comparisons of *Lochner* era governance to the minimalist "night watchman" state, wryly noting that "[i]f this was a night watchman state, then this night watchman had a very active thyroid." Cushman, *supra* note 100, at 102.

the overall Progressivist agenda draws on each of the federalism values in different respects: (1) some regard for checks and balances (in ambivalence about further expanding federal authority to drive reform efforts);[106] (2) the promotion of local autonomy and subsidiarity (in efforts to grant cities and municipalities home rule authority independent of the states);[107] (3) pragmatic problem solving (in eventually turning to national legislation when state legislation failed to accomplish needed reforms);[108] and perhaps most important, (4) accountable and participatory governance (in campaigns for citizen entitlement to nominate candidates in open primary elections, to vote on laws directly, to elect and recall judges, and for direct elections of U.S. senators).[109]

When the Progressives finally assumed the national stage through the election of presidents Theodore Roosevelt and Woodrow Wilson, the movement shifted allegiance from local autonomy to pragmatism in pursuit of its vision of accountable government—but reluctantly, and tempered with an ethic of subsidiarity after their due diligence in pursuing local reforms first. In this respect, although their legacy mixes landmark legislative accomplishments (e.g., women's suffrage and the direct election of senators) with discredited regulatory goals (e.g., Prohibition), the Progressives proceeded from a cognizable federalist ethic based especially on principles of accountable, participatory governance and subsidiarity.

The Supreme Court's most famous *Lochner*-era decisions proceeded from a strikingly different ethic, with different priorities.[110] The decisions invalidating state economic regulation on Fourteenth Amendment grounds elevated the federal role in the protection of individual rights (albeit primarily the right to contract), reflecting the check-and-balance role that the federal government would famously assume in later years in protecting civil rights against discriminatory state laws. Federal Progressive statutes attempting similar reforms were also invalidated, sometimes out of respect for the states' role as the competent regulators of labor and employment matters. This particular invocation of checks and balances seems dubious when state labor laws were suffering simultaneous judicial rejection, but the Court saw its mission as protecting the rights of individual economic actors against excessive sovereign interference.[111] To the extent invalidated laws addressed legitimate regulatory problems, the Court's decisions discounted state and federal legislative problem-solving efforts, taking judicial prerogative to determine that threats to contractual liberty were the more serious problem.

Invalidating state laws did not advance the accountability of state officials to their electorate, nor did it advance local autonomy. In fact, the Court dealt its most severe blow to localism values in adopting the "Dillon Rule" of municipal-state relations, which emphasizes the near-plenary power of the state over its local municipalities. In *Merrill v. Monticello*[112] and *Hunter*

---

[106] *See* Moreno, *supra* Chapter Two, note 7, at 733.

[107] *See* HOFSTADTER, *supra* note 67, at 262–63.

[108] *See* Moreno, *supra* Chapter Two, note 6, at 732–33.

[109] *See* HOFSTADTER, *supra* note 67, at 258–64.

[110] *Cf.* Barry Cushman, *Lochner, Liquor and Longshoremen: A Puzzle in Progressive Era Federalism*, 32 J. MAR. L. & COM. 1, 5 (2001) (characterizing *Lochner*-era decisions as the result of various antebellum beliefs, including northern free labor principles, distaste for special legislation, and enthusiasm for faction-free politics).

[111] *See supra* notes 96–97 and accompanying text.

[112] 138 U.S. 673 (1891) (upholding state power to consolidate municipalities, even against majority will).

v. Pittsburgh,[113] the Court held that states could abolish the charters of their municipal corporations at will. Its 1908 decision in Ex Parte *Young*—an end-run around sovereign immunity that enabled suits against state officials for unconstitutional acts—further curtailed state authority in favor of federal power, but once again, it did so to protect individual rights.[114]

C. The Great Depression and the New Deal

New federalism concerns would soon occupy the Supreme Court's foremost attention as the booming economy of the 1920s gave way to the Great Depression of the 1930s. In 1928, President Herbert Hoover was elected on a platform of regulatory noninterference and rugged individualism.[115] After the stock market collapse of 1929, Hoover urged private and local solutions to economic despair, opposing congressional efforts to provide food and humanitarian relief to the nation's growing ranks of unemployed.[116] The Depression worsened despite his regular exhortations to the public, local officials, and businesses to do their parts in reversing the economic downturn.[117] After leaving office, Hoover was quoted as summarizing his philosophy of government in strikingly subsidiarity-like terms:

> The humanism of our system demands the protection of the suffering and the unfortunate. It places prime responsibility upon the individual for the welfare of his neighbor, but it insists also that in necessity the local community, the State government, and in the last resort, the National government shall give protection to them.[118]

Toward the end of his presidency, he reluctantly conceded that the time had come for national intervention, and took modest steps toward involving the federal government in the ordinary economic lives of its citizens, establishing a federal bank to forestall home mortgage foreclosures and a finance corporation to bolster failing banks, corporations, and railroads.[119]

By 1932, states and localities had proved themselves powerless to resolve the crippling social and economic problems associated with the Depression, and nationwide social unrest appeared headed toward catastrophe.[120] In the summer of 1932, twenty thousand World War I veterans marched on Washington and clashed with police regarding their demands for prepayment of wartime bonuses not due until 1945; communists and unemployed masses staged hunger marches in Philadelphia, Chicago, New York, and other cities across the nation; and Iowan populists organized a "farm holiday" movement in which they threatened

---

[113] 207 U.S. 161 (1907) (reaffirming the "Dillon Rule" adopted in *Merrill v. Monticello*).

[114] 209 U.S. 123 (1908); Purcell, *supra* note 99.

[115] *Cf.* 10 ERNEST R. MAY ET AL., THE LIFE HISTORY OF THE UNITED STATES: BOOM AND BUST (1917–1932), at 129, 134–35 (1974).

[116] *Id.* at 135.

[117] *Id.* at 134–35.

[118] *Id.* at 135.

[119] *Id.*

[120] *Id.* at 136–37.

to cease shipments of food products to the cities unless commodity prices were raised.[121] Toward the end of the year, American industry was operating at less than half its 1929 volume and 25 percent of the labor force was unemployed.[122] At this point, President Franklin Delano Roosevelt was elected on a platform of federal intervention that would become known as the New Deal.[123]

Concluding that only the national government had the capacity to address the scope of the Depression and its sequelae of joblessness, homelessness, hunger, and social dislocation, Congress joined FDR in marshaling the nation's resources and directing regulatory programs into realms that were previously the sole regulatory purview of the states. Between 1932 and 1938, New Deal regulatory reforms included such federally sponsored jobs programs as the Works Progress Administration[124] and the Civilian Conservation Corps,[125] the Agricultural Adjustment Act[126] and other farm programs, the Emergency Banking and Bank Conservation Act,[127] the establishment of the Securities and Exchange Commission[128] and the Federal Deposit Insurance Corporation,[129] the Federal Emergency Relief Administration that became the precursor to modern Social Security,[130] and many others. Combining the reformist zeal of the Progressives with the power of central administration at a pivotal time of national crisis, the New Deal redefined the traditional spheres of state and federal regulatory concern.[131] Power that had been "trickling, then flowing" in the federal direction now "poured in, in a mighty torrent."[132]

---

[121] *Id.* at 137.

[122] 11 WILLIAM E. LEUCHTENBURG ET AL., THE LIFE HISTORY OF THE UNITED STATES: NEW DEAL AND GLOBAL WAR (1933–1945) 7–8 (1964).

[123] The name stems from the promise he made in accepting the Democratic nomination for president that he would seek "a new deal for the American People." MAY ET AL., *supra* note 115, at 136.

[124] Exec. Order No. 7034 (May 6, 1935).

[125] Civilian Conservation Corps Act of 1937, ch. 383, 50 Stat. 319 (repealed 1966).

[126] Agricultural Adjustment Act of 1933, ch. 25, 48 Stat. 31 (codified as amended in scattered sections of 7 U.S.C.).

[127] Emergency Banking and Bank Conservation Act of 1933, ch. 1, 48 Stat. 1 (codified as amended in scattered sections of 12 U.S.C.).

[128] Securities Exchange Act of 1934, ch. 404, 48 Stat. 881 (codified at 15 U.S.C. § 78 (2000)).

[129] Banking Act of 1933, ch. 89, 48 Stat. 162 (codified at 16 U.S.C. §§ 1811–1832 (2000)).

[130] Federal Emergency Relief Act of 1933, ch. 30, 48 Stat. 55, *replaced by* Social Security Act, ch. 531, 49 Stat. 620 (1935) (codified as amended at 43 U.S.C. §§ 301–1397 (2000)).

[131] Orly Lobel, *The Renew Deal: The Fall of Regulation and the Rise of Governance in Contemporary Legal Thought*, 89 MINN. L. REV. 342, 351–52 (2004) ("Responding to the burdens and risks of the Depression and two world wars, the New Deal instigated the creation of the modern regulatory and administrative state. The New Deal paradigm invoked three Rs—relief, recovery, and reform, but it was the legal developments that united all three under the umbrella of the big 'R' of regulation."). Notably, however, there is a split in the academic literature on the New Deal paradigm shift between "externalists," who assert that political reasons (such as the massive economic collapse of the Great Depression) caused the shift in federalism theory at this time, and "internalists," who emphasize doctrinal and intellectual causes in explaining constitutional change in tandem with external events. *E.g.*, Laura Kalman, *Law, Politics, and the New Deal(s)*, 108 YALE L.J. 2165, 2165–66 (1999).

[132] FRIEDMAN, LAW IN AMERICA, *supra* note 2, at 134.

As the Civil War had, the events of the Great Depression jolted political and judicial federalism interpreters into a new theoretical paradigm. But this federalism paradigm shift did not proceed without significant hesitation on the part of traditionalists, and it faced legal challenges at nearly every turn.[133] The Supreme Court did reject some early New Deal regulatory programs for exceeding enumerated federal powers, including the National Industrial Recovery Act of 1933 and the Agricultural Adjustment Act of 1933, by which the federal government had sought pricing and production controls.[134] Justice Brandeis was particularly concerned about the centralization of regulatory authority, reportedly warning one of FDR's political advisors to "tell the President that we're not going to let this government centralize everything."[135]

However, the Court ultimately approved most of the second wave of more carefully crafted New Deal legislation that came later, including the National Labor Relations Act and Social Security Acts of 1935,[136] and the later Fair Labor Standards Act of 1938[137]—which accomplished most of the regulatory goals of the first wave in a more piecemeal but narrowly tailored fashion.[138] As one historian notes, the Court at this time "abandon[ed] the two chief doctrinal limitations on government power": (1) the *Lochnerian* understanding of liberty-of-contract substantive due process by which it had constrained state regulatory authority; and (2) the preindustrial understanding of dual sovereignty by which it had constrained federal regulatory authority in the early New Deal years.[139] With broad local support, all three federal branches cooperated to expand federal authority for regulating economic problems under the Commerce Clause, no longer subject to the *Lochnerian* limits of economic substantive due process.

American federalism underwent a spectacular (some argue, a spectacularly misguided[140]) transformation during the New Deal era—but it hardly disappeared. The body politic remained one of dual sovereignty. Then, as now, "the bulk of American law [wa]s still state law, and overwhelmingly so."[141] States continued to manage the vast array of regulatory contexts in which the police power is deployed, from family law to local law enforcement to education. Moreover, the Supreme Court's staged acceptance of the New Deal legislation

---

[133] *See* Moreno, *supra* Chapter Two, note 7, at 737–38.

[134] A.L.A. Schechter Poultry Corp. v. United States, 295 U.S. 495 (1935) (invalidating the National Industrial Recovery Act), and United States v. Butler, 297 U.S. 1 (1936) (invalidating the Agricultural Adjustment Act).

[135] *See* Moreno, *supra* Chapter Two, note 7, at 738 (quoting PHILIPPA STRUM, LOUIS D. BRANDEIS: JUSTICE FOR THE PEOPLE 352 (1984)).

[136] The National Labor Relations Act is now codified at 29 U.S.C. § 151 et seq. (2010). Social Security is now codified at 42 U.S.C. § 301 et seq. (2010).

[137] United States v. Darby, 312 U.S. 100, 119 (1941) (abandoning the distinction between commerce and production in favor of a "substantial effects" test for valid federal commerce authority).

[138] *E.g.*, Barry Cushman, *Rethinking the New Deal Court*, 80 VA. L. REV. 201 (1994).

[139] Moreno, *supra* Chapter Two, note 7, at 738.

[140] *E.g.*, Richard A. Epstein, *The Cartelization of Commerce*, 22 HARV. J. L. & PUB. POL'Y 209, 214–17 (1998) (critiquing the expansion of federal power under the New Deal and urging a return to the pre-1937 approach).

[141] United States v. Morrison, 529 U.S. 598, 661 (2000) (Breyer, J., dissenting).

indicates that federalism controls were operating. The first wave of federal laws demanded too much unconstrained federal power for use in the interjurisdictional gray area of economic regulation. Now that historians have largely set to rest the "switch-in-time-that-saved-nine" mythos,[142] we understand the Court's acceptance of the second wave of New Deal programs as a principled decision by ambivalently progressive justices to approve urgently needed problem-solving legislation that had been sufficiently narrowly tailored to pass constitutional muster.[143]

Many disagreed with the Court's assessment that this expansion of federal power passed constitutional muster,[144] but then as now, such disagreement is really between competing theoretical models of federalism. Mature New Deal federalism, although faithful to the overall premise of dual sovereignty, exalted the problem-solving value above all other considerations. To the extent that citizens might be confused about the source of new economic regulations, accountability concerns were not given much consideration (although the overwhelming and repeated reelections of FDR suggest that citizens had a fairly certain idea of who was responsible for New Deal programs).[145] New Deal regulation proceeded with limited regard for localism values, and the vast expansion of federal power proceeded at direct cost to classical checks and balances. Although the New Deal Court also approved wider regulatory authority by the states,[146] as new regulatory targets became the legitimate subject of federal commerce authority, so state regulation in these areas became vulnerable to preemption under the Supremacy Clause.[147]

The regulatory ambit of the national government waxed substantially during this time, and to the extent the states' correspondingly waned, the balance between the problem-solving and anti-tyranny principles of federalism was threatened. Yet a federalism that enabled pragmatism to eclipse checks and balances during the Great Depression years seems well suited to the social facts of the time: massive unemployment, farmer uprisings and hunger marches, public rioting, and widespread fear of revolt.[148] If even Herbert Hoover—great champion of localism and laissez-faire economics—finally recognized that federal intervention was needed, surely most government actors would have come to the same conclusion.[149] New Deal federalism did not aggrandize the federal government's power for federal expansion's sake; it was in direct response to the states' demonstrated lack of capacity to overcome a nationwide economic collapse, and was thus ultimately faithful to the premise of subsidiarity. The Supreme Court subjected the New Deal programs to forgiving but meaningful

---

[142] *E.g.*, Cushman, *supra* note 138; Moreno, *supra* Chapter Two, note 7, at 738–39.

[143] Chief Justice Hughes and Justice Roberts became the reluctant new Progressives on the Court. *Id.*

[144] *See, e.g.*, JAMES M. LANDIS, THE ADMINISTRATIVE PROCESS 4 (1938) (describing "fulmination" among opponents).

[145] LEUCHTENBURG ET AL., *supra* note 122, at 57.

[146] *See* Gardbaum, *supra* note 82, at 486–87 (explaining how the states benefited from the New Deal cases).

[147] *See* Robert A. Schapiro & William W. Buzbee, *Unidimensional Federalism: Power and Perspective in Commerce Clause Adjudication*, 88 CORNELL L. REV. 1199, 1210–19 (2003); Lobel, *supra* note 131, at 794–95.

[148] MAY ET AL., *supra* note 115, at 137 (noting that nationwide, "people fearfully whispered the word 'revolution.'").

[149] *Cf. id.* at 134–35 (recounting Hoover's reluctance and eventual acquiescence to governmental intervention).

review, requiring that programs be narrowly tailored out of weakened but sincere respect for the maintenance of balance between state and federal power. A model of federalism that would have prevented a federal response under such circumstances would have (like Katrina multiplied exponentially) profoundly disserved the nation.[150]

In the political realm, New Deal federalism proved its authenticity as a principled model of federalism by virtue of being falsifiable. Libertarians may view the model as one of uncritical federal aggrandizement,[151] but most proponents used it to mediate what they saw as the proper relationship between state and federal power at the time, not as a blank check of power to a fully centralized sovereign. As the Supreme Court observed in 1938, the Constitution "presupposes the continued existence of the states."[152] New Deal federalism proponents continued to see the relationship as one of dual sovereignty, and federal problem-solving capacity was not the only matter of concern. At some point, even for those proponents, the pendulum had swung too far to the problem-solving side, and traditional localism and check-and-balance concerns began to draw them back. When FDR announced plans in 1937 to further entrench his vision of expansive federal power by adding justices to the Supreme Court, his public support waned, and he failed to win any further reform legislation in Congress after 1938.[153]

The legacy of New Deal federalism on the Court reached its apex shortly thereafter in 1941–42, when the Court held in *United States v. Darby* that Congress could legitimately regulate employment conditions[154] and in *Wickard v. Fillburn* that Congress could regulate even the intrastate production of wheat grown for private consumption if it affected interstate commerce in the aggregate.[155] The two cases are recognized as those in which the Court effectively relinquished its control over Congress's exercise of the commerce power, at least for the next sixty years.[156] But on December 7, 1941, the Japanese bombed the American naval base at Pearl Harbor, and World War II claimed the nation's focus from the New Deal. Nevertheless, even after the nation emerged from the war into the era of 1950s prosperity, Americans continued to embrace such New Deal innovations as Social Security and unemployment insurance, the Federal Housing Administration, and the Federal Deposit Insurance Corporation—all critical institutions of American governance that remain in force today.[157]

---

[150] Indeed, the Katrina emergency indicates how the New Deal changed public expectations about the federal regulatory role. Before the New Deal, Americans might not have expected the federal government to have provided much assistance. *Cf.* JONATHAN ALTER, THE DEFINING MOMENT: FDR's HUNDRED DAYS AND THE TRIUMPH OF HOPE 91–92 (2006) (describing federal involvement in aiding the needy as fairly "radical" before FDR took office).

[151] *E.g.*, Epstein, *supra* note 140.

[152] Helvering v. Gerhardt, 304 U.S. 405, 414 (1938).

[153] LEUCHTENBURG ET AL., *supra* note 122, at 70.

[154] 312 U.S. 100, 119 (1941) (upholding the Fair Labor Standards Act of 1938 against a Tenth Amendment challenge by finding it within Congress's commerce power).

[155] 317 U.S. 111 (1942) (upholding the Agricultural Adjustment Act of 1938).

[156] Barry Cushman, *The Securities Laws and the Mechanics of Legal Change*, 95 VA. L. REV. 927, 939 (2009).

[157] *Cf.* FRIEDMAN, LAW IN AMERICAN, *supra* note 2, at 137 (noting that post-war Republicans "left the core of the New Deal intact" because "they had to," and that "nobody dared touch Social Security").

D. The Civil Rights Era, the Great Society, and the Growth of Cooperative Federalism

The 1950s' era of prosperity also began a period for reflection on the implications of how the United States had reacted to the perceived threat of Japanese-Americans during World War II—by forcing them into internment camps. *Korematsu v. United States*[158] and other lawsuits challenging the forced internment of American citizens did not raise issues of state-federal relations directly, but they did test the nation's commitment to one of the fundamental purposes of federalism: the diffusion of governmental authority to protect individual rights. The nation's underwhelming performance in these tests, together with other brewing racial conflict, fueled the emerging Civil Rights Movement that would directly challenge early ideals about the respective roles of state and federal government.

Early civil rights decisions such as *Brown v. Board of Education*,[159] *Heart of Atlanta Motel v. United States*,[160] and others that upheld the constitutionality of federal civil rights laws and invalidated Jim Crow segregation laws implicated the relationship between state and federal power even more directly. The continued migration of black Americans northward, postindustrial immigration, and the aftereffects of two world wars had continued to spur demographic and economic changes across the nation through the 1950s and 1960s.[161] This led to further entrenchment of nativist and racist sentiments in public life, abetted by McCarthyist fears about communist infiltration.[162] Resistance to these latter trends culminated in an era of great cultural change over the 1960s and 1970s. The civil rights, women's rights, and other social movements were underway in the political sphere, forcing federalism theory among all three branches of government to evolve with the concerns of the times.

In the background of all this change, Dean Erwin Chemerinksy has described an important functional paradox in federalism that emerged between the end of the New Deal and the New Federalism decisions of the 1990s, contrasting the Supreme Court's use of federalism principles over this time to constrain federal judicial power but not federal legislative power.[163] Beginning in 1938, in *Erie Railroad Co. v. Tompkins*, the Court reversed its past course to require that federal courts sitting in diversity must apply state substantive law, thus preventing forum shopping and protecting the integrity of state law.[164] In the following decades, the Court would also affirm the principles of federalism and comity by announcing a series of deferential federal abstention doctrines that prevent federal courts from adjudicating certain questions of federal law before giving state courts the first opportunity. For example, in 1941 in *Railroad Commission v. Pullman*, the Court required all federal courts to abstain from deciding the constitutionality of potentially ambiguous state statutes until state

---

[158] 323 U.S. 214 (1944) (upholding the World War II era internment camps).

[159] 347 U.S. 483 (1954) (invalidating state laws mandating racially segregated schools).

[160] 379 U.S. 241 (1964) (mandating integration of local places of public accommodation).

[161] HALL AND KARSTEN, *supra* note 2, at 268–69.

[162] *Id.*

[163] CHEMERINSKY, *supra* Introduction, note 12, at 15.

[164] 304 U.S. 64 (1938).

courts have had an opportunity to interpret them (in a way that might avoid the constitutional claim).[165]

During the Civil Rights Movement, the Supreme Court experimented with decisions that
ran counter to this trend under the leadership of Chief Justice Earl Warren. In 1965, it held
in *Dombrowski v. Pfister* that plaintiffs could nevertheless access federal courts to challenge
their convictions under a facially unconstitutional state anticommunist law.[166] *Dombrowski*
and companion cases easing access to federal court by civil rights plaintiffs reflected the
Warren Court's distrust of southern state courts' ability to protect the constitutional rights
of African-Americans and civil rights activists.[167] However, the impact of *Dombrowski* was
sharply blunted by the *Younger* abstention doctrine that followed in 1971, in the early days of
the new leadership of Chief Justice Warren Burger.[168] In *Younger v. Harris*, the Supreme
Court barred federal review of civil rights tort claims by litigants still undergoing state prosecution from which the alleged tort arose.[169] The Court also articulated several discretionary
doctrines between 1940 and 1980 that enabled federal courts sitting in diversity jurisdiction
to defer to state courts on certain matters of state law, either because the states had greater
expertise or because federal determination could compromise state sovereignty.[170]

The judicial federalism abstention doctrines were expressly solicitous of state sovereignty
and the role of state courts in the overall administration of justice, prioritizing local autonomy and perhaps accountability (at least on the voter-confusion front, to the extent that
state court judges are often elected). Preserving the balance of state and federal judicial
power might also enhance the check-and-balance value, although Dean Chemerinsky's
work suggests that the objective of checks and balances—the protection of individual rights
through the diffusion of government power—is not well-served by making it harder for
litigants to obtain federal civil rights remedies while exhausting comparatively unfriendly
state processes.[171]

However, even as the Supreme Court acknowledged federalism principles as a check on
federal judicial power, it vigorously upheld the expanding uses of federal legislative power
against federalism challenges. This was most visible during the Warren Court era, when the
majority broadly expanded federal power at state expense for the purpose of protecting civil
rights. Most famously, in 1964 in *Heart of Atlanta Motel, Inc. v. United States*, the Court

---

[165] 312 U.S. 496 (1941) (setting forth the doctrine that would become known as "*Pullman* abstention").

[166] 380 U.S. 479 (1965); *see also* Fay v. Noia, 372 U.S. 381 (1963) (allowing federal adjudication of issues on habeas
review that were not presented in state court if there was no deliberate bypass of state procedures).

[167] *E.g.*, SETH STERN & STEPHEN WERMIEL, JUSTICE BRENNAN 228 (2010).

[168] *Id.*

[169] 401 U.S. 37 (1971).

[170] *E.g.*, Burford v. Sun Oil Co., 319 U.S. 315 (1943) (enabling federal abstention where state courts are likely to
have greater subject matter expertise in a complex area of state law); Louisiana Power & Light Co. v. City of
Thibodaux, 360 U.S. 25 (1959) (in deference to state sovereignty, enabling federal abstention to allow state
courts to decide issues of state law of significant public importance to that state); Colorado River Water
Conservation Dist. v. United States, 424 U.S. 800 (1976) (enabling federal abstention in parallel litigation to
determine the rights of parties with respect to the same questions of law).

[171] *Cf.* CHEMERINSKY, *supra* Introduction, note 12, at 31.

upheld a federal ban on private discrimination in places of public accommodation,[172] demonstrating the Warren Court's commitment to broad readings of the commerce power as necessary to protect civil rights.

On the same day, the Court upheld the Civil Rights Act of 1964 against Ninth and Tenth Amendment challenges,[173] rejecting historical precedent for using the Tenth Amendment as justification to defeat previous federal civil rights laws (and to protect slavery).[174] In 1966, the Court held that the Voting Rights Act of 1965, requiring federal approval of state changes to voting qualifications, was authorized by Congress's power under Section Two of the Fifteenth Amendment.[175] Even after establishing *Younger* abstention in the 1970s, the Court chipped away at state sovereign immunity to empower new federal policies, holding that state sovereign immunity could be abrogated with clear congressional intent[176] and that Congress has broad discretion to do so under the Fourteenth Amendment.[177] Some critiqued the Court for disrespecting state sovereignty through judicial activism,[178] while others praised its mission of protecting individual rights against the backdrop of hostile state law.[179]

In contrast to the *Lochner* era, the expansive view of federal power approved by the Warren Court worked hand in glove with the assertion of new federal power by the political branches. If New Deal federalism allowed for the expansion of federal power to protect individuals through economic reform, the Civil Rights Era model of federalism allowed for the expansion of federal power to protect individual rights directly, through ambitious federal laws such as the Civil Rights and Voting Rights Acts. Federal encroachment into state law realms vindicated the jurisdictional overlap view of checks and balances, enabling a federal regulatory backstop to some states' abdication of their obligation to protect civil rights. However, this evolving vision of the federal role in dual sovereignty also caused the Court to draw back from the extreme dormant Commerce Clause and preemption doctrines it had embraced beginning in the *Lochner* era. Instead, the Court committed to a "presumption against preemption" that deferred to the traditional exercise of state power in contexts of jurisdictional overlap unless Congress had intentionally or unambiguously preempted the state law at issue or the entire field of law, or if the state law posed a direct conflict.[180] This set the stage for the burgeoning jurisdictional overlap that would come to define the cooperative federalism model.

---

[172] 379 U.S. 241 (1964).

[173] Katzenbach v. McClung, 379 U.S. 294 (1964).

[174] William E. Leuchtenburg, *The Tenth Amendment over Two Centuries, in* THE TENTH AMENDMENT AND STATE SOVEREIGNTY 41, 43 (Mark R. Killenbeck ed., 2002).

[175] South Carolina v. Katzenbach, 383 U.S. 301 (1966).

[176] Edelman v. Jordan, 415 U.S. 651 (1974).

[177] Fitzpatrick v. Bitzer, 427 U.S. 445 (1976).

[178] *See, e.g.,* Patrick M. Garry, *Federalism's Battle with History: The Inaccurate Associations with Unpopular Politics,* 74 UMKC L. REV. 365, 375 (2005).

[179] *See, e.g.,* Jim Chen, *Come Back to the Nickel and Five: Tracing the Warren Court's Pursuit of Equal Justice under Law,* 59 WASH. & LEE L. REV. 1203 (2002).

[180] *See* Rice v. Santa Fe Elevator Corp., 331 U.S. 218, 230 (1947); CHEMERINSKY, *supra* Introduction, note 12, at 226.

President Lyndon Johnson further attempted to funnel the national optimism of the day into his administration's policy-making vision of the Great Society.[181] The New Deal had sought to lift the nation away from economic catastrophe, and now that most Americans were enjoying newfound affluence, Great Society programs were designed to reach those who had been left behind, through its twin goals of eliminating poverty and racial injustice. During the Johnson presidency, Americans also began to discover that clean air and water could no longer be taken for granted, prompting calls for antipollution regulations with teeth.[182] Ambitiously tackling issues of racism, urban slums, environmental ills, transportation, and inadequate education, President Johnson requested two hundred major pieces of legislation before his presidency was half over.[183] To manage the enormous agenda it had undertaken, his administration sought to involve states and municipalities in administering Great Society programs through a new form of state-federal collaboration that came to be known as "cooperative federalism."[184] In programs of cooperative federalism, state and federal actors would take responsibility for separate but interlocking components of a unified regulatory program.

Great Society programs further ushered federal authority toward regulatory realms traditionally managed by the states, including health care and education.[185] The Great Society was premised on the idea that persistent levels of intergenerational poverty, racial segregation, and urban decay had outpaced the capacity of state and local governments to protect their most vulnerable citizens. John Gardner, then-Secretary of the Department of Health, Education, and Welfare, described the cooperative federalism relationship the Johnson administration hoped to establish in broaching this new territory:

> That may be the most revolutionary single thing that we are doing today. It means that the Federal Government, far from trying to dominate, is trying increasingly to preserve the pluralism of our society. We are heading toward a new kind of creative federalism, toward the establishment of new relationships that will see us through not only the complexity of today but the increasing complexity of the decades to come.[186]

President Johnson also emphasized that Great Society goals required creative federalism rather than big governmental programs, anticipating that state and local partners would help implement his administration's big ideas with federal funds to make them possible.[187] However, the Great Society suffered criticism as a series of excessively top-down bureaucracies, run by secret panels of national experts who proposed legislative solutions without

---

[181] JOHN A. ANDREW III, LYNDON JOHNSON AND THE GREAT SOCIETY 16 (1998).

[182] FRIEDMAN, LAW IN AMERICA, *supra* note 2, at 138–39.

[183] ANDREW, *supra* note 181, at 13.

[184] *Id.* at 14.

[185] *See, e.g.*, Elementary and Secondary Education Act of 1965, Pub. L. 89–10, 79 Stat. 27, 20 U.S.C. ch. 70 (1965); Social Security Act of 1965, Pub. L. 89–97, 79 Stat. 286 (1965) (establishing Medicare benefits).

[186] ANDREW, *supra* note 181, at 16.

[187] *Id.*

sufficient local input.[188] Many programs were expanded under the subsequent Republican administrations of presidents Ford and Nixon, and some (such as federal education financing, Head Start, and Medicare) continue in force today—but the policy and economic pressure they placed on state and municipal governments would lay the groundwork for further transition.

Offering a neutral critique of the Great Society approach to cooperative federalism, economics professors Eli Ginzberg and Robert Solow focus on the key issue of problem-solving capacity in these contexts:

> Decategorization and decentralization of federal programs in education, manpower, health, urban development, and other areas are attractive goals once one realizes the inherent incapacity of the federal government to be directly involved in the delivery of services to millions of beneficiaries. But if the transfer of responsibility is a matter of political convenience and ideological rectitude, the weight of recent evidence should not be ignored. Most state and local governments must be substantially strengthened if they are to discharge their expanded functions effectively. In the meanwhile, and perhaps in perpetuity, the federal government must continue to insist on certain priorities, exercise surveillance over the execution of programs, and maintain financial control.[189]

Since then, cooperative federalism has remained the primary model of interjurisdictional problem solving in the United States. Over the subsequent decades, federal and state partners have attempted to adjust the model to improve on the top-down weaknesses of the original bureaucratic one of the 1960s. Ideally, regulators seek to harness the synergy between local and national capacity for addressing problems with both local and national components while incorporating more meaningful leadership from local partners. Still, some critics continue to see the same top-down problems in modern-day cooperative federalism that weakened the Great Society approach.[190]

The continuing involvement of the federal government in areas once managed solely by the states reflects both the expanded reach of the federal commerce power achieved during the New Deal era and continued popular expectations for federal regulatory solutions following the rights revolutions of the Civil Rights Era.[191] The incorporation of the Bill of Rights to be enforceable against the states imposed even stronger federal limits on state and

---

[188] *Id.*

[189] Eli Ginzberg & Robert M. Solow, *Some Lessons of the Great Society, in* THE GREAT SOCIETY: LESSONS FOR THE FUTURE 218 (Ginsberg and Solow eds., 1974).

[190] *See, e.g.,* Jonathan H. Adler, *Jurisdictional Mismatch in Environmental Federalism,* 14 N.Y.U. ENVTL. L.J. 130, 172–73 (2005).

[191] *See* William W. Buzbee, *Regulatory Reform or Statutory Muddle: The "Legislative Mirage" of Single Statute Regulatory Reform,* 5 N.Y.U. ENVTL. L.J. 298, 362 & n.210 (1996) (discussing the popular support for various environmental protection programs, such as the Endangered Species Act); Christopher Yeh, *Workplace Stereotypes: The Simultaneous Eradication and Reinforcement,* HAW. B.J., May 2002, at 6 (discussing public

local governments. However, cooperative federalism matches this expansive federal role with increased regard for state autonomy. Where New Deal programs virtually preempted state involvement in the newly federally regulated realms, programs of cooperative federalism afford roles for both state and federal regulators in the interjurisdictional gray area. For example, the Clean Water Act exemplifies the cooperative federalism approach in its congressional declaration of goals and policies:

> It is the policy of the Congress to recognize, preserve, and protect the primary responsibilities and rights of States to prevent, reduce, and eliminate pollution, to plan the development and use (including restoration, preservation, and enhancement) of land and water resources, and to consult with the Administrator in the exercise of his authority under this chapter. It is the policy of Congress that the States manage the construction grant program under this chapter and implement the permit programs under . . . this title. It is further the policy of the Congress to support and aid research relating to the prevention, reduction, and elimination of pollution and to provide Federal technical services and financial aid to State and interstate agencies and municipalities in connection with the prevention, reduction, and elimination of pollution.[192]

Although cooperative federalism thus remains rooted in the post–New Deal expansion of federal regulatory authority, it maintains more careful regard for the role of the states in a federal system.

Programs of cooperative federalism continue to dominate in many areas of modern law, especially in environmental contexts such as the Clean Air Act's division between standard-setting authority (to the federal government) and program design and implementation (to the state government),[193] or the Clean Water Act's invitation to the states to assume the Environmental Protection Agency's role as the in-state permitting authority for point-source discharges (an invitation that all but four states (New Hampshire, Massachusetts New Mexico, and Idaho) and the District of Columbia have accepted).[194] Between consciously designed partnership programs like these and the many legal realms boasting both state and federal law, cooperative federalism remains the predominant model of American governance in interjurisdictional arenas.[195]

Cooperative federalism has been championed by its proponents as "partnership federalism," enabling a collaboration in which each level of government takes responsibility for

---

support for Title VII); *supra* Chapter One, note 153 and accompanying text (detailing expectations for more federal intervention during Katrina).

[192] 33 U.S.C. § 1251(b) (2000).

[193] Clean Air Act, 42 U.S.C. §§ 7401–7671 (2010).

[194] Clean Water Act, 33 U.S.C. §§ 1251–1387 (2010); EPA, *National Pollution Discharge Elimination System (NPDES): State Program Status*, http://cfpub.epa.gov/npdes/statestats.cfm.

[195] *See infra* Chapter Four, notes 7–10 and accompanying text.

what it can do best.[196] Like the model of federalism that enabled the New Deal, cooperative federalism is heavily motivated by a commitment to interjurisdictional problem solving, attacking such problems as environmental degradation and persistently disparate educational opportunities that seem beyond the capacity (or concern) of more local levels of government. But its pragmatic approach in realms of jurisdictional overlap is tempered by more careful attention to localism and check-and-balance values than New Deal federalism, through its careful assignment of roles for both state and federal government and increased regulatory space for local autonomy. As shown by the elaborate partnerships in modern-day programs of cooperative environmental federalism, the quality of meaningful state and local participation has increased since the early days of the Great Society.[197]

In addition, although cooperative federalism may encourage less competition than a model of federalism that minimized central planning authority, some have favorably characterized it as affording greater competitive federalism benefits than the New Deal model, by enabling laboratory-style competition among states developing unique implementation strategies.[198] True to the federalism values associated with localized diversity, the laboratory element of cooperative federalism promotes regulatory innovation and interjurisdictional competition, while checking political power from becoming too concentrated around a fully centralized planning regime.

Meanwhile, the federalism considerations that motivated legislative enactment and judicial approval of the civil rights laws were driven by the check-and-balance value, if flipped in orientation from most previous eras. Strengthening federal power to protect civil rights provided a check against the lackluster commitment of many states to affirming rights the Constitution promises to all citizens. As after the Civil War, expanding federal civil rights authority accomplished exactly what checks and balances are intended to do—protecting individual rights through the diffusion of sovereign power.

Cooperative federalism thus saw the pendulum shift back from the extreme problem-solving side that it occupied during New Deal federalism toward the center, reflecting attention to each of the federalism values (though at greatest expense to the voter-confusion aspect of accountability). With judicial deference to federalism-sensitive lawmaking, the allocation of authority between the state and federal government is largely left to the political process. Known as the "political safeguards" model, the theory of federalism that

---

[196] *Cf.* Bruce Babbitt, *Federalism and the Environment: An Intergovernmental Perspective of the Sagebrush Rebellion*, 12 ENVTL. L. 847, 847, 857–58 (1982) (advocating joint decision making regarding public lands); Daniel C. Esty, *Revitalizing Environmental Federalism*, 95 MICH. L. REV. 570, 652–53 (1996) (arguing for collaborative intergovernmental environmental policy making); Bradley C. Karkkainen, *Collaborative Ecosystem Governance: Scale, Complexity, and Dynamism*, 21 VA. ENVTL. L.J. 189, 225–26 (2002) (same).

[197] For example, beginning in the 1970s, President Nixon oversaw a better differentiation of the roles of the federal and state governments in some of the ambitious national regulatory endeavors that characterized his administration, including the Clean Water Act and the Clean Air Act. *See supra* Chapter Ten (including primary reporting by state actors about their participation in programs of cooperative federalism).

[198] *E.g.*, Daniel J. Elazar, *Cooperative Federalism*, *in* COMPETITION AMONG STATES AND LOCAL GOVERNMENTS 65, 67–68 (Daphne A. Kenyon & John Kincaid eds., 1991); *cf.* John Kincaid, *The Competitive Challenge to Cooperative Federalism: A Theory of Federal Democracy*, *in* COMPETITION AMONG STATES AND LOCAL GOVERNMENTS 87, 88 (arguing that cooperation and competition are equally necessary in federalism).

underlies the Supreme Court's federalism jurisprudence in this era trusts the state-elected members of the national legislature to make the fundamental calls about the best boundary between state and federal policy making. As Herbert Wechsler famously argued in 1954, judicial supervision is unnecessary because of Congress's institutional design: legislators elected at the state level are presumed to represent local interests during federal lawmaking, protecting the balance of authority in the system of dual sovereignty.[199] The Court's various abstention doctrines, which enforce deference to state adjudication of certain questions otherwise available to federal litigants, partners further federal judicial modesty with a commitment to preserving the state judicial role.

Nevertheless, cooperative federalism has been the subject of vociferous criticism from opponents who object to its continued sanctioning of New Deal-expanded federal authority. It has also prompted anxiety among federalism scholars who identify theoretical questions unresolved by its pragmatic approach to interjurisdictional problem solving.[200] For example, Professor Philip Weiser has called attention to the need to better justify the authority of state agencies to implement federal law, and to ensure constitutionally adequate oversight by the federal executive of that implementation.[201] Professor Roderick Hills has raised questions regarding the unjustified preferential treatment by the Supreme Court of "generally applicable" federal laws that regulate states, as well as the unresolved permissibility of conditional preemption and federal "funded mandates" to states to implement federal law.[202] Dean Chemerinsky questions the underlying assumptions of the political safeguards model to the extent it justifies unfettered federal preemption of state law, and the underlying values of comity in judicial federalism to the extent they undermine rights-protective federal litigation.[203]

From the point of view of the states, the cooperative federalism model seems preferable to the most preemptive aspects of New Deal federalism, in which the federal government displaced state efforts in targeted arenas by crafting and staffing programs that extended all the way to the local level. Even so, cooperative federalism partnerships are often based on the federal spending power, by which Congress persuades states to participate in regulatory programs less directly tethered to its other enumerated powers. Some critics of cooperative federalism thus argue that it would be more accurately characterized as "coercive federalism," in which the federal government forces state cooperation on penalty of withholding needed

---

[199] Wechsler, *supra* Introduction, note 6, at 558 ("[T]he national political process in the United States—and especially the role of the states in the composition and selection of the central government—is intrinsically well-adapted to retarding or restraining new intrusions by the center on the domain of the states . . . our system . . . necessitat[es] the widest support before intrusive measures of importance can receive significant consideration, reacting readily to opposition grounded in resistance within the states.").

[200] *E.g.*, Jonathan H. Adler, *Judicial Federalism and the Future of Federal Environmental Regulation*, 90 IOWA L. REV. 377, 399 (2005) (arguing that administering federal programs through states obscures federal responsibility).

[201] Phillip J. Weiser, *Towards a Constitutional Architecture for Cooperative Federalism*, 79 N.C. L. REV. 663, 677–81, 713–19 (2001).

[202] Hills, *supra* Part I Introduction, note 5, at 916–26, 934–38.

[203] CHEMERINSKY, *supra* Introduction, note 12, at 27–29.

benefits or preempting independent state programs.[204] Most important, cooperative federalism provides no clearly theorized means of mediating between the competing federalism values in a way that affords meaningful protections for check-and-balance, localism, or accountability values, and no basis for judicial review in the event of errors. It accurately describes what American federalism *does* look like, but is more normatively reticent about what it *should* look like.

Frustration with cooperative federalism's solicitousness of federal authority, anxiety over its theoretical robustness, and flailing economic growth during the 1970s ultimately inspired the rise of New Federalism—first as a political movement in the 1970s and 1980s, and then as the judicial revolution of the 1990s. Both appealed rhetorically to classical dual federalism ideals as a means of restoring balance between state and federal power.[205] Nevertheless, Congress continues to rely heavily on the cooperative federalism model in crafting regulatory solutions to interjurisdictional problems such as wetlands regulation, products liability, bankruptcy, and national security.[206] The resulting disconnect between the predominant empirical model of state-federal regulatory relationships and the theoretical model that animates the Supreme Court's New Federalism jurisprudence has evoked calls for everything from a complete rejection of cooperative regulatory programs,[207] to the complete rejection of New Federalism,[208] to a revision of the Rehnquist Court's jurisprudence to better accommodate the cooperative federalism model.[209]

Concerns that the pendulum has swung either too far in favor of national or the local excess have also motivated proposals to adopt a cooperative model that affords greater functional protection for local authority;[210] a model of polyphonic federalism in which state and federal courts participate in jointly developing constitutional law;[211] a model of empowerment federalism that broadly empowers both sides to regulate in overlapping spheres;[212] and a model of integrated federalism in which regulatory partnerships would draw on more

---

[204] *Cf.* Adler, *supra* note 190, at 169–73; Baker, *supra* Chapter Two, note 7, at 217–19.

[205] New Federalism proponents often claim that dual federalism reflects the Framers' original intent, but the historical sources that support the claim are matched with equally as many that do not. *See* PURCELL, *supra* Introduction, note 11.

[206] *See infra* Chapter Five.

[207] *See, e.g.,* Michael S. Greve, *Against Cooperative Federalism,* 70 MISS. L.J. 557, 559 (2000); Joshua D. Sarnoff, *Cooperative Federalism, the Delegation of Federal Power, and the Constitution,* 39 ARIZ. L. REV. 205, 270–80 (1997).

[208] *E.g.,* CHEMERINSKY, *supra* Introduction, note 12; SCHAPIRO, *supra* Introduction, note 11.

[209] *See, e.g.,* Esty, *supra* note 196, at 571, 652–53; John R. Vile, *Truism, Tautology or Vital Principle? The Tenth Amendment Since* United States v. Darby, 27 CUMB. L. REV. 445, 531–32 (1997); Weiser, *supra* note 201, at 719–20; Kimberly C. Galligan, Note, ACORN v. Edwards: *Did the Fifth Circuit Squirrel Away States' Tenth Amendment Rights at the Cost of National Environmental Welfare?,* 9 VILL. ENVTL. L.J. 479, 508–09 (1998).

[210] Hills, *supra* Part I Introduction, note 5, at 816–17, 938–44.

[211] SCHAPIRO, *supra* Introduction, note 11; Robert A. Schapiro, *Polyphonic Federalism: State Constitutions in the Federal Courts,* 87 CAL. L. REV. 1409, 1466–68 (1999).

[212] CHEMERINSKY, *supra* Introduction, note 12.

individualized evaluations of local, state, and national capacity for addressing a given interjurisdictional problem.[213]

Even if cooperative federalism continues to dominate the legal landscape—and perhaps especially if it does—interpreters deserve more meaningful theoretical tools to cope with the thorny federalism decisions that invariably arise in the gray area. Previous scholars have noted that the political safeguards model on which cooperative federalism rests is not really a theory of federalism at all, but an empty-vessel theory of judicial review.[214] As Professor Schapiro observes:

> The political safeguards argument explains why courts should not draw lines between the state and federal government; instead, the courts should defer to congressional judgments. However, the theory does not tell Congress how it should make the allocational decisions. The political safeguards approach tells courts not to interfere with [a federalism-sensitive statute], but does not help Congress design the law.[215]

Indeed, a robust theoretical model of federalism does not just delineate who gets to interpret federalism, it assists the interpreter in allocating authority between the state and federal government. It provides a meaningful basis on which to decide, in the end, *who gets to decide*. To that end, this book sets out to improve upon what the competing cooperative and New Federalism approaches have already offered. But New Federalism does not suffer from the "undertheorized" critique that attaches to cooperative federalism. The more relevant question is whether its theory of federalism is the best we can do.

E. The New Federalism

If cooperative federalism swung the pendulum away from the problem-solving extreme of New Deal federalism, the New Federalism ideal swings it from the more central position staked out by cooperative federalism toward the dualist check-and-balance extreme. As both a political and judicial phenomenon, the New Federalism movement arose out of concern that cooperative federalism fails to adequately circumscribe federal authority.[216] Anxious to preserve classical checks and balances against further degradation, the New Federalism cases seem nostalgic for the separationist model of dual sovereignty that idealizes a clean boundary between exclusive zones of state and federal prerogative, together with judicial responsibility to enforce it.

As the preceding discussion demonstrates, the New Federalism is certainly not the first interpretive movement to herald the distinction, whose adherents include even such early

---

[213]   Nolon, *supra* Chapter Two, note 180, at 18–22.

[214]   *E.g.*, Hills, *supra* Part I Introduction, note 5, at 821.

[215]   SCHAPIRO, *supra* Introduction, note 11, at 87.

[216]   For its proponents, Congress's failure to state a clear jurisdictional nexus in the Gun-Free School Zones Act of 1990 epitomized the source of their frustration. *See* United States v. Lopez, 514 U.S. 549, 561–63 (1995).

champions of federal authority as Justice Oliver Wendell Holmes.[217] However, renewed political interest in the distinction arose in the 1970s, following the explosion of new federal civil rights and environmental laws and the Great Society regulatory apparatus that extended federal reach into education, urban renewal, transportation, and antipoverty programs. The war in Vietnam and the oil crisis of the 1970s punctured the era of economic growth that had enabled the ambitious cooperative federalism programs of the Great Society. Critics noted that as the size of the federal budget became a genuine political constraint, Congress became more willing to use established federal grant programs to coerce states toward federal policy objectives.[218] *South Dakota v. Dole* would later affirm broad federal authority under the spending power to condition federal grants to states on reasonably related objectives.[219] Block-grant programs initiated under presidents Nixon, Carter, and Reagan would increase state autonomy under federal grants programs, but did not markedly reduce the overall federal regulatory presence.

Fueling the fire in 1976, in *Kleppe v. New Mexico* the Supreme Court found broad federal authority under the Property Clause for the management of national public lands for discretionary federal purposes, including conservation.[220] This new assertion of federal power exacerbated conflict with western state interests, as protected federal lands are overwhelmingly located in the west.[221] The conflict deepened a few months later when Congress enacted the Federal Land Policy Management Act (FLPMA), establishing as the new federal policy that lands then owned by the national government would be retained in federal ownership.[222]

The policy behind the FLPMA had been brewing since the turn of the century, when President Theodore Roosevelt accelerated the protection of federal lands in national parks, monuments, and forests,[223] and it was further foreshadowed by the contested Wilderness Act of 1964, in which Congress prohibited resource development within designated wilderness areas on federal lands that had once been open for private extraction.[224] But the FLPMA represented the formal end to the policy from the earliest days of the republic that the national government would dispose of acquired lands and resources for the purposes of private economic development.[225] The Sagebrush Rebellion of the late 1970s followed, as western state legislators and activists mobilized to challenge federal conservation policies,

---

[217] *See* N. Sec. Co. v. United States, 193 U.S. 197, 402 (1904) (Holmes, J., dissenting) (noting that the federal government should refrain from regulating in traditional realms of state authority only tangentially related to commerce).

[218] *Cf.* Lynn A. Baker, *Federalism and the Spending Power from* Dole *to* Birmingham Board of Education, *in* THE REHNQUIST LEGACY 205, 205–06 (Craig M. Bradley ed., 2006).

[219] 483 U.S. 703 (1987).

[220] 426 U.S. 529 (1976).

[221] *E.g.,* Erik Larson, *Unrest in the West: Nevada's Nye County,* TIME, Oct. 23, 1995, at 7–9, 12, http://www.time.com/time/magazine/article/0,9171,983593,00.html.

[222] 43 U.S.C. § 1701(a) (1976).

[223] RASBAND ET AL., *supra* note 77, at 132.

[224] Pub. L. No. 88–577, 78 Stat. 890, 16 U.S.C. § 1131–36 (1964).

[225] RASBAND ET AL., *supra* note 77, at 115–128, 140.

seeking legislation to transfer federal lands to state ownership and engaging in acts of civil disobedience.[226] States' rights sentiments further gathered steam in the 1980s,[227] following President Carter's designation of large new tracts of national forests, monuments, and wildlife refuges and Congress's declaration of new national parks in Alaska.[228] President Carter's likeness was burned in effigy at a rally in Fairbanks,[229] and National Park Service employees were threatened.[230]

Following this period of growing anxiety over the changing balance of state and federal power, states' rights activism was galvanized into a national political movement during the presidency of Ronald Reagan. President Reagan vowed in his 1981 inaugural address "to curb the size and influence of the Federal establishment and to demand recognition of the distinction between the powers granted to the Federal Government and those reserved to the States or to the people."[231] The movement reached maturity during the mid-1990s, when Republican majorities were elected for the first time in four decades to both the House and Senate. In a "Contract with America," they promised to devolve regulatory authority that had come to rest with the federal government back to the state level.[232] This was the political context in which the Rehnquist Court began experimenting with new judicially enforceable federalism constraints during the 1990s.

Since 1992, the Supreme Court's New Federalism jurisprudence has come to represent the revival of national interest in federalism issues (perhaps even disproportionately to their actual influence on American governance).[233] The Rehnquist Court issued a controversial series of federalism decisions[234] (reviewed more fully in the next chapter) in which it limited the federal commerce power and the extent of Congress's power under the post-Civil War amendments. It expanded state sovereign immunity and made it more difficult for Congress to abrogate. Reinvigorating Tenth Amendment constraints after more than a half century of slumber, it curtailed Congress's ability to compel state activity and redefined an enforceable boundary between proper spheres of state and federal power.

---

[226] *Id.* at 156–58.

[227] Moreno, *supra* Chapter Two, note 7, at 741–42.

[228] RASBAND ET AL., *supra* note 77, at 145.

[229] Alaska Humanities Forum, *Modern Alaska: The Alaska National Interest Lands Conservation Act*, ALASKA HISTORY AND CULTURAL STUDIES (2004), http://www.akhistorycourse.org/articles/article.php?artID=256.

[230] *Id.*

[231] Ronald Reagan, First Inaugural Address (Jan. 20, 1981) (transcript available at http://reaganfoundation.org/pdf/Inaugural_Address_012081.pdf).

[232] *See* Chung-Lae Cho & Deil S. Wright, *The Devolution Revolution in Intergovernmental Relations in the 1990s: Changes in Cooperative and Coercive State–National Relations as Perceived by State Administrators*, 14 J. PUB. ADMIN. RES. & THEORY 447, 450–51, 464 (2004).

[233] *E.g.*, Marci A. Hamilton, *Nine Shibboleths of the New Federalism*, 47 WAYNE L. REV. 931, 940–41 (2001) (arguing that "[t]he new federalism is intellectually fascinating, and scholars have something wonderful to chew on, but the Court itself is nibbling" due to the limited impact of the decisions on general federal lawmaking practices).

[234] *See supra* Part I Introduction, note 2 (listing the cases), *infra* Chapter Four (discussing them).

The New Federalism cases were also partnered in time with a less famous set that pre-empted state and local governance out of the realms of jurisdictional overlap in which they had long regulated previously.[235] Together, the New Federalism and accompanying preemption decisions evoke the Court's theoretical debt to the nineteenth century dual federalism model, attempting stricter separation between local and national regulatory authority even in the face of overwhelming modern jurisdictional overlap. While this theoretical model is belied by continuing cooperative federalism partnerships and other instances of overlap, New Federalism idealism has powerfully altered the federalism discourse—permeating legal thinking in the making, interpreting, and teaching of law.

New Federalism's reinvigoration of judicial federalism safeguards also reflects its embrace of the classical dualist model. By the prevailing political safeguards theory, courts should leave interpretation of close federalism calls to the political process because the locally elected and deliberative body of Congress can best navigate competing federalism concerns through policy making.[236] However, citing unchecked federal expansion into traditional areas of state prerogative, the New Federalism movement rejected the assumption that political safeguards are sufficient to protect dual sovereignty.[237] The judicially enforceable constraints of the New Federalism canon not only redefined when state and federal government would get to decide policy—they powerfully redefined which branch would get to decide that.

The New Federalism agenda seemed to weaken in the waning days of the Rehnquist Court,[238] and the Court's transition to new leadership and membership in recent years leaves the legacy of the judicial New Federalism revival uncertain. In addition to President Bush's appointments of the new Chief Justice John Roberts, Jr., and Justice Samuel Alito to replace the late chief justice and the retiring Justice O'Connor, President Obama appointed justices Sonia Sotomayor and Elena Kagan to replace retiring justices Souter and Stevens respectively. But none of this necessarily portends change on issues of federalism, as each new justice is generally expected to approximate the jurisprudence of the one he or she has replaced.[239] In particular, the replacements of New Federalism pioneers Chief Justice

---

[235] *E.g.*, Chemerinsky, *supra* Introduction, note 12, at 225–45; *infra* Chapter Four, note 153.

[236] Wechsler, *supra* Introduction, note 6, at 547 ("To the extent that federalist values have real significance they must give rise to local sensitivity to central intervention; to the extent that such a local sensitivity exists, it cannot fail to find reflection in the Congress.").

[237] *E.g.*, Lynn A. Baker, *Putting the Safeguards Back into the Political Safeguards of Federalism*, 46 Vill. L. Rev. 951 (2001); Saikrishna B. Prakash & John C. Yoo, *The Puzzling Persistence of Process-Based Federalism Theories*, 79 Tex. L. Rev 1459 (2001); William W. Van Alstyne, *The Second Death of Federalism*, 83 Mich. L. Rev. 1709 (1985).

[238] For example, in Gonzales v. Raich, 545 U.S. 1 (2005), the Court upheld broad federal power under the Commerce Clause to regulate medical marijuana.

[239] The two chief justices are closely matched in their federalism sentiments, *infra* note 239, while Justice Alito has positioned himself to the right of Justice O'Connor in potentially relevant cases such as Citizens United v. Federal Election Commission, 558 U.S. 50 (2010) (striking down portions of the McCain-Feingold Bipartisan Campaign Reform Act). President Obama's liberal appointees, Justices Sotomayor and Kagan, are also expected to emerge slightly to the right of their predecessors. E.g., Peter Baker, *Kagan Nomination Leaves Longing on the Left*, N.Y. Times, May 10, 2010, http://www.nytimes.com/2010/05/11/us/politics/11nominees.html.

Rehnquist and Justice O'Connor by states rights' advocates Roberts and Alito suggest that the unstable federalism coalition may shift again toward a New Federalism interpretive alliance.[240]

In the first three years in which the new chief justice participated in the selection of cases, the Court did not agree to hear any cases directly involving issues at the heart of the Rehnquist Court's federalism revolution, leaving the New Federalism precedent intact.[241] The Roberts Court has differently engaged preemption and dormant Commerce Clause cases[242] and reopened interpretation of the Necessary and Proper Clause,[243] suggesting that these may be areas where the Court's federalism jurisprudence will evolve. In the meanwhile, the New Federalism cases remain the law of the land, and New Federalism ideals have galvanized the emerging Tenth Amendment movement at the level of grassroots politics.[244]

The Tea Party and the Tenthers have resurrected classical dualist idealism with a passion that exceeds even the New Federalism political movement of the 1970s and 1980s, when frustration with expanding federal reach stopped short of calls for state secession.[245] As reported in the Introduction, many state actors have responded to federal health insurance

---

[240] *See* Christopher Banks & John Blakeman, *Chief Justice Roberts, Justice Alito, and New Federalism Jurisprudence*, 38 PUBLIUS 576 (2008). A widely cited signal that Chief Justice Roberts would join the New Federalism interpretive alliance was his dissent as a D.C. Circuit judge from the court's denial of rehearing en banc a case upholding the constitutionality of the Endangered Species Act under the Commerce Clause. Rancho Viejo, LLC v. Norton, 334 F.3d 1158, 1160 (D.C. Cir. 2003) (Roberts, J., dissenting) (noting the panel decision's inconsistencies with *Lopez* and *Morrison*); *see also* 151 CONG. REC. S10481 (daily ed. Sept. 27, 2005) (statement of Sen. Reed) (noting that "Judge Roberts' short record raises troubling signs that he may subscribe to this new Federalism revolution"). Similarly, cues to Justice Alito's allegiance to the New Federalism cause could be found in the sole dissent he authored as a Third Circuit judge in United States v. Rybar, 103 F.3d 273, 286 (3d Cir. 1996). In *Rybar*, the court held that a federal law prohibiting the transfer or possession of machine guns did not offend the Commerce Clause. *Id.* at 285. Judge Alito contended that although Congress had the authority to regulate the interstate sale of machine guns, the intrastate sale of individual machine guns was beyond its reach. *Id.* at 291–94 (Alito, J., dissenting). Senator John McCain espressed confidence that the two would respect state decisions banning gay marriage for federalism reasons. Press Release, Senator John McCain, Statement on Marriage Protection Amendment (June 6, 2006), http://mccain.senate.gov/press_office/view_article.cfm?id=34.

[241] Dan Schweitzer, *Federalism in the Roberts Court*, National Association of Attorneys General, NAAGAZETTE, Nov. 6, 2007, http://www.naag.org/federalism_in_the_roberts_court.php.

[242] *E.g.*, Wyeth v. Levine, 129 S. Ct. 1187 (2009) (declining to preempt state tort claim under federal pharmaceutical labeling regulations); Altria Group v. Good, 555 U.S. 70 (2008) (declining to preempt a state law prohibiting deceptive tobacco advertising by federal regulation of cigarette advertising); United Haulers Ass'n v. Oneida–Herkimer Solid Waste Mgmt. Auth., 550 U.S. 330 (2007) (declining to preempt under the dormant Commerce Clause restrictive waste processing rules favoring state facilities).

[243] United States v. Comstock, 130 S. Ct. 1949 (2010) (affirming broad federal authority under the Necessary and Property Clause to civilly commit mentally-ill federal inmates beyond their prison sentences).

[244] *See supra* Introduction, notes 33–51 and accompanying text (discussing, *inter alia*, Tea Party and Tenther movements).

[245] By contrast, Texas Governor Rick Perry and Tennessee gubernatorial candidate Congressman Zach Wamp each floated the possibility of state secession in protest of federal overreach at Tea Party rallies in recent years. *E.g.*, W. Gardner Selby & Jason Embry, *Perry Stands By Secession Comments*, STATESMAN.COM, Apr. 17, 2009, http://www.statesman.com/news/content/region/legislature/stories/04/17/0417gop.html; Jimmy Orr,

reform and other federal laws with Tenth Amendment-based efforts to nullify them through state legislation or repeal them in litigation.[246] The Tenth Amendment has also been invoked in favor of liberal causes to protect state-based gay marriage rights and right-to-die legislation, and against national security policies alleged to burden privacy and civil rights.[247] But these claims often reflect an understanding of jurisdictional overlap as a rights-protective check-and-balance value.[248] By contrast, the separationist view of the Tenth Amendment is most often invoked in support of conservative efforts to cull federal involvement from areas of law where it was scarce before the New Deal. For example, Tea Party Tenth Amendment activists have argued that it should vitiate Medicaid and Medicare, federal financial reform efforts, and federally funded public education.[249]

Indeed, the straightforward New Federalism revival of classical dualism provides a historically grounded, intuitively attractive framework from which to test assertions of regulatory jurisdiction against concerns about the balance of local and national power. Its simplicity is compelling, and its intellectual appeal understandable. But in the messy reality of jurisdictional overlap, the separationist ideal does a poor job of vindicating federalism values beyond checks-and-balances for their own sake, and some accountability values that could be otherwise protected. Part II explores how this model proves ill-equipped to handle the dynamics that arise in interjurisdictional contexts, where the need for multiplicity and partnership can overwhelm the wall of separation that dual federalism seeks to preserve.

The New Federalism cases themselves are relatively few in number, and reasonable minds may differ on the extent of harm they have actually caused in the present. Yet the trajectory of their principles should concern us—especially given their passionate embrace in contemporary politics—both for the new doctrinal barriers they could inspire judicially and for the intellectual barriers they can inspire in policy making (demonstrated by the failures in leadership after Katrina). As described in Chapter Five, the uncertainty that hovers over efforts to cope with such serious environmental problems as water pollution, radioactive waste disposal, and climate change suggests the treacherous future of interjurisdictional problem solving in the ideological shadow of New Federalism.

Part II critiques the New Federalism model for these failures, but this part demonstrates why it was nevertheless a rational response to a legitimate set of concerns. The narrative of American history shows how the New Federalism model arose at the apex of one end of the freewheeling federalism pendulum that has long been swinging between the competing values that undergird the enterprise, propelled by new events and ideas that continue to challenge them. Recent decisions such as *Gonzales v. Raich*[250] (affirming federal commerce authority to prosecute the licensed, in-state production of medical marijuana) and *United*

Tennessee Gubernatorial Candidate Floats Secession, L.A. TIMES, July 24, 2010, http://latimesblogs.latimes.com/washington/2010/07/tennessee-gubernatorial-candidate-floats-secession-rival-calls-him-crazy.html.

[246] *See supra* Introduction, notes 33–46 and accompanying text.

[247] *See supra* Introduction, notes 41–48 and accompanying text.

[248] *Cf.* Schapiro, *supra* Introduction, note 48.

[249] *See supra* Introduction, notes 42–45 and accompanying text.

[250] 545 U.S. 1 (2005).

States v. Comstock[251] (affirming federal authority under the Necessary and Proper Clause to civilly commit mentally ill federal inmates) show that the pendulum continues to swing. Even if it ultimately swings past the New Federalism ideals now in place, we would do well to appreciate the problems with the dualist model so that we can escape the cycle in which it arises again and again.

Of course, that the theoretical framework of American federalism continues to evolve hardly means that its underlying principles are stale. The deep political divide made visible across the nation against the backdrop of expansive federal authority after 9/11 and Great Recession suggests that the importance of nurturing federalism's values—checks and balances that vindicate rights, accountable governance that enhances democratic participation, local autonomy that fosters innovation, and synergy between local and national regulatory capacity—remains as compelling as ever. Nevertheless, the rise of truly interjurisdictional problems, from new threats to national security to new environmental harms, signals this as a moment when the framework must adapt. The pendulum must continue to swing, at least until we adopt a federalism model that can cope with the tug of war within.

---

[251] 130 S. Ct. 1949 (2010).

The Interjurisdictional Gray Area

THIS PART EXPLORES the challenges of administering federalism in contexts of concurrent regulatory jurisdiction, and how the New Federalism theoretical model there falls short. Returning discussion to the present, Part II shifts it to the primary policy-making inquiry that federalism raises: in any given regulatory context, *who gets to decide*—the local or national government? When there are conflicts, whose decision should trump? Setting aside the critical meta-issue of who should make that call (the federalism safeguards debates addressed in Parts III and IV), Chapters Four and Five focus on vertical federalism at the level of policy-making authority, especially in contexts of jurisdictional overlap. I argue that the revival of classical dualism in the judicial and political realms does not account well for the values competition that is heightened in contexts of jurisdictional overlap. The New Federalism's renewed emphasis on jurisdictional separation—especially visible in its Tenth Amendment cases—bodes ill when society increasingly faces regulatory dilemmas that defy these idealized boundaries.

Challenging the simplistic premise that all regulatory issues *can* be clearly characterized as matters of either local or national jurisdiction, Part II demonstrates that some regulatory targets are better understood within a separate, interjurisdictional sphere that legitimately implicates both local and national responsibility. As defined here, an *interjurisdictional regulatory problem* is one whose meaningful resolution demands action from both state and federal regulatory authorities, either because neither has all of the jurisdiction necessary to address the problem as a legal matter or because the problem so implicates both local and national expertise that the same is true as a factual matter. Federalism practice has mastered the genre, but federalism theory must do better to understand these dilemmas. Cooperative federalism uncritically describes the phenomenon, while dual federalism doubts its legitimacy.

Establishing precise boundaries around this interjurisdictional gray area invites disagreement, ranging from dispute over whether a problem truly implicates both local and national concerns to dispute over whether the given problem is truly amenable to a regulatory solution.[1] Yet between these contested margins lie regulatory matters that warrant simultaneous state and federal response under any honest definition—such as the Great Depression, Hurricane Katrina, or the realms of ordinary regulatory law that invariably mix and match state and federal elements, such as bankruptcy.[2] In introducing my conceptual framework for jurisdictional overlap to the discourse, I avoid legitimate arguments at the margins of the model by focusing on a sample of regulatory issues that meet the criteria relatively uncontroversially. In recognition that not every social quandary will rank among the "regulatory problems" with which the model should concern itself, I focus on those associated with the classic targets of administrative law, such as market failures, negative externalities, and other collective action problems reasonably susceptible to efficient resolution by government activity. Analyzed in Chapter Five, examples that are sustained targets of local and national attention can be found among environmental and land use law, disaster management, public health, and national security law.

Dual federalism attempts to circumscribe state and federal regulatory responsibility by subject matter, which may have been possible in earlier times (although historical accounts cast doubt on the hegemony of this ideal even then).[3] Yet assigning responsibility for interjurisdictional problems to the exclusive attention of either the local or national government is an arbitrary endeavor. As discussed in Part III, the better criteria for consideration is whether regulation by either side in the gray area ultimately advances or detracts from the full panoply of federalism values that undergird the enterprise. Nevertheless, interjurisdictional problems pose special challenges because they exacerbate the inherent tension between federalism's regard for local autonomy and national uniformity, pitting the values of checks, accountability, localism, and problem solving against one another.

As catalogued in Chapter Three, the tug of war between them has been of no small consequence. The progression of federalism theory informing Supreme Court interpretation reflects an ongoing attempt to achieve better balance, with each model overcompensating for the excesses of its predecessor. When the Great Depression crippled local capacity, the New Deal model exalted problem solving over checks to expand federal reach. Cooperative federalism recovers some balance through its partnership approach, but it is criticized as an overly pragmatic model that insufficiently protects checks. Responding to concerns that cooperative federalism is, at best, undertheorized (and at worst, more coercive than collaborative),

---

[1] *See infra* Chapter Five, text between footnotes 15–16.

[2] Bankruptcy law is an enumerated federal power but relies on state law definitions of property in application. *See* Felicia Anne Nadborny, Note, *"Leap of Faith" into Bankruptcy: An Examination of the Issues Surrounding the Valuation of a Catholic Diocese's Bankruptcy Estate*, 13 AM. BANKR. INST. L. REV. 839, 889 (2005).

[3] *E.g.* PURCELL, *supra* Introduction, note 11.

New Federalism reasserts the supremacy of classical checks and balances, bolstering the boundary between state and federal authority against all pressures that would blur the line. Part II explores this challenge and the theoretical friction it has generated in the interjurisdictional gray area.

Demanding attention from both national and local actors, interjurisdictional problems do blur the dualist boundary, pitting concerns about tyranny and pragmatism against one another. But it is arguably the tension between the federalism values that has made our system such a robust form of government—enabling it to adjust for changing demographics, technologies, and expectations without losing its essential character. A model of federalism that engages these tensions is a model that can endure. However, dual federalism's focus on preserving the bright-line boundary above all else renders it unable to effectively mediate the competition, contributing to a governmental ethos that obstructs even needed regulatory activity in the gray area.

In this ironic respect, the New Federalism simply does what New Deal federalism did in the opposite direction—shortchanging the problem-solving value in the name of separationist checks and balances, which it mistakes for federalism generally. But New Federalism differs from New Deal federalism in its strident rhetorical emphasis, by which it lays claim to the essence of American federalism itself. The canonical New Federalism cases cast their approach as the only legitimate reading of federalism, when the Constitution really affords space for multiple interpretations. Like earlier models, the New Federalism approach vindicates some of these values to the exclusion of others, threatening regulatory efforts to cope with society's most pressing problems in adherence to a separationist vision that misses the full federalism target.

Modern-day dilemmas warrant a more sophisticated approach, driven by a theory of federalism that better accounts for the interjurisdictional complexity that marks federalism in practice. Good governance is threatened by uncertainty about how regulatory responses will fare under the current doctrine and uncertainty about how the doctrine will continue to evolve. Although cooperative federalism continues to predominate vast areas of American law, New Federalism idealism in the judicial and political sphere have posed a formidable challenge. Legal questions that seemed settled are again debated, and it remains unclear whether the New Federalism revival will soon taper or expand its reach.[4]

Chapter Four outlines the Supreme Court's New Federalism embrace of dual federalism under the leadership of Chief Justice William Rehnquist, focusing on its Tenth Amendment jurisprudence. Beginning with reflections on the problematic quest for jurisprudential absolutes, the chapter compares the contemporary Tenth Amendment cases to their predecessors, reviews dualist elements in other doctrinal areas of the New Federalism, and explores how the Rehnquist Court's federalism and preemption cases joined to reify greater separation between proper spheres of state and federal jurisdiction. It critiques the resulting model of federalism for failure to grapple with the values tug of war and the problem of jurisdictional overlap.

---

[4] *See supra* Chapter Three, notes 239–40 and accompanying text (discussing the likely impacts of new judicial appointments).

Chapter Five then probes the zone of jurisdictional overlap that belies the dual federalism ideal, where both the states and federal government hold legitimate regulatory interests or obligations. It explores water and air pollution, counterterrorism efforts, climate governance, and the Katrina response as examples of interjurisdictional regulatory problems. These examples highlight federalism's need for better theoretical tools to cope with the demands of jurisdictional overlap and the ongoing uncertainty it raises about who, in the end, should decide.

Ultimately, Part II sets the stage for my argument in Part III that we should take what lessons are worthy from the New Federalism experiment—perhaps the importance of "hard look" adjudication in certain gray area contexts—and move forward toward a model that enables effective interjurisdictional governance with a healthy balance of state and federal power. At the very least, a federalism framework that accounts for gray area tensions would facilitate the kinds of wrenching decisions called for in interjurisdictional crises like Katrina-devastated New Orleans. At best, it would provide procedural tools for mediating the tug of war in all areas of federalism-sensitive governance.

THE REHNQUIST REVIVAL OF JURISDICTIONAL SEPARATION

BUTTRESSED BY CASELAW in other doctrinal realms, this chapter focuses on the Supreme Court's Tenth Amendment jurisprudence to explore the Rehnquist Court's embrace of the dual federalism theoretical model. It begins with a brief reflection on the New Federalism's penchant for certainty in interpreting the conflict between state and federal power that has baffled Americans since the beginning. It then reviews the Court's unstable attempts to cope with dual sovereignty's boundary problem in its Tenth Amendment cases over the twentieth century, culminating in the New Federalism era. Touching on the revival of classical dualism in other areas of the New Federalism jurisprudence, it then describes a set of contemporaneous preemption decisions that further reinforce the model of jurisdictional separation.

Through the combined force of formal federalism doctrine and functional preemption decisions, the Rehnquist Court's federalism approach attempts to shift the baseline from the uncritical overlap of cooperative federalism to a model emphasizing more protected zones of exclusive state and federal power. The overarching implication is that the checks and balances of jurisdictional separation are the principal federalism value worthy of consideration. The New Federalism decisions do not reestablish nineteenth century dualism, but they create theoretical tension with the cooperative federalism baseline. They suggest an understanding of the Tenth Amendment as the arbiter of an idealized, bright-line boundary between proper state and national jurisdiction, even at the interjurisdictional margin that belies such clarity. The chapter concludes with reflections on the role cast for the Tenth Amendment within this model, and its inevitable clash with the reality of jurisdictional overlap.

A. The Jurisprudential Quest for Absolutes

In the standard litany of New Federalism decisions, the Rehnquist Court disqualified federal attempts to compel state participation in federal regulatory regimes under the Tenth Amendment,[1] championed state immunity from citizen suits under the Eleventh Amendment (despite congressional attempts to hold states accountable to federal antidiscrimination and other laws),[2] and asserted the limits of federal regulatory authority over activities that affect interstate commerce[3] and to enforce individual rights under Section Five of the Fourteenth Amendment.[4] Articulating the conviction that animates the New Federalism revival, Justice Scalia admonished in *Printz v. United States* that "[i]t is an essential attribute of the States' retained sovereignty that they remain independent and autonomous within their proper sphere of authority" from federal interference (without clarifying exactly what that "proper" sphere of authority is).[5]

Of course, debate over the precise boundaries of proper state and federal regulatory authority has preoccupied Americans since the founding of the republic. It continued through the Civil War era and its aftermath, during the Progressive/*Lochner* era and the New Deal, and into the post-World War II Civil Rights and Great Society eras of cooperative federalism.[6] What is novel about the New Federalism in modern times is the ease and

---

[1] Printz v. United States, 521 U.S. 898, 935 (1997) (holding that Congress may not compel state executive participation in a federal regulatory program), New York v. United States, 505 U.S. 144, 161 (1992) (holding that Congress may not compel state legislative action under a federal regulatory program); *but see* Reno v. Condon, 528 U.S. 141, 151 (2000) (finding that a federal law regulating state action did not commandeer state legislative and administrative process).

[2] *E.g.*, Bd. of Trs. v. Garrett, 531 U.S. 356, 374 n.9 (2001) (holding that Title I of the ADA does not abrogate state immunity from private citizen damage suits); Kimel v. Fla. Bd. of Regents, 528 U.S. 62, 78–79 (2000) (disallowing the ADEA from abrogating state sovereign immunity); Alden v. Maine, 527 U.S. 706, 712 (1999) (holding that Congress lacks Article I power to subject unconsenting states to citizen suits in state courts); Fla. Prepaid Postsecondary Educ. Expense Bd. v. Coll. Sav. Bank, 527 U.S. 627, 636 (1999) (same, in patent law context); Coll. Sav. Bank v. Fla. Prepaid Postsecondary Educ. Expense Bd., 527 U.S. 666, 691 (1999) (holding that Congress lacks Article I power to subject unconsenting states to citizen suits in federal courts); Idaho v. Coeur d'Alene Tribe, 521 U.S. 261, 287–88 (1997) (same, denying relief against individual officials); Seminole Tribe v. Florida, 517 U.S. 44, 47 (1996) (disallowing abrogation of sovereign immunity under the Indian Commerce Clause).

[3] United States v. Morrison, 529 U.S. 598, 627 (2000) (invalidating a section of the Violence Against Women Act of 1994 (VAWA) for exceeding the commerce power); United States v. Lopez, 514 U.S. 549, 551 (1995) (overturning the Gun-Free School Zones Act of 1990); *but see* Gonzales v. Raich, 545 U.S. 1, 32–33 (2005) (affirming federal authority to proscribe intrastate commerce in medical marijuana despite contrary state law).

[4] *E.g.*, *Garrett*, 531 U.S. at 374 (holding that the private damages remedy against states in Title I of the ADA exceeded Congress's power under Section Five of the Fourteenth Amendment); United States v. Morrison, 529 U.S. 598, 627 (2000) (finding the federal civil remedy under the VAWA went beyond Section Five); *Kimel*, 528 U.S. at 82–83 (deeming requirements on state and local governments by the ADEA to be beyond Section Five); City of Boerne v. Flores, 521 U.S. 507, 536 (1997) (striking application of the RFRA to the states for exceeding Section Five).

[5] Printz v. United States, 521 U.S. 898, 928 (1997). *See also* Jackson, *supra* Part I Introduction, note 21, at 2193 (noting that *Printz*'s recognition of a sphere of state sovereignty "begs the question of what that proper sphere of authority is").

[6] *Supra* Chapter Three; Barron, *supra* Chapter One, note 56, at 2085–87.

absoluteness with which its decisions purport to recognize the distinction (and the judicial prerogative in enforcing it), especially in the Tenth Amendment anti-commandeering cases and the combined force of its Eleventh and Fourteenth Amendment cases.

Doubts about the theoretical resilience of the boundary the cases suggest between "proper" spheres of state and federal regulatory authority have engendered both scholarly criticism and practical confusion. Some have argued that the New Federalism's invocation of classical separation reflects an anachronistic notion of federalism that ignores well-established realms of concurrent state and federal jurisdiction,[7] including commercial, consumer, and economic affairs,[8] criminal law,[9] and the environment.[10] Even if those realms were regarded as historically recent examples of federalism failure,[11] vast areas of state and federal law have long been closely intertwined. For example, the law of bankruptcy—explicitly delegated by the Constitution to the federal government[12]—relies heavily on state law definitions of property.[13] Confusion following the Supreme Court's charge to protect this disputed boundary has already spawned legal challenges and regulatory failures in interjurisdictional contexts.[14] Some opponents view the decisions as the purely partisan pursuit of a substantively conservative agenda.[15]

Meanwhile, proponents have applauded the New Federalism's boundary-drawing enterprise, stressing the need for judicially enforceable constraints to protect state sovereignty lest expanding Commerce Clause jurisdiction enables Congress to legislate on whatever subject it chooses (so long as the bill is cloaked in the disingenuous but legitimizing guise of a putative relationship to interstate commerce).[16] Some have even taken the Court to task for failing to perfect its project by limiting the spending power—arguing that the broad spending

---

[7] *E.g.*, Hills, *supra* Part I Introduction, note 5, at 831–32, 938–39 (deeming it "palpably untrue"); Jackson, *supra* Part I Introduction, note 21, at 2196 (discussing its "outmoded" basis); Deborah Jones Merritt, *Three Faces of Federalism: Finding a Formula for the Future*, 47 VAND. L. REV. 1563, 1564–66 (1994) (critiquing its "territorial" view).

[8] *E.g.*, Issacharoff & Sharkey, *supra* Chapter Two, note 128, at 1382–85 (describing jurisdictional overlap in products liability law); A. Brooke Overby, *Our New Commercial Law Federalism*, 76 TEMP. L. REV. 297, 299–300 (2003) (in commercial law); Ernest A. Young, *Dual Federalism, Concurrent Jurisdiction, and the Foreign Affairs Exception*, 69 GEO. WASH. L. REV. 139, 145 (2001) (in economic regulation).

[9] *E.g.*, Susan R. Klein, *Independent-Norm Federalism in Criminal Law*, 90 CAL. L. REV. 1541, 1553 (2002).

[10] *E.g.*, Hubert H. Humphrey III & LeRoy C. Paddock, *The Federal and State Roles in Environmental Enforcement: A Proposal for a More Effective and More Efficient Relationship*, 14 HARV. ENVTL. L. REV. 7, 13–14 (1990).

[11] *See, e.g.*, Adler, *supra* Chapter Three, note 190, at 131–33 (critiquing overfederalization in environmental law); Wayne A. Logan, *Creating a "Hydra in Government": Federal Recourse to State Law in Crime Fighting*, 86 B.U.L. REV. 65, 104–06 (2006) (in criminal law).

[12] U.S. CONST. art. I, § 8.

[13] Nadborny, *supra* Part II Introduction, note 2, at 889 ("It is in fact common for bankruptcy courts to look to state law for guidance in determining what constitutes property of the bankruptcy estate").

[14] *See infra* Chapter Five and Chapter Seven (discussing various examples).

[15] *E.g.*, William P. Marshall, *Conservatives and the Seven Sins of Judicial Activism*, 73 U. COLO. L. REV. 1217, 1255 (2002).

[16] Van Alstyne, *supra* Introduction, note 7, at 782–83, 797–98; *see also* Baker & Young, *supra* Introduction, note 7, at 128.

power doctrine enables Congress to sidestep all other federalism constraints by coercively bribing the states to enact preferred federal policies.[17] Others argue that the cases are more complex than the general literature has acknowledged, and that the fuss over their embrace of dualist elements obscures other important (and occasionally conflicting) themes.[18]

Either way, the New Federalism cases jarred decades of congressional complacency about the breadth of national power by rejecting a series of federal laws held to transgress this reinvigorated boundary between proper state and federal authority. The decisions have been variously characterized as a needed revival of judicially enforced constitutional structure,[19] an assault on constitutional antidiscrimination norms,[20] a renaissance of state sovereignty,[21] and an assertion of judicial supremacy.[22] They have attracted considerable attention among jurists, lawmakers, and scholars, and if they have not significantly altered the continued intermingling of state and federal jurisdiction in many areas of law, they have at least changed the way the American legal community thinks about federalism. The vocabulary of the New Federalism has altered the lexicon of the legislators (and their staff) who make new laws and the judges (and their law clerks) who interpret them, not to mention the vast ranks of the implementing agencies—and as an entrenched element of law school constitutional law curricula, it is likely to continue to do so for some time.[23]

The New Federalism's separationist project is evident in decisions contesting both the scope of Congress's affirmative powers and the negative structural limitations on federal power, but it is the Tenth Amendment that most directly invokes the dual sovereignty directive from which all other federalism doctrine originates. The primary tests for constitutional exercises of federal authority remain under such affirmative grants as the commerce power, the spending power, and Section Five of the Fourteenth Amendment, but the Tenth Amendment—affirming that powers not delegated to federal government are reserved to the states[24]—is the Constitution's most direct textual statement of the goals and indeterminacy that complicate American federalism.

As discussed in the Introduction, there is no separate theory of federalism underlying cases about the Tenth Amendment, the Commerce Clause, or any other doctrinal federalism

---

[17] *E.g.*, Lynn A. Baker & Mitchell N. Berman, *Getting Off the Dole: Why the Court Should Abandon Its Spending Doctrine, and How a Too-Clever Congress Could Provoke It To Do So*, 78 IND. L.J. 459, 499–500 (2003); Mitchell N. Berman, *Guillen and Gullibility: Piercing the Surface of Commerce Clause Doctrine*, 89 IOWA L. REV. 1487, 1523–26, 1531–32 (2004).

[18] *E.g.*, Young, *supra* Part I Introduction, note 3, Eid, *supra* Part I Introduction, note 3.

[19] *E.g.*, Baker, *supra* Chapter Three, note 237, at 951–52.

[20] *E.g.*, Jed Rubenfeld, *The Anti-Antidiscrimination Agenda*, 111 YALE L.J. 1141, 1142 (2002).

[21] *E.g.*, Michael B. Rappaport, *Reconciling Textualism and Federalism: The Proper Textual Basis of the Supreme Court's Tenth and Eleventh Amendment Decisions*, 93 NW. U.L. REV. 819, 821 (1999).

[22] *E.g.*, Larry D. Kramer, *The Supreme Court, 2000 Term—Foreword: We the Court*, 115 HARV. L. REV. 4, 14 (2001) (noting that the "Court no longer views itself as first among equals, but has instead staked its claim to being the *only* institution empowered to speak with authority when it comes to the meaning of the Constitution").

[23] *See, e.g.*, Allison H. Eid, *Teaching New Federalism*, 49 ST. LOUIS U. L.J. 875 (2005); MICHAEL KENT CURTIS ET AL., CONSTITUTIONAL LAW IN CONTEXT (2003) (addressing the "Rehnquist Revolution").

[24] U.S. CONST. amend. X.

realm.[25] In coping with the questions raised in each instance, judges and policy makers draw from a unified understanding about what federalism is for. The Court explicitly affirmed the uniformity underlying its federalism jurisprudence, including the relationship between the enumerated powers and the Tenth Amendment, in a 2011 decision holding that individuals have standing to raise certain federalism-based claims:

> There is no basis to support the Government's proposed distinction between different federalism arguments for purposes of prudential standing rules. The principles of limited national powers and state sovereignty are intertwined. While neither originates in the Tenth Amendment, both are expressed by it. Impermissible interference with state sovereignty is not within the enumerated powers of the National Government, and action that exceeds the National Government's enumerated powers undermines the sovereign interests of States.[26]

The limited number of Tenth Amendment cases in each generation enables especially clear insight into the Supreme Court's transitioning theory, because each case conferred an unusual opportunity to reshape the doctrine with relatively little precedential constraint (at least compared to expansive doctrinal areas such as commerce).[27] Accordingly, the Court's vacillating Tenth Amendment jurisprudence provides an excellent, narrowly tailored laboratory for exploring the overarching theoretical issues that federalism interpretation has demanded over time.

B. Dual Sovereignty and the Boundary Problem

The New Federalism cases lean toward the nineteenth-century reading of dual sovereignty, sympathizing with its emphasis not only on separate sources of state and federal power, but mutually exclusive realms in which they should be used. Justice Scalia explained the New Federalism understanding of dual sovereignty in *Printz v. United States*, which invalidated portions of the Brady Handgun Violence Prevention Act (Brady Act) that required state law officials to provide background check information on gun purchasers while the federal government compiled a national database.[28] In holding that these provisions violated the Tenth Amendment by compelling state participation in a federal program, he explained:

> It is incontestable that the Constitution established a system of "dual sovereignty." Although the States surrendered many of their powers to the new Federal Government, they retained "a residuary and inviolable sovereignty. . . ." [This r]esidual state

---

[25] *See supra* Introduction, notes 25–66 and accompanying text (explaining the book's Tenth Amendment focus). State sovereign immunity may pose an exception, based on the Rehnquist Court's incorporation of extraconstitutional elements into its Eleventh Amendment cases. Alden v. Maine, 527 U.S. 706, 712 (1999). Alternatively, one might argue that this simply represents a problem with those cases.

[26] Bond v. United States, No. 09-1227, 564 U.S. __, *13 (slip opinion) (2011), 2011 Westlaw 2369334 (U.S.).

[27] *See supra* Introduction, notes 52–54 and accompanying text.

[28] 521 U.S. 898 (1997).

sovereignty was also implicit, of course, in the Constitution's conferral upon Congress of not all governmental powers, but only discrete, enumerated ones, . . . which implication was rendered express by the Tenth Amendment[] . . . .

. . . The great innovation of this design was that "our citizens would have two polit-ical capacities, one state and one federal, each protected from incursion by the other"—"a legal system unprecedented in form and design, establishing two orders of government, each with its own direct relationship, its own privity, its own set of mutual rights and obligations to the people who sustain it and are governed by it."[29]

Indeed, the premise of American dual sovereignty is hardly controversial. Justice Scalia is clearly correct that the Constitution anticipates a system of government in which authority is housed at both the federal and state levels, and some reservoirs of state and federal powers do not overlap. However, the ongoing federalism debate in the United States proceeds from unresolved questions about the tricky margin between them—where it is, exactly, that state authority begins and federal authority ends (and vice versa) when a regulatory matter trig-gers attention in both spheres. Notwithstanding the cooperative federalism baseline in which it is enmeshed, the New Federalism revival resurrects the separationist view of dual sover-eignty, idealizing realms of state and federal authority that are protected from incursion by either side over a clearly defined boundary.

As discussed in Chapter One, the Constitution's presupposition that the states would sur-vive the Union falls short of providing a clear directive in this regard, nor does it establish the exact protocols in the relationship between state and federal authority when areas of legiti-mate national and local regulatory interest overlap.[30] The Supremacy Clause tells us that fed-eral law will prevail against conflicting state authority when it is enacted pursuant to constitutionally enumerated powers.[31] Moreover, *McCulloch v. Maryland* made clear that the state and federal governments are not "dual in the sense of *equal*,"[32] characterizing the respective sovereignties of the federal and state governments as that "between the laws of a government declared to be supreme, and those of a government which, when in opposition to those laws, is not supreme."[33]

However, the New Federalism Tenth Amendment cases suggest that even otherwise con-stitutionally enacted federal laws may not intrude upon a specially protected realm of "invio-lable" state sovereignty by commanding state agents (other than state judges) to execute federal laws.[34] It is noteworthy, both because it has not always been so, and also because it remains difficult to understand the boundaries between state authority that is inviolable

---

[29] *Id.* at 918–20 (citations omitted).

[30] *Supra* Chapter One, notes 4–33 and accompanying text; *cf.* Jackson, *supra* Part I Introduction, note 21, at 2191.

[31] U.S. CONST. art. VI, cl.2.

[32] Jackson, *supra* Part I Introduction, note 21, at 2196 (emphasis added).

[33] McCulloch v. Maryland, 17 U.S. (4 Wheat.) 316, 436 (1819).

[34] *E.g.,* Printz v. United States, 521 U.S. 898, 933 (1997). Of note, even cooperative federalism recognizes an area of "residuary and inviolable sovereignty," Garcia v. San Antonio Metro. Transit Auth., 469 U.S. 528, 550 (1985), but it presumes that checks and balances in the political process will define the contours. *Id.* at 550–52.

under the new rules and that which remains vulnerable (especially in the executive context). The Supreme Court's treatment of the Tenth Amendment over the last century demonstrates one of the most volatile areas of constitutional jurisprudence, precisely because the Court has not settled on a clear theory for understanding the nature of the boundaries that dual sovereignty implies.

The following section explores three episodes in the Court's attempts to grapple with this problem, drawing on the historical context in Chapter Three: (1) the early era from *Hammer v. Dagenhart* in 1918 to *Maryland v. Wirtz* in 1968, (2) the middle era of *National League of Cities* in 1976 and *Garcia* in 1985, and finally, (3) the New Federalism era that began with *New York* and *Printz* in the 1990s.

I. HAMMER V. DAGENHART *TO* MARYLAND V. WIRTZ: *FROM JUDICIAL TO POLITICAL SAFEGUARDS*

The Rehnquist Court's efforts to protect the boundary between state and federal regulatory authority reflect similar attempts earlier in the twentieth century to restrict the reach of the federal government into traditional realms of state power. These included decisions during the *Lochner* era invalidating early federal regulation of industrial child labor practices, in which the Supreme Court invalidated both state and federal legislation burdening industry.[35] While debate continues over the extent to which *Lochner* era decisions were based in the laissez-faire economic theory of the times,[36] several directly addressed the evolving relationship between state and federal power in regulating labor and employment.

For example, in 1918 in *Hammer v. Dagenhart*, the Court struck down a federal prohibition on the shipment in interstate commerce of certain goods manufactured by children under the age of fourteen, holding that Congress's authority to regulate interstate commerce did not extend to the realm of intrastate manufacturing reserved to the states by the Tenth Amendment.[37] Labor and employment law was the traditional purview of state law. Reflecting its continued embrace of nineteenth-century dualism, the Court explained that "[t]he grant of authority over a purely federal matter was not intended to destroy the local power always existing and carefully reserved to the States in the Tenth Amendment to the Constitution."[38] Congress next attempted to discourage child labor by levying a prohibitive federal tax on goods manufactured with underage labor, but the Court invalidated that law in *Bailey v. Drexel Furniture Co.* in 1922, finding it a disguised attempt to perforate the Tenth Amendment boundary between state and federal power it had so recently affirmed.[39]

The line of cases in which federal power was limited by judicially enforced Tenth Amendment constraints continued through the 1935 rejection of the National Industrial Recovery Act, a statute regulating agricultural pricing and production at the heart of FDR's legislative agenda. In *A.L.A. Schechter Poultry Corp. v. United States*, the Court unanimously

---

[35] *See supra* Chapter Three, notes 91–105 and accompanying text.

[36] *See supra* Chapter Three, notes 96–100.

[37] 247 U.S. 251 (1918).

[38] *Id.* at 274.

[39] 259 U.S. 20 (1922).

found that Congress's attempts to regulate industrial labor standards, production, and competition exceeded the bounds of federal power as protected by the Tenth Amendment.[40] Reaffirming the Court's continued commitment to dualism, the decision exclaimed that "[s]uch assertions of extraconstitutional authority were anticipated and precluded by the explicit terms of the Tenth Amendment."[41]

These decisions expose the conflict between the theoretical model of New Deal federalism that was driving congressional and executive lawmaking and the Court's continued adherence to the more formal, dualist model. Yet it was Congress's enactment of the Fair Labor Standards Act in 1938 that would lay the foundation for the most intense conflicts between interbranch federalism theory and the most profound instability in the Court's own federalism jurisprudence.[42] Pushing the margins of the dual federalism model that had brought down previous legislative efforts, the 1938 Fair Labor Standards Act set federal minimum wage and overtime standards for employment, but in deference to state sovereignty, specifically exempted state and local employees. The Court's acceptance of this federal move into labor law in *United States v. Darby* demonstrated its own transition to New Deal federalism in 1941.[43]

However, in 1966, Congress signaled further evolution in its own operative federalism theory (as President Johnson did in signing the bill into law) by amending the Fair Labor Standards Act to extend its protections to public school, hospital, and mass transit employees.[44] Legislative and executive willingness to transgress the ultimate boundary between state and federal law showcased the increasing embrace of the cooperative federalism model, inspired by the New Deal expansion of federal reach and the emerging Civil Rights Era recognition of the role of the federal government as a protector of individual rights. The Fair Labor Standards Act hardly preempted the field of labor and employment law, which remains a vibrant area of state leadership. Nevertheless, in setting a minimum floor for the protection of all workers, the federal government effectively asserted its authority to protect individual rights at the expense of state autonomy. Objections to federal encroachment on state sovereignty would center on the view that the move violated the classical checks and balances implied by the Tenth Amendment. Reminiscent of the Civil War example, defense of the move would hinge on the idea that the encroachment protected individuals, the very purpose of simultaneous sources of sovereign power.

In *Maryland v. Wirtz*, in the waning days of the Warren Court, the majority upheld the amendments against several states' assertion that they exceeded the scope of the Commerce Clause.[45] Writing for the Court, Justice Harlan observed that although the commerce power

---

[40] A.L.A. Schechter Poultry Corp. v. United States, 295 U.S. 495 (1935).

[41] *Id.* at 529.

[42] Fair Labor Standards Act of 1938, Pub. L. 75–718, ch. 676, 52 Stat. 1060 (codified as amended at 29 U.S.C. §§ 201 *et seq.* (2006)).

[43] 312 U.S. 100, 119 (1941) (abandoning the distinction between commerce and production in favor of a "substantial effects" test for valid federal commerce authority).

[44] Fair Labor Standards Amendments of 1966, Pub. L. 89–601, 80 Stat. 830, 29 U.S.C. § 203(d) (1964 ed., Supp. II).

[45] 392 U.S. 183 (1968).

is not unlimited, "valid general regulations of commerce do not cease to be regulations of commerce because a State is involved" when the state is acting not in its sovereign capacity as a regulator but as a participant in a market (here, for labor).[46] Reflecting cooperative federalism tolerance for jurisdictional overlap, he explained: "[i]f a State is engaging in economic activities that are validly regulated by the Federal Government when engaged in by private persons, the State too may be forced to conform its activities to federal regulation."[47] Joined by Justice Stewart, Justice Douglas dissented to argue that the change from allowing federal regulation of private employment to federal regulation of state government violated the principles of state sovereignty that they believed were protected by the Tenth Amendment.[48]

In a related 1975 case during the Burger Court years, *Fry v. United States*, the Court upheld federal authority to limit state employee wages during a time of inflation-driven national economic crisis.[49] Constrained by the broad understanding of commerce authority in *Maryland v. Wirtz*, the plaintiffs staked their claim on the affront posed by this regulation to the Tenth Amendment.[50] Justice Rehnquist accepted the plaintiffs' argument in his dissent,[51] but the majority reasoned that

> The Amendment expressly declares the constitutional policy that Congress may not exercise power in a fashion that impairs the States' integrity or their ability to function effectively in a federal system. Despite the extravagant claims on this score made by some amici, we are convinced that the wage restriction regulations constituted no such drastic invasion of state sovereignty.[52]

Disagreement thus centered on just how far federal law may incur into state functions before it impairs state integrity, foreshadowing the theme of volatility in the next era.

2. NATIONAL LEAGUE OF CITIES *AND* GARCIA: *THE RISE AND FALL OF THE SOVEREIGN FUNCTIONS TEST*

Signaling complete embrace of the new model, Congress again amended the Fair Labor Standards Act in 1974 (and President Ford signed it into law), this time extending its minimum wage and hour protections to almost all state employees.[53] Local governments argued that they were shielded from enforcement under the act by "intergovernmental immunity," and this time, the Supreme Court shifted course from its precedent in *Maryland* and *Fry*.

---

[46] *Id.* at 196–97.

[47] *Id.*

[48] *Id.* at 201 (Douglas, J., dissenting).

[49] 421 U.S. 542 (1975).

[50] *Id.* at 547 n.7.

[51] *Id.* at 550 (Rehnquist, J., dissenting).

[52] *Id.* at 547 n.7.

[53] Fair Labor Standards Amendments of 1974, Pub. L. 93–259, 88 Stat. 55, 29 U.S.C. § 203(d), (s), (x) (1970 ed., Supp. IV).

In a 1976 decision that would become its most significant precursor to the New Federalism revival, the Court held in *National League of Cities* that the Tenth Amendment prohibited the application of federal minimum wage and maximum hour laws to state employees.[54] Writing for a tight 5–4 majority, then-Associate Justice Rehnquist distinguished *Fry* as a temporary emergency measure, but flatly overruled the contrary precedent in *Maryland v. Wirtz*.[55]

Justice Rehnquist explained that even Congress's Commerce Clause authority is subjected to structural limitations implied by the Tenth Amendment,[56] which protect "integral government functions" as an inviolable aspect of state sovereignty: "Congress may not exercise that power so as to force directly upon the States its choices as to how essential decisions regarding the conduct of integral governmental functions are to be made."[57] Joined by Justices White and Marshall, Justice Brennan dissented, arguing that the majority's rationale dealt "a catastrophic body blow" at the federal government's ability to manage national affairs: "[e]ven if Congress may nevertheless accomplish its objectives—for example, by conditioning grants of federal funds upon compliance with federal minimum wage and overtime standards . . . —there is an ominous portent of disruption of our constitutional structure implicit in today's mischievous decision."[58]

Foreshadowing a subtle but important element of the approach the Rehnquist Court would later take in its Tenth Amendment cases, the *National League of Cities* decision articulated a "sovereign functions" test, requiring that adjudicators distinguish between ordinary activities of state government that could be made subject to federal law and the essentially sovereign activities that could not be. Congress could presumably require that state employees conform to federally mandated environmental laws and safety standards, but states could not be forced to pay their employees a federally mandated minimum wage.[59] In a short concurrence, Justice Blackmun emphasized that the Court's opinion "does not outlaw federal power in areas such as environmental protection, where the federal interest is demonstrably greater and where state facility compliance with imposed federal standards would be essential."[60] But in a separate dissent, Justice Stevens specified multiple other areas of authority where he believed the the federal government should be able to "require the State to act impartially," such as:

> when it hires or fires the janitor, to withhold taxes from his paycheck, to observe safety regulations when he is performing his job, to forbid him from burning too much soft coal in the capitol furnace, from dumping untreated refuse in an adjacent waterway,

---

[54] 426 U.S. 833 (1976). For an excellent comparison of the approaches taken in *National League of Cities* and the New Federalism cases, see Barron, *supra* Chapter One, note 56, at 2085–2100.

[55] 426 U.S. at 852–53.

[56] *Id.* at 842–43.

[57] *Id.* at 855.

[58] *Id.* at 880 (Brennan, J., dissenting).

[59] *Id.* at 847–52 (majority opinion).

[60] *Id.* at 856 (Blackmun, J., concurring).

from overloading a state-owned garbage truck, or from driving either the truck or the Governor's limousine over 55 miles an hour.[61]

The multiplicity of opinions displayed the conflicting federalism theory on the Court, and it also portended the difficulties that would attend the sovereign functions test in practice. In its first significant attempt to apply it thereafter, in the 1981 case of *Hodel v. Virginia Surface Mining & Reclamation Ass'n*, the Court upheld the Surface Mining Control and Reclamation Act's preemption of state mining law against Virginia's facial challenge.[62] The act provided states the choice of either enacting their own environmental and safety regulations that met minimum federal standards or submitting to direct federal regulation of surface mining.[63] The decision explicitly rejected "the suggestion that Congress invades areas reserved to the States by the Tenth Amendment simply because it exercises its authority under the Commerce Clause in a manner that displaces the States' exercise of their police powers."[64] Consistent with many modern programs of cooperative federalism, states are given the choice of regulating in harmony with the federal directive or forgoing the field of regulation to preempting federal rules.

In order to maintain harmony with *National League of Cities*, however, the Court also rejected the district court's finding that the law "operates to 'displace the States' freedom to structure integral operations in areas of traditional functions,' ... and, therefore, is in contravention of the Tenth Amendment."[65] To clarify the consistency of its holding with the sovereign functions test, the Court explained the significance that "Virginia presses its Tenth Amendment challenge to the act simply as another regulator of surface coal mining whose regulatory program has been displaced or pre-empted by federal law," conclusorily holding that "there are no Tenth Amendment concerns in such situations."[66] But this was confusing, because it is not clear what regulatory program would be preempted by federal law other than that of a state or one of its municipalities.

State and federal actors struggled to make sense of the sovereign functions test for another few years until 1985, when *National League of Cities* was dramatically overruled and the sovereign functions test abandoned in *Garcia v. San Antonio Metropolitan Transit Authority*.[67] In *Garcia*, a municipal transit agency sought a declaratory judgment that the Tenth Amendment shielded it from obligations under the Fair Labor Standards Act because metropolitan transit was a sovereign state function.[68] The district court had ruled in its favor, but several state and federal appellate courts had reached the opposite conclusion on similar sets of facts, showcasing the difficulties of applying the sovereign functions test.[69] The Supreme

---

[61] *Id.* at 880 (Stevens, J., dissenting).

[62] 452 U.S. 264 (1981).

[63] *Id.* at 269–72.

[64] *Id.* at 269, 291.

[65] *Id.* at 274 (quoting the district court's invocation of *National League of Cities*).

[66] *Id.* at 291 n.31.

[67] 469 U.S. 528 (1985).

[68] *Id.* at 534–36.

[69] *Id.* at 530.

Court reversed in an opinion poignantly authored by Justice Blackmun, the very justice who had "flipped" from the *National League of Cities* majority to create the new, equally narrow majority in *Garcia*.[70] Condemning the test as "unworkable," he wrote:

> Our examination of this "function" standard applied in these and other cases over the last eight years now persuades us that the attempt to draw the boundaries of state regulatory immunity in terms of "traditional governmental function" is not only unworkable but is also inconsistent with established principles of federalism and, indeed, with those very federalism principles on which *National League of Cities* purported to rest. That case, accordingly, is overruled.[71]

In describing the sovereign functions test as "inconsistent with established principles of federalism," Justice Blackmun formally rejected the dual federalism model on which the test was premised in favor of the cooperative federalism model that had come to characterize state-federal relations in practice. (Foreshadowing Part IV's discussion, the decision also rejected the need for judicially enforceable Tenth Amendment constraints for the same political safeguards it had been observing in other federalism doctrine since the end of the New Deal.)

The dissent, of course, saw things differently. Joined by Justices Rehnquist and O'Connor, Justice Powell warned that "by usurping functions traditionally performed by the States, federal overreaching under the Commerce Clause undermines the constitutionally mandated balance of power between the States and the Federal Government, a balance designed to protect our fundamental liberties."[72] In her own dissent, joined by Justices Powell and Rehnquist, Justice O'Connor was even more specific in invoking a theory of federalism to account for her disagreement with the majority:

> The problems of federalism in an integrated national economy are capable of more responsible resolution than holding that the States as States retain no status apart from that which Congress chooses to let them retain. *The proper resolution, I suggest, lies in weighing state autonomy as a factor in the balance when interpreting the means by which Congress can exercise its authority on the States as States.*[73]

Strikingly, Justice O'Connor's dissent appeared to recognize a role for balancing in federalism jurisprudence, implying an interpretive model of federalism in which the important values of local autonomy and national problem solving warrant relative consideration. But calling for balance when one's preferred concerns are in the minority is not quite as courageous as allowing for balancing when one is in command—and indeed, no further calls

---

[70] Molly Farrell, *The Blackmun Papers: Key Blackmun Opinions and Dissents*, PBS NEWSHOUR ONLINE, http://www.pbs.org/newshour/bb/law/supreme_court/blackmun/blackmun_opinions.html.

[71] *Garcia*, 469 U.S. at 531.

[72] *Id.* at 572 (Powell, J., dissenting).

[73] *Id.* at 588 (O'Connor, J., dissenting) (emphasis added).

for balance arose from the *Garcia* dissenters once they became the majority in the next wave of Tenth Amendment cases.

3. NEW YORK, PRINTZ, *AND* CONDON: *ANTI-COMMANDEERING AND THE RETURN OF JUDICIAL SAFEGUARDS*

Shortly after *Garcia* was decided, Justice Rehnquist was elevated to chief justice and Justices Antonin Scalia, Anthony Kennedy, and Clarence Thomas joined the Court. Together with Justice Sandra Day O'Connor, this reliable majority of five turned the Court's jurisprudence back toward the theory of federalism that Justice Rehnquist had advanced in *National League of Cities* and in dissent of *Garcia*. In comparison to these earlier attempts to create judicially enforceable federalism constraints under the Tenth Amendment, the New Federalism revival has been more ambitious—invalidating large numbers of federal laws under a wider variety of doctrines at an unprecedented rate. As Professor Leon Friedman describes,

> From the 1994–95 Supreme Court Term to the 1999–2000 Term, the Court has held twenty-five separate federal laws unconstitutional. . . . This rate is unprecedented in our history. The Supreme Court has nullified a total of 150 acts of Congress on constitutional grounds since *Marbury v. Madison* . . . an average of slightly less than one act per year. The recent trend in striking down an average of more than four statutes each year is exceptional.[74]

Yet the revival has also been more measured, in that it generally eschews the problems associated with the vague "sovereign functions" test for more easily administrable, rule-based constraints—at least in its affirmative federal power and state sovereign immunity jurisprudence.[75]

Nonetheless, the New Federalism Tenth Amendment cases preserve a key element of the earlier approach even within the simple, bright-line rule they adopt to forbid the commandeering of state entities to enforce federal laws. Although seemingly straightforward, the anti-commandeering rule proves more complicated in application, requiring renewed reliance on considerations evocative of the sovereign functions test to distinguish between appropriate federal compromise of state authority (such as that upheld in *Hodel* and *Reno v. Condon*[76]) and impermissible commandeering (such as that invalidated in *Printz* and *New York v. United States*[77]). As Professor David Barron notes, although their focus on commandeering distinguishes them from *National League of Cities*, "the Tenth Amendment cases 'raise the same conceptual difficulty posed by the sovereign functions test.'"[78]

---

[74] Leon Friedman, *Federalism, in* SUPREME COURT REVIEW 13, 15 (PLI Litig. and Admin. Practice, Course Handbook Series No. H0–009C 2000) (citations omitted). It is possible that this high rate of reversal might also be attributable to boundary-testing on the part of congressional lawmakers.

[75] *See* Barron, *supra* Chapter One, note 56, at 2095–98.

[76] 528 U.S. 141 (2000).

[77] 505 U.S. 144 (1992).

[78] Barron, *supra* Chapter One, note 56, at 2097–98.

In *New York v. United States*,[79] the Court set forth the anti-commandeering doctrine in overturning a provision of the Low-Level Radioactive Waste Policy Amendments Act of 1985 (which, of note, was enacted by Congress and signed into law by President Reagan after being unanimously negotiated by the states themselves).[80] Drawing on the model of choice upheld in *Hodel*, this part of the act required that states without adequate disposal facilities either locate an in-state facility in accordance with its terms or assume legal liability for harm associated with the waste (in lieu of in-state producers).[81] In its decision (analyzed more fully in Chapter Seven), the Court held that this provision gave states a false choice between equally unconstitutional alternatives, because either one impermissibly commandeered the "residuary and inviolable sovereignty . . . reserved explicitly to the States by the Tenth Amendment."[82] Conceding that the plaintiff New York State had actually lobbied Congress to pass both the original act and the offending amendments, the Court nevertheless concluded that the anti-commandeering doctrine could not be waived even by state consent, emphasizing the threat that commandeering poses to clear lines of accountable governance.[83]

Amplifying *New York*'s prohibition of legislative commandeering, in *Printz v. United States* the Court extended the anti-commandeering rule to protect state executive function, striking down the Brady Act's requirement that state police do background checks on potential gun purchasers during an interim in which the federal infrastructure to perform the checks would be created.[84] In *Printz*, the Court emphasized that "[i]t is an essential attribute of the States' retained sovereignty that they remain independent and autonomous within their proper sphere of authority."[85] Invoking the classical vision of dual sovereignty, the Court added that "[i]t is no more compatible with this independence and autonomy that their officers be 'dragooned' . . . into administering federal law, than it would be compatible with the independence and autonomy of the United States that its officers be impressed into service for the execution of state laws."[86] *Printz* conceded the concurrent authority that the federal and state governments hold over their common citizens, but maintained that this jurisdictional overlap did not abrogate the classical relationship between their sovereign authorities.[87]

---

[79] 505 U.S. 144 (1992).

[80] *See infra* Chapter Seven, notes 3–50 and accompanying text (detailing the history of the law).

[81] 505 U.S. at 153–54.

[82] *Id.* at 188 (quoting THE FEDERALIST, No. 39, at 245 (James Madison), *supra* Chapter Two, note 5.

[83] *Id.* at 182–83.

[84] 521 U.S. 898 (1997); see *supra* notes 28–29 and accompanying text (quoting from the decision).

[85] *Id.* at 928.

[86] *Id.* (citation omitted). Nevertheless, state and federal officers are frequently cross-deputized to assist one another in administering criminal and other law enforcement. *See infra* Chapter Eight, notes 75–80 and accompanying text.

[87] *Id.* at 919–20.

Despite the controversial facts that attended these cases,[88] the anti-commandeering rule that emerged seems at least more administrable than the *National League of Cities* sovereign functions test, and most observers have been content to distinguish them on this ground. As Justice O'Connor wrote in *New York*, "[w]hatever the outer limits of [state] sovereignty may be, one thing is clear: The Federal Government may not compel the States to enact or administer a federal regulatory program."[89] Nevertheless, the third decision in the New Federalism's Tenth Amendment trio belies the simplicity of the anti-commandeering rule.

In *Reno v. Condon*, the Court held that the Driver's Privacy Protection Act of 1994 (DPPA) did *not* commandeer state executive authority in forbidding state motor vehicle departments from making drivers' personal information available to interested parties in the free market.[90] Both *Printz* and *Condon* involved executive commandeering claims: the former by requiring state executive actors to exercise their sovereign authority in an undesired way (forcing them to conduct background checks), and the latter by requiring them to cease exercising sovereign authority in a way they desired (forcing them to stop selling drivers' personal information). The Court distinguished *Condon* from *Printz* not on the legally shaky grounds of an act/omission distinction,[91] but by finding that the federally regulated activities of the state motor vehicle agents were not within the protected sphere of inviolable state sovereignty.

Instead, the Court reasoned that the regulated activities were of a market-participant variety—even though the market is one in which the only vendors are state motor vehicle departments.[92] Only the states can compile such complete files of citizens' personal information, as only the state can compel citizens to relinquish such information in exchange for official identification and authorization to drive on public roads. Although such a motor vehicle department is clearly acting within a zone of authority available only to the state, it is apparently *not* within the zone of inviolable state authority that is protected by the Tenth Amendment. This confusing reasoning is evocative of the intellectual gymnastics the Court had performed to uphold the Surface Mining Act in *Hodel* under the sovereign functions test.

Justice O'Connor's concurrence in *Printz* suggests a similar distinction. Though she agreed that "[t]he Brady Act violates the Tenth Amendment to the extent it forces States and local law enforcement officers to perform background checks on prospective handgun

---

[88] *See infra* Chapter Seven for discussion of controversy over *New York* (stemming from facts that rendered the Tenth Amendment claim appear opportunistic). *Printz* drew controversy primarily for extending the commandeering doctrine from the more defensible legislative policy-making realm to the more marginal one of ministerial executive activity. *See Printz*, 521 U.S. at 926–33.

[89] New York v. United States, 505 U.S. 144, 188 (1992).

[90] 528 U.S. 141 (2000).

[91] *See* Erwin Chemerinsky, *Empowering States: A Rebuttal to Dr. Greve*, 33 PEPP. L. REV. 91, 93–94 (2005) (arguing that the act/omission distinction is unavailing in the context of the anti-commandeering inquiry); *cf.* Cass R. Sunstein & Adrian Vermeule, *Is Capital Punishment Morally Required? Acts, Omissions, and Life-Life Tradeoffs*, 58 STAN. L. REV. 703, 720–21 (2005) (rejecting the distinction between acts and omissions as untenable with respect to government regulation because "unlike individuals, governments always and necessarily face a choice between or among possible policies for regulating third parties" such that the distinction is neither intelligible, nor does it "make a morally relevant difference").

[92] *Condon*, 528 U.S. at 147, 150–51.

owners,"[93] she also made clear that "the Court appropriately refrains from deciding whether other purely ministerial reporting requirements imposed by Congress on state and local authorities pursuant to its Commerce Clause powers are similarly invalid."[94] For example, in Justice O'Connor's view, the *Printz* decision did not reach requirements such as those imposed on state and local law enforcement agencies to relay information about missing children to the U.S. Department of Justice, which coordinates interstate searches for abducted children.[95] But what distinguishes the "ministerial" nature of reporting on missing children from the sovereign function of reporting on criminal history?

At least one court struggling with the distinction concluded that it is *not* because the administration of criminal justice is a core feature of state sovereign power. In *American Civil Liberties Union of New Jersey, Inc. v. County of Hudson*, a New Jersey appellate court relied on *Condon* to overcome Tenth Amendment objections raised after promulgation of post-9/11 federal regulations requiring nondisclosure of detained terrorist suspects' identities.[96] Apparently, the rules had been designed specifically to preempt a New Jersey law requiring that names of such prisoners in state facilities be released. The court reasoned that the overriding federal law regulated New Jersey not as a sovereign state, but merely as the owner of a database of prisoners' personal information—just as the DPPA regulated the states as owners of databases about their citizens' personal information:

> If federal regulations restricting the release of information compiled by state motor vehicle departments pass constitutional muster, then regulations restricting the release of information compiled by state correctional facilities about INS detainees certainly do as well.[97]

Even then, the court observed, "while the states have traditionally administered and regulated the issuance of drivers licenses, they have never been empowered to regulate immigration and naturalization matters."[98]

Indeed they have not, but states have always been empowered to regulate the administration of criminal justice in accordance with state constitutional due process considerations that may exceed the federal floor. This conflict highlights the interjurisdictional nature of the problem (which may ultimately offer the more compelling rationale for the court's decision, if the federal interest in public safety legitimately outweighed the state's due process baseline in this particular corner of the gray area). But it also reveals how the anti-commandeering inquiry forces the adjudicator into a posture that is awkward at best (and disingenuous at worst), either evaluating whether the compromised sovereign function is worthy of Tenth Amendment protection or selectively characterizing the inquiry to obscure the task.

---

[93] *Printz*, 521 U.S. at 935–36 (O'Connor, J., concurring).

[94] *Id*. at 936.

[95] *Id*.

[96] 799 A.2d 629, 638–39, 654–55 (N.J. Super. Ct. App. Div. 2002).

[97] *See id*. at 655.

[98] *Id*.

Examples like these show that, while the New Federalism approach appears tidier than its predecessor, it nevertheless draws from the same conceptual realm as the *National League of Cities* zone of integral state authority.[99] In comparison to the sovereign functions test, the New Federalism Tenth Amendment cases focus on the more circumscribed prohibition against commandeering. Indeed, Professor Barron notes that the New Federalism anti-commandeering and state sovereign immunity doctrines are both evocative of the failed sovereign functions distinction, although both attempt to overcome the unworkability problem by focusing on a prohibited mechanism (e.g., commandeering, unpermitted citizen suit) rather than attempting to define the distinction itself.[100]

Yet in forcing adjudicators to somehow differentiate between the state activities with which federal interference constitutes commandeering and the rest, the Tenth Amendment decisions resurrect the classical dualist model, evoking exclusive state and federal spheres. Striking is the ease with which they purport to recognize the distinction between them that so troubled the Supreme Court in both *Garcia* and *National League of Cities*. Even *National League of Cities* failed to achieve true majority adherence to Justice Rehnquist's proposition that inviolable and violable state functions could be categorically distinguished: his majority required the vote of Justice Blackmun, but Justice Blackmun's concurrence clarified his belief that the distinction could be made, at best, through a balancing test.[101]

Especially in application to the murkier realm of state executive action, the anti-commandeering rule requires that courts distinguish between the truly sovereign areas of state authority that are inviolable by federal commands and the cheaper areas of state authority that remain vulnerable.[102] As the creative center of state government, legislative authority most defensibly warrants safeguards against federal compulsion. But the regulatory realms in which state executive agents wield authority—ranging from more substantive regulatory rulemaking to pure ministerial implementation—are much harder to differentiate. Perplexingly, state authority implicated in performing a background check on state citizens is protected, but state authority implicated in gathering and reporting information about state citizens (e.g., missing children to the federal government, or drivers' information to willing buyers) is not.

The Court explains that the distinction hinges on whether the federal law requires a state to regulate its own citizens as part of a federal regulatory program,[103] a consideration that certainly holds currency in the defense of dual sovereignty. Nevertheless, the degree of parsing required by the distinction becomes troubling when comparing (1) the protected activity in *Printz*, where the state would have provided information to its citizens (gun dealers) in

---

[99] *See* Barron, *supra* Chapter One, note 56, at 2097–98.

[100] *Id.*

[101] 426 U.S. 833, 856 (1976) (Blackmun, J., concurring) ("I may misinterpret the Court's opinion, but it seems to me that it adopts a balancing approach, and does not outlaw federal power in areas such as environmental protection, where the federal interest is demonstrably greater and where state facility compliance with imposed federal standards would be essential.")

[102] *Id.*

[103] *E.g.*, Reno v. Condon, 528 U.S. 141, 150–51 (2000) (citing South Carolina v. Baker, 485 U.S. 505, 514–15 (1988)).

accordance with the same federal law that tells those citizens to whom they may sell guns, and (2) the unprotected activity in *Condon*, where the state must refrain from disseminating information directly to its own citizens. Unless the two are distinguished as act and omission—a distinction so riddled with problems that it simply cannot bear the weight this constitutional discrimination calls for[104]—then it is hard to understand without some recourse to sovereign functions-like reasoning.

Taking the challenged federal law in *Printz* as an example of the act/omission problem, Dean Chemerinsky shows how the requirement that states run background checks before issuing firearms permits—which the case characterized as a congressional command—can be just as easily characterized as a prohibition against states issuing permits unless they run background checks. Moving on to the DPPA at issue in *Condon*, he explains that

> it seems that [the statute] is a prohibition against states from releasing driver's license information. The Driver's Privacy Protection Act of 1994 says that state Departments of Motor Vehicles cannot release certain information, such as home addresses, Social Security numbers, and driver's license information. [Some say] that is a prohibition. I think it just as easily can be understood as a command. Congress commanded the states to keep this information secret. Command or prohibition, I think they are inter-changeable. To me, what is important is when [to] allow the states to make the choices, and when not. And I think that we should empower the states to make choices unless there is clear congressional prohibition.[105]

To the extent the anti-commandeering rule invokes the same conceptual difficulties that undermined the *National League of Cities* sovereign functions test, the New Federalism Tenth Amendment cases leave an unsettled jurisprudential wake. The Supreme Court has not revisited the Tenth Amendment since *Condon*, aside from a cursory foray into Tenth Amendment standing in *Bond v. United States*[106] (although all ears anxiously await how the justices will cope with the Tenth Amendment issues in the health-care litigation currently making its way toward the Court). The cases also demonstrate how Tenth Amendment jurisprudence will inevitably do more than simply state a rule, such as the seemingly simple anti-commandeering rule. Rather, interpreting the Tenth Amendment puts flesh on the bones of constitutional dual sovereignty, providing contour to the theoretical model of federalism in play. As the principal representation of the dual sovereignty directive, the Tenth Amendment is the primary guardian of the federalism values implied by dual sovereignty, and in any given federalism model. New Federalism renders the Tenth Amendment justiciable in terms of the anti-commandeering rule, in service of the separationist checks and balances favored by the classical dualist ideal.

---

[104] *See* sources cited *supra* note 91.

[105] Chemerinsky, *supra* note 91, at 93–94 (footnotes omitted).

[106] No. 09-1227, 564 U.S. __ (2011), 2011 Westlaw 2369334 (U.S.).

4. JURISDICTIONAL SEPARATION THROUGHOUT THE NEW FEDERALISM

The separationist ideal that the New Federalism expresses in its Tenth Amendment jurisprudence is also evident in the rest of its federalism jurisprudence (excepting the spending power[107]), in cases interpreting the Eleventh Amendment, Section Five of the Fourteenth Amendment, and the Commerce Clause. In each realm, the Rehnquist Court established new, judicially enforceable constraints to better protect a boundary between proper state and federal spheres—carving out islands of dual federalism doctrine from the vast cooperative federalism baseline.

The Rehnquist Court's Eleventh Amendment sovereign immunity jurisprudence rivals the rhetorical force of its Tenth Amendment decisions in touting the inviolability of state sovereign authority. In the seminal 1996 case of *Seminole Tribe of Florida v. Florida*, the Court broke with precedent to disallow a suit by an Indian tribe under a federal law that required states to negotiate with tribes in good faith toward the formation of compacts to permit tribal gaming operations.[108] Pursuant to its authority under the Indian Commerce Clause, Congress afforded tribes a federal judicial remedy for nonperformance by the states. However, the Court disallowed it, holding that "[e]ven when the Constitution vests in Congress complete law-making authority over a particular area, the Eleventh Amendment prevents congressional authorization of suits by private parties against unconsenting States."[109] *Seminole Tribe* and its companion cases suggest that exceptions are permitted only under Section Five of the Fourteenth Amendment, because its later ratification implicitly limits the Eleventh Amendment in the same way that the later Eleventh Amendment implicitly limits Congress's authority under Article I.[110] (Of note, however, the Roberts Court gingerly allowed it in one other instance, under the Bankruptcy Clause.[111])

In subsequent cases, the Court articulated protections for state sovereign immunity even broader than those specified by the Constitution, which only prohibits suits against a state by citizens of another state or a foreign nation.[112] Instead, in cases such as *Alden v. Maine*, the Rehnquist Court drew on the Tenth Amendment's protection of the states' "residuary and inviolable sovereignty" to formalize protections for states against suits brought even by their own citizens—in this case, claims by state probation officers for overtime pay.[113] Quoting the the Tenth Amendment in full, the decision intoned,

---

[107] Notably, the Rehnquist Court declined at least two invitations to rein in the federal spending power as it did other sources of federal authority. *See* Sabri v. United States, 541 U.S. 600 (2004) (upholding a federal law prohibiting bribery of state or local officials of entitites that receive at least $10,000 in federal funds); Pierce County v. Guillen, 537 U.S. 129, 147–48 (2003) (affirming against a spending power challenge a federal statute restricting certain publicly collected information from use as trial evidence).

[108] 517 U.S. 44, 47, 66 (1996) (overruling Pennsylvania v. Union Gas Co., 491 U.S. 1 (1989), which had enabled abrogation of state sovereign immunity under the commerce power).

[109] *Id.* at 72.

[110] *Id.* at 59, 72–73.

[111] Cent. Va. Cmty. Coll. v. Katz, 546 U.S. 356, 363 (2006).

[112] U.S. CONST. amend. XI. *See also* cases cited *supra* note 2.

[113] 527 U.S. 706, 712–15 (1999).

Any doubt regarding the constitutional role of the States as sovereign entities is removed by the Tenth Amendment, which, like the other provisions of the Bill of Rights, was enacted to allay lingering concerns about the extent of the national power. The Amendment confirms the promise implicit in the original document: "The powers not delegated to the United States by the Constitution, nor prohibited by it to the States, are reserved to the States respectively, or to the people."[114]

Yet in removing states from the corrective reach of suits by their own citizens, these cases ironically strengthen the sphere of state autonomy protected by the new Tenth Amendment doctrine at the expense of the very accountability rationale the Court had used to justify it.

The Rehnquist Court also reinterpreted federal authority under Section Five of the Fourteenth Amendment, which authorizes Congress "to enforce, by appropriate legislation" the Amendment's guarantees of due process and equal protection against the states (and has also been interpreted to incorporate many other Bill of Rights protections against the states).[115] In the 1997 case of *City of Boerne v. Flores*, the Court invalidated Congress's attempt to require strict judicial scrutiny of state laws burdening religious exercise through the Religious Freedom Restoration Act.[116] The act had been designed to restore previously understood religious freedom that the Court had narrowed in a 1990 decision, *Employment Division v. Smith*.[117] *Smith* held that free exercise is not violated by neutral laws of general applicability that incidentally burden religion—such as a prohibition on peyote consumption, even for use in Native American religious ceremonies.[118]

An unconventional majority of the Court invalidated the Religious Freedom Restoration Act in *Boerne*, a decision with profound implications not only for the scope of federal authority under Section Five but for the relationship between the judicial and legislative roles in interpreting the Constitution.[119] Emphasizing the vertical federalism concerns implied by the use of federal power to burden state law, the Court narrowly interpreted Section Five as conferring only remedial congressional authority to enforce rights formally recognized by the Court, and not substantive authority to recognize rights beyond that baseline.[120] Emphasizing the horizontal separation of powers among the three federal branches, the Court sharply curtailed Congress's initiative under Section Five, specifying that Congress may only enforce Section Five rights that are recognized by the Court.[121] For the same reason, a more conventionally divided Supreme Court later held that Congress

---

[114] *Id.* at 713–14.

[115] U.S. CONST. amend. XIV, § 5.

[116] 521 U.S. 507, 536 (1997).

[117] 494 U.S. 872 (1990).

[118] *Id.* at 879–82.

[119] Justice Kennedy's majority opinion was joined by Chief Justice Rehnquist and Justices Scalia, Thomas, Stevens, and Ginsburg (although Justice Scalia declined to join part III-A). Justices O'Connor, Souter, and Breyer dissented.

[120] *Boerne*, 521 U.S. at 536.

[121] *Id.* at 519.

could not create a civil remedy under its Section Five enforcement authority for victims of domestic violence.[122]

In the discourse foreshadowing Part IV's discussion of judicial and legislative interpretive roles, many have criticized *Boerne* as establishing judicial interpretive supremacy beyond the requirements of constitutional design.[123] As Dean Chemerinsky has argued, the decision hinges on the ambiguous meaning of the word *enforce* in the text of Section Five, which could just as easily mean "to implement" the provisions of the Amendment—leaving more room for congressional initiative—as it does "to remedy" violations established by the Court.[124] Indeed, *Boerne* labored to distinguish the contrary reasoning in the leading Section Five case of *Katzenbach v. Morgan*, which upheld the Voting Rights Act's prohibition on state law literacy requirements against a Tenth Amendment challenge.[125] In *Katzenbach*, the Court found the statute legitimately enacted under Section Five, even though the act conflicted with a previous Supreme Court decision that had upheld the constitutionality of similar literacy requirements.[126] *Boerne* differentiated its conclusion by finding that the Voting Rights Act corrected well-established harms, while the Religious Freedom Restoration Act was a disproportionate response to (what it considered) a much less serious problem.[127]

The Court used this New Federalism understanding of limited Section Five authority, working hand in glove with its enhanced Eleventh Amendment doctrine, to invalidate or shield the states against new rights-protective federal statutes. Based on *Boerne* and *Seminole Tribe*, the Court ruled that a series of federal statutes enacted to protect various individual rights could not be enforced against the states because they exceeded Section Five authority to abrogate Eleventh Amendment sovereign immunity.[128] For example, in *Kimel v. Florida Board of Regents*, the Court held that state governments could not be sued for violating the Age Discrimination in Employment Act because neither the Fourteenth Amendment nor any in the Bill of Rights guarantees such protections.[129] For the same reason, *University of Alabama v. Garrett* held that states were immune from suit under Title I of the Americans with Disabilities Act, which prohibits disability-based employment discrimination and requires reasonable accommodations.[130] *Florida Prepaid Postsecondary Education Expense*

---

[122] United States v. Morrison, 529 U.S. 598, 627 (2000).

[123] *E.g.*, Kramer, *supra* note 22, at 142.

[124] CHEMERINSKY, *supra* Introduction, note 12, at 79–80.

[125] 384 U.S. 641, 646–47 (1966).

[126] *Id.* at 649 (finding "inapposite" the contrary holding in *Lassiter v. Northampton Bd. of Elections*, 360 U.S. 45 (1959)). The Court explained, "Lassiter did not present the question before us here: Without regard to whether the judiciary would find that the Equal Protection Clause itself nullifies New York's English literacy requirement as so applied, could Congress prohibit the enforcement of the state law by legislating under § 5 of the Fourteenth Amendment? In answering this question, our task is limited to determining whether such legislation is, as required by § 5, appropriate legislation to enforce the Equal Protection Clause," and finding in the affirmative. *Id.* at 649–50.

[127] City of Boerne v. Flores, 521 U.S. 507, 530–31 (1997).

[128] *See also* cases cited *supra* notes 2 and 4.

[129] 528 U.S. 62, 78–79 (2000).

[130] 531 U.S. 356, 374 (2001).

Board v. College Savings Bank prevented citizen suits against the states for patent infringement.[131]

In its final federalism decisions of significance, the Rehnquist Court allowed the abrogation of state sovereign immunity under Section Five in two closely watched civil rights cases. In *Nevada Department of Human Resources v. Hibbs*, it upheld a citizen suit against the state under the family leave provisions of the Family and Medical Leave Act.[132] In *Tennessee v. Lane*, it did the same under Title II of the Americans with Disability Act, which prohibits discrimination against people with disabilities in state services, including courts.[133] The Court reconciled these cases with the others by explaining that Section Five enables the abrogation of state sovereign immunity in statutes that proportionately remedy forms of discrimination that the Court has already designated for heightened scrutiny (such as race or gender discrimination),[134] or that proportionately remedy interference with rights that the court has already designated as fundamental (such as access to the courts).[135] Statutes that provide remedies for other forms of discrimination (such as age or disability discrimination in employment) or that provide remedies disproportionate to the harm (as it concluded the Religious Freedom Restoration Act had) remain vulnerable.

Indeed, Congress tried again to enact the failed provisions of the Religious Freedom Restoration Act, including a private right of action against culpable states, in the Religious Land Use and Institutionalized Persons Act of 2000—this time under its spending and commerce powers.[136] But in 2011, faithful to the Rehnquist Court's Eleventh Amendment jurisprudence, the Roberts Court invalidated the private right of action, holding that states do not consent to waive their sovereign immunity by accepting federal funding under the act.[137]

Despite the rare exceptions, the combined force of the Rehnquist Court's Eleventh Amendment and Section Five jurisprudence shifted these important doctrinal areas in the direction of dual federalism, reinforcing the inviolable boundary between state and federal power that the Tenth Amendment must police. Accomplishing this in the realm of the Commerce Clause is a project of an entirely different order, given the overlap that cooperative federalism has already enabled between state and federal laws that regulate different aspects of commercial channels and activity. Realms such as employment and environmental law are veritable thickets of intertwining state and federal rules whose relationships are mediated by entrenched understandings of expansive federal commerce authority.

Nevertheless, the Rehnquist Court made a dramatic effort to demonstrate that the federal commerce power is limited by the same principles that dictate the rest of its federalism

---

[131]   527 U.S. 627, 636 (1999).

[132]   538 U.S. 721 (2003).

[133]   541 U.S. 509 (2004).

[134]   *Hibbs*, 538 U.S. at 728–35.

[135]   *Lane*, 541 U.S. at 528–29. Pursuant to this distinction, for example, the Roberts Court enabled a wheelchair-bound prisoner to sue the state under Title II of the ADA when he could not access prison toilet or shower facilities. United States v. Georgia, 546 U.S. 151 (2006).

[136]   42 U.S.C. § 2000cc(2)(a).

[137]   Sossamon v. Texas, 131 S. Ct. 1651 (2011).

jurisprudence. In 1995, in *United States v. Lopez* the Court invalidated the Gun-Free School Zones Act's prohibition of guns within one thousand feet of a school[138]—the first time a federal law had been invalidated for exceeding the commerce power since the end of the New Deal. A sharply divided Court held that Congress had not satisfied its obligation to demonstrate a justifiable relationship between the prohibition and commerce.[139] Over dissenting objections that for the last sixty years, only rational basis review had been required,[140] the Court held that constitutional exercise of the commerce power is limited to regulation of the channels of interstate commerce, persons and things in interstate commerce, and activities that substantially affect interstate commerce.[141] In the closing paragraph of the decision, the Court acknowledged the decision's departure from precedent and affirmed its commitment to a different theory of federalism:

> To uphold the Government's contentions here, we would have to pile inference upon inference in a manner that would bid fair to convert congressional authority under the Commerce Clause to a general police power of the sort retained by the States. Admittedly, some of our prior cases have taken long steps down that road, giving great deference to congressional action. The broad language in these opinions has suggested the possibility of additional expansion, but we decline here to proceed any further. To do so would require us to conclude that the Constitution's enumeration of powers does not presuppose something not enumerated, and that there never will be a distinction between what is truly national and what is truly local. This we are unwilling to do.[142]

The decision thus ends with a nod to the nineteenth-century vision of jurisdictional separation, even in the realm of commerce doctrine where it is most irretrievable

When Congress later attempted to provide a federal remedy for victims via the Violence Against Women Act of 1994, it responded to the Court's holding in *Lopez* by including extensive findings about the financial costs of domestic violence in interstate commerce and its constraints on women's interstate travel.[143] Nevertheless, the Court invalidated the provision in *United States v. Morrison*, affirming the new test it had set forth in *Lopez* and clarifying that legitimately regulable activity must not only substantially affect interstate commerce when taken cumulatively, but the activity must also be itself economic in nature.[144] Chief Justice Rehnquist again closed the decision by invoking dualist idealism, reminding his audience that "[t]he Constitution requires a distinction between what is truly national and what is truly local."[145]

---

[138] 514 U.S. 549, 551 (1995).

[139] *Id.* at 561–64.

[140] *Id.* at 604 (Souter, J., dissenting), 617 (Breyer, J., dissenting).

[141] *Id.* at 558–59.

[142] *Id.* at 567–68 (citations omitted).

[143] United States v. Morrison, 529 U.S. 598, 629–36 (Souter, J., dissenting) (2000).

[144] *Id.* at 610–13.

[145] *Id.* at 617–18.

The ringing invocations of classical dualism in the rhetoric of the New Federalism Commerce Clause decisions are significant, notwithstanding the continuing predominance of the cooperative federalism model in most commerce doctrine. As the quoted text from *Lopez* explicitly acknowledges, these rhetorical gestures provide valuable insight into transitions in the Court's operative theoretical model (here, interesting precisely because it conflicts with the cooperative federalism baseline). Those who dismiss such rhetoric because dicta will not itself dismantle the baseline are either uninterested in theoretical transitions or untroubled that the Court's new model departs from the reality of governance, when I believe we should be neither.

Moreover, when the majority of the Supreme Court takes a clear normative position—even in dicta—the legal world pays attention. As every Supreme Court justice who has ever written a carefully constrained concurring opinion will attest, today's dicta is tomorrow's law (or at least an open invitation). The decade since *Morrison* was decided is a blip on the historical screen of the Court's continuing struggle to make sense of dual sovereignty. An important case in the final days of the Rehnquist Court, *Gonzales v. Raich*, reaffirmed broad commerce authority to prosecute state-licensed, intrastate medical marijuana cultivation—in a contested decision from which Chief Justice Rehnquist and Justices O'Connor and Thomas bitterly dissented, and with which Justice Scalia reluctantly concurred.[146] But *Raich* merely affirmed the old New Deal principle that purely intrastate economic activity in the aggregate may substantially affect interstate commerce,[147] and did not damage the new economic activity limitation of *Lopez* and *Morrision*. Taken together, the jurisprudence remains hot to the touch.

C. Federalism, Preemption, and the Reallocation of Authority into Mutually Exclusive Spheres

Despite varying emphases, most analytical accounts of the New Federalism decisions share the understanding that a unifying theme among them is the "vindication of state authority relative to the federal government."[148] Yet examination of them in the context of the Rehnquist Court's overall jurisprudence—especially its preemption cases over the same time period—suggests a broader ideal of differentiating mutually exclusive spheres of state and federal authority and defending each from incursion by the other side. While the federalism cases doctrinally protect a realm of state authority from federal incursion, the preemption cases functionally protect an expanded realm of federal authority from state incursion—despite

---

[146] 545 U.S. 1 (2005).

[147] Wickard v. Fillburn, 317 U.S. 111 (1942).

[148] Issacharoff & Sharkey, *supra* Chapter Two, note 128, at 1355; John O. McGinnis, *Reviving Tocqueville's America: The Rehnquist Court's Jurisprudence of Social Discovery*, 90 CAL. L. REV. 485, 487 (2002). *See also* Barron, *supra* Chapter Two, note 19, at 411–12 (noting that "even the critics assume that the [New Federalism] protects local autonomy").

the long-standing presumption against preemption in cases with significant federalism implications.[149]

In review of the Rehnquist Court's overall jurisprudence, it is not difficult to locate increased protection for the local sphere from national incursion. By the common wisdom, the Rehnquist Court resurrected political regard for state government as the best and most democratic champion of the will of the people, and invested with judicially enforceable clout the notion that public decision making should take place as locally as possible.[150] Accordingly, Professor Richard Garnett observes that the New Federalism has "brought back to the public-law table the notion that the Constitution is a charter for a [federal] government of limited and enumerated powers, one that is constrained both by that charter's text and by the structure of the government it creates and authorizes."[151]

In addition to the standard New Federalism cases, Professor Garnett points to several other areas of the Rehnquist Court's jurisprudence that further reflect an effort to protect a zone of state authority from federal incursion, including: (1) the Court's increasing use of the "avoidance canon," which exhorts judicial interpretations that avoid raising difficult constitutional issues (e.g., the scope of Congress's authority under the Commerce Clause); (2) the Court's body of habeas corpus cases, which "reflect New Federalism-style deference to state-law procedures, state-court determinations, and state legislatures' policy preferences;" and (3) the Court's evolving Establishment and Free Exercise Clause jurisprudence, which promote "more variation, experimentation, and accommodation by States and localities."[152]

However, a closer look at the entirety of the Rehnquist Court's decisions reveals a more complex jurisprudence that champions local government less consistently than suggested by analyses such as Professor Garnett's. The list of New Federalism cases that curtail federal authority in favor of the states are partnered with a less conspicuous litany of aggressive preemption decisions that effectively curtail traditional state and local authority in favor of expanded exclusive federal jurisdiction[153]—even in close cases involving areas of traditional

---

[149] *See* Medtronic, Inc. v. Lohr, 518 U.S. 470, 485 (1996) ("In all pre-emption cases, and particularly in those in which Congress has legislated . . . in a field which the States have traditionally occupied, we start with the assumption that the historic police powers of the States were not to be superseded by the Federal Act unless that was the clear and manifest purpose of Congress." (citation omitted)); Wis. Pub. Intervenor v. Mortier, 501 U.S. 597, 605–06 (1991) (applying presumption against preemption to protect a local regulation).

[150] *See, e.g.*, McGinnis, *supra* note 148, at 490–91; Barron, *supra* Chapter Two, note 19, at 378.

[151] Garnett, *supra* Chapter Two, note 25, at 12.

[152] *Id.* at 13–14 & n.63, 14–15. Curiously, Professor Garnett also points to the Court's preemption jurisprudence as an example of this trend, but his argument here is less persuasive and supported by reference to positions taken mostly in dissenting opinions. *Id.* at 14 & n.67.

[153] *E.g.*, Lorillard Tobacco Co. v. Reilly, 533 U.S. 525 (2001); Geier v. Am. Honda Motor Co., 529 U.S. 861 (2000); CSX Transp., Inc. v. Easterwood, 507 U.S. 658 (1993); Cipollone v. Liggett Group, Inc., 505 U.S. 504 (1992). *See also* David J. Barron, *Reclaiming Federalism*, DISSENT MAG., Spring 2005, http://www.dissentmagazine. org/article/?article=249 (noting the rise of preemption decisions by the Rehnquist Court in the consumer protection context); Barron, *supra* Chapter One, note 56, at 2112 (same); Issacharoff & Sharkey, *supra* Chapter Two, note 128, at 1356–58 (in the commercial law context); Keith R. Fisher, *Toward a Basal Tenth Amendment: A Riposte to National Bank Preemption of State Consumer Protection Laws*, 29 HARV. J.L. & PUB. POL'Y 981, 994–98 (2006) (in the context of state banking laws); Catherine M. Sharkey, *Preemption by Preamble: Federal Agencies and the Federalization of Tort Law*, 56 DEPAUL L. REV. 227, 237–42 (2007) (describing judicial

state prerogative, such as tort, health, and safety law.[154] While the federalism cases doctrinally enlarge an exclusive realm of state authority that is free from federal regulatory incursion, the preemption cases functionally enlarge a realm of federal authority that is free from state and local regulatory incursion.

Although neither set of cases has routed the cooperative federalism baseline in which jurisdictional overlap is still commonplace, the two round out the Court's theoretical embrace of the classical dualist ideal, in which the state and federal governments occupy exclusive subject-matter spheres. Voting coalitions are less coherent in the preemption cases (and some decisions more Solomon-like, preempting some but not all claims under review).[155] But within them, New Federalism concerns often appear oddly inverted: many of the justices most likely to protect state authority from federal incursion in the standard New Federalism decisions are also most likely to vote in favor of federal preemption of state and local law in preemption cases.[156]

Under the Supremacy Clause and the jurisprudential tools the Court has developed to interpret it, state laws are preempted when either Congress or an executive agency declares an express intention to do so ("express" preemption) or when a court implies preemption for

---

deference to preemption of traditional areas of state law by executive agencies). *See also* Daniel J. Meltzer, *The Supreme Court's Judicial Passivity*, 2002 SUP. CT. REV. 343, 369 (noting that "[t]he five Justices most protective of state autonomy in constitutional federalism cases are the Justices who most often join opinions finding state laws preempted"). One empirical study suggests "no clear decisional trend in preemption law," Michael S. Greve & Jonathan Klick, *Preemption in the Rehnquist Court: A Preliminary Empirical Assessment*, 14 SUP. CT. ECON. REV. 43, 47 (2006), but other authors suggest that trends are evident in the voting patterns of individual justices. *E.g.*, Issacharoff & Sharkey, *supra* Chapter Two, note 128, at 1366–67 n.42; Thomas W. Merrill, *The Making of the Second Rehnquist Court: A Preliminary Analysis*, 47 ST. LOUIS U.L.J. 569, 571, 611–12 (2003) (tracking the juxtaposition between Justice Scalia's states' rights positions in the New Federalism cases and pro-preemption positions in others).

[154] *See, e.g.*, Issacharoff & Sharkey, *supra* Chapter Two, note 128, at 1356–57, 1382–84, 1420–21 (noting the trend of preempting claims of products liability, medical malpractice, and punitive damages despite tort law being among the most traditional realms of state common law). This contrasts with past deference to traditional state authority to protect public health and safety. *See* Huron Portland Cement Co. v. City of Detroit, 362 U.S. 440, 442 (1960).

[155] *See, e.g.*, *CSX Transp.*, 507 U.S. at 673, 675 (finding that the Federal Railroad Safety Act of 1970 preempted negligence claims regarding excessive speed of the train but did not preempt claims for failure to warn); *Cipollone*, 505 U.S. at 530–31 (plurality opinion) (holding that the Federal Cigarette Labeling and Advertising Act preempted a common law failure to warn and a fraudulent misrepresentation claim but not all state law damages claims).

[156] For example, in *Cipollone*, New Federalism champion Justice Scalia wrote separately to find that *all* claims were preempted under ordinary principles of statutory interpretation, 505 U.S. at 548 (Scalia, J., concurring in the judgment in part and dissenting in part), while New Federalism opponent Justice Blackmun found that *none* of the claims was preempted. *Id.* at 531–32 (Blackmun, J., concurring in part, concurring in the judgment in part, and dissenting in part). New Federalism proponents also joined opinions favoring federal power in the famously aggressive preemption cases of *Geier*, 529 U.S. at 863 (Rehnquist, C.J., O'Connor, Scalia, Kennedy, JJ.), and *Lorillard Tobacco*, 533 U.S. at 530 (Rehnquist, C.J., O'Connor, Scalia, Kennedy, Thomas, JJ.). Justice Thomas is a notable exception, a faithful member of the New Federalism coalition who is also leery of preemption. *E.g.*, *CSX Transp.*, 507 U.S. at 676 (Thomas, J., dissenting in part) (arguing that none of respondent's claims was preempted).

one of three reasons: (1) the state law actually conflicts with federal law ("conflict" preemption); (2) federal law effectively occupies the regulatory field, leaving no room for additional state input ("field" preemption); or (3) the state law would pose an obstacle to execution of the federal law's objectives ("obstacle" preemption).[157] When federal law has not directly addressed the issue, preemption cases require the courts to interpret whether Congress had intended to preempt the field and how seriously the state law interferes with a federal program. The cursory review of cases that follows is not exhaustive of all preemption doctrine during the Rehnquist Court era, but it focuses on those decisions that were most controversial because of the way they appeared to invert the historical "presumption against preemption" in areas of traditional state prerogative.[158]

Of course, the Supremacy Clause clearly invests the federal government with superior power in the jurisdictional realms it is delegated by the Constitution,[159] and the preemption decisions—essentially statutory interpretation cases—cannot be understood as formal statements by the Court on the question of federalism. However, neither are they wholly insignificant in a review of the functional impact of the Court's decisions during the New Federalism revival.[160] In one sense, preemption cases ask the justices not to consider their own views about balancing state and federal power, but to determine what Congress intended in passing the federal statute at issue. Still, the Rehnquist Court's noted shift from the "legislative intent" to the "plain-meaning" approach to statutory interpretation empowers the Court at the expense of Congress in deciding what a statute should be taken to mean.[161] This becomes especially important when coupled with the Court's threshold decision of whether to allow federalism considerations to inform the statutory analysis.

For example, in *Gregory v. Ashcroft*, the Court began its analysis of a Missouri law mandating judicial retirement age with a famous statement of federalism principles that became the platform for the New Federalism.[162] The Court upheld the Missouri provision against the plaintiffs' claim that it violated the federal Age Discrimination in Employment Act and the Equal Protection Clause of the Fourteenth Amendment—but only after reviewing how the principles of federalism informed its interpretation.[163] "As every schoolchild learns," Justice O'Connor began, "our Constitution establishes a system of dual sovereignty between the States and the Federal Government," establishing a baseline of federalism

---

[157] *See* Gade v. Nat'l Solid Wastes Mgmt. Assn., 505 U.S. 88, 98 (1992).

[158] *See* Rice v. Santa Fe Elevator Corp., 331 U.S. 218, 230 (1947).

[159] U.S. CONST. art. VI, cl. 2.

[160] *Cf.* Gonzales v. Oregon, 126 S. Ct. 904, 939–41 (2006) (Thomas, J., dissenting) (suggesting the Court had disingenuously avoided the obvious federalism issues raised by its decision declining to preempt Oregon's Death With Dignity Act, especially in light of its previous decision preempting another state law in *Gonzales v. Raich*).

[161] *See* Michael Gadeberg, *Presumptuous Preemption: How "Plain Meaning" Trumped Congressional Intent in Engine Manufacturers Association v. South Coast Air Quality Managament District*, 32 ECOLOGY L.Q. 453 (2005) (arguing that in rejecting legislative history for the textualist approach, the Court empowered itself at the expense of Congress).

[162] 501 U.S. 452, 457 (1991).

[163] *Id.* at 473, 457–64.

concerns from which to consider the relationship between the competing state and federal laws.[164]

By contrast, the most controversial preemption cases that followed were decided without overt consideration of federalism principles—except in the vociferous dissents. For example, in its unusually broad endorsement of federal preemption in *Geier v. American Honda Motor Co.*, the Court held that a common law defective design claim for failure to equip an automobile with a driver-side airbag was preempted by a Federal Motor Vehicle Safety Standard.[165] Interestingly, Justice Breyer's pro-preemption majority opinion was joined by four of the most consistent champions of the New Federalism cases (Chief Justice Rehnquist and Justices O'Connor, Scalia, and Kennedy), while most of the usual New Federalism opponents dissented (Justices Stevens, Souter, and Ginsburg, along with New Federalism supporter Justice Thomas).[166] Writing for the dissent, Justice Stevens quoted from recent New Federalism cases in admonishing that "[t]his is a case about federalism, that is, about respect for the constitutional role of the States as sovereign entities."[167] He further explained that the Court's holding

> raises important questions concerning the way in which the Federal Government may exercise its undoubted power to oust state courts of their traditional jurisdiction over common-law tort actions. The rule the Court enforces today was not enacted by Congress and is not to be found in the text of any Executive Order or regulation. It has a unique origin: It is the product of the Court's interpretation of the final commentary accompanying an interim administrative regulation and the history of airbag regulation generally.[168]

Given that "[t]ort law in America is built on the bedrock of state common law,"[169] the majority's preemption finding indicates the importance it must have attached to the national interest in what has historically been an area of traditional state concern.

Like *Geier*, in *Lorillard Tobacco Co. v. Reilly*, an opinion written by Justice O'Connor and joined by Chief Justice Rehnquist and Justices Kennedy, Scalia, and Thomas, the Court held that state regulations prohibiting cigarette and cigar advertising on billboards within one thousand feet of a school or playground were preempted by the Federal Cigarette Labeling and Advertising Act (FCLAA).[170] Joined by Justices Ginsburg, Breyer, and Souter, Justice Stevens dissented, invoking a long line of precedent counseling judicial restraint before federal statutes are construed to preempt "the historic police powers of the States."[171] He argued

---

[164] *Id.* at 457.

[165] 529 U.S. 861 (2000).

[166] *Id.* at 863–64, 866 (Stevens, J., dissenting). *See supra* note 156 (noting Justice Thomas's voting record against preemption as a marked exception to the generalization at issue).

[167] *Id.* at 887 (citation omitted).

[168] *Id.*

[169] Robert L. Rabin, *Federalism and the Tort System*, 50 RUTGERS L. REV. 1, 2 (1997).

[170] 533 U.S. 525, 530, 550–51 (2001).

[171] *Id.* at 590 (Stevens, J., dissenting).

that the state law "implicate[s] two powers that lie at the heart of the States' traditional police power—the power to regulate land usage and the power to protect the health and safety of minors."[172]

Perhaps signifying the instability of this approach, in a Roberts Court 2009 preemption decision with facts similar to *Geier*, Justices Breyer and Kennedy abandoned the *Geier* majority to join the *Geier* dissenters in issuing a barely consistent ruling in *Wyeth v. Levine*.[173] In *Wyeth*, this time emphasizing the presumption against preemption in contexts of "the historic police powers of the States," the Court upheld a common law failure-to-warn claim based on a dangerous method of injecting a pharmaceutical that had satisfied FDA labeling regulations.[174] Still, it declined to overrule *Geier*—flimsily distinguishing the two cases on grounds that the preempting FDA regulations were only in the preamble, and thus lacked the true "force of law."[175] In the 2011 decision of *Williamson v. Mazda Motor*, the Court even more narrowly distinguished *Geier* to hold that the very same federal law would not preempt a state tort suit claiming that manufacturers should have installed lap-and-shoulder belts (rather than lap belts) on rear inner seats.[176]

One wonders whether the statutory interpretations in *Geier* and *Lorillard* might have proceeded differently had the Court begun with the same historical federalism inquiry with which it commenced its analysis in *Gregory*. Either way, *Gregory* itself provides a rationale to distinguish the cases that reinforces the New Federalism's resurrection of the hapless *National League of Cities* sovereign functions distinction. Writing for the Court, Justice O'Connor emphasized: "[t]he present case concerns a state constitutional provision through which the people of Missouri establish a qualification for those who sit as their judges. This provision goes beyond an area traditionally regulated by the States; it is a decision of the most fundamental sort for a sovereign entity."[177]

Again, the implication is that different state laws possess different degrees of sovereign integrity, warranting different levels of judicially enforceable federalism protection. In this

---

[172] *Id.* at 591 (internal quotation marks omitted). *See also* Engine Mfrs. Ass'n v. S. Coast Air Quality Mgmt. Dist., 541 U.S. 246, 258–59 (2004) (holding that local regulations requiring the purchase and leasing of fuel-efficient vehicles by state-connected fleet operators were preempted as an "emission standard" under the Clean Air Act). As the sole but passionate dissenter, Justice Souter argued: "[I]n all pre-emption cases, and particularly in those [where] Congress has legislated . . . in a field which the States have traditionally occupied, we start with the assumption that the historic police powers of the States were not to be superseded by the Federal Act unless that was the clear and manifest purpose of Congress. . . . The pertinence of this presumption against federal preemption is clear enough from the terms of the [Clean Air] Act itself: § 101 states that 'air pollution prevention (that is, the reduction or elimination, through any measures, of the amount of pollutants produced or created at the source) and air pollution control at its source is the primary responsibility of States and local governments.' . . . The resulting presumption against displacing law enacted or authorized by a State applies both to the question whether Congress intended any pre-emption at all and to questions concerning the *scope* of [the Act's] intended invalidation of state law." *Id.* at 260–61 (Souter, J., dissenting) (citations omitted).

[173] 129 S. Ct. 1187 (2009).

[174] *Id.* at 1194–98.

[175] *Id.* at 1200, 1203.

[176] Williamson v. Mazda Motor of America, 131 S. Ct. 1131 (2011).

[177] Gregory v. Ashcroft, 501 U.S. 452, 460 (1991).

realm, the "more sovereign" the state law, the more deferential to state interests the preemption analysis should be. Based on the importance of the accountability value to federalism, it would be reasonable to require greater federal deference to the Missouri election law than the tort claim at issue in *Geier*. But frustratingly, the Court provides no doctrinal basis on which to assess reasonableness. It simply asserts the difference in categorical terms, without much by way of useful explanation. Promisingly, early decisions from the Roberts Court suggest that it may be taking a different approach to preemption.[178]

Finally, the Rehnquist Court also famously preempted state laws held to transgress the exclusively federal sphere of foreign affairs. Because the conduct of foreign affairs is not a traditional area of state authority, these cases do not pose the same dilemma as those discussed above (although they do suggest the same judicial tendency to limit state authority beyond that demanded by prior precedent). Nevertheless, the facts in these cases bear the hallmark of interjurisdictionality that grates against the dualist model of jurisdictional separation at stake.

For example, in *Crosby v. National Foreign Trade Council*, the Court preempted a Massachusetts law that prohibited state and local actors from purchasing goods or services from companies doing business with the nation of Burma, also known as Myanmar.[179] The state legislature had voted to invest its taxpayers' dollars in indirect support of nations with more desirable human rights records than Burma—just as many state entities had once divested from business interests in South Africa in protest of apartheid. However, the Court held that federal legislation imposing sanctions on Burma preempted the Massachusetts law, even though the law did not facially conflict with the federal sanctions and the sanctions did not expressly preempt state law.[180] A state's ability to decide from whom it will purchase goods and services goes to the heart of whatever "residuary and inviolable sovereignty" the New Federalism's Tenth Amendment protects. Nevertheless, the Court unanimously held that the very existence of the law undermined the U.S. president's capacity for effective diplomacy, a central aspect of enumerated federal power.[181]

More troublingly, the Court preempted a California law mandating public disclosure of in-state insurance companies' Holocaust policies, which had been enacted so that consumers could patronize companies that had rectified Nazi-era practices (when many failed to honor Jewish policies).[182] In *American Insurance Ass'n v. Garamendi*, the Court resurrected a fifty-year-old, once-used preemption doctrine known as the "dormant foreign affairs power."[183] Like the dormant Commerce Clause, the doctrine enables preemption of state law that could interfere with the U.S. president's authority over international diplomacy—even when no

---

[178] *E.g.*, Wyeth v. Levine, 129 S. Ct. 1187 (2009); Altria Group v. Good, 555 U.S. 70 (2008) (declining to preempt a state law prohibiting deceptive tobacco advertising by federal regulations of cigarette advertising); United Haulers Ass'n v. Oneida–Herkimer Solid Waste Mgmt. Auth., 550 U.S. 330 (2007) (declining to preempt under the dormant Commerce Clause restrictive waste processing rules favoring state facilities).

[179] 530 U.S. 363 (2000).

[180] *Id.* at 388.

[181] *Id.* at 381.

[182] Am. Ins. Ass'n v. Garamendi, 539 U.S. 396 (2003).

[183] *Id.* at 417–20 (citing Zschernig v. Miller, 389 U.S. 429 (1968)).

formal federal action has yet been taken. Although other federal law expressly recognizes insurance as a subject of state regulation (in language specifically designed to limit preemption of state insurance law under the affirmative or dormant Commerce Clause), the Court held that directive inapposite when state law operates beyond its geographic boundaries.[184] The sharply divided Court concluded that the California law interfered with the president's conduct of foreign policy by placing more pressure on foreign companies than the president might intend.[185]

Garamendi demonstrates the interjurisdictional thorn in the dualist model even in the realm of foreign affairs where exclusive federal power seems most secure. While the president's authority to conduct foreign policy is plenary, states and localities increasingly make purchasing and policy decisions on issues of import to the broader international community, while foreign policy addresses a broader array of domestic issues.[186] Divestment from pro-apartheid South Africa was an early example, but states and municipalities now routinely regulate in areas with potentially diplomatic significance. The California law struck down in *Garamendi* did not engage foreign nations or even regulate businesses beyond the state's borders; it merely regulated companies doing business in the state, in a traditional area of state law, by requiring them to provide information about business practices that were relevant to state consumers. Moreover, it did so in the absence of contrary federal law. Read broadly, the reasoning in *Garamendi* could preempt virtually any state regulation dealing with any issue that was also the subject of potential foreign negotiations, such as women's rights, credit default swaps, or even climate change—a subject area in which state and local governments have long led.[187]

Partnered with the standard New Federalism cases, the Rehnquist Court's willingness to expand federal regulatory reach into traditional realms of state law while preempting traditional state activities that encroach on areas of federal law[188] suggests that its federalism project was not so simply about the vindication of state authority. The combined effect of this jurisprudence was to galvanize a particular assignment of separate regulatory roles evocative of dualist jurisdictional separation.

That the preemption cases carve out a zone of federal authority from incursion by the states is unsurprising; after all, preemption cases have always done this. Especially since the New Deal, the very nature of a preemption case recognizes arenas in which both levels may regulate until the federal government intentionally displaces state efforts under the Supremacy Clause. Still, preemption cases from the New Federalism era stand out, partly because they disregard the historic presumption against preemption and partly because they do so at the same time that the New Federalism decisions assert the inviolability of conceptually related realms of state sovereignty.

The Court's more strident rhetoric in the New Federalism cases is matched by more pragmatic tones in the majority preemption decisions, which have attracted less attention but

---

[184] *Id.* at 427–28 (discussing the McCarran-Ferguson Act).

[185] *Id.* at 427.

[186] *E.g.*, Resnik et al., *supra* Introduction, note 72.

[187] *See infra* Chapter Five, notes 133–203 and accompanying text (discussing state and local climate governance).

[188] *See supra* note 153.

sent equally powerful reverberations into the balance of state and federal power.[189] Indeed, the uptake in federal preemption has been characterized by one state legislator as "unwanted power grabs by the federal government [that] subvert the federal system, choke off innovation, and ignore diversity among states."[190] The Court's takings jurisprudence over the same time period shows a similar willingness to second-guess the regulatory judgment of state and local governments in the traditional state realm of land use law,[191] contrasting with the New Federalism rhetoric of inviolate state "dignity" in the state sovereign immunity cases.[192] The Roberts Court's unfolding treatment of preemption issues remains unclear, with decisions alternatively reinforcing and rejecting the path of its predecessor.[193]

Considered holistically, then, perhaps the best characterization of the Rehnquist Court's federalism legacy is that it not only seeks to protect a zone of local authority from national incursion, but also to *reallocate* powers between the states and the federal government into separate spheres according to a specific vision about the proper home for different kinds of regulatory authority.[194] Drawing these links between the New Federalism cases and the accompanying preemption and takings cases, Professor Barron observes that

---

[189] *Compare* United States v. Lopez, 514 U.S. 549, 557 (1995) (warning that the growth of federal regulatory jurisdiction must not "obliterate the distinction between what is national and what is local and create a completely centralized government" (quoting NLRB v. Jones & Laughlin Steel Corp., 301 U.S. 1, 37 (1937))), *with* Geier v. Am. Honda Motor Co., 529 U.S. 861, 886 (2000) (preempting traditional state tort law because "[t]he rule of state tort law for which petitioners argue would stand as an 'obstacle' to the accomplishment of [the federal standard]").

[190] Pendergrass, *supra* Chapter Two, note 129, at 8 (reporting on 2006 comments by Georgia State Senator Don Balfour).

[191] *See, e.g.*, Palazzolo v. Rhode Island, 533 U.S. 606, 627–30 (2001) (holding against state wetlands law); Dolan v. City of Tigard, 512 U.S. 374, 388–96 (1994) (holding against a municipal exaction); Lucas v. S.C. Coastal Council, 505 U.S. 1003, 1030–32 (1992) (holding against state coastal preservation statute); Nollan v. Cal. Coastal Comm'n, 483 U.S. 825, 838–42 (1987) (holding against a municipal exaction). *But see* Kelo v. City of New London, 545 U.S. 469, 489–90 (2005) (holding in favor of municipal condemnation for economic development); Tahoe-Sierra Pres. Council, Inc. v. Tahoe Reg'l Planning Agency, 535 U.S. 302, 341–43 (2002) (holding in favor of a temporary moratorium on regional development). Like the preemption cases, voting coalitions are reversed in the takings cases, with New Federalist champions most likely to reject state and local regulations as takings, and dissenters most willing to uphold them. Professor David Barron among others has observed the marked trend away from deference to state land use regulation by noting that "[b]y changing constitutional doctrine in this way, the Court departs from its view of states and localities as autonomous sovereigns entitled to respect." Barron, *Reclaiming Federalism*, *supra* note 153.

[192] *See supra* note 2 (listing the New Federalism state sovereign immunity cases).

[193] *Compare* Watters v. Wachovia Bank, 550 U.S. 1, 21 (2007) (holding that the National Bank Act preempted state efforts to regulate state-chartered subsidiaries of national banks engaging in real estate lending) *with* Cuomo v. the Clearing House Assn., 129 S. Ct. 2710, 2721-22 (2009) (declining to allow the same Act to preempt state efforts to judicially enforce state banking laws against national banks). *See also, e.g.*, Chamber of Commerce v. Whiting, 131 S. Ct. 1968 (2011) (declining to preempt under federal immigration law an Arizona statute allowing state revocation of licenses for businesses that knowingly employ unauthorized workers); AT&T Mobility, LLC v. Concepcion, 131 S. Ct. 1740 (2011) (upholding preemption under the Federal Arbitration Act of a state law prohibiting certain adhesion contracts, over a vigorous dissent arguing that federalism requires respect for state consumer protection laws).

[194] Barron, *supra* Chapter One, note 56, at 2116.

the current "federalism" revival does not simply protect states' rights. It reallocates powers between the federal government and state and local ones, simultaneously limiting and extending the scope of each.... When it comes to nonmarket social issues, the Court carves out a domain of state and local power that is immune to federal legislative interference because of the "economic" requirement.... With respect to market matters, by contrast, the Court consistently decides against "overreaching" by states and localities and legitimates business-backed federal efforts to curb state and local regulations. So, the Court finds that federal statutes trump state consumer protection laws or that local government land-use measures are unconstitutional.[195]

In this regard, the Rehnquist era can be at least partially understood as curtailing federal reach into subject matter areas considered the proper realm of state authority (e.g., certain state operations and social justice issues shy of Section Five's force) while also limiting the assertion of state authority into realms considered properly federal (e.g., foreign affairs and consumer products).[196] The theory motivating these efforts owes a debt to the nineteenth-century model of mutually exclusive spheres, but that model is now more at odds with the reality of modern governance than it was even when it last collapsed in 1938.

D. The Tenth Amendment as New Federalism's Line in the Sand

Whether viewed through the state-vindication lens preferred by Professor Garnett or the reallocation lens proposed by Professor Barron, Chief Justice Rehnquist's admonition that we must distinguish between the "truly national" and the "truly local" aptly captures the essence of the New Federalism as a project devoted to the boundary in between.[197] Haunted by the ghost of classical dualism, the cases effectively ask us to identify zones of properly local and national authority and protect each from incursion by the other, narrowing the expanse of permissible jurisdictional overlap. Reinforced by those decisions' preference for formal doctrinal rules that eschew consideration of functional consequences,[198] the enterprise is akin to "bright-line rule" jurisprudence, in which the judiciary articulates "clearly defined, highly administrable" lines separating permissible from impermissible activity.[199]

As the constitutional champion of dual sovereignty, it is the Tenth Amendment that stands watch over that line, earnestly if ambiguously promising that "[t]he powers not delegated to the United States by the Constitution, nor prohibited by it to the States, are reserved to the States respectively, or to the people." The Tenth Amendment tells us that

---

[195] Barron, *Reclaiming Federalism, supra* note 153; *see also* Barron, *supra* Chapter Two, note 19, at 377–80.

[196] Barron, *Reclaiming Federalism, supra* note 153.

[197] United States v. Morrison, 529 U.S. 598, 617–18 (2000).

[198] *See* CHEMERINSKY, *supra* Introduction, note 12, at 57–77 (discussing New Federalism formalism in detail).

[199] Duncan Kennedy, *Form and Substance in Private Law Adjudication*, 89 HARV. L. REV. 1685, 1685 (1976) (articulating the dichotomy between generally applicable bright-line rules and fact-responsive standards); Carol M. Rose, *Crystals and Mud in Property Law*, 40 STAN. L. REV. 577 (1988) (reviewing the cycle between rule-based and standard-based approaches).

there will be realms of respective state and federal authority, without squarely telling us what powers lie in which realm.[200] But the New Federalism cases read the text with new clarity, thanks to their dualist premise and the various bright-line doctrinal rules they have developed to help define the boundary.[201] Indeed, the decisions invoke the Tenth Amendment as the flip side of the affirmative limits they established on Congress's power, so organically related that bright lines in one realm suggest bright lines in the other. As Justice O'Connor explained in *New York*:

> The actual scope of the Federal Government's authority with respect to the States has changed over the years . . . but the constitutional structure underlying and limiting that authority has not. In the end, just as a cup may be half empty or half full, it makes no difference whether one views the question at issue in these cases as one of ascertaining the limits of the power delegated to the Federal Government under the affirmative provisions of the Constitution or one of discerning the core of sovereignty retained by the States under the Tenth Amendment. Either way, we must determine whether [the challenged law] oversteps the boundary between federal and state authority.[202]

Defining this boundary with precision has plagued jurists since the time of the framing, and in closer memory, since the Court's attempt to define it in *National League of Cities*.

On the surface, the small handful of New Federalism cases defines the Tenth Amendment as a simple rule against federal commandeering of state apparatus. They do not pose an explicit doctrinal barrier to all regulation within the interjurisdictional gray area. Yet the disjuncture between its application in *Printz* and *Condon*—not to mention the missing children reporting requirements distinguished in Justice O'Connor's *Printz* concurrence,[203] the preempted New Jersey rules of due process in criminal justice,[204] or the many other imaginable scenarios in which such differentiation becomes necessary[205]—suggest the more ambitious role required of the Tenth Amendment within the overall New Federalism project. It must do more than simply decide whether the federal government has compelled state participation in a federal regulatory program. It arbitrates between protected and unprotected realms of state authority, pulling federalism back toward the old model of mutually exclusive spheres while also framing the resolution of all other federalism inquiries.

The combined doctrinal and rhetorical force of the New Federalism canon constructs the Tenth Amendment as all models of federalism do: as the guardian of its operative model of dual sovereignty. In the New Federalism model, the Tenth Amendment stands watch over a critical line in the sand, even as we continue to struggle with mapping it. Meanwhile, the

---

[200] *See supra* Chapter One, notes 4–33 and accompanying text.

[201] *See supra* notes 107–145 and accompanying text.

[202] New York v. United States, 505 U.S. 144, 159 (1992).

[203] *See supra* notes 93–95 and accompanying text.

[204] *See supra* notes 96–98 and accompanying text.

[205] *See infra* Chapter Five, notes 64–67 and accompanying text (describing its role in adjudication of the CWA's stormwater regulatory efforts).

policy-making mind-set encouraged by this ethic discourages needed regulatory initiative in the gray area. If it has not settled this elusive boundary, the Rehnquist Court has at least reignited the debate.

Attention to the quandary has once again surged, fueled most recently by the Court's mixed signals in upholding expansive federal jurisdiction over medical marijuana while scaling back federal jurisdiction under the Clean Water Act (CWA).[206] Following the medical marijuana decision, some suggested that the New Federalism revolution may be over[207]—but the respective replacements of Chief Justice Rehnquist and Justice O'Connor by conservative jurists John Roberts and Samuel Alito (as well as their votes in the CWA cases) suggest that the eulogy may be premature.[208] Meanwhile, the Tenther and Tea Party Movements of the late 2000s have breathed new life into dual federalism ideals in the political sphere.

Though it may not produce the grail to end the quest, this inquiry reveals the true debate as one over the competing interpretive models that differently mediate the conflicting values underlying federalism. It critiques the theoretical underpinnings of the New Federalism boundary-drawing enterprise and disputes the singular claim its proponents lay to what the Court has called "Our Federalism."[209] Although some contend that a faithful reading of the Tenth Amendment requires the New Federalism approach,[210] others argue that neither its text nor its history does so, and that flexibility is preserved for interactive exercise of state and federal authority within meaningful constraints.[211] In service of the separationist ideal, the New Federalism honors a dualist vision of checks and balances that preserves a healthy balance by separating state and federal power. Yet it defines the check-and-balance value narrowly and privileges it at the expense of other good governance values that also undergird our federalism. Its relationship with accountability and localism is ambiguous, and the value of problem-solving synergy is shortchanged.[212]

Of course, if regulatory problem solving could effectively take place within the separate spheres idealized by this model, then this objection to dual federalism disappears.

---

[206] *Compare* Gonzales v. Raich, 545 U.S. 1 (2005) (medical marijuana) *with* Rapanos v. United States, 126 S. Ct. 2208 (2006) (wetlands).

[207] Among them was Justice O'Connor herself, who suggested in her dissenting opinion in *Raich* that the death knell had been sounded on the principles in *Lopez* and *Morrison* for which the New Federalism is best known. *Raich*, 545 U.S. at 46–47 (O'Connor, J., dissenting). *See also* John Yoo, Commentary, *What Became of Federalism?*, L.A. TIMES, June 21, 2005, at 13.

[208] Justice Scalia's plurality opinion cabining the scope of federal authority under the CWA was joined by both Chief Justice Roberts and Justice Alito. *Rapanos*, 126 S. Ct. at 2214. *See also supra* Chapter Three, notes 239–40 and accompanying text (discussing the impacts of new judicial appointments).

[209] Younger v. Harris, 401 U.S. 37, 44 (1971) (defining it as the idea that the federal government will perform best if "the States and their institutions are left free to perform their separate functions in their separate ways").

[210] *E.g.*, Printz v. United States, 521 U.S. 898, 918–20 (1997) (finding its result "incontestible" under a textual approach to the Constitution).

[211] *E.g.*, PURCELL, *supra* Introduction, note 11. *Cf.* Hills, *supra* Part I Introduction, note 5, at 942–43; Jackson, *supra* Part I Introduction, note 21, at 2237; Robert L. Stern, *That Commerce Which Concerns More States than One*, 47 HARV. L. REV. 1335, 1344–45, 1364–65 (1934).

[212] *See supra* discussion in the final section of Chapter Two, following note 181.

Governance could simply proceed from within the appropriate sphere, preserving the boundary against erosion and enabling both levels of government to perform the obligations with which they are charged by their respective constitutions. The clear boundary might encourage better regulatory performance all around—inspiring both sides to invest more in solving the problems for which they hold unequivocal responsibility, and discouraging them from abdicating responsibility on grounds of uncertainty. All would be well in this universe of clean lines and discrete regulatory problems—which well may constitute many that we confront. But what of those that remain—that is, those problems that do not fit cleanly within one sphere or the other, inhabiting the murky zone between?

5

THE INTERJURISDICTIONAL GRAY AREA

THIS CHAPTER PLUMBS the gray area that belies the dualist ideal of exclusive state and federal spheres motivating New Federalism theory. Focusing on examples from water and air pollution, counterterrorism efforts, disaster response, and climate governance, it demonstrates the reality of regulatory territory in which both the states and federal government hold unique authority, interests, obligations, and expertise.

Tensions between federalism values are especially heightened in these fields of environmental, land use, and public health and safety regulation—all legal realms that match compelling claims for the importance of local autonomy and/or expertise with equally compelling needs for national uniformity or federal capacity. Regulatory efforts here often reflect the identification of relatively new problems that lack a settled answer to the question of which side is the most appropriate regulator (such as cyberthreats and greenhouse gas reduction). Others address problems once presumed to be purely local in nature (such as land use planning, disease control, or waste disposal), although evidence increasingly shows their important interjurisdictional implications. As such, the "proper" level of regulatory authority in the classical sense is often contested.

The federalism analyses in these fields are especially fractured, but they are valuable to the inquiry precisely for these quirks—revealing federalism's fault lines in ways that mainstream economic regulation cannot. Just as there is no separate federalism theory for Tenth Amendment and Commerce Clause doctrine, there are not separate theories of federalism for environmental and other fields of law. (If there were, then perhaps the New Federalism ethos would not have thrown whole fields of environmental law into disarray—such as Clean

Water Act enforcement after two recent wetlands decisions,[1] discussed below.) Environmental federalism decisions such as these and *New York v. United States*, overturning an effort to cope with radioactive waste, may well have proven the canary in federalism's coal mine—indicating the critical need to better cope with jurisdictional overlap at the level of theory. But insights from environmental federalism are therefore significant for other legal arenas in which jurisdictional overlap is prevalent, such as national security, public health, immigration, the Internet, and others.

The chapter begins by illustrating the different reasons for jurisdictional overlap, exploring regulatory problems that merge local and national authority at both the legal and practical levels. It then reconceptualizes the boundary problem of dual sovereignty in terms of *regulatory crossover* into the interjurisdictional gray area. It discusses how uncertain federalism theory creates two kinds of risk for good gray area governance: (1) that fear of doctrinal liability may deter needed interjurisdictional efforts, and (2) that doctrinal uncertainty may invite self-serving regulatory abdication. The chapter then explores the benefits of regulatory overlap in the gray area through the detailed example of regulatory backstop in climate governance. Finally, it applies its framework of analysis to the Katrina experience, concluding with reflections on how federalism theory more sensitive to the gray area might have led to a different regulatory response.

A. Interjurisdictional Regulatory Problems

Against the idealized backdrop of a regulatory world neatly cleaved between the truly national and the truly local, this chapter asks how federalism theory can better account for the problems that straddle the boundary between them. Interjurisdictional regulatory problems—ranging from the environment to telecommunications to national security—simultaneously implicate areas of such national and local obligation or expertise that their resolution depends on authority at both levels of government. Theorizing this third sphere of interjurisdictional concern should facilitate the development of a more stable American federalism by revealing where the separationist premise of dual federalism inevitably fails.

When dualist approaches like New Federalism's try to segregate the local from the national, interjurisdictional problems monkey-wrench the system by being simultaneously *both*. This is so either because neither side has all the legal authority it needs to effectively solve the problem, or because compelling circumstances make a partnership approach necessary as a factual matter even if the federal government could fully preempt state involvement as a legal matter. In the latter case, the regulatory target so implicates an area of local concern or expertise that preemption would ultimately obstruct, rather than facilitate, meaningful resolution of the problem.

The legal concept of an interjurisdictional problem is nothing new, having been recognized in the United States at least since the early border-crossing cases involving

---

[1] *See* Solid Waste Agency of Northern Cook County v. U.S. Army Corps of Engineers, 531 U.S. 159 (2001) [hereinafter *SWANCC*]; Rapanos v. United States, 126 S. Ct. 2208 (2006).

interstate litigation,[2] criminal law enforcement,[3] air pollution,[4] water pollution,[5] waterway management,[6] and species protection.[7] However, the advancing reach of local impacts in the postindustrial era has also given rise to interjurisdictional problems that the Framers could never have foreseen—including such powerful environmental problems as storm-water pollution,[8] greenhouse gas emissions,[9] and mass extinctions,[10] but also such non-environmental problems as Internet and telecommunications law,[11] such public health crises as childhood obesity and pandemic flu,[12] and localized threats to national security and infrastructure, such as failures of the power grid or Internet backbone.[13]

Moreover, the growing economic interdependence that accompanied us into the new millennium has transformed many problems that might once have been purely local into the interjurisdictional variety. For example, when hurricanes hit New Orleans a century earlier, they would have triggered fewer national interests than Katrina did, because the Port of New Orleans was less central to the nation's economy, and its nearby nerve center of oil and gas infrastructure had yet to exist.[14] Professors Samuel Issacharoff and Catherine Sharkey identify this problem in the realm of products liability, where the

---

[2] *E.g.*, Erie R.R. Co. v. Tompkins, 304 U.S. 64 (1938) (requiring federal courts hearing state law claims under diversity jurisdiction to apply the substantive laws of those states).

[3] *E.g.*, Logan, *supra* Chapter Four, note 11, at 66–67 (examining federal use of state law in criminal justice contexts).

[4] *E.g.*, Gerald F. Hess, *The Trail Smelter, the Columbia River, and the Extraterritorial Application of CERCLA*, 18 GEO. INT'L ENVTL. L. REV. 1, 2–4 (2005) (discussing early Canadian-United States arbitration over air quality).

[5] *E.g.*, Milwaukee v. Illinois, 451 U.S. 304, 317–19 (1981) (resolving an interstate sewage discharge claim).

[6] *E.g.*, Willson v. Black-Bird Creek Marsh Co., 27 U.S. (2 Pet.) 245, 251–52 (1829) (acknowledging overlapping state and federal concern in upholding a state-authorized dam through a federally regulated waterway).

[7] *E.g.*, Migratory Bird Treaty Act, 16 U.S.C. §§ 703–711 (2000) (protecting interstate migratory birds).

[8] *E.g.*, John R. Nolon, *Katrina's Lament: Reconstructing Federalism*, 23 PACE ENVTL. L. REV. 987, 987–91 (2006) (examining the overlapping state and federal regulatory jurisdiction of stormwater runoff).

[9] Regional Greenhouse Gas Initiative, http://www.rggi.org/home (last visited Sept. 29, 2010).

[10] *E.g.*, Endangered Species Act of 1973, 16 U.S.C. §§ 1531–1544 (2000).

[11] *E.g.*, Philip J. Weiser, *Federal Common Law, Cooperative Federalism, and the Enforcement of the Telecom Act*, 76 N.Y.U.L. REV. 1692 (2001); Weiser, *supra* Chapter Three, note 201, at 675–77 (discussing telecommunications issues).

[12] *E.g.*, Elisabeth Rosenthal, *Recent Spread of Bird Flu Confounds Experts*, N.Y. TIMES, Mar. 6, 2006, at A6.

[13] *E.g.*, Seth Schiesel, *In Frayed Networks, Common Threads*, N.Y. TIMES, Aug. 21, 2003, at G1 (examining the vulnerabilities of the interconnected power networks that led to the largest blackout in history); David McGuire & Brian Krebs, *Large-Scale Attack Cripples Internet Backbone*, WASH. POST, Oct. 23, 2002, at E5 (describing a coordinated attack on computers that serve as master directories for networks and Web sites around the world).

[14] *See* Oliver Houck, *Can We Save New Orleans?*, 19 TUL. ENVTL. L.J. 1, 17–18 (2006) (explaining the development of Louisiana oil and gas infrastructure from the early 1900s on). *See also* Issacharoff & Sharkey, *supra* Chapter Two, note 128, at 1410–12 (discussing the increase in federalization of areas traditionally regulated by state law).

undertheorized attempts of federal courts (particularly the Supreme Court) to mediate the tensions between the claimed commitment to the states as sovereign overseers of the quotidian affairs of their citizens and the reality that the lives of citizens are increasingly accountable to broader market commands.[15]

Public servants at the federal, state, and municipal levels are working overtime to address regulatory problems that increasingly straddle local and national concerns—but the dualist leanings of the New Federalism movement leave them unclear on the appropriate rules for solving them.

This chapter sets forth a conceptual framework for understanding interjurisdictional regulatory problems and their relationship to dual sovereignty. But in articulating such a framework, I should first disclaim what I am *not* proposing to do. First, although I believe that we can meaningfully discuss "regulatory problems" in general terms, I offer no unifying theory about the features of problems that make them more or less susceptible to regulatory solutions, other than to note that I am generally referring to such classic regulatory targets as market failures, negative externalities, and collective action problems that respond favorably to administrative intervention. For example, while reliable law enforcement is a widely accepted basis for regulation in the United States, compliance with the tenets of religiously based faith would not be viewed the same way. An externalized harm that is poorly internalized through the free market (e.g., air pollution) is an uncontroversial regulatory problem, while outpaced demand for the supply of a particular manufacturer's widget would probably not be. The management of such public commons as navigable waterways and radio space qualifies, while such important societal problems as divorce rates, intergenerational conflict, and loneliness are less directly amenable to government intervention.

In the end, reasonable minds will differ about the margin between the set of problems resolvable by government and the set of those that are not, but this approach enables a conversation about the best decision rules for government actors navigating the federal system regardless of that margin. In other words, to continue the conversation from here, we need only agree that there is such a thing as "regulatory problems" in some shape or form, allowing individuals to substitute different constants for the variables in an otherwise stable equation.[16]

Much more important, reasonable minds will differ on the definition of legitimate "local and national concern." This is, of course, the central *who decides?* federalism quandary itself, and the fact that consensus has so long eluded us in the general debate suggests that it will not be easily forthcoming for the purposes of this conversation even if we can agree to acknowledge the existence of some set of interjurisdictional problems. I return to this quandary more fully in Part III, where I propose jurisprudential tools for differentiating between legitimate interjurisdictional regulation and constitutional violations, and in Part IV, where I propose a theory of intergovernmental bargaining to facilitate interjurisdictional

---

[15] Issacharoff & Sharkey, *supra* Chapter Two, note 128, at 1358.

[16] Some contend that no problems are truly solved by governmental methods, which only create new problems, ROTHBARD, *supra* Part I Introduction, note 19, at 73–78 (cataloging the ills of regulation), but this book takes a more mainstream view.

governance even without establishing precise boundaries. To the extent the gray area looms large, it suggests something important about the reality of jurisdictional overlap and the limitations of separationist conceptions of dual sovereignty. But at this point, I put off debate about the absolute margins of the gray area to make the relatively meek claim that there are at least some problems that truly implicate both local and national obligation in a way that warrants attention from both levels.

I believe this is an easy case to make; indeed, it has already been argued persuasively in federalism scholarship such as that by Dean Erwin Chemerinsky[17] and Professors Robert Schapiro,[18] William Buzbee,[19] Kirsten Engel,[20] Jody Freeman,[21] Judith Resnik,[22] Bradley Karkkainen,[23] and many others. We may yet lack a national consensus about the extent to which local regulation should be held vicariously accountable under the Endangered Species Act (ESA),[24] or to which the federal government should regulate gay marriage.[25] But few now argue that the federal government should not play a role in disaster management (an area of regulatory authority traditionally assigned to the states), or that state law enforcement should not do so in domestic efforts to prevent terrorist attacks abroad (a realm of foreign affairs by which the federal government could preempt state participation).[26] Similarly, the federal government was more often criticized for failing to address the 2006

---

[17] CHEMERINSKY, *supra* Introduction, note 12 (proposing broad jurisdictional overlap to empower multiple levels to act).

[18] SCHAPIRO, *supra* Introduction, note 11 (proposing a polyphonic federalism model that focuses on interaction rather than separation); Robert A. Schapiro, *Toward a Theory of Interactive Federalism*, 91 IOWA L. REV. 243, 248–49 (2005) (same); Schapiro, *Polyphonic Federalism, supra* Chapter Three, note 211, at 1416–17 (proposing intersystemic adjudication).

[19] PREEMPTION CHOICE: THE THEORY, LAW, AND REALITY OF FEDERALISM'S CORE QUESTION (William W. Buzbee ed., 2009); William W. Buzbee, *Contextual Environmental Federalism*, 14 N.Y.U. ENVTL. L.J. 108, 108–09 (2005) (explaining the benefits of regulatory overlap in cooperative federalism structures); William W. Buzbee, *Recognizing the Regulatory Commons: A Theory of Regulatory Gaps*, 89 IOWA L. REV. 1, 8–14 (2003) (examining the "regulatory commons problem" in interjurisdictional problems such as urban sprawl and global warming).

[20] Engel, *supra* Introduction, note 72 (arguing that the static allocation of authority obstructs environmental management).

[21] Jody Freeman, *Collaborative Governance in the Administrative State*, 45 UCLA L. REV. 1, 4–8 (1997) (proposing a model of collaborative governance that involves multiple levels of cooperation).

[22] Resnik et al., *supra* Introduction, note 72 (explaining transnational local governance); Resnik, *supra* Chapter Two, note 98 (same).

[23] Karkkainen, *supra* Chapter Three, note 196, at 225–26 (advancing intergovernmental ecosystem management).

[24] *E.g.*, Strahan v. Coxe, 127 F.3d 155, 161–66 (1st Cir. 1997) (holding a state agency responsible for takes of endangered whales because it authorized harmful commercial fishing gear near their feeding grounds).

[25] *Compare* Massachusetts v. U.S. Department of Health and Human Services, No. 1:09-cv-11156-JLT, 21–36 (D. Mass. July 7, 2010) (ruling that the federal Defense of Marriage Act violates the Tenth Amendment) *with* 152 CONG. REC. S5517 (daily ed. June 7, 2006) (statement of Sen. Byrd) (invoking federalism to support a constitutional amendment banning gay marriage on grounds that it would prevent border-crossing harms).

[26] *Cf.* ACLU of N.J., Inc. v. County of Hudson, 799 A.2d 629, 654–55 (N.J. Super. Ct. App. Div. 2002) (allowing federal law protecting the identities of terrorist suspects to preempt state law requiring their disclosure).

bird flu threat than it was for intruding on a classic realm of the state police power.[27] Few argue that the federal government should fully displace intrastate administration of the Clean Air and Clean Water Acts, which would vastly increase the size of the federal bureaucracy in an ironic move to protect the boundary between state and federal authority.[28]

The phenomenon of appropriately shared regulatory space is demonstrated by much of the overlapping governance that the cooperative federalism model has enabled, if uncritically, since the New Deal. Although opponents may not concede the entirety of this overlap as legitimate, even the architects of the New Federalism conceded jurisdictional overlap well beyond the nineteenth-century ideal. They had to: at the level of legal realism, it is the system they inherited. At the normative level, much of it reflects the promise of multiplicity that has always driven American federalism.[29] Indeed, although my ultimate proposals will bear differences from the cooperative federalism model, my project is less about dismantling the cooperative federalism baseline and more about refining it with conceptual justification for unresolved problems that have long plagued it at the level of theory.

Finally, I should flag the related premise that there are at least some areas of governance that are constitutionally committed at both the national and local levels. How large or small they are is the crux of the debate, but most debaters will at least concede an exclusive federal power to declare war, and exclusive state authority to manage elections.[30] (Beyond that, all bets are off.) But recognizing that no claim about the legitimate realms of state and federal regulatory authority will be without controversy, I hope the following discussion affords a sample of sufficiently uncontroversial examples that my assertion of *some* interjurisdictional gray area will enable the more important discussion that follows of its relationship to dual sovereignty. Even with disputed boundaries, the existence of a core gray area pierces the integrity of the nineteenth-century dualism that still haunts modern federalism theory. To continue the conversation from here, we need only agree that some interjurisdictional regulatory problems exist, in that their effective resolution depends on the exercise of regulatory authority by both a local and a national actor—for one of two reasons.

I. DE JURE INTERJURISDICTIONAL PROBLEMS

In the first instance, resolution depends on both local and national engagement because neither side has all the legal authority it needs to meaningfully address the problem. Examples of such "de jure" interjurisdictional problems include the management of coastal resources under the Coastal Zone Management Act (which recognizes distinct areas of state and

---

[27] *E.g.*, James Gerstenzang, *Bird Flu Warning Would Ravage U.S., White House Warns*, L.A. Times, May 4, 2006, at A6 (reporting on criticism of the administration for failing to better prepare for a possible flu pandemic).

[28] Some argue that more responsibility should be devolved to the states. *E.g.*, Adler, *supra* Chapter Three, note 190, at 135.

[29] *Cf.* LaCroix, *supra* Introduction, note 71.

[30] *Cf.* U.S. Const. art. I, § 8 (delegating the federal war power); *id.* at §§ 1–2, amend. XVII (describing state role in congressional elections); art. II, § 1, amend. XII (describing state role in presidential elections). *But see* Bush v. Gore, 531 U.S. 98 (2000) (holding limited to facts).

federal jurisdiction in the coastal zone and facilitates intergovernmental consultation),[31] the protection of wetlands (which may be subject to both federal water pollution regulations and state land use regulations),[32] and the intersection between the ESA and state wildlife regulation and land use laws.[33]

De jure interjurisdictional problems such as these often arise due to the intersection between a federally regulated interest, such as navigable waters or endangered species preservation, and local land use policy, the traditional province of state and municipal government.[34] They may also arise through overlap between the state's police-power obligation to protect public safety and related national interests in protecting national infrastructure and policing border-crossing harms. The *New York v. United States* problem of how to safely and equitably dispose of the nation's radioactive waste is a good example, mixing national authority over the interstate commerce aspects of waste production and transport with state authority over the land use and police power aspects of siting facilities.[35] The following discussion details the more common example of managing water pollution.

a. Water Pollution

Water pollution exemplifies the de jure interjurisdictional regulatory problem, because nearly all water passes through subsequent realms of state and federal jurisdiction on its hydrological journey from sky to sea. This is not simply a matter of rivers and lakes that straddle state boundaries; water moves through state and federal jurisdiction even within state lines. When rain hits the ground, it may fall directly into federal jurisdiction on federal lands, the sea, or other navigable waterways (which are federally regulated as channels of interstate commerce)[36]—but it most often falls on state or state-regulated private land first.

As this water makes its gravity-driven journey through increasingly larger watersheds back to the sea, it traverses surfaces subject to land use regulation by the states and their municipalities, which control the kinds of land-based contaminants rainwater encounters before draining into a lake or stream. The water will dissolve traces of motor oil and automotive fluids, lawn fertilizer and pesticides, household and chemical effluents, and whatever else it

---

[31] Coastal Zone Management Act, 16 U.S.C. §§ 1451–1465 (2006).

[32] *See SWANCC*, 531 U.S. 159, 171–72 (2001) (limiting federal infringement on traditional state land and water use authority); Rapanos v. United States, 126 S. Ct. 2208, 2224–25 (2006) (plurality opinion) (same).

[33] *See supra* note 24 and accompanying text (discussing "vicarious takes" by state agencies authorizing private activity that violates the ESA); Gibbs v. Babbitt, 214 F.3d 483, 499–504 (4th Cir. 2000) (addressing federalism concerns stemming from federal regulation of an intrastate population of listed red wolves inhabiting private land).

[34] *See* Petersburg Cellular P'ship v. Bd. of Supervisors, 205 F.3d 688, 705–06 (4th Cir. 2000) (discussing the clash between local land regulation and federal telecommunications law); Cape May Greene, Inc. v. Warren, 698 F.2d 179, 192–93 (3d Cir. 1983) (balancing state land use authority and federal interests in protecting floodplains).

[35] 505 U.S. 144 (1992).

[36] Several statutes regulate federal lands, the sea, or large bodies of water. *E.g.*, Coastal Zone Management Act, 16 U.S.C. §§ 1451–1465 (2006); Rivers and Harbors Appropriations Act of 1899, ch. 425, 30 Stat. 1121 (codified as amended in scattered sections of 33 U.S.C.); Clean Water Act, 33 U.S.C. §§ 1251–1387 (2000); Submerged Lands Act, ch. 65, 67 Stat. 29 (1953) (codified as amended in scattered sections of 43 U.S.C.).

comes across,[37] carrying the pollutants into the wetlands or small creeks that may fall under either local or national regulatory jurisdiction.[38] Eventually, all will flow or percolate into larger water bodies that clearly fall under federal Clean Water Act (CWA) jurisdiction—roughly speaking, any that are themselves navigable, are permanent tributaries of navigable waters, or that maintain a continuous surface connection to these.[39] Under the CWA, the Environmental Protection Agency (EPA) regulates the passage of pollutants into these waters by "point source" discharges, or those that enter through the end of a pipe, requiring them to be permitted under the National Pollutant Discharge Elimination System (NPDES).[40]

Say, then, that you want to clean up the Chesapeake Bay's infamously hypoxic "dead zone,"[41] or make it safe to eat fish caught in mercury-laced Lake Michigan,[42] or enable swimming in the enterococcus-rich Boston Harbor.[43] Assuming the EPA is able to perfectly regulate point source discharges under the NPDES program, should you then feel safe letting your children splash in Boston Harbor or eat fish from Lake Michigan? Not if you like your kids. NPDES regulation of conventional point source discharges has done much to improve water quality, but the greatest threat to the health of our nation's waters is now acknowledged to be from stormwater[44]—the diffuse surface water that rains down from the heavens and picks up whatever contaminants it meets on the ground while working its way toward these larger water bodies downstream. Until you can reduce the delivery of land-based contaminants into the hydrological chain, fishing and swimming remain dangerous, and state and federal agencies regularly advise against these activities.[45]

The problem in this scenario is that the accumulation of these contaminants on the surface of private and state lands is generally beyond the scope of federal regulatory jurisdiction.

---

[37] *See* Ryan, *supra* Chapter One, note 155, at 983 (discussing movement of land-based marine pollutants from land to sea).

[38] For EPA's report on how the *SWANCC* and *Rapanos* decisions have complicated its ability to distinguish the two, see EPA, CONGRESSIONALLY REQUESTED REPORT ON COMMENTS RELATED TO EFFECTS OF JURISDICTIONAL UNCERTAINTY ON CLEAN WATER ACT IMPLEMENTATION (2009), http://permanent. access.gpo.gov/LPS114021/LPS114021/www.epa.gov/oig/reports/2009/20090430-09-N-0149.pdf.

[39] *See* Rapanos v. United States, 126 S. Ct. 2208, 2235 (2006).

[40] 33 U.S.C. § 1342. *See also* William L. Andreen, *Delegated Federalism Versus Devolution: Some Insights from the History of Water Pollution Control*, in PREEMPTION CHOICE, *supra* note 19, at 257–76 (discussing the evolution of federal authority to regulate water pollution).

[41] *See* Ryan, *supra* Chapter One, note 155, at 1005–07 (describing this "region so polluted that it lacks sufficient oxygen to sustain marine life").

[42] The EPA has issued fish consumption advisories for fish caught in Lake Michigan as they show elevated levels of mercury, PCBs, dioxins, and chlordane. EPA, FACT SHEET: NATIONAL LISTING OF FISH ADVISORIES 3 (2004), http://www.epa.gov/waterscience/fish/advisories/factsheet.pdf.

[43] *See* Brian Fitzgerald, *The People's Harbor: Metropolitan College's Bruce Berman Charts the Boston Harbor Cleanup*, BOSTONIA, Fall 2004, http://www.bu.edu/alumni/bostonia/2004/fall/harbor/(reporting on frequent beach closures when bacteria exceed advisory levels and naming "[t]he culprit: filthy stormwater and sewage").

[44] *See* Envtl. Def. Ctr., Inc. v. EPA, 344 F.3d 832, 840–41 (9th Cir. 2003) ("*EDC II*") (*vacating and superceding* Envtl. Def. Ctr., Inc. v. EPA, 319 F.3d 398 (9th Cir. 2003) ("*EDC I*").

[45] *See supra* notes 42–43.

It is usually the states and municipalities that have authority over the local land uses that lead to such accumulation, as well as the storm sewer systems that channel collected stormwater into downstream rivers, lakes, and harbors. Some of the contaminated stormwater enters the chain at the top of the watershed, passing into the local streams and wetlands that ultimately flow to the bottom, while the rest enters after being collected in municipal storm sewers that discharge directly into the federally protected water bodies that drain the watershed. At present, no technology exists to remove these pollutants from stormwater at the point of municipal discharge, but even if it did, this would eliminate only one source of the problem. Land-based contaminants would still enter the chain at the top of the watershed, where stormwater passes into creeks and wetlands after running over polluted surfaces but before entering a municipal storm sewer.[46]

Moreover, the most powerful technology for removing stormwater contaminants before it enters free-flowing water bodies remains the natural filtration feature of wetlands, which (for this very reason) have become a bitter battleground between claims of state and federal jurisdiction.[47] The Supreme Court's recent wetlands cases have narrowed federal regulatory reach over the destruction of wetlands, leaving regulation of both the land uses that cause contamination and the fate of the wetlands that remove them from the hydrological chain in predominantly state jurisdictional hands.[48]

In this way, stormwater pollution is an especially tricky interjurisdictional problem, a cross-media one of local land-based pollution flowing into federally protected waters. Though most land and land uses causing water pollution are under state regulatory authority, the water bodies that ultimately drain polluted stormwater runoff are under federal regulatory authority. So long as municipalities drain storm sewers into federal waters, the stormwater pollution problem can only be solved by regulatory activity by both local actors (who govern where the pollution starts) and national actors (who govern where the pollution ends)—ideally in coordination.

b. *The Phase II Stormwater Rule and* Environmental Defense Center, Inc. v. EPA

For these reasons, Congress authorized the EPA to propose rules for regulating the discharge of collected stormwater under the CWA as a point source discharge.[49] Although stormwater

---

[46] Even if the EPA denied all NPDES permits allowing storm sewer discharges to federal waters, it could not prevent contamination of protected lakes, rivers, or coastal waters by non-navigable tributaries. Even if it regulates all point-source discharges to these tributaries, it cannot prevent their contamination by overland pollutants passively picked up by nonchanneled stormwater runoff. Regulation of land-based activities that commonly contribute to such contamination (e.g., real estate development, lawn pesticide use, and oil-leaking motor vehicles) is generally by state law. For this reason, the only effective way to prevent stormwater pollution is to pair state regulation of land-based activities that initiate the pollution cycle with federal regulation of water bodies that absorb the pollution. *See* City of Abilene v. EPA, 325 F.3d 657, 659–60 (5th Cir. 2003) (discussing state-federal stormwater regulation); S.F. BayKeeper v. Whitman, 297 F.3d 877, 879–80 (9th Cir. 2002) (discussing state-federal point source regulation). *See also* Nolon, *supra* note 8, at 1431–32 (describing an integrated local, state, and federal partnership).

[47] *See infra* note 86–96 and accompanying text.

[48] *Id.*; *supra* note 32.

[49] 33 U.S.C. § 1342(p)(4) (2000) (authorizing the "Phase I" and "Phase II" Stormwater Rules).

originates as nonpoint source diffuse surface runoff, it is converted to a point source discharge when it is collected in the storm sewer and then piped to the receiving river, lake, or harbor. At the end of the pipe, the discharge of collected stormwater looks like any other point source discharge into the lake—but these new regulations would be unlike previous NPDES permitting programs, which usually regulate industrial discharges.[50] By contrast, stormwater is almost exclusively collected and discharged by municipalities.[51]

Sensitive to the federalism implications of regulating state entities in performance of a traditional municipal function (the maintenance of storm sewers), the EPA convened a working group of stakeholders to collaborate on the development of a workable regulatory solution to this thorny interjurisdictional problem. The group included representatives from the National Governors' Association, the Environmental Council of the States, the Association of State and Interstate Water Pollution Control Authorities, and six state departments of natural resources.[52] After nearly a decade of negotiation, the EPA promulgated two phases of regulations that were endorsed by all working group participants. The first regulation applied only to the largest cities, while the second, the "Phase II Stormwater Rule," applied to the vastly larger number of small municipalities with populations of less than 100,000.[53]

To minimize the federalism problems associated with this unusual regulatory partnership, the Phase II Rule was designed to accomplish pollution controls while conferring as much discretion as possible to covered municipalities. The Rule enables states to seek coverage under a general permit that allows municipalities to discharge so long as they propose stormwater management plans ensuring that stormwater discharged to federal waters arrives as clean as possible.[54] Although the specifics of the management plans are left to each municipality, they must at least address a set of five primary concerns (the "minimum measures"), including a plan to discover and prevent illegal storm sewer discharges and a means of raising public awareness about the prevention of stormwater pollution.[55] However, one of the minimum measures required that municipalities mitigate construction-related pollution by issuing permits for construction projects that would require compliance with the overall municipal program.[56] Acting independently from the State of Texas, a group of

---

[50] *See id.* at § 1342(p)(3) (permitting regulation of industrial discharges).

[51] EPA, Permits for Municipal Separate Storm Sewer Systems (MS4s), http://www.epa.gov/region8/water/stormwater/municipal.html. Other dischargers include federal agencies, Indian tribes, and private dischargers operating large compounds, such as university or corporate campuses.

[52] OFFICE OF WATER, EPA, STORM WATER DISCHARGES POTENTIALLY ADDRESSED BY PHASE II OF THE NATIONAL POLLUTANT DISCHARGE ELIMINATION SYSTEM STORM WATER PROGRAM 1–22 (1995); Brief of Respondent-Intervenor Natural Resources Defense Council, Inc., at 50, *EDC II*, 344 F.3d 832 (9th Cir. 2003) (Nos. 00–70014, 00–70734, 00–70822) 2001 WL 34092891 (listing participants of the Phase II Subcommittee).

[53] OFFICE OF WATER, EPA, STORMWATER PHASE II FINAL RULE: FACT SHEET 2.1, at 2 (2005), http://www.epa.gov.npdes/pubs/fact2–1.pdf.

[54] OFFICE OF WATER, EPA, STORMWATER PHASE II FINAL RULE: FACT SHEET 2.9, at 3 (2005), http://www.epa/gov/npdes/pubs/fact2–9.pdf.

[55] *EDC II*, 344 F.3d 832, 845 (9th Cir. 2003).

[56] *Id.* at 845–46 & n.20.

Texas municipalities sued to invalidate the Rule on Tenth Amendment grounds, arguing that the construction measure required them to regulate their own citizens in violation of the New Federalism anti-commandeering rule.[57]

The Ninth Circuit ultimately upheld the Rule against the Tenth Amendment challenge, but not without controversy. Writing for the court in its initial decision, Judge James Browning found that the Tenth Amendment challenge failed because it compelled no state behavior; municipalities that objected to the terms of the general permit were free to seek permission to discharge under an individual permitting framework that, while more administratively onerous, omitted the construction permitting requirement.[58] However, Judge Browning volunteered the further possibility that the Tenth Amendment challenge would fail anyway for lack of coercion, because a municipality that did not like the terms of the general permit could simply choose *not* to engage in the federally regulated activity of discharging into the waters of the United States.[59]

Reasoning by analogy to the spending power (which enables Congress to condition discretionary federal funds on state action it could not otherwise compel),[60] Judge Browning suggested that the federal government is free to condition a privilege it is not obligated to provide on the performance of a related obligation it might not otherwise compel.[61] Municipalities remained free to dispense with collected stormwater by other means, such as the creation of wetlands, recycling facilities, or terminal evaporation basins, and the fact that these may be more expensive than simply discharging to the downstream water body does not alter the constitutional calculus.[62] They could also stop collecting stormwater altogether. Judge Richard Tallman dissented on this point, arguing that although the federal regulation was legitimately within the commerce power, the suggestion that the federal government could prevent municipalities from discharging stormwater in the direction of gravity, or from collecting it at all, was nonsensical.[63] To him, such reasoning would enable the federal government to encroach upon a realm of inviolate state sovereignty—the protection of property from damage by the management of local storm sewers.[64]

Although the panel denied the Texas municipalities' subsequent petition for rehearing, the court issued a second opinion that rescinded the alternative reasoning, this time with the consensus of Judge Richard Tallman.[65] That the court proceeded this way is unsurprising; otherwise the panel would have been forced to engage in the very sort of sovereign functions test that

---

[57] *Id.* at 843–45. The Phase II Rule was also challenged on other grounds by the National Association of Home Builders, the American Forest & Paper Association, and the Environmental Defense Center. *Id.* at 843.

[58] *EDC I*, 319 F.3d 398, 413–14, 416–19 (9th Cir. 2003).

[59] *Id.* at 414–16.

[60] South Dakota v. Dole, 483 U.S. 203 (1987).

[61] *EDC I*, 319 F.3d at 416.

[62] *Id.* at 415.

[63] *Id.* at 451–53 (Tallman, J., concurring in part and dissenting in part).

[64] *Id.*; *cf. SWANCC*, 531 U.S. 159, 174 (2001) (discussing traditional state roles regulating land and water use).

[65] *EDC II*, 344 F.3d 832, 847–48 & n.22 (9th Cir. 2003). Judge Tallman concurred in this portion of the opinion, but dissented in others. *Id.* at 880 (Tallman, J., concurring in part and dissenting in part).

plagued *National League of Cities*.[66] Is the municipal management of storm sewers a protected sovereign function like the performance of background checks by state officers in *Printz*, or is it the unprotected provision of a service like the personal information made available by the state motor vehicle department in *Condon*? Is the problem that the construction permitting process requires the municipality to directly regulate its own citizens? If so, then why did Judge Tallman not object to portions of the Phase II Rule that require the municipality to regulate illicit discharges by its citizens to storm sewers? Is one form of authority more "sovereign" than the other?

The Texas petitioners unsuccessfully sought Supreme Court review, and the Ninth Circuit's second decision was left standing.[67] But the evolving line of argument in the court's progression of decisions and dissents demonstrates the fretful task of interpreting interjurisdictional regulatory responses within the confines of separationist Tenth Amendment doctrine. The overall tenor of the decisions suggests that the panel considered the Phase II Rule a respectful means of navigating the state and federal considerations at issue. After all, it preserved local autonomy as much as possible in an accountable program of interjurisdictional problem solving. Still, classical checks and balances were threatened by blurring the lines of state and federal prerogative. Although the panel was inclined to uphold what appeared to them a reasonable regulatory partnership, doing so within the New Federalism framework proved tortuous.

2. DE FACTO INTERJURISDICTIONAL REGULATORY PROBLEMS

The second variety of interjurisdictional regulatory problems requires the exercise of authority by both a state and federal actor for prudential reasons. In some contexts, the federal government could hypothetically preempt state involvement under a clearly enumerated power, but the problem implicates a matter of such local concern and/or expertise that it invites state participation instead. In other contexts, the states could hypothetically fight federal incursion into a realm of historic police power, but federal resources and expertise are needed to cope with the problem at hand. In these "de facto" interjurisdictional regulatory contexts, the problem cannot be attacked at an exclusively national or local level without jeopardizing the mission.

a. Air Pollution

The management of air pollution under the Clean Air Act (CAA) offers a prime example of a de facto interjurisdictional problem.[68] Air pollution is a classic border-crossing harm, and so Congress authorizes the EPA to set ambient air quality management goals under the CAA.[69] However, the statutory scheme delegates design and enforcement authority to the

---

[66] *See supra* notes Chapter Four, 59–73.

[67] Tex. Cities Coal. on Stormwater v. EPA, 541 U.S. 1085 (2004) (denying the petition for certiorari).

[68] 42 U.S.C. §§ 7401–7671 (2000).

[69] *Id.* at § 7409(a).

states, which put into effect individually tailored State Implementation Plans (SIPs).[70] The federal government sets uniform air quality goals for the entire nation in order to avoid the negative externality problems that border-crossing air pollution implies. Otherwise, upwind states could choose high thresholds for pollution borne by downwind states, which would be powerless to stop the polluting activities in the upwind states. Preventing such negative externalities is a classic regulatory function of government, as is preventing the potential "race to the bottom" collective action problem if states competed for industry by progressively lowering pollution standards that could ultimately leave all worse off.[71]

Nevertheless, although the federal government could theoretically exert this legitimate authority from top to bottom of the regulatory endeavor, the state-federal consensus has clearly selected a partnership approach, in which each state decides how best to meet federal standards in light of its unique geographical and industrial features.[72] For example, the unique topography and weather patterns of the Los Angeles basin might lead to different regulatory features than a program designed for the flatlands of Houston, Texas—even though both cities face the kinds of serious air pollution problems that are the focus of the CAA.[73] Similarly, air pollution challenges related to the auto manufacturing industry in Michigan might require different design features than plans for resolving air pollution problems associated with coal mining in West Virginia.

The CAA's classic cooperative federalism partnership enables both levels of government to remain involved in regulating a problem of concern to each. Considered in terms of the core federalism values, it honors subsidiarity in matching localism with effective interjurisdictional problem solving, and it serves the check-and-balance value in that both levels of government backstop the other's commitment to protecting the public from air pollution harm. Still, the jurisdictional overlap threatens the separationist view of checks and balances, and accountability concerns may arise (especially when Congress requires state participation without sufficient funding).[74] Accordingly, although the Clean Air Act is a backbone of federal environmental law, it has not escaped criticism from the Tenther Movement.[75]

---

[70] *Id.* at § 7410(a).

[71] *See* Kirsten H. Engel & Scott R. Saleska, *"Facts Are Stubborn Things": An Empirical Reality Check in the Theoretical Debate over the Race-to-the-Bottom in State Environmental Standard-Setting*, 8 CORNELL J.L. & PUB. POL'Y 55, 60–61 (1998) (finding evidence of the phenomenon); Richard L. Revesz, *Federalism and Environmental Regulation: A Public Choice Analysis*, 115 HARV. L. REV. 553, 583–625 (2001) (suggesting a race to the top).

[72] *See* 42 U.S.C. § 7410(a)(1) (authorizing state implementation plans ("SIPS")); *id.* at § 7413(a)(2) (granting enforcement authority to EPA if a state fails to enforce or produce one). States uniformly prefer their own SIPs.

[73] *Cf.* 42 U.S.C. § 7401(a)(2) (2000) (including congressional findings about various sources of air pollution).

[74] *See supra* Chapter Two, notes 72–74 and accompanying text (discussing unfunded mandates).

[75] *E.g.*, Brian Roberts, *The EPA Can Go to Hell, and I Will Go to Texas*, TEXAS TENTH AMENDMENT CENTER (May 29, 2010), http://texas.tenthamendmentcenter.com/2010/05/the-epa-can-go-to-hell-and-i-will-go-to-texas/.

Other examples of de facto interjurisdictional regulatory problems include products liability,[76] some interstate criminal law enforcement,[77] enforcement of provisions in the Telecommunications Act,[78] and public health crises.[79] De facto problems often arise in contexts where externality-producing or interstate commercial activities of national concern are best matched with local enforcement media.

b. Domestic Counterterrorism Efforts

To complete the conceptual framework, some regulatory problems draw simultaneously on state and federal concerns in ways that reflect both de jure and de facto features, such as the maintenance of antiterrorism efforts and national security.[80]

As discussed in Chapter One, the Department of Homeland Security's National Response Framework anticipates cooperation between federal and state agencies.[81] In the de jure sense, this matches the states' police-power authority to protect the safety of their citizens with federal authority over interstate intelligence gathering and foreign affairs.[82] In the de facto sense, although federal preemption of local participation in preventing and responding to an act of terrorism is theoretically permissible,[83] it would be both counterproductive and absurdly inefficient.

Even if the federal government could preempt local involvement in domestic antiterrorism programs through its plenary power over international affairs, to what end? Especially in the post-9/11 world, national security must draw on *both* the global intelligence and expertise only available through the CIA *and* the local intelligence and expertise only available

---

[76] *See* Issacharoff & Sharkey, *supra* Chapter Two, note 128, at 1358 (noting that federal law defines standards but leaves remedies for violation to state law).

[77] *See* Logan, *supra* Chapter Four, note 11, at 66–67 (discussing federal criminal law reliance on state enforcement).

[78] Like the Clean Air Act, the Telecommunications Act merges federal standards with state implementation. *See* Weiser, *supra* Chapter Three, note 201, at 677 (noting that in its current form, the Telecommunications Act allows state agencies to engage in "measures that the agencies would not otherwise be authorized to do under state law").

[79] Public health crises implicate both state police power to regulate for public safety and federal responsibility for border-crossing harms and commercial impacts, as regards pandemic flu management and vaccine production. *See* Rosenthal, *supra* note 12 (discussing the potential global implications of avian flu).

[80] *National security* is an obvious national concern, but some commentators have noted that the term is rarely defined or given limiting contours. *See* Mariano-Florentino Cuéllar, *The Mismatch between State Power and State Capacity in Transnational Law Enforcement*, 22 BERKLEY J. INT'L L. 15, 37 (2004); Donald Kerwin, *The Use and Misuse of "National Security" Rationale in Crafting U.S. Refugee and Immigration Policies*, 17 INT'L J. REFUGEE L. 749, 750 (2005); David B. McGinty, *The Statutory and Executive Development of the National Security Exemption to Disclosure Under the Freedom of Information Act: Past and Future*, 32 N. KY. L. REV. 67, 80 (2005) (critiquing contemporary definitions of national security as "negligibly more helpful than no definition" at all). An overly open-ended definition could overwhelm federalism's check-and-balance value.

[81] *See* NATIONAL RESPONSE FRAMEWORK, *supra* Chapter One, note 96.

[82] *See* Whitley et al., *supra* Chapter One, note 62, at 4.

[83] *Cf.* 42 U.S.C. § 5191(b) (2000); *supra* Chapter One, notes 120–23.

at the municipal level.[84] Not only would complete federal preemption foreclose the value of local expertise and inefficiently duplicate efforts, it should not please the champions of dualist checks and balances. Nobody, it would seem, wants a federal government extensive enough to take the place of local police, firefighters, and other emergency service providers.[85] State agents are best able to provide the needed services due to their local placement and expertise—and the only way federal actors could match this would be to duplicate the entire state apparatus that generates these advantages.

B. Crossover into the Interjurisdictional Gray Area

This section reconceptualizes the boundary problem of dual sovereignty in light of the gray area, reframing the mutually exclusive state and federal spheres of the classical dual federalism model as three overlapping jurisdictional zones. It then highlights the risks of under-response and regulatory abdication that uncertain federalism theory creates for good interjurisdictional governance.

I. RECONCEPTUALIZING REGULATORY CROSSOVER

Interjurisdictional problems are troubling to dual federalism because they invite what might be deemed "regulatory crossover" between mutually exclusive state and federal spheres. In classical dualist terms, the relevant boundary is the line between proper state and federal authority, and crossover from one clearly defined side of this line to the other is impermissible. In a federalism model that understands the gray area, crossover is something more nuanced—describing regulatory choices to step beyond the settled realms of state or federal jurisdiction (whatever they may be at the time) and into the uncertain territory between them. Regulatory crossover is thus from the "uncontroversial sphere" of either state or federal authority into the gray area of interjurisdictional concern. (Once again, we can have the interesting part of this conversation regardless of disagreement over how to define the "uncontroversial spheres" of state and federal authority, so long as the forgoing discussion has satisfied doubts that there is at least some territory in between.) The difference can be demonstrated by controversial regulatory efforts on both sides, including federal efforts to prevent wetlands loss and state efforts to reduce harmful vehicular emissions.

For example, when the federal government protects water quality by regulating end-of-pipe discharges from a factory into the Wisconsin River, it is regulating within the uncontroversial sphere of its Clean Water Act (CWA) authority under the Commerce Clause. But when it protects water quality in the Wisconsin River watershed by regulating the filling of

---

[84] *Cf.* Christopher Dickey, *The Spymaster of New York*, NEWSWEEK, Feb. 9, 2009, at 40–41, http://www.newsweek.com/2009/01/30/the-spymaster-of-new-york.html (reporting on overlapping counterterrorism intelligence gathering by the CIA and NYPD).

[85] TASK FORCE ON FEDERALIZATION OF CRIMINAL LAW, ABA, REPORT ON THE FEDERALIZATION OF CRIMINAL LAW 27 (1998) (noting that Americans have innately distrusted "the concentration of broad police power in a national police force, and . . . have long resisted the evolution of such a broadly powerful national police force, as distinguished from specialized national police agencies").

a small seasonal pond on a private dairy farm (a so-called "hydrologically isolated intrastate wetland"), it has moved beyond the uncontroversial sphere of its CWA authority and crossed over into the gray area of state and federal concern. In the shadow of the New Federalism revival of dual federalism theory, regulatory crossover can be perilous. The Army Corps of Engineers is the federal agency that administers this part of the Clean Water Act, and it has been learning this very lesson the hard way, repeatedly, since 2001.

In *Solid Waste Agency of Northern Cook County v. U.S. Army Corps of Engineers* (*SWANCC*), the Court held that the Army Corps of Engineers had exceeded its statutory CWA authority in regulating isolated wetlands such as these.[86] As discussed above, the destruction of intrastate wetlands has serious consequences for the quality of the nation's waters, triggering legitimate federal concern.[87] However, the regulation of land use decisions involving isolated wetlands also triggers a core area of traditional state concern.[88] Writing for the Court in a decision redolent with federalism implications, Chief Justice Rehnquist narrowly interpreted the language of the statute to hold that Congress had not intended to regulate the non-navigable intrastate wetlands over which the Army Corp had asserted jurisdiction. Although it avoided deciding the constitutional issue, the Court suggested that the Army Corps' approach may even have exceeded the federal commerce power. The case sent shockwaves through the field of environmental law, leading to circuit splits and regulatory uncertainty.[89]

Rapanos v. United States, the most important wetlands decision since *SWANCC*, made things even worse for the Army Corps and EPA, which also implements the CWA.[90] Justice Scalia's plurality opinion explicitly invoked the New Federalism canon to cast doubt on federal assertions of CWA jurisdiction over wetlands connected to navigable waters by manmade channels (such as storm sewers) or separated by artificial berms.[91] There, a fractured Supreme Court invalidated new portions of the Army Corps' jurisdictional guidelines without reaching consensus on permissible alternatives—thus throwing the field into even further disarray.

The effects of CWA jurisdictional uncertainty after these decisions have been substantial. A major investigation in 2010, three years after *Rapanos* added force to the questions initially raised in *SWANNC*, reported that nearly 1,500 major water pollution investigations have

---

[86] 531 U.S. 159, 173–74 (2001).

[87] *See* Rapanos v. United States, 126 S. Ct. 2208, 2252 (2006) (Stevens, J., dissenting) (noting that wetlands adjacent to tributaries of navigable waters have an impact on the nation's waters by "providing habitat for aquatic animals, keeping excessive sediment and toxic pollutants out of adjacent waters, and reducing downstream flooding by absorbing water at times of high flow"); *see also SWANCC*, 531 U.S. at 174–75 (Stevens, J., dissenting) (explaining that the CWA was an extension of federal regulatory authority to combat severely polluted waters).

[88] *Cf.* Kelo v. City of New London, 545 U.S. 469, 482–83 (2005) (noting broad deference to state land use regulation).

[89] *E.g.*, Duane J. Desiderio, *Ditching It Out . . . But Can the Corps Take It?*, NAT'L WETLANDS NEWSLETTER, (Envtl. Law Inst., Washington, D.C.) May–June 2005, at 3, 3–4.

[90] 126 S. Ct. 2208 (2006).

[91] *Id.* at 2224 (rejecting the federal agency's interpretation of the CWA as infringing on traditional state control over land and water use and thus pushing the limits of congressional commerce power).

been dropped due to the difficulty of establishing jurisdiction after these decisions.[92] Mid-level EPA officials indicated that federal regulators may be "unable to prosecute as many as half of the nation's largest known polluters because officials lack jurisdiction or because proving jurisdiction would be overwhelmingly difficult or time consuming."[93] The report notes concerns raised by both state and federal regulators about the troubling regulatory consequences of this jurisdictional uncertainty:

> Thousands of the nation's largest water polluters are outside the Clean Water Act's reach because the Supreme Court has left uncertain which waterways are protected by that law, according to interviews with regulators. As a result, some businesses are declaring that the law no longer applies to them. And pollution rates are rising. Companies that have spilled oil, carcinogens and dangerous bacteria into lakes, rivers and other waters are not being prosecuted, according to Environmental Protection Agency regulators working on those cases, who estimate that more than 1,500 major pollution investigations have been discontinued or shelved in the last four years. . . .
>
> Some argue that such decisions help limit overreaching regulatory efforts. . . . But for E.P.A. and state regulators, the decisions have created widespread uncertainty. The court did not define which waterways are regulated, and judicial districts have inter-preted the court's decisions differently. As regulators have struggled to guess how vari-ous courts will rule, some E.P.A. lawyers have established unwritten internal guidelines to avoid cases in which proving jurisdiction is too difficult, according to interviews with more than two dozen current and former E.P.A. officials. . . . The E.P.A. said in a statement that it did not automatically concede that any significant water body was outside the authority of the Clean Water Act. . . . But midlevel E.P.A. officials said that internal studies indicated that as many as 45 percent of major polluters might be either outside regulatory reach or in areas where proving jurisdiction is overwhelmingly dif-ficult. And even in situations in which regulators believe they still have jurisdiction, companies have delayed cases for years by arguing that the ambiguity precludes prose-cution. In some instances, regulators have simply dropped enforcement actions.[94]

Indeed, in 2008, a House oversight committee reviewed an internal EPA memo quoting similar statistics on decreased enforcement after *Rapanos* due to jurisdictional uncertainty.[95] The House committee ominously concluded that uncertainty after *Rapanos* may be under-mining the "ability to maintain an effective enforcement program."[96]

The states are equally vulnerable to the perils of regulatory crossover in a federalism model leaning toward dualism. For example, when a state reduces asthma-causing auto emissions by

---

[92] Charles Duhigg & Janet Roberts, *Rulings Restrict Clean Water Act, Foiling EPA*, N.Y. TIMES, Feb. 28, 2010, at A1, http://www.nytimes.com/2010/03/01/us/01water.html?emc=eta.

[93] *Id.*

[94] *Id.*

[95] Jeff Kinney, *Internal EPA Memo Finds Enforcement Decreased Following Rapanos Decision*, 39 ENV'T REP. (BNA) 1392 (2008).

[96] *Id.*

constructing special parking lots and traffic lanes to encourage carpooling, it is acting within the uncontroversial sphere of its police powers to regulate land use and protect the health and safety of its citizens.[97] But when it reduces the same asthma-causing auto emissions by requiring state agents and contractors to select from an approved list of fuel-efficient vehicles when purchasing new "fleet" vehicles (e.g., police cars, garbage trucks)[98]—then it is regulating beyond the uncontroversial sphere of its reserved police powers and has crossed over into the interjurisdictional gray area.

A municipal agency in California has learned this over more than a decade of litigation challenging the fleet-purchasing rules it created to alleviate the hot spot of air pollution in the Los Angeles basin. In *Engine Manufacturers v. South Coast Air Quality Management District*,[99] Justice Scalia explained that even such "demand-side" state purchasing regulation may be too close in kind to the "supply-side" federal emission regulations that preempt state law under the Clean Air Act.[100] (The case is discussed more fully below.)

2. THE GRAY AREA AS REGULATORY "NO-MAN'S LAND"

The notion of "regulatory crossover" implies that a regulatory authority has crossed some kind of line—but it is important to isolate exactly what line this is. Again, classical dualism would characterize crossover in clear terms: (1) there is a subject-matter sphere of proper state concern for which it has reserved regulatory authority and a sphere of proper federal concern reflecting the enumerated powers; (2) targets of legitimate regulation fall within one or the other; and (3) the Tenth Amendment—affirming that the powers not enumerated to the national government are reserved to the states—protects this vision of dual sovereignty by policing the boundary between. In this model, "crossover" therefore implies that one side has transgressed the line differentiating federal and state realms—and by corollary, that it has violated the Tenth Amendment. (The Tenth Amendment violation may be in principle only; sometimes the doctrinal claim would arise under an affirmative power such as commerce, while the remedy for state transgression is normally preemption.) Chapters Three and Four detailed case after case in which exactly these kinds of claims were leveled against then-gray area regulations, ranging from the First Bank of the United States in 1791 to the Civil Rights Act of 1964 to the Phase II Stormwater Rule upheld in 2003.

Yet in the interjurisdictional gray area, the line between state and federal concern is not always so clear. As the wetlands regulation and vehicular pollution examples demonstrate, there is an area of overlap that implicates both state and federal concerns, such that regulatory

---

[97] *See* Engine Mfrs. Ass'n v. S. Coast Air Quality Mgmt. Dist., 541 U.S. 246, 260 (2004) (Souter, J., dissenting) [hereinafter *Engine Mfrs. Ass'n I*] (quoting the CAA's recognition of the primary role of the states in preventing air pollution "at its source").

[98] *Id.* at 249–50 (majority opinion).

[99] 541 U.S. 246 (2004).

[100] *Id.* at 254–56. Notably, his holding contradicted congressional intent (according to the ample legislative history on point) and violated the presumption against preemption of state law in traditional police power contexts unless Congress has done so explicitly. *See Engine Mfrs. Ass'n I*, 541 U.S. at 260–62 (2004) (Souter, J., dissenting); Gadeberg, *supra* Chapter Four, note 161, at 478–80, 483.

crossover is not necessarily from one clearly defined sphere of concern and authority into the other, but from one clearly defined sphere into the interjurisdictional gray area—and not necessarily in violation of dual sovereignty.[101] The descriptive cooperative federalism model implicitly recognizes the gray area, although it has not provided a satisfying theoretical account for managing the conflicts that arise there. However, the New Federalism cases have clouded the field of federalism theory with a revival of dualist idealism that makes gray area regulation even more fraught.

The separationist ideal chills regulation in the gray area by fostering a view of federalism that interprets departures from the uncontroversial spheres of state and federal authority as constitutional violations. Its binary model assumes that regulatory concerns must be addressed from within the properly local or national sphere, as informed by an enumerated powers analysis and history, without crossover.[102] But as shown in the preceding chapters, this strict-separationist approach is only one among many possible interpretations of dual sovereignty. The interjurisdictional gray area demonstrates that it is a bad choice, because it forsakes the important federalism values of localism and problem solving at the behest of a contested understanding of checks and balances. Discouraging regulatory activity in the gray area allows pressing interjurisdictional problems to fester, either because motivated regulators fear legal liability if they stray too far from their uncontroversial sphere, or because unmotivated regulators use the gray area as an excuse to abdicate responsibility.

The Los Angeles regional agency's attempts to regulate air pollution hot spots demonstrate the risk of liability, and radioactive waste management in the wake of *New York v. United States* highlights the problem of abdication.

a. *The Risk of Liability:* Engine Manufacturers Ass'n v. South Coast Air Quality Management District

In the shadow of this dual federalism revival, even the most motivated regulators might reasonably avoid the interjurisdictional gray area for fear of having to defend against legal challenge in an area of jurisprudential instability. Taking up the previous example, the regional agency that manages air pollution controls in the Los Angeles metropolitan area was concerned about the relationship between respiratory disease among its citizens and the exceedingly poor quality of its air.[103] Pollution levels in the Los Angeles basin are the worst in the nation, because its bowl-like geography traps emissions from extreme levels of traffic generated by the massive fleet of regional commuters and the constant stream of trucks and barges using the Port of Los Angeles shipping corridor.[104] It is the only region in the nation that has been designated an "extreme nonattainment area" for safe ozone levels as defined by the CAA.[105] Accordingly, the South Coast Air Quality Management District attempted to

---

[101] Parts III and IV take on the question of distinguishing between permissible and impermissible crossover.

[102] *See, e.g.,* Schapiro & Buzbee, *supra* Chapter Three, note 147, 1203–05.

[103] Engine Mfrs. Ass'n v. S. Coast Air Quality Mgmt. Dist., 158 F. Supp. 2d 1107, 1108–09 (C.D. Cal. 2001).

[104] *See id.* at 1109.

[105] *See Engine Mfrs. Ass'n I,* 541 U.S. at 259 n.1 (Souter, J., dissenting); Engine Mfrs. Ass'n v. S. Coast Air Quality Mgmt. Dist., 498 F.3d 1031, 1035 (9th Cir. 2007) [hereinafter *Engine Mfrs. Ass'n II*].

reduce harmful emissions by requiring that the operators of vehicular fleets purchase only low-emissions replacement vehicles. The Engine Manufacturers Association challenged the program as an emissions control preempted by federal Clean Air Act standards.[106]

The agency prevailed both at trial and on appeal to the Ninth Circuit, which affirmed that the agency had not set emission standards but merely regulated the purchasing choices by state agents and contractors of vehicles that were already in production and certified for sale within the state.[107] The decisions emphasized the agency's legitimate authority and regulatory obligation to protect its citizens from the disproportionate incidence of asthma and other respiratory health problems in the Los Angeles basin.[108]

However, the Supreme Court vacated the judgment and remanded, concerned that the District's standard was indeed preempted by the CAA, and that the agency had thus overstepped its permissible sphere of local authority.[109] Writing for the Court, Justice Scalia rejected the distinction the lower courts had accepted between purchasing rules that were not subject to preemption and manufacturing standards that were, but the opinion did not decide whether the rules were actually preempted.[110] The Court volunteered that it was "likely that at least certain aspects of the Fleet Rules are pre-empted," but remanded for further proceedings consistent with its opinion.[111] Only Justice Souter dissented, passionately invoking the presumption against preemption and the federalism concerns implied by yet another incursion into the state's police power to protect the health, safety, and welfare of its citizens.[112]

After several additional years of litigation on remand, the Ninth Circuit ultimately upheld the purchasing rules on the basis of the market participant exception, which protects state regulations from CAA preemption when the state is acting not as a regulator but in its proprietary capacity.[113] However, the Ninth Circuit remanded the case yet again for a final determination about whether unrelated aspects of the rules were preempted.[114] In the end, most of the agency's innovative fleet-purchasing rules are in effect, but litigation on the remaining issues is still pending a full decade after the rules were initially promulgated. Based on models like this one, a more risk-averse municipal agency would be extremely cautious before venturing into a potential interjurisdictional quagmire, especially an agency with fewer resources available than the powerful South Coast Air Quality Management District. Sadly, this would be so even if it strongly believed—as the agency has now been arguing for a decade—that it

---

[106] *Engine Mfrs. Ass'n I*, 541 U.S. at 249–51. Although the State of California may create separate emissions standards under a waiver from the EPA, municipal agencies within the state may not.

[107] Engine Mfrs. Ass'n v. S. Coast Air Quality Mgmt. Dist., 309 F.3d 550, 551 (9th Cir. 2002) (affirming Engine Mfrs. Ass'n v. S. Coast Air Quality Mgmt. Dist., 158 F. Supp. 2d 1107, 1109, 1117–20 (C.D. Cal. 2001)).

[108] *Id.*

[109] *See Engine Mfrs. Ass'n I*, 541 U.S. at 258–59.

[110] *Id.* at 249, 258.

[111] *Id.* at 258.

[112] *Id.* at 260–61 (Souter, J., dissenting); *see supra* Chapter Four, note 172 (quoting his argument at length).

[113] *Engine Mfrs. Ass'n. II*, 498 F.3d at 1039.

[114] *Id.*

was not only regulating within its proper sphere of authority, but obliged to do so to protect the health and safety of its citizens.

b. *The Risk of Abdication:* New York v. United States

Dual federalism's obfuscation of the gray area may also invite more self-serving behaviors by underachieving civil servants. An interjurisdictional problem may seem so expensive or politically unpalatable that the relevant actors on either or both sides of the line might prefer to pass it off as the other's problem to solve—thus abdicating responsibility under the cover of federalism. Indeed, some have offered this as the least charitable explanation for federal inaction in the aftermath of Hurricane Katrina, characterizing it as an abdication of responsibility in a no-win zone of interjurisdictional responsibility.[115] Another example with a more specific debt to New Federalism can be found in the wake of *New York v. United States*, the Tenth Amendment case that established the New Federalism anti-commandeering rule.[116] Chapter Seven tells this story in more detail, but it exemplifies the problem of regulatory abdication so powerfully that some foreshadowing here is warranted.

The policy-making protagonists in the *New York* story had been faced with the particularly unpalatable problem of low-level radioactive waste disposal. Because nobody seems to want a radioactive waste disposal facility in his or her backyard, almost none had been built, and so only two or three existing sites—one in South Carolina, one in Washington State, and at times, one in Nevada—existed for the disposal of all low-level radioactive waste produced and disposed of in all the other states.[117] When the Washington and Nevada sites temporarily closed, South Carolina's facility was left to accept all the hazardous waste in the nation, and its unhappy citizens threatened to stop accepting out-of-state shipments (though they would need congressional authorization to do so, given the dormant Commerce Clause implications of rejecting this stream of distasteful but undeniably interstate commerce).[118]

Congress considered mandating a federal solution, but the National Governors Association urged Congress to leave the problem to the states, and developed an interstate accord by which the sited states (South Carolina, Washington, and Nevada) agreed to continue accepting out-of-state shipments until 1986.[119] In the interim, the non-sited states would work in regional partnerships to develop local disposal sites that would relieve the unfair burden currently placed on the sited states.[120] At the request of the states, Congress ratified this agreement as the Low-Level Radioactive Waste Policy Act of 1980, thereby resolving the dormant Commerce Clause problem that would otherwise confound the sited states' plans

---

[115] *E.g.*, Peggy Noonan, Editorial, *The Scofflaw Swimmer: Government Takes Too Much Authority and Not Enough Responsibility*, WSJ.COM, Sept. 29, 2005, http://www.opinionjournal.com/columnists/pnoonan/?id=110007328 ("No one took charge. Thus the postgame commentary in which everyone blamed someone else: *The mayor fumbled the ball, the governor didn't call the play, the president didn't have a ground game.*").

[116] 505 U.S. 144 (1992).

[117] *Id.* at 150.

[118] *Id.*

[119] *Id.* at 150–51.

[120] *Id.* at 151.

to close their borders to waste shipments in 1986.[121] However, as 1985 ended, not a single new disposal site had been built. The states reconvened negotiations and urged Congress to amend the act with a new schedule of sanctions they had developed to incentivize compliance by the non-sited states.[122]

New York was among the states that lobbied Congress in support of the new penalties, and Congress passed the amendments without incident.[123] However, when New York later failed to persuade any of its localities to host the disposal facility it had agreed to site, it sued under the Tenth Amendment to be relieved of the obligations imposed by the new sanctions.[124] Despite New York's specific role in the design of the act, it persuaded the Supreme Court that Congress had moved beyond the uncontroversial sphere of its regulatory powers and commandeered state sovereign authority by requiring New York to either build a facility or take title to the waste.

The well-known outcome of the case is that New York prevailed, the Low-Level Radioactive Waste Policy Act was defanged, and the Tenth Amendment anti-commandeering doctrine was born. But as Chapter Seven describes more fully, the outcome less well-known is that in the fifteen years since that time, *not a single net-additional waste facility has been sited*.[125] The states have made no true progress in creating additional disposal sites for low-level radioactive waste; the nation remains tethered to a mere three overwhelmed facilities: Barnwell in South Carolina, Hanford in Washington State, and Clive in Utah (replacing the now defunct Nevada facility).[126] South Carolina continued to accept the bulk of waste generated in the eastern United States until 2008, when it formally closed its doors to states outside of its current compact.[127] Virtually nothing more has been done to address the crisis of limited low-level radioactive waste disposal facilities that set the states into a conflict requiring congressional mediation.

Considering the stakes involved, the lack of progress is shocking. South Carolina became so incensed over what it considered unfair exploitation by neighboring states that it engaged in a high-stakes constitutional standoff with North Carolina, from whom it decided to stop receiving shipments of waste in 1995 after North Carolina repeatedly failed its promises to the Southeast Compact to site its own facility.[128] The governor of North Carolina threatened to sue South Carolina under the dormant Commerce Clause,[129] though no suit was ever filed

---

[121]   *Id.* at 150–51.

[122]   *Id.* at 151.

[123]   *Id.* at 180–81.

[124]   *Id.* at 154.

[125]   *See* U.S. Nuclear Regulatory Commission, Locations of Low-Level Waste Facilities, http://www.nrc.gov/waste/llw-disposal/licensing/locations.html (last visited July 14, 2010).

[126]   *Id.*

[127]   *South Carolina's Barnwell Closes; Many without Rad. Waste Disposal*, Nuclear Waste News, July 7, 2008, at 1.

[128]   Mark Holt, Cong. Research Serv., Civilian Nuclear Waste Disposal 17 (2006), http://ncseonline.org/NLE/CRSreports/06Sep/RL33461.pdf.

[129]   *See* Jim Clarke, *N.C., S.C. at Odds Over Who Can Use Barnwell Landfill*, Charlotte Observer, June 26, 1995, *available at* 1995 WLNR 1767874.

(perhaps due to recognition by North Carolina of its own unclean hands, or perhaps because the Utah site became available to accept its waste around that time).[130] However, four other states in the Southeast Compact later sued North Carolina (unsuccessfully) for some $90 million in light of its various failures to comply with the terms of the Compact.[131]

South Carolina's plight suggests the dilemma of a gray area "hot potato problem" for which nobody wants to take responsibility. Congress can claim that it is respecting federalism by staying out of the regulatory arena that the states requested be left to them, while the non-sited states can claim that the Supreme Court invalidated (on federalism grounds!) their best attempt at handling the problem. Each side can point a finger at the other, abdicating regulatory responsibility in this interjurisdictional gray area of particularly radioactive concern.[132]

C. *The Benefits of Regulatory Backstop:* Climate Federalism

Of course, the most ominous interjurisdictional problem of them all is that of climate change, both domestically and internationally. In the United States, regulators venturing into this arena confront substantial risks of litigation under conditions of jurisprudential instability and uncertain federalism theory. They also risk that financial and intellectual capital invested in regulatory innovation will be squandered if their efforts are overturned or preempted by later governance at a higher level. For a long time, these daunting risks led to abdication on both sides. However, many have finally decided that the risk of taking no action to confront the problem is an even worse alternative.

The explosion of climate governance in the last decade—especially at the state and local level—demonstrates a chief benefit of jurisdictional overlap as a source of regulatory backstop. This is the view of checks and balances that departs from the separationist model, emphasizing how overlapping local and national authority protects individual rights and regulatory obligations against neglect by the other side.[133] This section describes climate governance as an interjurisdictional problem, reviews the risks of abdication and liability, and then explores the promising efforts of local and state governments to act in the face of these risks during a period of federal regulatory gridlock.

Scientific consensus about the looming changes in global climate suggest the need for interjurisdictional governance of a sort the world has not yet seen, involving both mitigation and adaptation measures domestically and internationally. Decades of study by the Intergovernmental Panel on Climate Change (IPCC), a joint effort by the United Nations Environment Program and the World Meteorological Organization, show "high confidence" in human contributions to climate change through the emission of carbon dioxide and other

---

[130] *LLW Compacts: Emerging Private Initiatives May Be Big News in New LLW Efforts*, NUCLEAR WASTE NEWS, Sept. 5, 1996, *available at* 1996 WLNR 3101706.

[131] Alabama v. North Carolina, 130 S. Ct. 2295 (2010).

[132] *Cf.* John Dinan, *Congressional Responses to the Rehnquist Court's Federalism Decisions*, 32 PUBLIUS 12 (2002) (arguing that there were viable options even after *New York*, because Congress could have tried to persuade states to act via its spending power, or to directly regulate waste producers under its commerce authority).

[133] *See supra* Chapter Two, notes 41–53 and accompanying text.

gases that trap heat in the atmosphere.[134] The atmospheric collection of these "greenhouse gases" is expected to create profound changes in world weather patterns.[135] If current trends continue, the IPCC predicts arctic warming and polar ice reduction, sea level rise leading to coastal flooding and land loss, changes in ocean salinity and wind patterns, widespread changes in global precipitation patterns, and increases in extreme weather, including droughts, drenching rains, heat waves, and more intense hurricanes.[136] Indeed, these changes are already upon us, suggested not only by the force of storms like Katrina, but by the catastrophic flooding that displaced tens of millions in Pakistan, the mudslides that killed thousands in China, and the Russian heat wave that set the countryside ablaze—all in just the summer of 2010.[137]

Regulatory responses are needed to mitigate the anthropogenic causes of further climate change and to adapt to the harms that are already inevitable. Mitigation efforts focus on reducing greenhouse gas emissions and increasing carbon sinks (to capture carbon dioxide and other greenhouse gases underground, in the ocean, or within expanses of protected forests.)[138] Adaptation efforts range from proposals to build protective levees around low-lying coastal areas like New York City to global geoengineering efforts that would introduce stratospheric aerosols into the atmosphere to reflect sunlight.[139] Even "climate skeptics" who contest the scientific consensus on the anthropogenic role in climate change[140] must concede the need for regulatory adaptation to the changes that are already observable. Nevertheless, both mitigation and adaptation are likely to raise the same hurdles that have complicated responses to other interjurisdictional environmental problems (such as wetlands loss and radioactive waste) and natural disasters (such as pandemic flu and hurricanes).

Climate is the overarching public commons, and coping with forecasted changes will require regulatory response from every point along the spectrum of political scale. After all, climate change connects the most local of all happenings—the decisions each of us makes about where we decide to live, how we get to work, and what we eat—with the most global of all happenings: shifts in planetary weather patterns that will decide, in larger terms, where whole populations can live, what they can grow for food, and what policies nation states will

---

[134] IPCC, 2007, *Summary for Policymakers, in* CLIMATE CHANGE 2007: THE PHYSICAL SCIENCE BASIS. CONTRIBUTION OF WORKING GROUP I TO THE FOURTH ASSESSMENT REPORT OF THE INTERGOVERNMENTAL PANEL ON CLIMATE CHANGE (S. Solomon et al., eds., 2007), http://www.ipcc.ch/pdf/assessment-report/ar4/wg1/ar4-wg1-spm.pdf.

[135] *Id.*

[136] *Id.*

[137] Allister Doyle, *Analysis: Pakistan Floods, Russia Heat Fit Climate Trend,* REUTERS, Aug. 9, 2010, http://www.reuters.com/article/idUSTRE6782DU20100809.

[138] J.B. Ruhl, *Climate Change Adaptation and the Structural Transformation of Environmental Law,* 40 ENVTL. L. 363, 365 (2010).

[139] *See also* Bruce Stutz, *New York City Girds Itself for Heat and Rising Seas,* ENVIRONMENT 360, Sept. 10, 2009, http://e360.yale.edu/content/feature.msp?id=2187 (discussing city plans for levees); Jason J. Blackstock et al., *Climate Engineering Responses to Climate Emergencies* (2009), archived online at: http://arxiv.org/pdf/0907.5140 (discussing the use of stratospheric aerosols).

[140] *See* Associated Press, *Stolen E-mails Embolden Climate Skeptics,* CBSNEWS, Dec. 10, 2009, http://www.cbsnews.com/stories/2009/12/10/tech/main5963892.shtml.

follow in pursuit of their changing interests. With the high costs of avoiding it and even higher costs of avoidance, climate change is the mother of all collective action problems.

Because greenhouse gases are produced locally but mix evenly in the atmosphere regardless of origin,[141] climate mitigation necessarily requires the exercise of authority from the local to the national to the international level (hopefully in meaningful coordination). Local efforts are necessary to cope, for example, with the impacts of countless personal commuting decisions through climate-sensitive land use planning and transportation initiatives. But national and international efforts are needed to cope with the interstate commerce and collective action features of the problem. Otherwise, action taken in one locale can be effectively negated by free riders in another, and regulated industries in one jurisdiction may relocate (or "leak") to less stringently regulated alternatives.[142] Climate adaptation governance will involve similar jurisdictional overlap, triggering local authority to cope with rapid changes in land use and public safety issues and the various national responsibilities implicated during the Katrina emergency.[143]

As with so many other interjurisdictional quandaries, then, the challenge of climate governance is to locate the ideal equipoise between two competing goods: (1) a strong centralized program that can achieve the needed cumulative results, and (2) continued room for the kind of vibrant local innovation and interjurisdictional competition that can provide new ideas and regulatory backstops in case of failed national policy. The same dilemma exists both internationally and domestically, although this discussion is limited to climate governance in the United States. And in U.S. climate policy, the potential for serious federalism conflict is everywhere. The ghost of classical dualism haunts climate governance both through the heightened risk of litigation associated with regulatory crossover and by encouraging regulatory abdication in the face of that uncertainty.

During a long period of federal abdication, state and local actors overcame the fears of liability and lost investment to enter the regulatory field in force. After a decade of federal inaction on climate governance, states have taken the lead in developing a broad variety of initiatives using their police powers to regulate for the health and welfare of their citizens.[144] Most climate regulatory efforts fall into two main categories: those that take aim at the supply and demand of electricity generation, and those that focus on the transportation sector. Initiatives targeting electricity supply and demand include state and regional carbon

---

[141] John Copeland Nagle, *Discounting China's CDM Dams*, 7 LOY. U. CHI. INT'L. L. REV. 9, 10 (2009).

[142] David E. Adelman & Kirsten H. Engel, *Reorienting State Climate Change Policies To Induce Technological Change*, 50 ARIZ. L. REV. 835, 842–46 (2008).

[143] *Cf.* Ruhl, *supra* note 138.

[144] Michele M. Betsill & Barry G. Rabe, *Climate Change and Multilevel Governance: The Evolving State and Local Roles*, *in* TOWARD SUSTAINABLE COMMUNITIES: TRANSITIONS AND TRANSFORMATIONS IN ENVIRONMENTAL POLICY 201 (Daniel A. Mazmanian & Michael E. Kraft eds., 2d ed. 2009); Engel, *supra* Introduction, note 79.

cap-and-trade markets;[145] renewable portfolio standards;[146] electric power plant carbon emission standards;[147] public benefit funds, tax credits, and other public subsidy programs;[148] net metering and green pricing;[149] energy efficiency resource and products standards;[150] building energy codes;[151] and local government initiatives such as installing energy-efficient lighting.[152]

The regional carbon caps are the most ambitious state-based programs (though perhaps more poetic than potent, given the dilemma of regional restraint in the global greenhouse gas arena). In creating and regulating new interstate markets, they are the most vulnerable to federal preemption. But as federalism innovators in the absence of national action, three regional groups and one state have instituted their own carbon cap-and-trade systems. In the Northeast and Mid-Atlantic regions, ten states have joined the Regional Greenhouse Gas Initiative (RGGI) and pledged to reduce carbon dioxide emissions from their power sectors by 10 percent by 2018.[153] RGGI states held their ninth carbon auction in September of 2010.[154] In the West, seven states joined four Canadian provinces to form the Western Climate Initiative, with plans to begin carbon trading by 2012.[155] In the Midwest, six states and one Canadian province formed the Midwest Greenhouse Gas Reduction Accord, pledging to establish a multisector cap-and-trade system to meet regional greenhouse gas reduction targets.[156] The State of California is creating its own state-wide program, with plans to adopt cap-and-trade regulations by 2011 and begin trading in 2012.[157]

---

[145]   Regional Greenhouse Gas Initiative, http://www.rggi.org/home (last visited Sept. 29, 2010); Western Climate Initiative, http://www.westernclimateinitiative.org/ (last visited Sept. 29, 2010); California Climate Action Registry, http://www.climateregistry.org/ (last visited Sept. 29, 2010); Midwestern Greenhouse Gas Reduction Accord, http://www.midwesternaccord.org/ (last visited Sept. 29, 2010). *See also* Robert B. McKinstry, Jr., John C. Dernbach, & Thomas D. Peterson, *Federal Climate Change Legislation As If the States Matter*, 22 NAT. RESOURCES & ENV'T 4 (Winter 2008) (describing regional partnerships).

[146]   Engel, *supra* Introduction, note 79, at 437 (highlighting programs in the District of Columbia and twenty-eight states).

[147]   *See e.g.*, CAL. CODE REGS. tit. 20, §§ 2900–2913 (2010).

[148]   Engel, *supra* Introduction, note 79, at 438.

[149]   Katherine N. Probst & Sarah Jo Szambelan, *The Role of the States in a Federal Climate Program* 6 (Resources for the Future Discussion Paper, Nov. 2009), http://www.rff.org/RFF/Documents/RFF-DP-09-46.pdf.

[150]   PEW CENTER ON GLOBAL CLIMATE CHANGE, CLIMATE CHANGE 101: STATE ACTION 5 (2009), http://www.pewclimate.org/docUploads/Climate101-State-Jan09.pdf; Daniel A. Farber, *Climate Change, Federalism, and the Constitution*, 50 ARIZ. L. REV. 879, 885 (2008).

[151]   Engel, *supra* Introduction, note 79, at 438.

[152]   *Id.* at 434; *see also* PEW CENTER ON GLOBAL CLIMATE CHANGE, CLIMATE CHANGE 101: LOCAL ACTION (2009), http://www.pewclimate.org/docUploads/Climate101-Local-Jan09.pdf.

[153]   Regional Greenhouse Gas Initiative, *supra* note 145.

[154]   Auction Results, Regional Greenhouse Gas Initiative, http://www.rggi.org/market/co2_auctions/results.

[155]   Western Climate Initiative, http://www.westernclimateinitiative.org/milestones (last visited Sept. 29, 2010).

[156]   Midwestern Greenhouse Gas Reduction Accord, http://www.midwesternaccord.org/ (last visited Sept. 29, 2010).

[157]   The California Warming Solutions Act of 2006 directed the California Air Resources Board to develop a plan to reduce greenhouse gas emissions to 1990 levels by 2020. Cap-And-Trade, California Air Resources Board, http://www.arb.ca.gov/cc/capandtrade/capandtrade.htm (last visited Sept. 29, 2010); Text of A.B. 32

Twenty-eight states and the District of Columbia are also reducing greenhouse gas emissions by regulating the electricity supply sector directly, including the establishment of renewable portfolio standards that require electric utility companies to generate a certain portion of their electricity from renewable sources.[158] For example, thanks to its vast wind resources, Texas was able to meet its initial renewable supply targets and then double them in a second round of legislation.[159] Other states directly limit the amount of greenhouse gasses their power plants emit. For example, the California Public Utility Commission established a greenhouse gas emission cap, then forbade in-state power plants from entering into long-term supply contracts that would violate the cap.[160] This controversial move has required careful navigation of the federalism and preemption concerns raised by the fact that California retailers often obtain power from out-of-state suppliers in interstate commerce.

States also use monetary incentives to promote emissions reductions, some through tax credits and direct subsidies to promote renewable energy and increased energy efficiency.[161] Approximately twenty-five states have established Public Benefit Funds for this purpose, funded by surcharges on consumer utility bills.[162] Some have also created programs to subsidize particular renewable technologies or encourage their use by consumers. For example, California has established a fund of $3.3 billion to subsidize installation of solar power systems in homes and businesses.[163] Eighteen states have enacted "net metering" programs, which allow consumers generating electricity through home-based solar or wind collectors to sell excess back to the grid.[164] Forty-one states allow "green pricing," which enable consumers to choose electricity generation from renewable sources by adding small premiums to their electric bills.[165]

States also regulate electricity on the demand side. Nineteen states are grappling with growing energy demand by establishing energy efficiency resource and product standards, encouraging more efficient production methods among generators by setting minimum energy-savings targets for electricity generation and heating fuels.[166] Eight states have established similar efficiency standards for consumer appliances as of 2008, generating further federalism controversy.[167] Electrical appliance standards are normally subject to federal

---

available at http://www.leginfo.ca.gov/pub/05-06/bill/asm/ab_0001-0050/ab_32_bill_20060927_chaptered.html.

[158] Engel, *supra* Introduction, note 79, at 437.

[159] *Id.* at 438.

[160] 20 CAL. CODE REGS. § 2902(b) (2010).

[161] Engel, *supra* Introduction, note 79, at 438.

[162] *Id.*

[163] *Id.*

[164] Probst & Szambelan, *supra* note 149, at 6–7. Distributing energy through a "Smart Grid" would facilitate net metering. AMY ABEL, CONG. RESEARCH SERV., SMART GRID PROVISIONS IN H.R. 6, 110TH CONGRESS 5 (2007), http://assets.opencrs.com/rpts/RL34288_20071220.pdf.

[165] Green Pricing: Utility Programs by State, U.S. Department of Energy, http://apps3.eere.energy.gov/greenpower/markets/pricing.shtml?page=1 (last visited Sept. 29, 2010).

[166] PEW CENTER ON GLOBAL CLIMATE CHANGE, CLIMATE CHANGE 101: STATE ACTION 5 (2009), http://www.pewclimate.org/docUploads/Climate101-State-Jan09.pdf.

[167] *Id.*

preemption, but the Department of Energy has proposed waiving preemption so that states can exceed federal minimum standards.[168] California estimates that it can save consumers $3 billion and eliminate the need for three new power plants just by improving product efficiency.[169]

States are also regulating the energy efficiency of buildings, in recognition of the fact that residential and commercial buildings use over 70 percent of electricity consumed in the United States.[170] Most states have building energy codes, though they generally set modest energy savings goals.[171] Thirty-one state and local governments also require or encourage compliance with voluntary green building rating systems, such as LEED (Leadership in Energy and Environmental Design) and Green Globe standards.[172] Colorado requires that any new or renovated building whose total project cost includes at least 25 percent in state funds must comply with "standards of an independent third-party green building certification system, such as LEED."[173] Boston was the first major U.S. city to require all buildings over fifty thousand square feet to be certifiable under LEED standards.[174] Local governments are also seeking to promote energy efficiency,[175] implementing municipal solid waste management programs that use less energy and recover landfill gasses, installing energy-efficient lighting, and adopting efficiency building codes.[176] Boulder, Colorado went even farther and adopted the nation's first energy tax in 2006.[177]

On the transportation side, some states are now regulating greenhouse gas emissions from motor vehicles. In another move that sparked substantial federalism controversy, California became the first state to directly target greenhouse gas emissions from passenger cars and light trucks, ultimately winning a contested waiver from EPA to exceed the national standard under the Clean Air Act.[178] Because other states are permitted to choose the alternative motor vehicle standards under the California waiver rule, fourteen states have now adopted California's new greenhouse gas emissions standards, and approximately eleven others have

---

[168] Farber, *supra* note 150, at 885; U.S. Energy Information Administration, *Annual Energy Outlook 2010 with Projections to 2035*, Report #: DOE/EIA-0383 (May 11, 2010), http://www.eia.doe.gov/oiaf/aeo/leg_reg.html (discussing room for state appliance standards under federal law).

[169] Farber, *supra* note 150, at 885.

[170] Engel, *supra* Introduction, note 79, at 438.

[171] *Id.*

[172] *Id.*

[173] *Id.*

[174] *Id.*

[175] See PEW CENTER ON GLOBAL CLIMATE CHANGE, CLIMATE CHANGE 101: LOCAL ACTION (2009), http://www.pewclimate.org/global-warming-basics/climate_change_101.

[176] Engel, *supra* Introduction, note 79, at 434.

[177] Press Release, Boulder Office of Environmental Affairs, "Boulder voters pass first energy tax in the nation," Nov. 8, 2006, http://ci.boulder.co.us/index.php?option=com_content&task=view&id=6136&Itemid=169.

[178] Assem. B. 1493, 2002 Reg. Sess., Cal. Statutes 2002, codified at CAL. HEALTH & SAFETY CODE § 43018.5(a) (directing the standard); California Air Resources Board, *Clean Car Standards - Pavley, Assembly Bill 1493*, Jan. 14, 2010, http://www.arb.ca.gov/cc/ccms/ccms.htm (requesting the waiver from the EPA).

indicated an interest.[179] California is now considering implementing a low-carbon fuel standard, perhaps launching a new national model.[180] Municipalities are also incorporating climate concerns into their land use planning decisions, revising transportation plans and investing in mass transit to reduce vehicle miles traveled, and encouraging carpooling and bicycle commuting.[181]

Finally, states have approached climate governance through more holistic measures. Thirty-eight states either already have or are creating statewide nonbinding climate action plans varying in specificity, baselines, and targets.[182] Seventeen states have statewide emission-reduction targets.[183] States also participate in several greenhouse gas emission registries, which develop uniform protocols for measuring, reporting, and verifying greenhouse gas emissions in several industrial sectors.[184] The largest is the Climate Registry, a not-for-profit organization representing forty states, eleven Canadian provinces, six Mexican states, and three tribal nations.[185] The California Climate Action Registry, formed by the state at the request of energy investors, provides a greenhouse gas registry for organizations to report their emissions and offsets.[186] The Climate Action Reserve is another program that sets standards for measuring carbon offsets for the purpose of credits, pricing, and trade.[187]

Nevertheless, this wealth of state activity may not be enough to cope with the problem, given substantial concerns about leakage and regulatory inefficiencies. Most advocates for climate governance argue that federal leadership is critical. Even state climate governance proponents tend to see regional efforts as a "next-best strategy in the absence of serious national leadership."[188] At the same time, successful state and local initiatives are exceedingly

---

[179] The fourteen states are Arizona, Connecticut, Florida, Maine, Maryland, Massachusetts, New Jersey, New Mexico, New York, Oregon, Pennsylvania, Rhode Island, Vermont, and Washington. JAMES E. McCARTHY & ROBERT MELTZ, CONG. RESEARCH SERV., CALIFORNIA'S WAIVER REQUEST UNDER THE CLEAN AIR ACT TO CONTROL GREENHOUSE GASES FROM MOTOR VEHICLES 4, n.13 (2009), http://ncseonline.org/ NLE/CRSreports/09Mar/RL34099.pdf; Emily Chen, *State Adoption Status on California Vehicle Emissions Control Requirements* (2008), http://www.westar.org/Docs/Business%20Meetings/Spring08/ParkCity/03. 2.2%20CAA%20177%20states.xls (listing states adopting CA emission standards and states considering adoption).

[180] Exec. Order No. S-01-07 by the Governor of the State of California, Jan.18, 2007, http://gov.ca.gov/ executive-order/5172/.

[181] Engel, *supra* Introduction, note 79, at 433–35.

[182] *Id.* at 437. PEW CENTER ON GLOBAL CLIMATE CHANGE, CLIMATE ACTION PLANS, July 21, 2010, http:// www.pewclimate.org/what_s_being_done/in_the_states/action_plan_map.cfm.

[183] PEW CENTER ON GLOBAL CLIMATE CHANGE, A LOOK AT EMISSIONS TARGETS, http://www. pewclimate.org/what_s_being_done/targets (last visited Sept. 29, 2010).

[184] Members of a registry agree to calculate, verify and publicly report their greenhouse gas emissions. THE CLIMATE REGISTRY, WHAT IS THE CLIMATE REGISTRY? 2 (2010), http://www.theclimateregistry.org/ downloads/Registry_Brochure.pdf.

[185] THE CLIMATE REGISTRY, http://www.theclimateregistry.org/(last visited Sept. 29, 2010).

[186] CALIFORNIA CLIMATE ACTION REGISTRY, http://www.climateregistry.org/about.html (last visited Sept. 29, 2010).

[187] CLIMATE ACTION RESERVE, ABOUT US, http://www.climateactionreserve.org/about-us/(last visited Sept. 29, 2010).

[188] *See, e.g.*, McKinstry et al., *supra* note 145, at 3.

vulnerable to preemption against a constitutional backdrop in which most of these initiatives overlap with potential exercises of the federal commerce, property, and foreign affairs powers.[189]

Now that Congress has finally shown some interest in regulating on climate, federalism and preemption issues are no longer hypothetical. The Waxman-Markey bill that passed the House in 2009[190] and the accompanying bills pending in the Senate[191] are all modeled on the existing local, state, and regional efforts, prompting formidable political struggle over how best to manage the overlap. Intersections between a national program and the local initiatives raise difficult issues about where overlap is desirable and where a fully centralized policy is necessary. Waxman-Markey and the corresponding Senate bills incorporate cap-and-trade programs modeled on the state and regional programs that would fully preempt the originals in the early years, on the assumption that a national market for credits and offsets with a single set of rules and oversight offers the best chance at a workable regulatory program.[192] However, broad savings clauses protecting state renewable portfolio standards and other complementary measures demonstrate congressional intent to preserve local initiatives unrelated to cap-and-trade.[193]

As this book goes to press, fluctuating party leadership in the House and partisan gridlock in the Senate render the future of these particular bills unclear. Nevertheless, any future federal attempt at climate legislation will confront the same federalism dilemmas. They ultimately boil down to two: (1) does Congress have the power to regulate all aspects of the problem, or are there realms (such as local land use planning or utility regulation) that are the exclusive purview of the states? And, (2) once federal legislation is passed, then what regulatory role will remain for the states in the realms Congress has legitimately acted? In these early drafts, Congress appears ready to preempt on cap-and-trade while preserving room for state regulation of complementary measures. But uncertainty remains about the extent to which competing state programs can coexist. (And depending on what Congress ultimately decides, there will be plenty of opportunities for field and conflict preemption challenges by regulated parties that may prefer one set of regulations over the other.)

Assuming federal climate legislation follows the model set by existing antipollution laws, valid federal provisions will almost certainly preempt similar state and local regulation less stringent than a designated standard, creating a national regulatory floor under which states cannot deviate downward.[194] But several states have indicated their desire to have the same "meet-or-exceed" flexibility under a greenhouse gas program that they do under most other

---

[189] U.S. Const. art. I, § 8 (commerce power); art. IV, § 3 (property power); art. II, § 2 (treaty power). *See also* Farber, *supra* note 150.

[190] American Clean Energy and Security Act, H.R. 2454, 111th Cong. (2009).

[191] *E.g.*, Clean Energy Jobs & American Power Act, S. 1733, 111th Cong. (2009) ("Kerry-Boxer").

[192] American Clean Energy and Security Act, H.R. 2454, 111th Cong. § 702 (2009).

[193] *Id.* at § 610(c)(1).

[194] William W. Buzbee, *State Greenhouse Gas Regulation, Federal Climate Change Legislation, and the Preemption Sword*, 1 San Diego J. Climate & Energy L. 23, 38 (2009).

environmental laws.[195] For these points of overlap, the questions will revolve around whether the national regulations create a preemptive ceiling as well as a floor.[196] Underscoring the point, the governors of twelve states wrote to President Obama in 2009, expressing their interest in regulating more stringently than a federal cap and advocating how they might do so even within a binding national cap-and-trade program.[197]

If Congress does enact cap-and-trade legislation like that in Waxman-Markey, proposals like these raise serious questions about the extent to which states could continue to regulate in indirect ways that might affect the national carbon market. For example, could states retire in-state credits allocated to them under the national plan, effectively reducing the overall allocation and raising the marginal price of carbon on the national market?[198] Could they regulate to restrict the release of "co-pollutants"—independently harmful substances that accompany greenhouse gas emissions but remain locally distributed—and thus indirectly reduce carbon emissions as well?[199] Could they charge a premium for each ton of carbon emitted within their borders?[200] Could states regulate sources and varieties of greenhouse gasses that are not addressed in the federal program?[201]

Overlapping renewable energy and portfolio standards also raise difficult questions, since the regulation of utilities is a traditional and entrenched area of state law, but Congress is considering a national market in renewable energy credits under its program.[202] Even if

---

[195] Attorneys general from Arizona, California, Connecticut, Delaware, and New Jersey sent a letter to Senate leaders in September 2009 opposing federal limits on states' ability to regulate greenhouse gas emissions. *Senate Urged to Let States Keep Climate Plans,* REUTERS, Sept. 2, 2009, http://www.reuters.com/article/ idUSTRE58064F20090902.

[196] Buzbee, *supra* note 194, at 38.

[197] *See* Letter from Offices of the Governors of California, Connecticut, Florida, Kansas, Maryland, Massachusetts, New Jersey, New Mexico, New York, Oregon, Washington, Wisconsin to the President (Jan. 29, 2009), http://www.governor.wa.gov/news/20090129_climate.pdf.

[198] Nicholas Bianco et al., *Allowing States to Retire Allowances without Affecting National Allowance Prices: A Straw Proposal* (World Resources Institute & The Nicholas Institute Working Paper, 2009), http:// nicholasinstitute.duke.edu/climate/policydesign/allowing-states-to-retire-allowances-without-affecting-national-allowance-prices-a-straw-proposal.

[199] William Buzbee & Victor B. Flatt, *Op-Ed: Tough Caps Would Likely Curb Pollution and Cool Warming,* ATLANTA J.-CONST., May 5, 2009, http://www.ajc.com/opinion/content/opinion/stories/2009/05/05/ proconed_0505.html.

[200] For example, states could decide that 1.1 federal allowances would satisfy compliance under state law for every one ton of carbon emitted by in-state sources, effectively lowering the cap. Catherine S. Hill & Margreta Morgulas, *Regional and State-Based Climate Change Initiatives in the United States,* 10 GOV'T L. & POL'Y J. 41 (2008), http://www.woh.com/img/document_files/State%20Based%20Climate%20Initiatives%20articl e.pdf. This proposal seems especially vulnerable to preemption under the proposed federal bills.

[201] For example, a state could mandate methane capture at all landfills, rather than allowing in-state landfills to trade on methane capture as an offset. *Cf.* Jim Tankersley, *Climate Negotiators Eye the "Forgotten 50%" of Greenhouse Gas Pollutants,* L.A. TIMES, Dec. 14, 2009, http://articles.latimes.com/2009/dec/14/world/ la-fg-climate-emissions14-2009dec14. *See also* Andrew G. Keeler, *State Commission Electricity Regulation under Federal Greenhouse Gas Cap-and-Trade Policy,* THE ELECTRICITY J., May 2008, at 19, 21 (discussing greenhouse gases not covered by the bills).

[202] *Cf.* Buzbee, *supra* note 194, at 37 (arguing against a uniform national approach).

Congress does not expressly preempt state initiatives, they remain vulnerable to various claims of conflict and field preemption under the dormant Commerce Clause and even the foreign affairs power—not to mention the limitations implied for federal reach by New Federalism Tenth Amendment ideals.

While some maintain that a centralized approach is the only way to prevent leakage and maximize efficiency, others argue that preserving climate jurisdictional overlap is our best hope for meaningful climate governance. For example, Professor William Buzbee argues that protecting the integrity of state climate programs is the best way to foster regulatory innovation and ensure the availability of state-based fail-safes if the national program stalls in litigation, is subject to interest group capture, or otherwise fails to accomplish its goals.[203] Indeed, despite Waxman-Markey's passage in the House, the lack of movement in the Senate suggests that the current patchwork of state efforts may be the closest thing to comprehensive U.S. climate governance for some time to come. But assuming national climate legislation eventually passes, federalism-based challenges are sure to ensue regardless of how Congress decides the preemption issues. Challenges will come from those who want either more or less centralization, respectively arguing for more or less preemption.

The challenge for climate governance will be how best to continue reaping the benefits of interjurisdictional innovation and regulatory backstop that local initiatives have thus far provided without undermining the national forces that may ultimately be necessary to produce satisfactory results. It will require implementing a strong centralized program without crippling the laboratories of ideas that have given us our most promising tools to date. The profound breadth of overlap implied by meaningful climate governance suggests that the ramifications of climate federalism will redound in both directions. Federalism will certainly influence the development of American climate policy. And by role modeling the reality and necessity of jurisdictional overlap, climate policy will—in turn—influence the development of American federalism.

3. THE AFTERMATH OF HURRICANE KATRINA

Climate change portends dramatically difficult challenges, but of course, we have already experienced the tragic consequences of poorly managed responses to interjurisdictional crises. Within this framework for understanding jurisdictional overlap, we can now return to the Katrina crisis described in Chapter One, understanding it as a colossal interjurisdictional regulatory problem of both the de jure and de facto variety. Especially in hindsight, it is hard to imagine a serious argument that preparation and response should have proceeded at an exclusively national or local level. Nevertheless, in the shadow of dualist idealism, the White House viewed the Katrina response as a properly state-led project, declining to take more aggressive federal initiative because it viewed avoiding interference with (let alone commandeering) state resources as its highest obligation.[204] Nothing could have proved this view more tragically simplistic than our actual experience in the aftermath of the hurricane.

---

[203] *Id.*

[204] *See supra* Chapter One, notes 104–30, 160–61 and accompanying text.

Katrina was clearly a local problem, demanding the protection of public health and safety and the maintenance of domestic law and order that lie at the heart of traditional state function.[205] State regulatory concern was implicated in the dispatch of first responders with localized expertise, the provision of humanitarian aid for intrastate evacuees, and the protection and salvage of state infrastructure and private property. However, to the extent that the crisis implicated the channels of interstate commerce, the national economy, and the care of interstate evacuees, it was also a matter of national concern.

The Port of New Orleans is the largest shipping port in the United States (measured by tonnage handled),[206] and a sizeable percentage of our domestic energy supplies are pumped, delivered, or shipped via its channels.[207] In addition, a network of twenty thousand miles of oil and gas distribution lines embedded in the New Orleans wetlands provides critical supplies to the rest of the nation,[208] lines so vital that the federal government tapped into the national oil reserves to make up for the shortfall when the network went offline.[209] Residents left homeless and destitute in the wake of the storm soon became refugees requiring assistance in countless other states.[210] Federal responsibility in the crisis may also attach to the federal role in constructing what the Army Corps of Engineers now itself concedes were structurally faulty levees.[211] One scholar has even argued that the anarchy following Katrina rendered federal intervention necessary to fulfill the Constitution's Guarantee Clause, which, in guaranteeing each state "a Republican Form of Government" implicitly promised federal action to preserve at least *some* functioning governance in New Orleans when state and local government had collapsed.[212]

For these reasons, responding to Katrina was indeed the state's obligation—but it was also the nation's obligation. Each possessed critical expertise, authority, and responsibility for different parts of the problem and its solution. Despite the National Response Plan's promise to protect lives, the relief effort failed the thousands of residents who died in their neighborhoods and nursing homes and the thirty-four who died in the Superdome and convention center.[213] Hundreds of thousands of evacuees sought shelter and employment in cities and

---

[205] *See* 16A AM. JUR. 2D *Constitutional Law* § 313 (2006) (noting that the "state cannot surrender, abdicate, or abridge its police power").

[206] Rip Watson, *New Orleans Port Opens to Relief Ships after Katrina*, BLOOMBERG.COM, Sept. 6, 2005, http://www.bloomberg.com/apps/news?pid=10000082&sid=adNXIjdn4Z8Q; Simon Romero, *A Barren Port Waits Eagerly For Its People*, N.Y. TIMES, Oct. 6, 2005, at C1 (noting its significance to the national economy).

[207] Thanks to the proximity of carbon-based fuels in the Gulf of Mexico to the Port, the region is perhaps the most important energy hub in the continental United States, supplying nearly 20 percent of domestic demand for oil and natural gas. Robert Viguerie, *Coastal Erosion: Crisis in Louisiana's Wetlands*, 51 LA. B.J. 85, 86 (2003).

[208] *Stemming the Tide: The Mississippi River Delta and the Davis Pond Freshwater Diversion Project*, LACOAST. GOV, http://www.lacoast.gov/programs/DavisPond/stemming-the-tide.htm (last visited Mar. 15, 2007).

[209] Jad Mouawad & Vikas Bajaj, *Gulf Oil Operations Remain in Disarray*, N.Y. TIMES, Sept. 2, 2005, at C1.

[210] *See supra* Chapter One, notes 138–139 and accompanying text.

[211] *See supra* Chapter One, note 156 (discussing the Army Corps' concession that levee designs were flawed).

[212] U.S. CONST. art. IV, § 4; Greenberger, *supra* Chapter One, note 118, at 123.

[213] *See supra* Chapter One, notes 131–32 and accompanying text.

towns across the nation, and federal expenditures on emergency housing for them amounted to millions of dollars each day. Oil spills and damaged infrastructure spiked the price of fuel nationwide, triggering fears ranging from a national recession to an increase in domestic terrorist activity. With up to 25 percent of New Orleans's housing stock condemned,[214] an epidemic of crime that has persisted more than a year after the storm,[215] and environmental hazards threatening health and safety into the foreseeable future,[216] there is no quick end to the crisis in sight.

In other words, everyone had a stake—but as we now well know, the bifurcated disaster response itself proved disastrous. As the stories of failure after failure in the relief effort unfolded, culpability fell on city, state, and federal agencies alike. The City of New Orleans should have considered how the 100,000 New Orleans residents without motor vehicles would heed Mayor Nagin's evacuation command. The State of Louisiana should have considered moving the National Guard headquarters that would coordinate hurricane response to higher ground before the storm. The federal government apparently failed to heed National Weather Service warnings about the scope of the storm, and failed to deploy FEMA resources appropriately before it. The federal government should have intervened sooner when it became clear (at least to the average American watching the nightly news) that local efforts to confront the hurricane aftermath were insufficient. And when it finally did intervene, it should have been able to impose a more effective chain of command to facilitate decision making in the midst of a thousands-of-lives-at-stake crisis, with or without Governor Blanco's help.

From the constitutional perspective, it is these last failures that are most troubling, given reports about the White House debate over the federalism implications of taking initiative, and former FEMA Director Michael Brown's congressional testimony explaining the reluctant federal response (whether disingenuously or not) in overtly separationist terms.[217] The New Federalism decisions themselves did not erect an explicit doctrinal barrier to the needed interjurisdictional response, but they define a trajectory pointing state and federal leadership toward the classical model of dual federalism that either convinced or confused them about the available regulatory choices. The fact that the crisis was a legitimate matter of state concern did not foreclose the fact that it was also a matter of legitimate federal concern, demanding proactive federal intervention from within the federalism order.

The Katrina debacle illustrated the risks of applying a binary decision rule in interjurisdictional contexts—characterizing matters as "either/or": if national, then not local; if local,

---

[214] See Adam Nossiter, *Thousands of Demolitions Near, New Orleans Braces for New Pain*, N.Y. TIMES, Oct. 23, 2005, at § 1 (noting that over fifty thousand of the city's 180,000 homes could be demolished).

[215] See Brandon L. Garrett & Tania Tetlow, *Criminal Justice Collapse: The Constitution after Hurricane Katrina*, 56 DUKE L.J. 127, 135–54 (2006) (describing the collapse of the New Orleans criminal justice system after Katrina); Adam Nossiter, *Storm Left New Orleans Ripe for Violence*, N.Y. TIMES, Jan. 11, 2007, at A24 (same).

[216] See EPA, Response to 2005 Hurricanes: Frequent Questions, http://www.epa.gov/katrina/faqs.htm (last visited Mar. 15, 2007) (forum to address health- and safety-related issues for the residents of the New Orleans area).

[217] See supra Chapter One, notes 160–61 and accompanying text.

then not national. Taken to its extreme, this approach obstructs effective governance by assigning jurisdiction over a matter requiring both a local and national response to *either* state *or* federal agents exclusively, and then zealously guarding the boundary against defensible (or even desirable) crossover by the other. But this is a nonsensical approach when the problem requires both local and national competencies. The dualist model regards regulatory activity as permissible if it fits neatly within the state or federal box anticipated by its test, and impermissible if it does not. But what if the problem is not with the activity, but with the limitations of a simple, two-box test?

If nothing else, Katrina has taught us that interjurisdictional regulatory problems require us, quite literally, to think outside the dual federalism boxes. Michael Brown memorably intoned (from squarely within the box) that the principles of federalism "should not be lost in a short-term desire to react to a natural disaster of catastrophic proportions," fretting that a more proactive federal response would have undermined the very foundations of dual sovereignty.[218] His testimony sadly demonstrates how dualist thinking failed Katrina victims not for lack of good intentions, but for lack of imagination.

Once the thirty-nine thousand refugees had left the "Third World hellhole" that became New Orleans in the days after the storm,[219] a pause for reflection enabled greater sympathy for how White House officials got mired in federalism theory. Faithful to the separationist ideals of the New Federalism movement, they hesitated to invoke potential Stafford Act authority to intrude upon the state's primary role as the provider of intrastate relief and law enforcement services. But the interjurisdictional nature of the Katrina emergency demonstrates how a problem shaped beyond the comprehension of the operative theoretical model can cause the entire system to crash. Interjurisdictional problems exacerbate the tension between underlying federalism values, and dual federalism is ill-equipped to handle them. Although symptoms had been evident in foundering responses to slower-unfolding problems beforehand (e.g., radioactive waste disposal and asthma in Los Angeles), the Katrina debacle brought home to the nation a clear message: a legal framework built around a theory misaligned with the real-world targets of regulatory response is not only unstable, but unsustainable.

It also suggested an alternative, at least in the Katrina response that most Americans collectively imagined was possible. In this vision, the federal government would have assessed the demand for regulatory crossover and weighed the costs of proactive intervention against each of the federalism values at stake. It would have considered its own obligations, the capacity of the state and local governments to respond, and the relative risks to dual sovereignty of crossing into the gray area. The state and local governments would have made a similar evaluation, at least to the extent of their respective capacities. Most Americans apparently believed that the federal interest in saving the lives and relieving the human suffering of its own citizens far overwhelmed the risks to inter-sovereign diplomacy,[220] but in any event,

---

[218] See *September 27 Katrina Hearing, supra* Chapter One, note 70, at 3 (statement of Michael Brown).

[219] Thomas et al., *supra* Chapter One, note 66, at 40.

[220] See *supra* Chapter One, note 153 and accompanying text (reviewing public disapproval of the federal response).

a conclusion would have been reached more efficiently and decisively if officials were freed from the paralysis of separationist idealism.

This paralysis reflects perhaps the most serious trap of binary thinking promoted by the New Federalism revival, which is its essential suggestion that we must choose between *either* federalism *or* interjurisdictional problem solving. Either we are faithful to the constitutional ideal of dual sovereignty, or we can effectively grapple with the collective action problems that we ask regulation to help us control. New Federalism frames this as the choice by positing its separationist vision of checks and balances as synonymous with federalism in general. But the check-and-balance value is only *one* of the principles of good government that undergird American federalism—and it may be enhanced by jurisdictional overlap as well as separation. Either way, it competes with the accountability, localism, and problem-solving values that are equally in tension. The interpretive model of federalism that we choose determines how we mediate these tensions, and the dualist solution privileges checks over all others. So does faithfulness to federalism require that we forsake interjurisdictional problem solving of the sort Katrina demanded? It depends on the operative federalism model. Some may suggest so, but the model proposed in this book suggests not.

Instead, federalism interpretation should draw on a theory that honors the balance of state and federal power while affording flexibility for government at all levels to address the problems we entrust to their care. If the New Federalism's model cannot accommodate the dimensions of the interjurisdictional gray area, then it must be adjusted until it can. Whether an act of regulatory crossover violates the Constitution should depend on consideration of all the values that inform our system of dual sovereignty—not just the strict separation of state and federal powers for its own sake. Once again, the choice is not between federalism or not, but rather *which theoretical model* encourages the best balance of the values that motivate federalism to begin with.

Balanced Federalism

A COHERENT MODEL of federalism that supports a healthy balance of local and national authority while enabling effective governance remains a central task of public law. To remedy the theoretical problems unresolved by cooperative federalism and those resurrected by the New Federalism revival, this part introduces an alternative—one that would foster more thoughtful balance among the federalism values that, through their network of tension, fortifies our system against the challenges of change. As elaborated in the chapters that follow, it would also balance the unique interpretive capacities that the different branches of government offer in support of these goals, and ultimately, the wisdom of both state and federal actors. In honor of these critical points of equipoise, I call this model "Balanced Federalism."

Balanced Federalism better mediates the core federalism conflicts and enables more transparent guidance for regulatory decision makers. It accounts for each of the federalism values and proposes jurisprudential tools to help actualize its goal of preserving both checks and balance in an interjurisdictional world. It proceeds from a more mature understanding of dual sovereignty, in which the Tenth Amendment is concerned not with protecting the bright line where it is illusory but with adjudicating unacceptable compromise to the federalism values on which dual sovereignty is premised. Importantly, it matches emphasis on balancing the core values with balancing the capacities of the three branches in safeguarding them, on both the state and federal sides. Although the model presumes that all governmental actors have a role to play, Chapter Six begins with judicial safeguards in narrative deference for Part II's focus on the New Federalism, saving fuller discussion of political safeguards for Chapter Seven and Part IV.

Balanced Federalism departs little from its predecessors in interpretation of the easy cases, where even cooperative federalism and New Federalism supporters often agree. However, it provides better means for coping with the more difficult cases through a new set of conceptual and operational tools. Unlike dual federalism, Balanced Federalism theory accounts for the interjurisdictional gray area that heightens federalism tensions. It forces interpreters to acknowledge each of the federalism values in any given conflict, and to justify interpretive choices that prioritize among them in an open and accountable way. Unlike cooperative federalism, Balanced Federalism provides more fully theorized justification for gray area regulation, and more meaningful safeguards through limited judicial review that protects all federalism values. Unlike modern New Federalism, it emphasizes the interpretive potential of the political branches and more tightly circumscribes judicial intervention in the political process.

This part articulates the theoretical approach of the new model and offers the first two stages for thinking about a transition toward more fully Balanced Federalism. The proposal is theoretically driven but pragmatically introduced, designed to displace as little operative doctrine as possible in order to place the possibility of adaption within realistic reach. Focusing on the judicial role, Chapter Six offers a proposal for reconstituting Tenth Amendment doctrine, replacing the anti-commandeering doctrine with a judicial balancing test that considers commandeering, preemption, and other federalism claims that may not be justiciable under existing doctrine (such as unfunded mandates). Regardless of the claim, the query is always whether the challenged regulatory governance ultimately advances or detracts from the values underlying federalism, taken as a whole. Chapter Seven focuses more specifically on the anti-commandeering rule, altering the remedy rule to enable a greater legislative role with more limited judicial review and taking fuller account of state input, bridging Part III to Part IV's fuller consideration of the role of the political branches at all levels of government. Because it most directly conveys the values-balancing heart of the Balanced Federalism project, however, I begin with the balancing test.

Chapter Six imagines how the judicially enforceable constraints resurrected by New Federalism would change under Balanced Federalism, focusing on the Tenth Amendment. Where dual federalism asks the Tenth Amendment to police the boundary between mutually exclusive spheres of state and federal authority from crossover, Balanced Federalism asks the Tenth Amendment to patrol regulatory activity within the gray area for impermissible compromises to federalism's underlying values. As the Tenth Amendment implicitly frames all other federalism doctrine, a more refined understanding should eventually yield greater clarity to all corners of federalism discourse. To enable formal adjudication, Chapter Six introduces the elements of a balancing test for interpreting Tenth Amendment claims in lieu of the New Federalism anti-commandeering doctrine. The chapter illustrates how the balancing test might work in four concrete examples, and concludes with a defense of judicial balancing as a tool of constitutional interpretation in the federalism context.

Nevertheless, the federal judicial discretion enabled under the balancing test is progressively moderated by the second and third stages of the Balanced Federalism proposal, which call for greater judicial deference to the interpretive activity of state and federal political actors. Chapter Seven proposes a modest modification to the anti-commandeering rule that would require judicial deference to consensual state-federal legislative bargaining over federalism entitlements. Using *New York v. United States* as a case study, it identifies the federalism entitlements that the Constitution creates and the remedy rules the Court has chosen to protect them. It shows how more consistent use of the property remedy rule could free intergovernmental legislative bargaining to advance Balanced Federalism goals in the way it is already free under the commerce and spending power doctrines. Such bilateral bargaining is uniquely structured to balance competing federalism values through the consensual exchange of state and federal interests and expertise. Chapter Seven's intermediate proposal for judicial deference to intergovernmental bargaining with federalism entitlements lays foundation for the full negotiated federalism proposal in Part IV.

THE ROLE OF THE COURTS: TENTH AMENDMENT BALANCING

THIS CHAPTER OFFERS a preliminary exploration of how Balanced Federalism theory would depart from the status quo, imagining the strongest judicial role within such a model. It sets forth the theoretical ideal, factors for judicial consideration, and mechanics of how judicially enforceable Balanced Federalism constraints could work in lieu of existing New Federalism Tenth Amendment doctrine. It illustrates a proposed judicial balancing test for Tenth Amendment claims through cursory application to four concrete federalism controversies: the regulation of stormwater pollution, climate governance, the Katrina response, and national health insurance reform.

Finally, the chapter rebuts the most powerful critiques of the balancing approach, including indeterminacy, untethered reasoning, judicial bias, and separation of powers. In a world with any judicial federalism constraints, explicit judicial federalism balancing is preferable because judicial values-balancing is inevitable—either covertly in application of another doctrinal rule, or through the initial act of judicial balancing that produced the doctrinal rule.

Legitimate concerns about expansive judicial discretion lay the foundation for discussion in Chapter Seven and Part IV of how the judiciary should work in tandem with—and in greater deference to—the federalism determinations of the political branches of both state and federal government. Although state and federal courts would both apply the balancing test, jointly fleshing out its ideals through incremental application over time, the U.S. Supreme Court would define its ultimate contours, diminishing state input in comparison to the intergovernmental partnerships emphasized in later chapters. Nevertheless, the judicial balancing test proposed here is a good way to introduce the Balanced Federalism model because of the way it so literally demonstrates the project of balancing the competing federalism values.

A. Toward a Balanced Federalism

Unlike dual or cooperative federalism, Balanced Federalism explicitly recognizes the competition among checks, accountability, localism, and problem-solving values, and provides a theoretically grounded means of mediating among them when conflicts arise. In addition, Balanced Federalism rejects the mutually exclusive spheres of dual federalism idealism for an understanding of dual sovereignty that includes an indeterminate gray area of overlapping, interjurisdictional concern. The model assumes that the jurisprudential consensus on the "uncontroversial" spheres of state and federal power will continue to shift as it has throughout history, but it also assumes a perpetual zone of overlap that implicates both local and national concern. The proposals in Parts III and IV provide administrable means of arbitrating dispute in the gray area whenever the times allege it.

Conflicting state law would continue to be preempted in the uncontroversial sphere of federal authority, but the preemption inquiry would shift in the interjurisdictional gray area, returning force to the long-standing presumption against preemption of traditional state police power unless Congress has explicitly and legitimately required it. (Among other benefits, requiring Congress to clearly express its intent to preempt state law would enhance its accountability to the electorate, rather than allowing such decisions to be politically diluted among agency and judicial interpreters.) Correspondingly, federal policy makers would continue to respect the primacy of state authority in its uncontroversial sphere and avoid regulatory encroachment into the gray area until interjurisdictional factors demand capacity available only at the national level.

Balanced Federalism dual sovereignty would also require a shift in the work of the Tenth Amendment. As described in Chapter Five, a state or federal actor threatens constitutional values under the classical dualist model whenever it regulates beyond its own uncontroversial sphere and into the interjurisdictional gray area at its margin. As construed in New Federalism, the Tenth Amendment implicitly polices this boundary, punishing transgressions from either side and framing other affirmative limits on federal power. In Balanced Federalism, such regulatory reach is conceived not as crossover from the permissible into the impermissible realm, but from the *unqualified* into the *qualified* realm of jurisdiction.[1] As now, crossover from one uncontroversial sphere past the gray area and all the way into the other would be immediately preempted (if by the state) or invalidated (if by the federal government)—but crossover into the gray area would require additional consideration. As construed in Balanced Federalism, the Tenth Amendment polices challenged regulatory activity in the gray area by either side, testing the potential threats and benefits of such crossover against the fundamental federalism values. Policy makers and adjudicators must balance the degree to which the advancement of one federalism value is or is not outweighed by harm to competing values.

Chapter Six imagines the most ambitious role that the judiciary might play in such a legal regime, contrasting judicially enforceable Balanced Federalism constraints against the judicially enforceable constraints reinvigorated by the Rehnquist Court. In Balanced Federalism,

---

[1] *See supra* "Reconceptualizing Regulatory Crossover," Chapter Five, Section B(1), text preceding note 86.

challenged activity in the gray area would be reviewed with heightened scrutiny for overall faithfulness to the panoply of federalism values for which the Tenth Amendment stands. Given their tug of war, this analysis would require more explicit judicial balancing than the status quo—the threat of which incentivizes careful balancing in ex ante policy making by political actors. However, the balancing test would force more transparency in judicial decision making about how balancing is effected, providing greater guidance to regulators. Conversely, judicial deference to explicitly reasoned balancing behind political decisions would encourage greater accountability and transparency in policy making as well.

Application of this model thus hinges on the development of a jurisprudential test for acceptable regulatory crossover within Balanced Federalism dual sovereignty. To reiterate a critical point, the judicial balancing test is only one tool among many for realizing a more Balanced Federalism—but in honor of Part II's critique of New Federalism judicial constraints, it is where Part III begins.

B. Judicially Enforceable Balanced Federalism Constraints

Although Balanced Federalism ideals could conceivably alter other judicially enforceable federalism doctrines, this exploration begins with the Tenth Amendment, that textual ambassador of the constitutional dual sovereignty that informs all other federalism inquiries. As the Tenth Amendment most encapsulates the dual sovereignty directive,[2] it is the proper point of departure for the evaluation of federalism threats that are not addressed by more specific federalism doctrines (such as the commerce power or state sovereign immunity). It would remain available as the primary means of evaluating allegations of commandeering, but could also afford a remedy against undue preemption, unfunded mandates, or any other federalism claim not more directly treated by other doctrine. Consideration would focus on whether the challenged governance ultimately serves or disserves Balanced Federalism as a whole, with reference to each of the foundational federalism values.

The articulation of such a standard would do for the Tenth Amendment what has already been done for nearly every other operative provision in the Bill of Rights, each of which has required the crafting of interpretative rules by which to administer the constitutional rule it sets forth. The Eighth Amendment tells us that cruel and unusual punishment is prohibited, but lacks specific direction as to whether the execution of minors is unconstitutional.[3] The Fourth Amendment prohibits unreasonable searches and seizures, but remains silent on the use of drug-sniffing dogs during traffic stops.[4] The Tenth Amendment tells us that powers not delegated to the federal government are reserved to the states, offering even fewer specifics than most of its nine predecessors.[5] As Chapter One explained, a penumbral reading of

---

[2] *See supra* Chapter One, notes 4–32 and accompanying text.

[3] U.S. CONST. amend. VIII.

[4] U.S. CONST. amend. IV.

[5] U.S. CONST. amend. X. The exception may be found in the Ninth Amendment. *See* U.S. CONST. amend. IX ("The enumeration in the Constitution, of certain rights, shall not be construed to deny or disparage others retained by the people."). The Ninth Amendment's textual vagueness has left it relatively off the table of constitutional interpretation, save for the efforts of Justice Goldberg to ground in the Ninth Amendment the

the Constitution confirms its structural premise that the state and federal governments would operate simultaneously from separate sources of authority, but the Tenth Amendment itself gives no direction on where the line between state and federal power lies (nor even about what kind of boundary it is).[6] Its directive is meaningful only in concert with other constitutional provisions enumerating federal powers and limitations—none of which has settled the long debate.

Indeed, it is not surprising that they don't, as the Constitution's resilience has so often flowed from the interpretive possibilities preserved by its brevity—just specific enough to convey the foundational rule of law, just flexible enough to allow for evolving rules of interpretation that mediate between the enduring principles and changing social facts. Formal amendment is required only when substantive textual commands must give way, for example, to outlaw slavery, enfranchise women, or permit the unapportioned federal income tax.[7] But none of the Bill of Rights has ever required amendment; indeed, it is doubtful that their directives could be improved upon without compromising their potency. In this way, the First Amendment made sense in 1789 and it makes sense today, despite ambiguous moments at the margins of interpretive turnover—such as the Tenth Amendment now invites.

The First Amendment has received attention from the judiciary for well over one hundred years, and the body of jurisprudential rules that have developed around it reflects this volume of consideration.[8] By contrast, Tenth Amendment dual sovereignty has been the focus of sustained judicial attention only three times in the last century, in only a handful of significant cases. It is not surprising that the Tenth Amendment lacks rules of interpretation to translate its underlying principle into an ascertainable directive amid the thicket of competing values that arise in real cases and controversies. Yet the Supreme Court periodically takes the affirmative step of providing needed guidance to governmental actors regarding complicated areas of law.[9]

---

penumbral right to privacy. Griswold v. Connecticut, 381 U.S. 479, 490–92 (1965) (Goldberg, J., concurring). *But see* Barnett, *supra* Introduction, note 62, at 80 (arguing that the Ninth Amendment should be read literally to "prohibit[] constitutional constructions . . . that infringe upon the unenumerated, natural, and individual rights retained by the people").

[6] *See supra* Chapter One, notes 4–34 and accompanying text.

[7] *See* U.S. CONST. amend. XIII (outlawing slavery); U.S. CONST. amend. XIX (enfranchising women); U.S. CONST. amend. XVI (permitting taxation without apportionment).

[8] *See* Reynolds v. United States, 98 U.S. 145, 162–67 (1878) (interpreting it to enable the outlawing of polygamy). The sophistication of First Amendment jurisprudence has led to various tests for different circumstances. *See, e.g.*, Brandenburg v. Ohio, 395 U.S. 444, 447 (1969) (per curiam) (articulating one standard for determining when the government may abridge freedom of speech); Clark v. Cmty. for Creative Non-Violence, 468 U.S. 288, 293 (1984) (articulating another permitting it by "reasonable time, place, or manner restrictions").

[9] For example, in Penn Central Transportation Co. v. New York City, 438 U.S. 104, 124, 128 (1978), the Court adopted a three-factor balancing test for interpreting the Fifth Amendment's taking prohibition in regulatory contexts (evaluating the character of state action, the extent of its interference with investment-backed expectations, and its overall economic impact). In Motor Vehicle Manufacturers Ass'n v. State Farm Mut. Automobile Ins. Co., the Court supplemented the Administrative Procedures Act's vague proscription of "arbitrary and capricious" agency action with a four-factor test to facilitate judicial review. 463 U.S. 29 (1983); *see id.* at 42–43.

Models for a Tenth Amendment jurisprudential standard are available among the rules of interpretation that have developed around the First, Fourth, Fifth, and Eighth Amendments and the Commerce Clause, bargaining rules that the Court has promulgated to constrain the federal spending power[10] and municipal regulatory exactions,[11] and such common law balancing tests as the Hand formula of tort law.[12] Moreover, prior scholarship has shown how to tailor such a standard to take account of the fact-rich scenarios that accompany specific constitutional dilemmas. Professor Michelman demonstrated this in identifying the elements that inform the regulatory takings balancing test adopted by the Court in *Penn Central Transportation Co. v. New York City*.[13] Close analysis of the tension between federalism values reveals a similar series of factors that warrant consideration when regulation crosses into the interjurisdictional gray area.

C. Factors for Consideration

As do the Court's balancing tests in *Penn Central*, *Pike v. Bruce Church, Inc.*,[14] and other areas of law that sport competing values, the Balanced Federalism Tenth Amendment standard would balance purpose and effects, considering the check-and-balance, accountability, localism, and problem-solving values explored in Chapter Two. It would enable appropriate redress whenever a plaintiff with standing shows that regulatory activity in the gray area unduly threatens the constitutional federalism directive.

A threshold consideration for the reviewing court would be whether the challenged regulatory activity is taking place within the interjurisdictional gray area or one of the uncontroversial spheres of state and federal authority retained in the Balanced Federalism model of dual sovereignty. As described above, Balanced Federalism recognizes three jurisdictional zones: the two settled areas of exclusive state and federal authority at the (contingent) extremes of the spectrum, and the (contingent) gray area between them, where regulatory matters implicate both state and federal interests or obligations. Facilitated by a gatekeeping inquiry, the initial determination would control which standard the court would apply to evaluate the challenged regulation.

---

[10] *E.g.*, South Dakota v. Dole, 483 U.S. 203, 207–08 (1987) (limiting it by three general restrictions and a separate constitutional bar).

[11] *See* Dolan v. City of Tigard, 512 U.S. 374, 386–91 (1994) (requiring "rough proportionality" between the municipal regulation and the intended use of property); Nollan v. Cal. Coastal Comm'n, 483 U.S. 825, 837 (1987) (requiring a demonstrable nexus between the regulation and the legitimate government purpose).

[12] *See* United States v. Carroll Towing Co., 159 F.2d 169, 173 (2d Cir. 1947); *see also* Ronald J. Allen & Ross M. Rosenberg, *Legal Phenomena, Knowledge and Theory: A Cautionary Tale of Hedgehogs and Foxes*, 77 CHI.-KENT L. REV. 683, 695 (2002) (discussing the Hand formula as a type of balancing approach).

[13] 438 U.S. 104, 124, 128 (1978); *see also* Frank I. Michelman, *Property, Utility, and Fairness: Comments on the Ethical Foundations of "Just Compensation" Law*, 80 HARV. L. REV. 1165, 1226–45 (1967) (proposing the elements that would form the basis of the Court's three-factor balancing test).

[14] 397 U.S. 137 (1970); *see id.* at 142, 145 (employing a balancing test to determine whether a legitimate state interest outweighed the nature of the burden imposed on interstate commerce).

To summarize the mechanics (discussed more fully below the factors), if the challenged activity takes place within the regulator's own settled sphere—for example, a federal patent regulation[15]—then the challenge fails to state a Tenth Amendment claim. If the challenged activity represents regulatory crossover fully into the uncontroversial sphere of the other side—for example, state patent regulation—then strict scrutiny is applied, and the Balanced Federalism Tenth Amendment standard is not needed, as the challenged regulatory activity fails constitutional requirements without further analysis. But if there is a nonfrivolous basis for characterizing the challenged activity as within the gray area, then the court applies the Tenth Amendment multifactor test. Of note, because the rough boundaries these zones imply are themselves contingent, application of the balancing test itself may move them over time.

In applying the test to evaluate challenged regulatory activity in the gray area, a court would consider to what extent the activity either supports or derogates: (1) checks and balances, (2) governmental accountability, (3) localism values, and (4) problem solving. After weighing these findings in consideration of the factual context of the crossover, the court would conclude whether, on balance, the challenged activity serves or disserves the principles of constitutional federalism. Were the Supreme Court to adopt a balancing test like this, incremental application of the test over time would reveal the most important factors for consideration. But as a point of departure, deliberation might take account of the following considerations, based on the concerns raised in the principal cases reviewed in Part II.

1. CHECKS AND BALANCES

In considering whether the challenged activity enhances or detracts from checks and balances, decision makers should consider such factors as consent or waiver by the adversely affected party, the scope and duration of the crossover, the nature of the crossover, and the degree to which the crossover is designed to prevent tyrannical abuse of sovereign authority or abdication of sovereign responsibility.

a. Waiver by Adversely Affected Party

Waiver by the adversely affected party merits attention in evaluating threats to the check-and-balance value, because consent should negate the fear of tyrannical abuses. For example, the *New York* holding was most persuasive to the extent it addressed an act of legislative commandeering, but least persuasive to the extent that the regulatory crossover had been invited by the state plaintiff. New York may well have waived its Tenth Amendment objection when, together with the other states, it asked Congress to engage in the challenged regulatory crossover by ratifying state consensus as federal law. The states did so based on a subsidiarity-informed conviction that they lacked the capacity to resolve their collective action problem by other means. In a move that seemed other than tyrannical, Congress declined to exercise available plenary federal authority to defer to the states' expressed preference for a more localist approach.

---

[15] U.S. CONST. art. I, § 8 (delegating patent and copyright regulation to Congress).

Especially troubling in the *New York* decision was Justice O'Connor's explanation that a state's consent is no defense to a Tenth Amendment violation, because the Tenth Amendment protects the rights of individuals, not state agents who might bargain away the individual rights of their citizens.[16] As detailed in Chapter Seven, her analysis leaves unclear what theory of representation is employed if citizens do not elect their agents to represent their interests. We should be able to assume that a state would not bargain for crossover against its interests, and that its consent preserves even the classical check-and-balance value against tyrannical assault. Waiver is thus a factor; a challenge leveled by one who has not consented should weigh more heavily than a challenge by one who has.

b. Scope of the Regulatory Crossover

The standard should also consider the scope of the crossover, measured over time or in degree of compromise. In *Printz*, Congress was held to have commandeered the executive authority of the states in temporarily requiring state police officers to perform background checks on would-be gun purchasers while the federal government established the facilities to run such checks itself.[17] The Supreme Court concluded that any amount of commandeering—admittedly, the most severe form of regulatory crossover—violates the Tenth Amendment,[18] no matter how small or how temporary. Whether or not the challenged federal law was correctly construed as commandeering, however, both the temporariness and degree of crossover should be relevant considerations in the balancing test. Obviously, longer and larger crossover has the potential to threaten the check-and-balance value more seriously than shorter and lesser crossover. The Court recognizes similar dimensions in measuring the degree of harm when it uses balancing to evaluate alleged regulatory takings.[19]

For example, Justice O'Connor distinguished the background checks required in *Printz* from the Department of Justice's missing children reporting requirement on the grounds that the latter was a more "ministerial" requirement, indicating one less severe in scope and thus less threatening to federalism.[20] However, the fact that the background checks was a temporary requirement while the missing child reporting requirements are permanent indicates that the background checks were less severe over time. Indeed, when coupled with a compelling short-term problem-solving need (for example, the immediate Katrina relief effort), a large, temporary crossover may be less threatening to the check-and-balance value than a small but permanent crossover, which could threaten a more pernicious slippery slope.

---

[16] *See* New York v. United States, 505 U.S. 144, 182–83 (1992).

[17] Printz v. United States, 521 U.S. 898, 933 (1997).

[18] *Id.* at 935.

[19] *See* Tahoe-Sierra Pres. Council, Inc. v. Tahoe Reg'l Planning Agency, 535 U.S. 302, 331–32 (2002) ("An interest in real property is defined by the metes and bounds that describe its geographic dimensions and the term of years that describes the temporal aspect of the owner's interest. Both dimensions must be considered if the interest is to be viewed in its entirety.").

[20] *Printz*, 521 U.S. at 936 (O'Connor, J., concurring).

c. Nature of the Crossover

The nature of the crossover is also an important consideration; compulsion and commandeering warrant stricter scrutiny than displacement or self-contained regulatory activity in the gray area. However, even the nature of an alleged act of commandeering warrants consideration. Legislative commandeering (such as that invalidated in *New York*) is the most severe form of crossover because it targets the creative center of state governance. Accordingly, it is rightly subject to the most searching scrutiny under the standard. By contrast, alleged executive commandeering requires more nuanced consideration, because federal regulation of state executive actors performing ministerial or market-participant activities is less threatening to checks and balances than federal regulation of executive rulemaking.

As the discussion of *Reno v. Condon* in Chapter Four suggests, persuasively differentiating the two will be difficult, hinging on consideration of all the factors in play.[21] Following Justice O'Connor's intuition in her *Printz* concurrence, the requirement that states report missing children to a federal database seems defensible, especially if there are no other means for resolving kidnappings that may cross state lines. The interference with state sovereign activity would be limited in scope to ministerial activity, while the problem of protecting kidnapped children vulnerable under purely intrastate enforcement is particularly compelling.

Following Justice O'Connor's other intuition, the requirement that state law enforcers report criminal background information to gun dealers as part of a federal program might exceed the acceptable strain on check-and-balance or accountability values if the federal government could fulfill the role directly within a reasonable time period. Alternatively, it might prove an acceptable strain if the federal government could not produce the database quickly and the risk of public safety during the time lag were substantial. Notwithstanding the right to bear arms, mass shootings by mentally ill citizens with legally purchased weapons—such as the 2007 Virginia Tech massacre and the 2011 Tucson shootings at a political rally for Congresswoman Gabrielle Giffords—intensify this question of fact.

d. Extent to Which Crossover Thwarts Exploitation of Sovereign Power against Individuals

Checks and balances protect citizens from the abuse and abdication of sovereign power by either the federal or state government. Accordingly, the extent to which crossover thwarts exploitation or abdication of sovereign power is also a valid consideration. Indeed, a legal realist interpretation of the disjuncture between *Reno v. Condon* and its predecessors suggests that these considerations may have already played a (perhaps subconscious) role in the Supreme Court's most recent Tenth Amendment case.

In *Condon*, the Court avoided finding commandeering on grounds that the Driver's Privacy Protection Act (DPPA) did not truly invade the states' sovereign authority.[22] Perhaps, although a more cynical interpretation of the decision is that the Court simply lacked sympathy for what South Carolina wanted to do with its citizens' personal data. As considered under the balancing test, the challenged federal law prevented the

---

[21] 528 U.S. 141 (2000).

[22] *Id.* at 151.

nonconsensual dissemination by states of citizens' personal data. This protected individuals against government exploitation when they sought official identification and permission to drive—two critical gateways to participation in modern society that only the state may grant. Regulatory crossover designed to protect individuals against the state, as the DPPA did, should fare better in the analysis than nakedly self-aggrandizing crossover.

2. ACCOUNTABILITY

The decision maker should consider the extent to which regulatory crossover enhances or detracts from governmental accountability, and the extent to which these problems can be effectively mitigated. The analysis should consider the potential for voter confusion and other negative impacts on citizens' participation in the democratic process. Crossover that meaningfully hampers citizens' ability to understand, oversee, and participate in their own governance at whatever level warrants serious scrutiny. The analysis should also consider the possibility that crossover enhances governmental accountability, if it enables policy making in the venue that best enhances democratic participation and oversight.

a. Potential for Mitigation

In some cases, crossover that threatens voter confusion might be salvaged by effective public explanation. If voters can be reasonably made to understand which regulators are responsible for which regulatory choices, then accountability concerns might be overcome. For example, the Phase II Stormwater Rule upheld in *Environmental Defense Center* partnered federal and municipal regulators in an effort to abate stormwater pollution, blurring lines of accountability in an already tricky interjurisdictional zone. However, it also included a public education campaign to ensure that citizens be given the tools to understood what the program was for, how it would work within each municipality, and who was responsible for which aspects of regulatory decision making in each locale. Similarly, the Obama administration's Open Government Initiative seeks to demystify federal regulation by publishing explanations and supporting data on the Internet.

b. Purpose and Effects

If accountability concerns cannot be effectively mitigated through transparency and communication, then they should weigh more heavily in the analysis. For example, crossover that shoulders the adversely affected party with significant financial or political burdens warrants additionally heightened scrutiny if it is purposefully done to obfuscate accountability. The adjudicator should scrutinize objections to an unfunded federal mandate to state governments if the cost-shifting mandate creates unavoidable voter confusion without a compelling rationale, or if it seriously undermines the state's ability to perform on other core regulatory obligations.

3. LOCALISM VALUES

The decision maker should consider the extent to which the regulatory crossover would assist or undermine federalism values associated with the protection of local autonomy, including the protection of localized diversity and the promotion of efficiency and innovation through interjurisdictional competition.

a. Extent to Which Crossover Protects Local Autonomy (Against Federal, State, or Other Local Power)

Some states apply a "home-rule" system that encourages local autonomy (e.g., New York), while others regulate in a more centralized manner (e.g., "Dillon Rule" states such as Virginia). When important localism values are under-protected at the state level, crossover by a municipality responding to a pressing localized problem may deserve greater deference. For example, despite broad federal authority over the regulation of air pollution, the South Coast Air Quality Management District may have acted defensibly in the gray area to protect the respiratory health of children vulnerable to the effects of unusually severe local air pollution.[23]

Conversely, even centralized regulatory crossover may warrant deference on localism grounds when it is the only means of accomplishing locally desired objectives obstructed by negative externalities from other localities.[24] For example, land use decisions relating to intrastate wetlands are typically made at the state level, but federal crossover may be defensible when needed to contain the border-crossing impacts of related water pollution on downstream localities. For the same reason, the local autonomy compromised by the Phase II Stormwater Rule's requirement that municipalities participate in a national effort to combat stormwater pollution may be offset by the local autonomy it protects in downstream areas.

b. Extent to Which Crossover Marginalizes or Discriminates Against Vulnerable Localities

The adjudicator should also consider the extent to which crossover marginalizes vulnerable states or localities. For example, Nevada has been fighting a federal decision to site the nation's most dangerous nuclear waste disposal facility at Yucca Mountain near Las Vegas.[25] Nevada's protest was effectively sidelined by consensus among representatives from other states in federal policy making. In 2010, Nevadans' vociferous protest finally resulted in suspension of the plan—yet other states now burdened with nuclear waste awaiting shipment to safer storage at Yucca Mountain are now protesting.[26] This is a particularly difficult collective action problem in which states want the benefits but not the burdens of nuclear power, and a central solution that burdens land use planning concerns within one or more states may be

---

[23] *See supra* Chapter Five, notes 103–14 and accompanying text.

[24] *See* Barron, *supra* Chapter Two, note 19, at 386–87; *see supra* Chapter Two, note 142 and accompanying text.

[25] *See* Chris Rizo, *NRC Rejects Nevada AG's Yucca Mountain Complaint*, LEGAL NEWSLINE (Aug. 22, 2008), http://www.legalnewsline.com/news/215102-nrc-rejects-nevada-ags-yucca-mountain-complaint (noting that 70 percent of Nevadans oppose the Yucca Mountain project, and describing efforts to fight it).

[26] President Obama withdrew federal support for the Yuccan Mountain plan—only to draw fire from other states still burdened with "homeless" high level waste, including South Carolina and Washington. Steve Tetreault, *Washington State Continues Push to Halt Yucca Shutdown*, LAS VEGAS REV. -J., Apr. 13, 2010, http://www.lvrj.com/news/washington-state-continues-push-to-halt-yucca-shut-down-90781169.html.

necessary. (Indeed, a related story involving radioactive waste of a lesser order is the focus of the next chapter.) However, if the decision making were challenged under the standard, the adjudicator should consider whether the process of allocating risk sufficiently safeguarded vulnerable localities.

4. PROBLEM SOLVING

The decision maker should consider the extent to which crossover enhances or detracts from effective regulatory response to an interjurisdictional problem that satisfies the criteria in Chapter Five. Careful attention to the conflict between pragmatism and anti-tyranny values is warranted, in order to ensure that the problem-solving interest does not automatically overcome checks whenever a legitimate interjurisdictional problem arises. Moreover, claims for problem solving should be tempered by subsidiarity's preference for localism. If capacity exists at both levels, the more local actor should be empowered to respond.

a. Capacity Analysis

A key aspect of the problem-solving analysis will be its ability to distinguish cases where one side or the other lacks capacity to cope exclusively with the problem. In assessing whether crossover is warranted, the decision maker should take a "hard look" at relative capacity. One starting point for evaluating the limits of state capacity to regulate effectively is the extent to which the matter implicates border-crossing harms or national markets. A starting point for evaluating the limits of federal capacity is the extent to which the matter disproportionately affects some localities over others, implicates local land use authority, requires continued regulatory innovation, or draws on other forms of local expertise and access unavailable at the federal level.

Evidence of a given party's past performance (or undue lack thereof) may also be relevant to an evaluation of its problem-solving capacity in a given scenario. For example, behind the veil of ignorance, we might assume that states would lack the capacity to form regional carbon cap-and-trade markets, a regulatory project uniquely suited to federal authority and expertise in managing interstate markets. Yet lifting the veil reveals that the state-based Regional Greenhouse Gas Initiative has now been operating for years with no federal competition. Such evidence weighs against federal capacity, even if only for the political barriers that have stalled similar federal legislative proposals. By contrast, the states of the RGGI and other regional associations have demonstrated unexpected capacity.

Creating a satisfactory metric for capacity is an important task in perfecting the standard. A poorly calibrated threshold for competency could allow a professed need for problem solving to unnecessarily dominate other considerations. The discourse reveals good starts on the project, including Justice Breyer's proposal in his *Morrison* dissent[27] and a theory of capacity separately proposed by Professors Donald Regan and Douglas Kmiec in interpreting the

---

[27] *See* United States v. Morrison, 529 U.S. 598, 663 (2000) (Breyer, J., dissenting) (suggesting that courts evaluate the rigor of congressional fact-finding when deciding whether Congress has impermissibly invaded a traditionally state-controlled area of regulation).

Commerce Clause.[28] In their work, Regan and Kmiec turn for inspiration to the sixth Virginia Resolution, a proposal for distinguishing between state and federal competencies that was approved by the Constitutional Convention on July 17, 1787.[29] The signatories were resolved:

> That the National Legislature ought to possess the Legislative Rights vested in Congress by the Confederation; and moreover, to legislate in all cases for the general interests of the union, and also in those to which the States are separately incompetent, or in which the harmony of the United States may be interrupted by the exercise of individual Legislation.[30]

The Virginia Resolution did not become part of the final text of the Constitution, but Regan notes that a proposal based on this text would "not rely on it for any proposition that we could not infer from the text of the Constitution itself."[31] But as with the Tenth Amendment itself, other than affirming that the states and federal government will possess different competencies, the text does not provide explicit tools for evaluating which sovereign is best suited for a specific regulatory target. Such a determination would likely hinge on the facts in each controversy, acknowledging that competencies may shift over time.[32]

The possibility of shifting competencies places important limits on the precedential effects of capacity-based determinations under the standard. Although the method for assessing capacity will have precedential effect, substantive capacity determinations should always be ripe for reexamination in later cases. For example, during the Katrina emergency, the federal government possessed superior response capacity to Louisiana (though not Mississippi). However, the Katrina experience might motivate Louisiana to improve its own capacity so that it is more capable during the next hurricane. Even had the federal government taken charge the first time and survived a challenge under the balancing test, a second act of identical crossover would warrant fresh scrutiny.

The sixth Virginia Resolution also suggests an important sand trap in the capacity analysis, which is the danger that how one characterizes the regulatory target might determine which side has the relevant capacity. In other words, if the regulatory objective is identified as "the need for a uniform approach" (because, in the words of the Resolution, the exercise of

---

[28] Regan, *supra* Chapter Two, note 106, at 557–58 (suggesting that differing state views should be protected and should not be infringed by Congress without sufficient justification); Douglas W. Kmiec, *Rediscovering a Principled Commerce Power*, 28 Pepp. L. Rev. 547, 561–62 (2001) (proposing that courts evaluate states' inability to rectify regulatory problems as one factor in determining the boundaries of the federal commerce power).

[29] Regan, *supra* Chapter Two, note 106, at 555.

[30] *Id.* at 555–56 (quoting James Madison, Notes of Debates in the Federal Convention of 1787 at 380 (W. W. Norton & Co. ed., 1966)).

[31] *Id.* at 556.

[32] The dualist vision suggests that the enterprise work in the opposite direction: if we assign roles ex ante, then all can develop the capacity required to manage respective responsibilities. Yet local, regional, and national expertise accumulate organically at the municipal, state, and federal levels—and interjurisdictional problems draw on them in ways beyond the anticipation of a rigid initial allocation of authority.

individual legislation would interrupt the harmony of the nation), then only the federal government will have the capacity to act as needed. It is critical therefore to begin the analysis by asking the right question, or identifying the core regulatory problem that demands redress. A problem characterized as "the need for a uniform approach" must always be probed several analytical levels deeper. Why the need? Are we concerned about a prisoner's dilemma in which the states, acting rationally alone, may nevertheless pursue an irrational end (for example, a race to the bottom in setting air pollution standards)? Or is the problem really one in which the need for fine-tuned regulatory solutions and local expertise are paramount (for example, policing local gang violence)? The former concern suggests a legitimate need for national capacity; the latter less so. Capacity determinations will inevitably require incremental, case-by-case development in concrete circumstances.

b. Extent to Which Federalism-Based Objections Are Pretextual

Finally, the standard might legitimately take into consideration whether federalism-based objections are merely pretextual, offering rhetorically appealing cover for baser motives. The State of New York's opportunistic arguments in *New York v. United States* drew this critique, as did Michael Brown's invocation of federalism in his post-Katrina congressional testimony, which some alleged were post-hoc rationalizations to cover for abdication.[33] The reviewing court should treat apparently pretextual invocations of federalism concerns with at least the level of skepticism it has applied to Congress's invocations of ties to interstate commerce in cases such as *Lopez* and *Morrison*. Neither the check-and-balance value nor any other principle of federalism should be opportunistically deployed as an excuse to avoid unpalatable or difficult gray area problem solving.

D. Mechanics

The mechanics of asserting federalism claims would remain similar to the current model in most respects. To avoid overuse of the balancing test, a gatekeeping inquiry at the outset would establish a two-track system of Tenth Amendment review, screening out challenges invoking the more settled spheres of state and federal authority and reserving application of heightened scrutiny under the balancing test to credible gray area controversies. Balanced Federalism applies ordinary review for challenges brought in either of the uncontroversial realms and the balancing test for challenges in the gray area. (Again, because the boundaries of these three zones are themselves contingent, application of the balancing test may itself move them over time.)

To clarify how this two-track standard of review differs from the dual federalism model critiqued in Chapter Four, consider that separationist dual sovereignty cleaves into two mutually exclusive realms, the properly local and the properly national. Balanced Federalism recognizes three possible zones: the uncontroversially local realm, the uncontroversially national realm, and the interjurisdictional gray area between them. All three zones are

---

[33] *See supra* Chapter One, notes 160–61 and accompanying text; Noonan, *supra* Chapter Five, note 115.

flexibly contingent on the jurisprudence of the times; the model works without making absolute claims about boundaries and anticipates shifting consensus. The purely prudential gatekeeping inquiry is designed to advance economy and administrability, avoiding application of the intensive balancing test in unnecessary cases, but courts should err on the side of fully entertaining credible claims to the gray area.

The gatekeeping baseline would thus designate the uncontroversial sphere of federal authority as extending as far as there is clear constitutionally delegated authority and Congress has expressly preempted further state regulation at the time—but if the state can raise a colorable claim as to why its action has not been preempted, then it will be treated as a gray area claim and adjudicated under the balancing test. For example, this is what the South Coast Air Quality Management District was effectively able to show in its second round of review by the Ninth Circuit in the *Engine Manufacturers* saga.[34]

The gatekeeping baseline might reciprocally define the uncontroversial sphere of state authority as extending as far as the Constitution has granted or not expressly denied it, and as far as it has not been expressly preempted by valid federal law. The first criteria are clear from the text itself. For example, the Constitution specifically delegates responsibility for the mechanics of elections to the states, while elsewhere preempting state authority to withhold voting rights on the basis of race. The latter is contingent on the specificity and validity of federal law at the time. A long-standing example of "uncontroversial" state authority of this sort would be state and local regulation of most land use planning.

If no colorable claim can be made that the challenged action falls within the gray area, then the matter is resolved according to the existing jurisprudence without recourse to the balancing test. A challenge to regulation that takes place within the regulator's own sphere fails to state a Tenth Amendment claim, and crossover fully to the sphere of the other side would be invalidated without recourse to judicial balancing. (Thus, a federalism-based challenge to Congress's declaration of war would fail to state a claim, while a challenge to Florida's declaration of war would succeed on summary judgment.) But if either party can set forth a nonfrivolous argument challenging either the clarity of the constitutionally delegated authority or the extent of congressionally intended preemption, the court proceeds to the four-factor test.

Otherwise, a Balanced Federalism Tenth Amendment challenge would be brought like any other. A party with standing would claim that a regulatory initiative should be invalidated on Tenth Amendment grounds. The reviewing court would apply the gatekeeping inquiry to establish, in essence, what level of scrutiny to apply: something akin to rational basis review if within the regulator's own uncontroversial sphere, intermediate scrutiny under the balancing test if within the interjurisdictional gray area, and strict scrutiny if crossover is to the uncontroversial sphere of the other sovereign. If a challenge merits heightened scrutiny under the jurisprudential standard, then the court tests the challenged regulation against the fundamental federalism values, heeding the factors articulated above, and weighs the results of its inquiry.

---

[34] *See supra* Chapter Five, notes 103–14 and accompanying text.

In this exploratory proposal, the Tenth Amendment standard would provide a means for evaluating only those controversies that could not be resolved under a more specific federalism inquiry, and the rest would be brought as before. For example, although Balanced Federalism theory has implications for cases involving the scope of federal authority under the Commerce Clause or Section Five of the Fourteenth Amendment, such challenges would not be adjudicated under the Tenth Amendment standard; they would be resolved on the basis of the most specifically relevant constitutional doctrines. Elaborated through application of the standard, the principles of Balanced Federalism dual sovereignty will probably bear on the continued, incremental unfolding of jurisprudence in other doctrinal areas, such as the Eleventh Amendment or dormant Commerce Clause. Under fully flourishing Balanced Federalism theory, it may be that some elements of the balancing test find traction in other areas. In this initial proposal, however, most existing doctrine need not be altered.

Nevertheless, Tenth Amendment challenges might be more readily available under Balanced Federalism than previous models. In contrast to cooperative federalism, Tenth Amendment claims would be justiciable at some level. In contrast to New Federalism, justiciable claims would include, but not be limited to, commandeering challenges. The gatekeeping inquiry is designed to avoid unnecessary recourse to the standard, but states might find in it a broader forum to challenge other alleged federal excess that threatens federalism values. For example, if it could survive the gatekeeping inquiry, a state might challenge federal preemption in the gray area, including dormant foreign affairs preemption or other questionable uses of dormant federal authority. If it could show unjustifiable harm to governmental accountability, a state might attempt to challenge an unreasonable unfunded mandate or an especially coercive use of the spending power.

Given easy recourse to the Supremacy Clause in contexts of overlap, federal actors are more likely to defend against Tenth Amendment challenges than bring them. However, the standard would provide additional guidance for ex ante policy making in anticipation of how a court might rule, as well as new defenses in litigation. For example, in extreme cases such as the Katrina response, the federal government might raise federalism problem-solving values in defense of an alleged check-and-balance violation. As with all doctrinal transitions, the new possibilities would probably lead to a bevy of federalism challenges in the short term—just as introduction of the new anti-commandeering rule did in the decade after *New York* and *Printz* were decided.[35] However, the doctrinal parameters would become settled

---

[35] In the fourteen years following the introduction of the anti-commandeering rule in *New York v. United States*, 505 U.S. 144, 188 (1992), seventy-three cases in total were decided in all of the federal courts of appeals (including the Supreme Court) in which *New York* was significantly cited in reference to a Tenth Amendment claim. During the first seven years after the *New York* decision (1993–1999), forty-four such cases were decided. During the second seven-year period (2000–2006), an additional twenty-nine such cases were decided, a reduction of about 34 percent over the first seven-year period. These figures are suggestive of the trend predicted in the main text, but even more so when the full set of seventy-three is winnowed to select for the most meritorious claims. After eliminating the twenty-six cases in which the novel anti-commandeering claim represented more of a "shot in the dark" or "kitchen-sink" argument than a persuasive application of the newly articulated doctrine, the remaining forty-seven cases span the fourteen-year period relatively evenly: twenty-six were decided between 1993 and 1999, and twenty-one between 2000 and 2006. (Research on file with author.) This suggests that a passing surge of cases attempted to capitalize on potential new claims available under the

through incremental application of the standard, and the volume of exploratory challenges would fall (just as commandeering challenges did after that initial decade).

E. Illustrations

Several cursory illustrations may help flesh out the proposal.

Stormwater Management. Consider, for example, the municipalities that challenged the Phase II Stormwater Rule in *Environmental Defense Center*. Among other features, the rule requires municipal stormwater dischargers to issue permits for local construction activity that could contribute to stormwater pollution. Municipal opponents of the rule could claim that it should be invalidated because it compels them—dare we say, commandeers them—in their sovereign capacity to participate in the federal management of stormwater pollution by regulating the conduct of their own citizens.[36] (To make this evaluation interesting, assume there is no alternative permitting scheme to enable a locality to opt out of this requirement, in contrast to the actual facts of the case.) As discussed in Chapter Five, the management of stormwater pollution is well within the interjurisdictional gray area, so the reviewing court would apply the Tenth Amendment standard with intermediate scrutiny.

The court would then test the regulation against the factors identified in the standard. It would consider the plaintiffs' claim that the Phase II Rule derogates from the check-and-balance value by enabling the federal government to compel state regulatory activity in a realm of traditional state authority. The rule might also erode accountability by embedding state and federal responsibility in a way that could confuse voters about which regulators are responsible for what policies. However, its incorporation of a public information campaign might alleviate accountability concerns by helping voters understand the nature of the federal-municipal partnership.

Similarly, enabling a centrally imposed plan to bind municipalities threatens local autonomy, but the court would also consider the ways in which the Phase II Rule advances localism values by couching its commands in terms that minimize federal preemption and maximize local initiative in a realm in which both central coordination and local expertise are crucial. The court might take note that the rule encourages local innovation, fostering the laboratory of ideas in which individual localities and the nation as a whole benefit from municipal experimentation in satisfying the broadly stated federal requirements.

Finally, the court would consider whether the Phase II Rule serves federalism's problem-solving value. Under the facts, problem solving makes a strong case for allowing the challenged crossover. Stormwater pollution is a pervasive collective action problem that cannot be managed by either the federal or the local government acting alone. The problem is closely tied to the management of local land uses that are the specialty of local government, and only local actors would have the relevant expertise to create a stormwater management plan adapted for unique local characteristics. Yet stormwater pollution is also a border-crossing

---

new doctrine, leaving a smaller and steadier stream of more appropriate claims after the Court used this first wave to clarify the parameters of the doctrine.

[36] *See supra* Chapter Five, notes 49–67 and accompanying text.

prisoner's dilemma, providing strong incentives for individual localities to take no precautions, even though all would eventually suffer if no precautions are taken. In this instance, the force with which the Phase II Rule advances problem solving and certain localism values might outweigh its admitted costs to separationist check-and-balance and accountability values. Indeed, this appears to be the calculus that the Ninth Circuit majority performed in its first analysis.

Climate Governance. If Congress were to enact comprehensive climate legislation similar to the Waxman-Markey bill that passed the House in 2009, it would expressly preempt state and regional carbon caps, but questions would remain about the degree of state discretion to regulate more stringently than the national cap.[37] Chapter Five noted several ways states might attempt to do this, of which three follow, each vulnerable to preemption under a Waxman-Markey model: (1) states might regulate to restrict the release of locally harmful "co-pollutants" that would indirectly reduce carbon emissions, (2) states might seek to retire the credits allocated to them as states under the national plan in order to reduce the overall allocation and raise the marginal price of carbon on the national market, and (3) states might seek to regulate sources and varieties of greenhouse gasses that are not addressed in the federal program.[38] States engaged in such efforts could invoke the balancing test to resist preemption, arguing that such preemption impermissibly burdens federalism values in the gray area. Without performing the full balancing test on any one proposal, we can note how each resounds with particular elements of the test.

Allowing states to effectively lower the national cap by regulating co-pollutants could threaten centralized control over the national market for carbon credits, and the regulation of national markets is an area in which federal power is at its strongest. But preempting states from regulating greenhouse gas co-pollutants that pose localized human health risks—such as airborne particulates that cause childhood asthma in such high-risk communities as Los Angeles[39]—would seriously undermine localism values in precisely the realm where state police power is strongest (in protecting against uniquely local threats to health and safety). It would take a strong showing that preemption was critical to the success of the national program to overcome the combination of localism and problem-solving values that weigh in favor of local control to protect children's respiratory health.

By contrast, allowing states to strategically retire credits to raise carbon prices on the national market would compromise centralized control over an important national market on the basis of a weaker claim for local autonomy. The state would argue that it should be free to control its own decisions about its carbon entitlements, emphasizing the value of local autonomy and its legitimate role in regulatory decision making. However, since greenhouse gases collect uniformly in the atmosphere, the claim for special local expertise or regulatory obligation is weaker than in the co-pollutant example. If the federal government can show that state frustration of its allocation and pricing mechanism would impede efficient functioning of the overall market, it may have the more compelling check-and-balance claim for state interference with its constitutionally delegated role in administering interstate

---

[37] *See id.* notes 194–203 and accompanying text.

[38] *See id.* notes 198–201 and accompanying text.

[39] *See id.* notes 103–06 and accompanying text.

commerce. Each side would invoke the problem-solving value: the federal government in support of its centralized plan to reduce greenhouse gas emissions, and the state in support of its attempt to reduce emissions even more aggressively. More precise factual evidence would be needed to evaluate the stronger claim.

Meanwhile, preempting states from regulating greenhouse gases that are not even covered by the national program would protect federal supremacy for its own sake alone. Neither checks, localism, nor problem solving would support preemption in this case. Accountability values seem a wash in each example, to the extent that any of these approaches could probably be adequately explained to voters through available channels. As discussed in Chapter Two, it may be that citizens are enabled a more meaningful opportunity to participate in the more local policy-making venues—but it may also be that the larger venues are less vulnerable to capture by special interests, a powerful concern in the climate context.

The Katrina Response. On another familiar front, had the federal government taken charge of the Katrina response effort without gubernatorial consent, placing state and local first responders already on the ground within the federal chain of command, this easily could have been challenged afterward as outright commandeering. It is hard to imagine a more serious breach of the check-and-balance value under any conception—a U.S. president wresting away command of a state's own militia without gubernatorial consent—but if it were demonstrably necessary to protect the lives of U.S. citizens and sufficiently constrained in time, then even this breach might have been overcome in the balancing analysis. Such federal crossover would have been large in scope but short in time, and possibly warranted in the calculus by the overwhelming need for an efficient response that might have saved thousands of lives, honored the express desires of the most local level of government in New Orleans, and forestalled grave externalities that were spun off throughout the rest of the nation. By contrast, the same federal commandeering after Katrina of Mississippi's state responders would have violated the Constitution, given the completely different factual predicates.

Health Insurance Reform. Finally, consider health insurance reform, an area of law generating enormous federalism controversy since passage of the Patient Protection and Affordable Care Act of 2010.[40] The extensive new statute includes, inter alia, expanded Medicaid eligibility and prescription drug coverage, subsidized insurance premiums, incentives for businesses to provide health care benefits to employees, the creation of health insurance exchanges to assist individuals ineligible for group coverage, requirements for preventative services such as immunizations and prenatal care, market reforms to enhance service and competition, and prohibitions on denying coverage based on age, preexisting medical conditions, or other criteria.[41] The law also includes opportunities for state flexibility relating to exchanges and for establishing alternative programs.[42] The costs of the substantial program are to be borne through a variety of new taxes, fees, and cost-cutting measures, and by expanded participation

---

[40] H.R. 3590, 111th Cong. (2010).

[41] For a thorough summary of the law's contents, see Bill Summary-H.R. 3590, http://thomas.loc.gov/cgi-bin/bdquery/z?d111:HR03590:@@@D&summ2=m&.

[42] *Id.* (describing §§ 1321–1324, 1331–1334, 2401).

in the health insurance market of previously uninsured Americans whose participation is now required.[43]

Indeed, the feature of the law that has generated the most controversy is this individual mandate, or the requirement that beginning in 2014, all individuals "maintain minimal essential health care coverage."[44] Those who fail to do so face a financial penalty unless they are exempt for such reasons as low income or personal objections to health care coverage on religious grounds.[45] Controversy over this particular element of the bill has helped inspire Tenth Amendment-based nullification bills and lawsuits from legislative and executive actors in well over half the states.[46] None of the nullification bills have become law, and only a few legal scholars predict that the litigation will go far under current precedent, given Congress's established authority to regulate the health insurance market as interstate commerce and to levy individual taxes.[47]

Nevertheless, after the first two federal district courts upheld the individual mandate in 2010, two others held that requiring individuals to purchase a product (health insurance) violates the Constitution—variously finding that it violates the Tenth Amendment as well as the Commerce, Tax, and Necessary and Proper Clauses.[48] As this book goes to press, all observers presume that the Supreme Court will ultimately rule on the constitutionality of the law. For the sake of argument, let us consider the Tenth Amendment objections raised to the law under the balancing test.

The claim would almost certainly pass the gatekeeping inquiry, since protection of citizens' health is arguably a primary source of the states' historic police powers, and the regulation of economic activity in the health insurance market is arguably within Congress's commerce authority even after *Lopez* and *Morrison*. In regulating this way, Congress has stepped out of its uncontroversial sphere of exclusive authority and into the interjurisdictional gray area where the state also has legitimate regulatory interests and obligations. Tea Party hopes to overturn the law as flatly unconstitutional under strict scrutiny would thus fail; only intermediate scrutiny under the balancing test is warranted. Applying the full

---

[43] *Id.* (describing, e.g., §§ 9001–9023).

[44] *See id.* (describing § 1501, as modified by § 10106).

[45] *Id.* Ironically, the individual mandate is not the part of the act most significant to the states qua states. The costs of expanding Medicaid would likely dwarf all other concerns, except that the states successfully lobbied federal lawmakers to pay the vast majority of the increased costs, beginning at 100% in 2014 and declining only to 90% in 2020 and subsequent years. *See* Metzger, *supra* Introduction note 73, at *5.

[46] *See supra* Introduction, notes 33–34 and accompanying text.

[47] *E.g.,* Randy E. Barnett, *Is Health Care Reform Constitutional?*, WASH. POST, Mar. 21, 2010, http://www. washingtonpost.com/wp-dyn/content/article/2010/03/19/AR2010031901470.html (suggesting ways that the law might be overcome, but conceding that Tenth Amendment-based nullification arguments will have political force without legal impact); Erwin Chemerinsky, *Health Care Reform Is Constitutional*, POLITICO, Oct. 23, 2009, http://www.politico.com/news/stories/1009/28620.html (arguing that objections to the bill have no basis in law).

[48] Commonwealth *ex rel.* Cuccinelli v. Sebelius, 728 F. Supp. 2d 768 (E.D. Va. 2010); Florida *ex rel.* Bondi v. U.S. Dept. of Health & Human Svcs., __F.Supp.2d__, 2011 WL 285683 (N.D. Fla., 2011); Kevin Sack, *Federal Judge Rules That Health Law Violates the Constitution*, N.Y. TIMES, Feb. 1, 2011, at A-1 (describing all four suits).

balancing test to this voluminous law is beyond the scope of this inquiry, but we can focus on those elements of the test most implicated by the controversial individual mandate.

Accountability concerns should be easily mitigated with sufficient public information about the new federal role in the field (and the extent of federalism controversy over the new law suggests that most observers are acutely aware of what level of government is responsible for the plan.) The nature of the crossover is not facially unreasonable, given Congress's long role in regulating national markets for health insurance under Medicaid and Medicare. The overall statute preempts much of the regulatory field of health insurance reform, but part IV of the law enhances interjurisdictional innovation and competition by allowing state flexibility to establish alternative programs, to seek waivers for specific statutory requirements, and to form health care choice compacts with other states, all of which would enhance the role of state policy making in administration of health insurance reform.[49] Preserving a policy-making partnership with the states honors localism and harnesses the check-and-balance value of jurisdictional overlap.

However, the real check-and-balance question raised by the individual mandate is whether the regulatory crossover ultimately threatens the individual rights that checks and balances are intended to protect. Objections to the individual mandate center on this aspect of the law. As Professor Randy Barnett wrote in a *Washington Post* Op-Ed on the eve of the bill's passage, the Supreme Court would probably view the regulation of health insurance as in line with other economic activities that substantially affect interstate commerce, and yet:

> the individual mandate extends the commerce clause's power beyond economic activity, to economic *inactivity*. That is unprecedented. While Congress has used its taxing power to fund Social Security and Medicare, never before has it used its commerce power to mandate that an individual person engage in an economic transaction with a private company. Regulating the auto industry or paying "cash for clunkers" is one thing; making everyone buy a Chevy is quite another. Even during World War II, the federal government did not mandate that individual citizens purchase war bonds. If you choose to drive a car, then maybe you can be made to buy insurance against the possibility of inflicting harm on others. But making you buy insurance merely because you are alive is a claim of power from which many Americans instinctively shrink.[50]

If checks and balances are to protect individual rights against government overreaching, then this could be an instance of regulatory crossover that undermines the purpose of the check-and-balance value. This is what the balancing test considers when it asks whether the crossover is related to undue exploitation by government of its sovereign power against individuals.

Conversely, Dean Erwin Chemerinsky argues that "no constitutionally protected freedom is infringed" because "there is no right to not have insurance," analogizing to state laws that require insurance before individuals are permitted to drive.[51] Professor Barnett

---

[49] *See* Bill Summary, *supra* note 41 (describing §§ 1331–1334).

[50] Barnett, *supra* note 47.

[51] Chemerinsky, *supra* note 47.

distinguishes the act of driving, which can cause harm to others, from the act of simply being alive—and the distinction weighs heavily. However, so does the fact those who would incur a financial penalty for refusing insurance under the law already incur indirect financial penalties in subsidizing the health care of the millions of previously uninsured Americans who seek treatment in emergency rooms around the country. Similarly, the assumption that one who chooses not to be insured poses no threat of harms to others is also questionable, since those who choose not to be insured for reasons other than religious conviction will not be denied health care, usually at public expense, when they really need it.

In this respect, the health insurance market begins to look like other interjurisdictional regulatory problems, such as climate governance or stormwater pollution, in which inaction by some individuals can externalize harms to others. Parallels may also be drawn to collective action problems regulated at the national level to forestall a race to the bottom among the states, if states that attempt holistic reforms suffer economic leakage to those that do not.[52] These are the regulatory problems that rightly warrant intervention, even to the detriment of a certain level of individual liberty. And while the liberty to not have health insurance counts for something, it would not weigh as heavily as the individual rights to free speech and religion (indeed, those with religious convictions against health care are exempted from the individual mandate).

The law thus makes a compelling case for needed interjurisdictional problem solving, requiring the capacity to manage national markets that only the federal government holds. The problem it addresses is serious beyond dispute: millions of previously uninsured Americans unable to obtain minimally adequate health care, skyrocketing health insurance costs for all, and the inexorable bankrupting of Medicaid and Medicare. Subsidiarity tells us that the problem should be solved as locally as possible, but this may be one of those instances in which the federal level is the most local level with actual capacity for doing so.

As with the Katrina response, balancing the federalism considerations implicated by the individual mandate triggers an especially powerful tug of war between check-and-balance and problem-solving values. Given the minimal burden on individual rights and the serious nature of the problem, at least this adjudicator would uphold the law as consistent with federalism values overall. But the level of judicial discretion required by doctrinal balancing indicates the wisdom of appellate panels with more than a single judge. Indeed, one of the most powerful critiques of the balancing test proposal will be the problem of indeterminacy that judicial balancing creates. Judge Barnett and Judge Chemerinsky might well reach very different conclusions in scrutinizing the health law under the test, just as the four federal district court judges reached different decisions in the first round of actual litigation. Nevertheless, the surprising variety among their findings applying *non*-balancing doctrine suggests two things: (1) judicial doctrine that does not require balancing is also substantially vulnerable to individual discretion, and (2) whether they realize it or not, these judges probably engaged in covert values balancing anyway.

---

[52] *See, e.g.*, Neil Siegel, *Free Riding on Benevolence: Collective Action Federalism and the Individual Mandate,* (forthcoming, 2011), available at http://ssrn.com/abstract=1843228 (discussing health reform); Andreen, *supra* Chapter Five, note 40 (discussing water pollution).

Acknowledging the problems of indeterminacy, I turn in subsequent chapters to proposals that shift the better part of balancing away from the judiciary and toward the political branches most suited to the demands of balancing in the course of normal policy making. However, I also argue that the judicial balancing test proposed here is still of value in comparison to existing judicial constraints, on grounds that it forces to the surface the implicit judicial balancing already in operation in less accountable ways. In comparison to pure political safeguards, it provides an important check on extreme and unilateral assertions of gray area power that are not moderated by bilateral state-federal input. The following section addresses concerns about judicial discretion in constitutional balancing and defends the Tenth Amendment balancing test against these concerns.

F. Defending the Balancing Approach: In Search of Checks and Balance

The Balanced Federalism standard would begin to rectify the separationist fallacy of New Federalism while grappling with the tensions that cooperative federalism glosses over. It would provide an inventory of federalism considerations to assist both ex ante policy making and ex post adjudication, forging a middle path between the critical but competing values that have thus far driven the federalism debate to extremes.[53] Indeed, it would require federalism adjudicators to do what they have always done, but for the first time, in a transparent, accountable way.

As the Chapter One excerpt from Justice Souter's 2010 speech explained, constitutional courts often turn to a balancing approach in uncertain interpretive contexts. The Supreme Court began balancing in its First Amendment jurisprudence as far back as the late 1930s and embraced more general balancing in the late 1960s; constitutional balancing was commonplace by the 1980s.[54] Doctrinal balancing tests are often used when evaluating tensions between orthogonal constitutional values like the federalism values. For example, in adjudicating dormant Commerce Clause challenges under the *Pike v. Bruce Church* test, the Court considers values relating to the state's obligation to protect its citizens and values relating to the nation's interest in efficient interstate commerce.[55]

Similarly, in adjudicating regulatory takings claims under the *Penn Central* multifactor test, the Court balances values relating to the legitimate protection of public interests and to the owner's private property rights.[56] The Court also uses the *Mathews v. Eldridge* balancing test to establish whether an individual has received due process of law, weighing the importance of the individual liberty or property interest at stake, the risk that the procedure used may erroneously deprive the individual of that interest, and the government's interest in

---

[53] *Cf.* Kathleen M. Sullivan, *Foreword: The Justices of Rules and Standards*, 106 HARV. L. REV. 22, 122 (1992) ("Ideological poles tend to attract rules. Standards tend to dive for the middle and split the difference between ideological poles.").

[54] Frank M. Coffin, *Judicial Balancing: The Protean Scales of Justice*, 63 N.Y.U.L. REV. 16, 18 (1988).

[55] 397 U.S. 137, 145 (1970).

[56] Penn Cent. Transp. Co. v. New York City, 438 U.S. 104, 123–25 (1978).

administrability.[57] In such cases, the Court is left with few useful alternatives to balancing, whether or not the justices admit it. Bright-line rules that pretend otherwise either drive judicial balancing underground[58] or perpetuate (even irrationally) a particular balance established by the judge who articulated the rule in the first place.[59]

The use of judicial balancing has generated substantial commentary over the years, often focusing on the problems of managing judicial discretion and weighing incommensurable factors.[60] Scholars have debated the extent to which constitutional balancing is desirable, unconscionable, or inevitable.[61] Champions of balancing stress that it is an inevitable and honest part of judicial interpretation, enabling resolutions more finely tailored to the particulars of justice in a given context.[62] Critics argue that judicial balancing invites the unconstrained exercise of policy preferences and reduces poorly to a prescriptive rule of law around which rational actors can plan.[63] Critics have also objected to its casual use in interpretive contexts where more formal tools would suffice, such as the application of precedent and the close analysis of text, history, and legislative intent.[64] The concern is that balancing invites lazy and sloppy judicial reasoning.

Perhaps most troubling, critics warn that constitutional rights may be inappropriately weighed against unconstitutional considerations, such as pragmatic consequences, implying that all are equally cognizable under the Constitution.[65] These scholars argue that the Constitution is a precommitment to certain values above others—for example, freedom of speech over ease of government administration—and that balancing threatens the dilution of constitutional rights. One way to protect against such balancing abuse is to ensure that

---

[57] 424 U.S. 319 (1976).

[58] Stephen E. Gottlieb, *The Paradox of Balancing Significant Interests*, 45 HASTINGS L.J. 825, 828 (1994).

[59] Kennedy, *supra* Chapter Four, note 199, at 1701; Joseph Singer, *Catcher in the Rye Jurisprudence*, 35 RUTGERS L. REV. 275, 278 (1983).

[60] *See, e.g.,* T. Alexander Aleinikoff, *Constitutional Law in the Age of Balancing*, 96 YALE L.J. 943 (1987) (critiquing the use of balancing in constitutional interpretation); Joseph Blocher, *Categoricalism and Balancing in First and Second Amendment Analysis*, 84 N.Y.U.L. REV. 375 (2009) (arguing that the Court's categorical approach in its new Second Amendment jurisprudence should, and inevitably will, evolve into the kind of balancing approach it has come to use in its First Amendment jurisprudence); Coffin, *supra* note 54 (arguing that judicial balancing, while problematic, is better than the alternatives); Gottlieb, *supra* note 58 (arguing that judicial balancing is impossible but also inevitable, but warning against balancing rights against incommensurable interests); Louis Henkin, *Infallibility under Law: Constitutional Balancing*, 78 COLUM. L. REV. 1022 (1978) (distinguishing between interpretive balancing and balancing tests, and arguing for greater judicial guidance in the latter); Iddo Porat, *The Dual Model of Balancing: A Model for the Proper Scope of Balancing in Constitutional Law*, 27 CARDOZO L. REV. 1393 (2006) (proposing jurisprudential tools to curb problems in judicial balancing); Michel Rosenfeld, *Judicial Balancing in Times of Stress: Comparing the American, British, and Israeli Approaches to the War on Terror*, 27 CARDOZO L. REV. 2079 (2006) (comparative analysis).

[61] *Id.*

[62] *See, e.g.,* Coffin, *supra* note 54, at 41 (as a First Circuit judge, noting that he is bothered by the problems with balancing until he looks for alternatives, and finding none, returns to balancing with "openness, candor, and sensitivity").

[63] Kennedy, *supra* Chapter Four, note 199, at 1688–89.

[64] Aleinikoff, *supra* note 60, at 987–90.

[65] *Id.* at 977.

factors in the balance are always of the same constitutional order, deserving the same level of protection. To this end, Professor Iddo Porat has proposed a model of judicial balancing that better differentiates between the appropriate judicial balancing among conflicting principles of the same order (for example, balancing two constitutional interests against one another, such as governmental administrability and economic stability) and the inappropriate balancing that should be discouraged between principles of differing orders (for example, balancing a constitutional interest against a full-fledged constitutional right, such as free speech, which should rightly trump the interest).

Still, most scholars acknowledge that balancing is a legitimate methodology in at least some constitutional circumstances,[66] and many concede that it is inevitable.[67] Federalism is one of these circumstances in both respects. Balancing is inevitable in interpreting federalism controversies because there is no alternative but to reckon with the tug of war within. The federalism values that pull in directions of checks and balances, localism, accountability, and problem solving are not always well-aligned, and for that reason, trade-offs are inevitable. Balancing is legitimate because the trade-offs are better made in careful consideration under a guided jurisprudential standard than under a categorical rule that arbitrarily establishes the same trade-off in every instance.

Moreover, the Balanced Federalism standard avoids many of the primary objections to constitutional balancing. Critics worry that balancing leads to undertheorized reasoning, but the Tenth Amendment balancing test proceeds from the painstakingly developed Balanced Federalism theory of what constitutional text and structure requires. By specifying the precise factors for balancing in the core federalism values, it excludes the possibility of diluting constitutional principles in casual trade-offs against factors of a lesser order. Indeed, the Tenth Amendment standard does not mix constitutional and nonconstitutional considerations. To the extent the balancing test considers practical consequences, it is only because the constitutional considerations identified under Balanced Federalism theory *include* a pragmatic element. As demonstrated in Chapter Two, federalism represents many things at once, and one of them—subsidiarity—incorporates the consideration of consequences, mediated by the preference for localism, into federalism's problem-solving value. Unlike the individual rights in the Constitution, structural federalism makes consequence a legitimately constitutional consideration. Yet in Balanced Federalism theory, it is carefully weighed against checks and balances, accountability, localism, and other aspects of synergy—all of which are also constitutional considerations at the same level.

The Tenth Amendment balancing test will not casually mix constitutional and nonconstitutional concerns, but it will confront the difficulty of balancing among incommensurable values. Professor Cass Sunstein defines incommensurable values as those that cannot be reduced to a similar scale of measure—such as wages and friendship—so that balancing among them requires necessarily subjective calculations.[68] Indeed, it is difficult to translate

---

[66] *See, e.g.*, Henkin, *supra* note 60, at 1028–32.

[67] *See, e.g.*, Gottlieb, *supra* note 58, at 843.

[68] Cass R. Sunstein, *Incommensurability and Valuation in Law*, 92 MICH. L. REV. 779 (1994) (explaining how the problem of valuing trade-offs between incommensurable goods inevitably leads to ad hoc intuitive balancing).

the federalism value of localism into the value of accountability, even though they are both related to ideals of good government. Critics contend that balancing thus becomes an interpretive "cheat"—an appeal to biased intuitivism that need not be explained outside the black box of the mind.[69] Nevertheless, judges have long proved expert in exactly this sort of balancing among incommensurable factors in performing the causation analysis at the heart of the negligence standard. Judges apply the Hand formula to assess whether a duty has been breached in tort by weighing the cost of precautions, the gravity of potential harm, and the likelihood that it will come to fruition—a foundational common law tradition that even critics of judicial discretion are happy to entrust to the judiciary.

Moreover, it is unlikely that Balanced Federalism would induce balancing where there is none presently. More likely, it would give overt expression to the value-laden balancing process already covertly in use by courts and policy makers when they reason their way through the inevitable conflict among federalism values, especially checks and problem solving. Evidence of this values-based assessment appears in the progression of the two *Environmental Defense Center* (Phase II Stormwater) decisions,[70] the New Jersey court's reasoning in *American Civil Liberties Union*,[71] and the court of public opinion regarding the Katrina response.[72] Perhaps even the apparent disconnect between *Gonzales v. Raich* (approving federal jurisdiction to prosecute in-state cultivation of medical marijuana as legalized under California law)[73] and *Gonzales v. Oregon* (disapproving federal jurisdiction to prosecute euthanasia as legalized under Oregon law)[74] can be explained this way. Similarly, despite Justice Scalia's strong appeal to federalism in his *Rapanos* plurality opinion,[75] Justice Kennedy's concurrence highlights the limitations of bright-line rules in his embrace of the ad hoc "case-by-case-basis" approach that is now the governing rule.[76]

If covert values balancing is really informing these decisions, far better to move that reasoning process to the surface, where it can be scrutinized and developed according to the mechanisms of the common law tradition.[77] A well-defined judicial balancing test will provide a rational means of inventorying the factors that judges should consider, while providing guidance for state and federal policy makers to formulate and defend regulatory choices about crossover in anticipation of the courts' calculus in the interjurisdictional gray area. The transition to the balancing approach will admittedly generate a period of exaggerated indeterminacy, as judges establish the contours of the test by applying it in new circumstances. However, sustained and incremental application of the test will generate a stable body of

---

[69] *See* Aleinikoff, *supra* note 60.

[70] *See supra* Chapter Five, notes 49–67 and accompanying text.

[71] *See supra* Chapter Four, notes 96–98 and accompanying text.

[72] *See supra* Chapter One, notes 57, 124–25, 152, and accompanying text.

[73] 545 U.S. 1 (2005); *see id.* at 9.

[74] 126 S. Ct. 904 (2006); *see id.* at 925.

[75] Rapanos v. United States, 126 S. Ct. 2208, 2224–25 (2006) (plurality opinion).

[76] *Id.* at 2249 (Kennedy, J., concurring).

[77] *Cf.* Alexandra B. Klass, *Common Law and Federalism in the Age of the Regulatory State*, 92 IOWA L. REV. 545, 582–84 (2007) (highlighting the benefits of common law decision making in arguing for an enhanced role for state common law in environmental regulation).

precedent to guide judicial discretion and provide greater certainty to policy makers over time.

Anxiety over indeterminacy demonstrates that the real problem is one of expectations about what legal rules can and should do. Balancing tests frustrate their critics because they fail to specify ex ante how the balancing ought to be done. But of course, that is not the point of the balancing test: it is designed to provide ground for further elaboration in individual contexts, where categorical rule-like choices will eventually be made among the competing values. Through the common law processes of judging, the balancing act takes on distinctive forms in distinctive contexts. Over time, it becomes clear that in one particular circumstance, protecting local autonomy for innovation will usually prevail, while in another, checking sovereign authority to serve rights must trump. Each outcome states a categorical rule about the appropriate balance in that particular context. Each rule becomes a snapshot of the balancing test as applied in a given circumstance. Each snapshot becomes a precedential guidepost for future decision making in similar contexts, mitigating the unpredictability of the standard while retaining enough suppleness to find justice in the individual case. By this incremental, iterative process of flexibility and order, the jurisprudential standard will foster a healthy balance of state and federal power.

Concerns about judicial bias in balancing appear further overstated when viewed in comparison to the alternatives. As Professor Duncan Kennedy has argued, balancing tests can actually dilute the impact of judicial bias in comparison to categorical rules, because a balancing test allows the alchemy of precedent and judgment to filter individual decisions through the prism of many different sets of bias, rather than the singular preferences of the judge who first created a categorical rule.[78] Professor Stephen Gottlieb argues that candid constitutional balancing constrains judicial bias by making judges publicly accountable for their choices.[79] He warns that the "Supreme Court does not tame interests when it stops writing about them; it merely hides them, making them even more powerful because, as hidden, they are not subject to scrutiny."[80]

Still others point to the inevitable layers of judicial discretion called for by most constitutional interpretation. Judge Frank Coffin of the U.S. Court of Appeals for the First Circuit observes that he is troubled by balancing until he considers the alternatives, concluding that "justice is something we approach better on a retail than a wholesale basis."[81] And as Justice Souter explained in his 2010 speech, "the Constitution is no simple contract . . . because its language grants and guarantees many good things, and good things that compete with each other and can never all be realized, all together, all at once."[82] In other words, all difficult constitutional judging requires balancing—even in contexts that purport otherwise.

There is, of course, an important difference between the interpretive balancing that Justice Souter describes and the doctrinal balancing called for by a multifactor test. Scholars

---

[78] Kennedy, *supra* Chapter Four, note 199, at 1701.

[79] Gottlieb, *supra* note 58, at 828.

[80] *Id.*

[81] Coffin, *supra* note 54, at 40 ("As a nation, we are, and have ever been, concerned with justice. To me, justice is something we approach better on a retail than a wholesale basis.").

[82] *Souter Speech, supra* Chapter One, note 34.

differentiate between exegetic judicial balancing that produces a categorical rule for future application and balancing that produces an ad hoc test requiring individualized balances in future cases. Exegetic balancing is part of an interpretive process to parse implicit constitutional tensions in service of an absolute result, while doctrinal balancing requires future decision makers to apply specific factors a previous adjudicator has identified.[83] While many acknowledge that some degree of exegetic balancing is necessary in constitutional interpretation,[84] others fear that the sloppy use of doctrinal balancing will add to uncertainty and inefficiencies in the regulatory marketplace.[85]

The Tenth Amendment balancing test proposed here incorporates both exegetic and doctrinal balancing. Federalism analysis requires the same sort of exegetic balancing that Justice Souter described in the First Amendment context,[86] in interpreting such federalism-related categorical rules as the implied limits of the federal commerce power, or the true meaning of the check-and-balance value. At the same time, the required consideration of identified federalism values engages the adjudicator in a doctrinal multifactor test. To allay concerns about sloppy ad hoc reasoning, doctrinal balancing should include guidance about the considerations that belong in appropriate balancing (territory into which this chapter has made an initial foray, though only a rough one). Indeed, to the extent that doctrinal balancing specifies the exact factors for balancing, then concerns about balancing incommensurable values are defused.

The Tenth Amendment balancing test also mitigates concerns about inefficiency, given the special nature of repeat-player interactions between the state and federal government. Scholars have researched how doctrinal balancing that could lead to inefficiencies in isolated, one-off transactions are well suited to flexible adjudication between repeat players, because they "mimic a pattern of post hoc readjustments that [the parties] *would* make if they were in an ongoing relationship with each other."[87] By contrast, the classic advantage of bright-line categorical rules in enabling efficient bargaining between governed parties evaporates in this context, given the Court's admonition in *New York* that the state may not bargain away a Tenth Amendment entitlement that essentially belongs to its citizens.[88] (In the next chapter, I therefore suggest abandoning that aspect of the rule.)

Unresolved judicial balancing problems remain, even within the carefully designed Tenth Amendment standard. The proposal heralds all the usual disadvantages associated with flexible standards in comparison to bright-line rules—enhancing the discretion of judicial decision makers, limiting certainty for regulated parties, promising mud instead of crystal.[89] It purposefully leaves the boundaries of the interjurisdictional gray area indistinct, a project

---

[83] Henkin, *supra* note 60, at 1023–28.

[84] *Id.* at 1047–48.

[85] Aleinikoff, *supra* note 60 (worrying that doctrinal balancing leads to judicial laziness).

[86] *See supra* Chapter One, notes 34–42.

[87] Rose, *supra* Chapter Four, note 199, at 602–03.

[88] *See* New York v. United States, 505 U.S. 144, 182 (1992).

[89] *See* Kennedy, *supra* Chapter Four, note 199, at 1687–89 (discussing advantages and disadvantages of rules and standards); Rose, *supra* Chapter Four, note 199, at 578–79 (likening clear-cut rules of decision to crystals and ambiguous rules to mud).

of ongoing jurisprudential consensus (although Part IV mitigates the issue by surfacing the role of intergovernmental bargaining at the margins). State and federal courts would jointly contribute to its incremental development in concrete application, but the U.S. Supreme Court would ultimately define the test (which would not differ from existing judicial safeguards, but which would diminish state input in comparison to Balanced Federalism intergovernmental partnerships). Precisely *how* to balance the competing inquiries would be committed to judicial discretion, distressing those who distrust the independent decision making of individual judges.

For these reasons, opponents of the uncertain Balanced Federalism approach may long for the comparative simplicity of New Federalism's bright-line rules. Canons of interpretation and precedential guidance notwithstanding, a balancing test like this one can never render the predictability that a categorical rule carves out of the interjurisdictional chaos. Nevertheless, a bright-line approach that fails to track the real world targets of adjudication is of no jurisprudential value. In the end, at least in the context of formal judicial review, a rough-edged balancing test that provides meaningful protections for federalism values and genuine guidance for decision makers is better than a crisp rule that obstructs good government and forces difficult considerations below the radar of accountability.[90]

Because it leads well into the following chapters, I end with consideration of the most intriguing charge against judicial constitutional balancing—that it threatens the intended separation of powers.[91] Intuitive balancing may be a mysterious process, goes the argument, but navigating through the incommensurable features of our world is the very essence of legislative policy making. Common law judges may indeed do this regularly, but common law judging is distinguishable from constitutional interpretation because the legislature can overrule a common law court's decision, while a constitutional court's decision binds the legislature.[92] Legislative judgments about constitutional questions can be second-guessed by the judiciary, but judicial constitutional judgments cannot be second-guessed by the legislature.[93] Giving judges this power is too dangerous, when balancing is neither reasonably explainable nor tethered to the legal text they are required to interpret.

Nevertheless, the Balanced Federalism standard is both tethered to constitutional text and susceptible to explanation. It may also be our best alternative for substantive judicial review of Tenth Amendment claims, given admonitions by Justice Souter, Judge Coffin, Professors Kennedy and Gottlieb, and others that judicial balancing is inevitable even in constitutional contexts (and that it will take place in less accountable forms if not held to

---

[90] For example, Professor Vicki Jackson argues that the rule drawn by *Printz* "is not well supported in constitutional history and is both underinclusive and overinclusive toward legitimate goals of protecting state governments and promoting political accountability." Jackson, *supra* Part I Introduction, note 21, at 2182. She further argues that "[d]espite the conventional association of the rule of law with more categorical approaches . . . a multifactored flexible standard is likely to provide more stability than the categorical (but insufficiently supported) rule of *Printz*, and better accords with both rule of law and federalism values." *Id.* at 2183.

[91] Aleinikoff, *supra* note 60, at 984–86.

[92] *See* Marbury v. Madison, 5 U.S. 137 (1803).

[93] *See* City of Boerne v. Flores, 521 U.S. 507, 511 (1997).

the open air this way).[94] While the constitutional interpretation of individual rights may be less amenable to doctrinal balancing, federalism interpretation is different, because—thanks to the tug of war within—it is already a balancing act by design. Rights are designed to be inefficient, serving purposes wholly unrelated to pragmatic ends. To be sure, there are also purposeful inefficiencies in the Constitution's structural design—for example, the bicameral legislature and required presidential signature that so burdens the process of federal lawmaking.[95] But American federalism was purposefully designed to balance the rights-protective inefficiencies of dual sovereignty with the pragmatic synergies it enables.[96]

In any event, the separation of powers critique helpfully opens the door to the other central question in federalism—that of political or judicial safeguards. This is the introductory question of *who decides who gets to decide?*—or which branch of government determines which level of government may make policy in a given subject-matter realm. The claim that judicial federalism balancing usurps the role of the legislature may be intended as an argument for more categorical judicial reasoning, but in the federalism context (where balancing is inevitable), it approaches the Wechslerian argument of pure judicial deference to legislative determinations about federalism limits. Indeed, between the New Deal and New Federalism eras, Congress was responsible for making the difficult trade-offs in federalism policy. Thus, one alternative to the problems caused by New Federalism judicial safeguards—categorically applying a preordained judicial balance—is simply to retreat to the prior system in which the Court left federalism interpretation to the political process without judicial oversight.

My contrary proposal rests on grounds partly theoretical and partly pragmatic. From the vantage point of theory, the pure political safeguards period of cooperative federalism was undertheorized. More descriptive than prescriptive, it lacked satisfying justification for uncritical jurisdictional overlap beyond the simple faith that if federalism really matters, Congress will see that it is taken care of.[97] Cooperative federalism has been rightly deferential to federal power in many circumstances over the last century, and it has spawned invaluable laboratories of collaborative interjurisdictional governance. Yet its uncritical federalism inquiry has so often defaulted to whether federal crossover is within the commerce power that we have failed to ask when that should not be the end of the inquiry as a normative matter.

The illustrations in Chapters Five and Nine show numerous instances in which good governance requires local involvement even in instances where there is preemptive federal authority. Balanced Federalism provides theoretical justification for retaining national strength in interjurisdictional governance where needed while enhancing local authority to resist casual or uncritical preemption. Even scholars sympathetic to the institutional

---

[94] *See supra* notes 78–82 and accompanying text.

[95] *E.g.*, INS v. Chada, 462 U.S. 919 (1983) (discussing these purposeful inefficiencies in overturning the one-house veto).

[96] *See supra* Chapters Two and Three; *cf.* LaCroix, *supra* Introduction, note 71; Purcell, *supra* Introduction, note 11.

[97] Even defenders of cooperative federalism practice have conceded the need for judicial constraints in cases where regulatory crossover was truly unaccountable. *E.g.*, La Pierre, *supra* Chapter Two, note 59, at 665.

competence of Congress and the pragmatic advantages of the cooperative model deserve more robust theoretical guidance about close federalism calls, and a clearer account of the respective roles of the three branches in making them.

From the pragmatic vantage point, it is worthwhile to consider why the political safeguards model was rejected in the New Federalism revival. This rejection began in the political sphere and matured in the judicial sphere due to building political sentiment that the model had failed to protect important federalism values. Rather than reviving a model that will only be rejected again through the inevitable backlash as the pendulum continues to swing between extremes, Balanced Federalism offers a framework in which both sides may find consensus about how to allocate responsibilities among all three branches. The Supreme Court's role in administering the Tenth Amendment balancing test would proceed naturally from its role as the New Federalism arbiter, although it is appropriately modified by the subsequent proposals.

Indeed, to achieve true balance, decisions about federalism should not be the sole province of the judiciary. In many cases, more trustworthy balancing can be achieved through ex ante policy making, especially when it is the product of joint state and federal expertise. Balanced Federalism thus also recognizes the interpretive potential of the political branches at all levels of government, subject to more narrowly tailored standards of judicial review. The next chapter begins that exploration.

7

LEGISLATIVE BALANCING THROUGH INTERGOVERNMENTAL

BARGAINING

THE TENTH AMENDMENT balancing test provides a good introduction to the Balanced Federalism theoretical model because it so clearly frames the inquiry as one seeking balance between the competing core federalism values. However, it consolidates substantial discretion in the federal judicial branch, and would require a wholesale rejection of current doctrine that could take generations to realize. This chapter proposes a simultaneous means of moving toward the Balanced Federalism ideal, through a simple jurisprudential fix that would facilitate greater balance even from within the existing paradigm.

Discussion proceeds from the premise that the Constitution's federalism directives can be viewed as default rules that confer jurisdictional entitlements to state and federal actors. When breaking legal rules into their component parts, we find that the normative entitlement of the rule (such as a grant of policy-making jurisdiction) is matched with a subordinate infrastructural component that designates how and whether the normative entitlement can be shifted.[1] Chapter Seven explores the extent to which federalism doctrine allows the consensually negotiated exchange of these entitlements, such as waiver of Eleventh Amendment state sovereign immunity, or state waiver of the implied limitations on the enumerated powers when accepting spending power deals conditioned on loosely related federal policies.

---

[1] *See* Calabresi & Melamed, *supra* Introduction, note 67. *See also* Erin Ryan, *Federalism at the Cathedral: Property Rules, Liability Rules, and Inalienability Rules in Tenth Amendment Infrastructure*, 81 U. COLO. L. REV. 1, 4, 14–18 (2010).

In *New York v. United States*, when the Rehnquist Court created the normative anti-commandeering entitlement that states hold against Congress, it did not allow for consensual intergovernmental bargaining to shift the entitlement. Using the story of the *New York* decision as a case study of gray area intergovernmental bargaining, this chapter proposes that Tenth Amendment entitlements be harmonized with the rest of the federalism doctrines to enable consensual legislative bargaining. Professor Guido Calabresi and Douglas Melamed describe this aspect of legal architecture as "property rule" protection—enabling the holder of a legal entitlement to bargain with it as if it were an item of personal property.[2] Notwithstanding the provocative nature of using this private law vocabulary to discuss a central facet of public law, it usefully distinguishes legal entitlements from the rules that govern their exchange, and the second part of the chapter adopts this vocabulary to discuss its proposal.

By leaving the normative part of the anti-commandeering rule in place but enabling states to bargain with this entitlement in intergovernmental partnerships, the Court could open up new possibilities for values-balancing interjurisdictional governance while leaving the most protective aspects of the rule intact. The nature of bilateral legislative exchange ensures that the negotiated balance reflects the wisdom and interests of both state and federal actors. Enabling it would tap unique legislative resources for balancing federalism values in the fact-intensive contexts of policy making, where legislatures usually outperform courts. By incorporating state and federal legislative judgment, such bargaining would go beyond the unilateral assertions of federal power or deference to state prerogative that characterize traditional political safeguards. Judicial oversight only for bargaining abuses provides limited judicial safeguards that respect the superior capacity of legislative balancing in ex ante policy-making contexts—especially that which incorporates state perspective directly, rather than as filtered through Congress. The proposal for judicial deference in Chapter Seven thus trumps the Chapter Six balancing test if the balancing test were called upon to adjudicate an instance of consensual commandeering. In so doing, Chapter Seven also begins to shift attention from the federalism quandary of when state or federal law should trump to the equally pressing quandary of who should make that call.

The chapter begins by reviewing the facts of the *New York* saga and the decades of regulatory abdication that have followed in the field of radioactive waste disposal. It then critiques the Court's justification of its anti-bargaining approach, adopting the Calabresi-Melamed vocabulary to propose an alternative that would facilitate state-federal legislative partnerships to balance competing federalism values in the gray area. In so doing, it builds the theoretical foundations for Part IV's recognition of the role that intergovernmental bargaining already plays in enabling fully bilateral values balancing.

---

[2] *Id.*

A. *The Saga of* New York v. United States

New York v. United States inaugurated the Supreme Court's New Federalism era in 1992,[3] setting forth the Tenth Amendment anti-commandeering doctrine in a decision that invalidated parts of the Low-Level Radioactive Waste Policy Act Amendments of 1985.[4] The most forceful component of the Act's penalty structure was held unconstitutional for commandeering state legislative authority, even though the states had collaboratively crafted the law and lobbied Congress for its passage over a competing proposal that would have preempted the field with federal regulations.[5] But in an effort to make its own rhetorical point about federalism, the Court specified that Congress lacked the authority to bind a state's participation in federal law even if state officials had waived Tenth Amendment-based objections during consensual negotiations.[6] In the decades that have followed, the crisis of safely and equitably siting radioactive waste among the states has only worsened, prompting renewed rounds of litigation and legislative attempts to solve the problem. This section shares the history of the *New York* saga, which foreshadows the interjurisdictional difficulties that the decision has perpetuated.

I. THE LOW-LEVEL RADIOACTIVE WASTE POLICY ACT

The Low-Level Radioactive Waste Policy Act and the *New York* decision involved a constitutional crisis over the disposal of radioactive waste.[7] As the Supreme Court explained, commercially and scientifically produced radioactive waste is both dangerous and ubiquitous:

> Radioactive waste is present in luminous watch dials, smoke alarms, measurement devices, medical fluids, research materials, and the protective gear and construction materials used by workers at nuclear power plants. Low-level radioactive waste is generated by the Government, by hospitals, by research institutions, and by various industries. The waste must be isolated from humans for long periods of time, often for

---

[3] 505 U.S. 144, 161 (1992).

[4] Low-Level Radioactive Waste Policy Amendments Act of 1985, Pub. L. No. 99–240, 99 Stat. 1842 (1986) (codified as amended in 42 U.S.C. § 2021).

[5] Low-Level Radioactive Waste Policy Amendments Act of 1985 § 5(d)(2)(C), Pub. L. No. 99–240, 99 Stat. 1842, 1850, *vacated in part by* New York v. United States, 505 U.S. 144 (1992). *See* Neil Siegel, *Commandeering and Its Alternatives: A Federalism Perspective*, 59 VAND. L. REV. 1629, 1660–64 (2007) (arguing that in thwarting the state-based solution, the decision was ultimately more destructive to state sovereignty than the alternative).

[6] 505 U.S at 182.

[7] Generated from medical, scientific, and commercial applications, these low-level radioactive waste products include debris, rubble, soils, paper, liquid, metals, and clothing that have been exposed to radioactivity, and sealed radiological sources that are no longer useful. GOVERNMENT ACCOUNTABILITY OFFICE, LOW-LEVEL RADIOACTIVE WASTE MANAGEMENT: APPROACHES USED BY FOREIGN COUNTRIES MAY PROVIDE USEFUL LESSONS FOR MANAGING U.S. RADIOACTIVE WASTE 1 (2007), http://www.gao.gov/new.items/d07221.pdf. High-level waste from weapons and spent nuclear reactor fuel is dealt with separately, though also controversially. *Supra* Chapter Six, notes 25–26.

hundreds of years. Millions of cubic feet of low-level radioactive waste must be disposed of each year.[8]

Most Americans, it appears, prefer not to live near radioactive waste disposal facilities, and so the increasing use of commercial technologies involving radioactive materials over the 1970s and 1980s was not matched by an increase in disposal facilities to deal with their waste products.[9] By 1979, after half the nation's disposal sites had either filled up or closed for water management problems, only three low-level radioactive waste facilities remained in the United States to handle the entire nation's waste stream: the Beatty site in Nevada, the Richland site in Washington, and the Barnwell site in South Carolina.[10] Nationwide, all waste that could not be stored safely at its site of generation was trucked to one of these three facilities, frustrating the citizens of Nevada, Washington, and South Carolina.[11]

The states with disposal facilities (the "sited states") faced a dilemma. They could not simply close their borders to interstate shipments of waste and continue to site in-state produced waste without running afoul of the dormant Commerce Clause, which forbids the states from discriminating against interstate commerce.[12] For constitutional purposes, shipments by paying customers for the disposal of low-level radioactive waste created in other states represent a stream of interstate commerce otherwise indistinguishable from the preferred in-state shipments. Accordingly, the sited states had two options: trigger a constitutional standoff to make their point (but likely lose in court), or simply close their facilities down, forcing the rest of the nation out of its collective stupor and into action regarding the radioactive waste capacity crisis.

One by one, they chose the latter option. Nevada and Washington temporarily closed their sites starting in 1979, leaving South Carolina's Barnwell site as the only available disposal facility in the country.[13] After South Carolina then threatened to close Barnwell, the prospect of no disposal capacity finally jump-started a national political conversation to resolve the inequities faced by the sited states while protecting the public from unsafe exposure to harmful radioactive waste products.[14]

---

[8] 505 U.S. at 150–51.

[9] *Id.* at 182.

[10] *Id.* at 151.

[11] Audeen W. Fentiman et al., *Legislation Governing Disposal of Low-Level Radioactive Waste*, Ohio State University RER-60, http://ohioonline.osu.edu/~rer/rerhtml/rer_60.html (last visited July 14, 2008).

[12] For example, Washington tried to refuse out-of-state shipments in 1981, but failed when a federal court determined that it would violate the dormant Commerce and Supremacy Clauses. *State's Nuclear Waste Ban Is Ruled Unconstitutional*, ASSOCIATED PRESS, June 27, 1981, *available at* http://query.nytimes.com/gst/fullpage.html?res=9503E6D91138F934A15755C0A967948260.

[13] *New York*, 505 U.S. at 150. *See Nevada A-Dump Closed*, 519 WORLD NEWS DIGEST A2, July 13, 1979. After reopening and closing several times, Nevada closed the site permanently in 1992. *See* Richard R. Zuercher, *Nevada Accord Closes Beatty LLW Facility Permanently*, 34 NUCLEONICS WEEK 6, November 11, 1993; *see also Squeeze on Wastes*, CHEMICAL WEEK, April 12, 1978, at 21 (discussing tense state relations over site closures).

[14] *New York*, 505 U.S. at 151; Thomas O'Toole, *President Seeking Permanent Sites To Store Atomic Waste, Spent Fuel*, WASH. POST, February 12, 1980, at A1 (discussing alternatives as Barnwell grew less accessible).

To accomplish these objectives, Congress considered mandating a national regulatory program that would preempt state decision making.[15] However, the states unanimously negotiated an alternative proposal through the National Governors Association and lobbied hard for Congress to adopt what came to be known as the "state-based" solution.[16] Underscored by the general policy that each state should be responsible for its own waste,[17] the states' regional approach embodied a compromise between the sited states (frustrated at bearing more than their fair share of the nation's toxic waste) and the non-sited states (desperate for more time to prepare for the point at which they would no longer be able to use the sited states' facilities).[18]

In this approach, states would be responsible for disposing of their own waste, either alone or within regional interstate compacts formed for the purpose of low-level radioactive waste disposal.[19] Each compact would choose a state to host the compact's disposal facility for a designated period, or otherwise provide for waste disposal, as by contractual arrangement with another compact for use of its facility.[20] After a reasonable period in which non-sited states could build new disposal facilities, the sited states would be authorized to close their borders in 1986 to interstate shipments of waste if they chose, or to admit waste generated only from within their own regional compacts.[21]

The plan would alleviate the unfair burden on the sited states while protecting all Americans from the hazards associated with the cross-country transportation of low-level radioactive waste on public highways. However, the states could not implement the plan completely on their own; they needed Congress's formal blessing to head off the dormant Commerce Clause problem otherwise created by the controls on interstate waste shipments after the 1986 deadline.[22] In acknowledgment of the states' hard-fought consensus, Congress

---

[15] *New York*, 505 U.S. at 192.

[16] LLW Forum, *Supporting a State and Regional Approach to a Complex Environmental Issue*, www.llwforum.org (noting that both the original 1980 legislation and the 1985 amendments "were endorsed by the Governors of the 50 states"). *See also New York*, 505 U.S. at 189–90 (White, J., dissenting) ("To read the Court's version of events . . . one would think that Congress was the sole proponent of a solution to the Nation's low-level radioactive waste problem. [But the Act] resulted from the efforts of state leaders to achieve a state-based set of remedies to the waste problem. They sought not federal pre-emption or intervention, but rather congressional sanction of interstate compromises they had reached" (citations omitted)).

[17] 505 U.S. at 190–91 (White, J., concurring and dissenting) ("In May 1980, the State Planning Council on Radioactive Waste Management submitted the following unanimous recommendation to President Carter: 'The national policy of the United States on low-level radioactive waste shall be that every State is responsible for the disposal of the low-level radioactive waste generated by nondefense related activities within its boundaries and that States are authorized to enter into interstate compacts, as necessary for the purpose of carrying out this responsibility.' This recommendation was adopted by the National Governors' Association a few months later.").

[18] *Id.* at 181 (majority opinion) (noting that "the Act embodies a bargain among the sited and unsited States").

[19] *Id.* at 150–51.

[20] *Id.* at 151–52; Fentiman et al., *supra* note 11.

[21] *New York*, 505 U.S. at 151.

[22] *Id.* (noting that ratification by Congress was necessary for states to restrict interstate shipments by compact).

unanimously adopted the state-based approach in the Low-Level Radioactive Waste Policy Act of 1980 (LLRWPA).[23]

Despite such national consensus before its passage into law, the plan was plagued by widespread noncompliance.[24] The initial act was toothless;[25] Congress had honored the states' request that it include no federal penalties for violations in the first few years, giving the states time to evaluate how best to perfect their plans without federal interference.[26] However, this deference did not serve the LLRWPA's goal of rapid progress toward the creation of additional disposal capacity, as no new facilities had been built even by 1985.[27] The act permitted the sited states to refuse out-of-state shipments beginning in 1986, a fast-approaching deadline that was now certain to leave many states without any means of disposing of this hazardous waste. The looming crisis was reminiscent of that in 1979, when the sited states had first threatened to close their facilities, except that now they could do so without violating the dormant Commerce Clause.

Anxious to forestall a top-down federal solution, the states returned to the negotiating table to hammer out a new proposal, which the National Governors Association persuaded Congress to pass as the Low-Level Radioactive Waste Policy Act Amendments of 1985.[28] The new compromise extended the deadline by which non-sited states could continue to ship waste to sited states until 1992, but included harsher penalties for noncompliance with a timetable of regulatory milestones requiring states to take specific steps toward the ultimate goal of disposal self-sufficiency.[29] States that failed to meet milestones before 1992 could be forced to pay steep surcharges for access to existing disposal facilities in increasing increments over time, and denied certain access.[30]

---

[23] Low-Level Radioactive Waste Policy Act, Pub. L. No. 96–573, 94 Stat. 3347 (1980).

[24] New York, 505 U.S. at 151.

[25] Id. ("The 1980 Act included no penalties for States that failed to participate in this plan.").

[26] Id. at 191–92 (White, J., concurring and dissenting). Justice White quoted from the Governors' Task Force recommendation to Congress that it: "defer consideration of sanctions to compel the establishment of new disposal sites until at least two years after the enactment of compact consent legislation. States are already confronting the diminishing capacity of present sites and an unequivocal political warning from those states Governors. If at the end of the two-year period states have not responded effectively, or if problems still exist, stronger federal action may be necessary. But until that time, Congress should confine its role to removing obstacles and allowing the states a reasonable chance to solve the problem themselves." Id.; see also id. at 195 (Congress "could have pre-empted the field by directly regulating the disposal of waste pursuant to its powers under the Commerce and Spending Clauses, but instead it unanimously assented to the States' request for congressional ratification of agreements to which they had acceded").

[27] Id. at 151 (majority opinion).

[28] Low-Level Radioactive Waste Policy Amendments Act of 1985, Pub. L. 99–240, 99 Stat. 1842. See New York, 505 U.S. at 151 (noting the role of the National Governors Association in preparing the terms of the law).

[29] New York, 505 U.S. at 151–53. Among these milestones: by 1986, each state was to have ratified legislation either joining a regional compact or indicating intent to develop a disposal facility within the state; by 1988, each unsited compact was to have identified the state in which its facility would be located, and each compact or standalone state was to have developed a siting plan for the new facility; by 1990 each state or compact was to have filed a complete application for a license to operate the disposal facility (or certified that the state would be able to dispose of all in-state generated waste after 1992). Id. at 152–53.

[30] Id. at 152–53.

The most severe penalty under the new plan, and that most expected to motivate compliance, was the "take-title" penalty—by which a state that had not met the terms of the LLRWPA by 1996 would, at the request of the waste's producers, be held to "take title" to any low-level radioactive waste produced within its borders.[31] The take-title provision essentially meant that a state would assume legal liability for any damage associated with low-level radioactive waste produced within its borders for which it had not made disposal arrangements, either by building its own facility or gaining access to a site with sufficient capacity through membership in a willing regional compact. As a quid pro quo for the extended deadline that the sited states were granting, the non-sited states were thus promising to make genuine progress toward self-sufficiency or face real and dire consequences.

2. NEW YORK STATE'S CHALLENGE

Over the following seven years, Congress approved nine regional compacts encompassing forty-two states, three of which included the sited states of South Carolina, Washington, and Nevada.[32] The six non-sited compacts and four of the unaffiliated states met the first few milestones required under the amended LLRWPA, among them New York State—one of the largest state producers of low-level radioactive waste in the nation.[33] Anxious for prolonged access to existing facilities until it could make other arrangements, New York had supported both the state-based plan that the National Governors Association initially brought to Congress and the secondary compromise in the penalty-bearing Amendments, actively lobbying for their passage into federal law.[34] With so much in-state waste production, New York especially benefited from the additional twelve years of access under the law, and it made good faith efforts to build its own facility during that time.[35] Although it enacted legislation providing for the siting and financing of a facility and identified five potential locations in Allegany and Cortland Counties, the surrounding communities each strenuously objected to the construction of a radioactive waste disposal site in its vicinity.[36]

With the 1992 deadline fast approaching and no contingency for disposing of the waste that could soon be refused by the sited states, New York and its two counties sued to overturn the LLRWPA on various grounds, including violation of their rights under the due process clause, the Tenth Amendment, the Eleventh Amendment, and the Guarantee Clause.[37] After New York lost at the district and appellate court levels, the Supreme Court granted certiorari to hear its Tenth Amendment and Guarantee Clause issues.[38] The Court was interested in New York's claim that the statute's penalty structure commandeered its retained reservoir of state sovereign authority, most dramatically through the take-title

---

[31] *Id.* 153–54.

[32] *Id.* at 154.

[33] *Id.*

[34] *Id.* at 180–81.

[35] *Id.* at 154.

[36] *Id.*

[37] *Id.* at 154.

[38] *Id.*

provision.[39] New York argued that under the Tenth Amendment, Congress could neither force a state to build a radioactive waste disposal facility nor compel it to assume liability for the waste of in-state producers, and so the false choice required under the LLRWPA rendered it an unenforceable act of federal coercion.[40]

The sited states intervened as defendants in New York's suit. They agreed with the United States' position that the act did not violate the Tenth Amendment, but added that whether or not some other state could successfully object on these grounds, New York—of all states— could hardly state a Tenth Amendment claim of coercion when it had so clearly consented to the very terms it now challenged.[41] Even if, arguendo, the LLRWPA really interfered with a state's Tenth Amendment rights in the abstract, they argued that New York had waived the relevant entitlement not only through its participation in the National Governors Association process, but by its independent efforts to get the act and its amendments passed into federal law.[42] As Justice White summarized in his dissent,

In my view, New York's actions subsequent to enactment of the 1980 and 1985 Acts fairly indicate its approval of the interstate agreement process embodied in those laws within the meaning of Art. 1, § 10, cl. 3, of the Constitution, which provides that "[n]o State shall, without the Consent of Congress, . . . enter into any Agreement of Compact with another State." First, the States—including New York—worked through their Governors to petition Congress for the 1980 and 1985 Acts. As I have attempted to demonstrate, these statutes are best understood as the products of collective state action, rather than as impositions placed on States by the Federal Government. Second, New York acted in compliance with the requisites of both statutes in key respects, thus signifying its assent to the agreement achieved among the States as codified in these laws. After enactment of the 1980 Act and pursuant to its provision in § 4(a)(2), New York entered into compact negotiations with several other northeastern States before withdrawing from them to "go it alone."

Indeed, in 1985, as the January 1, 1986 deadline crisis approached and Congress considered the 1985 legislation that is the subject of this lawsuit, the Deputy Commissioner for Policy and Planning of the New York State Energy Office testified before Congress that "New York supports the efforts of Mr. Udall and the members of this Subcommittee to resolve the current impasse over Congressional consent to the proposed LLRW compacts and provide interim access for states and regions without sites. *New York has been participating with the National Governors' Association and the*

---

[39] *Id.* at 174–77.

[40] *Id.* at 175–76.

[41] *Id.* at 180–81 ("The sited state respondents . . . correctly observe that public officials representing the State of New York lent their support to the Act's enactment. A Deputy Commissioner of the State's Energy Office testified in favor of the Act. Senator Moynihan of New York spoke in support of the Act on the floor of the Senate. Respondents note that the Act embodies a bargain among the sited and unsited States, a compromise to which New York was a willing participant and from which New York has reaped much benefit.")

[42] *Id.* at 180–81.

other large states and compact commissions in an effort to further refine the recommended approach in HR 1083 and reach a consensus between all groups."

Based on the assumption that "other states will not continue indefinitely to provide access to facilities adequate for the permanent disposal of low-level radioactive waste generated in New York," the state legislature enacted a law providing for a waste disposal facility to be sited in the State . . . [listing New York's compliance with various provisions of the Act]. As it was undertaking these initial steps to honor the interstate compromise embodied in the 1985 Act, New York continued to take full advantage of the import concession made by the sited States, by exporting its low-level radioactive waste for the full 7-year extension period provided in the 1985 Act. By gaining these benefits and complying with certain of the Act's 1985 deadlines, therefore, New York fairly evidenced its acceptance of the federal-state arrangements—including the take title provision.[43]

The sited states claimed that New York could not make out a commandeering challenge after specifically asking to be bound by the terms of a legislative bargain, one in which it had participated just long enough to reap the intended benefits of twelve additional years of access to the sited states' facilities. Surely, they urged, New York's actions seeking federal ratification of the interstate deal it had helped negotiate should vitiate a later claim that Congress had violated its state sovereignty. In support of this claim, Justice White cited the Court's estoppel decision in *Dyer v. Sims*, denying West Virginia's claim that it lacked authority to enter into a compact it had already joined and upon which other states had relied.[44]

To be sure, there were compelling arguments on both sides of the debate as to whether New York's actions leading up to the passage of the challenged provisions should have estopped its subsequent Tenth Amendment challenge. Its enthusiastic support for federal passage of the act and its amendments certainly made New York seem less like the victim of federal coercion and more like an opportunistic litigant, one seeking any possible legal foothold before a Court eager to hold forth on matters of federalism.[45] Similarly, waiver might be discernable from its manifested intent to abide by the terms of the law until the time of its challenge—at least insofar as to take full advantage of the period of extended access.[46]

On the other hand, Tenth Amendment waiver had never previously been addressed by the Court, so whether New York's action actually constituted waiver would have been a question of first impression. States have always been able to waive their Eleventh Amendment immunity from lawsuits, but there is no such thing as "implied" or "constructive" Eleventh Amendment waiver; it must be made explicitly.[47] If Tenth Amendment waiver is comparable,

---

[43] *Id.* at 196–97 (White, J., concurring and dissenting) (emphasis in original).

[44] *Id.* at 199 ("Estoppel is not often to be invoked against a government. But West Virginia assumed a contractual obligation with equals by permission of another government that is sovereign in the field. After Congress and sister States had been induced to alter their positions and bind themselves to terms of a covenant, WV should be estopped from repudiating her act.") (citing *Dyer v. Sims*, 341 U.S. 22, 34 (1951)).

[45] *See, e.g.*, Gregory v. Ashcroft, 501 U.S. 452 (1991).

[46] *New York*, 505 U.S. at 196–98 (White, J., concurring and dissenting).

[47] Coll. Sav. Bank v. Fla. Prepaid Post-Secondary Educ. Expense Bd., 527 U.S. 666, 680 (1999).

then New York's actions—though suggestive and even self-serving—were still probably too indirect to have qualified as waiver. Even if the National Governors Association could be held to have spoken for New York, its recommendation to Congress did not have the force of a binding agreement by the states, it was not separately consented to by the state legislatures, and it certainly fell short of an explicit waiver of protected constitutional rights. Neither could statements of support for the legislation by higher-level New York officials be construed as express consent to waive a constitutional right. That New York took advantage of open disposal facilities also may not have manifested a clear enough intent to surrender its Tenth Amendment rights, at least if the appropriate metric were the Eleventh Amendment model.[48]

In the end, the well-known outcome of the case is that New York prevailed on its Tenth Amendment claim with regard to the take-title penalty, the penalty was stricken, and legal history was made as the New Federalism's Tenth Amendment anti-commandeering doctrine was born.[49] The Court was clear that although Congress could preempt state authority to directly regulate the interstate market for low-level radioactive waste disposal, and though it can also wield the spending power to persuade states to voluntarily accede to a federal regulatory program, "[t]he Federal Government may not compel the States to enact or administer a federal regulatory program."[50] In other words, the Tenth Amendment creates an entitlement to the states for a zone of federal noninterference, which, inter alia, forbids the federal government from using—or "commandeering"—state government as an apparatus within a national regulatory program.

As discussed in Chapter Six, there is compelling force behind the idea that Congress be limited from coercing state legislative performance rather than regulating directly. Yet for the purposes of this inquiry, the significant part of the decision is not the normative anti-commandeering rule itself, but the infrastructural component of the rule that disallows even the possibility that a state might choose to participate in such an arrangement.[51] If the anti-commandeering rule confers an enforceable entitlement to the states against federal commandeering, it is unclear why preventing states from consensually waiving that entitlement furthers the goals of the rule, or of federalism more generally.

Permitting states to bargain with their entitlement would not offend the touchstone of Tenth Amendment jurisprudence, which even the decision cites as the prevention of federal coercion.[52] Enabling a state to decide for itself whether to waive its entitlement serves the values of local autonomy (locating decisional authority at the local level), interjurisdictional innovation (allowing for the diversity of response that engenders the federalism "laboratory of ideas"), and subsidiarity-tempered problem solving (fostering the creation of intergovernmental partnerships as needed to solve interjurisdictional problems). It would offer sufficient protection for even the classical view of checks and balances, because a state will not bargain

---

[48] *New York*, 505 U.S. at 183.

[49] *Id.* at 187–88.

[50] *Id.* at 188.

[51] *Id.* at 180–82.

[52] *Id.* at 166–69 (1992).

against its powerful interest in maintaining the balance of state and federal power unless the offsetting problem-solving values justify the trade-off.

Indeed, this was the conclusion that all of the states came to when they negotiated the terms of the LLRWPA with each other and with Congress. The history of the act demonstrates that both the state and federal legislatures carefully balanced the competing considerations and negotiated a regulatory partnership that they believed represented the best equipoise from the perspective of local and national policy making. This question is whether the states should have been able to make this choice, and then bind themselves to it through the best available medium of federal law. Federal enforceability contains the collective action problem we can anticipate between states that rationally consent behind the veil of ignorance about who will be the eventual winners and losers under the plan, but then try to repudiate once the veil is lifted and they find themselves losers.

However, *New York* removed the possibility that state and federal legislatures might collaborate in balancing competing federalism values through this sort of consensual negotiation, even in gray area dilemmas in which the initial allocation of state and federal authority is itself unclear. Ironically, allowing state-federal bargaining around the bright line that separates New Federalism Tenth Amendment entitlements could alleviate some of the obstacles to problem solving that have otherwise plagued the gray area. As Coase predicts, bargaining protects us against errors in assigning the initial legal entitlement under conditions of uncertainty,[53] and uncertainty is a serious concern when drawing a line of jurisdictional separation through the haze of jurisdictional overlap. As with all bright-line rules, one potential advantage of jurisdictional line drawing is the clarity it creates about *who has what* for the purposes of state-federal bargaining. Whether or not the line is correctly drawn, at least the parties are on clear notice about which level of government has been designated which jurisdictional entitlements. Applying Coasian insight, even this artificial clarity might facilitate negotiation of the intergovernmental partnerships needed to cope with gray area problems. *New York* thus renders impotent the one architectural feature of the dual federalism revival that could be made useful for interjurisdictional governance.

In the ex ante policy-making arenas in which legislatures outperform courts, intergovernmental bargaining may be the best means of balancing checks, accountability, localism, and synergy values to cope with an interjurisdictional problem like this one. Bargaining between state and federal legislatures further ensures protection for the federalism values most vulnerable to unilateral legislative balancing: those of checks and localism. Part IV takes on the question of intergovernmental bargaining more fully, but the remainder of this chapter explores the idea in the specific context of commandeering bargaining that is freely initiated by the states as an alternative to more preemptive forms of federal gray area regulation. But first, in testimony for the need for a different approach, it reviews the devastating practical consequences of the *New York* decision for radioactive waste disposal in the decades that have followed.

---

[53] R. H. Coase, *The Problem of Social Cost*, 3 J.L. & ECON. 1, 15 (1960) (arguing that efficient results are obtainable when parties can bargain, if transaction costs are low).

3. THE AFTERMATH: RADIOACTIVE WASTE DISPOSAL
IN INTERJURISDICTIONAL LIMBO

The coordination of safe and equitable radioactive waste disposal is among the more stubborn regulatory problems that have become stranded in the interjurisdictional gray area. The *New York* saga reveals it as a matter that concerns both the states and the federal government, and one whose resolution requires the unique capacity that each can offer. It is a textbook national collective action problem requiring a federal umpire, in that none of the states wants to site the hazardous facility that all of them nevertheless need, with each state hoping to "free ride" on another's sacrifice.[54] After all, Congress became involved only after the states, acting separately, were fast approaching one of two unacceptable outcomes (either South Carolina would remain the unwilling bearer of all other free-riding states' costs, or it would close its site altogether and leave the entire nation without safe disposal options).

At the same time, it is a textbook example of a local land use problem about which surrounding communities have profoundly unique interests. Siting a hazardous waste facility implicates the very governmental decision making about land use planning that is the hallmark province of state and local government—and for good reason, bearing as it does on issues of property law, public health and safety, community stability, and other equitable matters of uniquely local concern.[55] Even the Court conceded this jurisdictional overlap by its recognition that both the states and federal government are empowered to regulate there.[56] As with many such gray area problems, an intergovernmental partnership is appropriate, desirable, and possibly the only effective means of proceeding.

Moreover, the fact that this one was negotiated by the state and federal legislatures ensured that federalism concerns were balanced in the calculus in a structural way that exceeds the political safeguards of a locally elected Congress. Although the most serious environmental justice questions were preserved for the ultimate siting decisions,[57] the state-based approach promised at least a rough environmental justice among the states, protecting individuals in guaranteeing that the burden of environmental risk would be shared throughout the nation. By forcing all states to internalize costs previously externalized to the three sited states, the LLRWPA would have realigned the interests of voters and lawmakers nationwide toward

---

[54] Another solution is to outlaw production of this waste altogether, but that has not gained political traction.

[55] For example, several states require local voter approval of new or renewed licenses for low-level radioactive waste facilities, consistent with the traditional municipal role in approving land uses that affect neighboring homes and businesses. *E.g.*, UTAH CODE ANN. § 19–3-105 (2008); VT. STAT. ANN. tit. 10, § 7012(f); ME. REV. STAT. tit. 38, §1493. The hurdles created by these statutes indicate tension between accountable governance and the parochialism that can accompany local land use decisions. While acknowledging the traditional land use planning role of local government, the statutes also exacerbate the NIMBY ("not in my backyard") phenomenon that has obstructed the development of fairly distributed capacity to handle the nation's unavoidable waste load. For this reason, an interjurisdictional approach is needed that can honor local interests while refereeing the nationwide collective action problem at hand (in which all communities would prefer to free ride on another neighborhood's risk taking).

[56] New York v. United States, 505 U.S. 144, 188 (1992).

[57] Low-income and minority neighborhoods disproportionately host hazardous waste facilities, which can contribute to high rates of asthma and other health problems. *See* Anna Kuchment, *Into the Wilds of Oakland Calif.: Young Pollution Sleuths and Community Activists Fight for Healthier Air*, NEWSWEEK, Aug. 11, 2008, at 50.

more accountable regulatory decision making about the use and production of materials none wished to host as waste. Local communities would be given more voice under the state-based solution than a fully federalized approach. Enacting the state plan as federal law avoided the constitutional hurdle and solved the collective action enforcement problem, harnessing the synergy between state and federal capacities. The states were willing to accept the limited federal interference in the take-title penalty because they preferred it to the alternative—by which Congress might rely on its commerce authority to craft a federal solution that preempted state input from top to bottom.[58]

Yet in the three decades since the *New York* decision removed this alternative, complete regulatory stagnation has exacerbated the problem of safe and equitable low-level radioactive waste disposal. As noted in Chapter Five, the states have made no net progress in creating additional disposal sites. There are still only three facilities for processing the entire nation's low-level radioactive waste.[59] Not a single new facility has been built as part of the regional compacts created by the LLRWPA.[60] Only one new facility has come on line since the permanent closure of the Beatty, Nevada site—a private facility in Clive, Utah.[61] Because the Clive facility is licensed to accept only the least hazardous class of radioactive waste, its addition does not alleviate the deficit in capacity exacerbated by the loss of the Beatty site.[62]

Furthermore, the Clive facility generated additional controversy when it contracted to accept low-level radioactive waste from Italy, which would hasten when the site would fill to capacity (currently anticipated in about twenty years).[63] Utah and the other members states

---

[58] No state voted against the solution proposed at the 1980 meeting of the National Governor's Association, which the Association then took to a unanimous vote in Congress. LLW Forum, *supra* note 16. Had a state initially opposed the state-based plan and then sued to invalidate the LLRWPA as applied to it, that suit would have presented a much more persuasive claim against federal commandeering. For this reason, the bargained-for-commandeering approach taken in the LLRWPA is most useful with broad ex ante state consensus.

[59] *See* U.S. Nuclear Regulatory Commission, Locations of Low-Level Waste Facilities, http://www.nrc.gov/waste/llw-disposal/licensing/locations.html (last visited July 14, 2010).

[60] A facility in West Texas may become the first new disposal site created within one of the regional compacts. Waste Control Specialists received a license in 2009 to dispose of low-level radioactive waste from the federal government, Texas, and Texas's compact partner, Vermont. *WCS Gets Final License*, ODESSA AMERICAN, Sept. 10, 2009, http://www.oaoa.com/articles/andrews-36577-waste-low.html. However, pending litigation has delayed construction of radioactive waste-compatible facilities. Kathleen Thurber, *Court of Appeals Agrees with District Court's Decision on Andrews County Election Case*, MIDLAND REPORTER-TELEGRAM, Apr. 16, 2010, http://www.mywesttexas.com/news/top_stories/article_27d55e5d-d9b1-52fd-af10-c79eb31c4e78.html. The company is also seeking—over vociferous local protest—to receive shipments from other states. Anna M. Tinsley, *Texas Reworking Plan for Radioactive Waste Shipments*, STAR-TELEGRAM, June 28, 2010, http://www.star-telegram.com/2010/06/28/2299720/texas-reworking-plan-for-radioactive.html.

[61] U.S. Nuclear Regulatory Commission, *supra* note 59.

[62] Clive's disposal facility is only licensed to accept "Class A" waste. U.S. Nuclear Regulatory Commission, Fact Sheet on Energysolutions' Proposal to Import Low-Level Radioactive Waste from Italy, http://www.nrc.gov/reading-rm/doc-collections/fact-sheets/energysolutions.html (last visited July 24, 2008).

[63] Rep. Bart Gordon & Rep. Jim Matheson, *Importing Nuclear Waste Is in EnergySolutions' Best Interests, But Not America's*, Op-Ed, SALT LAKE TRIB., April 5, 2008 (noting the nineteen-year figure was based on low estimates and did not include foreign shipments). The Government Accountability Office reports that we do not even know how much waste is currently awaiting storage, and that the burden will increase if more nuclear plants are licensed. *Id.*

of the Northwest Compact protested,[64] but the private site operator fought to preserve what was likely to be a lucrative contract, given that Europe faces an even greater shortage of disposal options.[65] Before ultimately abandoning plans to permanently store the Italian waste in Utah,[66] the operator unsuccessfully sued to establish that the states lacked authority to interfere with the Italian contract because its facility is not contractually bound by the Northwest Compact.[67] Meanwhile, alarmed at the prospect of further eroding capacity for domestic waste, both houses of Congress proposed bills to forbid domestic sites from accepting international shipments of radioactive waste (although neither bill emerged from committee).[68]

South Carolina's Barnwell site continued to accept the bulk of waste generated in the Eastern United States until July 1, 2008, when it finally acted on the authority conferred in the LLRWPA to close its doors to shipments of waste from outside its regional compact.[69] Although the take-title penalty was overturned in *New York*, the act's remaining penalty structure permitted the sited states to exclude others after the deadline. South Carolina continued to provide access to the many members of the Southeast Compact (including, for a time, New York—which had negotiated its way into the compact after its judicial victory because it still lacked disposal options for its in-state producers), but it eventually withdrew from the Southeast Compact when it became clear that its partner states were not progressing on their compact obligations to share disposal responsibilities.[70] South Carolina eventually joined the much smaller Atlantic Compact with New Jersey and Connecticut, and as of 2008, Barnwell now accepts interstate shipments only from these two states.[71]

Barnwell's closure to the rest of the nation has finally triggered the crisis that commanded the attention of Congress and the National Governors Association during the 1980s. As a nation, we are arguably in an even worse situation than before the LLRWPA and its amendments were passed. There are still only three low-level radioactive waste facilities nationwide. Richland accepts waste only from the Northwest and Rocky Mountain Compacts, and Barnwell accepts only from the two other states in the Atlantic Compact. Only Clive will

---

[64] *See* Charlotte E. Tucker, *Dwindling Capacity in US to Handle Low-Level Waste Prompts Import Questions*, 31 Int'l Envtl. Rep. (BNA) 495 (2008) (reporting on a Northwest Compact resolution seeking to block the imports).

[65] *Cf. Warning on Nuclear Waste Disposal*, BBC NEWS, April 4, 2005, http://news.bbc.co.uk/2/hi/science/nature/4407421.stm (discussing severe shortage of disposal sites in England).

[66] Tripp Baltz, *EnergySolutions Drops Plans to Store Low-Level Radioactive Waste at Utah Facility*, 41 Envtl. Rep. (BNA) 1580 (2010) (reporting that waste will still be processed in Tennessee but returned to Italy for storage).

[67] EnergySolutions, Inc. v. Utah, (10th Cir., No. 09–4122, Nov. 9, 2010) (holding that the regional compact is authorized to exclude low-level radioactive waste from within its member states' borders).

[68] *See* Mike Ferullo, *Radioactive Waste: Congressmen Offer Bill to Ban Import of Foreign-Generated Low-Level Waste*, 39 Env't Rep. (BNA) 562 (2008) (discussing H.R. 5632); S. 3225, 110th Cong. (2008) (the Senate version).

[69] *South Carolina's Barnwell Closes; Many without Rad Waste Disposal*, 28 NUCLEAR WASTE NEWS 1 (2008).

[70] *See* Andrew Meadows, *Governor-Elect Wants South Carolina to Rejoin Nuclear-Waste Group*, THE STATE, Dec. 16, 1998, at B1 (reporting on South Carolina's departure from the Southeast Compact).

[71] *See Barnwell Closure Results in Revised Storage Guidance*, NUCLEAR NEWS, July 2008, at 19.

accept shipments from any producer in the entire nation, but Clive accepts only the least hazardous "Class A" forms of waste, which degrade over a period of one hundred years.[72]

Hoping to resolve that particular aspect of the capacity crisis with the stroke of a pen, nuclear industry lobbyists asked the Nuclear Regulatory Commission to reconsider its waste classification system.[73] The Commission received public comment on the proposal in 2010, which would allow holders of low-level radioactive waste to blend the more hazardous Class B and C wastes (which can take up to five hundred years to degrade) with Class A waste, and classify the resulting product simply as Class A.[74] If adopted, the new system would enable the Clive site, approved only for Class A waste, to begin accepting the more hazardous forms without taking additional safety precautions, a point which met with resounding protest from nearby Utah residents.[75] In addition, Clive is poised to devote a portion of its available capacity to importing nations such as Italy, further hastening its projected fill date.

Accordingly, the Nuclear Regulatory Commissioner publicly acknowledged in 2007 that "the low-level waste compact process has not been quite as successful as we would have hoped"[76]:

> While the NRC has developed national standards for low-level radioactive waste disposal in its regulations the agency does not currently regulate any of the disposal sites in the United States. The current disposal facilities are all regulated by states. . . . The Low-level Radioactive Waste Policy Acts of 1980 and 1985 were supposed to ensure a reliable and predicable means of disposing of low-level radioactive waste. The acts made each state responsible for providing for waste disposal, but I do not believe that the overarching objectives of the acts will ever be realized.[77]

Indeed, the citizens of South Carolina, Washington, and Utah remain unhappily burdened with an unfair share of the entire nation's hazardous waste, all citizens remain at risk for waste transportation accidents over long stretches of public highways, and the nation is that much

---

[72] Patty Henetz, *Huntsman Signs Waste-Ban Measure*, SALT LAKE TRIB., Feb. 26, 2005 at A6 (explaining this, and that Utah has banned the more toxic Class B and C forms of waste).

[73] *See* Judy Fahys, *Industry Recipe: Diluted N-Waste*, SALT LAKE TRIB., June 28, 2008, http://www.sltrib.com/news/ci_9726810 (reporting on the industry effort to access Clive with more toxic wastes).

[74] *Id*; U.S. Nuclear Regulatory Commission, Blending of Low-Level Radioactive Waste http://www.nrc.gov/waste/llw-disposal/llw-pa/llw-blending.html (last visited Sept. 29, 2010); Thomas Burr, *Energy Solutions: State OK Not Needed for Blending Radioactive Waste*, SALT LAKE TRIB., Jan. 14, 2010.

[75] *See, e.g.*, Editorial, *Radioactive Cocktail: Blending Waste Won't Lessen the Danger*, SALT LAKE TRIB., July 1, 2008. Utahns were already concerned about attracting more radioactive waste to the state, given reports that Clive had accepted ninety-three percent of all government radioactive waste destined for domestic commercial facilities between 1998 and 2003. Judy Fahys, *Guv Says "N-O' to N-dump Times Two*, SALT LAKE TRIB., Nov. 11, 2005 at A1.

[76] Gregory B. Jaczko, Commissioner, U.S. Nuclear Regulatory Commission, Remarks at the International Low-Level Waste Conference and Exhibit Show: The Need for Alternatives in Low-Level Radioactive Waste Disposal (June 26, 2007), http://www.nrc.gov/reading-rm/doc-collections/commission/speeches/2007/S-07-033.html

[77] *Id*.

closer to running out of available disposal capacity without further options. The one silver lining to this continued failure is that the increasing costs of low-level radioactive waste disposal has somewhat dampened supply, slowing the pace of the looming crisis, but also the pace of potentially life-saving medical research.[78] But fluctuating oil prices and concerns about climate change have renewed national interest in nuclear power, and erecting more nuclear power plants—which produce significant quantities of both high-level and low-level radioactive waste—would significantly exacerbate the problem.[79]

The 1980s' collaboration between the states and Congress used a variety of carrots and sticks to incentivize non-sited states to take responsibility for their fair share of risk, but *New York* dissolved the most persuasive stick, and carrots have proved insufficient. The states have lost any incentive to resolve the collective action problem without a means of enforcing the needed interstate bargain.[80] Congress, having been judicially disciplined on federalism grounds for an attempt made with due respect for state autonomy, has lost all incentive to impose a top-down solution that (even if legal) will engender serious federalism friction. In a classic case of abdication, neither Congress nor the states have meaningfully wrestled with the resulting regulatory "hot potato" since then, each side apparently conceding from its respective loss in court that the status quo is really the other's problem.[81]

Yet solving the problem of equitable radioactive waste disposal cannot be the exclusive province of one or the other side alone; it is an interjurisdictional problem best tackled with the unique regulatory capacities that both Congress and the states bring to bear. The partnership they negotiated in the LLRWPA might have been the means to break the collective action deadlock. Even conceding the problems with truly coercive legislative commandeering, consensual bargaining with the anti-commandeering entitlement should be treated differently.

---

[78] *See id.* In 2001, a National Academies study found that disposal costs were a substantial hurdle for medical research, concluding that medical facilities already stressed to capacity could not proceed with needed research if additional site closures further restricted storage options. COMM. ON THE IMPACT OF LOW-LEVEL RADIOACTIVE WASTE MGMT. POL'Y ON BIOMEDICAL RESEARCH IN THE UNITED STATES, BOARD ON RADIATION EFFECTS RESEARCH, NAT'L RESEARCH COUNCIL, THE IMPACT OF LOW-LEVEL RADIOACTIVE WASTE MANAGEMENT POLICY ON BIOMEDICAL RESEARCH IN THE UNITED STATES (2001), http://www.nap.edu/catalog.php?record_id=10064.

[79] Although some waste can temporarily be stored on-site, all must be processed at a proper disposal facility when the plant is eventually decommissioned. INTERNATIONAL ATOMIC ENERGY AGENCY, CLIMATE CHANGE AND NUCLEAR POWER (2000), http://www.iaea.org/Publications/Booklets/ClimateChange/climate_change.pdf.

[80] South Carolina could have forced other states to internalize their share of economic externalities by taxing incoming waste shipments, but this would not resolve its distributional fairness concerns about allocating safety risk.

[81] *See supra* Chapter Five, notes 115–32 and accompanying text. However, the Obama administration may be taking up the gauntlet. *See* Judy Fahys, *Obama Panel Examines Nation's Nuclear Waste Issues*, SALT LAKE TRIB., Apr. 4, 2010. In addition, Utah, Maine, and Vermont have each asserted new authority over waste production within their borders, requiring new and relicensing nuclear facilities to obtain approval from governors, legislatures, and/or voters—although one author suggests this violates the Supremacy Clause. Melissa B. Orien, *Battle over Control of Low-Level Radioactive Waste: Some States Are Overstepping Their Bounds*, 1–2005 BYU L. REV. 155, 156 (2005).

B. The Court's Rationale: Checks and Accountability

The Supreme Court justified its decision to disallow commandeering bargaining—even when initiated by the states—on two separate grounds, neither of them satisfying. First, it analogized to other individual rights that the state may not waive on behalf of individuals and to the immobility of other structural constitutional features, such as the horizontal separation of powers among Congress, the president, and the federal judiciary. It also justified the rule on grounds of accountability, worrying that the interests of a state's citizens and their elected representatives might differ too much to allow the latter to waive on behalf of the former in state-federal negotiations. Finally, it undermined both lines of reasoning by suggesting that the same elected officials who should not be able to waive their citizens' entitlement in negotiations with the federal government might nevertheless be able to solve the same problem in negotiations with another state of an interstate compact.

In defending the choice not to allow waiver, the Court first appealed to the important federalism value of checks and balances. It analogized to the horizontal separation of powers among the three federal branches,[82] which is (weakly) vindicated by the nondelegation doctrine that prevents Congress from abdicating its role to the executive[83] and the jurisprudential *Chevron* doctrine of administrative law that prevents the judiciary from encroaching on executive and legislative decision making.[84] But even assuming strong protection for the horizontal separation of powers, the analogy fails in comparison with the vertical separation of state and federal power.

Though appealing at first blush, the comparison is ultimately unsatisfying when considered in the full context of federalism entitlements that are treated as tradable. As discussed more fully below, the same state sovereign authority considered sacrosanct under the *New York* rule is the subject of bargaining elsewhere, especially amid the waivable reciprocal entitlements to regulatory noninterference that are created in the interplay between the grants and limits on federal power.[85] When the states yielded to a nationally mandated speed limit in exchange for federal highway funds, they bargained away an entitlement to a particular zone of sovereign authority free of federal interference.[86] When they accepted federal education funding in exchange for instituting a battery of standardized tests, they bargained away another such entitlement.[87] If constitutional law permits state-federal bargaining around

---

[82] *See* Lujan v. Defenders of Wildlife, 504 U.S. 555, 559–60 (1992) (noting that the horizontal separation of powers "depends largely upon common understanding of what activities are appropriate" to each branch).

[83] The Court has not enforced the nondelegation doctrine for over sixty years, upholding all recent delegations to administrative agencies. ERWIN CHEMERINSKY, CONSTITUTIONAL LAW: PRINCIPLES AND POLICIES §3.10.1 (3d ed. 2006). *E.g.*, Whitman v. Am. Trucking Ass'n, 531 U.S. 457, 472 (2001) (upholding EPA's air quality standards).

[84] Chevron U.S.A., Inc. v. NRDC, Inc., 467 U.S. 837, 838 (1984).

[85] *See infra* notes 156–59 and accompanying text.

[86] South Dakota v. Dole, 483 U.S. 203, 211 (1987).

[87] *See* No Child Left Behind Act of 2001, 20 U.S.C. §§ 6301–6578 (2000).

Tenth Amendment-defined zones under the spending power, why should the states' Tenth Amendment anti-commandeering entitlement be different?[88]

Perhaps conscious of this weakness in its characterization of the Tenth Amendment entitlement as an immutable structural feature of the constitution, the Court also characterized it as an individual right—reasoning that the entitlement is inalienable in state-federal bargaining because it belongs not to the state as a state, but to the individuals within the state. After acknowledging that the challenged terms of the LLRWPA constituted a regulatory bargain in which New York was a willing beneficiary, the Court asked and then answered its own rhetorical question in terms of the individual interests in state sovereign authority. Writing for the Court, Justice O'Connor reasoned:

> How can a federal statute be found an unconstitutional infringement of state sovereignty when state officials consented to the statute's enactment? The answer follows from an understanding of the fundamental purpose served by our Government's federal structure. The Constitution does not protect the sovereignty of States for the benefit of the States or state governments as abstract political entities, or even for the benefit of the public officials governing the States. To the contrary, the Constitution divides authority between federal and state governments for the protection of individuals. State sovereignty is not just an end in itself: "Rather, federalism secures to citizens the liberties that derive from the diffusion of sovereign power."[89]

Indeed, no one would argue that the Tenth Amendment does not protect individuals in this way, but the argument proves too much—because ultimately, *all* constitutional directives exist to protect individuals. Indeed, this is the very purpose of the Constitution; it is what each of its elements is designed, directly or indirectly, to accomplish.

That it benefits individuals, then, is an unremarkable feature of the Tenth Amendment entitlement. But by invoking its relationship to individuals, the Court implicitly compared the entitlement to others in the Bill of Rights that establish clear individual rights, such as the Sixth Amendment right to jury trial, the Fourth Amendment right against unreasonable search and seizure, or even the First Amendment right to free speech.[90] Still, even the fact that a constitutional entitlement protects individuals does not justify the non-waiver rule, since most constitutional rights—including each of those mentioned above—are waivable.[91] Citizens frequently bargain away their right to jury trial for a plea agreement that better meets their interests,[92] as well as their rights against unreasonable searches when they choose

---

[88] Noting this inconsistency, some scholars argue that the others are under-protected. *See infra* note 163.

[89] New York v. United States, 505 U.S. 144, 180–82 (1992). *Accord* Bond v. United States, No. 09-1227, 564 U.S. __, *9–10 (slip opinion) (2011), 2011 Westlaw 2369334 (U.S.).

[90] U.S. Const. amends. VI, IV, and I.

[91] *E.g.*, Richard H. Seamon, *The Asymmetry of State Sovereign Immunity*, 76 Wash. L. Rev. 1067, 1135 n.325 (2001) (observing that constitutional rights are presumptively protected by property rules).

[92] In 2003, out of 83,530 defendants in U.S. District Courts, 74,850 were convicted, 72,110 of whom entered pleas of guilty or nolo contendere. United States Dept. of Justice, Bureau of Justice Statistics, Sourcebook of Criminal Justice Statistics 423 (2003), http://www.albany.edu/sourcebook/pdf/t522.pdf. *See also* Thomas W. Merrill, *The Constitution and the Cathedral: Prohibiting, Purchasing, and Possibly*

to cooperate with warrantless police,[93] and their rights to free speech when they accept government employment.[94] Is there something else about the nature of Tenth Amendment state sovereign authority that justifies the difference?

Most constitutional rights that are waivable are not usually waived by the *state*, which makes sense because they are mostly rights held by individual citizens *against* the state. The First Amendment entitles individuals to speak free from state interference, the Fourth Amendment entitles them to be free of unreasonable search and seizure by the state, and the Sixth Amendment guarantees them a fair trial before facing state punishment. But the Court's facile invocation of this principle in *New York* is dubious, because the Tenth Amendment entitlement—though it may exist to protect individuals—is not like these other individual rights. The entitlement at issue in *New York* was not held by citizens against New York or the state officials who might have waived it; if it was held against anything, that would have been the federal government. The states' Tenth Amendment entitlement, the mirror image of its reciprocal federal counterpart, benefits individuals by delineating a zone of sovereign authority protected against federal incursion. In this respect, it seems far less like the First or Fourth Amendment entitlement than it does its neighboring entitlement, the Eleventh Amendment one to state sovereign immunity—a medium of state sovereign authority that the Court acknowledges a state *can* waive.[95]

Disallowing waiver of the Tenth Amendment entitlement to state sovereign authority is difficult to reconcile with the freely alienable Eleventh Amendment entitlement to the same constitutional medium. The Tenth Amendment protects a zone of local regulatory authority, and the Eleventh Amendment protects the fiscal integrity of that level (and perhaps more in some philosophically significant way, in vindicating the state as a sovereign not subject to private suit[96]). While each benefits individuals by empowering them locally within a federal system, neither is cognizable except as it attaches to the state as an institution of government. An individual citizen has no divisible interest in state regulatory authority, or in a state's treasury, except as stakeholders within that state.

The Tenth and Eleventh Amendments are thus better understood (as, indeed, they usually are[97]) as conferring collective rights, meaningfully administered by the states qua states, and not to individuals. Indeed, in a recent case establishing Second Amendment rights at the individual level, the Court distinguished its understanding that the Tenth Amendment's reservation of sovereign authority to "the people" refers to them only in their corporate

---

Condemning Tobacco Advertising, 93 Nw. U L. Rev. 1143, 1144 (1999) (noting that a property rule governs the Sixth Amendment).

[93] See Miranda v. Arizona 384 U.S. 436, 477–78 (1966) (noting that citizens may willingly provide information that may aid a law enforcement effort); cf. Erik G. Luna, *The Models of Criminal Procedure*, 2 Buff. Crim. L. Rev. 389, 436 (1999) (arguing against a liability rule approach in the Fourth Amendment context).

[94] See, e.g., Snepp v. United States, 444 U.S. 507 (1980) (holding that a contract between the CIA and one of its employees was valid, even though it restricted his ability to publish a book about his work for the agency).

[95] See e.g., Lapides v. Bd. of Regents of U. Ga., 535 U.S. 613, 614 (2002); Coll. Sav. Bank v. Fla. Prepaid Postsecondary Educ. Expense Bd., 527 U.S. 666, 681, n.3 (1999); Pennhurst State Sch. v. Halderman, 465 U.S. 89, 99 (1984); Ex parte State of New York No. 1, 256 U.S. 490, 497 (1921).

[96] See Alden v. Maine 527 U.S. 706, 713 (1999).

[97] E.g., Fry v. United States, 421 U.S. 542, 557 (1975) (citing the two as conveying the Framers' intention to recognize that the states, while subject to some federal authority, were not to be regulated like ordinary citizens).

capacity, as the collective body that forms the citizenry of a government: "the term unambiguously refers to all members of the political community, not an unspecified subset."[98] Tenth and Eleventh Amendment claims are thus conventionally grouped together under the banner of "States' Rights," even though their underlying purposes may be to protect citizens from losing locally based legislative authority and from being forced as taxpayers to satisfy federal court judgments against their states. If state sovereign authority is alienable by state officials in the Eleventh Amendment context, it is hard to understand why it should not be in the Tenth Amendment context as well.[99]

Were the relationship to individual interests really the proper yardstick for waiver that the Court proposes in *New York*, then the most logical arrangement would be the reverse: the Eleventh Amendment should receive more protection, since that one can be much more closely connected with the protection of discrete individuals' interests than the Tenth Amendment entitlement. Discrete individual taxpayers bear the brunt of legal liability for judgments against their states, and all else being equal, it is safe to predict that all citizens would prefer lower rather than higher taxes—so at least all taxpayers would have a substantially parallel interest in how the Eleventh Amendment entitlement is used or waived. It is much harder to trace a direct relationship between use or waiver of the sovereign authority protected by the Tenth Amendment and the interests of discrete individuals due to the inevitable policy dissensus among them about how that authority is used. (Demonstrating the breadth of conflicting interests among statewide electorates is the perfect absence of unanimous elections and referenda at the state level.)

Moreover, though all citizens may have a parallel interest in protecting local authority, it is disputable that preventing waiver of the entitlement at issue in *New York* even did so. Where the rubber of that entitlement really hits the road in each case depends on the specific authority and how it would be used or traded, which will always be different. Citizens' interests are much more uniform under the Eleventh Amendment, where they are unified around issues of finances and judicial process. Supporting this distinction is the litany of recent cases following *Seminole Tribe's* characterization of the Eleventh Amendment as protecting individual taxpayers,[100] while *New York* remains the only Tenth Amendment decision to characterize the entitlement as a protection for individuals that states may not waive.[101]

---

[98] District of Columbia v. Heller, 128 S. Ct. 2783, 2790–91 (2008).

[99] One might try to justify the difference on grounds that the Eleventh Amendment is framed as a limit on federal power (which the states can waive) and the Tenth as affirming some reserve of state power (which the state cannot waive)—but the distinction fails. The Tenth also represents a limit on federal power by affirming that reservoir of authority not delegated to the federal government. Indeed, each amendment's phrasing creates a similarly reciprocal set of "Hohfeldian" rights and duties. Wesley Newcomb Hohfeld, *Some Fundamental Legal Conceptions as Applied in Judicial Reasoning*, 23 YALE L.J. 16 (1913). The Eleventh Amendment limitation on federal judicial power is what creates the meaningful state entitlement to sovereign immunity, just as the Tenth Amendment's reciprocal affirmations set forth distinct sources of state and federal authority.

[100] *See, e.g.*, Seminole Tribe of Florida v. Florida, 517 U.S. 44, 58 (1996) (noting that one of its primary purposes is to protect "individual taxpayers" from satisfying federal court judgments against their states).

[101] *New York* cites to *Coleman v. Thompson*, 501 U.S. 722, 759 (1991), as precedent for this proposition, but the case provides dubious support; *Coleman* dealt with the ability of federal courts to grant habeas relief that had been denied by state courts, and the cited statement is part of the dissenting opinion.

The Court's other main justification for disallowing waiver hinged on federalism's account-ability value, highlighting the problems of trust that can arise between citizens and their agents in government. First, the majority worried that enabling state legislators to bargain with Congress this way would undermine citizens' ability to monitor the effectiveness of their representation in government and take corrective action as needed.[102] The Court explained that when state legislators bind themselves under federal law in negotiations with Congress, both sides potentially evade responsibility for policy making. Constituents will have a harder time knowing whom to hold accountable for the resulting laws. As discussed in Chapter Two, however, this argument has been roundly criticized for resting on the unsup-ported empirical premises that (1) voters cannot tell what level of government is to blame for a given policy, and (2) state and local officials are unable to tell them when the fault truly lies in Washington.[103] The Court's reasoning assumes that voters are either unable to understand interaction between the federal and state governments and/or that they cannot voice correc-tive preferences through their federal representation, though evidence suggests otherwise.[104]

More significant was the majority's deep concern that state officials cannot be trusted with the power to waive an entitlement that truly belongs to the citizens, who might have interests distinct from their elected representatives.[105] This is a more formidable concern, as the per-sonal interests of elected officials and those of the constituents they represent can never be completely aligned. Nevertheless, while this gap between the interests of principals and agents is endemic in all fields where primary interest holders are represented by others, the gap is actually *less* problematic in the anti-commandeering context than in others that the Court seems to accept as a consequence of our representational democracy.

The problem that the *New York* decision identifies—that state representatives may not faithfully execute the best Tenth Amendment interests of their citizens[106]—is a species of the well-researched genera of what negotiation and economic theorists call the principal-agent tension.[107] The principal-agent tension is created by the subtle disconnects between the personal interests of the principal and his or her bargaining agent that pervade all negotiations carried on by representatives.[108] Reflecting insights from the public law analog of public choice theory, the principal-agent tension focuses more directly on the relationships

---

[102] New York v. United States, 505 U.S. 144, 168 (1992).

[103] *Cf.* Moulton, *supra* Chapter Two, note 74, at 877.

[104] *Supra* Chapter Two, notes 74–76 and accompanying text.

[105] 505 U.S. at 182–83 (noting the "possibility that powerful incentives might lead both federal and state officials to view departures from the federal structure to be in their personal interests").

[106] *Id.*

[107] *See* Robert Mnookin et al., Beyond Winning: Negotiating to Create Value in Deals and Disputes 69 (2000) (describing the principal-agent tension); Joseph Schumpeter, Capitalism, Socialism and Democracy 287 (1987) (describing how elections can distort incentives for representa-tives in government); McGinnis & Somin, *supra* Chapter Two, note 4, (arguing that elected officials may consent to federalism violations against the interests of their constituents, though conceding that this prob-lem is least severe in the anti-commandeering context).

[108] *See, e.g.,* Mnookin et al., *supra* note 107, at 69.

in representational bargaining contexts.[109] For example, an agent paid by the hour may proceed more deliberately than if paid a flat fee, even if the principal is more interested in speed in the first case or care in the second. Voters' interests may best be served by tackling a thorny dilemma as soon as possible, but their elected official might ignore opportunities until after the election in order to mitigate the personal costs of any political fallout. Thus, although this aspect of the agent-accountability problem is a valid concern, it is also one that applies to *all* legislative products of elected representation (including the sorts of state legislative decision making that the Court approves in opposition to Tenth Amendment bargaining).[110] Should this particular context of state-federal bargaining be different?

The Court clearly believed so, heralding the vertical separation of powers as a cornerstone of American federalism, but closer analysis belies the proposition. If anything, this context is the one in which we can *least* fear the distorting effects of the principal-agent tension, because the nature of Tenth Amendment state sovereign authority affords the greatest overlap between the private interests of individual citizens and their elected representatives, whose only claim to power lies in that very authority. Both citizens and state officials benefit by retaining as much local authority as possible, except when the problem they wish to resolve requires as constrained a sacrifice in this authority as possible.[111] But state representatives will be particularly jealous of Tenth Amendment protected state authority; if they were too free in bargaining away these entitlements, they would soon find themselves out of work. (If anything, we might fear the reverse problem—in which the citizens would benefit from waiver of an entitlement that the representative refuses to alienate—but this was clearly not the Court's concern.)

Meanwhile, we trust elected state representatives to make legislative trade-offs against all sorts of other constitutionally protected interests that are valued much differently at the individual and state levels, where the principal-agent tension is much more pronounced. State legislatures can pass laws that constitutionally burden individual citizens' free speech (as narrowly tailored time, place, and manner restrictions), even though those are speech rights specifically held against the government.[112] They can also enact neutral rules of general applicability that burden their citizens' free exercise of religion, although that is also a right held against the state.[113] State legislatures pass laws that burden their citizens' equal protection interests all the time, and they can do so on any rational basis, so long as no protected

---

[109] Public choice theory is used most powerfully to show how small groups with concentrated interests exert disproportionate pressure on the public process in comparison to larger groups with more dispersed interests. *E.g.,* DANIEL A. FARBER & PHILIP P. FRICKEY, LAW AND PUBLIC CHOICE: A CRITICAL INTRODUCTION (1991). Though it works well to explain the influence of special interests in confounding the accountability of representational governance, it focuses less directly on this narrower representational tension in public bargaining.

[110] 505 U.S. at 168 (arguing that Congress should not compel but rather negotiate with states to achieve federal goals).

[111] *See* CHARLES FRIED, CONTRACT AS PROMISE: A THEORY OF CONTRACTUAL OBLIGATION 9–11, 14–16 (1981) (explaining that contractors compromise their autonomy in promises when the benefits outweigh the compromise).

[112] *See* Grayned v. City of Rockford, 408 U.S. 104, 115–18 (1972).

[113] *See* Employment Div. v. Smith, 494 U.S. 872 (1990).

class is implicated.[114] It is much more likely that there could be a gap between the interests of individual citizens and their state representatives in vindicating these more classic individual rights because, once again, these are rights that individual citizens hold *against* the state. Yet in these contexts, where the principal-agent tension is that much more palpable, we do not hesitate to allow the state to burden them by the legislative decision making of elected representatives.

By contrast, when legislators bargain with their state's sovereign authority—the precious commodity that is the basis for their own authority to legislate anything about anything—we can feel comparatively secure that they will share their constituents' interests in conservatism. The principal-agent concern will always be most pressing when the right in question is one exercised by individuals one at a time against the state, and less so as the right is more cognizable as a collective one, such as those described by the Tenth and Eleventh Amendments. An entitlement to legislative decision making seems far from the prerogative of any one individual citizen, even though individual citizens benefit from it collectively. Even scholars who defend the need for judicial federalism constraints on principal-agent grounds acknowledge that the lack of potential for officials' personal gain in negotiating around commandeering constraints makes the threat much less pressing than in other federalism contexts.[115] Although they favor the Court's current approach, Professors John McGinnis and Ilya Somin have explained that:

> In practice, commandeering is not nearly as great a danger to federalism as the Spending power and the Commerce power. State governments often have strong incentives to resist uncompensated commandeering because, by definition, it deprives them of resources without any offsetting benefits. For this reason, state governments routinely use their political power to resist commandeering and other "unfunded mandates."[116]

By extension, they are unlikely to choose *not* to resist commandeering unless it promises substantial offsetting benefits.

Whether the Tenth Amendment entitlement protects an individual or a collective right, the close overlap between citizen and representative interests in their states' sovereign authority means that Tenth Amendment bargaining will be more resistant to the distorting effects of the principal-agent tension than most other legislative arenas in which elected officials make trade-offs against constitutionally protected rights. The Court also suggests that the better alternatives for coping with an interjurisdictional problem of this variety can be found in spending power deals or cooperate-or-be-preempted choices—which invite the very same principal-agent conflicts in negotiations that also strain accountability.

Finally, the majority's defense of the rule on both checks and accountability grounds was substantially undermined by dicta implying that even though New York State could not waive its citizens' entitlement to the federal government in negotiating a resolution to the crisis, it might have succeeded in doing so had it joined an interstate compact and waived the

---

[114] *See* McGowan v. Maryland, 366 U.S. 420 (1961).

[115] *See* McGinnis & Somin, *supra* Chapter Two, note 4, at 119.

[116] *Id.*

same sovereign authority directly to other states.[117] The decision suggests (without deciding) that the disputed take-title provision—which the majority considered part of the law requiring the formation of interstate waste disposal compacts but not part of the interstate compacts themselves[118]—might have been binding had New York promised to abide by the provision within the actual terms of an interstate compact it joined pursuant to the act:

> Nor does the State's prior support for the Act estop it from asserting the Act's unconstitutionality. While New York has received the benefit of the Act in the form of a few more years of access to disposal sites in other States, New York has never joined a regional radioactive waste compact. Any estoppel implications that might flow from membership in a compact thus do not concern us here. The fact that the Act, like much federal legislation, embodies a compromise among the States does not elevate the Act (or the antecedent discussions among representatives of the States) to the status of an interstate agreement requiring Congress' approval under the Compact Clause. That a party collaborated with others in seeking legislation has never been understood to estop the party from challenging that legislation in subsequent litigation.[119]

The Court's conclusion that the states' earlier negotiations did not rise to the level of a compact is unremarkable, but the implications of the passage are striking. The suggestion that New York's lawsuit might have been estopped had the state bargained away its sovereign authority with other states rather than the federal government betrays the heart of the Court's rationale that state officials may not waive an entitlement that does not belong to them. If sovereign authority cannot be waived by state officials to Congress because it really belongs to individual citizens, how could it nevertheless be waived by state officials to the officials of another state?[120] If a constitutional entitlement belongs to the citizens, what difference does it make whether the sovereign to whom their elected officials waive it is the federal or a separate state government?[121]

---

[117] New York v. United States, 505 U.S. 144, 182–83 (1992).

[118] Even this is a disputed point; in his dissent, Justice White interpreted the relevant interstate compacts as incorporating the Act's take-title provision by reference. *Id.* at 195–96 (White, J., concurring and dissenting).

[119] *Id.* at 183 (majority opinion) (citations omitted).

[120] Consider the perverse implications were the Court to enforce consistency by holding that a state could not waive sovereign authority in *either* context: compacts such as the ones embedded in the Act would be impermissible, no matter the need. Yet the proposition is undermined by the existence of hundreds of interstate compacts in which states do waive some degree of Tenth Amendment sovereignty to other states or to an interstate commission. *E.g.,* Klamath River Basin Compact, Pub. L. No. 85–222, 71 Stat. 497 (1957); Interstate Compact for Adult Offender Supervision, MINN. STAT. §243.1605 (2007); Interstate Compact for Juveniles, NEV. REV. STAT. § 62I.010 (2008). *See also* Michael L. Buenger & Richard L. Masters, *The Interstate Compact on Adult Offender Supervision: Using Old Tools to Solve New Problems,* 9 ROGER WILLIAMS U.L. REV. 71 (2003) (discussing how states use interstate compacts to work together on national issues while preserving autonomy).

[121] Note that *New York* did not definitively hold that a state *could* waive Tenth Amendment-protected sovereign authority by joining a compact; it merely suggested that it *might* have been able to. The decision suggests that had New York joined a compact in which the take-title penalty was an explicit part, then its bid for release

The discrepancy casts doubt on the Court's assertion that its rationale protects individuals. It is unclear why a state could waive an individual's entitlement to sovereign authority by joining a compact that requires congressional approval, but not after negotiating for the same waiver in direct congressional legislation independent of the compact. The same rights are at stake in both contexts, and the interstate compact medium certainly does not enable states to waive other constitutional entitlements held by individuals. For example, even with congressional consent, the New England states could not form an interstate compact to deny residency status to minorities, nor could the southeastern states compact to deny members of the Republican Party the right to speak in a public forum. But that is the absurd implication of the suggestion that the result of the case might have been different had New York followed the other of the two permissible paths outlined by the Act: joining a compact that required it to site a facility rather than attempting to site an in-state facility on its own.

The best counterargument is probably that the relevant Tenth Amendment entitlement is not really a positive one for a zone of state sovereign authority but a negative one against federal interference with that authority. If this were so, the state could waive the same sovereign authority in allowing interference by another state without triggering the separate entitlement against federal interference. Under this analysis, the question really becomes one about the content of the Tenth Amendment entitlement: regardless of who has the power to waive it, is the entitlement really to a zone of state authority that cannot be breached by any outside sovereign, including another state (we can call this the "positive entitlement"), or is it a specific prohibition on federal interference in state affairs ("the negative entitlement")?

Yet neither depiction of the entitlement truly stands without the other. Indeed, the Court tells us exactly this in *New York*, identifying these positive and negative Tenth Amendment entitlements as "mirror images of each other."[122] As it reaffirmed in *Bond v. United States*,

> The principles of limited national powers and state sovereignty are intertwined. While neither originates in the Tenth Amendment, both are expressed by it. Impermissible interference with state sovereignty is not within the enumerated powers of the National Government, and action that exceeds the National Government's enumerated powers undermines the sovereign interests of States.[123]

---

from the bargain might have been vitiated by an estoppel claim unavailable in this context (though it remains unclear why).

[122] 505 U.S. at 156. See also *id.* at 155–159, 177 ("In the end, just as a cup may be half empty or half full, it makes no difference whether one views the question at issue in these cases as one of ascertaining the limits of the power delegated to the Federal Government under the affirmative provisions of the Constitution or one of discerning the core of sovereignty retained by the States under the Tenth Amendment. Either way, we must determine whether any of the three challenged provisions of the [Act] oversteps the boundary between federal and state authority."). See also supra note 99 (discussing the reciprocal Hohfeldian framing of the Tenth Amendment).

[123] Bond v. United States, No. 09-1227, 564 U.S. __, *13 (slip opinion) (2011), 2011 Westlaw 2369334 (U.S.). See also *United States* v. *Lopez*, 514 U. S. 549, 564 (1995).

The existence of the positive entitlement's zone of state authority thus implies a presumption of federal noninterference, while the negative entitlement's restriction is meaningless unless it refers to noninterference with a specific zone of positive state authority.

Any answer to this question must therefore include both components, and the only question is whether the negative component protects state sovereign authority from interference by any outside sovereign or only the federal government. In Balanced Federalism, the best understanding of the Tenth Amendment entitlement is that it confers on each side a positive zone of sovereign authority coupled with a negative presumption against interference by the other that may be overcome in the gray area where state and federal zones overlap. By this view, the entitlement to noninterference is strongest at the two uncontroversial ends of the jurisdictional spectrum, but weakest in the gray area.[124] The central inquiry would seem to be the same in analyzing jurisdictional competition from beyond the state-federal continuum: whether waiver would advance or detract from the fundamental federalism values that the Tenth Amendment protects.

Regardless, the Court's own reasoning in *New York* fails to resolve the problem. If a state may not waive its citizens' entitlement to sovereign authority to the federal government but it may to another state, the Court must assume that the only relevant entitlement is the negative entitlement to federal noninterference. But as established above, this elides the positive entitlement to a zone of state sovereign authority that must accompany it. If the state can still trade on the positive entitlement with the right bargaining partner, then this contradicts the Court's own stated characterization of the entitlement as being not a state prerogative but a right belonging to individual citizens—one which would seem to deserve protection from trade to either the federal government or any another sovereign state.

On a pragmatic level, it is also worth noting that limiting a state's ability to bargain with its sovereign authority to the sole arena of interstate compacts would make it harder for the resulting compacts to be effective, because interstate compacts (like international laws) are easy to exit and hard to enforce. State default on compact obligations is what inspired the take-title penalty in the first place, and including the penalty directly into the compacts would be fraught with peril for the same reasons. In theory, most compacts can include terms that can be enforced like contracts, but even then, notorious enforcement hurdles make them an unreliable mechanism for binding state agreement in comparison to what the Act would have accomplished.[125] Unlike straightforward federal judicial interpretation of federal law such as the LLRWPA, the special challenges of litigating compacts between sovereign states often requires the appointment of a special master and decades of multiple-iteration litigation to reach a resolution.[126] In many cases, states can simply withdraw from the agreement by

---

[124] *Cf. supra* discussion surrounding Chapter Six, note 34 (explaining the three contingent zones of balanced federalism).

[125] *See* Caroline Broun et al., THE EVOLVING USE AND THE CHANGING ROLE OF INTERSTATE COMPACTS: A PRACTITIONER'S GUIDE 29–30 (2006) (describing the practical problems of enforcing compacts against sovereign entities and concluding that "to a large degree, the effectiveness of a compact continues to rest on the willingness of the member states to actually abide by the terms and conditions of the agreement notwithstanding its contractual nature").

[126] For example, the litigation by South Carolina and its fellow compact members against North Carolina for failure to abide by the terms of their LLRWPA compact is taking the better part of a decade to resolve under

repealing their own enacting state legislation, leaving compacting states vulnerable to strategic bargaining moves that may ultimately undermine the accomplishment of interstate bargaining goals.[127]

Indeed, this is exactly what New York State sought to do in the case of the Low-Level Radioactive Waste Policy Act: it took advantage of the Act's initial benefits (extended deadlines enabling it to use South Carolina as a low-cost radioactive waste dumping ground for an additional twelve years) until the bargain no longer seemed appealing, then left its partner states holding the proverbial bag. The unfairness of New York's behavior offends common law contract sensibilities, which may be why the Court held open the possibility that New York might be held to account for its strategic behavior by a state within the breached compact, even if not by the federal government suing for violation of the underlying federal law.[128] And indeed, when the Act's compacts were uncoupled from the independently enforceable take-title threat, it failed to deliver on its goal of creating a national network of disposal sites.

Removing the externally enforceable penalty thus defeated the intentions of the states that designed the system adopted by the Act. If penalties are limited to the language of interstate compacts because Congress cannot enact them even with states' consent, then enforcement problems could undermine interstate compacting goals altogether. A separately enforceable provision with teeth may be necessary to contain the collective action problems that inhibit full participation and enforcement. Indeed, freeloading and holdout are exactly the sort of collective action problems that motivated the influential analysis by Professor Calabresi and Douglas Melamed of how legal rules allow and disable entitlement shifting.[129] The following section describes their framework and demonstrates its application in constitutional contexts, enabling us to review the problems with the *New York* rule at the level of legal infrastructure.

C. The Infrastructure of Legal Rules: The Calabresi & Melamed Cathedral Framework

In their iconic Harvard Law Review article, *Property Rules, Liability Rules, and Inalienability: One View of The Cathedral*, Guido Calabresi and Douglas Melamed describe legal rules as the pairing of an entitlement—designating which of the conflicting parties will prevail in a given scenario of legal conflict—with a second-order rule indicating how that entitlement will be

---

the supervision of a special master, and the most recent iteration casts further doubt on meaningful enforceability of compacts. Alabama v. North Carolina, 130 S. Ct. 2295 (2010) (declining to hold North Carolina liable for damages and sanctions after it withdrew from the compact, even though it had accepted $80 million from the plaintiff states in anticipation of its performance). Similarly, Texas sued in 1974 to resolve the terms of a water allocation compact in *Texas v. New Mexico*, 462 U.S. 554, 562 (1983), and the case continued under the supervision of a special master for fifteen years until the dispute was finally resolved in 1988. Texas v. New Mexico, 485 U.S. 388 (1988).

[127] *Cf. Alabama*, 130 S. Ct. 2295 (affirming a state's right to freely depart a compact).

[128] New York v. United States, 505 U.S. 144, 183 (1992).

[129] Calabresi & Melamed, *supra* Introduction, note 67, at 1093–98.

vindicated if challenged.[130] Their conceptual vocabulary sheds important light on how the Supreme Court could have gotten the substantive part of the anti-commandeering rule right and the infrastructural part that prevents bargaining wrong.

This *Cathedral* Framework draws from tort, property, and criminal law in clarifying the different approaches available for protecting the assignment of legal entitlements.[131] Legal rules mediate between parties with conflicting interests in some legal sphere, and the rule's first task is to decide which of the parties' interests will be privileged as a substantive matter. In so doing, the rule confers on the privileged party a legal entitlement, or a right to do or to have something—be it the entitlement to exclude others from private property, or to use a crosswalk without being run over by lawful automobile traffic, or to regulate interstate commerce. The second, lesser-celebrated job of the legal rule is to structure the scope of permissible transactions involving this entitlement once it is assigned.

To this end, as between the privileged holder and those with competing interests, the law will vindicate the entitlement in one of three ways. If the entitlement is protected under a *property rule*, its holder has absolute power to convey the entitlement away for a satisfactory price. This approach treats the entitlement like an item of property, enabling the holder to protect it against all challengers or trade it on the open market at will. It represents the most common remedy rule in property law—for example, governing most private real estate transactions, where owners sell their homes in the marketplace only if they so desire, and then on their own terms.[132]

If the entitlement is protected under a *liability rule*, it may be purchased at an objectively determined price by the competitor even without the holder's consent.[133] This is the most common remedy rule in tort law—where accident victims are not usually given the ex ante opportunity to bargain away their entitlement not to be victims of negligently inflicted harm, but in which the law compensates them for the loss of that entitlement by requiring the competitor (here, the tortfeasor) to compensate them in the form of objectively determined damages. The Law and Economics school, which suggests that legal rules promote general utility over individual autonomy in cases where holdouts or other collective action problems derail socially desirable outcomes, has embraced the use of liability rule remedies in other areas of law that feature these problems, such as private nuisance.[134]

The final approach is one of *inalienability*, by which the entitlement is held to rest where it is initially laid by the law, rendering any attempted transfer by either party unenforceable.[135] This is a common remedy rule in criminal law (where consent is not a defense to murder or statutory rape),[136] but it is also found in other areas of law.

---

[130] *See generally id.*

[131] *Id.* at 1089.

[132] *Id.* at 1092.

[133] *Id.*

[134] *E.g.,* Boomer v. Atlantic Cement, 257 N.E.2d 870 (N.Y. 1970); RESTATEMENT (SECOND) OF TORTS § 822 cmt. d.

[135] Calabresi & Melamed, *supra* Introduction, note 67, at 1092–93.

[136] For example, Florida prohibits murder even when the victim consents. FLA. STAT. § 782.08 (2007). Oregon does not allow persons under age eighteen to consent to a sexual act. OR. REV. STAT. § 163.315(1) (2007).

For example, the implied warranty of habitability in property law establishes an entitlement to renters for a minimum standard of safety and sanitation in rental housing that cannot be negotiated away even between a willing landlord and tenant happy to bargain for less safety at less rent.[137] As argued below, by disallowing waiver of the anti-commandeering entitlement, the Court effectively protected the substantive anti-commandeering entitlement with an inalienability rule.

Calabresi and Melamed propose various reasons for using property, liability, and inalienability rules to accomplish the goals of well-ordered legal rules. For example, they suggest that property rules be used whenever the cheapest cost avoider can be identified, because it enables interparty bargaining that ensures the entitlement ultimately reaches the most efficient destination even if an error is made in the initial assignment.[138] Liability rules are useful when there is uncertainty at the outset about the identity of the cheapest cost avoider, and where transaction costs or collective action problems would impede efficient bargaining over the entitlement.[139] In either case, the liability rule ensures that a socially desirable transaction may proceed even if the entitlement holder protests[140]—as does the law of eminent domain, which enables the government to condemn land for highways and airports by paying fair market value even if one or more of the owners of targeted properties would rather not sell.[141]

Inalienability rules ensure specific outcomes to protect what Calabresi and Melamed call a "moralism," by which they mean a strong policy-making consensus preferring some desired outcome despite the resulting efficiency and autonomy losses that the assignment of an inalienability rule inevitably implies.[142] In this way, inalienability may be used to serve a policy of paternalism (to protect legal actors under some kind of disability, such as minors with regard to statutory rape), or to achieve a preferred distributional preference in light of some compelling public policy (such as affirmative action).[143] For example, the implied

---

[137] *E.g.*, Academy Spires, Inc. v. Brown, 111 N.J. Super. 477, 482 (N.J. Dist. Ct. 1970).

[138] Calabresi & Melamed, *supra* Introduction, note 67, at 1118. Of course, the choice of whom to assign the initial entitlement is still important, as it may create significant distributional consequences for the parties. Projections are also subject to the usual caveats of the Coase theorem's limiting assumptions, so property rules can lead to inefficiencies when transaction costs are high, as with multiple parties and collective action problems. *Id.* at 1119.

[139] *Id.*

[140] In theory, liability rules ensure efficient results regardless of initial allocation, because if a competitor values the entitlement more than the initial holder, he or she may purchase it even over the holder's dissent. *Id.* at 1107–10.

[141] *Id.* at 1120. Still, liability rules can also lead to troubling distributional effects, because the efficient result is partly determined by the parties' relative ability to pay. They can also mar efficiency when personal valuations are not approximated by market prices. *See* United States v. 564.54 Acres of Land, More or Less, 441 U.S. 506, 511 (1979) (discussing undercompensation of idiosyncratic owners in eminent domain); RICHARD A. EPSTEIN, TAKINGS: PRIVATE PROPERTY AND THE POWER OF EMINENT DOMAIN 183 (1985); Michael Heller & Roderick Hills, *Land Assembly Districts*, 121 HARV. L. REV. 1465, 1474 (2008).

[142] Calabresi & Melamed, *supra* Introduction, note 67, at 1111–12, 1123–24.

[143] *Id.* at 1113–14. Professor Thomas Merrill proposes a variation to better describe entitlements in the public law context, in which he suggests an alternate basis for inalienability rules. Merrill, *supra* note 92, at 1144 (applying the framework in the context of federal efforts to reduce smoking). He suggests that inalienability is

warranty of habitability reflects a societal consensus about minimum levels of residential safety, despite its frustration of bargains that some landlords and tenants might otherwise reach for less expensive, less safe housing.

From the standpoint of Law and Economics, the problem with inalienability rules is that they prioritize other policy concerns over economic efficiency[144] (if, as is often the case, these subjective concerns cannot be reliably measured in economic terms[145]). From the libertarian standpoint, the problem with inalienability rules is that they prioritize other policy concerns over individual autonomy. If there is not perfect consensus about the public policy privileged by the inalienability rule, then those who disagree with the policy may acutely object to this loss of all transactional control over the entitlement. From the standpoint of interjurisdictional governance, the problem is that regulatory authority in the gray area may be mistakenly allocated in the first instance, and inalienability rules prevent corrective negotiation.

1. *THE* CATHEDRAL *IN THE PUBLIC LAW CONTEXT*

Many authors have employed the *Cathedral* framework of analysis to critique underperforming legal rules in the common law contexts that Calabresi and Melamed addressed directly,[146] but others have shown that the framework proves robust at describing the infrastructure of constitutional rules.[147] From ongoing friction over the explicit liability rule in the Fifth Amendment takings clause (enabling the state to condemn private property for public use so long as market value is paid)[148] to debate over the coercive overuse of property rule-enabled plea bargains (alleged to distort the criminal law bargaining process to the point of vitiating the Sixth Amendment right to jury trial)[149]—many of today's most compelling constitutional controversies involve the second-order, remedial aspect of the operative legal rule.

---

useful whenever keeping the entitlement where it is initially allocated is worth more to the public than it is to the holder of the initial allocation—thus preventing socially undesirable transfers of publicly valuable allocations. It is a useful way of understanding the *Cathedral* "moralism" in public law contexts, but it ultimately breaks down to the same understanding used here: a policy-making consensus about a desired outcome that outweighs the efficiency and autonomy losses implied by the inalienability rule.

[144] That said, inalienability rules are not always used in opposition to efficiency; they can occasionally avoid the wasteful costs of setting up a market to shift an entitlement for which there is little actual demand. Calabresi & Melamed, *supra* Introduction, note 67, at 1123–24.

[145] Some authors describe these as "public goods." *E.g.*, David S. Brookshire & Don L. Coursey, *Measuring the Value of a Public Good: An Empirical Comparison of Elicitation Procedures*, 77 Am. Econ. Rev. 554 (1987); Sameer H. Doshi, *Making the Sale on Contingent Valuation*, 1 Tul. Envt'l. L.J. 295, 296 (2008).

[146] *E.g.*, Stewart E. Sterk, *Property Rules, Liability Rules, and Uncertainty about Property Rights*, 106 Mich. L. Rev. 1285 (2008); Henry Smith, *Property and Property Rules*, 79 N.Y.U. L. Rev. 1719 (2004); Ian Ayres & J. M. Balkin, *Legal Entitlements as Auctions: Property Rules, Liability Rules, and Beyond*, 106 Yale L.J. 703,748 (1997).

[147] *E.g.*, Eugene Kontorovich, *The Constitution in Two Dimensions: A Transaction Cost Analysis of Constitutional Remedies*, 91 Va. L.R. 1135, 1138 (2005); Merrill, *supra* note 92, at 1144.

[148] *E.g.*, Heller & Hills, *supra* note 141, at 1474 (critiquing the eminent domain liability rule that undercompensates owners for property they did not wish to part with at market rates in the first place).

[149] *E.g.*, Robert E. Scott & William J. Stuntz, *Plea Bargaining as Contract*, 101 Yale L.J. 1909, 1909–10 (1991–92); Tracey L. Meares, *Rewards for Good Behavior: Influencing Prosecutorial Discretion and Conduct with Financial*

The *Cathedral* framework is particularly useful in analyzing the infrastructural problems that can arise when courts must jurisprudentially infer what remedy rule should attach to an otherwise clearly stated normative rule. Some constitutional entitlements, such as individual rights, are easily analogized to the standard private law entitlements to do or have something. Other constitutional entitlements allocate jurisdictional authority to different governmental actors, and assign limits to that authority. Although these more structural entitlements stray farther from the original *Cathedral* inquiry, the framework remains surprisingly powerful in clarifying what happens when they are challenged, and offers useful analytical tools for courts that must determine remedies jurisprudentially.

The scholarly consensus is that most constitutional entitlements are protected under a property rule,[150] although Professor Eugene Kontorovich has recently demonstrated many instances of hidden liability rules.[151] Still, all three varieties can be found in constitutional law, some specified in the text and others jurisprudentially. For example, a defendant's Sixth Amendment right to jury trial is treated as protected by a property rule, since it can be bargained away with the state in exchange for a plea agreement that the defendant would prefer. Although land is generally protected under a property rule in the private market, an owner's Fifth Amendment right against government appropriation for public use is protected under an explicit liability rule, since the state may take it over the owner's dissent so long as just compensation is paid.[152] Meanwhile, the Thirteenth Amendment prohibition of slavery confers an entitlement to freedom zealously guarded by an inalienability rule, since even a consensual agreement to sell oneself into slavery will be legally unenforceable.[153]

Incentives, 64 FORDHAM L. REV. 851, 864 (1995–1996); Joseph P. Fried, *New York Judge Rejects Death Penalty Plea Deal*, N.Y. TIMES, Aug. 7, 1997 (reporting on concerns that death penalty law coerces guilty pleas).

[150] *E.g.*, AKHIL REED AMAR, THE CONSTITUTION AND CRIMINAL PROCEDURE: FIRST PRINCIPLES 115 & n.112 (1997); Kontorovich, *supra* note 147, at 1138; Vicki C. Jackson, *The Supreme Court, the Eleventh Amendment, and State Sovereign Immunity*, 98 YALE L.J. 1, 93–94 (1988); David Luban, *The Warren Court and the Concept of a Right*, 34 HARV. CR.-CL. L. REV. 7, 19–20 & n.36 (1999); Luna, *supra* note 93, at 436; Seamon, *supra* note 91, at 1135 n.325 (all suggesting that constitutional rights are presumptively protected by property rules).

[151] Kontorovich, *supra* note 147, at 1138; Eugene Kontorovich, *Liability Rules for Constitutional Rights: The Case of Mass Detentions*, 56 STAN. L. REV. 755 (2004).

[152] Professor Kontorovich has also coined the "pliability rule" combination of property and liability rules in certain areas of constitutional law, including takings, since the liability rule for public-use takings is paired with a property rule for nonpublic use takings. Kontorovich, *supra* note 147, at 1138. Another pliability rule can be found in the Third Amendment proscription on quartering troops on private property during peace time without permission—an explicit property rule paired with an implied liability rule protecting the entitlement in wartime. *Id.*

[153] Another example is the Guarantee Clause, promising each state a republican form of government. U.S. CONST. art. IV, §4. However, inalienability may be all bark and no bite, given the Court's long tradition of treating claims under this clause as nonjusticiable. *E.g.*, Luther v. Borden, 7. How. 1 (1849); New York v. United States, 505 U.S. 144, 184–85 (1992).

2. *FEDERALISM AT THE* CATHEDRAL

The Supreme Court's recent federalism jurisprudence shows the same array of choices among remedy rules for protecting assigned entitlements. Like other constitutional entitlements, most created by the rules of constitutional federalism are protected under a property rule. For example, a state's Eleventh Amendment entitlement to sovereign immunity from citizen suit is protected by a property rule, because the state can choose to waive it by consenting to an otherwise barred suit. In the New Federalism era, the Supreme Court has defended its strong protection of a state's rights under the Eleventh Amendment by characterizing the entitlement to sovereign immunity as a core attribute of statehood—one that cannot be casually abrogated without posing dire consequences for the success of the state as an enterprise of government.[154] However, in keeping with its general approach of protecting entitlements under a property rule, the Court has also consistently held that the Constitution does not prohibit a state from trading away this entitlement on its own accord.[155]

Similarly, much of the scope of federal regulatory jurisdiction under the Commerce Clause and other federally enumerated powers is protected by a property rule, as demonstrated by the Court's concomitant Spending Clause jurisprudence. Although the Commerce Clause grants a zone of positive jurisdictional authority to the federal government, the entitlement can be also be understood as a reciprocal entitlement to the states for federal regulatory noninterference beyond its designated limits (and as discussed in Chapter Four, it is this aspect that has most informed the New Federalism revival).[156] However, the federal government frequently uses its spending power to negotiate with the states for expanded regulatory jurisdiction beyond the limits of the commerce or other enumerated powers.[157] When this happens, a state is essentially bargaining away its constitutional entitlement to federal noninterference in the relevant regulatory zone,[158] much as an individual defendant might trade away his or her property rule-protected Sixth Amendment entitlement to jury trial in a plea agreement with the prosecution. For example, the federal government was able to persuade most states to reduce their speed limits during the gas crisis of the 1970s by conditioning their receipt of federal highway funds on the adoption of a 55-mph. maximum on interstate highways.[159]

---

[154] *E.g.,* Seminole Tribe of Fla. v. Florida, 517 U.S. 44, 54 (1996).

[155] *See supra* notes 95 and accompanying text.

[156] U.S. CONST. art. I, § 8, cl. 3.

[157] *E.g.,* South Dakota v. Dole, 483 U.S. 203, 211 (1987).

[158] For example, even as the Court held that Congress lacked constitutional authority to require the states to take the challenged actions, it noted that Congress remained free to persuade the states to do so using its power under the Spending Clause. *New York,* 505 U.S. at 166–67.

[159] See Zachary Coile, *Speier Seeks National Speed Limit to Save Gas,* SAN FRANCISCO CHRON., July 11, 2008, at A1. A contentious modern example is the "No Child Left Behind" program, by which the Bush Administration effectively mandated national elementary school performance standards, *e.g.,* David Nash, *Improving No Child Left Behind: Achieving Excellence and Equity in Partnership with the States,* 55 RUTGERS L. REV. 239, 253 (2002–2003), even though public education is beyond Congress's enumerated powers. United States v. Lopez, 514 U.S. 549, 565 (1995) (noting that the commerce power does not authorize Congress to mandate a national school curriculum).

In the background of these reciprocal federal and state entitlements lurks the Tenth Amendment, promising a system of dual sovereignty in which the state and federal governments play distinct roles. As discussed in Chapter Two, it is the penumbral effect of the Tenth Amendment that creates the reciprocal state entitlement whenever the Constitution grants a limited power to the federal government, such as the federal power to regulate interstate commerce, and the reciprocal state entitlement for federal noninterference beyond the limits thereby implied (such as the regulation of domestic violence or hydrologically isolated wetlands).[160] Indeed, although the New Federalism revival promotes a casual understanding of the Tenth Amendment entitlement as one against federal commandeering of state power,[161] the better characterization—acknowledged directly in the *New York* decision—is that the Tenth Amendment creates these very state and federal entitlements to reciprocal jurisdictional zones. To this point, writing for the majority in *New York v. United States*, Justice O'Connor explained that:

> [i]n a case like these, involving the division of authority between federal and state governments, the two inquiries are mirror images of each other. If a power is delegated to Congress in the Constitution, the Tenth Amendment expressly disclaims any reservation of that power to the States; if a power is an attribute of state sovereignty reserved by the Tenth Amendment, it is necessarily a power the Constitution has not conferred on Congress.[162]

In its commerce jurisprudence, the Court has interpreted these reciprocal state entitlements as protected under a property rule enabling waiver in spending power deals. In its Eleventh Amendment jurisprudence, the Court has allowed the states to trade on an entitlement to sovereign immunity that it has described as an essential attribute of state sovereignty. But in *New York*, the Court chose to protect Tenth Amendment entitlements under the inalienability alternative that prevents any kind of waiver, even as it allows a parallel sort of waiver in spending power cases.[163]

3. APPLICABILITY OF THE CATHEDRAL FRAMEWORK

Before critiquing this choice, however, I pause to defend the suitability of the *Cathedral* framework for doing so. Some public law scholars will chafe at the application of this private law bargaining analysis to constitutional law in general, and structural federalism in particular. Some suggest that it is heretical to speak of remedies for constitutional violations at all, because it implies that unconstitutional acts are permissible so long as they are remedied

---

[160] *See* United States v. Morrison, 529 U.S. 598, 605 (2000); *SWANNC*, 531 U.S. 159, 162 (2001).

[161] *See* Printz v. United States, 521 U.S. 898, 935 (1997).

[162] 505 U.S. 144, 156 (1992).

[163] For the argument that it is the spending doctrine that wrongly undermines the rest of the New Federalism cases, see Baker, *supra* Chapter Three, note 218, at 205–06; Baker & Berman, *supra* Chapter Four, note 17, at 499–500; Somin, *supra* Chapter Two, note 28.

appropriately.[164] But using the framework to understand these foundational legal rules does not undermine constitutional limits when it simply reveals the inherent limits built into the underlying constitutional entitlements. In other words, speaking of the liability rule protecting private property against condemnation for public use does not cheapen the Fifth Amendment right to private property; it merely accurately characterizes the remedy rule effectively built in to the constitutional grant.[165]

I am sympathetic to the concern that private law vocabulary can cause conceptual friction with public law ideals, especially in analogizing constitutional law to commodities in a market for exchange.[166] I do not reduce, nor do I mistake, federalism values for actual items of personal property. However, the familiar conceptual framework helpfully distinguishes between the substantive and infrastructural aspects of legal rules in a way that especially advances conversation about negotiated governance. I proceeded in the firm belief that there is much to be gained from intradisciplinary exchange between one area of legal thought and another—even when there are rough edges to the enterprise—because it can illuminate old problems with the clarity of a new vantage point, and unpack seemingly daunting new problems with the benefit of proven conceptual tools.

Moreover, the dynamics of state-federal bargaining approximate marketplace bargaining even more closely than other forms of negotiation in which government is a party. Intergovernmental bargaining suffers even more acutely from the very private law bargaining problems and collective action hurdles that Calabresi and Melamed urge are best resolved by the use of property and liability rules.[167] Political bargaining, involving the authoritative allocation of resources, is often distinguished from the price-regulated allocation of resources in economic bargaining.[168] Political bargaining is necessary when high transaction costs prevent market-efficient bargaining. But similar problems relating to collective action and "signaling" (to communicate leverage, proposals, and concessions) occur in both private and political bargaining, except that they are exacerbated in political bargaining, which generally involves a greater variety of interests and players.[169] Compared with private negotiations, governmental negotiations are complicated by multiple constituents' interests, public participation, and open meeting requirements.[170]

---

[164] *E.g.*, Kontorovich, *supra* note 147, at 1138 (discussing this objection).

[165] Either way, as Professor Kontorovich argues, the distinction is ultimately about whether negotiation over entitlement shifting happens ex ante (property rules) or ex post (liability rules), or not at all (inalienability). *Id.*

[166] *Cf.* Margaret Jane Radin, *Market-Inalienability*, 100 HARV. L. REV. 1849 (1987) (discussing the limits of commodification).

[167] Calabresi & Melamed, *supra* Introduction, note 67, at 1118–20.

[168] *See* GIDEON DORON & ITAI SENED, POLITICAL BARGAINING: THEORY, PRACTICE, & PROCESS (2001); David B. Spence & Lekha Gopalakrishnan, *Bargaining Theory and Regulatory Reform: The Political Logic of Inefficient Regulation*, 53 VAND. L. REV. 599 (2000).

[169] *See* Benjamin L. Snowden, *Bargaining in the Shadow of Uncertainty: Understanding the Failure of the ACF and ACT Compacts*, 13 N.Y.U. ENVTL. L.J. 134, 179–80 (2005) (in the context of a multi-state water compact, using bargaining theory to explore the issues that complicate political negotiations among multiple sovereigns).

[170] *Id.* at 176–80.

State-federal political bargaining is even more like private economic bargaining than conventional political bargaining between participants in the same pool of sovereign authority. Where sovereign authority is truly divided (as between federal and state government), rather than nested (as between state and municipal governments), it will be more like price-regulated private bargaining, because neither side can compel the other to perform against its will. Although this holds less true in contexts where the federal government has field-preempted under an enumerated power, the analogy is strongest in the gray area, where sovereign authority is divided and yet both kinds are necessary to effectively regulate. Even where power disparities exist between the parties (and the federal government is not always the more powerful party[171]), this reflects the inherent inequalities of bargaining power that pervade private bargaining. For example, Professor Roderick Hill has argued that states behave "exactly like private firms" in negotiating federal-state partnerships under the spending power.[172]

As do all negotiations, state-federal bargaining takes place "in the shadow of the law,"[173] and federalism uncertainty poses the biggest obstacle to efficient intergovernmental bargaining in the gray area. The primary source of uncertainty is the substantive question of who actually holds which jurisdictional entitlement.[174] But infrastructural uncertainties also pervade the law of intergovernmental bargaining—for instance, and especially after the *New York* decision, whether a given entitlement is even a legitimate medium of exchange. In addition, parties negotiate with an eye toward what negotiation theorists call their "BATNA" (best alternative to the negotiated agreement),[175] but uncertainty about the reach of judicial intervention after the negotiation concludes can undermine the parties' efforts to understand their true alternatives, further compromising bargaining efficiency.[176]

To facilitate intergovernmental bargaining, then, the single most valuable adjustment would be to reduce the legal uncertainties in the gray area. Shedding light on actual gray area bargaining will help generate better bargaining rules, which is the purpose of the case study in this chapter and Part IV generally. Some uncertainty will always pervade federalism-sensitive governance, but even if the substantive aspect of intergovernmental bargaining remains confusing, the overall enterprise would be improved by clarifying the procedural rules that help parties understand the available media of exchange and their best alternatives to agreement. The *New York* inalienability rule does this by forbidding bargaining altogether,

---

[171] As discussed more fully in Chapter Nine, leverage accrues to the party who loses least from reaching no deal. The federal government would likely be the bigger loser were the states to withdraw from many cooperative federalism enterprises as it would then have to find ways to provide the needed regulatory services without the substantial assets of local government infrastructure. *See also* Hills, *supra* Part I Introduction, note 5.

[172] *Id.* at 870 (also arguing that the anti-commandeering rule usefully constrains spending power bargaining).

[173] Robert H. Mnookin & Lewis Kornhausert, *Bargaining in the Shadow of the Law*, 88 YALE L.J. 950 (1979).

[174] For example, in the multi-state compact Snowden studied, uncertainty regarding the extent of federal claims on the river basin ultimately brought down the entire seven-year negotiation. Snowden, *supra* note 169, at 184.

[175] ROGER FISHER & WILLIAM L. URY, GETTING TO YES: NEGOTIATING AGREEMENT WITHOUT GIVING IN 100 (1991).

[176] Snowden shows how uncertainties regarding the potential for congressional apportionment and the unlikely prospect of judicial intervention helped undermine the Compact negotiations. Snowden, *supra* note 169, at 188.

but gray area uncertainty about the initial allocation of regulatory entitlements mitigates in favor of a different approach.[177] Enabling consensual bargaining could facilitate interjurisdictional progress even when mistakes are made in the initial allocation—or more accurately, in a court's best interpretation of the allocation.

D. Enabling Intergovernmental Bargaining with Tenth Amendment Entitlements

In *New York*, the Court articulated a reasonable entitlement to federal noninterference protected by an unreasonable inalienability rule. As discussed below, prohibiting state government from bargaining with the entitlement creates an inalienability rule, because any number of collective action problems would prevent the negotiated transfer of the entitlement *except* through representation by elected officials. It is unreasonable, because the intergovernmental partnerships thus thwarted would help resolve pressing interjurisdictional problems without offending the Tenth Amendment. Indeed, underlying values that give meaning to the Tenth Amendment would be better served by allowing a state to decide for itself whether to hold or trade its entitlement. With the benefit of the *Cathedral* framework, this section explores how the New York decision effectively created an inalienability rule, and proposes the Court modify the doctrine with a property rule.

1. ANTI-COMMANDEERING INALIENABILITY

Rather than deciding, as well it might have, that New York's actions simply did not rise to the needed level for waiving the Tenth Amendment entitlement against federal commandeering, the Court decided that the entire waiver question was moot. There was no need to decide whether New York's actions met the criteria for waiver because, simply put, there *is* no such waiver in the Tenth Amendment context. As described above, the decision expressly declared that a state may not waive its Tenth Amendment entitlement because it protects the interests of individual citizens in state sovereignty:

> The sited state respondents focus their attention on the process by which the Act was formulated. They correctly observe that public officials representing the State of New York lent their support to the Act's enactment. . . . Respondents note that the Act embodies a bargain among the sited and unsited States, a compromise to which New York was a willing participant and from which New York has reaped much benefit. Respondents then pose what appears at first to be a troubling question: How can a federal statute be found an unconstitutional infringement of state sovereignty when state officials consented to the statute's enactment?
>
> The answer follows from an understanding of the fundamental purpose served by our Government's federal structure. The Constitution does not protect the sovereignty of States for the benefit of the States or state governments as abstract political entities,

---

[177] Calabresi & Melamed, *supra* Introduction, note 67, at 1120.

or even for the benefit of the public officials governing the States. To the contrary, the Constitution divides authority between federal and state governments for the protection of individuals. State sovereignty is not just an end in itself: "Rather, federalism secures to citizens the liberties that derive from the diffusion of sovereign power." . . . Where Congress exceeds its authority relative to the States, therefore, the departure from the constitutional plan cannot be ratified by the "consent" of state officials.[178]

By this reasoning, state actors can *never* waive the Tenth Amendment entitlement against federal commandeering. Even if the New York state legislature had explicitly signaled its intent to waive any Tenth Amendment objections to the requirements of this or any other federal law, said the Court, it would have no legal consequence because elected officials may not waive a constitutional entitlement intended to protect individual citizens. For the purposes of legislative and executive action, then, the Tenth Amendment entitlement is inalienable as a matter of constitutional law.

Moreover, game theory decisively indicates that the entitlement would be inalienable even by the citizens supposedly empowered by the Court's rationale *except* through legislative or executive action. Whether a state's citizens could directly waive the entitlement was not addressed by the decision, but even if the majority had intended this odd contingency, any number of collective action problems make the needed universal consensus both theoretically and pragmatically impossible.[179] In reasoning that the entitlement cannot be waived by state officials because it protects individual citizens, the Court analogizes to others in the Bill of Rights that cannot be legislatively waived, but as discussed above, these protect a waivable autonomy that can only inhere in separate individuals, while the Tenth Amendment protects something singular and external in which all citizens hold equal interests collectively.

For citizens to waive their collectively held Tenth Amendment entitlement would thus require universal assent by each individually consenting citizen, but scholars of collective action agree that universal consensus in so large a group is all but impossible—not only due to inevitable policy dissensus among statewide electorates, but to the classic collective action problem of holdout, where a minority wields its veto power to "hold out" for special treatment by a majority anxious for their agreement.[180] A single naysayer could cancel the will of all other voters, creating overwhelming incentives for the obstacles that game theory predicts in such environments (and for which liability rules are often used to defuse),[181] foreclosing

---

[178] *Id.* at 180–82.

[179] MANCUR OLSON, THE LOGIC OF COLLECTIVE ACTION: PUBLIC GOODS AND THE THEORY OF GROUPS (1971).

[180] *E.g.*, SIMON M. LORNE & JOY MARLENE BRYAN, ACQUISITIONS AND MERGERS: NEGOTIATED AND CONTESTED TRANSACTIONS, § 9:39 (2005) (discussing holdout in mergers); Richard A. Epstein, *Notice and Freedom of Contract in the Law of Servitudes*, 55 S. CAL. L. REV. 1353, 1366–67 (1982) (discussing holdout in real estate). Even beyond holdout, members of a large group with common interests will almost never agree on the best way to further the group's interest. OLSON, *supra* note 179, at 8.

[181] The law of eminent domain employs a liability rule for exactly this purpose. *See* W.A. FISCHEL, REGULATORY TAKINGS: LAW, ECONOMICS, AND POLITICS 68 (1995).

the possibility that citizens could ever reach the universal agreement needed to alienate.[182] In addition are the daunting pragmatic problems implied by the statewide referendum needed to accomplish such agreement. Historically poor voter turnout at even critical elections[183] and acknowledged underinclusive census-taking[184] suggests that it would be impossible to hold an election or census that would actually count the vote of each entitlement holder.

Yet if we were to settle for something other than a perfect accounting of universal consensus to waive the entitlement—for example, supermajority vote at a standard statewide referendum—then why not by vote of majority-elected state officials as proxies for the people's will in the first place? *New York* purported to protect citizens by limiting intergovernmental bargaining to conditional federal spending or preemption because these methods enable "the residents of State [to] retain the ultimate decision as to whether or not the State will comply"—presumably by electing representatives who will exercise their preferred policies.[185] But if electing state representatives to express citizens' will regarding Tenth Amendment entitlements suffices in these contexts, why can't the same representatives act as faithful agents of their citizens in bargaining over the anti-commandeering entitlement? Both seem to reflect the theory of representative democracy on which the republic is founded; it is not clear why the first way constitutionally protects citizens' Tenth Amendment interests and the second does not.

---

[182] The buyout of the tiny polluted town of Cheshire, Ohio (population 221) provides one example of a multiparty transaction that overcame the holdout obstacle. *See* Gideon Parchomovsky & Peter Siegelman, *Selling Mayberry: Communities and Individuals in Law and Economics*, 92 CAL. L. REV. 75, 91 (2004). Yet universal consensus at the state level requires impossible consensus among populations ranging from Wyoming's 522,000 to California's 36,000,000. *Cf.* JOHN G. MATSUSAKA, FOR THE MANY OR THE FEW: THE INITIATIVE, PUBLIC POLICY, AND AMERICAN DEMOCRACY 143 (2004); OLSON, *supra* note 179, at 8.

[183] Even the most popular presidential elections boast participation rates of barely half the electorate. *E.g.*, Amie Jamieson, Hyon B. Shin & Jennifer Day, *Voting and Registration in the Election of November 2000*, U.S. CENSUS BUREAU 2 (Feb. 2002), http://www.census.gov/prod/2002pubs/p20-542.pdf (reporting that only fifty-five percent of those eligible voted in the 2000 election). Even among those who vote, volumes of ballots are cast but not counted for various reasons. Bush v. Gore, 531 U.S. 98, 103 (2000) (citing statistics showing that two percent of cast ballots fail to register a vote); Don Van Natta Jr., *Gore to Contest Recount Result in Palm Beach*, N.Y. TIMES, Nov. 25, 2000, http://www.nytimes.com/2000/11/25/politics/25PALM.html (reporting on ten thousand sworn affidavits by voters denied assistance, given bad instructions, or confused by the butterfly ballot design). Not all citizens are even registered or entitled to vote (children, some felons), but *New York* associates the entitlement with *citizenship*, not voting status.

[184] Federal acknowledgment that the census regularly misses millions of Americans (and disproportionately among them, the poor and politically disenfranchised) led to a national debate about whether to supplement the 2000 Census's raw enumeration with figures derived from statistical sampling. Joan Biskupic & Barbara Vobejda, *High Court Rejects Sampling in Census; Ruling Has Political, Economic Impacts*, WASH. POST, Jan. 26, 1999, at A1.

[185] 505 U.S. 144, 168 (1992). Justice O'Connor explained: "If a State's citizens view federal policy as sufficiently contrary to local interests, they may elect to decline a federal grant. . . . Where Congress encourages state regulation rather than compelling it, state governments remain responsible to the local electorate's preferences; state officials remain accountable to the people." *Id.*

2. SPENDING POWER INALIENABILITY

Sliced theoretically or pragmatically, then, the Tenth Amendment entitlement described in *New York* is inalienable by officials and citizens alike. But is this really so? Given the extent to which states regularly do waive such sovereign authority in negotiations with Congress and other states, it is hard to understand how this could be without rejecting nearly a century of settled constitutional law. States routinely waive their Eleventh Amendment entitlement to sovereign authority to private litigants, their Tenth Amendment sovereign authority to other states in interstate compacts, and their Tenth Amendment-protected jurisdictional territory to the federal government in commonplace state-federal bargaining via the spending power[186]—which even *New York* heralded as an available alternative to trading on the Tenth Amendment entitlement.[187] One might counter that the anti-commandeering rule protects federalism values of a different order than these others, but the underlying values of federalism do not change depending on which constitutional design feature is protecting them.[188]

Enabling alienation of the same state sovereign authority in spending power deals especially undermines the rationale for inalienability in *New York*. In fact, one federalism scholar suggests that the availability of state-federal bargaining under the Spending Clause converts the entire anti-commandeering enterprise into a property rule-protected regime.[189] Professor Roderick Hills has identified the *New York* entitlement as protected under a property rule, correctly observing that it gets stronger protection than it would under a liability rule because the states may withhold their services from the federal government even if the federal government were to fully compensate them.[190] However, his analysis considers only the two choices—property or liability rule—missing the third potential leg of the *Cathedral* stool. By contrast, Professor Ilya Somin invokes Calabresi and Melamed to more precisely specify that the anti-commandeering doctrine protects state autonomy "by an 'inalienability rule' that prevents it from being violated even through the voluntary agreement of the states themselves."[191]

Regardless of semantics, the proposition that needed interjurisdictional collaboration can always take place through spending power negotiations contests the foregoing analysis of inalienability.[192] If the same kind of state sovereign authority can be alienated by other means, then isn't it at least waivable in some form, and isn't that enough? The answers, respectively, are *yes* and *no*. The spending power enables one way in which states may waive sovereign authority, but the *Cathedral* framework appropriately directs our attention not just to the

---

[186] *See supra* notes 95 (sovereign immunity), 120 (interstate compacts), note 163 (spending power).

[187] 505 U.S. 144, 158–59 (1992). *See also* Siegel, *supra* note 5, at 1655–57 (noting that the Court's spending power alternative compromises the same federalism values claimed in support of the anti-commandeering rule).

[188] *See* Siegel, *supra* note 5, at 1660–64.

[189] Hills, *supra* Part I Introduction, note 5, at 822–23.

[190] *Id.*

[191] Somin, *supra* Chapter Two, note 28, at 482 (2002). *See also* McGinnis & Somin, *supra* Chapter Two, note 4, at 94 n.14.

[192] Congress may also bargain with the states by conditioning their action on the preemption power, but this does not raise the same issues as Tenth Amendment and spending power bargaining because Congress already possesses the jurisdictional entitlement when it bargains with a state's interest in not being preempted.

undifferentiated pool of sovereign authority, but to the relevant entitlement—that particular stick in the bundle of state sovereignty—that becomes the subject of bargaining. The argument that the spending power converts the *New York* inalienability rule into a property rule conflates the relevant entitlements, misses the important ways in which commandeering bargaining can resolve collective action problems that spending power bargaining cannot, and presumes that the dance of state-federal negotiation should always be within the control of the federal government.

The entitlement to a particular slice of sovereign authority waived in spending power deals is distinct from the more specific anti-commandeering entitlement. First, the state's waived authority in spending power deals may only be purchased for cash, not traded for in-kind regulatory benefits as a waivable anti-commandeering entitlement might be. This precludes all varieties of intergovernmental bargains that would trade waiver of a state's anti-commandeering entitlement to enable compensatory regulatory benefits, benefits that could be justified in federalism terms and would be otherwise unrealizable.[193] In the LLRWPA example, the state-based solution preserved state autonomy against preemption but needed federal ratification—which would have required a very difficult negotiation under the spending power. The consenting states would have had to replace the straightforward anti-commandeering waiver they offered Congress (i.e., "we have come to an interstate agreement and need your help to make it enforceable by binding us to our promises") with an invitation to a conditional spending bargain that might look more like: "we have come to an interstate agreement that needs your help to become enforceable, so please do that for us and also give us some money." Would those bargains really look the same to Congress? Perhaps Congress would prefer to just preempt the field, which might not benefit the state sovereign authority purportedly protected in this decision.

In addition, spending power deals do not afford the tools for negotiating around collective action problems that negotiated waiver of the anti-commandeering entitlement enables. Again taking the *New York* facts as illustration, the state-based solution was designed to resolve a collective-action problem that required measures to bind states early on, when nobody yet knew who would benefit most or least. By forging a federally enforceable agreement behind the contract veil of ignorance, the states could create a meaningful regulatory system free of fair-weather bargaining partners, who might (as New York State did) free ride on the continued sacrifice of the sited states and then renege when it became their turn to pay. In a spending power deal, states are free to join and leave the program as they see fit, simply by accepting and then refusing funds. Although this freedom may appear to advance the federalism value of local autonomy, that value is ultimately undermined by the wisdom of the contract law premise that we are most free when we can choose to be bound by our own promises.[194] State compacts uncoupled from federal penalties suffer from the same defect because they are so hard to enforce. *New York* makes it difficult for states to truly bind themselves to their promises, and all others know it.[195]

---

[193] *Cf.* Siegel, *supra* note 5 (discussing how the rule limits state autonomy in derogation of federalism).

[194] *See supra* note 111.

[195] The lawsuit between North Carolina and its former LLRWPA compact partners further illustrates the point. Alabama v. North Carolina, 130 S. Ct. 2295 (2010). North Carolina withdrew midway through the compact's

Moreover, limiting state-federal bargaining to deals based on conditional spending confers a leadership role on the federal government at all times, precluding the kind of local initiative and novel problem-solving synergy that the states sought to effect in the LLRWPA. It assumes that Congress is the only party who would initiate intergovernmental bargaining, empowers federal actors in the negotiation by assigning them first offer rights, and reduces the role of the states to accepting or rejecting the terms of a financial trade-off. Indeed, the fact that the spending power has *not* been the chosen medium in the intergovernmental negotiations that have encountered anti-commandeering challenges suggests something about the limits of conditional spending negotiations. Similarly, that the same states and Congress that had unanimously approved the LLRWPA did not simply turn to a spending power alternative after *New York* suggests substantive or practical differences in the spending power approach that differentiate the entitlements at issue.

3. THE CONSENSUAL BARGAINING ALTERNATIVE

When the anti-commandeering rule made *New York* the celebrated inaugural of the New Federalism revival, the inalienability rule tucked in to protect it garnered far less attention. The Supreme Court has never revisited this aspect of the rule, and the relevant language in *New York* has never been cited in a subsequent case, favorably or otherwise. But what the inalienability rule lacks in charisma, it makes up for in potency: the states and Congress have never again attempted to replicate the partnership lawmaking model that produced the ill-fated LLRWPA. In the name of federalism, state-federal bargaining has been confined to the conditional spending and preemption models, despite their foreclosure of state-leadership opportunities and collective action resolution.

Of course, it could be that the bargained-for commandeering model was so flawed that its short-lived influence is well-deserved. On the other hand, the states and Congress have not since produced a meaningful alternative for the safe and equitable disposal of radioactive waste in interstate commerce. But for New York's self-serving challenge, an idea that had received unanimous state and federal approval seemed poised to succeed where nothing else has, raising the fair question whether preventing this kind of intergovernmental bargaining is truly what federalism demands. Neither the normative nor remedial element of the anti-commandeering rule is specified in the text of the Tenth Amendment itself, but even if we stipulate that the substance of the rule is constitutionally required, the remedial aspect is as open to interpretation as those attaching to the Sixth or Eleventh Amendments. In the absence of a clear textual directive or entrenched precedent on the matter (and as shown in Chapter Four, the Court's Tenth Amendment jurisprudence is anything but entrenched), the determination invites interpretive considerations about whether inalienability is sufficiently consistent with all of federalism's values.

---

plans to create a new waste disposal facility. The Court upheld the state's ability to leave the compact with impunity amid concerns about state sovereignty, even though partner states lost millions of dollars they had fronted toward the new site. A compact including a clearer financial penalty for withdrawal might have had more teeth, *id.* at 2307, but enforcement would remain a formidable obstacle even then. *See supra* note 126.

The Chapter Six balancing test would adjudicate this after the fact, but intergovernmental legislative bargaining could perform the same balancing analysis during ex ante policy making, protecting federalism values through the very structure of the exchange. State-federal bargaining of the sort the LLRWPA represented would shift the values balancing from the judicial sphere to the legislative sphere, with minimal judicial oversight to ensure consensual bargaining in appropriate contexts. More important, it would shift the balancing to the joint discretion of legislatures at *both the state and federal levels*, providing insurance against federalism abuse unavailable when political safeguards are operating at the federal level alone. Intergovernmental negotiation of this sort allows state and federal legislators to jointly prioritize among competing considerations of checks, accountability, localism, and synergy in the fact-intensive policy-making contexts where legislative capacity outperforms the judiciary.

Federal commandeering of state legislative power raises serious concerns under each of the federalism values, but consensual commandeering does not when jointly determined by state and federal balancing through intergovernmental bargaining. A modest jurisprudential adjustment to enable this kind of bargaining could preserve most of what the Court intended in *New York* while encouraging these intergovernmental partnerships when needed in the gray area. Without upsetting the substance of the Tenth Amendment anti-commandeering rule, the Court could simply replace the infrastructural inalienability rule with a property-rule remedy.

The property rule approach distinguishes itself from the others in the *Cathedral* framework by enabling the parties to shift entitlements through consensual bargaining. Liability rules allow competitors to shift the entitlement over the holder's protest, and inalienability rules force the parties to live with the initial distribution even if both would prefer otherwise. In the interjurisdictional gray area, the inalienability approach frustrates the problem-solving value of federalism, while a liability rule that would enable the nonconsensual usurpation of state legislative authority would threaten checks and balances under any definition. However, a property rule that enables the state to decide for itself how to manage its entitlement would satisfy all federalism values. It would advance the problem-solving value by facilitating the negotiation of regulatory partnerships needed to solve interjurisdictional problems. It would advance the values associated with local autonomy by preserving decision-making authority to the states. And it would respect even the classical vision of checks and balances, protecting the fundamental order of American dual sovereignty, by reserving veto rights over waiver to the states.

A property rule would also take advantage of a primary architectural feature of the New Federalism's dualist revival. The bright-line rule approach to jurisdictional separation critiqued in Part II heralds at least one potential advantage for interjurisdictional governance, which is that bright lines can help facilitate efficient bargaining where bargaining is desirable. Ideally, bright lines delineate the relevant parameters of a bargaining environment[196]—who holds which entitlement, what are the available media of exchange, and how both parties evaluate their best alternatives to agreement. The pro-bargaining potential of

---

[196] *See* Rose, *supra* Chapter Four, note 199.

the separationist approach reveals the great irony of the *New York* rule: The substantive anti-commandeering element of the rule enhances state autonomy by preventing federal coercion, drawing a line in the sand between state and federal entitlements that could facilitate consensually negotiated partnerships around that line in the gray area. Then the remedial element undermines state autonomy by preventing the very bargains facilitated by the bright-line substantive element.

The inalienability approach also exacerbates inherent problems with the line-drawing enterprise to begin with. The Coase theorem teaches that bargaining protects against errors made in the initial assignment of legal entitlements under conditions of uncertainty.[197] Uncertainty pervades the initial allocation of regulatory jurisdiction under the dualist paradigm of mutual exclusivity, at least in what Chapter Five identifies as the interjurisdictional gray area. When the regulatory target implicates both state and federal obligations, any assignment of the jurisdictional entitlement exclusively to *either* the state *or* the federal government is essentially arbitrary. As discussed in Chapter Five, the New Federalism's protection of these arbitrary assignments has variously led to regulatory uncertainty, gridlock, litigation, and abdication in the bellwether fields of environmental law and public health and safety regulation, such as that which has plagued not only the regulation of radioactive waste, stormwater pollution, and wetlands, but even governmental response to threats of terrorism and natural disasters.

By contrast, property-rule protection for Tenth Amendment entitlements would enable states to engage in the very bargaining that Coase, Calabresi, and Melamed predict will facilitate efficiency when uncertainty muddles the initial allocation.[198] By their reasoning, when there is uncertainty about which initial distribution would best maximize benefits and minimize costs, the best alternative is to allow entitlement shifting until the optimal allocation is reached.[199] Assigning regulatory jurisdiction to either the state or federal government in the interjurisdictional gray area is a project of uncertainty by definition, refereed by well-intended but fallible human beings. To then defend these entitlements with an inalienability rule fixes errors in the arbitrary initial assignment forever. The property rule would protect the division of state and federal power while empowering both levels of government to take the needed steps in negotiating the kinds of partnerships that can effectively cope with interjurisdictional quagmires.

Key is the property rule's element of choice. In empowering the entitlement holder to decide for itself whether or not to bargain, the property rule approach enhances state

---

[197] Coase, *supra* note 53, at 15.

[198] *See id.*; Calabresi & Melamed, *supra* Introduction, note 67, at 1093–95.

[199] Calabresi & Melamed, *supra* Introduction, note 67, at 1093–95 (arguing that law can maximize efficiency by assigning entitlements to reflect Pareto optimality, yielding the most overall societal value and fewest overall societal costs). When there is uncertainty about the initial distribution of entitlements, the authors suggest that the law allocate costs to the party that can best perform the needed cost-benefit analysis (or most cheaply avoid costs), and if it is too difficult to determine the least cost avoider, then to the party that can most cheaply act in the market to correct disparities in the distribution (since they expect that our imperfect markets will, in fact, create transaction costs). *Id.* at 1096–97. However, they add that economic efficiency is not the only basis on which the law should choose; additional considerations include "other justice reasons" and societal distributional preferences. *Id.* at 1098–1105.

sovereignty by supporting local autonomy—a federalism value on par with checks and balances. The Tenth Amendment cases are predicated on the idea that states should not be compelled to participate in a federal regulatory program,[200] but where the states invite federal regulation—if only to enforce their own agreement against corrosive collective action problems—there is no coercion. The consensual element inherent in property rule protection means that states will not cede sovereign authority unless they elect it—just as they elect to waive sovereign authority in spending power deals that expand federal authority beyond the initial entitlements.[201] Even federalism theorists worried that state officials will elect to collude with the federal government in undermining federalism constraints have conceded that the anti-commandeering context is least vulnerable to this concern.[202]

If the Court were to eliminate the inalienability constraint, the mechanics of commandeering bargaining would be straightforward. A state's legislature, representing the people in their corporate capacity,[203] could directly waive the state's anti-commandeering entitlement or statutorily authorize the governor to negotiate on behalf of the people as needed. If there were no waiver, the anti-commandeering entitlement would remain with the state and could be judicially enforced against federal overreaching.[204] Commandeering bargaining could be supervised by meaningful but deferential judicial review to limit it to legitimate gray area contexts in which the initial allocation of sovereign authority is uncertain. If bargaining were challenged, the court would evaluate it based on the litigants' showing that bargaining is consensual and appropriately within the gray area, applying the gatekeeping inquiry proposed in Chapter Six.[205] If the bargaining meets these criteria, the court should give substantial deference to the outcome negotiated by the state and federal legislative partnership.

This deferential judicial review limits the potential scope of commandeering bargaining to the gray area, preventing state and federal legislatures from bargaining away any aspect of their sovereign authority—for example, federal jurisdictional entitlements over the military, or state jurisdictional entitlements over municipal government. Allowing bargaining while placing the burden of persuasion on the bargainers shows proper deference to classical checks and balances while preventing them from overshadowing all other considerations of good federalist governance. To avoid difficult questions about enforcing bargained-for commandeering, in-kind penalties for violation should ideally be specified in the terms of the negotiated agreement itself. For example, in the context of the LLRWPA, the remedy for

---

[200] *E.g.*, Hodel v. Va. Surface Mining & Reclamation Ass'n, Inc., 452 U.S. 264 (1981); New York v. United States, 505 U.S. 144 (1992); Envtl. Def. Ctr., Inc. v. United States EPA, 344 F.3d 832, 847 (9th Cir. 2003).

[201] Notably, if all the states but one agree on a policy and the majority persuades Congress to pass a commandeering rule, then the property rule allows the dissenting state to challenge the law as applied to it.

[202] McGinnis & Somin, *supra* Chapter Two, note 4, at 119.

[203] *Cf.* District of Columbia v. Heller, 128 S. Ct. 2783, 2790–91 (2008).

[204] In this respect, even under the property rule approach, the defendants in *New York* may not have been able to satisfy their burden that New York State had waived its entitlement. Analogously, the federal government might not have been able to defend against the *Printz* commandeering challenge under the property rule if states had not been given a prior opportunity to opt in or out. However, were the waiver rule available and clear, then the parties could structure their behavior to secure a legally adequate waiver beforehand where intended.

[205] *See supra* discussion in "Mechanics" section following Chapter Six, note 33.

violating the commandeering agreement was wisely set forth within the negotiated statute itself. A consenting state would absorb legal liability for any harm caused by improperly stored radioactive waste, as enforceable under the "take title" provision (in addition to the other penalties in the statute).

Of course, a future Congress could always repudiate the bargain struck in a statute like the LLRWPA, and all must account for that risk in the initial calculus. However, the results of such bargaining will be sturdy if it strikes the needed balance between state and federal expertise in resolving an interjurisdictional problem. Congress should hold up its end of the regulatory partnership not because it has lost its preemptive authority, but because the solution is better than the alternatives. Federal enforceability is present to curb state, not federal, opportunism, so Congress has little incentive to renege on its end of the deal unless there are material changes. Meanwhile, from the perspective of the states, commandeering bargains enable more state leadership in design than the fully preemptive alternative.

Adopting the property rule approach would be a relatively simple jurisprudential fix, as the inalienability rule has not been visited by the Court since its articulation in *New York*. Reversing the inalienability rule would leave other federalism precedent fully intact while affording flexibility for intergovernmental bargaining that should not offend them. In the end, the *New York* rule simply went further than necessary. By contrast, intergovernmental legislative bargaining under Balanced Federalism forges a middle path between the insights of both the political and judicial safeguards proponents. Enabling legislative bargaining resonates with Justice Blackmun's argument in *Garcia v. San Antonio Metropolitan Transit Authority* that states' rights are protected by the political process in which state actors play an important role.[206] However, the continued enforceability of the anti-commandeering entitlement when it is *not* waived (and limited judicial review of the bargaining parameters when it is) preserves judicial oversight to police for extreme abuses. In this respect, the approach balances the extremes of the Court's erstwhile vacillating Tenth Amendment jurisprudence. (It also provides groundwork for Chapter Ten, which proposes additional tools to evaluate broader forms of intergovernmental bargaining.)

4. FEARS OF "LIABILITY"

The property rule approach also frees the federal government to waive its reciprocal Tenth Amendment entitlement—but that already happens with so much frequency and so little ado that affirming it is of almost no consequence except to bring the system back into symmetry. The intertwining folds of the federalism marble-cake, representing the innumerable places across the regulatory landscape where federal and state jurisdiction really do overlap, include much territory where the federal government *could* but *declines* to fully preempt state involvement.[207] This is visible not only in formal programs of cooperative federalism such as the Clean Air and Clean Water Acts, but in the concurrent jurisdictional fabric of American law more generally.[208] The federal government's frequent waiver of its Tenth

---

[206] 469 U.S. 528 (1985).

[207] GRODZINS, *supra* Introduction, note 4, at 8.

[208] *See supra* Chapter Five.

Amendment entitlement has attracted little judicial attention—presumably because the Court has not been concerned about threats to the overall federal project posed by retained state power.

Needless to say, the reverse is true: the Court clearly considers unchecked federal power a threat to the overall project of retained state sovereign authority. It is for this reason that the Court protected the states' Tenth Amendment entitlement so purposefully (and for this reason that this chapter addresses only the state entitlement, though the argument applies equally well to its federal counterpart.) The Tenth Amendment inalienability rule misses the mark, but the concerns that drove the choice suggest what the Court was really afraid of: the third leg in the *Cathedral* stool. What the majority truly sought to prevent was the adoption of a liability rule, under which a state's Tenth Amendment entitlement would be vulnerable to the very kind of federal aggrandizement that the majority most feared. Protecting the Tenth Amendment entitlement under a liability rule would shift decision-making power about the entitlement to the jurisdictional competitor—empowering the federal government to condemn the entitlement even over a state's protest (so long as the loser was somehow "made whole" by the appropriator).

The *Cathedral* authors recommend liability rules when there is both uncertainty about the initial allocation and high transaction costs that prevent otherwise desirable entitlement shifting (an apt description of interjurisdictional governance in the shadow of classical dual federalism). But allowing nonconsensual shifting of state entitlements would advance problem solving at too great a cost to other important federalism values, such as local autonomy and checks and balances. Better simply to remove some of the bargaining obstacles that create high transaction costs in the gray area, which would bring the scenario more in line with those that the *Cathedral* authors recommend for property rule protection.

One could imagine rare circumstances in which a liability approach might be appropriate—perhaps where a serious interjurisdictional emergency renders the bargaining process impossible (or intolerably harmful), as may have happened in the wake of Hurricane Katrina.[209] As Chapter One discussed, many have argued that the president should have federalized the Louisiana National Guard and assumed command of local first responders with or without consent, because the emergency was so incapacitating that the relevant state actors could not take the needed steps to evaluate and instigate a waiver.[210] Professor Neil Siegel has posed a similar thought problem about a future terrorist attack on the scale of 9/11, where the substantive anti-commandeering rule could prevent the president from assuming command of local first responders without gubernatorial consent, even if needed to coordinate a centralized response.[211] Another provocative case that some argue could warrant a liability approach has materialized in the slower-motion emergency context of catastrophic injury to children in automobiles.[212]

---

[209] Siegel, *supra* note 5, at 1687–88.

[210] *See* Yoo, *supra* Chapter One, note 119, at M5; Greenberger, *supra* Chapter One, note 118, at 114–19.

[211] Siegel, *supra* note 5, at 1684–86.

[212] The National Transportation Safety Board (NTSB) has urged states to require children aged four to eight to use booster seats because most are too large for the infant restraints already required by law but too small for conventional seatbelt protection. Adam Hochberg, *NTSB Puts Heat on States without Booster Seat Laws*

Yet even in such compelling circumstances, nonconsensual federal commandeering would be contentious.[213] For all who argued that the federal government should have acted more forcefully after Katrina, others argued passionately that the federal government must not violate state sovereignty.[214] A liability rule could stress the check-and-balance value beyond its breaking point, defensible in only the most egregious circumstances (and better defended under the ex-post judicial balancing test than implied permissible by ex-ante legislative policy making). We can safely presume that in almost all imaginable circumstances, a state that really needed federal assistance to protect public safety would simply ask for it—waiving its entitlement to federal noninterference just as the property rule would encourage. Indeed, it was the specter of federal override of state sovereign authority that galvanized the New Federalism revival in the first place. But the property rule approach honors state autonomy and protects against federal coercion by keeping veto power in the hands of the entitlement holder—the states.

If consent is the touchstone, however, the other fear raised by the property-rule approach is the question of whether anything limits consensual intergovernmental bargaining about anything, even beyond commandeering. If the anti-commandeering entitlement is the proper subject of bargaining, does that mean that states should be able to bargain away any fundamental aspect of sovereignty? Of course not, and limited judicial review reinforces the point. Ultimately, the Court should evaluate whether a federalism entitlement should be waivable on the same terms as any other constitutional entitlement: if allowing remedial waiver would undercut the purpose of the normative element of the rule, then the entitlement should be treated as inalienable. For example, allowing a state to waive its equal suffrage in the Senate would undercut the representational ethic of Article I. Allowing Congress to redraw state boundaries would undermine dual sovereignty in any model of federalism. But allowing remedial waiver of the anti-commandeering entitlement—at least in the interjurisdictional gray area—advances those values more faithfully than the alternatives.

(NPR radio broadcast Sept. 30, 2009), http://www.npr.org/templates/story/story.php?storyId=112884532& ft=1&f=1003. NTSB estimates that these children are nearly sixty percent more likely to suffer catastrophic injury in a car accident when they are not using a booster seat. *Id.* In light of these statistics, all states have passed laws requiring booster seats except Florida, Arizona, and South Dakota. State representatives in Florida and Arizona are attempting to pass booster seat legislation in the coming year, but the governor of South Dakota recently vetoed his own legislature's successful booster seat bill on grounds that such decisions should be left to the family—despite "heart-rending testimony" from parents of injured children who had not used booster seats because they were following the requirements of child restraint laws that they had assumed were designed for maximum protection. *Id.* When a governor vetoes a demonstrated means of halting preventable child deaths in legislation that has been duly approved by the state legislature, which expression of Tenth Amendment sovereignty should prevail? At the formal level, the answer is simple: state legislation must yield to the governor's veto, and a displeased electorate may vote out the governor at the next election cycle. Still, the families of children injured in the intervening years may later consider it the sort of emergency that should have warranted NTSB override under an anti-commandeering liability rule.

[213] *Cf.* Hills, *supra* Part I Introduction, note 5, at 891–908 (decrying commandeering as inefficient, unjust, and forced speech).

[214] *See supra* Chapter One, note 158.

E. Tenth Amendment Inalienability and the Gray Area

Weak on its own theoretical terms, the Court's appeal in *New York* to an inalienability rule is ultimately best explained in *Cathedral* terms. Calabresi and Melamed suggest that an inalienability rule is often only justifiable to vindicate a strong "moralism"—a policy-making consensus about some value so important that it is worth protecting in spite of resulting efficiency and autonomy losses.[215] The Tenth Amendment inalienability rule has proven costly in efficiency and autonomy terms, but it faithfully protects the moralism that underlies the New Federalism's dualist paradigm. As it effectively acknowledged in *New York*, the authoring majority considered the line between state and federal authority so important that it must be protected even when the parties wish to bridge it, at whatever practical cost.[216] Consistent with the rest of the New Federalism jurisprudence, the inalienability approach exalts separationist checks and balances over all other federalism considerations, including local autonomy, interjurisdictional innovation, and interjurisdictional problem solving.

Federalism values certainly represent a legitimate moralism in the Tenth Amendment context, but checks are only part of the whole. Bilateral legislative bargaining honors the most critical values simultaneously—from checks to localism to problem solving—because a state would not waive sovereign authority against its own interests. Voter confusion can be mitigated to preserve accountability values. Moving to property-rule protection would take advantage of the New Federalism's revival of jurisdictional separation by using bright lines for what they are good at: facilitating bargaining. The change would also reconcile the Tenth Amendment entitlement with other federalism entitlements protected by a property rule. In all, allowing states to bargain with their entitlements—and significantly, to lead in the intergovernmental negotiating process—strengthens the role of the states in the federal system while opening up regulatory possibilities for dealing with issues in which neither side can be the proverbial "least cost avoider" on its own.

Safely and equitable managing radioactive waste is a single example of many in this variety. Because *New York* rendered commandeering bargaining illegal, it is hard to know how frequently it might have been used otherwise, but potential candidates abound from the fields where interjurisdictional conflict is most stark.[217] Consider another recent example in the controversy that threatened the Clean Water Act's Phase II Stormwater Rule. As described in Chapter Five, a decade of deliberations preceded EPA's promulgation of the rule, during which the states and federal government collaborated in the design of a national-local regulatory partnership ideally suited to the task of protecting the nation's waters from local

---

[215] *Id.*; *cf.* Merrill, *supra* note 92.

[216] 505 U.S. 144, 181 (1992) ("Just as the separation and independence of the coordinate branches of the Federal Government serves to prevent the accumulation of excessive power in any one branch, a healthy balance of power between the States and Federal Government will reduce the risk of tyranny and abuse from either front.").

[217] *See* John D. Tortorella, Note, *Reining in the Tenth Amendment: Finding a Principled Limit to the Non-Commandeering Doctrine of* United States v. Printz, 28 SETON HALL L. REV. 1365, 1381 (1998) (arguing that the anti-commandeering rule will impede important policy objectives); *cf.* Esty, *supra* Chapter Three, note 196, at 623–24 (discussing the need for overlap in environmental law); Weiser, *supra* Chapter Five, note 11, at 1733–34 (in telecommunications law).

stormwater pollution.[218] Protecting navigable waters is a matter of federal jurisdiction, but most land uses that are the source of stormwater pollution are under state and local jurisdiction.[219]

Recognizing this intersection, EPA invited the states and their localities to participate in the creation of a regulatory program, which—like the state-based solution in *New York*—departed from the conditional spending and preemption models to empower municipalities directly in designing localized pollution controls that satisfied EPA's baseline requirements. Nevertheless, the local construction permitting required under the Phase II Rule was challenged as commandeering local government. The Ninth Circuit narrowly upheld the permitting program, but only by painstakingly establishing that municipalities could avoid the challenged oversight by invoking an alternative under a different section of the Clean Water Act.[220] It took the panel two opinions over several years to establish this.[221] Without the inalienability rule, the court might have more simply concluded that participating states waived their Tenth Amendment entitlement in consenting to the collaboration they helped design. Although the Phase II Rule ultimately survived challenge, this lengthy anti-commandeering litigation has likely chilled other attempts at non-spending power bargaining to cope with other interjurisdictional crises.

Climate governance poses an even more likely instance in which commandeering bargaining could prove important. As discussed in Chapter Five, legislators at the state and federal level are struggling to reconcile the potential for federal climate initiatives with the many state and local laws enacted while federal attention to the issue was unforthcoming. Over most of the past decade, state and municipal governments have led the charge to reduce Americans' greenhouse gas emissions.[222] They are uniquely situated to regulate many causes of greenhouse gas production through police powers over public health, safety, and land use regulation, and to tailor state-based policies to regional differences in access to renewable sources of energy, transportation issues, and the like.[223] But the regulatory road remains treacherous for state leaders on climate governance. For example, states that followed California's lead in regulating greenhouse gas emissions by automobiles were confronted with (ultimately unsuccessful) lawsuits by the automobile industry claiming that the standards were preempted.[224]

---

[218] *See supra* Chapter Five, notes 52–57 and accompanying text.

[219] *See id.* notes 36–67 and accompanying text.

[220] *EDC II*, 344 F.3d 832 (9th Cir. 2003) (confirming its original holding in *EDC I*).

[221] *Id.*

[222] *See supra* Chapter Five, notes 144–87 and accompanying text.

[223] McKinstry et al., *supra* Chapter Five, note 145, at 3.

[224] *E.g.*, Lincoln-Dodge, Inc. v. Sullivan, 588 F. Supp. 2d 224, 227–28 (Dist. R.I. 2008) (affirming decisions in Vermont and California that neither the Clean Air Act nor the Energy Policy and Conservation Act, which set mile-per-gallon standards for motor vehicles, preempted state greenhouse gas emission standards); Marc Lifsher & John O'Dell, *Automakers Challenge States' Emissions Laws*, L.A. TIMES, Mar. 23, 2007, at C-2 (describing the suit against Vermont's tailpipe standards for greenhouse gases, based on a California standard that has been adopted by ten other states; the lawsuit was ultimately dismissed). The new administration is taking a more aggressive approach to tailpipe emissions and showing greater willingness to allow states to lead.

Even proponents of state-based programs urge a uniform approach to overcome issues of holdout and leakage, and that national standards would benefit regulated parties that operate in more than one state.[225] Yet national climate leadership continues to flounder, occasionally on federalism grounds. Congress considered seven different comprehensive climate change bills in 2007 that would have applied to all sectors of the economy, but each was criticized for failing to better collaborate with existing state programs or leverage state expertise, and none made it to the president's desk.[226] Even after the Obama administration took climate governance on as a national priority and legislative proposals showed greater deference to state initiatives, Congress has been unable to agree on the terms of a plan.[227] Despite House passage of the Waxman-Markey bill in 2009, the Senate considered a series of proposed bills over 2009–2010 that never made it to the floor.[228]

If political gridlock in Washington prevents Congress from articulating a national plan, perhaps the states that have already shown leadership on the matter could craft consensus on a uniform baseline to which other states could bind themselves through bargained-for legislative commandeering. So far, states have shown the only serious willingness to take on this most serious of all interjurisdictional problems, and allowing them to craft a state-based solution could provide an important regulatory backstop to a federal legislative logjam with no end in sight. But without the binding force of federal law, a state-based plan would suffer from the same collective action enforcement problems that took down the LLRWPA. State sovereignty should include the ability to bargain for that alternative.

Unifying vertical federalism entitlements under property rule protection would thus enable the states to lead while retaining the bulwark against coercion implied by the anti-commandeering rule—a combination that could facilitate regulatory partnerships to solve critical interjurisdictional problems. The *New York* inalienability rule removes a potentially fruitful tool from a toolbox with few others—one to which state and federal regulators must increasingly turn to combat our most difficult regulatory problems. Allowing legislative intergovernmental bargaining over commandeering partnerships and others would relieve the tension building in the gray area under the dual federalism revival, and it would begin to harness the contributions of the political branches. To that end, it might help to show how much federalism-sensitive governance is *already* the product of bilateral bargaining with federalism entitlements—the subject of the final part of this book.

Janet Raloff, *California May Yet Get the First Greenhouse Gas Limits for Cars*, SCIENCENEWS, Feb. 6, 2009, http://www.sciencenews.org/view/generic/id/40664.

[225] McKinstry et al., *supra* Chapter Five, note 145, at 4–5.

[226] *Id.* at 3–4. *See* Climate Stewardship and Innovation Act of 2007, S. 280,110th Cong. (2007); Global Warming Pollution Reduction Act, S. 309, 110th Cong. (2007); Climate Stewardship Act of 2007, H.R. 620, 110th Cong. (2007); Global Warming Reduction Act of 2007, S. 485, 110th Cong. (2007); Safe Climate Act of 2007, H.R. 1590, 110th Cong. (2007); Low Carbon Economy Act of 2007, S. 1766, 110th Cong. (2007); America's Climate Security Act of 2007, S. 2191, 110th Cong. (2007).

[227] Jim Tankersley, *Bowing to Political Reality, Senate Democrats Drop Broad Energy Bill*, L.A. TIMES, July 23, 2010, http://articles.latimes.com/2010/jul/23/nation/la-na-energy-democrats-20100723.

[228] *See supra* Chapter Five, notes 190–93 and accompanying text.

4

Negotiating Federalism

THIS PART TURNS fully to the roles of the political branches in implementing Balanced Federalism, exploring how federalism-sensitive governance is already a project of bilateral balancing through widespread state-federal bargaining. It reviews the consensually negotiated exchange of federalism entitlements within various statutory and constitutional frameworks, and the ramifications of this exchange for the federalism safeguards debate. Contemporary federalism theory is stranded between the undertheorized model of cooperative federalism safeguarded by political constraints and the ill-theorized model of New Federalism safeguarded by judicial constraints. In splitting that difference, this part provides theoretical justification for the political safeguards currently doing constitutionally valid work while defining a clearer role for more limited judicial oversight. In establishing principled means by which political actors lead in the navigation of federalism-sensitive governance, it also clarifies the reduced field of interjurisdictional contexts in which more rigorous judicial review is needed.

Parts I and II focused primarily on the original federalism inquiry: *who gets to decide—the state or federal government?* Where the Constitution has clearly enumerated or proscribed federal power, the answer is often facially clear. But as Chapter Five demonstrates, the interjurisdictional gray area complicates matters. In de jure interjurisdictional contexts, uncertainty persists about whose assertion of jurisdiction trumps as a legal matter, as it has in the context of wetlands regulation since *SWANCC* and *Rapanos*.[1] In de facto interjurisdictional contexts, practical uncertainty revolves around whose assertion of jurisdiction *should* trump in service of federalism goals, even if enumerated federal power could support preemption.[2] Whether for reasons of de jure or de facto uncertainty, jurisdictional authority remains contested for many issues of great policy consequence.

Yet if the primary federalism inquiry is which level of government will decide substantive policy, the meta-federalism inquiry becomes: *who gets to decides that?* Federalism thinkers have wrestled for centuries with the question of which branch of the federal government best determines the relationship between state and federal power.[3] Should we trust the decision to Congress, as cooperative federalism has, considering the political safeguards of institutional design? Should the decision rest with the Supreme Court, operating through judicially enforceable constraints of the sort New Federalism has reinvigorated? The federal executive has historically received little credence in the federalism safeguards debate, although even that is changing with new consideration of the role of administrative agencies. Meanwhile, the entire discourse has presumed that federalism safeguards operate only at the federal level, acknowledging state input only through the institution of locally-elected representatives to national governing bodies.

Balanced Federalism moves beyond this historic debate about the unilateral roles of the Court, Congress, and federal executive in interpreting federalism by recognizing the *bilateral* interpretive roles that all three branches play, at both the state and federal levels. Building on the values-balancing project of Chapter Six and the proposal for bargaining with federalism entitlements in Chapter Seven, Part IV now fully embraces the interpretive possibilities of intergovernmental partnerships among all branches of all levels of government. It answers federalism's ultimate meta-inquiry with the reality that *all* governmental actors are participating in the deciding, in different ways, all the time. These partnerships draw on the balancing potential in what each branch does best—legislative policy making, executive implementation, and judicial evaluation. By incorporating the interests of local, state, and federal actors into negotiated balance, these partnerships safeguard federalism values on levels beyond the comprehension of the unilateral discourse.

Indeed, even as theorists remain mired in debate over how to resolve regulatory competition, the regulators who actually work in contested contexts have learned to confront jurisdictional uncertainty simply by negotiating through it. Working directly or

---

[1] Solid Waste Agency of Northern Cook County v. U.S. Army Corps of Engineers, 531 U.S. 159 (2001); Rapanos v. United States, 547 U.S. 715 (2006).

[2] *E.g.,* PREEMPTION CHOICE, *supra* Chapter Five, note 19 (detailing the variety of architectural choices by which federal preemption decisions can be limited to allow for the benefits of institutional and regulatory diversity).

[3] *E.g.,* Wechsler, *supra* Introduction, note 6, at 588 (articulating the "political safeguards" theory that trusts federalism constraints to Congress); GRODZINS, *supra* Introduction, note 4, at 60–153 (describing the cooperative federalism model based on the political safeguards theory); Baker, *supra* Chapter Three, note 237, at 952 (endorsing the move toward judicially enforceable constraints in the New Federalism model); Thomas W. Merrill, *Preemption and Institutional Choice*, 102 Nw. U.L. Rev. 727, 755–56, 759 (2008) (arguing that executive agencies do not warrant the same deference as Congress in preempting state law); Brian Galle & Mark Seidenfeld, *Administrative Law's Federalism: Preemption, Delegation, and Agencies at the Edge of Federal Power*, 57 DUKE L.J. 1933, 1940 (2008) (making the opposite argument).

indirectly with counterparts across state-federal lines, legislative, executive, and even judicial actors reach consensus about sharing or dividing authority in order to move forward with gray area governance. When they do so in processes that are consistent with fair bargaining principles and the federalism values themselves, then they are deciding *who decides?* in a manner that vindicates constitutional goals. They are balancing the competing federalism values at the procedural level—doubly reinforced against federalism abdication at the structural level— because of the way that bilateral negotiation necessarily incorporates the preferences, expertise, and concerns of both state and federal actors.[4] They are constraining the activities of government to be consistent with constitutional directives. They are, in short, interpreting federalism.

The state-federal bargaining in the Low-Level Radioactive Waste Policy Act failed, but even a cursory look at American governance shows the vast extent to which contested authority is allocated through various processes of intergovernmental negotiation. Opponents of the 2010 Medicaid expansion invoke familiar tropes when they decry the move as a gross federal overreach,[5] but state and federal regulators in the trenches of health-care law know that the truth is more nuanced—that the Medicaid program really represents a site of extensive negotiation between state and federal actors about the specifics of each state plan, set within purposefully broad federal boundaries.[6] Similarly, those who opposed the 2009 Stimulus Bill on federalism grounds[7] discounted the substantial role of state actors in negotiating the terms of the federal law.[8] And those who challenged the Clean Water Act's stormwater regulations on federalism grounds missed the pivotal role state and municipal actors played in negotiating the terms of the rule—which itself became a forum for ongoing negotiation between state and federal regulators about how each municipality would ultimately comply.[9]

Such instances of intergovernmental bargaining offer a means of understanding the relationship between state and federal power that differs from the stylized model of zero-sum federalism that has dominated the discourse to this point, emphasizing winner-takes-all antagonism within bitter jurisdictional competition.[10] Contemporary judicial doctrine presents a similarly wooden view of sovereign antagonism within American federalism.[11] But countless real-world examples show that the boundary between state and federal authority is

---

[4] Structural reinforcement is solid unless state and federal actors were to collude against the interests of their constituents, a problem discussed *supra* at Chapter Seven, notes 106–16 and accompanying text. Under the procedural criteria in Chapter Ten, collusion would undermine the accountability value, and the resulting bargaining would not warrant interpretive deference.

[5] *See, e.g.*, Press Release, Tex. Office of the Governor, Statement by Gov. Rick Perry on Passage of Federal Health Care Bill (Mar. 21, 2010), http://governor.state.tx.us/news/press-release/14396/.

[6] *See infra* Chapter Eight, notes 225–41 and accompanying text.

[7] *See, e.g.*, *Some State Lawmakers Fighting Federal Stimulus*, Ariz. Republic, Mar. 2, 2009, http://www.azcentral.com/news/articles/2009/03/02/20090302stimulus-stateso302-ON.html (reporting on efforts to "fight against decades of federal overreach, culminating in the stimulus package").

[8] *See infra* Chapter Eight, notes 57–62 and accompanying text.

[9] *See supra* Chapter Five, notes 52–57, *infra* Chapter Eight, notes 180–87 and accompanying text.

[10] *E.g.*, Hornick, *supra* Introduction, note 10.

[11] *E.g.*, United States v. Morrison, 529 U.S. 598, 617–18 (2000) (distinguishing local and national spheres).

actually negotiated on scales large and small, and on a continual basis. Working in a dizzying array of regulatory contexts, state and federal actors negotiate over both the allocation of policy-making entitlements and the substantive terms of the mandates policy making will impose. Intergovernmental balancing takes place both in realms plagued by legal uncertainty about whose jurisdiction trumps, and in realms unsettled by uncertainty over whose decision *should* trump, regardless of legal supremacy. Reconceptualizing the relationship between state and federal power as one heavily mediated by negotiation demonstrates how federalism practice departs from the rhetoric, and offers hope for moving beyond the paralyzing features of the zero-sum discourse.

The final chapters of this book explore the role of intergovernmental bargaining in allocating contested authority within contexts of jurisdictional overlap. Using the negotiation theorist's definition, they broadly understand intergovernmental bargaining as "an iterative process of joint decision-making,"[12] encompassing conventional political haggling (as over the terms of proposed legislation), formalized methods of collaborative policy making (as in certain programs of cooperative federalism), and even more remote signaling processes by which state and federal actors share responsibility for public decision making over time (as they have over medical marijuana and immigration enforcement). I use the word *substantive* to refer to the substance of a legal rule or negotiated outcome, and *procedural* to refer to the process by which that rule or outcome was reached. Because "state-federal intergovernmental bargaining at all levels of the jurisdictional spectrum" is a mouthful, I use the term *federalism bargaining* to refer collectively to the forums in which state and federal actors engage in joint decision making, focusing on the vertical federalism relationship within each given array of participants.[13]

The structural incorporation of national and local interests creates protection for federalism values in joint policy making and enforcement, lending a degree of constitutional gravity to negotiated federalism that is unavailable in unilateral efforts. To be clear, Balanced Federalism does not discount the importance of meaningful unilateral balancing by political actors on only the state or federal side. Indeed, as suggested by the analogous reasoning in Chapter Six, it presumes that all federalism-sensitive governance requires such balancing, implicitly or explicitly. The same balancing takes place in all unilateral governance under the cooperative federalism model that is not subject to judicial review, and in all judicial interpretation of governance subject to review under New Federalism doctrine. In the end, the only question is the source and quality of the balancing.

The transparency of Balanced Federalism would improve the entire enterprise, stabilizing both policy making and judicial interpretation. As elaborated in this part, the theoretical arc

---

[12] Adopting the definition of negotiation theorists, I define bargaining as any iterative process of communication by which two or more parties seek to influence the outcome of a joint decision. FISHER & URY, *supra* Chapter Seven, note 175, at xvii; RICHARD SHELL, BARGAINING FOR ADVANTAGE: NEGOTIATION STRATEGIES FOR REASONABLE PEOPLE 6 (1999); *infra* Chapter Eight, note 46 and accompanying text.

[13] For simplicity, I treat municipal participants in intergovernmental bargaining as state actors, consistent with the Supreme Court's inclusion of municipal activity in its Tenth Amendment jurisprudence. For a discussion on how independent municipal activity further complicates the analysis, *see infra* Chapter Eight, notes 28–31 and accompanying text.

of the model is toward greater judicial federalism deference to the substance of all political balancing that meets the criteria of federalism procedurally, with limited review for abuses. Yet Part IV's primary contribution is the recognition that bilaterally negotiated balancing warrants deference of a different order from even solid unilateral efforts by virtue of its structural support for federalism values. Federalism will always be in contest with other substantive concerns in policy making and enforcement, but negotiated federalism is more likely to advance federalism goals for structural reasons that transcend the first-order policy concerns of participants. Because it represents a synthesis of state and federal perspectives in reaching regulatory consensus, intergovernmental bargaining strengthens checks, localism, and problem-solving values by design. When it also enhances democratic participation, it represents the kind of interjurisdictional governance that federalism should foster. Not all bargaining will do so, but when it satisfies the procedural criteria premised on Chapter Two, elaborated in Chapter Six, and applied in Chapter Ten, then the outcome warrants interpretive deference.

Chapter Eight demonstrates how the final Balanced Federalism proposal alters the federalism safeguards debate, showing how the unilateral discourse has missed the potential for bilateral federalism interpretation by missing the significance of the federalism bargaining enterprise. To remedy this, it surveys the basic opportunities for federalism bargaining within constitutional and statutory frameworks, charting the varied landscape into three overarching categories: conventional bargaining, negotiations to reallocate authority, and joint policy-making bargaining. The survey begins with familiar forms of negotiation used in lawmaking, negotiations over law enforcement, negotiations under the federal spending power, and negotiations for exceptions under otherwise applicable laws. It then considers more interesting forms of negotiated policy making, including negotiated federal rulemaking with state and local stakeholders, federal statutes that share policy design with states, and even intersystemic signaling negotiations by which independently operating state and federal actors trade influence over the direction of evolving interjurisdictional policies.

Mapping this landscape provides examples and vocabulary for analysis in Chapter Nine of the structural safeguards of bilateral balancing, based on the bargaining norms and media of exchange that accompany the trade in federalism entitlements. Federalism bargaining operates where each party wants something from the other, and negotiated results honor federalism goals by incorporating both local and national input. Negotiators trade on various aspects of the governing capacity available to them, including legal authority, financing, resources and expertise to accomplish specific regulatory goals, and release from inhibiting legal obligations that one side may hold over the other. Notably, the normative power of federalism itself forms important leverage at the bargaining table—often by clever statutory design—further constraining the results of negotiations in which participants are also motivated by other concerns. Chapter Nine includes compelling anecdotal testimony by primary source practitioners about their experiences balancing competing federalism values during intergovernmental bargaining.

This positive account ultimately provides the foundation for Part IV's critical normative claim: that federalism bargaining is not only a pragmatic solution to a problem of doctrinal uncertainty, but can *itself* be a legitimate way of interpreting federalism, when federalism interpretation is understood as a way of constraining public agencies to act consistently with constitutional directives. Federalism bargaining achieves interpretive status when it procedurally incorporates not only the consent principles that legitimize bargaining in general, but also the fundamental federalism values that should guide federalism interpretation in any forum. After all, the core federalism values are essentially realized through good governance procedure: (1) the maintenance of checks and balances to protect individuals against sovereign excess or abdication; (2) the protection of accountability and transparency to ensure meaningful democratic participation; (3) the preference for process that fosters local innovation, variation, and competition; and (4) the cultivation of regulatory space for harnessing synergy between local and national capacity when needed to cope with interjurisdictional problems.

Incorporating these values into the bargaining process allows negotiators to interpret federalism directives procedurally when consensus on the substance is unavailable. The more that federalism bargaining incorporates legitimizing procedures founded on mutual consent and federalism values, the more it warrants deference as a means of federalism interpretation. Interpretive bargaining becomes less legitimate as factual circumstances depart from the assumptions of mutual consent—in other words, when bargainers cannot freely opt out, cannot be trusted to understand their own interests, or cannot be trusted to faithfully represent their principals—and when procedures contravene core federalism values. Drawing on the procedural application of fair bargaining and core federalism values, bilaterally negotiated governance opens possibilities for filling the inevitable interpretive gaps left by judicial and legislative mandates. Indeed, it has been doing so all along. This analysis provides the missing pieces to explain when intergovernmental bargaining offers not only pragmatic—but also interpretive—potential.

Differentiating itself from previous process-based claims, Chapter Ten provides new theoretical justification for the interpretive work that federalism bargaining has always provided, and calls for greater judicial deference to qualifying examples. Courts adjudicating federalism-based challenges to the results of qualifying bargaining should defer to the substance of the negotiated outcome. At a minimum, courts should consider procedural federalism factors when deciding the appropriate level of deference to extend to both bilateral and unilateral governance. In this respect, the Chapter Ten proposal expands on the proposal for judicial deference to legislative commandeering bargaining in Chapter Seven, effectively subsuming it.[14] Its deferential standard of review would trump the Chapter Six balancing test if it were invoked to challenge the products of valid intergovernmental bargaining.[15] Chapter Ten concludes by analyzing the forms of federalism bargaining most likely to yield interpretive results and offering recommendations for structurally engineering more successful interpretive bargaining forums.

---

[14] The two could theoretically coexist, with the Chapter Seven test trumping for challenges to commandeering bargaining, but as they would yield the same result, the cleanest solution is for the Chapter Seven proposal to yield.

[15] In this case, the court would first apply the Chapter Ten procedural review, and only proceed to the Chapter Six balancing test if the procedural criteria were not met. Unilateral governance would remain subject to the Chapter Six balancing test and other judicial federalism doctrines. Yet review should be tempered with the judicial modesty implied by Balanced Federalism's normative regard for the interpretive potential of the political branches, taking account of how effectively even unilateral governance meets the procedural criteria of federalism values.

8

THE ROLE OF THE POLITICAL BRANCHES:

NEGOTIATING FEDERALISM

NOTWITHSTANDING THE RHETORIC of zero-sum federalism, the boundary between state and federal authority is actually the project of ongoing negotiation, in which federalism values are jointly balanced by local and national actors. More interesting still are the possibilities for federalism bargaining to fill interpretive gaps through recourse to procedural principles. This chapter situates these two normative claims within the existing federalism discourse and explains how a better understanding of federalism bargaining can contribute to the overall federalism interpretive endeavor. It summarizes the federalism safeguards debate and introduces the contributions of negotiated federalism as a supplement to other means of interpreting federalism directives. Most importantly, Chapter Eight surveys the most common forms of federalism bargaining, highlighting opportunities for intergovernmental balancing among all branches of government.

In federalism bargaining, federalism entitlements are consensually negotiated between partners, honoring anti-tyranny concerns while affording the check-and-balance values of jurisdictional overlap. Negotiated governance involves local authority rather than displacing it, and remains accountable at multiple levels. By engaging both local and national perspectives about problem solving, federalism bargaining becomes a joint project of balancing the various federalism values and competing policy considerations in each instance, offering structural protection for federalism concerns regardless of the subjective considerations of the participants.

Shifting focus from unilateral judicial balancing to bilateral political balancing, Part IV often uses the shorthand of *bargaining* to describe the relevant activity. However, all forms of balancing perform the same basic task of mediating between competing values, federalism and otherwise (again, the only question is the quality of the work). The examples of bilateral bargaining surveyed below all offer support for federalism values at the structural level, although procedural features discussed in Chapter Ten make some more reliable than others at the interpretive level. Reverse engineering the most successful examples would reveal the very considerations built into the Chapter Six test—rendering bilateral bargaining by the political branches the functional ex ante equivalent of the ex post balancing analysis contemplated there. However, the purpose of this chapter is simply to reveal the uncharted enterprise of federalism bargaining, setting the stage for subsequent discussion of how it should forever change the federalism safeguards debate.

A. Interpreting Federalism

By whatever means, federalism interpretation constrains public behavior so that it is consistent with constitutional values. Since the nation's founding, jurists and scholars have debated the roles the three branches of government should play in interpreting the constitutional promise of federalism. The courts explicitly interpret federalism directives in judicial opinions, while political actors implicitly interpret federalism whenever they take action implicating federalism concerns. Superficially, the protection of vertical federalism is viewed as a matter of ensuring that the respective exercise of authority by national and local government honors constitutional directives. This book, of course, grounds the task of safeguarding federalism in protecting the core federalism values: checks and balances, transparent and accountable governance, localized diversity and innovation, and interjurisdictional problem-solving synergy. Faithfulness to these values should be the touchstone when adjudicating difficult jurisdictional issues that raise questions of federalism—a principle that should hold true regardless of whether the decision maker is judicial, legislative, or executive.

Through most of American history, the debate over which branch should be the final federalism arbiter has centered on whether Congress or the Supreme Court is best positioned to defend these values in governance. In the early years of the new century, attention has shifted toward the role of the executive branch. The debate has remained lively over time precisely because there are strong arguments to be made for the critical contributions of each branch. However, the discourse has focused exclusively on how the branches interpret federalism *unilaterally*—on one side of the federal system or the other—when they decide whether to pass a law in contested regulatory space, whether to uphold it when challenged, and how to implement or enforce it. Acting unilaterally, branch actors interpret federalism by deciphering text, applying precedent, and formulating substantive answers to precise questions about state and federal power: *"Is this federal statute within Article I authority?" "Is this state statute legitimately preempted?"*

Yet Balanced Federalism understands that actors within each branch also participate in *bilateral* federalism interpretation, negotiating the allocation of contested policy-making authority and policy terms with others across the state-federal line. In the spaces between unilaterally articulated substantive interpretation, state-federal bargaining offers bilateral interpretive tools to realize constitutional meaning procedurally. They work by procedurally yoking the allocation of federalism entitlements to the principles that legitimize bargaining generally and federalism specifically. As discussed in Chapter Ten, bargaining confers procedural legitimacy on outcomes when the prerequisites of genuine mutual consent are met: when parties sufficiently understand their interests, can meaningfully opt out of the agreement, and are faithfully represented at the negotiating table. Federalism bargaining confers further interpretive legitimacy when negotiations are procedurally consistent with the core federalism values of checks, accountability, innovation, and synergy. By its very nature, federalism bargaining is a project of jointly balancing the competition among these values in each individual instance.

Until now, the discourse has failed to account for the full federalism implications of state-federal bargaining. Filling this important gap in the literature, this treatment explores the possibilities raised by intergovernmental bargaining to help navigate public decision making in contexts fraught with federalism concerns, such as environmental law, financial regulation, and public health. It assesses how bargaining helps bridge the pockets of uncertainty that remain after the more conventionally understood forms of federalism interpretation are exhausted, allocating contested authority and shepherding interjurisdictional collaboration. It also considers the dangers for federalism values posed by problems of representation, transparency, and autonomy that may attend certain negotiations. This chapter begins with a review of the federalism safeguards controversy that federalism bargaining alters, highlighting the unilateral focus of the discourse already in progress about which branch most faithfully interprets federalism.

I. THE FEDERALISM SAFEGUARDS DEBATE

As reviewed in Chapter Three, the general view prevailed after the New Deal that Congress is the ideal guardian of federalism, operating within a political process that ensures local concerns are considered during national lawmaking. Herbert Wechsler argued in 1954 that judicially enforceable constraints were unnecessary because of Congress's institutional design.[1] Legislators are elected at the state level, they are understood to represent local interests during federal lawmaking, and they demonstrate keen awareness of issues that matter to constituents (exemplified by the prevalence of local "earmark" legislation within national statutes).[2] Even after senators were elected by popular vote rather than by state legislatures, they continued to answer to state-based constituencies.[3]

Because Congress is a large, deliberative, locally elected body, the "Political Safeguards" view holds that courts should leave interpretation of close federalism calls to the political process.[4] Echoed in judicial decisions such as *Garcia v. San Antonio Metropolitan Transit*

---

[1] Wechsler, *supra* Introduction, note 6, at 558 ("[T]he national political process in the United States—and especially the role of the states in the composition and selection of the central government—is intrinsically well-adapted to retarding or restraining new intrusions by the center on the domain of the states . . . the inherent tendency in our system . . . necessitat[es] the widest support before intrusive measures of importance can receive significant consideration, reacting readily to opposition grounded in resistance within the states.").

[2] *Id.* at 558; *see* John Dinan & Dale Krane, *The State of American Federalism, 2005: Federalism Resurfaces in the Political Debate*, 36 PUBLIUS 327, 343–44 (2006) (discussing clashes over earmarks in legislation).

[3] U.S. CONST. amend. XVII.

[4] Wechsler, *supra* Introduction, note 6, at 547 ("To the extent that federalist values have real significance they must give rise to local sensitivity to central intervention; to the extent that such a local sensitivity exists, it cannot fail to find reflection in the Congress.").

Authority,[5] this approach assumes that Congress is properly equipped to (unilaterally) interpret constitutional federalism directives through the federal lawmaking process, and underlies the cooperative federalism model that informed Supreme Court interpretation until the New Federalism era. Later scholarship has contributed additional process-based theories of federalism.[6]

Nevertheless, others critiqued the assumption that political safeguards are sufficient to protect federalism, fearing unchecked federal expansion into traditional areas of state prerogative.[7] As federal regulatory programs grew more ambitious regarding civil rights and environmental objectives, a political movement blossomed in the 1980s urging judicial intervention.[8] This would ultimately influence the Rehnquist Court's resurrection of judicially enforceable federal constraints, empowering the judiciary to (unilaterally[9]) interpret federalism constraints through jurisdictional boundary-setting doctrines institutionally amenable to judicial oversight.[10] For example, departing from the previous era of deferral to congressional fact-finding about a law's relationship to interstate commerce, the Rehnquist Court articulated an "economic activity" limitation on the commerce power, enabling the judiciary to establish definitively whether a regulatory target was within Congress's regulatory reach.[11]

Even as proponents of cooperative and New Federalism sparred over whether Congress or the courts should lead, most agreed that the executive should be last in line.[12] The unelected nature of most executive agents and branch capacity for swift, decisive federal action runs counter to the legislative features that persuade political safeguards adherents that judicial constraints are unnecessary.[13] Concerns especially revolve around the scope of executive

---

[5] 469 U.S. 528 (1985). More recently, the political safeguards theory appeared in the dissenting opinions of Justices Breyer and Souter in United States v. Morrison, 529 U.S. 598 (2000). *Id.* at 660 (Breyer, J., dissenting), 647 (Souter, J, dissenting).

[6] *E.g.*, CHOPER, *supra* Introduction, note 6 at 175–76; Stephen Gardbaum, *Rethinking Constitutional Federalism*, 74 TEX. L. REV. 795, 799–800 (1996); Larry D. Kramer, *Putting the Politics Back into the Political Safeguards of Federalism*, 100 COLUM. L. REV 215 (2000); Young, *supra* Introduction, note 70, at 1364; Jackson, *supra* Part I Introduction, note 21, at 2240–42. *See also* JOHN HART ELY, DEMOCRACY AND DISTRUST 87 (1980) (articulating a general process-based theory of constitutional interpretation).

[7] *E.g.*, Lynn A. Baker, *Putting the Safeguards Back into the Political Safeguards of Federalism*, 46 VILL. L. REV. 951 (2001); Saikrishna B. Prakash & John C. Yoo, *The Puzzling Persistence of Process-Based Federalism Theories*, 79 TEX. L. REV 1459 (2001); William W. Van Alstyne, *The Second Death of Federalism*, 83 MICH. L. REV. 1709 (1985).

[8] *See supra* Chapter Three, notes 217–32 and accompanying text.

[9] Importantly, the political safeguards/New Federalism debate evokes a separate contest over unilateral federalism interpretation, with each school advocating exclusive interpretive control by Congress or the Court, respectively. For the purposes of my larger analysis here, however, I use the term *unilateral* interpretation to refer to interpretive activity that takes place exclusively on either the state or federal side of the system.

[10] *See supra* Part I Introduction, note 2 (listing the New Federalism canon); *see also supra* Chapter Four, notes 107–45, 197–99 and accompanying text (discussing cases and analyzing jurisdictional separation).

[11] United States v. Morrison, 529 U.S. 598, 610 (2000).

[12] *E.g.*, Cass Sunstein, *Law and Administration after Chevron*, 90 COLUM. L. REV. 2071, 2072–73 (1990).

[13] *E.g.*, *id.*; Merrill, *supra* Part IV Introduction, note 3, at 755–56.

authority to preempt state law through agency rulemaking.[14] More recently, however, the scholarly community has divided over executive federalism. Some maintain that political safeguards cannot apply to agencies, which operate less accountably and less deliberatively, and that have institutional focuses on narrow areas of concern.[15] But an emerging literature makes the opposite claim, suggesting that agencies are the preferred guardians due to their own institutional capacity.

For example, Professors Brian Galle and Mark Seidenfeld argue that agencies are better defenders of federalism than Congress because their subject matter expertise and frequent experience working with related state agencies makes them *more* deliberative and transparent than Congress.[16] Professor Gillian Metzger advocates administrative law as a subconstitutional surrogate for addressing federalism concerns,[17] noting that procedural and substantive safeguards in administrative law offer useful avenues for judicial federalism review that are unavailable for review of legislation.[18] She also observes that agencies are often better equipped to deal with core federalism concerns, which generally arise in specific policy-making contexts in which agency experts are best positioned to investigate state interests.[19] Professor Catherine Sharkey adds that President Clinton's Federalism Executive Order provides an excellent framework for making agencies accountable to federalism concerns, and argues that it should be made enforceable.[20]

These "administrative safeguards" authors skillfully highlight the institutional features that make agencies more responsive to state interests. They show the federalism benefits that follow intergovernmental interaction by demonstrating the respect for state concerns that federal agents gain from consistent contact.[21] Thus, even though the arguments for administrative safeguards are implicitly framed in unilateral terms, the suggestion that the executive branch offers the last, best hope for protecting federalism is predicated on the volume of

---

[14] *See* Geier v. Am. Honda Motor Co., 529 U.S. 861, 864 (2000) (upholding preemption of tort law by agency rule); Wyeth v. Levine, 129 S. Ct. 1187, 1200–01 (2009) (allowing similar tort but declining to overrule *Geier*).

[15] *E.g.*, Nina Mendelson, *A Presumption against Agency Preemption*, 102 Nw. U.L. Rev. 695, 699 (2008); Merrill, *supra* Part IV Introduction, note 3, at 755–56, 759; Sunstein, *supra* note 12, at 2111–15.

[16] Galle & Seidenfeld, *supra* Part IV Introduction, note 3, at 1955–59; *see also* Catherine M. Sharkey, *Federalism Accountability: "Agency-Forcing" Measures*, 58 Duke L.J. 2125, 2146–55 (2009).

[17] Metzger, *supra* Introduction, note 8, at 2063–69 (discussing Massachusetts v. EPA, 549 U.S. 497, 521 (2007), conferring state standing to raise climate change, and Gonzales v. Oregon, 546 U.S. 243, 263–64 (2006), declining to preempt state law legalizing assisted suicide).

[18] *Id.* at 2086–88; *see also* Sharkey, *supra* note 16, at 2128–31. *But see* Wayne Logan, *The Adam Walsh Act and the Failed Promise of Administrative Federalism*, 78 Geo. Wash. L. Rev. 993, 994–95 (2010) (contesting these claims).

[19] Metzger, *supra* Introduction, note 8, at 2073–74; *see also* Sharkey, *supra* note 16, at 2146–55.

[20] Sharkey, *supra* note 16, at 2128–31, 2156–73 (discussing Exec. Order No. 13,132, 64 Fed. Reg. 43,255 (Nov. 4, 1999)).

[21] Professor Sharkey observes that agencies engaged in programs of cooperative federalism with state partners better heed federalism concerns than those administering programs without state collaboration. *Id.* at 2155–72. For example, the EPA, which works closely with states in administering the Clean Air and Water Acts, has shown much greater deference to state interests than the Federal Drug Administration, whose regulations have preempted state common law without much sensitivity. *Id.* at 2159–61; *cf.* Metzger, *supra* Introduction, note 8, at 2078.

executive rulemaking, implementation, and enforcement that is effectively negotiated in consultation with state partners.

2. NEGOTIATING FEDERALISM

The federalism safeguards debate is contentious, but the voices are uniform in considering only the federalism implications of unilateral branch activity at the federal level[22]—even though a substantial amount of governmental activity is better understood as moves made within bilateral state-federal negotiation. The federal bias of the safeguards debate reflects the fact that state interpretations of federal constitutional law are subordinate to federal interpretations at both the judicial and political levels. Nevertheless, the role of state and local actors in bilaterally negotiated governance challenges this paradigm. The disconnect is especially stark for the political branches, where negotiations are most apparent.

It is easier to understand the unilateral bias in certain regulatory contexts. For example, the Supreme Court acts fairly unilaterally by design—consulting only the Constitution and precedent—and so we naturally expect unilateralism along the state-federal line when it decides cases with important federalism implications. It acts unilaterally when interpreting constitutional constraints, as it did in articulating the "economic activity" test limiting the commerce power,[23] and in upholding laws against federalism challenges, as it did in affirming supremacy of federal drug laws over state medical marijuana laws.[24] The debate over Congress's role also presumes unilateral action, alternatively referencing unilateral choices to legislate to the broadest reach of its enumerated powers—such as its failed attempt to expand protection for religious expression under the Religious Freedom Restoration Act,[25] or to exercise restraint of the sort envisioned by the political safeguards model.

The executive branch may have the greatest institutional freedom to act unilaterally in every sense of the word, given the single individual at the top of the decision-making apex.[26] Nevertheless, it also holds the greatest potential to act bilaterally across state-federal lines, with responsibilities ranging from policy making to implementation and enforcement. Especially in the realms of implementation and enforcement, federal executive activity becomes less unilateral and more negotiated with state and other stakeholders. This high

---

[22] *See supra* note 9 (distinguishing the contest over interpretive unilateralism between federal branches from the federal/state-side unilateralism on which this analysis is focused).

[23] *See* United States v. Morrison, 529 U.S. 598, 610 (2000).

[24] *See* Gonzales v. Raich, 545 U.S. 1, 9 (2005).

[25] *See* Pub. L. No. 103–141, 107 Stat. 1488, invalidated by City of Boerne v. Flores, 521 U.S. 507, 511 (1997) (partially overturning the act for exceeding congressional authority to regulate state government); *see also* 42 U.S.C. § 2000bb(b)(1) (2006) (restoring some protections for religious activity burdened by neutrally applicable regulations in the wake of contrary Supreme Court precedent).

[26] *See* William G. Howell, *Unilateral Powers: A Brief Overview*, 35 PRESIDENTIAL STUD. Q. 417, 418 (2005) (discussing controversial executive decisions); Elena Kagan, *Presidential Administration*, 114 HARV. L. REV. 2245, 2331–46 (2001) (discussing the benefits of presidential control over administrative process); Matthew Stephenson, *Optimal Political Control of the Bureaucracy*, 107 MICH. L. REV. 53, 73 (2008) (critiquing the unitary executive theory on the basis of accountability).

degree of involvement between some federal agencies and state partners substantiates the arguments for administrative safeguards.

Yet executive agents are hardly the only federal bargainers. Sometimes Congress participates by engaging its spending power to negotiate with states, creating statutory forums for more nuanced intergovernmental bargaining, or enacting laws by state invitation through a negotiated political process. One scholar even describes how the Supreme Court effectively bargains with state courts over the future direction of federal law (though even this novel work fails to recognize the indirect bargaining process that negotiation theorists understand as intersystemic signaling).[27] Some forms of federalism bargaining are relatively straightforward, as when state actors negotiate for specific policies within federal lawmaking. Others partner different federal, state, and local actors from across the different branches on both sides of the line in an elaborate process with multiple stages of iterative exchange—such as negotiated federal lawmaking over policy, which leads to negotiated rulemaking over the details of implementation, which, in turn, leads to a general permit system that itself becomes a site for continued negotiation over the details of individual compliance.

As demonstrated in the following section all three branches of government participate across state-federal lines in the iterative process of joint decision making that—whether or not they realize it—is the hallmark of bargaining. They do so in a profound variety of contexts, and with a startling array of participants. Although negotiations often match executive actors at the highest state and federal levels, they just as often match federal, executive, or legislative actors at various points along the authoritative continuum with even more local actors, representing individual cities, discrete municipal agencies, or national organizations of local governance actors.[28] For the sake of simplifying an already complex theoretical inquiry, I focus on the "bilateral" vertical federalism relationship between state and federal participants, unfortunately submerging the more multilateral matrix of inter- and intrastate and federal interests concealed behind that line.[29] Indeed, though the conceit of monolithic state and federal actors clarifies my analysis without violating its premise, a fuller treatment of federalism bargaining should take even better account of the horizontal and diagonal dimensions of federalism relationships,[30] and better emphasize the ways in which municipal actors operate independently from the states.[31]

Because federalism scholars habitually see the issue in unilateral terms along the state-federal axis, the bilateral interpretive enterprise of intergovernmental bargaining is missing from the federalism safeguards discourse. But recognizing how much federalism practice is

---

[27] Frederic M. Bloom, *State Courts Unbound*, 93 CORNELL L. REV. 501, 509–47 (2008) (discussed *infra* notes 289–93 and accompanying text).

[28] *See* Resnik et al., *supra* Introduction, note 72, at 739–48 (describing the role of the "Big 7" and other translocal organizations in the adaptation of legal norms).

[29] Certainly, different federal agents can have a conflict over a negotiated outcome, as can states on the other side, and localities within states. *See, e.g.*, Osofsky, *supra* Introduction, note 72 (describing diagonal federalism relationships).

[30] *See id.*; Resnik, *supra* Chapter Two, note 98 (disaggregating state and local interests in horizontal federalism terms).

[31] *See* Davidson, *supra* Chapter Two, note 95 (discussing municipal-federal partnerships that bypass the state level).

suffused in negotiation opens up new possibilities for managing federalism controversies, and new theoretical tools for analyzing them.

Negotiation theory offers well-developed conceptual frameworks for understanding the dynamics and dilemmas of federalism bargaining, including issues of representation, commitment, leverage, sources of trade, competition, collaboration, and ethics.[32] Negotiation theorists have harnessed insights from law, economics, game theory, psychology, and organizational behavior to build an extensive and interdisciplinary vocabulary for discussing the mechanics of bargaining, analyzing them simultaneously within frameworks of decision theory, societal norms, economic exchange, group dynamics, and cognitive science.[33] In addition, negotiation theory offers negotiated governance new means to accomplish effective democratic participation, incorporate contingent and revisable decision making, manage barriers to consensus, and maximize integrative (rather than purely distributive) solutions to resource allocations whenever possible.[34]

Negotiation theory becomes especially valuable when disaggregating federalism bargainers into the matrix of separate local, state, and federal actors that may have independent interests behind the state-federal line. The multilateral characteristics of federalism bargaining align with many of the central problems with which multiparty negotiation theorists have long wrestled,[35] including group behavior,[36] coalition dynamics,[37] process management,[38] and representation and agency tensions.[39] Negotiation theorists' application of game theory,

---

[32] *E.g.*, FISHER & URY, *supra* Chapter Seven, note 175; DAVID A. LAX & JAMES K. SEBENIUS, THE MANAGER AS NEGOTIATOR: BARGAINING FOR COOPERATION AND COMPETITIVE GAIN (1986); HOWARD RAIFFA, THE ART AND SCIENCE OF NEGOTIATION: HOW TO RESOLVE CONFLICTS AND GET THE BEST OUT OF BARGAINING (1982); THE CONSENSUS BUILDING HANDBOOK: A COMPREHENSIVE GUIDE TO REACHING AGREEMENT (Lawrence E. Susskind et al. eds., 1999); Carrie Menkel-Meadow, *Toward Another View of Legal Negotiation: The Structure of Legal Problem Solving*, 31 UCLA L. REV. 754 (1984). For an excellent collection of essays reviewing the practical insights of negotiation theory in specific dispute resolution contexts, see THE HANDBOOK OF DISPUTE RESOLUTION (Michael L. Moffitt & Robert C. Bordone eds., 2005).

[33] *See* sources cited, *supra* note 32; *see also* Carrie Menkel-Meadow, *Roots and Inspirations: A Brief History of the Foundations of Dispute Resolution, in* THE HANDBOOK OF DISPUTE RESOLUTION, *supra* note 32, at 13.

[34] *E.g.*, Carrie Menkel-Meadow, *Getting to "Let's Talk": Comments on Collaborative Environmental Dispute Resolution Processes*, 8 NEV. L.J. 835, 836 (2008). In negotiation theory, an integrative solution is one that incorporates as much interest-based value into the decision as possible, uncovering potentially beneficial trades between parties' differing interests that may never be realized during conventional haggling between positions. FISHER & URY, *supra* Chapter Seven, note 175, at 40–80.

[35] *See* LAWRENCE E. SUSSKIND & LARRY CRUMP, MULTIPARTY NEGOTIATION (2008).

[36] *See* Cass R. Sunstein, *Deliberative Trouble? Why Groups Go to Extremes*, 110 YALE L.J. 71 (2000).

[37] *See* James Sebenius & David Lax, *Thinking Coalitionally: Party Arithmetic, Process Opportunism, and Strategic Sequencing, in* NEGOTIATION ANALYSIS 153 (H. Peyton Young ed., 1991); James Sebenius, *Sequencing to Build Coalitions: With Whom Should I Talk First?, in* WISE CHOICES: DECISIONS, GAMES, AND NEGOTIATIONS (Richard Zeckhauser et al. eds., 1996).

[38] *See, e.g.*, David Strauss, *Managing Meetings to Build Consensus, in* THE CONSENSUS BUILDING HANDBOOK, *supra* note 32, at 287. *See* LAWRENCE SUSSKIND & JEFFREY CRUIKSHANK, BREAKING ROBERT'S RULES (2006).

[39] *See, e.g.*, MNOOKIN ET AL., *supra* Chapter Seven, note 107, at 178–203.

decision analysis, and behavioral economics could shed light on perverse incentives and irrational outcomes in federalism bargaining contexts, as well as means for overcoming multiparty process impediments such as exclusion and holdout.[40] The multilateral nature of federalism bargaining offers unexplored possibilities for interest linkages and the kind of integrative value creation that negotiation theorists have demonstrated among multiple dovetailing interests.[41] Federalism bargainers would also do well to heed research by negotiation theorists on the powerful heuristic biases that compromise negotiations.[42] The architects of federalism bargaining forums could especially learn from the emerging field of dispute systems design, which applies negotiation theory in organizational structures to reduce the drag of conflict on institutional goals,[43] and from new governance theorists' experimentation with process pluralism and iterative self-assessment criteria.[44]

Drawing insights from this literature, the analysis here fords new theoretical territory to assess how intergovernmental bargaining contributes to the overall federalism interpretive project, and how it can deliver on the promise of Balanced Federalism. Building on previous negotiated governance scholarship,[45] it reconceptualizes the boundary between state and federal power as a project of ongoing negotiation across the regulatory spectrum. It shows how government actors navigate the challenges of federalism not by virtue of unilateral good (or bad) faith, but through bilateral exchange with counterparts across the divide. It explores how procedural bargaining tools can supplement other interpretative methods to fill the inevitable gaps, advancing the core values that give federalism meaning.

But to fully understand the collaborative project of American federalism and the tools intergovernmental negotiation yields for navigating it, the first step is to explore the

---

[40] *See* LEIGH L. THOMPSON, THE MIND AND HEART OF THE NEGOTIATOR 189–94, 198–203 (2d ed. 2001). *See* R. DUNCAN LUCE & HOWARD RAIFFA, GAMES AND DECISIONS: INTRODUCTION AND CRITICAL SURVEY (1957); HOWARD RAIFFA, DECISION ANALYSIS: INTRODUCTORY LECTURES ON CHOICES UNDER UNCERTAINTY (1997).

[41] *See, e.g.*, FISHER & URY, *supra* Chapter Seven, note 175, at 40–80; LAX & SEBENIUS, *supra* note 32, at 88–116; RAIFFA, *supra* note 32, at 131–47; *see also* Michael L. Moffitt, *Disputes as Opportunities to Create Value, in* THE HANDBOOK OF DISPUTE RESOLUTION, *supra* note 32, at 173 (summarizing the literature). Indeed, for conflicts amenable to non-zero-sum solutions, increasing the number of parties at the table can provide even more opportunities for value creation. For federalism bargaining that appears predominantly zero-sum, negotiation theory offers promising new aspiration points.

[42] *See* Russell Korobkin & Chris Guthrie, *Heuristics and Biases at the Bargaining Table, in* THE NEGOTIATOR'S FIELDBOOK 351 (Andrea Kupfer Schneider & Christopher Honeyman eds., 2006). *See* MAX H. BAZERMAN & MARGARET A. NEALE, NEGOTIATING RATIONALLY (1992); BARRIERS TO CONFLICT RESOLUTION (Kenneth Arrow et al. eds., 1995); THOMPSON, *supra* note 40.

[43] *E.g.*, Khalil Z. Shariff, *Designing Institutions to Manage Conflict: Principles for the Problem Solving Organization*, 8 HARV. NEGOT. L. REV. 133, 133–57 (2003). *See* WILLIAM URY ET AL., GETTING DISPUTES RESOLVED: DESIGN SYSTEMS TO CUT THE COSTS OF CONFLICT (1993).

[44] *See* sources cited *infra* note 51.

[45] *See, e.g.*, Bruce Babbitt, *ADR Concepts: Reshaping the Way Natural Resources Decisions Are Made, in* 19 ALTERNATIVES TO HIGH COST OF LITIGATION 13, 13 (2001); Freeman, *supra* Chapter Five, note 21, at 4, 8–31 (proposing a model of collaborative governance as an alternative to the model of interest representation); Karkkainen, *supra* Chapter Three, note 196 (discussing the emergence of a new model of collaborative ecosystem governance).

previously uncharted federalism bargaining landscape. The rest of this chapter provides that introduction.

B. A Taxonomy of Federalism Bargaining

State-federal bargaining is endemic to American governance and pervasive in many substantive areas of law. This section identifies the primary ways in which state and federal actors negotiate with one another, focusing on opportunities for federalism bargaining within the structure of specific constitutional and statutory laws. Negotiations take place over both the allocation of policy- or decision-making authority and the content of policies made pursuant to that authority. Many negotiations are of the standard variety, neatly bookended in space and time and conducted among self-identified participants. However, some of the most interesting examples evoke a broader understanding of negotiation because they take place over longer periods of time, with a broader array of participants, or otherwise depart from the bounded exchange conjured by conventional images of the negotiating table. This analysis adopts the broad definition of bargaining that negotiation theorists prefer: an iterative process of communication by which multiple parties seek to influence one another in a project of joint decision making.[46] Unified by this definition, this section sketches a continuum of negotiating formats that range from familiar forms of face-to-face bargaining to remote exchanges between separately deliberating groups.

State-federal negotiations that follow the conventional model are easily recognizable. For example, state and federal executive actors frequently negotiate in a conventional manner over the details of federal law that may impact the states, about law enforcement matters in which both hold interests, and over administrative details within cooperative programs that include state and federal participation. In addition, Congress frequently uses its spending power to bargain with state policy makers in areas of law traditionally associated with state prerogative, such as education, family law, and health policy.

Other forums for intergovernmental negotiation have conventional features, but are more deeply buried within other legal frameworks. For example, within some spending power-based programs of cooperative federalism, Congress invites further state-federal bargaining by creating statutory invitations for states to propose innovations to existing federal programs, the details of which are often heavily negotiated with the overseeing federal agencies. In addition, some federal agencies invite state stakeholders to the negotiating table early in the process of administrative rulemaking, affording them a greater opportunity to influence the process than under traditional notice-and-comment rulemaking.

Still other forms depart even further from the conventional model, and may be overlooked as state-federal bargaining entirely. For example, states have occasionally negotiated with Congress to become bound by enforceable federal laws (as demonstrated in Chapter Seven),

---

[46] *See, e.g.,* FISHER & URY, *supra* Chapter Seven, note 175, at xvii (describing it as "back-and-forth communication designed to reach agreement" whenever parties have both shared and differing interests); SHELL, *supra* Part IV Introduction, note 12, at 6 (describing it as the "interactive communication process" that takes place when parties want things from each other).

and Congress has occasionally created forums for long-term, iterative sharing of policy-making authority with states. In the most exotic examples, participants may not have even recognized what they were doing as negotiation at all—such as the "iterative federalism" provisions of the Clean Air Act's two-track vehicular emissions program,[47] or the intersystemic signaling between state and federal policy makers that is currently underway regarding medical marijuana.[48] Nevertheless, they meet the criteria of joint consensus that sets negotiated decision making apart from other forms of state-federal interaction.

Defining negotiated governance so broadly invites the fair question of what acts of governance would *not* be considered some move within a larger negotiation. If intersystemic signaling between state and federal lawmakers over medical marijuana policy counts, what about amicus briefs by state actors in federal court, or even less formal means by which state and federal actors influence one another's decisions? In fact, our tradition of deliberative democracy within a federal system creates an almost infinite array of possibilities for federalism bargaining. The taxonomy shows just how variegated and entrenched such bargaining really is—although only the most formalized methods (those most amenable to procedural constraints, public scrutiny, and judicial review) will be candidates for the interpretive deference discussed in Chapter Ten.

Indeed, one normative purpose in fleshing out the details of federalism bargaining is to call attention to how much federalism-sensitive governance is already negotiated, belying the zero-sum tenor of the overall federalism discourse. Yet this should not be surprising, given the negotiation features built into the very structure of American government. The bicameral nature of the legislature, the presidential veto, and even the subtle invitation to iterative policy making afforded by judicial review—prompting Congress to try again to meet constitutional muster, or signaling the concerns future legislators must heed[49]—all speak to the way American governance is, by design, an iterative process of joint decision making. The interest group representation model of democratic governance itself anticipates how lawmaking will reflect the results of bargaining between competing interest groups.[50] But even beyond these features of the American system (and in contrast to the more privately bargained-for governance advocated by the New Governance movement),[51] it is striking how

---

[47] *See infra* notes 249–55 and accompanying text.

[48] *See infra* notes 267–279 and accompanying text.

[49] For example, Congress designed the Religious Land Use and Institutionalized Persons Act of 2000 (RLUIPA) in response to the U.S. Supreme Court's 1997 invalidation of the Religious Freedom and Restoration Act (RFRA) as exceeding legislative authority under the Fourteenth Amendment. RLUIPA, Pub. L. No. 106–274, 114 Stat. 803 (2000) (codified as amended at 42 U.S.C. §§ 2000cc-1 to -5 (2006)); RFRA, Pub. L. No. 103–141, 107 Stat. 1488 (1993), *invalidated by* City of Boerne v. Flores, 521 U.S. 507, 511 (1997).

[50] Freeman, *supra* Chapter Five, note 21, at 18 & n.48.

[51] *See* William H. Simon, *Toyota Jurisprudence: Legal Theory and Rolling Rule Regimes*, in LAW AND NEW GOVERNANCE IN THE EU AND THE US 37 (Grainne de Burca & Joanne Scott eds., 2006) (articulating the principles of the New Governance movement); Amy J. Cohen, *Negotiation, Meet New Governance: Interests, Skills, and Selves*, 33 LAW & SOC. INQUIRY 503 (2008) (examining the New Governance and negotiation literature and points of convergence between them); Michael C. Dorf & Charles F. Sabel, *A Constitution of Democratic Experimentalism*, 98 COLUM. L. REV. 267 (1998) (discussing a decentralized model of governance in which actors utilize local knowledge); Lobel, *supra* Chapter Three, note 131 (contrasting the New Deal and

much federalism-implicating governance is accomplished bilaterally, whether by conventional or dialogic processes. Examples are especially prevalent in environmental and land use law, where jurisdictional overlap is particularly acute and where the federalism discourse is most driven to extremes.[52]

The following survey reviews ten basic ways that state and federal actors negotiate, roughly organized into the three overarching categories of conventional examples, negotiations to reallocate authority, and joint policy-making negotiations. The many subject-matter examples substantiate my claim that the boundary between state and federal authority is more porous than political rhetoric suggests, and more contingent than federalism jurisprudence has acknowledged. They also provide supporting data for the analysis in Chapters Nine and Ten.

The conventional group includes examples in which the iterative process most resembles colloquial understandings of bargaining as a simple exchange, or a purposeful and time-bounded collective deliberation. These include: (1) interest group representation bargaining, by which state actors lobby federal lawmakers; (2) enforcement negotiations, including those over individual enforcement cases, state-federal enforcement partnerships, and enforcement matters within programs of cooperative federalism; and (3) negotiations over more administrative details, resource allocation, or settlement of litigation. (Spending power deals and negotiated rulemaking also reflect conventional bargaining, but they are addressed in categories that focus on their more interesting features.)

Negotiations to reallocate authority, or to depart from an otherwise established legal order, take place in contexts of overlap in which a constitutional or statutory provision provides an initial answer to the question of who gets to decide, but the parties choose to bargain around that line. Examples include: (4) spending power bargains, in which the federal government negotiates to extend its regulatory reach into zones otherwise constitutionally reserved to the states; (5) bargained-for encroachment and commandeering, two closely related (but occasionally unconstitutional) forms in which states bargain to assume federal power or become bound by federal law; and (6) negotiations for various exceptions and permissions within frameworks of statutory law.

The final and most theoretically interesting category draws elements from the prior two, partnering local and national actors in negotiations that lead to new substantive policies. Joint policy-making forms include: (7) negotiated rulemaking under the Administrative Procedure Act; (8) policy-making laboratory negotiations by which federal laws create "fill-in-the-blank" state policy-making zones and otherwise invite state proposals to modify federal law; (9) iterative policy-making negotiations, which create a limited forum for shared state-federal policy making over time; and (10) intersystemic signaling negotiations, by which separately deliberating state and federal actors trade influence over the direction of shared policy. Negotiations within this final category receive the most

---

New Governance regulatory models). In contrast to federalism bargaining between state and federal actors, the New Governance movement advocates devolution of national command-and-control regulation to locally mediated negotiation among private stakeholders.

[52] *See, e.g.,* New York v. United States, 505 U.S. 144 (1992) (adjudicating overlap in radioactive waste siting); Rapanos v. United States, 547 U.S. 715 (2006) (adjudicating overlap in wetlands regulatory jurisdiction).

.

sustained attention because they hold the most meaningful promise for bilaterally balanced federalism interpretation.

1. CONVENTIONAL FORMS OF FEDERALISM BARGAINING

The most familiar examples of federalism bargaining may be the most frequently used. The first category encompasses these most conventional examples, where the iterative process best resembles colloquial understandings of bargaining as a simple exchange or a time-bounded collective deliberation. These can include interest group representation bargaining, by which state actors lobby federal lawmakers; enforcement negotiations, including those over individual enforcement cases, state-federal enforcement partnerships, and enforcement matters within programs of cooperative federalism; and negotiations over more administrative details or resource allocation, or in settlement of litigation. This section highlights the interest group representation and enforcement bargaining types, with examples from negotiations over the Stimulus Bill, financial services reform, criminal law enforcement, and enforcement within programs of cooperative federalism.

The conventional negotiations involve a wide array of participants and variously address policy making, implementation, and enforcement. Although the result of these negotiations usually becomes a matter of public record, the process itself may be hidden from public view, such that details are ascertainable only through firsthand accounts. In that regard, though these familiar forms of federalism bargaining may raise the fewest eyebrows, they may also be the most vulnerable to accountability concerns about transparency, inclusion, third-party impacts, and principal-agent tensions.

a. Interest Group Representation: The Stimulus and Financial Services Reform

Though hardly unique to federalism bargaining, state agents negotiate with federal policy makers just like any other lobby to protect the state's interests during federal lawmaking. These negotiations reflect the normal workings of our interest group representation model of governance, in which stakeholders leverage their representation to accomplish their preferences during the legislative process.[53] In these conventional negotiations, state actors voice concerns, rally supporters, and pressure representatives to secure favorable legislative outcomes. Although Congress retains the ultimate decision to enact a law (and the president retains veto power), the sausage-making process by which a bill is created and shepherded through passage is always an elaborate multiparty negotiation among the various stakeholders and their representatives.[54]

The mechanics of this conventional form of bargaining would be familiar to any dealmaker, but interest group negotiations present interesting questions about who best represents state interests. As collective bargainers have long understood, leverage often follows clout, and states often work together to accomplish common legislative preferences in Congress

---

[53] Freeman, *supra* Chapter Five, note 21, at 18.
[54] *Id.*

through national organizations such as the National Governors Association (NGA), the National Conference of State Legislatures (NCSL), the National Association of Attorneys General, and the United States Conference of Mayors.[55] Nevertheless, consensus is often hard fought even within those organizations.[56] When interests diverge among the states, state actors lobby or otherwise negotiate with federal lawmakers independently, as demonstrated by the special interests taken by New York State in federal financial services regulation, or by California in federal environmental policy. In this context, negotiations are usually initiated by state interests, sometimes to spur desired federal policy, and other times in response to federal movement toward undesired policies.

2009 Stimulus

For example, the states shared fairly uniform interests in President Obama's $787 billion stimulus proposal, and played a formidable role in designing the resulting American Recovery and Reinvestment Act of 2009.[57] Although the policy decisions associated with the stimulus package are usually attributed to the Obama administration, extensive lobbying by the NGA and NCSL secured the substantial provision of direct relief to support state infrastructure and public education.[58] The NGA lobbied Congress to fund state projects that could quickly channel stimulus money into jobs,[59] while NCSL urged the president to aid fiscally hemorrhaging states, because their need to cut spending and raise taxes (to meet state constitutional balanced-budget requirements) would inevitably worsen the national slump.[60] In the end, the Stimulus Bill included over $250 billion in direct assistance to states,[61] approximately one-third of the total funds allocated.[62]

Financial Services Reform

Some states with unique financial regulatory interests have also negotiated tenaciously with federal lawmakers over recent proposals to regulate banking and financial services in the wake of the 2008 crisis. For instance, the recently passed Restoring Financial Stability Act of

---

[55] *E.g.*, Resnik et al., *supra* Introduction, note 72, at 726–69.

[56] Telephone Interview with Melissa Savage, Policy Officer, National Council of State Legislatures (Jan. 15, 2010).

[57] Pub. L. No. 111–5, 123 Stat. 115 (codified as amended in scattered sections of 6, 19, 26, 42, and 47 U.S.C.).

[58] ROBERT JAY DILGER, CONG, RESEARCH SERV., STATES AND PROPOSED ECONOMIC RECOVERY PLANS 7–8 (2009), http://assets.opencrs.com/rpts/R40112_20090116.pdf.

[59] Letter from Governors Edward Rendell & James Douglas, Nat'l Governors Ass'n, to Senators Harry Reid and Mitch McConnell and Representatives Nancy Pelosi and John Boehner concerning a proposed Economic Recovery Package (Oct. 27, 2008), http://www.nga.org/portal/site/nga/menuitem.cb6e7818b34088d18a2781 1050101oa0/?vgnextoid=147053975ef2d110VgnVCM1000001a01010aRCRD.

[60] DILGER, *supra* note 58, at 1–2 (quoting Letter from Representative Joe Hackney, NCSL President, to Barack Obama concerning the Economic Stimulus Package (Nov. 12, 2008), http://www.ncsl.org/print/statefed/ Transition_Stim111308.pdf).

[61] NAT'L GOVERNORS ASS'N, STATE IMPLEMENTATION OF THE AMERICAN RECOVERY AND REINVESTMENT ACT 2 (Mar. 10, 2009), http://www.nga.org/Files/pdf/ARRASTATEIMPLEMENTATION.pdf.

[62] *The Road to Recovery: Is Obamanomics a Boom or a Bane?*, NEWSWEEK, Nov. 30, 2009, at 46–47 (quoting Professor Allan Meltzer).

2010 creates both a Financial Stability Oversight Council and a new Consumer Financial Protection Agency housed within the Federal Reserve.[63] States lobbied hard to accomplish their legislative preferences in the crafting of these proposals, which could dramatically impact their own regulatory jurisdiction (as the former could wrest regulatory control from dozens of state and federal agencies, and the latter would set consumer protection standards that could alternatively undergird or preempt existing state laws).[64] Some negotiations evidence jealous battles for regulatory turf[65] while others demonstrate the potential for effective collaboration in areas of jurisdictional overlap.[66]

For example, New York State regulators have collaborated with federal counterparts to bilaterally regulate such hot-button financial issues as executive compensation.[67] In praise of a joint plan to do so, the state attorney general observed that "[o]ur cooperative efforts set a perfect example for how federal and state authorities should be working together on behalf of taxpayers."[68] The plan nicely demonstrates the potential for bilateral state-federal balancing of competing federalism values, jointly determining just how much national uniformity should yield to local autonomy even in an economic regulatory sphere that ordinarily favors federal preemption.

b. Enforcement Negotiations: Criminal Law and Cooperative Federalism

State and federal executive actors frequently negotiate over matters of enforcement where jurisdiction overlaps—ranging from individual criminal cases to enforcement responsibilities within complex programs of cooperative federalism. Ongoing state-federal partnerships have been negotiated to cope with chronic enforcement issues involving gun violence and child pornography, and to extend federal enforcement authority through negotiated memoranda of understanding to state actors in contexts where states possess critical enforcement capacity, such as immigration law,[69] and point source permitting under the Clean Water Act.[70] State and federal actors also negotiate over enforcement policy and individual

---

[63] Pub. L. No. 111–203, 124 Stat. 1376 (2010).

[64] Damian Paletta, *Consumer-Agency Bill Moves in House*, WALL ST. J., Oct. 23, 2009, at A5; Karey Wutkowski, *Dodd's Super Bank Cop Faces Tough Battle*, REUTERS, Nov. 11, 2009, http://www.reuters.com/article/idUSTRE5A94T520091110.

[65] Sarah H. Burghart, *Survey: Overcompensating Much? The Impact of Preemption on Emerging Federal and State Efforts to Limit Executive Compensation*, 2009 COLUM. BUS. L. REV. 669, 673 (2009).

[66] Press Release, Office of N.Y. Attorney Gen., Statement from Attorney General Andrew Cuomo Regarding New Developments in Investigation of Merrill Lynch Bonuses and Bank of America (Jan. 27, 2009), http://www.oag.state.ny.us/media_center/2009/jan/jan27a_09.html (describing collaborative state-federal regulatory efforts).

[67] *Id.*

[68] *Id.*

[69] *See, e.g.*, Immigration and Nationality Act, 8 U.S.C. § 1357(g)(1) (2006) (detailing the "ACCESS" program, whereby the Attorney General can "enter into a written agreement with a State . . . pursuant to which an officer or employee of the State . . . who is determined by the Attorney General to be qualified to perform a function of an immigration officer . . . may carry out such function.").

[70] 33 U.S.C. § 1342 (outlining the National Pollutant Discharge Elimination System permitting regime). When a state elects to assume NPDES permitting authority, it negotiates a Memorandum of Agreement with the EPA

enforcement actions arising within cooperative federalism programs, such as the Clean Air, Clean Water, and Superfund Acts.

Criminal Law

State and federal law enforcement agencies regularly negotiate responsibility for investigating and prosecuting criminal activity punishable under both state and federal law, often involving drug trafficking, alien smuggling, racketeering, or conspiracy cases.[71] Federal agencies usually become involved only after criminal activity has exceeded state and local law enforcement capacity.[72] Negotiations then begin early, because decisions about where the case will be prosecuted determine the allocation of resources and investigative responsibilities.[73] In contrast to state-federal competition over policy-making jurisdiction, state actors usually welcome federal intervention in criminal enforcement matters, especially those involving terrorism and immigration issues, because the deployment of federal resources frees up scarce state resources for other cases.[74] In addition, state and federal agencies occasionally negotiate collaborative "strike force" agreements, a cooperative enterprise for investigating and prosecuting interjurisdictional crime.[75] State district attorneys and lawyers from the state attorney general's office are occasionally deputized to act as U.S. Attorneys in order to collaborate in these interjurisdictional partnerships.[76]

Collaborative state-federal programs have been especially popular in efforts to combat gang violence.[77] Building on successful pilot programs in Virginia and Massachusetts, the Department of Justice has joined with the National District Attorneys Association and the International Association of Chiefs of Police to administer the Project Safe Neighborhoods program, which partners regional U.S. Attorney's offices with corresponding State Attorney's offices, the FBI, ATF, state and local police, and state probation and parole officers to coordinate the deterrence, investigation, and prosecution of gun violence in metropolitan areas.[78] Nearly all such initiatives also involve local government and community representatives,

---

that sets forth the details about how the permitting program will be implemented. Differences range from varying time periods for review to significantly different allocation of permitting authority in various contexts. For example, in otherwise similar agreements, the EPA retains authority to review any permits issued by the State of Maine but waives review of draft wastewater, stormwater, and sewage sludge permits in Texas. *Compare* NPDES MEMORANDUM OF AGREEMENT BETWEEN THE STATE OF MAINE AND THE UNITED STATES EPA REGION 1 (2000), http://www.maine.gov/dep/blwq/delegation/moa.pdf, with MEMORANDUM OF AGREEMENT BETWEEN THE TEXAS NATURAL RESOURCE CONSERVATION COMMISSION AND THE U.S. EPA REGION 6 (1998), http://www.epa.gov/region6/water/npdes/docs/texas-moa.pdf.

[71] Interview with Paul Marcus, Professor of Criminal Law, William & Mary Law School, Williamsburg, Va. (Oct. 16, 2009).

[72] *Id.*

[73] *Id.*

[74] Telephone Interview with Roscoe Howard, former U.S. Attorney for the District of Columbia (Jan. 4, 2010).

[75] *Id.*

[76] *Id.*

[77] *Cf.* Eric Holder, Attorney Gen., U.S. Dep't of Justice, Remarks at the California Cities Gang Prevention Network (May 10, 2010) (discussing partnership approaches for managing violent crime).

[78] *About Project Safe Neighborhoods*, http://www.psn.gov/about/index.html.

with explicit recognition of the benefits of drawing on both local and national capacities.[79] Similar enforcement partnerships have been established to combat child predation through the Internet Crimes Against Children Task Force Program.[80]

Cooperative Federalism Enforcement

Copious negotiation also takes place during individual enforcement cases that arise within complex programs of cooperative federalism. For example, the EPA often negotiates with state counterparts in prioritizing and implementing enforcement actions against in-state violations under the Clean Air and Water Acts.[81] In one recent instance, EPA collaborated with the Pennsylvania Department of Environmental Protection (DEP) in an attempt to bring a Pennsylvania foundry into compliance with Clean Air Act emissions standards, prompting the Department of Justice to file a federal suit against the foundry on behalf of the EPA and Pennsylvania DEP.[82] Congress also amended the Clean Water Act in the 1970s to require EPA to follow a state list of priority water pollution clean-up projects rather than allowing it to create its own list based on need and public health dangers. As a result, the EPA must negotiate with states about which treatment facilities to build where and when.[83] (Allocation by the Clean Air and Water Acts of state implementation responsibilities also engendered a distinct form of policy-making bargaining discussed under the policy-making laboratory category, infra.)

Similarly, the Superfund Act[84] effectively requires state-federal negotiation over enforcement priorities by mandating that states pay at least 10 percent of the costs of remedial action to qualify for certain federal clean-up funds.[85] Because EPA cannot force a state to pay more than it is willing to spend, states are effectively empowered to negotiate the priority and intensity of proposed cleanups by limiting costs to what the relevant state is willing to pay.[86]

---

[79] *Id.* (including "a commitment to tailor the program to local context" in acknowledgement of interjurisdictional variation). Nearly two billion dollars have been committed to the program since 2001. *Id.*

[80] *Internet Crimes Against Children Task Force Program*, DEP'T OF JUSTICE OFFICE OF JUVENILE JUSTICE & DELINQUENCY PREVENTION, http://ojjdp.ncjrs.org/Programs/ProgSummary.asp?pi=3. Since 1998, over 230,000 law enforcement officers, prosecutors, and other professionals have been trained through the program, which has reviewed more than 180,000 complaints resulting in over 16,500 arrests. *Id.*

[81] Clean Air Act, 42 U.S.C. § 7413 (2006); Clean Water Act, 33 U.S.C. § 1319 (2006).

[82] Press Release, Complaint against Erie Coke for Clean Air Act Violations Filed Today by the U.S. Attorney for EPA and Pa. DEP (Sept. 22, 2009) (reporting on the complaint and state-federal cooperation); Press Release, Pa. Dep't of Envtl. Prot., DEP, EPA Begin Joint Inspection of Erie Coke with Coke Oven Expert (Jan. 12, 2009).

[83] *See* 33 U.S.C. § 1296 (2006) (providing that states control priority). At least one scholar recalls resulting negotiations that may not have advanced the ultimate objectives of the Act. Emails from Howard Latin, Professor, Rutgers Law Sch., to author (July 2, 2009 & Dec. 31, 2009) (recalling political patronage negotiations in which "efforts to grasp a large pot of money triumphed over technical efforts to achieve water pollution control").

[84] Comprehensive Environmental Response, Compensation, and Liability Act of 1980, Pub. L. No. 96–510, 94 Stat. 2767 (codified as amended at 42 U.S.C. §§ 9601–9675 (2006)).

[85] 42 U.S.C. § 9604(c)(3)(C) (2006).

[86] Emails from Howard Latin to author, *supra* note 83.

2. NEGOTIATIONS TO REALLOCATE AUTHORITY

The second category includes negotiations to reallocate authority that is already delegated to one side or the other under an established constitutional or statutory order. In many of these negotiations, the parties bargain over clearly delineated federalism entitlements to sovereign authority, as discussed in Chapter Seven. When such bargaining is genuinely consensual and accountable, it may hold considerable interpretive potential, on grounds that the parties would not cede sovereign authority unless offsetting values were well-served. By the same token, because sovereign authority is at issue, consent and accountability in the bargaining process become especially important.

The best known example is spending power bargaining, in which the federal government negotiates to extend its regulatory reach into zones otherwise constitutionally reserved to the states. However, states also bargain to expand their jurisdiction into federal territory and to reallocate authority in favor of the federal government. In the LLRWPA example discussed in Chapter Seven, states attempted to engage in "bargained-for commandeering" to limit their own regulatory authority under binding federal law. The courts have looked more favorably on "bargained-for encroachment," in which states seek to exercise otherwise federal authority in interstate compacts with one another and Congress. Finally, state and federal actors also negotiate for permissions and exceptions within otherwise applicable statutory frameworks involving exchanges of statutorily based authority. This section illustrates these forms with examples from the Energy Independence and Security Act, the No Child Left Behind Act, interstate water compacts, the Endangered Species Act, and hydroelectric dam licensing.

a. Spending Power Deals: Energy Independence and Security Act and No Child Left Behind

The most recognized form of federalism bargaining is that which takes place between the federal and state governments under Congress's Article I spending power.[87] By conditioning the offer of federal funds on federally desired state action, Congress may extend its regulatory reach beyond that of its other enumerated powers.[88] Bargaining with the spending power this way has become a standard congressional tool for influencing regulatory policy in areas of interjurisdictional concern since the New Deal.[89] Examples pervade the regulatory landscape, ranging from simple exchanges sought by "federal funds with strings" to elaborate programs of cooperative federalism.

Of all federalism bargaining forms, spending power bargaining has received the most direct judicial and scholarly attention. As discussed above, some scholars have critiqued spending power bargaining as an unbounded exercise of federal authority that cannot be reconciled with the New Federalism limits on federal power.[90] They urge that spending power deals allowing federal reach into state jurisdiction cannot be considered fair simply

---

[87] U.S. Const. art. I, § 8.

[88] *See* South Dakota v. Dole, 483 U.S. 203, 206 (1987); *infra* notes 370–88 and accompanying text).

[89] *See* Lynn A. Baker, *The Spending Power and the Federalist Revival*, 4 CHAP. L. REV. 195, 196, 213 (2001).

[90] *See supra* Chapter Seven, note 163.

because states consent, because the bargaining leverage so favors the federal side that state participation is effectively coerced.[91] States dependent on federal funding cannot realistically opt out, they argue, so resulting deals are as flawed as a contract made under duress.[92] However, the Supreme Court has not been receptive, reasoning that, as do contracting individuals at common law, states hold the ultimate authority to decide whether their interests are best served by taking or rejecting the proffered deal.[93] The Court has never invalidated a deal meeting its modest spending doctrine constraints, and it rejected invitations to extend New Federalism constraints to that doctrine in the late Rehnquist years.[94]

On the surface, spending power deals are exclusively at the invitation of Congress, extended to the state executive or legislative actors empowered to act on the deal. Yet the negotiation process usually begins in interest group bargaining over terms before the deal is formally proffered—and Congress does not always initiate this bargaining.[95] For that reason, spending power bargains are not always federally force-fed policy directives to states; some represent the wishes of state advocates.[96]

Energy Independence and Security

For example, state actors were instrumental in the genesis of the Energy Independence and Security Act of 2007 (EISA),[97] which authorized the Energy Efficiency Conservation Block Grant program (EECBG) as part of a national clean energy legislative effort.[98] Thanks to state leadership in the design of the program, federal grants under the EECBG program offer funds to state, tribal, and municipal governments in exchange for their development and implementation of community-based projects to improve energy efficiency, reduce energy use, and reduce carbon emissions.[99] Congress proposed $2 billion in annual funding for the EECBG program in the EISA, with 2 percent going to tribal programs, 28 percent to states, 68 percent to large cities and counties, and an additional 2 percent for a competitive program for small cities and counties.[100]

---

[91] *E.g.*, Baker & Berman, *supra* Chapter Four, note 17, at 467–70, 520–21.

[92] *Id.* at 487.

[93] *Dole*, 483 U.S. at 207–08.

[94] Pierce County v. Guillen, 537 U.S. 129, 146 (2003); Sabri v. United States, 541 U.S. 600 (2004).

[95] *E.g.*, New York v. United States, 505 U.S. 144, 150 (1992) (discussing Congress's reliance on a report by the National Governors Association in drafting the Low-Level Radioactive Waste Policy Amendments Act of 1985); Anonymous Interview, U.S. Senate, Wash., D.C. (Nov. 24, 2009) [hereinafter Senate Interview] (describing how state actors often initiate spending power legislation through interest group negotiations with federal lawmakers, such as the Energy Efficiency Conservation Block Grant Program).

[96] *See* Senate Interview, *supra* note 95.

[97] Pub. L. No. 110–140, 121 Stat. 1492 (2007) (codified at 42 U.S.C. §§ 17001–17386).

[98] *See* 42 U.S.C. §§ 17151–17158.

[99] *Weatherization and Intergovernmental Program: Efficiency Conservation Block Grant Program*, Energy Efficiency & Renewable Energy, http://www.eecbg.energy.gov/ (noting that the DOE has already awarded $1.6 billion in grants to over 1,400 projects).

[100] Energy Efficiency and Conservation Block Grant Program—State, Local and Tribal Allocation Formulas, 74 Fed. Reg. 17461(Apr. 15, 2009); *see also* U.S. Conference of Mayors, The Energy Efficiency and

No Child Left Behind

On the other hand, other spending power deals are more clearly driven by federal policy makers, and some are unpopular even among the states that choose to bargain. For example, the No Child Left Behind Act of 2001[101] is a standards-based education reform law that trades federal education funding for states' agreement to focus on bringing their most disadvantaged students up to a federally mandated level of achievement. Although few question the value of its goals, and no states chose to forgo needed federal funds, the act's assessment policies have proved controversial. For example, many school systems argue that the act forces unbeneficial "teaching to the test," uneccesarily usurps local authority, and penalizes already struggling school systems.[102]

b. Bargained-For Encroachment and Commandeering:
Interstate Water Compacts and LLRWPA

On the flip side of spending power bargaining are states' occasional attempts to bargain around constitutionally designated lines of authority by negotiating to expand their jurisdiction at the expense of federal prerogative, or to be bound (or "commandeered") by federal law. In bargained-for encroachment, states negotiate for federal approval of interstate compacts that derogate federal power. Interstate compacts (which can also involve federal parties) represent the converse of spending power bargaining, in that states here seek federal permission to encroach on federal jurisdiction.[103] As a doctrinal matter, congressional approval is required whenever such an agreement would increase the power of states at the expense of the federal government,[104] effectively reallocating the initial distribution of regulatory authority.

Bargained-For Encroachment: Interstate Water Compacts

For example, between 2001 and 2005 eight states negotiated the Great Lakes-St. Lawrence River Basin Compact out of fear that proposals from the Army Corps of Engineers to divert Great Lakes waters to the high plains might trigger further federal mandates to funnel Great Lakes waters to arid western states.[105] The compact, like many similar interstate water compacts, won congressional approval despite clear Supreme Court precedent establishing federal supremacy in the allocation of interstate waters.[106] Notwithstanding, the compact

---

CONSERVATION BLOCK GRANT (EECBG) 2, http://usmayors.org/climateprotection/documents/eecbghandout.pdf.

[101] Pub. L. No. 107-110, 115 Stat. 1425 (enacted Jan. 8, 2002) (codified as amended in scattered sections of 20 U.S.C.).

[102] Sam Dillon, *Obama to Seek Sweeping Change of the "No Child" Law*, N.Y. TIMES, Feb. 1, 2010, at A1 (noting criticisms of the Act); Krista Kafer, *No Child Left Behind: Where Do We Go from Here?*, BACKGROUNDER (The Heritage Found., Wash., D.C.), July 6, 2004, http://www.heritage.org/research/education/bg1775.cfm (full state participation).

[103] DAN TARLOCK, LAW OF WATER RIGHTS AND RESOURCES § 10:24 (2009).

[104] *Id.*

[105] *Id.* § 10–32.

[106] Sporhase v. Nebraska *ex rel.* Douglas, 458 U.S. 941, 953–54, 959–60 (1982).

makes it difficult to divert water from the basin, empowering state decision making at the expense of federal prerogative.[107] Congressional consent also saves interstate compacts that might otherwise encroach on Congress's exclusive authority over interstate commerce.[108] For example, the terms of the Yellowstone River Compact contravene the Commerce Clause by requiring that Montana, North Dakota, and Wyoming consent to any water diversions outside the water basin,[109] but the Ninth Circuit has affirmed that congressional approval of the compact immunized this consent requirement from objections under the dormant Commerce Clause.[110]

Bargained-For Commandeering: Low-Level Radioactive Waste

More controversially, states may also negotiate to be "commandeered" by the federal government. In bargained-for commandeering, states agree to limit their own regulatory discretion under binding federal law that reflects state preferences (usually to referee a collective action problem among the states without losing state policy leadership). As in the Low-Level Radioactive Waste Policy Act (LLRWPA) example discussed at length in Chapter Seven, when state actors have initiated this kind of bargaining, it is generally because they prefer the solution they are proposing to a fully preemptive solution imposed top-down from federal lawmakers.[111] State consensus is often developed through the activities of a national state interests group, such as the National Governors Association, which then bargains directly with federal actors on behalf of its constituency.[112] Federal involvement is often necessary to make these state-initiated agreements enforceable, because state compacts are too easily abandoned by states that later repudiate the deal.[113]

Securing federal enforcement of a plan collectively chosen by the states behind the regulatory veil of ignorance allows the parties to fairly chart a course of consensus both horizontally and vertically before history determines the plan's eventual winners and losers.[114] But of course, the Supreme Court rejected this kind of bargaining in *New York v. United States* for violating the allocation of state and federal power protected by the Tenth Amendment.[115] Nevertheless, as demonstrated by the Clean Water Act's Phase II Stormwater Rule, weaker "modified commandeering bargains" have enabled similar forms of

---

[107] TARLOCK, *supra* note 103, § 10–32.

[108] *Id.* § 10–26.

[109] YELLOWSTONE RIVER COMPACT COMM'N, http://yrcc.usgs.gov/ (last visited Nov. 25, 2010).

[110] Intake Water Co. v. Yellowstone River Compact Comm'n, 769 F. 2d 568, 570 (9th Cir. 1985).

[111] Low-Level Radioactive Waste Policy Act, Pub. L. No. 96–573, 94 Stat. 3347 (1980) (as amended *by* Low-Level Radioactive Waste Policy Amendments Act of 1985, Pub. L. No. 99–240, 99 Stat. 1842 (1986)) (current version at 42 U.S.C. §§ 2021b-2021j (2006)); discussed *supra* Chapter Seven.

[112] *See* MITCHEL N. HERIAN, GOVERNORS AND THE NATIONAL GOVERNORS ASSOCIATION (NGA): EXAMINING THE FEDERAL LOBBYING IMPACT OF THE NGA 31 (2008) (finding that the NGA has a good success rate in achieving the outcomes for which it lobbies on behalf of its state-based constituencies).

[113] *See supra* Chapter Seven, notes 125–28 and accompanying text; Alabama v. North Carolina, 130 S. Ct. 2295 (2010).

[114] *See supra* Chapter Seven, notes 52–53 and accompanying text.

[115] *See* 505 U.S. at 174–75.

intergovernmental bargaining to move forward when individual state actors are enabled to opt out.[116]

c. Exceptions Negotiations: Endangered Species Act and Hydroelectric Dam Licensing

State and federal actors also negotiate for exceptions under otherwise applicable statutory law. Most of the time, these negotiations feature state executive actors seeking release from federal executives who administer federal laws that apply to state activity (or private activity of economic interest to the state), such as the Endangered Species Act (ESA). Other times, the federal government must negotiate release under statutory provisions that empower the states, as in licensing hydroelectric dams and offshore oil drilling. States also trade power with the federal government in the negotiation of federal enclaves carved out of existing state lands, in which states often cede power in exchange for desired federal policies—such as the creation of a wanted National Park, or the application of the Assimilative Crimes Act, 18 U.S.C. § 13(a) (2006) (allowing the borrowing of state law when there is no applicable federal statute).[117]

Endangered Species Act
The ESA[118] forbids public and private actions that would harm plant and animal species listed under the statute as threatened or endangered.[119] State actors must heed listed species protections both in maintaining state infrastructure[120] and in regulating private activity.[121] Nevertheless, although the statute prohibits human actions that harm (or "take") listed species, it provides a window to negotiate exceptions for certain activities that might cause unintentional harm if that harm is sufficiently mitigated.[122] When applicants create a "Habitat Conservation Plan" (HCP) to compensate for any harm, they can seek an "Incidental Take Permit" (ITP) that exempts them from ESA liability.[123] States have used this provision to negotiate exceptions for both development and conservation-oriented projects.

---

[116] For discussion of this example, *see supra* Chapter Five, notes 49–67, and Chapter Seven, notes 218–21, and accompanying text.

[117] For more on federal enclaves, see INTERDEPARTMENTAL COMM. FOR THE STUDY OF JURISDICTION OVER FEDERAL AREAS WITHIN THE STATES 7–11 (1956), http://www.constitution.org/juris/fjur/1fj1–3.htm. Another interesting arena of criminal law bargaining is the cross-deputization agreements between the federal government and Indian tribes expanding the jurisdiction of each side without compromising either's sovereignty. Joseph P. Kallt & Joseph W. Singer, *Myths and Realities of Tribal Sovereignty: The Law and Economics of Indian Self-Rule* 11 (KSG Faculty Research Working Paper No. RWP04–16, 2004), http://papers.ssrn.com/sol3/papers.cfm?abstract_id=529084.

[118] 16 U.S.C. § 1531–1544 (2006).

[119] *Id.* § 1538.

[120] *E.g.*, NATOMAS BASIN CONSERVANCY, http://www.natomasbasin.org/.

[121] *E.g.*, Strahan v. Coxe, 127 F.3d 155, 158 (1st Cir. 1997) (holding that state fishing permits allowing fixed nets in Northern Right whale breeding habitat constituted a vicarious take).

[122] 16 U.S.C. § 1539.

[123] *See id.* Applicants must submit a conservation plan specifying the likely impact from the taking, why alternatives are not preferable, and steps to minimize and mitigate negative impacts. *Id.* § 1539(a)(2)(A).

For example, California and federal agencies negotiated the complex Natomas Basin HCP in 2003 to enable the Sacramento Area Flood Control Agency to protect the city with a needed levee system that nevertheless placed habitat for listed species within the redirected floodplain.[124] Similarly, several northwest states have participated in the negotiation of complex HCPs to enable large-scale timber harvest on state forestlands.[125] Sometimes (as in the Natomas Basin example), states bargain in their sovereign capacity as local regulators; elsewhere (as with state timber sales), they act as ordinary regulated parties in their proprietary capacity as landowners (a distinction that may fairly warrant different interpretive scrutiny).[126] Negotiated HCPs have been lauded as striking a pragmatic balance between environmental and economic needs, but they have also been criticized for undermining the preservation principle behind the ESA[127]—demonstrating both the benefits and risks of negotiated balancing.

States have also negotiated ESA exceptions to enable even more ambitious conservation programs. For example, in the early 1990s, California passed the Natural Community Conservation Planning Act (NCCP), a voluntary conservation program to protect intact ecosystems rather than individual species.[128] The program sought to accommodate compatible land use and prevent the regulatory "gridlock" that can accompany listing decisions by engaging interested parties before species became threatened.[129] The NCCP was thus more ambitious in scope than both the ESA and the California Endangered Species Act, which only protect individual species that have already significantly declined.[130] However, the NCCP's "all carrots and no stick" approach did not marshal broad participation.[131]

---

[124] *See* NATOMAS BASIN CONSERVANCY, *supra* note 120. The levee required a federal permit that could not issue because habitat for twenty-two listed species would be drowned by the redirected flood. *Id.* However, a complex deal among federal agencies, state regulators, and private parties enabled an ITP on the basis of an HCP in which private landowners surrounding the levee protected additional habitat. *Id.*

[125] For example, proposals to list the northern spotted owl and marbled murrelet as endangered in Washington State prompted state-federal negotiation of a multispecies HCP to enable logging while mitigating harm. *See* Craig Hansen & William Vogel, *Forest Land HCPs: A Case Study*, ENDANGERED SPECIES BULL., July/Aug. 2000, at 18, 18–19, www.fws.gov/endangered/esa-library/pdf/18–19.pdf.

[126] *Cf.* Klump v. United States, 30 F. App'x 958, 961 (Fed. Cir. 2002) (adjusting scrutiny of a takings claim against a state acting not as a sovereign regulator but as a riparian landowner).

[127] 16 U.S.C. §1533(1)(A) (specifying that listing determinations be made "solely on the basis of the best scientific and commercial data available," without cost-benefit analysis). For the argument that HCPs simply "nickel-and-dime species toward extinction," see Gregory A. Thomas, *Where Property Rights and Biodiversity Converge, Part I: Conservation Planning at the Regional Scale*, 17 ENDANGERED SPECIES UPDATE 139, 140 (2000), http://deepblue.lib.umich.edu/bitstream/2027.42/39357/1/als9527.0017.006.pdf.

[128] CAL. FISH & GAME CODE §§ 2800–2835 (West 2003).

[129] *Natural Community Conservation Planning*, CAL. DEP'T OF FISH & GAME, http://www.dfg.ca.gov/habcon/nccp/.

[130] *Id.*

[131] BRUCE BABBITT, CITIES IN THE WILDERNESS: A NEW VISION OF LAND USE IN AMERICA 66 (2005); Mara A. Marks et al., *The Experimental Metropolis: Political Impediments and Opportunities for Innovation*, *in* UP AGAINST THE SPRAWL: PUBLIC POLICY AND THE MAKING OF SOUTHERN CALIFORNIA 353, 353 (Jennifer Wolch et al. eds., 2004).

The state labored to procure participation until the ESA listing of the California gnatcatcher threatened the NCCP's viability, because actions permitted under the NCCP (as consistent with preserving the birds' overall habitat) could still violate specific ESA protections for the birds (if individual birds were actually harmed or harassed).[132] State regulators understood that the conflict was fatal to the NCCP, and federal regulators were open to suggestions, as corresponding federal conservation efforts had been hamstrung without the legal authority and regulatory capacity available only at the state and local levels.[133] Under the leadership of Interior Secretary Bruce Babbit, state and federal wildlife agencies harnessed the needed interjurisdictional synergy in negotiating a framework to enable accomplishment of both state and federal goals without risk of NCCP participant prosecution under the ESA.[134] Through an extensively negotiated ITP, developers of targeted habitat were required to participate in the NCCP,[135] but actions taken in compliance with an NCCP permit were formally exempted from ESA liability.[136]

Bargaining is also commonplace over ESA listing decisions and recommendations for alternatives when proposed state-federal action might impact listed species. For example, Maine negotiated a five-year opportunity to experiment with state-based conservation efforts before its Atlantic salmon run was ultimately listed, and eleven midwestern states used a negotiated reprieve from a black-tailed prairie dog listing to successfully increase breeding populations while staving off the negative economic consequences of an ESA listing.[137] California agencies have long negotiated with the U.S. Fish and Wildlife Service (FWS) and the National Oceanic and Atmospheric Association Fisheries (NOAA Fisheries) over consultations that impact state water projects.[138]

---

[132] BABBITT, *supra* note 131, at 66; DeAnne Parker, Comment, *Natural Community Conservation Planning: California's Emerging Ecosystem Management Alternative*, 6 U. BALT. J. ENVTL. L. 107, 129–30 (1997).

[133] BABBITT, *supra* note 131, at 70 ("We had legal authority, yet there was no practical way to use it without the active cooperation of city and county governments willing to use their traditional zoning powers to regulate land use.").

[134] *Id.* at 64–72.

[135] Marks et al., *supra* note 131, at 353.

[136] John M. Gaffin, *Can We Conserve California's Threatened Fisheries through Natural Community Conservation Planning?*, 27 ENVTL. L. 791, 793 (1997).

[137] *See* John Elmen, *Swimming Upstream: A Legal Analysis of Listing Atlantic Salmon as an Endangered Species*, 9 OCEAN & COASTAL L.J. 333, 334 (2004). After FWS's 1995 determination that Maine's population was threatened, state-federal negotiations delayed formal listing to enable state-led management efforts, *Proposed Threatened Status for a Distinct Population Segment of Anadromous Atlantic Salmon (Salmo Salar) in Seven Maine Rivers*, 60 Fed. Reg. 50530, 50539 (Sept. 29, 1995) (codified at 50 C.F.R. pt. 17 & 425), but the species was ultimately listed as endangered in 2000. *Id. See also* RASBAND ET AL., *supra* Chapter Three, note 77, at 344 (discussing the prairie dog example). FWS determined that the species warranted listing in 2000, but, after successful state-based management efforts, found that the listing was no longer warranted in 2009. *12-Month Finding on a Petition to List the Black-Tailed Prairie Dog as Threatened or Endangered*, 74 Fed. Reg. 63343, 63366 (Dec. 3, 2009) (codified at 50 C.F.R. pt. 17).

[138] PERVAZE SHEIKH & BETSY CODY, CONG. RESEARCH SERV., CALFED BAY-DELTA PROGRAM: OVERVIEW OF INSTITUTIONAL AND WATER USE ISSUES 7 (2005), http://www.nationalaglawcenter.org/assets/crs/RL31975.pdf (describing state-federal negotiations over regulating project operations to protect water quality and listed species).

Hydroelectric and Offshore Drilling Licensing

The ESA presents a statutory forum for federalism exceptions bargaining that empowers the federal government against the states. However, other instances of exceptions bargaining reveal statutory forums that empower the states over the federal government. For example, hydroelectric licensing decisions by the Federal Energy Regulatory Commission (FERC) are negotiations for permission to violate the otherwise applicable federal navigational servitude.[139] Similarly, many federal decisions to license offshore oil drilling projects must receive permission from states participating in Coastal Zone Management Act programs.[140] Both represent unusual cases in which the states can hold the legally trumping authority.

Hydroelectric licensing decisions regularly feature state-federal bargaining because the Clean Water Act's Section 401 certification process gives states a regulatory hook over an otherwise federal process.[141] This provision authorizes states and tribal governments to review and approve, condition, or deny all federal permits or licenses that might result in a discharge to state or tribal waters, including wetlands.[142] The major federal licenses and permits subject to Section 401 are FERC hydropower licenses, Rivers and Harbors Act Section 9 and 10 permits, and CWA Sections 402 and 404 permits in the few states that have not assumed NPDES permitting authority.[143]

States wield their authority to ensure that the activity will comply with state water quality standards and other state water resource regulations.[144] When an applicant requests a license from FERC, either to relicense an existing dam or for new construction, the state determines whether state standards will be attainable if the license is granted, and what conditions may be required in the CWA Section 401 certification to ensure that the standards will be met.[145] Because these conditions are incorporated into the ultimate FERC license, states are effectively able to dictate some of the terms of the federal license—an ability that invites a limited process of state-federal logrolling.[146] States have particularly strong bargaining leverage when

---

[139] *See* Fed. Power Comm'n v. Niagara Mohawk Power Corp., 347 U.S. 239, 249 (1954) (describing how the Commerce Clause creates a dominant servitude to regulate navigation).

[140] *See infra* notes 200–24 and accompanying text.

[141] 33 U.S.C. § 1330 (2006); *see also* George Coggins & Robert Glicksman, Public Natural Resources Law § 37:41 (2d ed. 2009) (noting that the state certification process "represents the states' best opportunity to significantly affect the licensing process for hydroelectric facilities on waters within federal jurisdictions").

[142] 33 U.S.C. § 1330.

[143] 16 U.S.C. § 797(e) (2006) (authorizing FERC to license hydroelectric facilities); 33 U.S.C. §§ 401, 403 (2006) (regulating construction in navigable waters); 33 U.S.C. § 1342 (outlining the "National Pollutant Discharge Elimination System" permitting regime); Debra L. Donahue, *The Untapped Power of Clean Water Act Section 401*, 23 Ecology L.Q. 201, 219–20 (1996).

[144] *Section 401 Certification and Wetlands*, EPA, http://www.epa.gov/owow/wetlands/facts/fact24.html (last visited Nov. 26, 2010).

[145] *See* PUD No. 1 v. Wash. Dep't of Ecology, 511 U.S. 700, 710 (1994) ("The court concluded that § 401(d) confers on States power to 'consider all state action related to water quality in imposing conditions on section 401 certificates.'").

[146] *Id.* at 711–12 (holding that the CWA authorizes state conditions on section 401 certifications to enforce compliance with state water quality standards, conferring state negotiating leverage); California v. Fed.

the project implicates a state's proprietary water rights,[147] or when the project is governed under the Reclamation Act, which requires the Bureau of Reclamation to use project water in conformity with state law absent contrary congressional directives.[148]

In another example of state-empowered exceptions bargaining, the Coastal Zone Management Act (CZMA)[149] invites states to participate in the protection of coastal zones in which both the federal and state governments have significant interests. When a state elects to participate by creating a federally approved management plan, approval authority for federal activities within the zone shifts to the states.[150] For this reason, the Department of Interior often must receive state approval before issuing federal leases for offshore drilling on the outer continental shelf (OCS).[151]

3. JOINT POLICY-MAKING BARGAINING FORMS

The last and most theoretically interesting category are the joint policy-making negotiations, which often incorporate elements from previous categories. These generally take place in regulatory contexts in which the federal government could fully preempt state participation under a clearly enumerated power, but state authority or capacity is needed to effectively cope with the interjurisdictional problem at hand. Joint policy-making forums include negotiated rulemaking under the Administrative Procedures Act, "policy-making laboratory" negotiations, by which federal laws invite state proposals to create or modify federal law; "iterative policy-making" negotiations, which create staggered dialogues of state-federal policy-making; and intersystemic signaling negotiations, by which separately deliberating state and federal actors trade influence over the direction of shared policy over time.

In contrast to the more conventional forms of negotiation where only the results become matters of public record, the process of negotiation used in joint policy-making is often as available for public scrutiny as the results, moderating negotiated governance concerns that hinge on transparency and accountability.[152] Although conventional federalism bargaining often arises spontaneously, joint policy-making bargaining is usually the result of premeditated design, affording legislative opportunities to engineer support for federalism considerations into the process, even when participants are distracted by more immediate goals.

Energy Regulatory Comm'n, 495 U.S. 490, 496 (1990) (reaffirming preemption of other state minimum flow requirements).

[147] COGGINS & GLICKSMAN, *supra* note 141, § 37:8–10.

[148] *Id.* § 36:15; California v. United States, 438 U.S. 645, 677–79 (1978) (requiring that the New Melones Dam so conform).

[149] 16 U.S.C. §§ 1451–66 (2006).

[150] 15 C.F.R. pt. 930 (2010).

[151] BRANCH OF ENVTL. ASSESSMENT, *Environmental Programs: Coastla Zone Mgmt. Act*, BUREAU OF OCEAN ENERGY MGMT., REGULATION & ENFORCEMENT, http://www.boemre.gov/eppd/compliance/czma/index.htm. Federal interests may override state objections in limited circumstances, but program policy is to resolve differences with states, by mediation if necessary. *Id.*

[152] *Cf.* Telephone Interview with Lawrence Susskind, Professor, Mass. Inst. of Tech. (Feb. 19, 2010) (explaining that the transparency within stakeholder participation leads to stability, thereby reducing the need for future revisitation of issues because stakeholders already understand why the process reached the given outcome).

The structural incorporation of state and federal interests advances the checks of jurisdictional overlap, local innovation and diversity, and problem-solving synergy. Because these forms hold the most interpretive promise, I treat them in greater detail, reviewing each type with examples from the Clean Water Act's Phase II Stormwater Rule, the Real ID Act, Medicaid, the Coastal Zone Management Act, the Clean Air Act, and medical marijuana enforcement.

a. Negotiated Rulemaking: The Clean Water Act's Phase II Rule
and the REAL ID Act

Although it is the most conventional of the policy-making forms, "negotiated rulemaking" between federal agencies and state stakeholders is a sparingly used tool that holds promise for facilitating sound administrative policy-making in disputed federalism contexts, such as those implicating environmental law, national security, and consumer safety.

Under the Administrative Procedures Act, the traditional "notice and comment" administrative rulemaking process allows for a limited degree of participation by state stakeholders who comment on a federal agency's proposed rule. The agency publishes the proposal in the Federal Register, invites public comment critiquing the draft, and then uses its discretion to revise or defend the rule in response to comments.[153] Even this iterative process constitutes a modest negotiation, but it leaves participants so frequently unsatisfied that beginning in the 1970s, many agencies started informally using more extensive negotiated rulemaking.[154] In 1990, Congress passed the Negotiated Rulemaking Act, amending the Administrative Procedures Act to allow a more dynamic and inclusive rulemaking process,[155] and a subsequent executive order required all federal agencies to consider negotiated rulemaking when developing regulations.[156]

Negotiated rulemaking allows stakeholders much more influence over unfolding regulatory decisions. Under notice and comment, public participation is limited to criticism of well-formed rules in which the agency is already substantially invested.[157] By contrast, stakeholders in negotiated rulemaking collectively design a proposed rule that takes into account their respective interests and expertise from the beginning.[158] The concept, outline, and/or text of a rule is hammered out by an advisory committee of carefully balanced representation from the agency, the regulated public, community groups and NGOs, and state and local governments.[159] A professional intermediary leads the effort to ensure that all

---

[153] 5 U.S.C. § 553 (2006).

[154] Bertram I. Spector, *Negotiated Rulemaking: A Participative Approach to Consensus-Building for Regulatory Development and Implementation*, TECHNICAL NOTES (U.S. Agency for Int'l Dev., Wash. D.C.), May 1999, at 2, http://www.usaid.gov/our_work/democracy_and_governance/publications/ipc/tn-10.pdf. *See* DAVID M. PRITZKER & DEBORAH S. DALTON, NEGOTIATED RULEMAKING SOURCEBOOK (1995).

[155] 5 U.S.C. §§ 561–570.

[156] *See* Exec. Order No. 12,866, 58 C.F.R. § 190 (1993).

[157] *See* Spector, *supra* note 154, at 1.

[158] *See id.*.

[159] *Negotiated Rulemaking Fact Sheet*, EPA, http://www.epa.gov/adr/factsheetregneg.pdf.

stakeholders are appropriately involved and to help identify problem-solving opportunities.[160] Any consensus reached by the group becomes the basis of the proposed rule, which is still subject to public comment through the normal notice-and-comment procedures.[161] If the group does not reach consensus, the agency proceeds through the usual notice-and-comment process.[162]

The negotiated rulemaking process, a tailored version of interest group bargaining within established legislative constraints, can yield important benefits.[163] The process is usually more subjectively satisfying for all stakeholders, including the government agency representatives.[164] More cooperative relationships are established between the regulated parties and the agencies, facilitating future implementation and enforcement of new rules.[165] Final regulations include fewer technical errors and are clearer to stakeholders so that less time, money, and effort is expended on enforcement.[166] Getting a proposed rule out for public comment takes more time under negotiated rulemaking than standard notice and comment, but thereafter, negotiated rules receive fewer and more moderate public comment, and are less frequently challenged in court by regulated entities.[167] Ultimately, then, final regulations can be implemented more quickly following their debut in the Federal Register, and with greater compliance from stakeholders.[168] The process also confers valuable learning benefits on participants, who come to better understand the concerns of other stakeholders, grow invested in the consensus they help create, and ultimately campaign for the success of the regulations within their own constituencies.[169]

Negotiated rulemaking offers additional procedural benefits because it ensures that agency personnel will be unambiguously informed about the full federalism implications of a proposed rule by the impacted state interests. Federal agencies are already required by executive order to prepare a federalism impact statement for rulemaking with federalism implications,[170] but the quality of state-federal communication within negotiated rulemaking enhances the likelihood that federal agencies will appreciate and understand the full extent of state concerns. Just as the consensus-building process invests participating

---

[160] Gerard McMahon & Lawrence Susskind, *Theory and Practice of Negotiated Rulemaking*, 3 YALE J. REG. 133, 155 (1985).

[161] *Id.* at 137.

[162] *Id.*

[163] Jody Freeman & Laura I. Langbein, *Regulatory Negotiation and the Legitimacy Benefit*, 9 N.Y.U. ENVTL. L.J. 60, 60–64 (2000); McMahon & Susskind, *supra* note 160, at 137–38; Joshua Secunda & Lawrence Susskind, *The Risks and the Advantages of Agency Discretion: Evidence from EPA's Project XL*, 17 UCLA J. ENVTL. L. & POL'Y 67, 112–16 (1999).

[164] PRITZKER & DALTON, *supra* note 154, at 3–5; Spector, *supra* note 154, at 2.

[165] *Cf.* Freeman & Langbein, *supra* note 163, at 62; Cornelius M. Kerwin & Laura I. Langbein, *Regulatory Negotiation versus Conventional Rule Making: Claims, Counterclaims, and Empirical Evidence*, 10 J. PUB. ADMIN. RES. & THEORY 599, 610, 625 (2000).

[166] PRITZKER & DALTON, *supra* note 154, at 3–5; Spector, *supra* note 154, at 2.

[167] Spector, *supra* note 154, at 2.

[168] *Id.*

[169] McMahon & Susskind, *supra* note 160, at 161–65.

[170] Exec. Order No. 13132, 64 Fed. Reg. 43255, 43257–43258 (Aug. 10, 1999).

stakeholders with respect for the competing concerns of other stakeholders, it invests participating agency personnel with respect for the federalism concerns of state stakeholders.[171] State-side federalism bargainers interviewed for this project consistently reported that they always prefer negotiated rulemaking to notice and comment—even if their ultimate impact remains small—because the products of fully informed federal consultation are always preferable to the alternative.[172]

Nevertheless, the limitations of negotiated rulemaking also warrant attention. Some critics argue that the process does not always deliver the goods it promises because consensus cannot always be won.[173] To facilitate consensus, a substantial amount of pre-negotiation consultation occurs, which can helpfully advance the negotiated rulemaking but may compromise transparency.[174] There may also be rulemaking subjects that are simply inappropriate for negotiation, such as those that implicate fundamental rights. For example, it would be unwise to trust the legitimate interests of vulnerable and insular minorities to negotiated decision making by unsympathetic majorities.[175]

Another potential pitfall of negotiated rulemaking is deciding which stakeholders will be represented on the advisory committee, and by whom they will be represented. The process breaks down if there are too many negotiators involved, so agents must be selected to represent large groups of occasionally diverse stakeholders (such as the fifty states, hundreds of large cities, and countless smaller municipalities).[176] Among stakeholders who feel poorly represented, the rule will lack the legitimacy that often makes the results achieved by negotiated rulemaking more effective than the standard process. Nor will absent stakeholders amass the learning benefits or become the rule evangelists that make negotiated rules less vulnerable to challenge, less likely to be violated, and generally less expensive to implement and enforce. The transparency of the negotiation process will be especially important for concerned stakeholders who do not participate directly.

---

[171] *Cf.* Anonymous Interview, U.S. EPA, Office of the Administrator, Wash., D.C., (Jan. 4, 2010) [hereinafter EPA Interview] ("Early consultation is an important way of avoiding 'process fouls,' where someone says, 'hey you never asked us about that!' Consultation can help with buy-in to the rules, but even where it doesn't help with buy-in to the rules, it helps get buy-in to the process. It's much easier to move forward with that.").

[172] *E.g.,* Telephone Interview with Melissa Savage, *supra* note 56.

[173] Cary Coglianese, *Assessing Consensus: The Promise and Performance of Negotiated Rulemaking,* 46 DUKE L.J. 1255, 1261, 1321–34 (1997). *But see* Philip Harter, *Assessing the Assessors: The Actual Performance of Negotiated Rulemaking* 9 N.Y.U. ENVTL. L.J. 32, 39–44, 54–57 (2000) (challenging Coglianese's methodology and arguing that negotiated rulemaking has lived up to its promise).

[174] EPA Interview, *supra* note 171 (noting that the most protracted part of all state-federal bargaining is about "what the opening gambit will be" when the formal negotiation begins, but also that this facilitates progress and that, "when we're doing our job, there are lots of conversations like these early on in the process").

[175] *C.f.* Owen Fiss, *Against Settlement,* 93 YALE L.J. 1073, 1076 (1984). Nevada faced this problem when Yucca Mountain was selected for nuclear waste disposal over its citizens' vociferous protest. *See supra* Chapter Six, notes 25–26 and accompanying text.

[176] *Cf.* Robert Stavins, *Another Copenhagen Outcome,* EU ENERGY POL'Y BLOG (Jan. 6, 2010, 11:38 EST), http://www.energypolicyblog.com/2010/01/06/another-copenhagen-outcome-serious-questions-about-the-best-institutional-path-forward/ (discussing multiparty gridlock in Copenhagen climate negotiations).

Negotiated rulemaking is initiated by federal agencies, and can involve the participation of state actors from all levels of government and from national organizations advocating state interests.[177] The EPA is the most frequent federal user, followed by the Department of Labor, the Department of the Interior, and the Department of the Treasury.[178] Nevertheless, in the first thirteen years surrounding passage of the Negotiated Rulemaking Act, only fifty federal rules were produced through negotiated rulemaking—as little as 1 percent of the total number of rules promulgated over this period.[179] Standard notice-and-comment rulemaking clearly remains the dominant form of executive rulemaking.

Phase II Stormwater Rule

Negotiated rulemaking can be used to forge uniform regulations that best meet the interests of a large variety of stakeholders, or to forge regulations conferring wide discretion on regulated parties. For example, EPA used negotiated rulemaking to forge the complex regulations needed to implement the Clean Water Act's Phase II Stormwater program, discussed in Chapter Five.[180] Situated vexingly at the crossroad between land uses regulated locally and water pollution regulated federally, contaminated stormwater is mostly discharged to federally protected waters by municipalities that collect it through curbside stormdrains.[181] The Phase II negotiated rulemaking advisory committee included thirty-five members representing municipal, environmental, and industrial stakeholder groups.[182] Reached through a decade of intense negotiation, the final rule[183] empowers municipalities to tailor regulatory efforts as individually as possible while still accomplishing the overall federal goal, as reduced to a short list of minimum criteria.[184] Dischargers may develop any program that: (1) educates the public about stormwater hygiene, (2) incorporates public participation, (3) prevents illicit discharges, (4) controls construction debris, and (5) manages pollutant runoff from municipal operations.[185]

The rule's flexibility reflects the impact of multiple perspectives during the rulemaking process, in which participants recognized that circumstances differed too widely for

---

[177] *See* 5 U.S.C. §§ 562(8), 563(a) (2006). Many state agencies are also frequent users, as are agencies in other countries. Spector, *supra* note 154, at 2.

[178] Spector, *supra* note 154, at 2.

[179] *Id.* at 2 (noting fifty cases between 1982 and 1995); Coglianese, *supra* note 173, at 1336–41 (listing negotiated rules). This estimate is based on reports that federal agencies promulgated an average of five hundred rules per year during the early 2000s. *See* John Graham, Adm'r, White House Office of Info. & Regulatory Affairs, Speech at the Kennedy School of Government (Sept. 25, 2003), http://www.whitehouse.gov/omb/inforeg_speeches_030925graham/.

[180] EPA Office of Water, Overview of the Storm Water Program 8 (1996), http://www.epa.gov/npdes/pubs/owm0195.pdf; discussed *supra* Chapter Five, notes 49–67 and accompanying text.

[181] *See* Envtl. Def. Ctr., Inc. v. EPA, 344 F.3d 832, 840–41 (9th Cir. 2003) ("*EDC II*")

[182] *Id.* at 864.

[183] The Phase II Final Rule was published in the *Federal Register* on December 8, 1999. Regulations for Revision of the Water Pollution Control Program Addressing Storm Water Discharges, 64 Fed. Reg. 68722 (Dec. 8, 1999) (codified at 40 C.F.R. pts. 9, 122, 123, 124).

[184] *EDC II*, 344 F.3d at 847–48.

[185] 40 C.F.R. § 122.34(b) (2010).

consensus on requirements more specific than the minimum measures.[186] Although the rule nevertheless endured legal challenges from several plaintiffs unsatisfied with different aspects of the rule, it withstood challenge on almost every point, including a federalism-based claim.[187] Considering the massive number of municipalities it regulates, the fact that the rule was challenged by only a handful of Texas municipalities (in a lawsuit the State of Texas did not join) testifies to the strength of the consensus through which it was created.

The REAL ID Act

But the value of negotiated rulemaking to federalism bargaining may be best understood in relief against the failure of alternatives in federalism-sensitive contexts. Particularly informative are the strikingly different state responses to the two approaches Congress has recently taken in tightening national security through identification reform—one requiring regulations through negotiated rulemaking, and the other through traditional notice and comment.

After the 9/11 terrorist attacks, Congress ordered the Department of Homeland Security (DHS) to establish rules regarding valid identification for federal purposes (such as boarding an aircraft or accessing federal buildings).[188] Recognizing the implications for state-issued driver's licenses and ID cards, Congress required DHS to use negotiated rulemaking to forge consensus among the states about how best to proceed.[189] States leery of the staggering costs associated with proposed reforms participated actively in the process.[190] However, the subsequent REAL ID Act of 2005 repealed the ongoing negotiated rulemaking and required DHS to prescribe top-down federal requirements for state-issued licenses.[191]

The resulting DHS rules have been bitterly opposed by the majority of state governors, legislatures, and motor vehicle administrations,[192] prompting a virtual state rebellion that cuts across the red state/blue state political divide.[193] No state met the December 2009 deadline initially contemplated by the statute, and over half have enacted or considered legislation prohibiting compliance with the act, defunding its implementation, or calling for its repeal.[194] In the face of this unprecedented state hostility, DHS has extended compliance deadlines even for those that did not request extensions, and bills have been introduced in

---

[186] *See* 64 Fed. Reg. at 68754 ("EPA has intentionally not provided a precise definition of MEP [maximum extent possible] to allow maximum flexibility in MS4 permitting.").

[187] *EDC II*, 344 F.3d at 840 (finding, among other things, that the EPA had the authority to impose the NPDES rule and that the EPA properly consulted with state and local officials).

[188] National Security Intelligence Reform Act of 2004, Pub. L. No. 108–458, 118 Stat. 3638.

[189] *Id.*

[190] Sharkey, *supra* note 16, at 2151 (noting that DHS's detailed federalism impact statement included a three hundred-page transcript of input from the NGA, NCSL, and many individual governors and state agencies).

[191] Pub. L. No. 109–13, 1198 Stat. 302 (codified at 8 U.S.C. § 1778 (2006)).

[192] The History of Federal Requirements for State-Issued Drivers Licenses and ID Cards, Nat'l Conference of State Legislation (NCSL), http://www.ncsl.org/Default.aspx?TabId=13581.

[193] ACLU, *Anti-REAL ID Legislation in the States*, http://www.realnightmare.org/news/105/.

[194] *Id.*

both houses of Congress to repeal the act.[195] Efforts to repeal what is increasingly referred to as a "failed" policy have won endorsements from organizations across the political spectrum.[196] Even the Executive Director of the ACLU, for whom federalism concerns have not historically ranked highly, opined in *U.S.A. Today* that the REAL ID Act violates the Tenth Amendment.[197]

b. Policy-Making Laboratory Negotiations: Coastal Zone Management Act and Medicaid

Particularly powerful fora for federalism bargaining are "policy-making laboratory negotiations," which harness the promise of federalism as a national laboratory of state-based ideas and experimentation. In these negotiations, the federal government invites the states to propose innovations and variations within existing federal laws that address realms of concurrent jurisdiction. Sometimes, Congress explicitly authorizes bargaining in a statute that invites states to lead local policy-making in support of national objectives. Other statutes invite states to experiment with local improvements on the general federal approach, realizing the "laboratory of ideas" promise of federalism. Still others invite states to design implementation policy in support of federally mandated standards. Federal agencies may use a similar process in articulating rules to implement congressional statutes. These negotiations usually take place in the context of a spending power-based program of cooperative federalism.

In some policy-making laboratory negotiations, the federal government articulates the overall goals of an interjurisdictional regulatory policy and invites states to "fill in the blanks" on how best to get there, based on unique economic, environmental, topographical, or demographic factors that vary regionally. For example, although the Phase II Stormwater Rule was created through a process of negotiated rulemaking, the resulting rule itself creates policy-making zones in which individual municipalities craft unique management programs meeting minimum federal criteria.[198] The Coastal Zone Management Act, in which Congress agreed to subordinate federal prerogative to an unprecedented degree of state control, creates an even more intriguing example.[199]

Coastal Zone Management

The CZMA[200] is a voluntary cooperative federalism program designed to protect coastal resources from intense development pressures that isolated local land use planning could no

---

[195] Identification Security Enhancement Act of 2007, S. 717, 110th Cong.; The REAL ID Repeal and Identification Security Enhancement Act of 2009, H.R. 3471, 111th Cong.

[196] Declan McCullagh, *Congress Rethinks the REAL ID Act*, CNET News (May 8, 2007), http://news.cnet.com/Congress-rethinks-the-Real-ID-Act/2100-1028_3-6182210.html.

[197] Anthony Romero, Opinion, *Repeal REAL ID*, USA TODAY, Mar. 6, 2007, http://www.usatoday.com/news/opinion/2007-03-05-opposing-view_N.htm.

[198] *See* 64 Fed. Reg. 68722 (Dec. 8, 1999) (codified at 40 C.F.R. pts. 9, 122, 123, 124).

[199] Pub. L. No. 92–583, 86 Stat. 1280 (1972) (codified as amended at 16 U.S.C. §§ 1451–1466 (2006)).

[200] 16 U.S.C. §§ 1451–1466.

longer contain.[201] The act offers federal funding and technical assistance for voluntary state management programs that protect resources in coastal waters, submerged lands, and adjacent shorelands.[202] Unlike other environmental laws that promise federal control if states choose not to participate in administration, the act establishes no mandatory compliance standards[203] and does not authorize the federal government to develop programs for states that choose not to participate.[204] States have responded enthusiastically, welcoming both federal support and national recognition of the need for comprehensive coastal management.[205] Thirty-four of thirty-five eligible states have approved coastal management plans, and Illinois, the remaining state, is presently composing one.[206] The act also provides for extensive participation from local and municipal governments.[207]

Perhaps most significant, once a coastal zone management plan receives federal approval, all federal action directly or indirectly affecting the coastal zone (generally extending three miles seaward from a state's coastal boundary) must then receive approval by the state for "consistency" with the plan.[208] The Department of Commerce describes the consistency provision as "a limited waiver of federal supremacy and authority,"[209] allowing states to review not only those activities conducted by or on behalf of a federal agency, but also activities that require a federal license or permit, activities conducted pursuant to an Outer Continental Shelf Lands Act exploration plan,[210] and any federally funded activities that may impact the coastal zone.[211] States may disapprove activities that "affect any land or water use or natural resource of the coastal zone" unless they are "consistent to the maximum extent practicable" with accepted state management programs.[212] In this way, the CZMA uniquely designates

[201] *Id.* § 1451(i); 136 Cong. Rec. 26030, 26030–67 (1990) (statement of Rep. Walter B. Jones); S. Rep. No. 92–753 (1972), *reprinted in* 1972 U.S.C.C.A.N. 4776, 4778.

[202] 16 U.S.C. § 1453(1).

[203] *Summary of Coastal Zone Management Act and Amendments*, EPA, http://epa.gov/oecaagct/lzma.html#Summary%20of%20Coastal%20Zone%20Management%20Act%20and%20Amendments.

[204] 136 CONG. REC. 26030, 26030–67 (1990) (statement of Rep. Walter B. Jones); *see also* Jeffrey H. Wood, *Protecting Native Coastal Ecosystems: CZMA and Alaska's Coastal Plan*, 19 NAT. RESOURCES & ENV'T 57 (2004).

[205] Wood, *supra* note 204, at 57; S. Rep. No. 92–753.

[206] Office of Ocean & Coastal Res. Mgmt., Coastal Zone Management Act Performance System 2 (2006), http://coastalmanagement.noaa.gov/resources/docs/npmsupdate.pdf.

[207] Wood, *supra* note 204, at 57.

[208] BRANCH OF ENVTL. ASSESSMENT, *supra* note 151.

[209] Coastal Zone Management Act Federal Consistency Regulations, 71 Fed. Reg. 787 (Jan. 5, 2006) (codified at 15 C.F.R. pt. 930).

[210] A common example is the administration of federal leases for offshore drilling on the outer continental shelf. BRANCH OF ENVTL. ASSESSMENT, *supra* note 151.

[211] 16 U.S.C. § 1456(c) (2006); Coastal Zone Management Act Federal Consistency Regulations, 71 Fed. Reg. at 789–90.

[212] 16 U.S.C. § 1456(c)(1)(A). A federal agency may override objection only if it demonstrates its activity is consistent to the maximum extent practicable. *Id.*

concurrent state and federal jurisdiction for the zone between state-regulated lands and federally regulated waters.[213]

The CZMA consistency provision thus creates a rare instance in which the federal government must seek *state* permission before taking action affecting the interjurisdictional zone, opening the door for federalism bargaining and regulatory variation.[214] It provides a mandatory but flexible mechanism for resolving potential conflicts between state and federal priorities, and in so doing fosters early consultation and negotiated coordination.[215] Legislative history indicates that "the intent of [the bill] is to enhance state authority by encouraging and assisting the states to assume planning and regulatory powers over their coastal zones," with "no attempt to diminish state authority through federal preemption."[216] Indeed, Congress amended the CZMA in 1990 to be even more protective of state interests, clarifying that the consistency determination applied not only to federal activity within the designated boundaries of the coastal zone but to any activities conducted anywhere that affect resources within the coastal zone.[217]

None of this is to say that conflicts do not persist, or that states always prevail. Disputing states and federal agencies may seek mediation by the Secretary of Commerce to resolve serious federal consistency disputes,[218] and, if consensus fails, the state may request judicial mediation or seek other relief in federal court.[219] Finally, if a federal court decides that the proposed federal agency activity does not comply with a state management program, and the secretary certifies that mediation will not result in compliance, the secretary may request that the president make an exemption for the federal agency action if the action is "in the paramount interest of the United States."[220] The presidential exemption has been used exceedingly sparingly, however, and possibly only once—when President George W. Bush controversially used it in 2008 to override California's objection to the Navy's use of sonar in training exercises.[221]

---

[213] 43 U.S.C. § 1301 (2006) (referring to the general three-mile boundary designated by the Submerged Lands Act).

[214] KIM DIANA CONNOLLY ET AL., WETLANDS LAW AND POLICY: UNDERSTANDING SECTION 404, 344–45 (2005) (noting that the CZMA is "implemented differently in each state").

[215] 16 U.S.C. § 1456; *see also Coastal Zone Management Act*, FLA. DEP'T OF ENVTL. PROT., http://www.dep. state.fl.us/secretary/oip/czma.htm.

[216] S. Rep. No. 92–753, at 1 (1972), *reprinted in* 1972 U.S.C.C.A.N. 4776, 4776.

[217] Pub. L. No. 101–508, 104 Stat. 1388-307 (1990) (codified as amended at 16 U.S.C. §§ 1455b, 1456c, 1460 (2006)); *see also* 136 Cong. Rec. 26030, 26035, 26038 (1990) (explaining the decision to strengthen consistency after contrary Supreme Court precedent).

[218] 16 U.S.C. § 1456(h)(2).

[219] *See, e.g.*, California v. Norton, 311 F.3d 1162, 1167 (9th Cir. 2002).

[220] 16 U.S.C. § 1456 (c)(1)(B); FLA. DEP'T OF ENVTL. PROT., *supra* note 215 (noting that the exemption applies only to agency activities, not federally funded or permitted activities).

[221] Joseph Romero, *Uncharted Waters: The Expansion of State Regulatory Authority over Federal Activities and Migratory Resources under the Coastal Zone Management Act*, 56 NAVAL L. REV. 137, 146 (2008). The military use of sonar in these exercises was ultimately upheld in Winter v. NRDC, 129 S. Ct. 365, 370 (2008), but the consistency exemption was not a part of the case that reached the Supreme Court. The district court had questioned the constitutionality of the exemption on separation of powers grounds, as the president had

Nevertheless, the vast majority of state-federal interaction under the CZMA is harmonious, and federal consistency determinations are usually administered without controversy.[222] NOAA reports that "[w]hile States have negotiated changes to thousands of federal actions over the years, States have concurred with approximately 93%–95% of all federal actions reviewed."[223] Even before the act was amended in 1990 to improve state leverage in consistency negotiations, in 1983 states concurred with 93 percent of the four hundred proposed federal activities, 82 percent of the 5,500 proposed federal licenses and permits, 99 percent of the 435 submitted plans for outer continental shelf exploration, and 99.9 percent of the two thousand proposals for federal funding and assistance.[224]

Without access to the actual decision makers over this time period, it is hard to know exactly how to interpret such high levels of consensus. It is possible that they reflect the federal ability to override state protest through the presidential exemption, which could reduce a state's incentive to expend resources fighting a battle it expects to lose. However, given that the presidential trump has been used so sparingly—only once, and years after these statistics—a more likely explanation is that the consistency process itself moderates what federal agencies seek. Understanding that federal action will require state approval may promote greater federal deference to state interests in the very spirit intended by the CMZA. After all, the process that must be navigated after a state objects is costly to resource-poor federal agencies as well.

The CZMA thus establishes a program with three separate stages of intergovernmental bargaining. First, the federal government negotiates with its spending power to invite the states to the policy-making bargaining table. Next, the act enables interagency negotiations over the details of the state plan before federal approval. Once the plan is approved, the leverage flips, and the federal government then negotiates for state permission to take action that might impact resources protected by the plan. The model creates a forum for ongoing consultation and exchange between state and federal actors over coastal zone policy-making—potentially ad infinitum—that nicely matches local and national expertise in a particularly interjurisdictional zone. It seems to be a useful model for joint policy-making in gray area contexts where local land use authority is a particularly salient feature.

Medicaid
Another version of policy-making zones arises under the various federal statutes that allow states to propose variations on generally applicable standards within programs of cooperative

---

effectively overturned the order of an Article III court when he enjoined the Navy from using the challenged sonar. NRDC v. Winter, 527 F. Supp. 2d 1216, 1233–34 (C.D. Cal. 2008) ("Since the grounds for [the] President's exemption are the same as the grounds for the Court's injunction, the exemption 'reviews and overturns an order of an Article III Court.'"). However, under the doctrine of constitutional avoidance, the district court never ruled on the issue because it was not necessary to do so to reach its ultimate result. *Id.* at 1237–38.

[222] 136 CONG. REC. 26030, 26034 (1990) (statement of Rep. Walter B. Jones).

[223] Coastal Zone Management Act Federal Consistency Regulations, 71 Fed. Reg. at 789.

[224] 136 CONG. REC. 26030, 26034 (1990) (statement of Rep. Walter B. Jones).

federalism, often through demonstration waiver programs.[225] The Social Security Act includes several demonstration waiver programs that enable states to propose variations to standard federal entitlement programs, including the State Children's Health Insurance Program, Medicaid, and other forms of assistance to needy children and families.[226] Medicaid remains the leading site of state-federal negotiated social welfare policy.

The Medicaid law invites states to apply for "demonstration waivers" and "program waivers" that allow them to depart from the otherwise applicable terms of the law to pursue an objective coincident with the goals of the federal program.[227] The Medicaid program was initially designed as a classic spending power-based program of cooperative federalism through which Congress offered the states incentive funding to provide for the health-care needs of vulnerable populations. The baseline legislation and corresponding rules identified the populations that would be covered (children living in poverty, certain expectant mothers, and many other groups),[228] the services that would be covered (inpatient hospital and outpatient physician services),[229] and additional guidelines for state programs funded by Medicaid.[230] Congress had previously enabled states to propose beneficial departures from Social Security Act rules via a demonstration waiver program,[231] and Congress extended the waiver program to Medicaid in 1965.[232]

The Medicaid demonstration waiver programs were to function as the hallowed federalism laboratory of ideas would intend: the goal was to allow a limited degree of flexibility so that each state could experiment in a way that would yield learning benefits to the overall program. Over time, however, the waiver program has become the standard way that Medicaid is administered, as most states now use the waiver provisions to individually tailor the terms of their own Medicaid programs.[233] The application process is extensively negotiated with the Department of Health and Human Services, with executive agents on both

---

[225] *See, e.g.*, 42 U.S.C. §§ 1315, 1396n (2006) (inviting states to apply for "demonstration waivers" and "program waivers").

[226] Ann Laquer Estin, *Sharing Governance: Family Law in Congress and the States*, 18 CORNELL J.L. & PUB. POL'Y 267, 293 (2009).

[227] 42 U.S.C. §§ 1315, 1396n; Frank J. Thompson & Courtney Burke, *Executive Federalism and Medicaid Demonstration Waivers: Implications for Policy and Democratic Process*, 32 J. HEALTH POL., POL'Y & L. 971, 973–74 (2007).

[228] Colleen M. Grogan, *"Medicaid": Health Care for You and Me?*, in HEALTH POLITICS AND POLICY 329 (J. Morone et al. eds., 2008); ELICIA J. HERZ, CONG. RESEARCH SERV., MEDICAID: A PRIMER 1 (2008), http://aging.senate.gov/crs/medicaid1.pdf (listing categories of covered groups).

[229] HERZ, *supra* note 228, at 7 (listing examples of mandatory benefits for most groups).

[230] Federal guidelines establish services that states *may* provide and *must* provide, allowing states to define specifics within guidelines mandating sufficient care, equal treatment, and patient choice. *Id.* at 3–4.

[231] Public Welfare Amendments of 1962, Pub. L. No. 87–543, tit. I, sec. 122, tit. XI, § 1115, 76 Stat. 172, 192 (codified as amended at 42 U.S.C. § 1315 (2006)).

[232] Health Insurance for the Aged Act, tit. XI, § 1115, 79 Stat. 352 (1965) (codified as amended at 42 U.S.C. § 1315); Judith M. Rosenberg & David T. Zarin, *Managing Medicaid Waivers: Section 1115 and State Health Care Reform*, 32 HARV. J. ON LEGIS. 545, 547 (1995).

[233] Thomas Gais & James Fossett, *Federalism and the Executive Branch*, in THE EXECUTIVE BRANCH 509 (Joel D. Aberbach & Mark A. Peterson eds., 2005).

sides dickering back and forth over proposal terms before the application receives federal approval.[234]

Results of the waiver programs suggest that the policy-making laboratory of ideas can work.[235] Though not every waiver proposal has been a success, many of the proposals Congress is now considering in health reform efforts began as experimental terms in state waivers.[236] For example, Massachusetts used a demonstration waiver to extend health insurance to all residents,[237] and North Carolina used a programmatic waiver to experiment with a community care program that the Obama administration may emulate.[238] As one observer described, "Doctors like it, patients stay healthier, and the state saves hundreds of millions of dollars."[239] Another state-based innovation that has altered the overall Medicaid program includes the increased movement of covered populations into managed care.[240] Additional waivers have expanded the populations covered under original program rules in the hopes that preventative care to vulnerable populations will forestall more serious (and expensive) emergency care later.[241]

Similarly, in many programs of cooperative federalism, such as the Clean Air and Water Acts, Congress allocates rulemaking authority to a federal agency but invites the states to implement and enforce those rules. Delegating the design of statewide implementation and enforcement programs vests an important degree of policy-making discretion in the states, which wield substantial creative authority in deciding how to accomplish federal technical standards. Under the Clean Air Act (CAA), EPA sets overall standards for permissible levels of air pollutants, and the states generally develop individualized implementation plans to realize them given their unique economic, geographic, and demographic circumstances

---

[234] *Id.*

[235] That said, bad ideas are also tested through the waiver programs. Interview with Lawrence Palmer, Professor of Health Law & Bioethics, William & Mary Law School, Williamsburg, Va. (June, 2009). Although this can provide useful lessons nationally, the subjects—sick poor people—may have preferred not to be experimented on.

[236] *Id.*

[237] Thompson & Burke, *supra* note 227, at 971 (describing how Medicaid waiver negotiations between federal and state officials led to health coverage for all Massachusetts residents); Kay Lazar, *Mass. Gets $10.6b for Healthcare Insurance*, BOS. GLOBE, Oct. 1, 2008, at A1, http://www.boston.com/news/local/articles/ 2008/10/01/mass_gets_106b_for_healthcare_insurance (describing subsequent waiver negotiations leading to additional federal support for the state's expanded coverage).

[238] *Medicaid Waivers and Demonstrations List, Details for North Carolina ACCESS HealthCare Connection 1915(b)*, U.S. DEP'T OF HEALTH & HUMAN SERVS. CTRS. FOR MEDICARE & MEDICADE SERVS., http:// www.cms.hhs.gov/MedicaidStWaivProgDemoPGI/MWDL/list.asp; Rose Hoban, *N.C. Program A Model For Health Overhaul?*, NPR, Oct. 15, 2009, http://www.npr.org/templates/story/story.php?storyId= 113816621 (reporting on White House consultation over North Carolina's Community Care program after financial analysis showed it saves Medicaid $170 million annually).

[239] Hoban, *supra* note 238.

[240] Gais & Fossett, *supra* note 233, at 509 (noting that waivers are the primary drivers of health policy change, especially in shifting low-income clients into managed care); Thompson & Burke, *supra* note 227, at 985 (finding evidence of state policy diffusion in the nine-fold proliferation of major managed care initiatives during the 1990s).

[241] Lazar, *supra* note 237.

(otherwise, they must submit to a federal implementation plan).[242] EPA must approve the state implementation plans, however, and the process reportedly involves a fair amount of negotiation back and forth with state counterparts.[243] Similarly, states theoretically have some flexibility in setting water quality standards under the Clean Water Act's Total Maximum Daily Load (TMDL) program,[244] but EPA retains final approval authority. States often use their clout to push—sometimes successfully and other times less so—for EPA approval of relaxed standards.[245] Conversely, federal negotiators use their approval authority to push, also sometimes successfully and other times not, for more stringent standards.[246]

c. Iterative Policy-Making Negotiations: Clean Air Act Motor Vehicle Emissions and Climate

In contrast to the formal zones and waivers of policy-making laboratory federalism, another type of joint policy-making negotiation happens so slowly that it is possible to miss as a form of negotiation at all. Labeled "iterative federalism" by Professor Ann Carlson,[247] it takes place within a regulatory regime in which the federal and state governments share authority for creating regulatory policy in a precise and limited way. The federal government creates a uniform national plan while allowing a selected state to develop a competing standard—and then allows the other states to choose between the federal and single-state alternatives. By allowing states to choose between the two, iterative federalism programs—such as the CAA's regulation of motor vehicle emissions—create a dynamic of regulatory innovation and competition by which state choices influence federal standards over time.

Iterative federalism strikes a wise compromise in regulatory marketplaces where legitimate concerns over stagnating regulatory monopoly compete with legitimate economic needs for regulatory uniformity. Regulated parties never have to cope with more than two sets of regulatory standards at a time, but enabling the regulatory competitor to coexist with the federal baseline allows room for at least some innovation.[248] Over time, this often means that as states gravitate toward the state alternative, the federal law adjusts itself toward the state alternative in a slow, iterative form of state-federal negotiation.

---

[242] 42 U.S.C. §7410(a)(1) (2006). The overwhelming majority of states choose to create their own SIPS under the Act. Siegel, *supra* Chapter Seven, note 5, at 1676.

[243] *Cf.* Dave Owen, *Probabilities, Planning Failures, and Environmental Law*, 84 Tul. L. Rev. 265, 280–87 (2009); EPA Interview, *supra* note 171.

[244] 33 U.S.C. § 1313(d)(1)(C) (2006) (authorizing state TMDLs for waters prioritized under § 1313(d)(1)(A)).

[245] Robert Glennon & John Thorson, *Environmental Restoration Initiatives: An Analysis of Agency Performance and the Capacity for Change*, 42 Ariz. L. Rev. 483, 517–19 (2000) (discussing state-federal negotiations to reverse deteriorating conditions in the Bay Delta).

[246] *Cf. id.*

[247] Ann Carlson, *Iterative Federalism and Climate Change*, 103 Nw. U.L. Rev. 1097, 1099 (2009) (coining the term to describe "repeated, sustained, and dynamic lawmaking efforts involving both levels of government").

[248] *See* William W. Buzbee, *Asymmetrical Regulation: Risk, Preemption, and the Floor/Ceiling Distinction*, 82 N.Y.U.L. Rev. 1547, 1590–92 (2007) (showing how, in comparison to more narrowly tailored floor-preemption, "unitary federal choice" ceiling-preemption leads to poorly tailored regulation and public-choice process distortion).

Clean Air Act

Under the CAA, the EPA creates national standards for emissions from mobile sources,[249] saving the auto manufacturing industry from the crippling multiplicity of standards that might ensue if states were able to regulate independently. Nevertheless, Congress allowed the State of California to set an alternative standard deviating upward from the national floor.[250] The "California" exception was initially created out of respect for California's leadership in the field, and also because air quality in parts of the state so exceeded national averages that more stringent motor vehicle regulations were necessary to meet other CAA obligations.[251]

Congress later modified the CAA to permit other states to choose between EPA's standards or California's.[252] This critical structural change enabled a loose but powerful forum to conduct state-federal bargaining over the ultimate path of national emissions regulation, thus beginning an iterative process of subtle but joint state-federal decision making. Over time, more and more states lined up behind California instead of EPA, such that by 2009, fourteen states had adopted the more stringent standards[253] and up to twelve others had expressed interest in doing so.[254] This trend has exerted pressure on EPA to raise its standards even as California has continued to raise its own, together exerting pressure on other important standard setters, including auto manufacturers.[255] The overall effect, as states continue to vote with their regulatory feet, has been an upward migration in the nation's vehicular emissions standards.

Iterative policy making provides a unique means of balancing competing needs for federalism innovation and economic uniformity in the national market for automobiles. Automobile manufacturers may prefer a single set of emissions standards, but building for two sets of standards is preferable to coping with fifty. States may prefer to set their own standards, but the ability to choose between two levels of stringency is preferable to no choice at all. Meanwhile, the iterative dimension of the process enables the operation of a limited level of regulatory innovation and competition with demonstrated effect in the regulatory marketplace. A more uniform, traditional command-and-control regulation imposed from the top down may not have been so responsive.

The iterative policymaking structure also protects state innovators that invest in efforts to resolve their share of an interjurisdictional problem before the rest follow. These states would

---

[249] 42 U.S.C. § 7543 (2006).

[250] *Id.* § 7543(b)(1) (so authorizing California, as the single state with an emissions program before 1966).

[251] DAVID WOOLEY & ELIZABETH MORSS, CLEAN AIR HANDBOOK § 5:11 (2009).

[252] 42 U.S.C. § 7507 (2006); NAT'L RESEARCH COUNCIL COMM. ON STATE PRACTICES IN SETTING MOBILE SOURCE EMISSIONS STANDARDS, STATE AND FEDERAL STANDARDS FOR MOBILE-SOURCE EMISSIONS 70–71 (2006) (explaining that Congress did so in response to state requests for more tools to meet ambient air standards).

[253] MCCARTHY & MELTZ, *supra* Chapter Five, note 179, at 4 n.13.

[254] Emily Chen, *State Adoption Status on California Vehicle Emissions Control Requirements*, W. STATES AIR RESOURCES COUNCIL (Feb. 2008), http://www.westar.org/Docs/Business%20Meetings/Spring08/ParkCity/03.2.2%20CAA%20177%20states.xls (listing states considering adoption of California standards).

[255] David E. Adelman & Kirsten H. Engel, *Adaptive Federalism: The Case against Reallocating Environmental Regulatory Authority*, 92 MINN. L. REV. 1796, 1840 (2008) (explaining the dissemination of California's standards).

suffer disproportionately if forced to abandon path-breaking regulatory infrastructure to conform to a preemptive federal standard. Moreover, a purely preemptive policy would disincentivize states from taking needed action early on—at the most efficient opportunity for intervention—lest their investments prove wasted when the federal government eventually gets around to regulating. The model seems to be a good one for joint policy-making contexts in which the need for market uniformity is a particularly salient feature of an interjurisdictional problem—for example, a national market for carbon emission credits.

Climate Federalism

Scholars such as Professor Carlson have proposed that the CAA's model of iterative federalism policymaking may also be a useful means of navigating federalism concerns in climate policy making.[256] The suggestion may have merit, given the role states have already played in early rounds of policy-making negotiations over climate regulation[257] and the collective action problems necessarily implied.[258] As discussed in Chapter Five, nearly all of the proposals considered in recent federal climate bills—including renewable energy and portfolio standards, power plant emissions standards, net metering, and building codes—are already in place among many states,[259] including the carbon cap-and-trade centerpiece of the federal legislation proposed in 2009–2010.[260] The Northeast Regional Greenhouse Gas Initiative held its ninth auction in September 2010, the Western Climate Initiative is currently negotiating targets among several western states and Canadian provinces, and states and provinces in the Midwest are doing the same via the Midwest Greenhouse Gas Reduction Accord.[261]

By these initiatives, a handful of states have organized regional policy making, in part to put pressure on the federal government to regulate carbon emissions.[262] Success is apparent in the climate bill that passed the House in 2009, and is suggested by the others that have made it to the Senate.[263] Congress's proposal to preempt regional cap-and-trade for the first five years of a national market[264] demonstrates that it is heeding conventional economic wisdom that a national carbon market offers the best chance of achieving cost-efficient

[256] Carlson, *supra* note 247, at 1099.

[257] *See supra* Chapter Five, notes 144–87 and accompanying text.

[258] *See* Robert L. Glicksman & Richard E. Levy, *A Collective Action Perspective on Ceiling Preemption by Federal Environmental Regulation: The Case of Global Climate Change*, 102 Nw. U.L. Rev. 579, 579–80 (2008).

[259] Engel, *supra* Introduction, note 79, at 432; Probst & Szambelan, *supra* Chapter Five, note 149, at 3–8.

[260] American Clean Energy & Security Act of 2009, H.R. 2454, 111th Cong. (as passed by the House, June 26, 2009) [hereinafter Waxman-Markey]. The Clean Energy Jobs and American Power Act, S. 1733, 111th Cong. (2009) [hereinafter Kerry-Boxer] and American Clean Energy Leadership Act, S. 1462, 111th Cong. (2010) [hereinafter Bingaman], are pending in the Senate. *See* Press Release, RGGI Inc., RGGI States Complete Sixth Successful CO2 Auction (Dec. 4, 2009), http://www.rggi.org/docs/Auction_6_Results_Release_MMrep.pdf.

[261] *See supra* Chapter Five, notes 153–57.

[262] Engel, *supra* Introduction, note 79, at 432; Probst & Szambelan, *supra* Chapter Five, note 149, at 3.

[263] *See* Waxman-Markey, *supra* note 260; Kerry-Boxer, *supra* note 260.

[264] Waxman-Markey, *supra* note 260, tit. III, § 335; Kerry-Boxer, *supra* note 260, tit. I, § 125.

economy-wide reductions.[265] Nevertheless, after five years, a two-track iterative system could offer an innovation-preserving alternative to the hurdles that could arise if multiple cap-and-trade programs operated simultaneously. The bills also show congressional sensitivity to the federalism implications of enacting federal legislation in a field dominated by state leadership: beyond cap-and-trade, they foreclose preemption of state programs meeting the federal floor.[266]

d. Intersystemic Signaling Negotiations: Medical Marijuana, Immigration, and Courts

Iterative federalism negotiations such as the CAA's are created by intentional legislative design. However, indirect state-federal policy-making negotiations can approximate iterative bargaining in unintentional contexts. In these situations, state actors use sovereign capacity to influence federal lawmakers regarding federal policies that they disapprove through intersystemic signaling. Intersystemic signaling negotiations arise when separately deliberating state and federal actors influence one another's outcomes through indirect iterative exchange. This usually occurs in interjurisdictional regulatory contexts where each is vying for policy-making control in the face of regulatory dissensus. The Supremacy Clause notwithstanding, it is not always the federal government that prevails—as demonstrated by the arc of national policy regarding medical marijuana and immigration enforcement, and by a provocative analysis of intersystemic signaling between state and federal courts.

Medical Marijuana and Immigration Enforcement Policy

For example, several states have legalized the use of marijuana for medical treatment,[267] even though federal law does not distinguish between marijuana consumed for medical or recreational purposes.[268] In a celebrated case litigating the standoff between California and the federal government on this issue, the Supreme Court recently reaffirmed the supremacy of the federal law over conflicting state laws in *Gonzales v. Raich*, a decision with significant federalism implications due to its broad interpretation of the federal commerce power.[269] Nevertheless, states and municipalities have continued to pass contrary laws,[270] and the conflict has prompted unusual judicial decisions that appear to favor state over federal laws in individual cases, even in federal court. In turn, these contrary state laws and confusing

---

[265] Probst & Szambelan, *supra* Chapter Five, note 149, at 15.

[266] Waxman-Markey, *supra* note 260, tit. III, §334; Kerry-Boxer, *supra* note 260, tit. I, § 124.

[267] *Active State Medical Marijuana Programs*, NORML, http://norml.org/index.cfm?Group_ID=3391 (detailing legalization in thirteen states).

[268] *Drug Fact Sheet: Marijuana*, U.S. DRUG ENFORCEMENT ADMIN., http://www.justice.gov/dea/pubs/abuse/ drug_data_sheets/marijuana_DrugDataSheet.pdf (defining marijuana as a "Schedule 1" drug with no accepted medical use).

[269] 545 U.S. 1, 22 (2005).

[270] For example, Breckenridge, Colorado, recently legalized possession of small amounts of marijuana, despite contrary state and federal law. *Colorado Ski Town Legalizes Pot*, WASH. TIMES, Nov. 4, 2009, http://www. washingtontimes.com/news/2009/nov/04/colo-ski-town-could-push-pot-legalization/.

federal cases have prompted federal legislators to consider federal legislation to bridge the gap between state and federal law.[271]

In one notable example, the federal government brought charges against Ed Rosenthal in 2003 for cultivating marijuana, despite the fact that he had been duly authorized by the City of Oakland to distribute the drug for medicinal purposes under California state law.[272] Rosenthal was not able to present this information as a defense at his trial, however, because federal law does not recognize state laws legalizing medicinal marijuana.[273] Without the benefit of this potentially exculpatory information, Rosenthal was convicted by a jury of an offense that required a mandatory minimum five-year prison term.[274] Nevertheless, the judge sentenced him to only one day, based on the "unique circumstances of the case" (a decision the government is appealing).[275] In response to cases like this one, federal legislators have introduced the Truth in Trials Act[276] (still pending), which would enable federal drug offenders to raise the affirmative defense of acting in compliance with applicable state medical marijuana laws.[277]

Even as such legislative proposals languish in Congress, the pressure of the conflict between state and federal law has successfully moved federal policy making at the executive level. The Obama administration recently announced that the Department of Justice would not pursue enforcement cases against medical marijuana users or distributors in states where such use is legal.[278] With no record for review in intersystemic signaling, it is difficult to definitively establish the causal link between state action and federal reaction in this situation—and there are certainly contrary examples.[279] Nonetheless,

---

[271] *Cf.* Gerken, *supra* Introduction, notes 69, 81 (framing state and municipal decisions to purposefully contravene legally superior doctrine as a legitimate and sometimes successful method of political dissent).

[272] United States v. Rosenthal, 266 F. Supp. 2d 1091, 1098 (N.D. Cal. 2003); *see also* Michael O'Hear, *Federalism and Drug Control*, 57 VAND. L. REV. 783, 787 (2004) (discussing *Rosenthal*).

[273] O'Hear, *supra* note 272, at 787.

[274] *Rosenthal*, 266 F. Supp. 2d at 1093.

[275] *Id.* at 1099. The Ninth Circuit ultimately overturned Rosenthal's conviction in 2006 because a confused juror (probably confused about the state/federal law conflict) had improperly contacted a lawyer for advice during deliberations. Bob Egelko, *Pot Advocate Convicted on Three Charges, But "Ganga Guru" Won't Face Further Punishment*, SAN FRAN. CHRON., May 30, 2007, http://www.sfgate.com/cgi-bin/article.cgi?f=/c/a/2007/05/30/BAGTPQ420H5.DTL. However, Rosenthal was reindicted a few months later and convicted by the same judge after he was once more prevented from presenting evidence that he was acting pursuant to state law. Nevertheless, the judge would not sentence Rosenthal beyond the day he had already served, and so his conviction resulted in no additional prison time. *Id.*

[276] H.R. 1717, 108th Cong. (2003) (reintroduced as H.R. 3939, 111th Cong. (2009)).

[277] O'Hear, *supra* note 272, at 787 n.16.

[278] David Stout & Solomon Moore, *U.S. Won't Prosecute in States That Allow Medical Marijuana*, N.Y. TIMES, Oct. 19, 2009, at A1, http://www.nytimes.com/2009/10/20/us/20cannabis.html.

[279] *E.g.*, Judith Resnik, *Lessons in Federalism from the 1960s Class Action Rule and the 2005 Class Action Fairness Act: "The Political Safeguards" of Aggregate Translocal Actions*, 156 U. PENN. L. REV. 1929 (2008) (arguing that national lawmakers preempt state-based decisions they disapprove of by federalizing rights). Federal enforcers have also used supremacy to undermine contrary state policies by prosecuting crimes permissible under state law, such as the previous practice of prosecuting medical marijuana. O'Hear, *supra* note 272, at 810–11.

circumstantial evidence of the success of such dialogic processes is compelling, and could soon include climate change.[280]

In another coalescing example, Arizona's aggressive new immigration law—the most stringent in the nation—may be viewed as an attempt at intersystemic signaling with Congress in an effort to change national immigration policy.[281] The most aggressive portions of the law have been enjoined pending suit by the U.S. Attorney General, claiming that Arizona's foray into new immigration policy is preempted by federal law.[282] But in an unlikely coincidence, after years of inaction and within only weeks of the date that Arizona's new law went into force, Congress returned from an August recess to pass an immigration enforcement bill funding greater security measures along the southwestern border.[283] Adding force to the signaling process, legislative leaders in at least six other states have announced plans to propose similar state legislation, notwithstanding the pending challenge to Arizona's law.[284]

The flurry of state laws limiting the use of eminent domain for private economic development after the Supreme Court's decision in *Kelo v. City of New London*[285] provides another example of this fascinating dialectic.[286] The *Kelo* decision anticipated that states could legislate more stringently than the constitutional floor it described.[287] However, the widespread state response—often more rhetorically charged than legally meaningful—has been viewed as a means of rejecting the federal interpretation in the political sphere.[288]

---

[280] *See* Engel, *supra* Introduction, note 78; discussed *supra* Chapter Five, notes 134–203.

[281] Randal C. Archibold, *Arizona Enacts Stringent Law on Immigration*, N.Y. TIMES, APR. 24, 2010, at A1, http://www.nytimes.com/2010/04/24/us/politics/24immig.html (reporting that the law requires immigrants to carry immigration documentation at all times and allows (or requires) police to question anyone of uncertain citizenship). *See also* Chamber of Commerce v. Whiting, 131 S. Ct. 1968 (2011) (upholding against a federal preemption claim an Arizona law allowing the state to revoke the licenses of businesses that knowingly hire unauthorized aliens). Federal law expressly preempts state civil or criminal sanctions for employing unauthorized workers, other than through "licensing and similar laws." *Id.* at 1973.

[282] Press Release, Dep't of Justice Office of Pub. Affairs, Citing Conflict with Federal Law, Department of Justice Challenges Arizona Immigration Law (July 6, 2010), http://www.justice.gov/opa/pr/2010/July/10-opa-776.html (arguing that the Arizona law exceeds a state's role with respect to aliens, interferes with the federal government's balanced administration of the immigration laws, and critically undermines U.S. foreign policy objectives). *See also* Randal C. Archibold, *Judge Blocks Arizona's Immigration Law*, N.Y. TIMES, July 28, 2010, at A1, http://www.nytimes.com/2010/07/29/us/29arizona.html?_r=1&ref=immigration-and-emigration (reporting that a federal judge blocked the most controversial provisions requiring documentation and affirmative police stops).

[283] Julia Preston, *Obama Signs Border Bill to Increase Surveillance*, N.Y. TIMES, Aug. 13, 2010, at A10, http://www.nytimes.com/2010/08/14/us/politics/14immig.html.

[284] Julia Preston, *Political Battle on Illegal Immigration Shifts to States*, N.Y. TIMES, Dec. 31, 2010, at A1, http://www.nytimes.com/2011/01/01/us/01immig.html?_r=2&nl=todaysheadlines&emc=tha2 (reporting on proposed bills in Georgia, Mississippi, Nebraska, Oklahoma, Pennsylvania, and South Carolina).

[285] 545 U.S. 469 (2005) (holding that the Public Use Clause of the Fifth Amendment does not prohibit this use of eminent domain).

[286] *Cf.* Ilya Somin, *The Limits of Backlash: Assessing the Political Response to Kelo*, 93 MINN. L. REV. 2100, 2114–48 (2009) (listing state legislative responses).

[287] 545 U.S. at 488–90.

[288] *Id.*

State and Federal Courts

Although this project primarily analyzes negotiations between the political branches, a compelling research project identifies a pattern of intersystemic signaling negotiations by which state courts have sought to alter binding rulings by the U.S. Supreme Court.[289] Challenging the idea of the Court's interpretive monopoly, Professor Frederic Bloom has described a dynamic by which state courts have occasionally defied binding Court precedent in order to signal the need for its reversal.[290] Moreover, Professor Bloom argues that in these cases, the Court has effectively signaled its willingness to be influenced by state courts in unsettled areas of its jurisprudence:

> Nearly all of [the Court's calls for state-court disobedience] come in coded legal whispers—about strategically unsettled constitutional substance and over generous decision-making procedures—instead of dramatic doctrinal shouts. But quietly and methodically, the Supreme Court has encouraged state courts to ignore binding Court precedent—to act, in other words, as "state courts unbound." We should hardly be surprised when state courts agree.[291]

If Professor Bloom is right, then even the seemingly remote judicial branches participate in federalism bargaining, and to worthwhile effect. By Professor Bloom's account, state courts have succeeded at renegotiating U.S. Supreme Court precedent in the areas of matrimonial domicile, criminal sentencing reforms, and juvenile death sentencing.[292] Even the implicit conversations between federal and intermediate state courts under the *Erie* doctrine (over uncertain state precedent in federal cases) might be understood as negotiation.[293]

---

[289] Bloom, *supra* note 27, at 503.

[290] *Id.* at 504.

[291] *Id.*

[292] *Id.* at 516, 533, 544.

[293] Erie R.R. Co. v. Tompkins, 304 U.S. 64, 77–78 (1938) (establishing that a federal court in diversity must apply substantive state law). For a more overt example of judicial bargaining in a different context, see Linda Greenhouse, *Clarence Thomas, Silent but Sure*, OPINIONATOR (Mar. 11, 2010, 9:37 PM), http://opinionator. blogs.nytimes.com/2010/03/11/clarence-thomas-silent-but-sure/ (describing a series of invitations within Justice Thomas's dissents to challenge various Supreme Court precedents). *See* Gerald Frug, *The Judicial Power of the Purse*, 126 U. PA. L. REV. 715 (1978) (describing executive and judicial collusion in adversarial proceedings seeking judicial decrees that would require legislative authorization and funding for legal and social reform).

9

THE STRUCTURAL SAFEGUARDS OF FEDERALISM BARGAINING

AS SUGGESTED BY the examples in Chapter Eight, negotiated federalism is a project of bilateral balancing—incorporating wisdom from all levels of government about how to prioritize competing federalism values and exogenous considerations in each individual circumstance. Federalism bargaining ensures the active engagement of federalism goals through its very design—regardless of the competing policy concerns or the subjective considerations of participants—by balancing local and national interests in the substance of actual governance. Bilateral balancing thus affords protection for federalism on a structural level that surpasses the political safeguards available at a purely unilateral level.

Furthering the positive account of federalism bargaining, this chapter incorporates data from the taxonomy and interviews with a limited sample of primary sources to analyze the norms and sources of trade in federalism bargaining, with special attention to the currency of federalism values themselves.[1] Precious few generalizations apply to so diverse an array of intergovernmental bargaining, but useful commonalities can be drawn about the currencies with which participants bargain, and the legal constraints and uncertainties that restrict them. All bargaining is premised on the negotiation of various entitlements to sovereign authority and resources, and the parties explicitly and implicitly engage in balancing to determine when and how to exchange them. In addition to the shifting of authority, fiscal

---

[1] My small, nonstatistical sample included five state agents and five federal agents who regularly engage in federalism bargaining, as well as five legal scholars who research regulatory overlap, and five who research some of the relevant bargaining venues. Several requested anonymity to avoid the appearance of making official pronouncements.

resources, other governance capacity, and credit, the normative leverage of federalism values can be a powerful factor in federalism bargaining.

Understanding the dynamics in federalism bargaining helps demonstrate the structural safeguards that bilateral balancing affords. The exchange of state and federal preferences in this bargaining—even when it is over purely substantive policies—encourages negotiated governance to honor federalism even when individual negotiators are thinking about other things. As with other federalism safeguards, the structural encouragement of federalism values is powerful but not infallible. Leverage dynamics, failed relationships, competitions for credit, and bargaining abuses can overcome them in some cases. Chapter Nine's analysis thus provides empirical support for Chapter Ten's normative proposal to distinguish between federalism bargaining that warrants interpretive deference and that which does not.

A. Federalism Bargaining Norms

The following analysis reveals soft generalizations about the norms that operate in state-federal bargaining, including participation, rites of initiation, bargaining mechanics, negotiating leverage, and the uncertainty about roles and limits that can compromise federalism bargaining.

I. PARTICIPATION: EXECUTIVE DOMINANCE, WITH EXCEPTIONS

Most federalism bargaining takes place between the executive actors on either side of the state-federal divide; it is axiomatic in enforcement negotiations and in most permitting and licensing negotiations. For example, the EPA and state environmental agencies generally negotiate the terms of state implementation programs under the Clean Air Act,[2] while HHS and state health and social service agencies negotiate the terms of Medicaid demonstration waivers.[3] When federal executive agencies initiate negotiated rulemaking with state input, state participants are usually members of the executive branch.[4] That executive actors lead in many instances of state-federal bargaining is not surprising, given that they are charged with the details of statutory implementation and possess the most reliable substantive expertise about what each side can accomplish. Although high-ranking executive officials can play important roles in the process, the most important players are often the career agency staff on both sides.[5]

That said, there are many exceptions. For example, Congress is the federal negotiator in all spending power deals, in most policy-making laboratory and iterative federalism negotiations, and in much interest group representation bargaining. Sometimes Congress convenes the process of negotiated rulemaking by statute, as it initially required under the

---

[2] *See supra* Chapter Eight, notes 242–43 and accompanying text.

[3] *See id.* notes 227–41 and accompanying text.

[4] *E.g.,* Endangered Species Act (ESA) § 9, 16 U.S.C. § 1538 (2006), discussed *supra* Chapter Eight, notes 118–38 and accompanying text.

[5] Telephone Interview with Melissa Savage, *supra* Chapter Eight, note 56.

REAL ID Act.[6] Congress was also the federal partner in the LLRWPA negotiation with the states,[7] and it is the intersystemic signaling partner targeted by states that have organized regionally on climate change initiatives.[8] We might even consider the indirect negotiating roles played by judicial actors—not only as envisioned by Professor Bloom,[9] but even that of lower court judges like the one who sentenced Ed Rosenthal to one day in prison (rather than the federal mandatory five-year minimum) for cultivating medical marijuana under a state license.[10] Understanding federalism bargaining in its broadest forms, all branch actors may engage in it at one time or another.

2. INITIATION: FEDERAL DOMINANCE, ON THE SURFACE

The federal government most often initiates negotiations, especially when federal supremacy or the spending power plays an important role. The Clean Air and Water Acts, Medicaid, and No Child Left Behind Act all offer good examples, although even these statutory bargaining forums may obscure important state roles in interest group negotiations leading up to the statute's enactment.[11]

That said, sometimes states are the clear initiators. States often initiate by taking the policymaking lead in a way that evolves toward federalism bargaining—either formally (e.g., vehicular emissions)[12] or informally (e.g., medical marijuana enforcement).[13] Other times, states initiate more straightforwardly, engaging Congress either in a spending power deal they have designed, as they did by lobbying for the Energy Efficiency Block Grant Program,[14] or in bargained-for-commandeering negotiations, such as those that occurred between the NGA and Congress in enacting the LLRWPA.[15] In each of these cases, the states seek a particular form of federal capacity that they need to implement their own policy preferences—either financial resources, freedom from otherwise operative legal rules, or legal authority to resolve a collective action problem among the states.[16] Political scientist John Nugent has provided an especially powerful account of how states protect their interests in federal policy-making, often through interest-group, implementation, and intersystemic signaling bargaining.[17] Federalism bargaining thus arises from both ends of the state-federal divide.

---

[6] *See supra* Chapter Eight, notes 188–97 and accompanying text.

[7] Discussed *supra* Chapter Seven.

[8] *See supra* Chapter Five, notes 134–203 and accompanying text.

[9] *See supra* Chapter Eight, notes 289–92 and accompanying text.

[10] *See* O'Hear, *supra* Chapter Eight, note 272, at 787.

[11] *See* NUGENT, *supra* Introduction, note 71, at 54–76, 115–67 (describing the state-based lobby in federal policy making).

[12] *See supra* Chapter Eight, notes 249–55 and accompanying text.

[13] *See id.* notes 267–79 and accompanying text.

[14] *See id.* notes 97–100 and accompanying text.

[15] *See supra* Chapter Seven.

[16] For a more detailed treatment of when federal preemption is and is not an appropriate response to state collective action problems, see Glicksman & Levy, *supra* Chapter Eight, note 258, at 591–603.

[17] *See generally* NUGENT, *supra* Introduction, note 71.

3. MECHANICS: FORUM-DEPENDENT

The mechanics of state-federal bargaining vary depending on the forum, indicating various opportunities for federalism engineering in their design.

Sometimes Congress explicitly invites negotiation by statute, even if it leaves the particulars of the negotiating process to executive agencies. Congress took this approach in the Medicaid demonstration waiver programs, which invite states to propose exceptions,[18] and the Clean Water Act, which required that the EPA consult with states in developing the Phase II Stormwater Rule.[19] In other examples, Congress enacts a statute that implicitly necessitates state-federal bargaining, as it did in authorizing the formation of memoranda of understanding between state and federal agencies in allocating enforcement authority for immigration violations under the ACCESS program[20] and permitting pollutant discharges under the NPDES program.[21] Elsewhere, state and federal actors bargain under statutory provisions that enable more explicit negotiations, such as state-federal negotiations for Incidental Take Permits under the ESA.[22]

These various legislative arrangements may take advantage of the different institutional competencies of each branch to account for federalism concerns. For example, Congress may create explicit avenues for state-federal bargaining when it intends to engage the highest level of state government in policy design, while leaving executive agencies to manage the details of bargaining in individual circumstances where specialized expertise and particular relationships among federal and state negotiators will be useful.

In addition, federal statutes and rules incorporate features that cleverly motivate state-federal bargaining and collaboration where it is especially needed. For example, although seized criminal assets become state property and enter the general treasury under most state forfeiture laws, federal forfeiture laws remand most seized assets directly to state law enforcement agencies.[23] This creates a powerful incentive for state law enforcers to collaborate with federal agencies in investigating criminal activity in areas of jurisdictional overlap, motivating them to share information that may lead to more effective enforcement and more efficient allocation of scarce funding.[24] The Superfund Act includes a similar feature to encourage

---

[18] *See supra* Chapter Eight, notes 227–41 and accompanying text.

[19] *See supra* Chapter Five, notes 49–67; *see also supra* Chapter Eight, notes 180–87 and accompanying text.

[20] *See* Immigration and Nationality Act, 8 U.S.C. § 1357(g)(1) (2006) and related discussion, *supra*, Chapter Eight, note 69.

[21] *See* 33 U.S.C. § 1342(b); *supra* Chapter Eight, note 70.

[22] *See supra* Chapter Eight, notes 118–36 and accompanying text.

[23] Telephone Interview with Roscoe Howard, *supra* Chapter Eight, note 74; *see, e.g.*, 28 U.S.C. § 524 (2006) (establishing the DOJ Assets Forfeiture Fund); Eric D. Blumenson & Eva S. Nilsen, *Contesting Government's Financial Interest in Drug Cases*, 13 CRIM. JUST. 4, 5 (1999) (contrasting federal and state asset forfeiture laws).

[24] Telephone Interview with Roscoe Howard, *supra* Chapter Eight, note 74 ("It's a purposefully designed deal-making tool, and it works very well: bring us your big cases with federal import, and we'll give you the money!").

state-federal remediation partnerships.[25] If a state partners with EPA under the Natural Resources Damages Assessment program, recovered funds go to restoring the local resource—but if EPA acts alone, then 40 percent of recovered funds go into the U.S. operating budget.[26]

4. LEVERAGE: FEDERAL SUPREMACY, STATE CAPACITY

The conventional wisdom is that the federal government possesses substantially more leverage in state-federal negotiations, by combined force of the Supremacy Clause[27] and superior fiscal resources. Federalism bargaining participants confirm this view in many areas of governance.[28] One state agency attorney noted that "states lack leverage at the table . . . because they aren't as cohesive as they could be, notwithstanding the National Governors Association."[29] He explained, "Political differences between states mean that they aren't always on the same side, so they cannot get it together enough to lobby effectively as a single force—they care about different things, so they cannot really leverage effectively based on their collective capacity."[30] Despite the suspicion that leverage favors the federal government, however, state bargainers defend negotiation vigorously as a preferred tool of inter-jurisdictional governance.[31] As a National Conference of State Legislatures source noted, "even if the states lack leverage, [bargaining] is still the best, fairest process."[32]

Participants are also quick to note exceptions to the rule in both political and policy-making contexts. For example, state governors have formidable political leverage over their state's federal legislators by virtue of a governor's superior local access to state media.[33] The governor can generate serious political consequences for a legislator's career by manipulating popular opinion through statements to the press. State actors also possess more powerful leverage when they are the primary implementers of bargained-for policies.[34]

Although the conventional wisdom about favorable federal leverage should not be underestimated, negotiation theory helps unpack bargaining leverage in ways that highlight easily missed state advantages. In whatever form, leverage tracks influence in deal making.

---

[25] CERCLA, 42 U.S.C. § 9628 (2006); Interview with Mike Murphy, Director of Environmental Enhancement, Virginia Department of Environmental Quality (DEQ), Richmond, Virginia (Jan. 25, 2010).

[26] Interview with Mike Murphy, *supra* note 25.

[27] U.S. CONST. art. VI, cl. 2.

[28] Telephone Interview with Jeff Reynolds, Staff Attorney, Virginia DEQ (Jan. 4, 2010); Telephone Interview with Melissa Savage, *supra* Chapter Eight, note 56; Senate Interview, *supra* Chapter Eight, note 95.

[29] Telephone Interview with Jeff Reynolds, *supra* note 28.

[30] *Id.* Subject-specific state alliances, such as the Environmental Council of the States, are more successful at lobbying federal policy makers because member concerns are more unified. Interview with Mike Murphy, *supra* note 25.

[31] *E.g.*, Interview with Rick Weeks, Chief Deputy Dir. of Virginia DEQ, in Richmond, Va. (Jan. 25, 2010) ("Things typically work pretty well and leverage is not a real concern of ours.").

[32] Telephone Interview with Melissa Savage, *supra* Chapter Eight, note 56.

[33] Senate Interview, *supra* Chapter Eight, note 95.

[34] *See* Hills, *supra* Part I Introduction, note 5; NUGENT, *supra* Introduction, note 71, at 168–212 (describing state implementation of federal policy as an important safeguard of federalism).

The party with the most leverage is best positioned to secure its preferred terms, assuming the leverage is effectively deployed. Conversely, the party with the least leverage usually has the most to lose if a deal is not reached. But leverage really arises in three different forms: negative, positive, and normative.[35] Most obvious to the naked eye, negative leverage is power held by one side that the other does not want it to use—such as a state governor's ability to generate negative local press about a senator. By contrast, a party exerts positive leverage in wielding power or resources that the other side *does* want it to use—such as that Congress wields in spending power bargaining. Finally, normative leverage is morally based power, compelling the parties in a certain direction based on shared authoritative norms, such as fairness, consistency, patriotism, honesty, and any other values that might apply more locally.

Federal actors often hold the most important negative leverage, given their ability to preempt state law under the Supremacy Clause, and at times, powerful positive leverage in the form of federal funds. However, states often possess the most important positive leverage, given their generally superior capacity for enforcement, implementation, and innovation (and reciprocal negative leverage when they can credibly threaten to withhold it).[36] States occasionally deploy formidable negative leverage in their ability to frustrate federal regulatory plans through litigation or politically strategic threats of disobedience.[37] And as detailed in Section IV.B., states also benefit from the powerful normative leverage that constitutional norms and federalism principles exert on the federalism bargaining process.

In federalism bargaining, the negative leverage of federal preemption is often balanced by the positive leverage of state capacity. The more the implicated realm of governance depends on state capacity, the more power state negotiators wield at the table.[38] For example, negotiating leverage is more closely matched in many environmental negotiations because participants understand that the programs of cooperative federalism on which the big federal environmental statutes depend would implode without the good-faith participation of state environmental agencies.[39] In theory, the EPA assumes the roles that states choose not to fulfill, but participants understand that the agency could never realistically assume responsibility for localized implementation in each state, or even a handful at any given time.[40] As a result, state agents occasionally hear EPA threats of preemption as hollow, and occasionally

[35] SHELL, *supra* Part IV Introduction, note 12, at 40–57 (discussing leverage).

[36] *Cf.* NUGENT, *supra* Introduction, note 71.

[37] *See, e.g.*, Kate Galbraith, *Texas Leads Resistance to EPA Climate Action*, THE TEXAS TRIBUNE, Sep. 23, 2010, http://www.texastribune.org/texas-state-agencies/attorney-generals-office/texas-leads-resistance-to-epa-climate-action/ (reporting on state pledges to challenge EPA climate regulations through litigation and to actively resist them even if unsuccessful in court). In a letter to EPA, the state attorney general explained: "We write to inform you that Texas has neither the authority nor the intention of interpreting, ignoring or amending its laws in order to compel the permitting of greenhouse-gas emissions." *Id.*

[38] EPA Interview, *supra* Chapter Eight, note 171; Interview with Jeff Reynolds, *supra* note 28; Telephone Interview with Melissa Savage, *supra* Chapter Eight, note 56; Senate Interview, *supra* Chapter Eight, note 95.

[39] *See, e.g.*, enforcement under the Clean Air Act, 42 U.S.C. § 7413 (2006), and under the Clean Water Act, 33 U.S.C. § 1319 (2006); EPA Interview, *supra* Chapter Eight, note 171; Interview with Mike Murphy, *supra* note 25.

[40] EPA Interview, *supra* Chapter Eight, note 171; Telephone Interview with Melissa Savage, *supra* Chapter Eight, note 56.

expect that it is more likely to support failing state programs with additional funding and technical assistance than it is to assume control.[41] Where meaningful state participation is critical to federal success, state bargaining power waxes.[42]

Criminal law negotiations present the opposite scenario, because federal law enforcement agencies hold the capacity advantage in realms of jurisdictional overlap. Lacking legal supremacy and with fewer resources to allocate over a broader array of enforcement obligations, state negotiators should have measurably less leverage in criminal enforcement bargaining. Nevertheless, some sources indicate that leverage conflicts are muted in this arena because conflicting interests are infrequent.[43] According to Roscoe Howard, former U.S. Attorney for the District of Columbia, criminal enforcement federalism bargaining proceeds with surprisingly little controversy because the incentives toward cooperation on both sides are powerfully aligned:

> There are very practical reasons for the copious amount of state-federal bargaining that goes on in the criminal realm. It's unbelievably helpful, and without it, both systems would bog down. . . . States may have less leverage in terms of fiscal and legal resources, but it doesn't really amount to much, because it's not really a zero-sum game. When we cooperate, everyone wins because a threat is taken off the street. The only contentious issue is credit—that's usually when there is competition for jurisdiction. But state prosecutors, sheriffs, and commonwealth attorneys are usually elected, and very sensitive to public image. They need credit. The federal guy at the table is always appointed. So it's usually easy to manage that.[44]

Aside from rare, high-profile cases, interjurisdictional criminal matters are seldom tried in both state and federal forums, so credit usually rests with whoever prosecutes.[45] (Of course, it is unlikely that all federalism bargaining is equally as harmonious, especially in regulatory contexts in which incentives are not so cleanly dovetailed.)

---

[41] Anonymous Interview with State Agency Official (Jan. 15, 2010) [hereinafter State Agency Interview]. State agencies generally assume the EPA is more likely to assist failing state programs than to terminate them, as may happen now that Michigan has requested to return delegated CWA authority due to Michigan's budget crisis. Interview with Mike Murphy, *supra* note 25 (explaining that it would cost the EPA more to issue individual permits than to fund failing state programs); *see Key Corps Official Faults States' Push to Oversee Wetlands Permits*, Inside the EPA, Apr. 24, 2009, 2009 WLNR 7604929 (reporting on Michigan's request).

[42] EPA Interview, *supra* Chapter Eight, note 171; Telephone Interview with Melissa Savage, *supra* Chapter Eight, note 56.

[43] Telephone Interview with Roscoe Howard, *supra* Chapter Eight, note 74.

[44] *Id.* (adding that bargaining proceeds smoothly "at least 90% of the time").

[45] The high-profile "D.C. Sniper" case offers the rare counterexample of multi-jurisdictional competition over prosecution rights. Virginia and Maryland competed over trying the defendants, and the FBI (which held the defendants after making the arrests) was ready to have them prosecuted federally if the states could not agree. Virginia ultimately convicted both defendants in the first trials, but Maryland also prosecuted one defendant to ensure against death penalty procedural issues. FBI BEHAVIORAL ANALYSIS UNIT, SERIAL MURDER: MULTI-DISCIPLINARY PERSPECTIVES FOR INVESTIGATORS (2008), http://www.fbi.gov/stats-services/publications/serial-murder/serial-murder-july-2008-pdf/.

Admittedly, it can be problematic to analyze leverage according to a binary state-federal metric, when policy-making leverage often shifts between coalitions of different state and federal actors. For example, one U.S. Senate attorney described how state-federal negotiations over "cap-and-trade" policy were complicated by the fact that state legislators did not want federal law to put all delegated state power into the hands of state governors.[46] Battles over the REAL ID Act reveal similar dynamics of cross-party alliances within federalism bargaining. According to one source, DHS Secretary Janet Napolitano agreed with the state criticism of the act, but her only leverage to pressure congressional amendment was to allow the December 31, 2009 deadline to expire without extensions in the face of massive state noncompliance.[47] She reportedly seriously considered this tactic, by which she hoped to shame her federal peers in Congress into revising the law, but she ultimately issued the extensions to avoid stranding millions of holiday travelers unable to board aircrafts without federally valid ID.[48] The complex interplay of independent municipal actors further complicates federalism bargaining dynamics.[49]

5. RELATIONSHIPS AND CONSULTATION: KEY BUILDING BLOCKS

Participants report that positive working relationships with counterparts are the bedrock of successful federalism bargaining.[50] Whether bargaining takes place in a collaborative enforcement context or in a policy-making context fraught with preemption conflict, frequent communication, mutual concern for shared interests, and mutual respect for differing interests are the key ingredients for progress. As an attorney within the EPA Administrator's Office explained,

> We spend a lot of time communicating with people in the field. It's so much harder to negotiate without that investment. If you haven't spent time getting that information and building those relationships, then the likelihood that you'll end up arguing over the shape of the table is much higher.[51]

As Rick Weeks, Chief Deputy Director of Virginia's Department of Environmental Quality, explained about his negotiations with federal partners, "[T]here usually is not a clear right answer—both parties can be right [about who should do what], so we look for solutions that

---

[46] Senate Interview, *supra* Chapter Eight, note 95 (describing how different state-side negotiators can compete with one another by negotiating directly with federal policy makers rather than as a unified block).

[47] Telephone Interview with Melissa Savage, *supra* Chapter Eight, note 56.

[48] *Id.*

[49] *See* Chapter Eight, notes 29–31 and accompanying text.

[50] Telephone Interview with Melissa Savage, *supra* Chapter Eight, note 56 ("To make these efforts work, it's all about relationship building.... [Who] matters most is the local career folks at both the state and federal levels."); Telephone Interview with Roscoe Howard, *supra* Chapter Eight, note 74; Interview with Laurie Ristino, USDA Gen. Counsel's Office, Wash., D.C. (Dec. 31, 2009); Interview with Rick Weeks, *supra* note 31.

[51] EPA Interview, *supra* Chapter Eight, note 171.

work for everybody."[52] When asked for the most important item in his negotiation toolbox, former U.S. Attorney Roscoe Howard said, "Knee pads—very useful when asking for things!"[53]

Subjects uniformly highlighted the importance of frequent consultation with counterparts.[54] Most praised their negotiating relationships as critical to the success of interjurisdictional governance, and agreed that more consultation was always preferable to less. Interview subjects believed the system works well as it stands, and were hesitant to suggest improvements (even when prompted, and even anonymously).[55] Several opined that altering the federalism bargaining marketplace with additional constraints or requirements was a bad idea, even considering negotiations in which they did not achieve their preferred results.[56] On the other hand, all agreed that consultation was only helpful when it was genuine, and several suggested revision of requirements that reward "hoop-jumping" over substantive communication.[57]

Subjects generally agreed that implementation and enforcement negotiations are the smoothest, because they involve a level of consultation considered optimal by both sides.[58] State participants noted that policy-making negotiations present a greater challenge, because there is less consultation than they believe is needed.[59] These negotiations are more difficult by nature, because states are usually reluctant to cede authority to the federal programs implicated—but many state participants do acknowledge the need for national leadership in

---

[52] Interview with Rick Weeks, *supra* note 31.

[53] Telephone Interview with Roscoe Howard, *supra* Chapter Eight, note 74.

[54] *E.g.*, EPA Interview, Part IV, Chapter Eight, note 171 ("The effectiveness of regulatory structure depends on [stakeholders] believing that the regulations are needed, make sense, and will be administered fairly—so if you have important stakeholders, be in frequent contact with them.").

[55] *E.g.*, Interview with Jeff Reynolds, *supra* note 28 and accompanying quote; Telephone Interview with Melissa Savage, *supra* Chapter Eight, note 56 ("I'd say that things are pretty good the way they are ... basically, bargaining is better than the alternative, and changes could always make things worse.").

[56] *E.g.*, EPA Interview, *supra* Chapter Eight, note 171; Interview with Jeff Reynolds, *supra* note 28; Telephone Interview with Melissa Savage, *supra* Chapter Eight, note 56 (no matter how unsatisfying the result, "any kind of negotiation is preferable to the top-down approach, because the states come in too many different shapes and sizes for the 'one-size-fits-all' approach to work well").

[57] *E.g.*, Telephone Interview with Melissa Savage, *supra* Chapter Eight, note 56 (noting that more consultation requirements "could slow down an already slow process," but that "mak[ing] sure Congress is at least well-informed is a good idea"). Another interviewee distinguished between "real give and take" ensuring that stakeholders are actually heard, and "listening sessions" where "a series of state stakeholders make a five minute speech about what they want while the federal people eat lunch, so they can check the box that says they listened." See EPA Interview, *supra* Chapter Eight, note 171. This source would not support "ineffective consultation requirements that end up costing time and resources disproportionate to the purpose they should serve, or that make it impossible to do work in real time." *Id.*

[58] *E.g.*, Interview with Mike Murphy, *supra* note 25; Interview with Jeff Reynolds, *supra* note 28; Interview with Rick Weeks, *supra* note 31.

[59] Interview with Mike Murphy, *supra* note 25; Telephone Interview with Melissa Savage, *supra* Chapter Eight, note 56; Interview with Rick Weeks, *supra* note 31.

appropriate regulatory realms, and note the helpfulness of a federal regulatory backstop in contexts where local enforcement is difficult or unpopular.[60]

A more common theme of concern among state participants is that federal policy makers underestimate the financial burden of new federal laws on states, and most prescribe greater consultation as the remedy.[61] Federal agencies often project the costs of new programs based on an assumption of full compliance at the outset, even though states almost always face significant enforcement expenses in bringing the regulated community up to new compliance standards.[62] After a recent lobbying effort by state interest groups, at least one source sees encouraging signs that federal agencies understand the need to be better informed by state partners.[63] For example, the Environmental Council of the States persuaded the EPA to form a "Cost of Rules Regulatory Workgroup" consisting of EPA and state representatives to recommend reforms to address this problem.[64]

6. UNDERLYING LEGAL UNCERTAINTY

A final feature warranting analysis is the substantive legal uncertainty that pervades many federalism bargaining forums about respective roles and legal limits (or who, in the end, should get to decide).[65] Negotiations take place in realms of overlapping state and federal jurisdiction where both governments have regulatory interests to protect, authority to wield, and obligations to fulfill.[66] Previous chapters identify the special obstacles for policy making in these realms posed by the Rehnquist Court's resurrection of classical dual federalism

---

[60] EPA Interview, *supra* Chapter Eight, note 171 ("[T]he flip side is that [states] are closer to the people, who, to them, are voters—so sometimes they ask us to take the hard line because it's politically safer to have us do it."); Interview with Jeff Reynolds, *supra* note 28; Interview with Jeff Weeks, *supra* note 31 ("Having the 800-pound gorilla in the closet is helpful!").

[61] Senate Interview, *supra* Chapter Eight, note 95 (acknowledging the concern); Telephone Interview with Melissa Savage, *supra* Chapter Eight, note 56 (emphasizing that greater state consultation would help); Interview with Mike Murphy, *supra* note 25 (same); Interview with Jeff Reynolds, *supra* note 28 ("Unfunded mandates cause good ideas to fail. . . You can see it in failing underfunded environmental programs. States could give federal agencies a realistic assessment of what the new law will require to make it work. States are different, and they have different resources—they have to be able to talk about this when the rule is being made, or else states end up in a bind, unable to get things done.").

[62] Interview with Mike Murphy, *supra* note 25.

[63] *Id.* (noting that he serves on this new committee as one of four state agency delegates).

[64] *Id.*; Information Management, Environmental Council of States, http://www.ecos.org/section/committees/information_management (last visited Nov. 29, 2010) (providing information on ECOS's Data Management Work Group, which coordinates with EPA to build information systems regarding, among other things, cost of compliance).

[65] *See supra* Chapter Eight, notes 1–21 and accompanying text.

[66] *See, e.g.,* Clean Water Act § 303, 33 U.S.C. § 1313(d) (2006) (governing water quality standard setting), discussed *supra* Chapter Eight, notes 244–46 and accompanying text; 33 U.S.C. § 1342(b) (governing pollution permitting), discussed *supra* Chapter Eight, note 70 and accompanying text; Clean Air Act, 42 U.S.C. § 7507 (providing states the choice between national or California emissions standards), discussed *supra* Chapter Eight, notes 249–55 and accompanying text; 42 U.S.C. § 7410(a)(1) (2006) (governing state implementation plans), discussed *supra* Chapter Eight, notes 242–43 and accompanying text

elements. Friction between the interjurisdictional reality in which governance takes place and the theoretical model animating the Court's adjudication of conflicts creates uncertainty about the kinds of federalism bargaining that are enforceable (and even desirable). As Professor Coase predicts, such uncertainty threatens bargaining optimality as an additional transaction cost.[67] If federalism bargaining plays such an important role in already challenging realms of jurisdictional overlap, then optimizing results by reducing uncertainty should be a priority.

Yet even as academics fret over the conflict, participants report that they rarely worry about it.[68] They may not be entirely certain about legal constraints in the background, but they report that this uncertainty does not impact most negotiations, where the shared objective is usually to solve a clearly shared problem.[69] As one state attorney reported,

> Nobody is thinking about the New Federalism cases, or at least I'm not anymore. I know they were supposed to rein in federal law, but that hasn't really happened. [I work with a] problematic law, and the boundaries are confusing. But everyone ploughs ahead with it anyway: "Forget whether we have the authority—we're just going to press ahead and do it because it's the right thing to do. . . ." Let the chips fall where they may.[70]

A federal attorney similarly explained, "federalism constraints operate in the background, but they are not usually on the minds of most legislative bargainers; the first priority . . . is to solve the problem and get a bill passed that can do it."[71] When I asked one state official whether he ever thinks about the lines of jurisdictional separation that the New Federalism cases draw, he responded simply: "No—because there are no bright lines [in this realm]! So no, we do not really give them much thought."[72] He then observed that the state attorney general's office might have a different answer, nodding humorously to the plain disjuncture between the focus of unilateral and bilateral federalism interpretation.[73]

---

[67] Coase, *supra* Chapter Seven, note 53, at 15–19.

[68] Telephone Interview with Roscoe Howard, *supra* Chapter Eight, note 74; Interview with Mike Murphy, *supra* note 25; Telephone Interview with Melissa Savage, *supra* Chapter Eight, note 56; Senate Interview, *supra* Chapter Eight, note 95; Interview with Rick Weeks, *supra* note 31.

[69] Senate Interview, *supra* Chapter Eight, note 95; *see also* Interview with Jeff Reynolds, *supra* note 28 ("As for awareness about federalism concerns—I think it goes over everyone's heads, at least in the terms you're using, but they are thinking about them in other language . . . it's on people's minds, but they just don't know what to do with it.").

[70] State Agency Interview, *supra* note 41; *see also* Telephone Interview with Melissa Savage, *supra* Chapter Eight, note 56 (reporting that although NCSL is mindful about federalism, "court cases aren't usually the first thing we're thinking of. . . . We try to stay up to date . . . but honestly, in that whole process, the New Federalism cases are pretty remote").

[71] Senate Interview, *supra* Chapter Eight, note 95 (adding, "most aren't thinking about whether things will be litigated for federalism reasons; maybe they did a little bit after [*Lopez* and *Morrison*], but that was years ago").

[72] Interview with Mike Murphy, *supra* note 25.

[73] *Id.*

Other subjects reported that genuine federalism issues do arise during intergovernmental bargaining, even if they are not regarded in those terms.[74] These include questions about which side must yield on a given implementation issue, or concerns about the appropriate degree of consultation in policy making.[75] Demystifying legal constraints would thus be an important way of bettering the federalism bargaining enterprise.[76] And to the extent that participants do not actively consider legal constraints during negotiation, careful design of the legal frameworks that provide opportunities for federalism bargaining is important.

B. Sources of Trade

Having identified many of the forums in which federalism bargaining takes place and many of the norms that operate within them, we reach the meat of the actual intergovernmental exchange. This section analyzes what it is, exactly, that federalism bargainers are trading on, and evaluates what constitutional or jurisprudential rules constrain these various media of exchange. Chapter Seven analyzed the exchange of Tenth Amendment entitlements to sovereign authority, an especially important chip at the federalism bargaining table. This section explores some of the other sources of trade in federalism bargaining.

In all bargaining, each side possesses something the other side wants or needs, and these become the sources of trade for negotiation. Things in demand are the unique currency within any given deal, and there is usually more than one form operating at any given time. The medium of exchange can be a tangible resource, an intangible legal authority, or adherence to a normative principle that motivates the choices made in negotiation. To be sure, the details that motivate the parties will vary in each specific context. But the media exchanged in most state-federal negotiations are of the following types: fiscal resources; regulatory authority, permissions, and other governance capacity; credit; and principle (the normative leverage that federalism values themselves exert on the negotiation). And though the legal constraints on some forms of trading are clear, others remain murky.[77]

I. THE POWER OF THE PURSE

When money is the most salient federal-state medium of exchange, it is likely a spending power deal. Federal dollars were the critical negotiating currency when Congress used highway funds to bargain with states for a national drinking age,[78] matched state funds to

---

[74] *Id.*; Interview with Jeff Reynolds, *supra* note 28; Senate Interview, *supra* Chapter Eight, note 95.

[75] For example, Jeff Reynolds reports ongoing state-federal conflict over waivers of sovereign immunity under various permitting provisions of the CAA, CWA, and RCRA. Interview with Jeff Reynolds, *supra* note 28.

[76] *Cf.* Coase, *supra* Chapter Seven, note 53, at 43 ("A better approach would seem to be to start our analysis with a situation approximating that which actually exists").

[77] *See, e.g., infra* notes 105–12, 119–24, and accompanying text (discussing the uncertain legal constraints regarding capacity and permissions trading).

[78] *See* South Dakota v. Dole, 483 U.S. 203, 206 (1987).

provide health insurance for poor citizens through Medicaid,[79] and conditioned education funds on the adoption of national standards in No Child Left Behind.[80]

South Dakota v. Dole articulated a set of loose constraints on how Congress may bargain through conditional spending: conditions must (1) promote the general welfare, (2) be unambiguous, (3) relate to the federal interest or program, and (4) not offend other constitutional requirements.[81] In other words, Congress may wield the power of its purse when there is a reasonable nexus between the strings attached to federal money and a legitimate federal purpose. Underscored by invalidation of the LLRWPA bargained-for commandeering, negotiating states must have genuine choices about whether to participate— although participation will be deemed voluntary even when agreed to under enormous economic pressure.[82] Finally, the deal cannot otherwise violate the Constitution—for example, Congress cannot bribe states to restrict free speech.

Congress thus bargains with a relatively free hand under the spending power, but the doctrine still yields points of uncertainty—as demonstrated by a recent series of federal circuit court cases challenging No Child Left Behind.[83] Although all states have chosen to participate in the program (in order to continue receiving federal educational funds),[84] ten school districts around the country recently sued over an NCLB provision they argued failed to meet *Dole's* unambiguousness requirement.[85]

In 2009 in *School District of the City of Pontiac v. Secretary of the Department of Education*, the U.S. Court of Appeals for the Sixth Circuit considered whether states could escape a spending deal they claimed was ambiguous, when the alternative interpretation was not one they could reasonably have believed at the time the deal was made.[86] The plaintiffs argued that NCLB included a provision that could be read to prohibit federal enforcement of state action (such as hiring or purchasing) that would require funding beyond what was provided under the act, even if the disputed action were necessary to meet the federal standards designated by the act.[87] The Department of Education (DOE) insisted that the provision merely prohibited federal actors from applying more stringent standards than specifically

---

[79] 42 U.S.C. §§ 1315, 1396n and related discussion, *supra* Chapter Eight, notes 225–46 and accompanying text.

[80] *See supra* Chapter Eight, notes 101–02 and accompanying text.

[81] 483 U.S. at 207–08.

[82] *See* Jim C. v. United States, 235 F.3d 1079, 1082 (8th Cir. 2000) ("[H]ere, the Arkansas Department of Education can avoid the requirements of Section 504 simply by declining federal education funds. The sacrifice of all federal education budget, approximately $250 million or 12 percent of the annual state education . . . would be politically painful, but we cannot say that it compels Arkansas's choice.").

[83] *See supra* Chapter Eight, notes 101–02 and accompanying text.

[84] Kafer, *supra* Chapter Eight, note 102 ("So far, no state has refused to participate, although a few isolated districts have pulled out; apparently the money is too good to pass up.").

[85] *See* Sch. Dist. of Pontiac v. Sec'y of Dept. of Educ., 584 F.3d 253 (6th Cir. 2009) (en banc) (school districts receiving federal funds under No Child Left Behind sued unsuccessfully for a declaratory judgment stating compliance with the act's provisions was not required if compliance led to increased costs not covered by federal funds).

[86] *Id.* at 259.

[87] *Id.* at 259–60. 20 U.S.C. § 7907(a) (2006) states: "General Prohibition. Nothing in this Act shall be construed to authorize an officer or employee of the Federal Government to mandate, direct, or control a State, local

mandated in the act.[88] The DOE argued that the provision was unambiguous in the context of the full statutory bargain, which clearly indicated that Congress was trading a set amount of funding for states' agreement to meet the stated federal standards by whatever means.[89]

Strikingly, this seemingly generic statutory interpretation case failed to produce a majority opinion from the Sixth Circuit, sitting en banc.[90] Sixteen judges split evenly over whether the case should be dismissed, embroiled in contrary positions about how the spending power's "clear notice" requirement should comport with the interpretation of the "core bargain" under consideration in a spending power deal.[91] The case thus asked the judges not only to evaluate ordinary statutory language, but also, in negotiation theory terms, the core elements of a state-federal bargain. For example, Judge Jeffrey Sutton favored dismissal because the plaintiffs' ambiguity argument would undermine the Act's "central tradeoff": providing states funds and flexibility to develop their own educational programs in exchange for accountability to federal standards.[92] Indicating the significance of this question for federalism bargaining more generally, a similar debate arose among the Supreme Court justices deciding *New York v. United States* over how to interpret the LLRWPA without vitiating the "core bargain" that the states had reached with Congress over its enactment.[93]

The Sixth Circuit's astonishing failure to win even a narrow judicial consensus in *Pontiac School District* indicates the sensitivity with which judges must employ tools of statutory interpretation within the federalism bargaining context. Although statutory interpretation tools are no different in spending power cases, the court struggled with the federalism implications of releasing states from bargained-for federal obligations on an alleged technicality that half the judges believed would void the core essence of the bargain the states had struck when they agreed to take the funds.[94]

In addition, and contrary to popular criticism of the spending doctrine, the decision indicates the seriousness with which the judiciary will evaluate clear notice questions. A similar

---

educational agency, or school's curriculum, program of instruction, or allocation of State or local resources, or mandate a State or any subdivision thereof to spend any funds or incur any costs not paid for under this Act."

[88] *Pontiac*, 584 F.3d at 284 (Sutton, J., concurring) (noting that plaintiff "must identify a *plausible* alternative interpretation").

[89] *Id.* at 272–76.

[90] *En Banc Sixth Circuit Rebuffs Panel, Affirms Dismissal of "No Child" Challenge*, 78 U.S.L.W. 1241 (Oct. 27, 2009). The district court voted to dismiss for failure to state a legitimate spending power claim; an appellate panel reversed, and the panel's decision was vacated when the Sixth Circuit reconvened to review the case en banc. Without a majority consensus, the district court's dismissal stands. *Id.*

[91] Seven judges voted to allow the claim on the merits, an eighth judge rejected their rationale but voted to remand, six judges voted to dismiss on the merits, and two judges voted to dismiss as nonjusticiable—yielding a tie on whether to dismiss. *Id.*

[92] *Pontiac*, 584 F.3d at 285–86 (Sutton, J., concurring) (noting that plaintiff's interpretation "fail[ed] to account for, and effectively eviscerate[ed], numerous components of the Act," and "would break the accountability backbone of the Act").

[93] *Compare* New York v. United States, 505 U.S. 144, 181 (1992), *with Pontiac*, 584 F.3d at 199 (White, J., concurring and dissenting).

[94] *See Pontiac*, 584 F.3d at 255–56 (describing the various parts of the opinions that each of the en banc judges did or did not join).

case is now pending in the Second Circuit,[95] indicating states' continuing dissatisfaction with NCLB. As this book goes to press, another important spending power question is working its way toward the Supreme Court in litigation challenging the 2010 health insurance reform law. Florida argued that the law's expansion of the Medicaid program is so coercive that it violates all five of the *Dole* factors, and though the district court overturned the law, it upheld it against the spending power challenge.[96] All observers assume that the Supreme Court will ultimately review the case, which offers an open invitation to revisit the factors in *Dole* to account for what the state alleges is an unprecedented Hobson's choice.

2. CAPACITY TRADING

The spending power is often the most salient medium of exchange in a deal, but spending power deals are always also about a less obvious, equally important source of trade: state regulatory capacity. Sometimes the federal government buys state cooperation to advance a regulatory agenda exceeding clearly enumerated powers (e.g., a national drinking age).[97] Elsewhere, Congress creates programs of cooperative federalism in commerce-related realms it could constitutionally manage from top to bottom but chooses not to, because the federal government lacks the sovereign authority, local expertise, boots on the ground, or perceived legitimacy—in short, the *capacity*—that state government can provide.[98]

Regulatory capacity is the power to make things happen—by whatever resources or institutional feature enables either side to accomplish an objective that the other cannot do as well. In spending power deals, Congress trades federal fiscal capacity for state regulatory capacity to implement goals it lacks the expertise or resources to implement alone (for example, in regulating stormwater or insuring poor children).[99] The states thus wield powerful leverage in spending power negotiations because they control a reservoir of legal authority, expertise, and enforcement resources that federal counterparts cannot replicate (at least without replicating the very structure of local government that creates this capacity).[100] The previously underappreciated power of the states in spending deals—first analyzed by Professor Roderick Hills[101]—has become increasingly appreciated. Bargaining participants generally understand federal dependence on state cooperation, especially in the environmental context.[102]

---

[95] *See* Connecticut v. Duncan, 612 F.3d 107 (2d Cir. 2010).

[96] Florida *ex rel.* Bondi v. U.S. Dept. of Health & Human Svcs., __F.Supp.2d__, 2011 WL 285683 (N.D. Fla., 2011) (finding the law unconstitutional but upholding it against the spending power challenge).

[97] *See* South Dakota v. Dole, 483 U.S. 203, 206 (1987).

[98] *See e.g.*, Coastal Zone Management Act, discussed *supra* Chapter Eight, notes 200–24 and accompanying text.

[99] *See id.*; Medicaid demonstration waivers, discussed *supra* Chapter Eight, notes 225–41 and accompanying text.

[100] NUGENT, *supra* Introduction, note 71, at 168–212; *cf. supra* Chapter Five, notes 80–85 and accompanying text.

[101] *See* Hills, *supra* Part I, Introduction, note 5.

[102] EPA Interview, *supra* Chapter Eight, note 171; Telephone Interview with Melissa Savage, *supra* Chapter Eight, note 56; State Agency Interview, *supra* note 41.

State capacity is not only important in spending power deals, as Bruce Babbit understood when he negotiated a partnership with California to link the independent ESA and NCCP regulatory programs.[103] In negotiating a straight exchange of state and federal capacity, he realized that the success of both programs would require combining federal multijurisdictional vision and authority with the local land use authority and outreach that only the state commanded:

> The jurisdiction of local officials ends at the municipal or county boundary; while developers continually threaten to pack up and go across that boundary to the next jurisdiction down the road where local officials will be more pliable and willing to accommodate their demands. Pondering how to engage with the community in the face of these realities, we circled back to the state government. . . . It was becoming excruciatingly clear that neither of us could make this work without the other. Though we had provided California with the missing ingredient of [an enforceable] development moratorium, only California could provide us with the necessary credibility, capacity for outreach to local communities, and planning capabilities. It was time to reach across partisan lines and try for a working partnership with the state.[104]

In other examples, federal regulatory capacity is the more important currency of exchange. For example, the states sought federal authority when they asked Congress's blessing to violate the dormant Commerce Clause through the LLRWPA, or when they embraced the EPA's ability to mediate the collective action problem of stormwater management under the Phase II Rule. When states lobby for federal leadership on climate policy, they are seeking federal capacity at levels of both legal authority and superior informational and financial resources.

At first blush, federal capacity trading seems innocuous, or at least no more troubling than the exchange of federal fiscal capacity for state regulatory capacity that regularly takes place under the spending power. Nevertheless, the U.S. Supreme Court's decision in 1992 in *New York v. United States* suggests that the parties may actually be less free to bargain over federal capacity than they are to bargain over federal money, a situation creating additional uncertainty about legal constraints.[105]

In *New York*, the Court constrained capacity bargaining more tightly than spending power bargaining, at least in the bargained-for-commandeering context.[106] After striking down the federalism bargain at the heart of the LLRWPA, the Court expressly opined that if Congress really wanted to bind states to their promises to take responsibility for their radioactive waste, then it should do so in a spending power deal rather than binding them directly.[107] But the decision misses the critical point that it was the states, not Congress, that initiated the negotiation. As Chapter Seven argues, a spending power deal could not have replicated the

---

[103] *See supra* Chapter Eight, notes 128–36 and accompanying text.

[104] BABBITT, *supra* Chapter Eight, note 131, at 70–71.

[105] *See* 505 U.S. at 182.

[106] *Id.*

[107] *Id.* at 158–59.

result the states sought, nor would the deal seem as palatable to Congress if proposed that way (i.e., "Please use your regulatory capacity to allow us to negotiate among ourselves without violating the dormant Commerce Clause, and by the way, also give us some money"!).[108]

New York is the only Supreme Court precedent directly on point (although *Printz v. United States* reiterated the Court's commitment to the anti-commandeering rule in prohibiting a similar directive to state executives).[109] However, *New York* clearly differentiated between the wide scope of permissible bargaining available when the medium of exchange is federal dollars and the narrower scope when the medium is federal regulatory capacity—even when the states consent, and the regulatory result is similar.[110] In both cases, the states negotiate for a different aspect of federal capacity: fiscal or regulatory. But the Court was clear that, even when asked, Congress does not have the same latitude to agree when money is not the medium.[111] As a result, lower courts face uncertainty in interpreting other federalism bargains that trade on federal capacity.[112]

3. THE POWER OF THE PERMIT

As a subset of capacity bargaining over legal authority, the medium of exchange can also be permission for one side to do something the other could prohibit. Although permission most often runs from federal to state actors, the taxonomy reveals a few interesting contrary examples.[113]

Sometimes, permission is negotiated through an explicit permitting program designed by Congress, such as ESA provisions allowing Incidental Take Permits in exchange for a qualifying habitat conservation plan.[114] Medicaid demonstration waivers present a hybrid between negotiations under the powers of the purse and the permit because they begin within a spending power deal, but involve subsequent negotiations for state permission to deviate from standard Medicaid requirements.[115] Other times, states might seek permission to modify federal law beyond the confines of a specific statute, as occurred when the states asked Congress to waive the dormant Commerce Clause through federal passage of the state-based solution in the LLRWPA.[116]

Occasionally, the power of the permit can broker trading in the opposite direction: the federal government negotiates for state permission to do something that the state could

---

[108] *See supra* Chapter Seven, notes 192–94 and accompanying text.

[109] Printz v. United States, 521 U.S. 898, 935 (1977). *But see* Reno v. Condon, 528 U.S. 141, 150–51 (2000).

[110] *See New York*, 505 U.S. at 166–67, 168.

[111] *See id.* at 168 (noting that "[w]here Congress encourages state regulation rather than compelling it, state governments remain responsive to the local electorate's preferences," without recognizing how bargained-for commandeering parallels spending power bargaining in a way that strains the compulsion analysis).

[112] *See infra* notes 119–24 and accompanying text (discussing the Phase II Stormwater Rule challenge).

[113] *See supra* Chapter Eight, notes 208–17 and accompanying text (CZMA consistency); *supra* Chapter Eight, notes 141–48 and accompanying text (FERC relicensing).

[114] *See supra* Chapter Eight, notes 122–36 and accompanying text.

[115] *See supra* Chapter Eight, notes 225–46 and accompanying text.

[116] *See supra* Chapter Seven, notes 12–23 and accompanying text.

otherwise prohibit. The Coastal Zone Management Act presents the clearest example, in that federal activity must receive state approval when it takes place within the three-mile zone of concurrent coastal jurisdiction.[117] Similarly, thanks to state-protecting features in the Clean Water Act, applications for federal licensing of hydroelectric dams often require final authorization from state actors that the project will not compromise water quality.[118]

As a subset of capacity bargaining, federal bargaining with the power of the permit suffers the same uncertainty in constraints that attends federal capacity bargaining in general. The point has never been litigated directly, but the two iterations of the Ninth Circuit's handling of a federalism challenge to the CWA's Phase II Stormwater Rule demonstrate the delicacy of the question.[119]

As discussed previously, when the Phase II Stormwater Rule was challenged in 2003 for violating the Tenth Amendment in *Environmental Defense Center v. EPA*, the Ninth Circuit needed two tries to securely uphold the modified bargained-for commandeering in the construction-permitting measure.[120] On its first try, it analogized the deal to spending power bargaining—reasoning that plaintiffs had waived their Tenth Amendment objections (as they would in a spending power deal) when they bargained to regulate construction pollution in exchange for permission to discharge polluted stormwater into federal waters.[121] When challenged on rehearing, the panel withdrew its analogy between spending and capacity bargaining, which lacked direct support in any Supreme Court precedent. Instead, it upheld the provision on the safer basis that the rule was not coercive because it allowed dissenters to opt out in favor of a separate permitting program for larger cities.[122] The Supreme Court declined to hear the case.[123]

Environmental Defense Center demonstrates just how unclear the law is regarding the power to bargain for permission in the absence of more specific Supreme Court precedent. The Court could conceivably find the reach of permission bargaining to be indistinguishable from spending power bargaining, as many of the reasons that justify the freewheeling power of the purse could also justify a freewheeling power of the permit.[124] Yet other considerations suggest that the Court may not tolerate as broad a reach for permissions bargaining. Permitting authority may be more vulnerable to bargaining abuse, because inherent political limitations on use of the spending power may not apply to permissions bargaining. (After all, though Congress must enact politically unpopular taxes to amass negotiating currency under the spending power, it costs comparatively little to create permitting currency by passing new

---

[117] *See supra* Chapter Eight, notes 200–24 and accompanying text.

[118] *See supra* Chapter Eight, notes 141–48 and accompanying text.

[119] *See supra* Chapter Five, notes 49–67; *see also supra* Chapter Seven, notes 218–21 and accompanying text. *See* Envtl. Def. Ctr., Inc. v. EPA (*EDC I*), 319 F.3d 398 (9th Cir. 2003), *vacated* 344 F.3d 832 (9th Cir. 2003); Envtl. Def. Ctr., Inc. v. EPA (*EDC II*), 344 F.3d 832 (9th Cir. 2003) (confirming *EDC I*'s affirmation of the rule against a Tenth Amendment challenge).

[120] *Id.*

[121] *EDC I*, 319 F.3d at 411–19.

[122] *EDC II*, 344 F.3d at 847–48.

[123] *See* Tex. Cities Coal. on Stormwater v. EPA, 541 U.S. 1085, 1085 (2004) (denying certiorari).

[124] *Cf.* South Dakota v. Dole, 483 U.S. 203, 206–07 (1987).

federal limits that states must negotiate their way out of.) Without greater clarity on the permissible scope of capacity bargaining, courts may continue to duck the issue as the Ninth Circuit did, adding to the environment of legal uncertainty in which federalism bargainers negotiate.

4. THE NORMATIVE LEVERAGE OF FEDERALISM VALUES

The powers of the purse, the permit, and the power to get things done represent the mainstay of federalism bargaining currency, but there is another important medium of exchange that motivates decisions at the table. State and federal negotiators are not only driven by issue-specific needs such as funding, authority, or other forms of regulatory capacity. Sometimes bargaining results are influenced by regard for the American system of federalism itself—the desire to reach an outcome that respects the constitutional design and that harnesses the ways in which divided local and national authority serve the ultimate purposes of government. This more ethereal currency may best be understood as regard among the participants for the values of federalism themselves, and it is often present even when negotiators are not using the specific vocabulary of federalism to define it.[125]

For example, Laurie Ristino of the U.S.D.A. General Counsel's Office described how she approaches negotiations with state actors:

> As a federal attorney, you have an extra burden, you have this public trust. You're an advocate for the federal government, but you're also a public servant, so you have to think about how to uphold the law and act in a way that really advances the public benefit. You understand that this is a shared system of power, and that you have to be careful, and that preemption is not the favored approach. Sometimes you have to throw down the gauntlet of federal power, but as soon as you do, you lose the ability to get compromise, to bring the situation to a point where everyone feels like they're getting what they need and can move on.
>
> I was taught to watch my use of the Supremacy stick, to try to avoid using the word "preemption" or bring out the big guns. We work hard to find a compromise based on common ground, and only bring out big guns if [absolutely necessary]. We recognize that state actors may feel like the "little-guy" when they have to go up against the federal government with all its resources and legal supremacy. They may feel like they're going to get run over, so we try not to act in ways that justify those fears.[126]

On the state side, Jeffords Reynolds, staff attorney at the Virginia Department of Environmental Quality, describes his own approach to intergovernmental bargaining:

> I consider myself a trench lawyer. I'm in the trenches. I started out in JAG as a federal criminal attorney, then I was in private practice on oil and gas matters, and now I work

---

125. *E.g.*, EPA Interview, *supra* Chapter Eight, note 171; Interview with Jeff Reynolds, *supra* note 28; Interview with Rick Weeks, *supra* note 31.

126. Interview with Laurie Ristino, *supra* note 50 (composite quote).

with the state at DEQ. I've been an environmental attorney for fifteen years. Federalism issues were raised for me [early on in my practice], and I've always been sensitive to them. Federalism issues are extremely important in environmental realms because of the boundary-crossing problems in environmental law, like the Chesapeake. . . .

If it weren't for federal intervention, we wouldn't have so much critical [protection]. Where industry is involved, you really need the federal government to be forceful to achieve meaningful national standards. Technological and environmental changes have changed federalism, broken down some of the local prerogative. Environmental law is one area where federal strength is needed and appropriate. . . . The conventional wisdom is true that states lack leverage at the table. But do I think this means that the process is flawed? Not really. Things are as they should be, except that state finances need to be taken account of.[127]

Both lawyers indicate how the positions they take in intergovernmental bargaining are moderated by the values they associate with the proper roles of state and federal government within the American system. In this way, federalism values operate as an important motivator at the table, normatively impacting negotiators' choices just as the more material forms of currency do. They are especially evident in negotiations in which federal restraint or state cooperation goes beyond the strict limitations of capacity, based on constitutional and political considerations of role.[128]

As discussed above, negotiation theorists recognize this type of currency as "normative leverage," or the application of norms or standards that are persuasive to the other side for reasons that may be unrelated to the specific interests at stake.[129] Conventional examples of normative negotiating leverage include the do-unto-others principle, fair market value, respect for the rule of law, the persuasive value of precedent, and the consistency principle.[130] In the context of state-federal bargaining, negotiators' own regard for federalism values is a powerful source of leverage when it influences the outcome in ways unrelated to the individual interests at stake in the deal. Though participants concede that they rarely consider federalism at the level of specific Supreme Court precedents,[131] they report conscientious regard for the proper relationship between state and federal regulatory efforts during bargaining.[132] In other words, even without the formal vocabulary of federalism, they are moved by the fundamental values of federalism.

Federalism values help explain the motivation of both sides to engage in negotiated rulemaking and policy-making laboratory negotiations—even those within cooperative

---

[127] Interview with Jeff Reynolds, *supra* note 28 (composite quote).

[128] For example, the federal government could regulate interstate water allocation and external threats to federal lands much more than it currently does. *E.g.*, Interview with Laurie Ristino, *supra* note 50.

[129] SHELL, *supra* Part IV Introduction, note 12, at 3–4 (discussing normative leverage).

[130] Individuals prefer to see themselves as principled and consistent, rendering their previous statements and practices effective normative leverage if they attempt to negotiate a contrary result. *Id.* at 43–46 (discussing the normative leverage of the consistency principle).

[131] *See supra* notes 68–73 and accompanying text.

[132] *See, e.g., supra* note 126, *infra* note 135.

federalism programs—rather than alternatives that speak to contrary interests on both sides. Federal regulators have more control over administrative rulemaking through notice and comment, just as Congress could legislate more efficiently without state input in such policy-making laboratory contexts as Medicaid and the Coastal Zone Management Act. However, the value of state participation outweighs the federal interest in control. State influence over the formulation of federal law flows from the formidable subject matter expertise states hold and their interests as ultimate stakeholders in the given policy arena. Federal agencies want to hear from state participants so that they can establish solid, workable policies that respect the federalism issues that inevitably attend concurrent regulatory realms. As a source in the EPA Administrator's Office noted,

> We're thinking about the role and interest of the states in virtually everything we do, because the states are critical in everything we do. We don't use the word "federalism" to describe what we're thinking about, but there's almost nothing that we do in the field that doesn't involve state, local, and regional input. So thinking about [federalism] is a matter of agency culture by design.[133]

Meanwhile, states want input into federal policy making for the same reasons. Neither negotiated rulemaking nor cooperative federalism programs compel state participation. States are never required to negotiate, but the benefits of doing so include greater influence over the final result. States could opt for a Federal Implementation Plan administered by the EPA rather than designing and enforcing their own State Implementation Plans under the Clean Air Act, but their interests in regulatory participation generally outweigh contrary interests in frugality.[134]

Of course, some federal policies threaten financial or regulatory impacts that incentivize state participation without regard to respect for federalism (such as the imposition of unfunded mandates or preemption of state police power). Nevertheless, most values that make federalism good for governance—including checks, localism, and synergy—are in especially high relief in negotiated rulemaking and cooperative federalism programs. These values inform negotiations over the way that federal policies should take account of state interests—and vice versa—as both levels of government work to solve common problems. Deputy Director Rick Weeks of Virginia DEQ described his agency's regard for federalism values in these terms:

> We don't think about federalism so much in the generic terms. But we think about it in terms of who is really the right agency to be doing what. There are some things that really only the national government can do. For example, you need a national program to deal with air emissions, because of the way they move across state boundaries. This is less of an issue for water resources, which are more local—but then you have the

---

[133] EPA Interview, *supra* Chapter Eight, note 171.

[134] *See* 42 U.S.C. § 7410(a)(1) (2006); Siegel, *supra* Chapter Seven, note 5, at 1676 (discussing the fact that the majority of states create their own implementation plans, despite the option of relying on a federal implementation plan).

Chesapeake Bay situation. . . . And industry needs some certainty, which is hard to get without a national program. [There are other things that states do better.][135]

Nevertheless, at least one participant commented on the way that the normative leverage of federalism values can also be used, disingenuously, to manipulate decision makers.[136] The Senate attorney described the use of normative federalism leverage in interest group negotiations over a bill Congress had recently considered to protect aquatic species against invasives by authorizing the Coast Guard to regulate ballast water.[137] The new law might have preempted CWA provisions that also regulate invasive aquatic species, and the environmental community split over whether to support the new bill.[138] As the Senate attorney explained,

> We could have passed a bill, with industry support, that would have imposed much stricter national standards through the Coast Guard, and would have been much more likely to actually solve the problem [than the existing CWA provisions]. But some in the environmental community were unwilling to see any preemption of the CWA. They argued hard against the bill on grounds that preempting the CWA would dissolve the important state-federal program of cooperative federalism in the CWA, and touted how valuable that was. And they ultimately won the day by appealing to federalism this way . . . but *they* didn't really care about federalism! All they cared about was preserving their rights to litigate under the CWA.[139]

Congress thus manipulated normative federalism leverage in persuading others to reach their preferred outcome, even though (according to this source) they were not personally interested in federalism at all. The success of the gambit demonstrates the real normative power of federalism—but also how vulnerable it can be to opportunism. That said, the same problem holds true for all other ideals that exert normative leverage at the bargaining table, including legal precedent and even the do-unto-others principle, which are occasionally used by unscrupulous negotiators to manipulate an outcome desired for other reasons.[140]

Negotiations in which respect for federalism is a primary currency require few additional constraints. No precedent addresses this bargaining currency except cases praising federalism values themselves as worthy of legal protection.[141] Some scholars have reviewed

---

[135] Interview with Rick Weeks, *supra* note 31.

[136] Senate Interview, *supra* Chapter Eight, note 95.

[137] *Id.*; *see also* Brian Laskowski, *Coast Guard Considers New Rules to Regulate Ballast*, Great Lakes Echo, Oct. 8, 2009, http://greatlakesecho.org/2009/10/08/coast-guard-considers-new-rules-to-regulate-ballast-takes-up-where-congress-left-off/ (discussing the failure of the bill at issue, which passed the House but not the Senate).

[138] See Environmental Impact Statements, 73 Fed. Reg. 79473 (Dec. 29, 2008) for the proposed CWA regulations.

[139] Senate Interview, *supra* Chapter Eight, note 95.

[140] *E.g.*, Shell, *supra* Part IV Introduction, note 12, at 56–57 (discussing the negotiating ramifications of the fact that there are often two reasons people do things—"a good one and the real one").

[141] *See, e.g.*, United States v. Morrison, 529 U.S. 598 (2000); United States v. Lopez, 514 U.S. 549 (1995); Gregory v. Ashcroft, 501 U.S. 452 (1991); *supra* Part I Introduction, note 2.

the historic problem of federalism opportunism, or the invocation of federalism values as cover for unrelated policy goals.[142] However, Balanced Federalism proposes tools to help distinguish between bargaining that is truly consistent with federalism values and that which is disingenuous.[143]

5. CREDIT

Finally, credit represents a form of negotiating currency that triggers no legal analysis but can politically motivate federalism bargainers. In contexts of jurisdictional overlap, state and federal actors may compete for credit in situations in which it is difficult to share. For example, leverage dynamics in state-federal interest group bargaining are impacted by competition between governors and federal legislators from their states over credit for regulatory programs the legislator enacts that the governor implements.[144]

Similarly, in the criminal enforcement context, contests over credit are the principal driver of otherwise rare jurisdictional competition.[145] Credit is harder to share in the criminal context because arrests and trials are usually only made once, in either state or federal hands. Although federal law enforcers are appointed, state law enforcers are usually elected, and thus more sensitive to matters of credit and favorable publicity. Thus, under-resourced state prosecutors who are usually happy to cede cases to federal partners may balk when asked to cede a high-profile case that could impact public opinion, preferring to keep the investigation, arrests, and trial within the state system.[146] At least one former federal prosecutor notes that federal actors are sensitive to this dynamic and work hard to protect the interests of their state partners.[147] Nevertheless, many federal prosecutors also have career ambitions hinging on credit,[148] and at least one former state official recalls vivid state resentment over issues of credit and federal intervention in settling enforcement cases under the Clean Air Act's New Source Review program during the early 2000s.[149]

---

[142] *E.g.*, Devins, *supra* Chapter Two, note 8, at 133–35; *supra* Chapter 1, notes 160–61 and accompanying text and Noonan, *supra* Chapter Five, note 115 (discussing Michael Brown's invocation of federalism to defend his agency after Hurricane Katrina).

[143] *See supra* Chapter Six (proposing criteria for balancing); *infra* Chapter Ten (proposing criteria for deference).

[144] Senate Interview, *supra* Chapter Eight, note 95 ("States also have leverage because they tend to get the credit for programs that are funded with federal money their federal legislators have brought home to them. Governors get credit for programs that a Senator worked hard to pass—which can be very frustrating for senators!").

[145] *See* Telephone Interview with Roscoe Howard, *supra* Chapter Eight, note 74 ("The only contentious issue is credit—that's usually when there is competition for jurisdiction. But state prosecutors, sheriffs, and commonwealth attorneys are usually elected, and very sensitive to public image. They need credit. The federal guy at the table is always appointed. So it's usually easy to manage that.").

[146] *Id.*

[147] *Id.*

[148] For example, Attorney General Eric Holder and Homeland Security Secretary Janet Napolitano began their careers as U.S. Attorneys.

[149] Interviews with Anonymous Official, State Attorney General's Office (May 18, 2010 & July 2, 2010).

Because of its potential to impact the personal careers of participants, negotiating credit stands apart from the other sources of trade as the most vulnerable to disjuncture between a federalism bargainer's personal interests and his or her constituents' interests. For this reason, negotiations in which credit forms an important medium of exchange may raise comparatively more serious principal-agent concerns than others—an issue of import for the following interpretive analysis.

10

THE PROCEDURAL TOOLS OF INTERPRETIVE BALANCING

THE TAXONOMY AND participant reports establish that federalism bargaining is widespread in areas of jurisdictional overlap, affording procedural response to the uncertain question of *who decides*. The boundary between state and federal power is far more contingent and collaboratively determined than acknowledged by conventional federalism rhetoric. But the fact that federalism bargaining is frequently used does not resolve whether or when it accomplishes the objectives of Balanced Federalism.

With the preceding positive account and conceptual vocabulary of federalism bargaining in place, Chapter Ten advances to the final stage of the Balanced Federalism proposal: the interpretive potential of intergovernmental bargaining (and the lessons it bears even for unilateral balancing). The role of the political branches articulated here rounds out the equipoise that Balanced Federalism seeks not only among the competing values of federalism, but in the contributions of the three branches—at all levels of government—in locating the appropriate balance in each instance. Understanding that even the structural safeguards of federalism bargaining may be overcome, it provides tools to distinguish between processes of ordinary political deal making and that in which genuinely bilateral decision making accomplishes constitutional goals.

In exploring the procedural basis for interpretive legitimacy and the role of judicial review, this chapter argues that negotiated governance is not just a de facto response to regulatory uncertainty about who should decide. When it meets the threshold criteria, it can be—in and of itself—a constitutionally legitimate way of deciding. More than just a means to an end, carefully crafted federalism bargaining can be a *principled* means of allocating state and federal authority in realms of concurrent interest. As such, federalism bargaining can be part of the solution to the interpretive quandary that has preoccupied jurists over generations, affording checks and balance in interbranch federalism interpretation as well as vertical federalism policy making. This analysis provides the needed theoretical justification to explain the critical role that federalism bargaining already plays in constitutional terms.

As discussed in Chapter Eight, the conventional federalism discourse has probed how the three federal branches unilaterally interpret federalism directives by defining the contours, goals, and limits implied by the American system of dual sovereignty. However, scholars have alternatively worried that legislative political safeguards operate intermittently, and that judicial constraints are ill-suited to navigating the porous boundaries of jurisdictional overlap. The role of executive actors has been poorly understood until recently, and the discourse has virtually ignored the potential for state input beyond the provision of locally-elected federal representatives. However, properly designed federalism bargaining supplements unilateral approaches by interpreting, bilaterally, who should decide within the pockets of uncertainty unresolved by conventionally understood forms of interpretation. Sometimes these pockets reflect legal uncertainty about which side is entitled to act, and other times they reflect pragmatic uncertainty about how best to allocate authority to advance the overall federalism project.[1] Either way, as described in Chapter Five, persistent uncertainty about who decides can lead to litigation, regulatory stagnation, and even abdication.

To resolve this uncertainty, unilateral federalism interpretation deciphers meaning from legal text, applies precedent, and yields substantive answers to precise questions about where federal authority ends and state authority begins. Unilateral interpretive tools are useful in many contexts—but where they fall short, bilateral bargaining fills the substantive gaps with procedural interpretive tools. Intergovernmental bargaining grounds the legitimacy of its outcome in the legitimacy of its process, when that process is consistent with the principles of fair bargaining on the one hand, and federalism values on the other.

The procedural principles of fair bargaining are the necessary prerequisite, and procedural consistency with federalism values—themselves procedural values of good governance—are the ultimate criteria for interpretive deference. Once again, the values-based theory of federalism on which this inquiry is predicated locates the central purpose of federalism in the good governance values that it fosters: checks and balances, accountability and transparency, local autonomy and innovation, and the problem-solving synergy available between local and national regulatory capacity.[2] Federalism bargaining that is procedurally faithful to these values constrains public behavior to be consistent with constitutional goals, just as federalism interpretation intends.

Although the federalism literature has previously entertained process-based theories of federalism that eschew judicial review of substantive rules,[3] it is now realizing the benefits of partnering selected substantive rules with more flexible procedural constraints that can

---

[1] As discussed in Part II, legal uncertainty involves the reach of state or federal authority—for example, over intrastate wetlands regulation after *SWANNC* and *Rapanos*, or in gray area preemption cases such as *Geier* or *Garamendi*. Practical uncertainty revolves around the best allocation of national and local authority where both are needed (for example, in a national climate regulatory policy).

[2] *See supra* Chapter Two.

[3] *See supra* Chapter Eight, notes 1–6 and accompanying text.

enforce federalism norms within uncertain factual contexts.[4] Because negotiated governance process is often more amenable to assessment by federalism criteria than the substantive outcome itself, bilateral bargaining can do interpretive work where unilateral tools are unavailing. Still, legislative and executive interpretive bargaining is appropriately checked by limited judicial review that scrutinizes procedure, and if satisfied, defers to substance. If bargaining challenged on federalism grounds meets the procedural criteria, then the court defers to the negotiated results; if it fails the test, then the court reviews the substance of the deal de novo. Qualifying examples are thus shielded from judicial interference, while federalism bargaining abuses remain subject to judicial oversight. (Judicial review of nonfederalism challenges—including faithfulness to other constitutional or statutory requirements—are untouched by the proposal.)

Federalism bargaining is hardly collapsing from judicial interference; the taxonomy demonstrates a healthy variety of bargaining notwithstanding doctrinal constraints. Nevertheless, Chapters Nine and Ten also reveal several examples of judicial federalism doctrine and insensitivity that frustrate certain forms of intergovernmental bargaining. The anticommandeering doctrine chills strong forms of bargained-for commandeering,[5] and sovereign immunity doctrine can interfere with certain bargaining between state and federal agencies.[6] The *Pontiac School District* case suggests how judicial insensitivity to bargaining dynamics within negotiated governance could result in unnecessary invalidation of potentially qualifying bargaining.[7] Underlying legal uncertainty about the permissible scope of federalism bargaining could also pose obstacles to potentially fruitful bargaining if participants are sufficiently unnerved by litigated examples, or by the lack of clarity discussed in Chapter Nine about what legal rules operate in constraint of available sources of trade.[8]

The following analysis thus focuses on those forms of federalism bargaining that are most amenable to public scrutiny, judicial challenge, and procedural review. Less formal versions of federalism bargaining (such as intersystemic signaling or amicus brief writing) may serve valuable purposes within the system, but they do not invite interpretive deference because they do not yield a record that would enable procedural review. Review of even unilateral federalism balancing that is markedly faithful to the procedural federalism criteria may suggest a degree of related judicial deference—although it will be necessarily weaker, given the absence of the structural safeguards that bilateral balancing affords. The chapter concludes by evaluating examples from the Chapter Eight taxonomy against the new interpretive criteria, and by offering recommendations for engineering even greater structural support for federalism values in federalism-sensitive governance.

---

[4] *See, e.g.*, Erin Ryan, *Negotiating Federalism*, 52 B.C. L. Rev. 1 (2011) (from which this part of the book is drawn); Ashira Pelman Ostrow, *Process Preemption in Federal Siting Regimes*, 48 Harv. J. on Legis. 289 (2011).

[5] *See supra* Chapter Seven; *see also supra* Chapter Eight, notes 111–16 and accompanying text.

[6] *See supra* Chapter Nine, note 75.

[7] *See supra* Chapter Nine, notes 84–95 and accompanying text.

[8] *See supra* Chapter Nine, notes 77–149 and accompanying text. In Coasian terms, such uncertainty creates transaction costs that could cost marginal utility from underutilized bargaining. *See supra* Chapter Nine, note 67 and accompanying text.

A. Procedural Tools of Interpretation

Bargaining brings two important sets of procedural tools to federalism interpretation, the former common to all forms of negotiation and the latter specific to federalism bargaining: respectively, the legitimizing principle of mutual consent, and the procedural constraints of federalism values.

1. THE LEGITIMIZING PRINCIPLE OF MUTUAL CONSENT

Bargaining has always been the last resort for bridging dissensus—the time-honored means of moving toward "the good" in the absence of agreement about the perfect.[9] Dissensus pervades the historical discourse about how the Constitution adjudicates jurisdictional competition—and as negotiation theorists have long recognized, when consensus on a substantive outcome is elusive, next best is consensus on a procedure for moving forward.[10] In the absence of agreement over the precise contours of federalism directives in a given regulatory context, bargaining thus offers invaluable procedural tools. In the federalism context, as in others, the primary procedural tool offered by negotiated resolution is the fundamental fairness constraint of mutual consent.

For thousands of years, human cultures worldwide have turned to procedurally based negotiated outcomes to resolve persistent substantive disagreements,[11] essentially substituting procedural consensus for the missing substantive consensus. Negotiators defer to bargained-for results on the simple grounds that, even without a more convincing substantive rationale, the results must hold merit if all parties are willing to abide by them. In other words, even if the parties cannot agree on a rationale that explains *why* the negotiated result is the right outcome, if they can actually agree on some outcome that they all prefer to a stalemate—then, goes the wisdom of bargaining, that outcome must be a worthy choice. If it was reached through a fair process of exchange, then it holds decisional gravity that exceeds random chance or a forced alternative, and warrants deference in the future.

---

[9] *Cf.* Lee Anne Fennell, *Hard Bargains and Real Steals: Land Use Exactions Revisited*, 86 Iowa L. Rev. 1, 26–27 (2000) (recognizing the bargaining environment generated by the modern zoning model); Carol M. Rose, *Planning and Dealing: Piecemeal Land Controls as Problem of Local Legitimacy*, 71 Cal. L. Rev. 837, 849 (1983) (discussing use of bargaining in land use development proposals); Erin Ryan, *Zoning, Taking & Dealing, The Problems and Promise of Bargaining in Land Use Planning Conflicts*, 7 Harv. Negot. L. Rev. 337, 348 (2002) (advocating bargaining as a "rational strategy for pursuing the public good under conditions of substantive uncertainty about its shape or meaning").

[10] *E.g.*, Fisher & Ury, *supra* Chapter Seven, note 175, at 56–80; Susan Carpenter, *Choosing Appropriate Consensus Building Techniques and Strategies, in* The Consensus Building Handbook, *supra* Chapter Eight, note 32, at 61–97; Dwight Golann & Eric E. Van Loon, *Legal Issues in Consensus Building, in* The Consensus Building Handbook, *supra* Chapter Eight, note 32, at 495–522. *See also* John Dewey, Reconstruction in Philosophy (1920) (outlining a philosophy of pragmatism); William James, Pragmatism (1907) (same); William H. Simon, *Solving Problems v. Claiming Rights: The Pragmatist Challenge to Legal Liberalism*, 46 Wm. & Mary L. Rev. 127 (2004). Indeed, the resort to procedural solutions on substantive dissensus is demonstrated by the simplest of all negotiating tools—the "split-the-difference" principle.

[11] *Cf.* Shell, *supra* Part IV Introduction, note 12, at 5.

Mutual consent ensures fairness, on the theory that no deal is reached unless all parties agree, and reasonable negotiators will not bargain for results that contravene their best interests. If negotiators truly understand their own interests and pursue them faithfully, we can trust that they will not consent to terms that undermine their interests. And as long as they can truly walk away from the bargaining table when no beneficial deal is possible, then we can also trust that the terms they negotiate benefit all parties more than no agreement at all. Lacking substantive consensus about why the outcome is legitimate, the parties thereby substitute procedural consensus in agreeing to defer to the results of fair bargaining.

The principle of mutual consent underlies our faith in the bargaining process, conferring legitimacy on negotiated results so long as these three underlying assumptions are met: (1) bargaining autonomy, (2) interest literacy, and (3) faithful representation. First, the parties must have a genuine opportunity to walk away from the bargaining table, or the fact of agreement cannot substantiate its value as preferable to the alternatives. Similarly, to be confident that negotiated results are truly preferable to the status quo, we must be confident that the parties really understand their best interests and are not operating under a personal or situational disability causing substantial misinformation or misunderstanding. Finally, we must be confident that the agents involved in the bargaining process are faithfully representing the interests of the principals on whose behalf they are negotiating, rather than contrary personal interests.

When these prerequisites are met, bargaining can be a valuable means of resolving a jurisdictional contest where governance must press forward despite legal or practical uncertainty (such as that clouding environmental, public health, and financial regulatory law). The more the facts in a given negotiating scenario support these core assumptions, the more confidence in the legitimacy of the bargained-for result. However, when any of these assumptions are unduly stressed by the facts in the scenario, less legitimacy is conferred. In this regard, federalism bargaining legitimacy can suffer from points of vulnerability on each of the three assumptions of mutual consent.

First, there may be instances in which unequal bargaining power unduly compromises bargaining autonomy. For example, some critics argue that spending power deals strain the assumption of bargaining autonomy. They urge that state consent cannot justify the legitimacy of spending power deals because the balance of leverage far favors the federal government, with its daunting control over fiscal resources on which state programs rely.[12] The leverage imbalance is arguably similar in non-spending power contexts, such as negotiated rulemaking, where the federal government has trumping legal authority and superior fiscal resources, and is often empowered as the scribe of the proceedings.

Courts have consistently rejected the argument that spending power deals are akin to federal contracts of adhesion, holding fast to the view that states are free to forgo federal funds if they really prefer that alternative.[13] As the Ninth Circuit has observed, establishing a workable metric for spending power coercion is daunting:

---

[12] *See* Baker & Berman, *supra* Chapter Four, note 17, at 517–21.

[13] *See* South Dakota v. Dole, 483 U.S. 203, 207 (1987); Jim C. v. United States, 235 F.3d 1079, 1082 (8th Cir. 2000).

Does the relevant inquiry turn on how high a percentage of the total programmatic funds is lost when federal aid is cut-off? Or does it turn . . . on what percentage of the federal share is withheld? Or on what percentage of the state's total income would be required to replace those funds? Or on the extent to which alternative private, state, or federal sources of highway funding are available? . . . [S]hould the fact that Nevada, unlike most states, fails to impose a state income tax on its residents play a part in our analysis? Or, to put the question more basically, can a sovereign state which is always free to increase its tax revenues ever be coerced by the withholding of federal funds— or is the state merely presented with hard political choices? The difficulty if not the impropriety of making judicial judgments regarding a state's financial capabilities renders the coercion theory highly suspect as a method for resolving disputes between federal and state governments.[14]

Both contract law and negotiation theory generally hold parties responsible for their choices when choice is available, and both differentiate between strong leverage and true coercion.[15] Even when the stronger party crafts terms without input from the weaker party, the latter can still decide whether its interests are better served by taking or leaving the proffered deal.

In addition, the argument may elide the considerable leverage states wield in controlling the regulatory capacity that federal spending power bargainers seek, thus mitigating the concern.[16] Much of the prior analysis proceeds from the premise that the reason state and federal actors bargain with one another is because they need each other. When bargaining occurs in contexts of overlap, it is because neither the federal nor state government has all the tools needed to address a given problem. The more the states possess capacity that the federal government needs to accomplish a desired objective, the more leverage the states have in bargaining, and the less likely the federal government can deny them meaningful bargaining authority. Thus, at least in the regulatory realms where federalism bargaining is most needed, it is least likely to be unfair.

That said, as the ability of the weaker party to meaningfully impact the negotiated outcome wanes, so too does the force of the constraint in conferring procedural legitimacy. Even deals that satisfy constitutional scrutiny under spending power doctrine may be understood as warranting more or less interpretive deference on procedural grounds, depending on the degree to which individual facts stress the assumptions of bargaining autonomy. Spending power bargaining in which states have more genuine input—such as the joint policy-making forms—may confer more interpretive legitimacy than those in which states consent as a legal matter but under substantial economic pressure. For example, states participating in spending power deals under Medicaid or the Coastal Zone Management Act seem relatively satisfied

---

[14] Nevada v. Skinner, 884 F.2d 445, 448 (9th Cir. 1989).

[15] See 17A C.J.S. CONTRACTS § 176 (2010) ("[O]ne may not avoid a contract on the ground of duress merely because he or she entered into it with reluctance, the contract is very disadvantageous to him or her, the bargaining power of the parties was unequal, or there was some unfairness in the negotiations.").

[16] See supra Chapter Nine, notes 97–112 and accompanying text; NUGENT, supra Introduction, note 71; Hills, supra Part I Introduction, note 5.

with their autonomy, but many have expressed frustration at their perceived inability to walk away from deals under the No Child Left Behind Act, unable to reject the proffered federal educational funds for fiscal reasons even when they dislike other terms in the deal.[17] Using this lens of analysis, state agreement to No Child Left Behind may be seen as warranting less procedurally based interpretive deference than state agreement to the terms of the Coastal Zone Management Act.

Mutual consent as a meaningful procedural constraint must also contend with the representation-based critique that state and federal agents may reach consensus in collusion with one another against the true interests of their principals, the citizens.[18] The concern that elected state officials might betray the interests of their constituents was among Justice O'Connor's chief rationales for the anti-bargaining holding in *New York v. United States*.[19] The tension between citizen principals and their elected agents in government is endemic to representational democracies, but as demonstrated in Chapter Seven, the danger of federalism collusion is least pressing when the medium of exchange is the sovereign authority at the heart of all federalism bargaining.[20] Indeed, when government agents bargain with their own regulatory authority, their interests are more aligned with those of their constituents than in many legal realms where government agents freely negotiate against constituents' interests (i.e., in setting time, place, and manner restrictions on citizens' exercise of free speech rights).[21] Both state and federal agents are unlikely to trade the basis of their power unless it is clearly justified by offsetting benefits (although, as noted in Part IV, bargaining in which credit is a particularly salient medium of exchange may warrant closer scrutiny[22]).

Nevertheless, the assumption that federalism bargainers faithfully represent their constituents underlies the principle of mutual consent as foundationally as do the assumptions that they act autonomously and in appreciation of their own interests. The more the facts depart from any of these assumptions, the less legitimate the resulting bargain. This is why an important prerequisite for legitimate federalism bargaining must be that the process remains sufficiently transparent for monitoring to ensure that the interests of principals and agents remain well-aligned (enabling citizens to hold representatives accountable for decisions made on their behalf).[23] Public law scholars have long worried about the undue sacrifice of transparency and accountability in the settlement of private litigation in order to promote the flexibility and creativity that accords negotiated dispute resolution.[24] However, scholars of negotiated governance have shown that there is no need to sacrifice transparency or

---

[17] *See supra* Chapter Eight, notes 200–224 (CZMA), 101–02 (NCLB), and accompanying text; *see also supra* Chapter Nine, notes 83–95 (NCLB) and accompanying text.

[18] *See* McGinnis & Somin, *supra* Chapter Two, note 4, at 90 (warning that states may collude with the federal government in undermining federalism constraints).

[19] *See* 505 U.S. 144, 182–83 (1992) (worrying that "powerful incentives" might lead bargaining officials to betray their principals), and related discussion, *supra* Chapter Seven, notes 102–05 and accompanying text.

[20] *See supra* Chapter Seven, notes 105–16 and accompanying text.

[21] *Id.*

[22] *See supra* Chapter Nine, notes 144–49.

[23] *Cf.* Telephone Interview with Professor Lawrence Susskind, *supra* Chapter Eight, note 152.

[24] *See* Fiss, *supra* Chapter Eight, note 175, at 1078–82.

accountability in intergovernmental negotiation when the relevant stakeholders are appropriately involved and both final and draft documents become part of the record.[25] Moreover, judicial review remains available to enforce basic due process norms if any are threatened by a particular instance of bargaining.

Finally, any legitimacy conferred on federalism bargaining by the principle of mutual consent must confront the concern that federalism-related interests may be overwhelmed by competing nonfederalism interests during deal making, or that negotiators may not fully understand their interests. The more there is reason to doubt that negotiators understood their own interests, the less legitimacy is conferred on the bargain—and it is for that reason that we give less effect to contracts negotiated under conditions of legal disability such as infancy or mental illness. Federalism bargainers are unlikely to suffer from those conditions, but if an analogous circumstance were somehow to arise, it would surely weaken the binding effect of mutual consent.

However, the concern that federalism interests may be overcome by other substantive concerns proves less pressing in the context of bilateral governance. Long-sighted negotiators are unlikely to underestimate the importance of their federalism interests, as thorough consideration puts values of the constitutional order in their rightful place. Even so, what about negotiators preoccupied by more immediate needs? For example, consider the criminal enforcement negotiation in which state actors agree to cede jurisdiction over a case to federal agents because it will free up scarce local resources to investigate other cases lacking a federal nexus. Does the fact that both parties believed this result was in their best interest really mean that the result was consistent with their federalism-related interests? In fact, does this agreement really have anything to do with federalism at all?

The answer is yes, demonstrated by the structural safeguards of bilateral bargaining introduced in Chapter Nine. Structural safeguards perform even when bargainers are not subjectively considering federalism, because the incorporation of state and federal input into the negotiated outcome intrinsically advances most of the values that federalism stands for in the first place. At a minimum, federalism bargaining engages the values of checks, localism, and interjurisdictional synergy, structurally reinforcing most federalism values beyond what unilateral safeguards can accomplish. But while bilateral safeguards are powerful, they are not infallible, especially if there is insufficient transparency to ensure faithful representation and meaningful democratic participation. As ultimately revealed below, the federalism coherence of examples like the criminal enforcement exchange can be further scrutinized through

---

[25] See, e.g., SUSSKIND & CRUIKSHANK, supra Chapter Eight, note 38, at 176; Carrie Menkel-Meadow, The Lawyer's Role(s) in Deliberative Democracy, 5 NEV. L.J. 347, 348–49 (2005); Lawrence E. Susskind, Deliberative Democracy and Dispute Resolution, 24 OHIO ST. J. ON DISP. RESOL. 395, 399–401 (2009); Lawrence E. Susskind, Keynote Address: Consensus Building, Public Dispute Resolution, and Social Justice, 35 FORDHAM URB. L.J. 185, 192, 202 (2008). The notion that legislation and litigation provide greater transparency is also flawed, given how much decision making takes place beyond the reach of the stenographer. Telephone Interview with Professor Lawrence Susskind, supra Chapter Eight, note 152. See Amy J. Cohen, Revisiting against Settlement: Some Reflections on Dispute Resolution and Public Values, 78 FORDHAM L. REV. 1143 (2009) (arguing that Fiss's procedural critique is really embedded in a substantive vision advocating a particular form of public morality).

federalism bargaining's other procedural tools of interpretation—those that inhere in the specific context of federalism-sensitive governance.

2. THE PROCEDURAL CONSTRAINTS OF FEDERALISM VALUES

When substantive federalism interpretation fails to resolve jurisdictional contest, federalism bargaining's second set of procedural constraints can bridge interpretive gaps in ways that parallel the procedural benefits of generic bargaining. Just as bargaining procedurally legitimizes negotiated results in the absence of substantive agreement, these procedural constraints legitimize interpretive bargaining in the absence of substantive federalism consensus. The constraints of mutual consent continue to operate, but validly interpretive federalism bargaining also affords procedural consistency with the fundamental federalism values of checks, accountability, localism, and synergy.

Interpretive process proves invaluable when substantive federalism interpretation becomes stymied, because achieving procedural consistency with federalism values is both easier to accomplish and easier to assess. Why? Critically, because the federalism values *themselves* are essentially about process. Consider the values explored in Chapter Two. At the end of the day, they don't tell us much about the actual substance of good government or policy decisions, at least not directly. Rather, they tell us about the *process* by which good governance is conducted. The check-and-balance value advocates governance processes in which multiple sources of power (or capacity) counter and backstop one another's influence, ensuring a balance of political leverage. Accountability seeks transparency in governance, requiring process conducted openly enough to ensure that informed citizens can participate meaningfully at all levels of the democratic process. The localism value champions processes of governance that enable local variation and innovation of the sort promised by the great "laboratory of ideas." The problem-solving value advocates process that enables us to harness the interjurisdictional synergy between the unique capacities of local and national government where both are needed.

Checks, accountability, localism, and synergy are not coextensive with all purposes of government, but they do align federalism with the fundamentals of good governance that extend to international norms (and beyond domestic "states' rights" rhetoric).[26] Moreover, as demonstrated in Chapter Two, these values are in tension, such that fortifying one can weaken another in a given scenario. Thus, just as no theory of bargaining can forecast the outcome of every case, no theory of federalism bargaining can guarantee the best balance in each instance.[27] Constitutional federalism sets the structural baselines through which good governance values will be realized in practice, but controversial substantive outcomes are ultimately debated in policy spheres beyond the reach of the federalism project. For that reason, this inquiry stops short of distinguishing between rightly and wrongly decided outcomes in individual cases. Instead, it distinguishes between rightly and wrongly conducted processes.

---

[26] *Cf.* Galle & Seidenfeld, *supra* Part IV Introduction, note 3, at 1942.

[27] *But see* SOL ERDMAN & LARRY SUSSKIND, THE CURE FOR OUR BROKEN POLITICAL PROCESS (2008) (arguing that consensus-building processes in political negotiations *do* produce substantively superior outcomes).

Procedural consistency with federalism values helps ford the impasse caused by interpretive uncertainty just as fair bargaining principles ford generic substantive impasse. Certain areas in federalism jurisprudence are plagued by dissensus, as demonstrated by the volume of controversy over recent Supreme Court federalism decisions in contexts of overlap, especially in environmental law. The federalism canon demonstrates how frequently reasonable legal minds disagree about whether a given outcome is consistent with constitutional federalism (for example, Justice White believed the LLRWPA was consistent, while Justice O'Connor did not).[28] Part of the problem, as suggested in Chapter Three, is that different adjudicators may be relying on different theories of federalism—but another factor is that there are simply so many considerations operating in addition to federalism concerns that it can be difficult to disentangle them at the level of the substantive outcome.[29] By contrast, and especially when the challenged governance was negotiated, it is much easier to assess whether the federalism bargaining *process* was consistent with federalism values, thus redirecting the federalism inquiry to more fruitful territory.

To be sure, the process values implied within federalism can be understood in relation to more substantive constitutional norms—for example, the importance of procedural checks and balances are rooted in the importance of protecting individual rights against government, and the importance of governmental accountability and transparency is rooted in democratic ideals. Early process-based theories of constitutional interpretation were critiqued for their failure to account for the Constitution's clear commitment to such substantive norms as protections for human rights, free press, and private property, and for eliding how good constitutional process is but a means to constitutionally sanctioned substantive ends.[30] For this reason, claims to protect individual rights properly trump conflicting claims to protect structural federalism, as they have in various chapters of the nation's struggle to achieve civil rights.[31] However, in evaluating a federalism bargaining challenge unencumbered by an independent rights claim—for example, a claim about whether the state or federal government should determine a given environmental policy—evaluating whether the negotiation process honored checks, accountability, localism, and synergy gets as close to what we ask of the federal system as evaluating the policy outcome itself. (Again, recall that the federalism claim is not about the policy itself—just *who decides* the policy.)

In contrast to adjudicating rights, a substantive realm in which the Constitution's directions are relatively clear, the adjudication of federalism draws on penumbral implications in the text that leave much more to interpretation.[32] The boundary between state and federal authority is implied by structural directives such as the enumeration of federal powers in

---

[28] New York v. United States, 505 U.S. 144, 181–83, 189–90 (1992).

[29] Tension between federalism values at the substantive level further compounds interpretive difficulties.

[30] *Cf.* Laurence H. Tribe, *The Puzzling Persistence of Process-Based Constitutional Theories*, 89 YALE L.J. 1063, 1065–72 (1980) (critiquing John Ely's process-based theory of interpretation in DEMOCRACY AND DISTRUST, *supra* Chapter Eight, note 6, and emphasizing the Constitution's substantive commitment to human rights and individual dignity).

[31] *See supra* Introduction, notes 80–89 and accompanying text; *cf.* CHOPER, *supra* Introduction, note 6, at 176 (differentiating constitutional protections for individual rights and structural federalism).

[32] *See supra* Chapter One, notes 1–33 and accompanying text.

Article I and the retention of state power in the Tenth Amendment,[33] but neither commands the clarity of commitment that the Constitution makes to identifiable individual rights.[34] Setting aside marginal uncertainty about the extent that "no law" really means *no law* in the First Amendment context, the Constitution is comparatively clear in its substantive commitment to free speech and free exercise.[35] It is equally clear on the allocation of certain state and federal powers, such as which is responsible for waging war (the federal government) and which is responsible for locating federal elections (the states).[36] But the document gives less guidance about the correct answers to the federalism questions that become the subject of intergovernmental bargaining, such as how to balance local and national interests in coastal zone management, or how to allocate state and federal resources in criminal law enforcement.[37] For these reasons, negotiated federalism is not only inevitable but appropriate, and arguably constitutionally invited—at least when negotiations take place within the boundaries of federalism values that are most directly understood as procedural directives.

Bargaining that procedurally safeguards rights, enhances participation, fosters innovation, and harnesses interjurisdictional synergy accomplishes what federalism is designed to do—and what federalism interpretation is ultimately for. As such, it warrants interpretive deference from a reviewing court, or any branch actor interrogating the result. Of course, not all federalism bargaining will do so. Bargaining that allocates authority through processes that weaken rights, threaten democratic participation, undermine innovation, and frustrate problem solving is not consistent with federalism values and warrants no interpretive deference. The more consistency with these values of good governing process, the more interpretive deference is warranted; the less procedural consistency with these values, the less interpretive deference is warranted.

Just as not all federalism bargaining warrants deference, it bears emphasis that not all regulatory matters warrant federalism bargaining. Many regulatory arenas are not ripe for state-federal bargaining at all, as they involve clearly designated areas of state or federal jurisdiction about which there is no legitimate claim for overlap.[38] Even in contexts of legitimate

---

[33] U.S. CONST. art. I, § 8; amend. X.

[34] *See* Jesse H. Choper, *The Scope of National Power vis-à-vis the States*, 86 YALE L.J. 1552, 1554–57 (1977).

[35] U.S. CONST. amend. I.

[36] U.S. CONST. art. I, sec. 8 (empowering Congress to declare war); art. I, sec. 4 (delegating responsibility for the location of congressional elections to the state legislatures).

[37] *Cf.* Choper, *supra* note 34, at 1556 ("The functional, borderline question posed by federalism disputes is one of comparative skill and effectiveness of governmental levels. . . . Whatever the judiciary's purported or self-professed special competence in adjudicating disputes over individual rights, when the fundamental constitutional issue turns on the relative competence of different levels of government to deal with societal problems, the courts are no more inherently capable of correct judgment than are the companion federal branches. Indeed, the judiciary may well be less capable than the national legislature or executive in such inquiries, given both the highly pragmatic nature of federal-state questions and the forceful representation of the states in the national process of political decisionmaking.").

[38] For example, except in the most indirect intersystemic signaling sense, state actors would not normally bargain with the federal government over the prosecution of a war, or over foreign policy—and when they have, they have faced foreign affairs preemption. *See* Am. Ins. Assoc. v. Garamendi, 539 U.S. 396, 429 (2003) (preempting a California law requiring insurers doing business in the state to disclose Holocaust era insurance policies);

overlap, federalism bargaining need not trump all other means of federalism interpretation or values balancing; it merely adds tools where unilateral activity is less competent.[39] The more a given federalism question can be resolved through conventional interpretive means, the weaker the need for bilateral interpretive tools. Still, these are powerful interpretive tools for use by all branches of government. Ex ante, consistency with federalism values, including respect for clearly delineated authority, can be engineered into the bargaining process. Ex post, federalism bargaining can be judicially reviewed for procedural consistency with these values.

Indeed, the important interpretive roles by political actors in vertical federalism bargaining are enhanced by the horizontal check of judicial review. The availability of limited judicial review strengthens the institution of federalism bargaining in a variety of ways. The potential for neutral judicial oversight smooths leverage imbalances and due process problems that could otherwise frustrate mutual consent, compromise checks and balances, and hinder local participation. Judicial review gives procedural requirements for accountability and transparency enforceable bite. Just as parties to a contract bargain more efficiently when secure in the knowledge that fair bargaining norms are protected by contract law, so too will federalism bargaining parties negotiate more productively when secure that the process must be consistent with constitutional and fairness norms.[40] Contrasted with pure political safeguards, interpretive work by the political branches that is made falsifiable by judicial review will command greater political respect. Moreover, to the extent that the carrot of judicial deference provides meaningful incentive to engineers and participants, the proposal will encourage intergovernmental bargaining that better harmonizes with federalism values, thus advancing the goals of federalism itself.

Nevertheless, judicial review of federalism-related challenges to the products of legitimate bargaining should be limited by a threshold inquiry for interpretive integrity—sheltering instances where the bargaining process itself offers the best realization of federalism values. The reviewing court's first task should be to scrutinize the bargaining process for consistency with the procedural principles of fair bargaining and federalism values. If process passes muster, then the outcome warrants deference as a legitimate way of determining who gets to decide. The court should not interpret the allocation of rights as though legitimate federalism bargaining never took place (as, for example, the Supreme Court did in *New York v. United States*).[41] When federalism and fair bargaining principles are honored this way, we can trust that the process is achieving constitutional goals, and that the need for negotiation itself provides important structural safeguards.

Crosby v. Nat'l Foreign Trade Council, 530 U.S. 364, 373–74 (2000) (preempting a Massachusetts law limiting state entities and contractors from doing business with Myanmar). Similarly, federal actors would not normally bargain with states over the establishment of local governments, or the provision of local fire service.

[39] *See supra* note 1 (discussing uncertainty remaining after conventional methods).

[40] In this respect, the security afforded by judicial review confers a sort of forward-looking exit valve to substantiate the "walk-away" principle of genuine consent, as participation may be more meaningfully consensual when parties agree from this position of relative security.

[41] 505 U.S. at 174–75; *supra* Chapter Seven (discussing this example of failed bargained-for commandeering).

Of course, if the threshold inquiry shows that the bargaining process is not consistent with the requisite criteria, then the reviewing court should be free to assess the substance of the negotiated outcome de novo under whatever judicial federalism doctrine is raised. Negotiations that, on balance, violate federalism values should be rejected as interpretive devices. Negotiations that fail one or more of the assumptions underlying mutual consent also confer weakened interpretive legitimacy. Some of these failures may require less of a binary scale and more of a sliding one; for example, even a bargain that is consensual for legal purposes may slide uncomfortably down the legitimacy scale as the assumptions that underlie mutual consent are stressed. Bargaining that strains the consensual nature of agreement, that excludes relevant stakeholders, or in which participants may not fully understand implicated interests all require more careful scrutiny.

Judicial review of federalism bargaining would thus be unlimited in three circumstances. First, if the challenged intergovernmental bargaining takes place beyond the defensible realm of jurisdictional overlap, it receives no interpretive deference. Second, if the challenged bargaining fails the court's threshold procedural review, then the court reviews the substance of the outcome de novo, applying its own interpretive judgment on the federalism-related challenge. Third, nonfederalism-related challenges to the products of valid interpretive-federalism bargaining warrant ordinary judicial scrutiny—limiting judicial deference only to federalism challenges, and not other claims of constitutional or statutory violation. Otherwise, however, judicial review should be limited to scrutiny of the bargaining process regarding fairness and federalism principles, deferring to results in a procedural analog to rational basis review.[42] This enables an interpretive partnership between the political and judicial branches that harnesses what each best contributes to federalism implementation while honoring the premise of *Marbury v. Madison*.[43]

Accordingly, judicial deference to interpretive legislative and executive bargaining need not undermine judicial supremacy in protecting the rights of insular minorities against the majoritarian impulses of the political branches, or in enforcing nonfederalism-related statutory commands against state or federal administrative agencies. Imagining its application to the Phase II Stormwater Rulemaking demonstrates the precision of the proposed procedural test: the Tenth Amendment challenge that entangled the rule in years of additional litigation would have been dismissed from judicial consideration upon satisfaction of the procedural criteria, but challenges alleging specific failures under the Clean Water Act would have been independently judicially resolved (as they were in the initial case).[44]

---

[42] United States v. Carolene Prods. Co., 304 U.S. 144 (1938) (distinguishing rational basis review from strict scrutiny).

[43] 5 U.S. 137 (1803) (affirming judicial review as a constitutional check on the political branches).

[44] *See supra* Chapter Five, notes 49–67 and accompanying text; Chapter Six, discussion surrounding note 36; Chapter Seven, 218–21 and accompanying text (discussing the Phase II Rule); Envtl. Def. Ctr., Inc. v. EPA, 344 F.3d 832, 855–58 (9th Cir. 2003) (remanding two parts of the Phase II Rule to ensure compliance with specific Clean Water Act requirements).

In administering procedurally based deference, courts could draw from that which is applied to agency decision making under the Administrative Procedures Act[45] (and state analogs), and the interpretive deference federal courts give to agency statutory interpretation under *Chevron v. NRDC*.[46] New Governance scholars have also proposed theories of judicial review that position courts to monitor and incentivize problem-solving processes rather than adjudicate substantive disputes.[47] Review of bargaining autonomy, interest literacy, and faithful representation would rely on familiar judicial tools from contract law, agency law, and due process interpretation, and courts could draw from established federalism jurisprudence and scholarship in articulating the tests for procedural consistency with federalism values.[48] For example, the Chapter Six judicial balancing test, though more focused on the substantive implications of good federalist process, provides a road map of analogous considerations for procedural review.[49]

At a minimum, courts reviewing for consistency with checks and balances should ensure that the process did not violate other rights, that neither party was coerced or undermined during negotiations, and that any long-term impacts of the bargain on future intergovernmental relations were adequately considered. Accountability review should ensure that the process by which a bargain was reached was sufficiently transparent, produced an adequately reviewable record, followed any established protocols, maximized opportunities for public participation, and meaningfully involved affected stakeholders. Localism review should ensure that local interests were represented, that the process maximized opportunities for subsidiarity-based innovation through local variation and competition, and that there was adequate opportunity for interjurisdictional experimentation prior to the implementation of a national solution. Synergy review should ensure that the process maximized opportunities to assess and exploit comparative advantages in allocating and coordinating authority. Federalism bargaining that yields little record for procedural review, such as intersystemic signaling, warrants little judicial deference.

Articulating a role for judicial review raises the fair question of whether the need for policing bargaining abuse is worth the risk that courts will misassess procedure during their review. As with all legal innovations, the transition period may yield difficult cases as the judiciary settles into a new pattern of precedent. However, the overall thrust of the proposal is to

---

[45] Administrative Procedures Act, 5 U.S.C. §§ 551–559 (2006) (requiring deference to administrative action taken in accordance with the requirements of the statute).

[46] 467 U.S. 837, 842–43 (1984) (holding that courts should defer to an agency's reasonable interpretation of the statute it administers if statutory ambiguity requires interpretation). Notably, the doctrine of *Chevron* deference evolved to limit judicial interference in agency interpretation, but courts maintain substantial discretion in deciding the threshold issue of statutory ambiguity. Judicial review of federalism bargaining could take a similar turn, highlighting an area of uncertainty in how the proposal might evolve and an opportunity for further theorizing.

[47] *See, e.g.*, Simon, *supra* Chapter Eight, note 51; Susan Sturm & Joanne Scott, *Courts as Catalysts*, 13 COLUM. J. EUR. L. 565 (2007).

[48] For example, courts might assess whether the bargaining results were distorted by an abusive power imbalance, critical but unavailable information, inadequate stakeholder representation, inadequate public oversight, or non-impartial mediators, or by bargaining agents' private financial interests or desire for personal credit.

[49] *Cf.* Chapter Six, text accompanying notes 14–33.

reduce judicial interference with federalism bargaining. It does so primarily by providing theoretical justification for the role intergovernmental bargaining already plays in interpreting federalism quandaries, offering guidance, security, and encouragement to the engineers and practitioners of worthy examples. It also adds a new layer of defense against whatever existing doctrinal challenges may threaten its results. At a minimum, shifting emphasis from substantive to procedural review renders less onerous the problems of judicial discretion in federalism interpretation discussed in Chapter Six.

In contrast to previous process-based proposals, judicial oversight of federalism bargaining is available but limited in comparison to the status quo. Outcomes challenged on federalism grounds are assessed for procedure before substance; if the bargaining process satisfies the criteria, then the court defers to the substance of the negotiated result. The proposal thus amplifies the thrust for limited judicial review in Chapter Seven and potentially short-circuits other judicial challenges to federalism bargaining—including the judicial balancing test proposed in Chapter Six, if the challenged governance is the product of federalism bargaining. It is designed to prevent the judiciary from invalidating the results of challenged federalism bargaining that is ultimately faithful to federalism values, even if it does so in ways vulnerable to traditional judicial doctrine (as was the bargaining over the LLRWPA and the Phase II Stormwater Rule). Yet it does not provide any new grounds for challenging federalism bargaining in court. The proposal thus provides a new defense against negotiated federalism challenges without offering additional sources of doctrinal challenge—reducing the overall impact of judicial constraints while preserving courts' ability to police for abuses.

Because the Chapter Six judicial balancing test is also designed to adjudicate faithfulness to federalism values, the two tests might yield similar results in many cases. However, the Chapter Six balancing test asks the judiciary to evaluate governance at the substantive level, while this proposal asks the judiciary to evaluate it at the procedural level first—ideally a cleaner and less subjective task. To clarify how they would work together, if an instance of federalism bargaining were challenged on Tenth Amendment grounds (or indeed, on any federalism doctrinal grounds), the court should begin with the limited procedural review described here. If the challenged bargaining fails the criteria for procedural deference, then the court would go on to apply substantive review. Because it should reach the same results as the intermediate Chapter Seven proposal for deference to consensual commandeering (and provides more refined criteria for evaluating mutual consent), the Chapter Ten proposal for deference subsumes the Chapter Seven standard. Federalism challenges to unilateral governance (such as the Tenth Amendment or preemption claims discussed above) remain intact under the Chapter Six balancing test or other applicable federalism doctrine.

Returning at last to the criminal enforcement example, recall the negotiation in which state actors cede a case to interested federal agents in order to direct scarce resources to cases without a federal nexus (and assume it follows the model described in the taxonomy).[50] Applying the above analysis shows that procedure and outcome resonate with both fairness and federalism values. The bargaining takes place in a realm of legitimate jurisdictional overlap, and the bargaining parties satisfy the requirements of mutual consent by agreeing freely

---

[50] *See supra* Chapter Eight, notes 71–80 and accompanying text.

to an outcome that advances the legitimate law enforcement interests of their principals. Checks are satisfied because both parties meaningfully participate in the decision to allocate authority this way, constitutional guarantees of other implicated rights remain in force, and the bargain does not threaten other sovereignty concerns in the state-federal relationship. If we assume case files are adequately prepared and relevant rules of criminal procedure are followed, the bargain poses no significant trade-offs against accountability values. It honors localism values by involving state participation in the decision making and by shifting to a federal approach only after adequate local experience indicates the value of the trade. Finally, the regulatory partnership harnesses synergy in allocating authority along lines of comparative advantage.

Thus, in a world of scarce resources, what looks like a straightforward cost-benefit analysis proves not only a reasonable way to allocate contested jurisdiction, but a wise one that takes advantage of the capacity each has to offer. The deal ensures that the case at hand is investigated (federally) while increasing the likelihood that other cases get better attention from the only available (state) authority. Were the same decision rule applied in all such cases—such that federal enforcement interests in an area of concurrent jurisdiction effectively removed it from state reach without benefit of public process—the quantifiably different trade-offs against checks and localism values would warrant closer examination. But real-world law enforcement officials seem to understand the difference, because state actors are generally unwilling to cede this kind of blanket authority for cost-saving purposes,[51] and federal actors that do focus on whole categories of cases work hard to create collaborative enforcement programs that share planning, oversight, and credit with state partners.[52]

Importantly, whether bargaining is consistent with federalism is not an inquiry into the bargainer's subjective considerations. A procedurally legitimate bargain advances federalism values even if negotiators never think about federalism during the process. As in many areas of law, the focus is not on the black box of the mind, but on objective manifestations. If the negotiation process safeguards individual rights, enables democratic participation, fosters jurisdictional innovation, and harnesses problem-solving synergy—or if it does so on balance more than it detracts from those values—then the process is consistent with constitutional federalism regardless of what the participants thought about while negotiating. Solid federalism engineering in design of bargaining forums can thus facilitate constitutional objectives just as *Miranda* warnings engineer behavior consistent with Fourth Amendment values regardless of the subjective views of individual police officers.[53]

Moreover, as discussed above, the structural dimensions of federalism bargaining ensure protection for federalism values that transcends the subjective considerations of participants. The bilateral nature of negotiations—forging consensus that necessarily balances state and federal interests in resolving the first-order policy issue at hand—should advance checks, localism, and synergy almost by definition. When bargaining is engineered to enhance democratic participation, it can also satisfy the criteria of accountability. In this way, federalism bargaining offers structural support for federalism values that is independent of participant

---

[51] Telephone Interview with Roscoe Howard, *supra* Chapter Eight, note 74.

[52] *See supra* Chapter Eight, notes 78–80 (discussing gun violence and child pornography collaborations).

[53] Miranda v. United States, 384 U.S. 436, 441–42 (1966).

motivations and unavailable at the level of unilateral balancing. That said, even unilateral governance that procedurally honors the federalism values may warrant some lesser degree of judicial deference when challenged on federalism grounds. Still, although unilateral policy making may herald interpretive potential in proportion to its satisfaction of similar criteria, negotiated governance provides structural support to federalism values that unilateral regulation can never truly replicate.

To reiterate the critical caveats, the interpretive potential within federalism bargaining does not mean that every bargain between state and federal actors will always be faithful to federalism, nor does it mean that all federalism-sensitive governance should be negotiated. Scholars have already shown that some instances of state-federal bargaining are more consistent with these values than others, demonstrating variable interpretive potential.[54] By corollary, federalism bargaining that fails this test is not inherently bad; it just cannot confer interpretive legitimacy. Fortunately, both judicial review and the political process afford able mechanisms for flushing out true violators. In the most egregious cases, bargains that violate federalism principles will reallocate authority even beyond the pockets of uncertainty in existing jurisprudence. In these cases, bad federalism bargaining will be weeded out judicially by a court applying clear precedent independent of procedural review. Alternatively, bargained-for-results in legitimate contexts of overlap that are reached in contravention of good governance procedures are likely to distinguish themselves as bad governance. An otherwise legal bargain reached in a process that blurs boundaries, obfuscates accountability, undermines localism, and harnesses no meaningful problem-solving synergy is as unlikely to survive long politically as it is to withstand judicial review.

This evaluation of bargaining procedure operates from the ex ante perspective, enabling the proposed procedural review and suggesting the potential for engineering interpretive federalism bargaining forums. In other words, when the bargaining process is designed to safeguard rights, participation, innovation, and synergy, the proposal assumes that federalism bargaining will harmonize with federalism as a procedural matter without reference to the substantive results. Of note, however, bargained-for results that advance federalism values at the more challenging substantive level are further evidence of good federalism process. To this end, the negotiation literature offers encouraging empirical evidence that correlates the use of similar procedural tools with outcomes that are highly consistent with federalism values.[55] For example, Professor Lawrence Susskind has empirically evaluated volumes of governance outcomes against criteria of fairness, efficiency, stability, and wisdom,

---

[54] *See, e.g.*, Alejandro E. Camacho, Lawrence E. Susskind & Todd Schenk, *Collaborative Planning and Adaptive Management in Glen Canyon: A Cautionary Tale*, 35 COLUM. J. ENVTL. L. 1 (2010) (critiquing an example of suboptimal federalism bargaining for failure to allow meaningful stakeholder participation).

[55] *See* Carrie J. Menkel-Meadow, *San Francisco Estuary Project*, in THE CONSENSUS BUILDING HANDBOOK, *supra* Chapter Eight, note 32, at 818. *See, e.g.*, LAWRENCE SUSSKIND & OLE AMUNDSON, USING ASSISTED NEGOTIATION TO SETTLE LAND USE DISPUTES: A GUIDEBOOK FOR PUBLIC OFFICIALS (1999) (analyzing the results of 105 cases); Kirk Emerson et al., *Environmental Conflict Resolution: Evaluating Performance Outcomes and Contributing Factors*, 27 CONFLICT RESOL. Q. 27 (2009) (analyzing the outcomes of sixty different mediated agreements among local, state, and federal governments); Freeman & Langbein, *supra* Chapter Eight, note 163 (reporting on empirical data in studies of collaborative governance).

and his results suggest that negotiated governance consistently outperforms alternatives.[56] He convincingly argues that these criteria closely align with federalism values, noting that the problem-solving qualities of negotiation naturally advance localism and synergy values, while representation is the key to successful accountability and transparency.[57]

B. Evaluating Interpretive Bargaining

Application of this interpretive framework to the taxonomy indicates those forms in which the bargaining process itself may prove more protective of federalism than judicially enforceable doctrine—and those in which it may not. Not coincidentally, interpretive integrity closely tracks the primary sources of trade, anointing bargaining in which federalism values provide important normative leverage as the most reliable. This section evaluates which forms of federalism bargaining hold the greatest interpretive potential for allocating authority or shepherding collaboration, and identifies circumstances in which each form is most and least useful. It begins with a review of general regulatory features that indicate when federalism bargaining is most promising and those that should raise red flags of concern.

In general, the more a regulatory context draws on complementary state and federal capacities, the more opportunities there are for productive integrative exchange. Regulatory problems characterized by rapidly changing data, which may benefit from adaptive management or other incremental and contingent policies, are also good candidates for intergovernmental bargaining. When regulatory approaches to new interjurisdictional problems have yet to be proven, the potential for local innovation and interjurisdictional competition render federalism bargaining approaches a good option. Governance involving public goods and common pool resources are also amenable to regulatory bargaining, especially when policy making or implementation requires multiple points of intervention along the jurisdictional scale. Regulatory matters that match a need for state land use authority or other basic police powers with spillover concerns requiring federal oversight are especially ripe for federalism bargaining, given the important interest linkages, complementary regulatory capacities, and comparatively even positive and negative leverage. The more evenly balanced the leverage and well-represented the stakeholders, the more freely the rest of the bargaining may proceed.

Other regulatory features suggest where federalism bargaining may not be the best approach. Strong incentives that might lead state and federal bargainers to collude in opposition to constitutional or statutory commands should raise red flags that bargaining not foster

---

[56] Lawrence Susskind & Jeffrey Cruikshank, Breaking the Impasse: Consensual Approaches to Resolving Public Disputes 14 (1987). *See* sources cited *supra* note 55.

[57] Telephone Interview with Professor Lawrence Susskind, *supra* Chapter Eight, note 152. Professor Susskind explained: "These criteria are indistinguishable to me from the federalism values [of checks, accountability, localism, and synergy]. Preserving fairness is what checks and balances are for. Wisdom is about local innovation—allowing parties to apply all the information at hand to do the best thing possible in their unique circumstances. Stability is bound up with accountability—you don't have to keep revisiting the issue, because stakeholders were involved in the process and approved the result. Problem-solving synergy is bound up with efficiency." *Id.*

opportunities to evade public oversight or erode the rule of law. Bargaining should proceed cautiously, if at all, when regulatory matters pit individual rights against majoritarian interests. Where it is impossible to provide effective representation of all relevant stakeholders at the bargaining table, unilateral policy making may be preferable to federalism bargaining. Where uniformity is critical and efficiency is at a premium, unilateral efforts may also be preferable. Where intergovernmental relationships have irretrievably broken down, federalism bargaining may not function well. Unyielding dissensus behind the state line (leading to holdouts and other transaction costs) limits the scope of productive bargaining, as do uncertainties regarding legal bargaining entitlements. The more leverage gaps or participation concerns strain mutual consent, the more other procedural constraints are needed to preserve bargaining legitimacy.

I. THE NORMATIVE LEVERAGE OF FEDERALISM VALUES

Unsurprisingly, bargaining in which the normative leverage of federalism values heavily influences the exchange offers the most reliable interpretive tools, smoothing out leverage imbalances and focusing bargainers' interlinking interests.[58] Negotiations in which participants are motivated by shared regard for checks, localism, accountability, and synergy naturally foster constitutional process and hedge against nonconsensual dealings. All federalism bargaining trades on the normative values of federalism to some degree, and any given negotiation may feature it more or less prominently based on the factual particulars.[59] Yet the taxonomy reveals several forms in which federalism values predominate by design, and which may prove especially valuable in especially fraught federalism contexts: negotiated rulemaking, policy-making laboratory negotiations, and iterative federalism.[60] These examples indicate the potential for purposeful federalism engineering to reinforce procedural regard for state and federal roles within the American system.

Negotiated rulemaking between state and federal actors improves upon traditional administrative rulemaking in fostering participation, localism, and synergy by incorporating genuine state input into federal regulatory planning.[61] Most negotiated rulemaking also uses professional intermediaries to ensure that all stakeholders are appropriately engaged and to facilitate the search for outcomes that meet parties' dovetailing interests.[62] For example, after discovering that extreme local variability precluded a uniform federal program, Phase II stormwater negotiators invited municipal dischargers to design individually tailored

---

[58] *See supra* Chapter Nine, notes 125–43 and accompanying text.

[59] *See* Interview with Laurie Ristino, *supra* Chapter Nine, note 50; *see also* Interview with Jeff Reynolds, *supra* Chapter Nine, note 28.

[60] See *supra* Chapter Eight, notes 152–293 (discussing, inter alia, the Phase II Stormwater Rule, which was devised via negotiated rulemaking; the Coastal Zone Management Act, which was drafted using policy-making laboratory negotiations; and emissions standards under the Clean Air Act, which were developed following a process of iterative federalism).

[61] *See supra* Chapter Eight, notes 153–97 and accompanying text.

[62] McMahon & Susskind, *supra* Chapter Eight, note 160, at 154–55.

programs within general federal limits.[63] Considering the massive number of municipalities involved, the fact that the rule faced legal challenge from only a handful of Texas municipalities testifies to the strength of the consensus through which it was created.

By contrast, the iterative exchange within standard notice-and-comment rulemaking— also an example of federalism bargaining—can frustrate state participation by denying participants meaningful opportunities for consultation, collaborative problem solving, and real-time accountability. The contrast between notice-and-comment and negotiated rulemaking, exemplified by the two phases of REAL ID rulemaking, demonstrates the difference between more and less successful instances of federalism bargaining.[64] Moreover, the difficulty of asserting state consent to the products of the REAL ID notice-and-comment rulemaking (given the outright rebellion that followed) limits its interpretive potential.

Negotiated rulemakings take longer than other forms of administrative rulemaking, but are more likely to succeed over time. Regulatory matters best suited for state-federal negotiated rulemaking include those in which a decisive federal rule is needed to overcome spillover effects, holdouts, and other collective action problems, but unique and diverse state expertise is needed for the creation of wise policy. Matters in contexts of overlap least suited for negotiated rulemaking include those in which the need for immediate policy overcomes the need for broad participation—but even these leave open possibilities for incremental rulemaking, in which the initial federal rule includes mechanisms for periodic reevaluation with local input.

Among all federalism bargaining forms, policy-making laboratory negotiations offer the richest resources for productive bargaining and procedurally harnessing federalism values. They foster both checks and localism by maximizing state autonomy within national regulatory programs, and accountability because they proceed by formal operation of law. Advancing localism and synergy—and capitalizing on federalism's promise of the "laboratory of ideas"—they allow for localized innovation to confer learning benefits on the entire system, and locally tailored solutions that reflect unique state circumstances. For example, Medicaid demonstration waivers enable states to share policy-making design with both Congress and the DHS, harnessing the energy of state and local regulators to address unique circumstances while disseminating innovation throughout the system. North Carolina's Community Care program has thus received attention not only from other states but also from the Obama administration as a potential innovation for national health reform.[65]

Because they represent purposeful legislative design, policy-making laboratory negotiations also offer the greatest opportunities for premeditated federalism engineering, as recommended below. They are available for use by both political branches, and they are initiated by congressional statute, such as the Coastal Zone Management Act's creation of state policy-making zones for coastal management, or by administrative rule, such as the Phase II Stormwater Rule's creation of municipal policy-making zones for stormwater management.

Policy-making laboratory negotiations are the grandest of federalism bargaining enterprises, requiring formidable regulatory architecture on the front end and considerable time

---

[63] *See supra* Chapter Eight, notes 180–87 and accompanying text.

[64] *See supra* Chapter Eight notes 188–97 and accompanying text.

[65] *See* Hoban, *supra* Chapter Eight, note 238.

periods before both horizontal and vertical learning benefits can be fully realized. Matters best suited for policy-making laboratory negotiations include those in which federal needs for comprehensive regulation are closely matched by the benefits of state regulatory autonomy. Matters least suited include those in which the need for national uniformity (for reasons of economic efficiency or justice) overwhelms the benefits of local autonomy.

A subset of policy-making laboratory negotiations, iterative policy-making negotiations allow for balance between reasonable uniformity to enable commercial development and critical flexibility to foster competitive and adaptive policy making. For example, the Clean Air Act's two-track system for regulating automobile emissions allows states to choose between the federal or more stringent California standard, preventing regulatory stagnation, hedging against capture, and maximizing state autonomy without unduly compromising industrial needs.[66] Similar measures have been suggested to modify federal carbon cap-and-trade proposals lest a fully national program fall prey to the pitfalls of regulatory monopoly.[67]

Iterative policy-making negotiations offer the best means of splitting the difference between the costs and benefits of policy-making laboratory negotiations. They are most appropriate when clear leadership by a state or regional partnership warrants exceptional status as a co-policy maker with the national government, and least appropriate when conferring different levels of policy-making status would threaten values of equity among the states.

2. TRADING ON CAPACITY

As discussed in Part II, one focus of contemporary negotiation theory has been to facilitate the formation of integrative agreements, which exploit linkages between the parties' broadly construed interests to uncover value-creating trades, bridge leverage imbalances, and break negotiating deadlocks.[68] Federalism bargaining that trades on the different parties' unique capacities has great integrative potential, enabling the kinds of Pareto-superior trades that skilled negotiators capitalize on, and allowing the accomplishment of regulatory objectives that neither side could realize alone.[69]

For this reason, capacity-based federalism bargains, including those to reallocate federal authority, seem especially useful in advancing interjurisdictional synergy within the bounds of mutual consent. When both sides trade on unique capacity, each possesses a meaningful opportunity to impact the outcome. Results are less vulnerable to leverage imbalance because unique capacity is a powerful form of positive leverage that holders wield over those seeking access. Examples of capacity-based trading from the taxonomy include negotiations within cooperative federalism programs, negotiations for exceptions, and enforcement negotiations.

---

[66] *See supra* Chapter Eight, notes 249–56 and accompanying text.

[67] *See supra* Chapter Eight, notes 256–66 and accompanying text.

[68] *See supra* Chapter Eight, note 34 and accompanying text.

[69] *See, e.g.,* FISHER & URY, *supra* Chapter Seven, note 175, at 40–80; MNOOKIN ET AL., *supra* Chapter Seven, note 107, at 325.

Cooperative federalism negotiations harness valuable synergy between state and federal institutional capacity. For example, the Coastal Zone Management Act (CZMA) incentivizes states to use local land use planning authority that the federal government pointedly lacks in order to protect critical coastal resources of both local and national importance.[70] It does so while substantially protecting local policy-making authority and erecting unprecedented checks through the limited waiver of federal supremacy in the consistency provision.

The CZMA draws strong legitimacy from the principle of mutual consent because states have wide control over the degree and nature of their own participation. Other cooperative federalism programs put slightly more strain on that principle. For example, the Clean Air and Water Acts occasionally prompt state complaints about their Hobson's choice between expensive implementation obligations or submission to federal permitting by agents lacking expertise and investment in the local economy.[71] Nevertheless, states have ably wielded their capacity within these bargaining forums, negotiating air quality implementation plans, water quality standards, and NPDES permitting agreements. States retain substantial leverage in these negotiations because they alone possess the capacity to bring federal policies to fruition (deflating many threats of preemption).[72]

Regulatory matters allowing space for variation over uniform regulatory floors are good candidates for programs of cooperative federalism, such as the Clean Air and Water Acts, especially when regulatory targets require state implementation capacity. These afford less state influence on federal policy making than full-blown policy-making negotiations (like the CZMA), but more space for negotiation than full-blown command-and-control regulations (like the REAL ID Act). Poor candidates for cooperative federalism programs involve regulatory matters in which there is no space for local variation or nexus with state police powers, or in which state and federal actors cannot reach basic agreement on policy goals, making partnership unworkable.

Negotiations for exceptions can also yield fruitful collaborations in areas of concurrent jurisdiction, reallocating authority in support of localism and synergy values. For example, the Interior Department and the State of California broke regulatory ground in harmonizing the ESA and Natural Communities Conservation Program.[73] State and federal officials have continued to collaborate, negotiating additional Incidental Take Permits to harmonize ESA and NCCP requirements regarding state water projects, such as the Bay Delta Conservation Plan.[74] Exceptions negotiations open possibilities for productive exchange whenever the initial allocation of authority is not purposefully and properly assigned to one side under a statutory or constitutional inalienability rule (such as federal coinage, or state elections).

Enforcement negotiations speak directly to the problem-solving synergy value of federalism. Unified by the shared desire to avoid public harm, participants in contexts from

---

[70] *See supra* Chapter Eight, notes 200–24 and accompanying text.

[71] Adler, *supra* Chapter Three, note 190, at 169–73.

[72] *See supra* Chapter Nine, note 41 (discussing EPA's "hollow threats").

[73] *See supra* Chapter Eight, notes 128–36 and accompanying text.

[74] *What Is the BDCP?*, BAY DELTA CONSERVATION PLAN, http://baydeltaconservationplan.com/ BDCPPlanningProcess/AboutBDCP.aspx (last visited Dec. 27, 2010).

criminal to environmental law tend to cooperate smoothly and infrequently compete for jurisdiction.[75] Collaborative criminal law enforcement partnerships have been especially adept at linking a wide variety of local and national expertise, such as the Project Safe Neighborhoods program.[76] Enforcement negotiations are widespread and generally uncontroversial because they generally herald the hallmarks of both mutual consent and federalism values.

3. SPENDING POWER DEALS

Spending power deals are an important means of navigating jurisdictional overlap within the American system of dual sovereignty.[77] They are among the best understood, most popular, and least constrained form of federalism bargaining. Ironically, they may also rank among the least legitimate for interpretive purposes, in that state consent is not always as free as negotiation theory would prefer. Examples vary widely, from programs where state consent is unquestioningly genuine, such as the Coastal Zone Management Act, to examples notoriously fraught with consent-based controversy, such as the pending suits over the No Child Left Behind Act.[78]

No Child Left Behind provides a good example of federalism bargaining that strains the principle of mutual consent, because states felt coerced by profound needs for federal educational funding, and the act has struggled for legitimacy in federalism terms. However—and attesting to the force of at least some political safeguards in the process—the act is currently under modification in light of state dissatisfaction.[79] The Obama administration's new approach seems promising, adopting many of the federalism engineering devices of the successful policy-making laboratory negotiations in offering additional funds and policy-making discretion to states that compete on the strength of individual proposals.[80]

For this reason, spending power deals should be evaluated on the basis of their particulars and not as an entire category. The least worrying spending power deals for interpretive purposes involve the states in participatory partnerships that afford genuine consultation and synergy of the sort enabled in the joint policy-making forums. The most worrying are those that afford the least discretion to states and invite the least meaningful participation. That said, even spending power deals that fail the requirements of interpretive legitimacy may be legal (and even worthwhile) bargains; they simply warrant a different level of interpretive deference when challenged on federalism grounds.

---

[75] Interview with Roscoe Howard, *supra* Chapter Eight, note 74; Interview with Mike Murphy, *supra* Chapter Nine, note 25; Interview with Rick Weeks, *supra* Chapter Nine, note 31.

[76] *See supra* Chapter Eight, notes 77–80 and accompanying text.

[77] *See* South Dakota v. Dole, 483 U.S. 203, 206 (1987); discussed *supra* Chapter Eight, notes notes 87–102 and accompanying text.

[78] *See supra* Chapter Nine, notes 86–95 (discussing *Pontiac School District* and the new pending suit).

[79] Dillon, *supra* Chapter Eight, note 102.

[80] *Id.*

C. Toward Better Bilateral Balancing

The previous discussion identifies how certain forms of intergovernmental bargaining can serve the purposes that federalism sets out to accomplish. Identifying the criteria for this assessment opens up new possibilities for engineering and conducting federalism bargaining to accomplish better values-balancing partnerships. Although some forms are more promising than others in their ability to navigate federalism challenges, much can be done to further enhance interpretive bargaining at a variety of intervention points. This final section offers suggestions for how legislators, stakeholders, negotiators, and adjudicators can help facilitate more effective and legitimate federalism bargaining, advancing the Balanced Federalism objective of harnessing the contributions of state and federal political actors in federalism interpretation.

I. LEGISLATIVE AND ADMINISTRATIVE DESIGN

Legislators and administrators should draw from the lessons of federalism engineering in creating forums for state-federal bargaining. They should seek opportunities to reduce transaction cost barriers to interpretive bargaining through legal structures that could increase information flow, reduce strategic behavior, and build working relationships between bargaining participants.[81] Congress could consider more explicitly empowering agencies to negotiate directly with states in appropriate contexts, mirroring its endorsement of negotiated rulemaking more generally.[82] Executive agencies could consider institutional reforms to realign internal culture toward negotiating norms, self-assessing against positive baselines set by model agencies.[83] Lawmakers should carefully consider how their pronouncements will function as intergovernmental bargaining defaults, clarifying whether or not they should be subject to renegotiation. They should develop clear baseline entitlements and legal endowments, clarifying bargaining power and enabling better advocacy by participants.[84] Where needed in bargaining to resolve collective action problems, specific remedies for breach should be identified in the negotiated agreement itself.

The bilateral nature of federalism bargaining ensures that federalism values will be part of the calculus as a matter of overall structure, but to the extent that bargainers are tempted to stray from federalism concerns, legislators and administrators can shepherd regard for federalism values through purposeful procedural design. For example, Congress should consider requiring greater use of negotiated rulemaking in statutes requiring regulations that preempt state authority or impose significant costs, or about which states hold special expertise. Negotiating agencies' use of professional intermediaries can also reinforce procedural regard for federalism values by ensuring that stakeholders are adequately represented during the process, fortifying bargaining against concerns about transparency and accountability.

---

[81] *See cf.* Clayton P. Gillette, *Regionalization and Interlocal Bargains*, 76 N.Y.U. L. REV. 190 (2001) (discussing institutional tools for reducing bargaining costs in the regional context).

[82] *See supra* Chapter Eight, notes 155–56 and accompanying text.

[83] Sharkey, *supra* Chapter Eight, note 16, at 2159–61; Metzger, *supra* Introduction, note 8, at 2078.

[84] Menkel-Meadow, *supra* Chapter Eight, note 34, at 852.

Congress could also require transparency measures to alleviate concerns about principal-agent tensions in federalism bargaining, such as requiring that draft agreements be included in the public record after final agreement is reached.

A significant contribution of negotiation theorists is the importance of process pluralism, which emphasizes the value of variability and flexibility in process design to allow tailoring for individual circumstances.[85] Although Congress should heed this wisdom, successful federalism bargaining forums may provide appropriate models for imitation in related regulatory contexts. For example, policy-making laboratory forums such as Medicaid, the Coastal Zone Management Act, and those with state implementation plans provide procedural assists to strengthen local input in spending power negotiations that might otherwise strain the assumptions of mutual consent. The Clean Air Act iterative federalism device for regulating automobile emissions provides an ingenious tool for moderating between the benefits of jurisdictional competition and uniform industrial standards, a model that could prove useful in contexts facing similar tensions. Similar provisions in the Superfund Act and federal forfeiture laws incentivize useful intergovernmental enforcement partnerships; the same tool may prove useful in other contexts as well.[86]

Congress could also enact a statutory framework to facilitate its own creation of future policy-making negotiation forums by establishing templates to streamline future lawmaking. For example, Congress could create a uniform policy-making laboratory template based on Social Security Act demonstration waivers or the Coastal Zone Management Act, easing the way for process differentiation after establishing successful baseline terms.

Finally, Congress should consider ways to maintain a meaningful role for states as partners in spending power deals where exit is less politically available. Although not appropriate in every instance, the joint policy-making forums enable especially valuable spending power partnerships. The emerging field of Dispute Systems Design may be a fruitful source of federalism engineering innovations to respond to persistent state concerns about consultation during policy making.[87] The new behavior economics literature on suggestive policy making may also provide tools,[88] as may important advances in multiparty negotiation theory[89] and collaborative governance theory.[90]

2. SEARCHING OUT OPPORTUNITIES

Stakeholders should be made familiar with the most effective tools of federalism bargaining and the procedural constraints that confer interpretive legitimacy, empowering them to

---

[85] *Id.* at 850.

[86] *See supra* Chapter Nine, notes 23–26 and accompanying text.

[87] *See supra* Chapter Eight, note 43.

[88] *See, e.g.,* RICHARD THALER & CASS SUNSTEIN, NUDGE: IMPROVING DECISIONS ABOUT HEALTH, WEALTH, AND HAPPINESS (2008).

[89] *See, e.g.,* 2 LAWRENCE E. SUSSKIND & LARRY CRUMP, MULTIPARTY NEGOTIATION, THEORY AND PRACTICE OF PUBLIC DISPUTES RESOLUTION (2008).

[90] *See, e.g.,* Karkkainen, *supra* Chapter Three, note 196; Menkel-Meadow, *supra* Chapter Eight, note 34.

participate more meaningfully. As it once did through the Negotiated Rulemaking Act,[91] Congress could statutorily encourage use of specific forms by executive agencies. But to improve upon the lackluster impact of that act, Congress could further require that executive agencies give written guidance about specified forms to state stakeholders, enabling them to advocate their use in appropriate circumstances. Given the rarity of negotiated rulemaking even after the Negotiated Rulemaking Act, Congress should begin there.[92]

Once state and federal actors better understand alternatives for productive bargaining, they should search actively for opportunities. With recommendations by executive agencies, Congress could identify specific zones of jurisdictional overlap where valid interpretive bargaining could optimize collaboration. Even if Congress chooses not to mandate negotiated governance in these realms, it could require more meaningful consultation with state partners to inform federal lawmakers, emphasizing genuine rather than box-checking exchange.

Executive agencies should also identify opportunities for promising federalism bargaining independently of congressional mandates. Federal executive agencies should choose negotiated forms of policy making in contested federalism arenas, such as those intersecting federal safety regulations and state tort law. Where federal agencies extend genuine invitations to states to negotiate, state counterparts should make reasonable efforts to participate. Meanwhile, state actors need not wait for federal initiative. State executive agencies should reach out to regional federal partners in setting statewide policy on matters of interjurisdictional concern, strengthening regulatory relationships and policy resiliency. National organizations of state actors, such as the National Governors Association, the National Conference of State Legislatures, and the Environmental Council of States, can lobby on behalf of their constituents for a greater role in negotiating regional and federal policy making.

In general, complex regulatory arenas that would benefit from contingent agreements with flexible terms, incremental process, and built-in reevaluation mechanisms should signal the potential value of forums for federalism bargaining, collaborative regulatory planning, and adaptive management between state and federal actors.[93]

3. LEVERAGING LEVERAGE

One way of facilitating the interpretive potential of federalism bargaining is to ensure that both sides meaningfully influence the outcome by helping them understand the full array of leverage and exchange in play. Federal powers of the purse and the permit seem well understood, but some participants may not appreciate the leverage conferred by various forms of state and local capacity, or the normative power of federalism values. Effective use of these negotiating endowments can preserve healthy checks and balances during negotiations to enhance localism, problem-solving, and even accountability values.

---

[91] *See* 5 U.S.C. §§ 561–570 (2006).

[92] *See supra* Chapter Eight, note 179 and accompanying text.

[93] Menkel-Meadow, *supra* Chapter Eight, note 34, at 833–34.

Negotiation theory suggests that negotiations in which leverage is more evenly matched will produce the most integrative, value-encompassing results.[94] Although federal negotiators will always be able to leverage legal supremacy and superior fiscal resources, the preceding discussion reveals the significant leverage that states wield based on unique land use authority, local expertise, public outreach, and normative federalism leverage. If state actors more effectively leveraged the leverage they brought to the table, this might facilitate the development of more optimal alternatives within synergistic collaborations. At the very least, it would alter unfavorable negotiating dynamics.

Negotiation theorists also advise that parties study their best alternative to negotiated agreement and seek to improve it during the course of negotiations if possible.[95] States have demonstrated their willingness and ability to do this by creating regional cap-and-trade governing partnerships when the federal government has refused to bargain. For example, the states forming the Northeast Regional Greenhouse Gas Initiative and Western Climate Initiative have materially altered states' leverage in interest group negotiations with federal lawmakers over the direction of national climate policy.[96] If state actors better understood their alternatives to a proffered federal deal, as well as the force of federal need for state capacity in that deal, it could mitigate doubts about the "mutual consent" underlying some spending power deals.

Skilled intermediaries and better negotiation training for participants could help the parties fully understand their alternatives, enabling them to identify unappreciated leverage and linkages that can motivate earnest trade even in the presence of power imbalances.[97] To that end, both the pragmatic and interpretive potential of federalism bargaining would likely improve if state and federal participants received formal negotiation training. Training can help even skilled intuitive negotiators identify opportunities for productive bargaining, understand leverage and alternatives, and manage the mechanics of difficult multiparty negotiations.[98] (And for the many Americans intimidated by negotiation in general, it can make an even more profound difference.)[99]

Negotiation skills training confers many benefits, but among the most important are an enhanced sensitivity to opportunities for productive exchange and the tools to transform opportunities into mutually beneficial solutions. Training also enhances sensitivity to the

---

[94] This result is because parties evenly matched in leverage are more likely to fully exploit the integrative stage of negotiation (in which a variety of potential alternatives are explored before agreement is reached) than they are in negotiations in which one party can prematurely force the other into the distributive stage toward a favorable but Pareto suboptimal outcome. *Cf.* FISHER & URY, *supra* Chapter Seven, note 175, at 177–87 (discussing leverage dynamics in negotiation); MNOOKIN ET AL., *supra* Chapter Seven, note 107, at 325 (discussing Pareto optimality in negotiating outcomes); SHELL, *supra* Part IV Introduction, note 12, at 101–05, 113; *see also* SHELL, *supra* Part IV Introduction, note 12, at 220 (noting the greater risk of unethical behavior in negotiating contexts of leverage imbalance).

[95] FISHER & URY, *supra* Chapter Seven, note 175, at 97–106; SHELL, *supra* Part IV Introduction, note 12, at 101.

[96] *See* Erin Ryan, *Federalism Lessons for Climate Policy* (forthcoming 2012).

[97] Menkel-Meadow, *supra* Chapter Eight, note 34, at 848.

[98] *See, e.g.*, SHELL, *supra* Part IV Introduction, note 12, *id.* at xvii–xviii (summarizing the benefits of training).

[99] *Cf. id.* at xvi, 7 (discussing the nagging anxiety that average people, including professional students in all disciplines, feel about negotiating).

negotiation dynamics of social interaction, behavioral economics, game theory, and organizational behavior that can impede the formation or functioning of otherwise valuable collaboration. Federalism bargaining can trigger a surprisingly powerful subset of these "soft" negotiating obstacles, including in-group/out-group identity dynamics, affiliation and status sensibilities, and enforcement hurdles.[100] Better still, agency leaders should consider strategies to build institutional negotiating competency beyond individual skills, with the potential for transforming entire agency cultures toward more collaborative norms.[101]

4. JUDICIAL ROLE

Finally, the judiciary can help support the role of political federalism interpretation by clarifying and refining legal constraints as needed, acknowledging bargaining dynamics when judicially interpreting negotiated results, and deferring to the federalism interpretation of other governmental actors when it meets the procedural criteria of the federalism values.

Although spending power bargaining is well treated in judicial opinion, other forms of federalism bargaining remain murky without judicial elaboration, especially federal capacity bargaining.[102] Of course, without recourse to advisory opinion, the Supreme Court cannot elaborate until an appropriate case arises. But the Court's past precedent is responsible for some of this anxiety (especially *New York v. United States*[103]), demonstrating its lack of sensitivity to federalism bargaining at the time.[104] The justices should heed this error when they encounter future cases that raise similar issues. In particular, the overly broad proscription against "bargained-for commandeering" should be modified to allow consenting states to negotiate for binding federal terms to resolve state collective action problems.[105]

Adjudicators should also give deeper consideration to the bargaining factors present in Judge Sutton's analysis in *Pontiac School District*[106] and Justice White's in *New York*.[107] In cases interpreting federalism bargaining results, courts should evaluate the bargain at the heart of the transaction in deciding whether results are voidably ambiguous (as alleged in *Pontiac School District*) or voidably nonconsensual (as held in *New York*). Just as context from elsewhere in a statute (or others in related fields) are used to resolve ambiguity in conventional statutory interpretation, so should the "core bargain" illuminate its terms. Otherwise, plaintiffs will opportunistically renege on clearly understood terms, reaping

---

[100] *See, cf.,* DANIEL SHAPIRO & ROGER FISHER, BEYOND REASON: USING EMOTIONS AS YOU NEGOTIATE (2005) (discussing strategies for addressing various emotional hurdles that arise within negotiations).

[101] *See, e.g.,* HAL MOVIUS & LAWRENCE SUSSKIND, BUILT TO WIN: CREATING A WORLD CLASS NEGOTIATING ORGANIZATION (2009) (arguing that successful multiparty negotiations require institutional competence).

[102] *See supra* Chapter Nine, notes 119–23 and accompanying text.

[103] 505 U.S. at 149.

[104] *See supra* Chapter Nine, notes 77–96, 105–12 and accompanying text.

[105] *See supra* Chapter Eight, notes 103–10 and accompanying text; *see also* discussion accompanying Chapter Seven, notes 177–228, and Chapter Ten, notes 1–57 (proposing alternatives).

[106] *See supra* Chapter Nine, notes 83–95 and accompanying text.

[107] 505 U.S. at 196–98 (White, J., dissenting), discussed *supra* Chapter Seven, notes 41–46 and accompanying text.

benefits without delivering on their own promises. Interpreting state-federal bargaining by statute—in which states that choose to participate play a role beyond mere compliance with congressional dictates—thus demands a level of scrutiny one degree more complicated than ordinary statutory interpretation.

Finally, adjudicators should adopt the deferential interpretive scrutiny advanced above when intergovernmental bargaining is challenged on federalism grounds. Courts should defer to the allocation of authority in negotiated governance that meets the basic procedural requirements of fair bargaining and constitutional federalism, and consider the procedural criteria when evaluating unilateral political decisions. They should not defer to challenged governance that fails the constitutional criteria, and they should facilitate consequences for bargaining that violates due process or fundamental fairness by stressing mutual consent past the breaking point. Courts should discourage potential harm not by outlawing whole categories of federalism bargaining (such as spending power deals or commandeering bargaining), but by scrutinizing alleged harm in individual instances, enforcing transparency requirements or due process norms as appropriate. Above all, they should interpret bargained-for results in the context of bargaining, and not as though consensual negotiations had never taken place.

More work is needed to assess the full implications for judicial review of federalism bargaining (including, for example, issues of standing). Advancing from this proposal will require even more detailed attention to how courts could actually assess the outcomes of varying forms of bargaining for fealty to federalism values. Like the judicial transition to the Chapter Six balancing test, the transition to the Chapter Ten procedural criteria would unleash a period of indeterminacy as the incremental common law process of adjudication under the new standard would begin its work. Nevertheless, this treatment provides a starting point by recognizing the enterprise of bilateral intergovernmental balancing, building a framework of analysis, and articulating a theory of procedural interpretation. Most important, it provides the missing theoretical justification for the interpretive work that federalism bargainers do every day under clouds of doctrinal uncertainty.

After all, federalism is negotiated not only between the proclamations of the Court and the statutory will of Congress, but also in the day-to-day activities of individual actors in all branches of government. Recognizing how interpretive bargaining helps allocate authority at the uncertain margins of state and federal power provides a new lens for understanding the uniquely collaborative process of American governance. The structural safeguards of bilateral exchange ensure that the negotiated balance reflects the input of both national and local participants. Bargaining that fully satisfies the procedural criteria advances federalism by giving expression to its core values as a procedural matter, and by leveraging the unique capacity that all governmental actors bring to federalism interpretation and implementation.

When federalism bargaining honors federalism values through fair and falsifiable process, intergovernmental bargaining is itself a constitutionally legitimate way of allocating authority in contexts of jurisdictional overlap. In contrast to the judicial interpretive supremacy implied by New Federalism, the proposal demonstrates instances in which the very process of intergovernmental bargaining proves more able to preserve constitutional values than judicial or legislative decisions alone. In contrast to cooperative federalism and pure political safeguards, it preserves a limited role for judicial oversight of unilateral and procedural abuses. Here in the middle, perhaps, lies wisdom.

Conclusion

Toward Balance in Federalism

THE ACCELERATING INTERDEPENDENCE of modernity has applied renewed pressure on the enduring constitutional questions about how best to balance local and national power. Federalism has become a site of heated political contest over questions of which should trump where, and who should decide. To some, the boundary-blurring political safeguards of cooperative federalism impermissibly threaten state sovereignty. To others, New Federalism's nostalgia for judicially enforced jurisdictional boundaries impossibly threatens resolution of our most pressing societal problems. Deepening conflicts over climate change, health reform, national security, and other interjurisdictional challenges highlight the need for a theory of federalism that can better cope with these competing considerations.

The Balanced Federalism proposal here thus seeks to mediate the tensions within federalism on three dimensions. First, it encourages more thoughtful and transparent balancing between the competing values of good governance at the heart of American federalism. In addition, it more effectively leverages the distinct functional capacities of the judiciary, legislature, and executive branch in interpreting federalism directives in both abstract and concrete circumstances. Finally, it maximizes the input of local and national actors, not only through the conventional political safeguards of unilateral governance, but through the structural federalism safeguards of bilateral intergovernmental bargaining.

In suggesting these normative metrics, the book explores possibilities for how American federalism might move closer toward the balance around which it has oscillated for ages. While the Constitution provides a sturdy structural framework of American dual sovereignty, its federalism directives are sufficiently indeterminate to allow the development of multiple theoretical models to account for gaps in the text. All visions of American federalism share a commitment to the core values of good governance that federalism is designed to accomplish: (1) the checks and balances that protect individuals against sovereign overreaching or abdication, (2) transparent and accountable governance that enables meaningful democratic participation at all levels, (3) protection for local autonomy and innovation that enables the laboratory of ideas, and (4) the ability to harness interjurisdictional synergy between the unique capacities that local and national government offer for coping with the different parts of interjurisdictional problems. But these values are suspended in tension with one another, fueling a perpetual tug of war within federalism itself. How we prioritize among conflicting values is a choice with high stakes for actual governance, as demonstrated in the regulatory response to Hurricane Katrina.

Over history, Americans have put flesh on the bones of our federalism in contrasting ways, developing theoretical models of federalism that balance tension among the values according to the social and ideological demands of the times. As a result, American federalism theory and practice have both vacillated wildly over time, often out of sync, as reflected in the Supreme Court's constantly changing federalism jurisprudence. The tug of war was especially apparent in the competing models of federalism that informed the Court's federalism jurisprudence over the twentieth century. Theoretical transitions are evident from the nineteenth-century dual federalism that continued into the Progressive/*Lochner* era, to the New Deal model after the Great Depression, to the cooperative federalism model that emerged during the Civil Rights Era and predominates today, despite the formidable challenge by the Rehnquist Court's revival of dual federalism ideals and judicially enforceable constraints. The Court's Tenth Amendment jurisprudence especially reflects these fluctuating theoretical models.

The New Federalism challenge originated as a political phenomenon of the 1970s and 1980s, took root in the Rehnquist Court's federalism jurisprudence, and gathers force in the contemporary political Tea Party and Tenther movements. Distrustful of the political safeguards that enabled expanding federal reach during the cooperative federalism era, the Rehnquist Court reasserted judicial interpretive supremacy over the political branches and revived elements of dualist jurisdictional separation in many of its most important federalism and preemption cases. However, the theoretical model implied by these cases imposes a judicially mandated balance among federalism values that privileges some at the expense of others, sometimes without justification. In service of classical checks and balances, it strives for jurisdictional separation that can compromise competing values of localism and problem solving, and in some cases, accountable and participatory governance. It does so even in contexts that demand overlapping local and national authority to cope with complex regulatory challenges.

The tug of war is especially intense in the areas of environmental, land use, and public health and safety regulation. Such areas of law expose an interjurisdictional gray area that simultaneously implicates local and national responsibility, confounding the dual federalism model of jurisdictional separation. Where jurisdictional overlap is especially stark, the fault lines between the core federalism values are most revealed—exposing the conflict between federalism's regard for local autonomy in some instances and national uniformity in others. The descriptive model of cooperative federalism enables regulatory partnerships and crossover in the gray area, but provides few limits or theoretical tools of justification beyond faith in the political process. New Federalism rejects that faith, and its dualist revival threatens to exacerbate gray area regulatory challenges with additional confusion, hesitation, and litigation. Those who govern and adjudicate in federalism-sensitive contexts would be well-served by a theoretical model that provides better justification for gray area governance, tools for managing the competing federalism values, and guidance for mediating among the various claims to interpretive supremacy.

I offer the Balanced Federalism proposal in service of these goals. Balanced Federalism recognizes contingent zones of state and federal prerogative and the gray area of overlap between them where state-federal interaction is both unavoidable and desirable. It prepares policy makers and adjudicators to accountably consider each of the federalism values when determining the proper balance. It also draws on the specialized capacity of each branch of government—on both the state and federal levels—to participate in interpreting the appropriate balance in each instance. Using the Tenth Amendment as a starting point for modifying current federalism doctrine, the book proposes three stages for moving American federalism toward Balanced Federalism ideals.

In narrative deference to the New Federalism's revival of judicial safeguards, Chapter Six imagines the shift from New to Balanced Federalism judicially enforceable constraints, beginning with the Tenth Amendment. To demonstrate the literal project of balancing among competing federalism values, I propose a judicial balancing test for interpreting federalism, preemption, and other orphaned federalism claims under the Tenth Amendment. The balancing test asks the adjudicator to consider whether a challenged regulatory activity in the gray area ultimately serves or disserves the goals of American federalism, taken as a whole, by requiring consideration of how the activity advances or detracts from each independent federalism value along a spectrum of potential considerations. I defend judicial balancing as an appropriate interpretive device, given its inevitability in any regime of judicial federalism constraints—either overtly (as proposed) or covertly (as exists). However, the subsequent stages of the proposal mitigate the problem of judicial discretion by carving out substantial realms of political decision making that warrant judicial deference.

In the intermediate proposal, Chapter Seven requires judicial Tenth Amendment deference to values balancing reached through intergovernmental legislative policy making. The example of the negotiated Low Level Radioactive Waste Policy Act, defeated under the New Federalism anti-commandeering rule, shows how bilaterally negotiated partnerships between state and federal legislatures enable more sophisticated balancing than unilateral judicial decree. The discussion demonstrates how the Constitution's federalism directives can be understood as conferring jurisdictional entitlements, and proposes that states be as free to negotiate with their Tenth Amendment entitlements as is the federal government. This proposal trumps the balancing test over consensual commandeering challenges, and it builds a theoretical bridge to the final stage of the Balanced Federalism proposal.

Part IV fully engages the role of intergovernmental bargaining—by all branches, at all levels of government, and in all doctrinal areas—in helping to navigate the federalism challenges that invariably arise in the gray area. Under Balanced Federalism, values balancing by the political branches holds constitutional gravity when it takes place bilaterally, through intergovernmental bargaining that applies the core federalism principles as a procedural matter. When reviewing federalism challenges to such bargaining, the judicial role shifts to deferential oversight for bargaining abuse and procedural criteria. The book shows that intergovernmental bargaining with federalism entitlements is widespread throughout the regulatory spectrum. While not all governance should be negotiated and not all of this bargaining meets the procedural criteria, that which does represents a constitutionally cognizable way of answering the central question—*who gets to decide?*—warranting deference from other federalism interpreters. In ensuring that public agencies act in accordance with constitutional directives, the political branches thus participate in interpreting federalism itself.

The final proposal provides theoretical justification for the interpretive role that the political branches are already playing in countless instances of intergovernmental bargaining under cooperative federalism. Federalism bargaining engages federalism values at the structural level, surpassing the political safeguards available through unilateral policy making. The bilateral nature of the exchange balances state and federal interests in first-order policy concerns, protecting federalism values in a way that transcends the subjective considerations of participants. Federalism bargaining thus provides structural support for federalism that is simply unavailable through unilateral safeguards.

Because it would reach the same results as the intermediate proposal for deference to consensual commandeering, the Chapter Ten proposal for deference subsumes the Chapter Seven standard and trumps the Chapter Six balancing test when it is called upon to adjudicate negotiated governance. If regulatory bargaining were challenged under the balancing test (or any other judicial federalism constraint), the court would first apply procedural review and consider the doctrinal merits of a federalism challenge only if the negotiated governance did not meet the requisite criteria. The balancing test would remain available for challenges to unilateral governance in the gray area, although judicial review should be tempered by Balanced Federalism's regard for the interpretive capacity of the other branches. Indeed, even unilateral gray area decision making will warrant judicial federalism deference in proportion to the degree that the procedural criteria of federalism are satisfied—although negotiated governance reinforces federalism values at a structural level that unilateral regulation cannot approach.

These initial proposals for actualizing Balanced Federalism theory thus draw on the insights of the political safeguards school by deferring to political federalism determinations that incorporate state and local perspectives. They draw on the instincts of the judicial safeguards school in preserving a limited role for judicial review to police for extreme abuses. The tailored dialectic between judicial and political safeguards would thus facilitate legislative and executive implementation of Balanced Federalism where the political branches are most able, backstopped by modest judicial review that will finally ask the right questions. The same judicial modesty should ultimately suffuse other judicially enforceable federalism constraints, deferring to federalism-sensitive governance that proves faithful to the core federalism values and reserving judicial correction only for clear abuses. Meanwhile, judicial challenges to nonfederalism aspects of both unilateral and bilateral governance remain unimpeded, preserving robust judicial enforcement of other constitutional and statutory requirements.

This initial foray into Balanced Federalism theory has heavily emphasized the Tenth Amendment, guardian of our system of dual sovereignty and philosophical ambassador of constitutional federalism.[1] The analysis sheds light on the other federalism doctrines that hinge on the same theory of dual sovereignty, such as the commerce and spending powers, Section Five of the Fourteenth Amendment, Eleventh Amendment sovereign immunity, and preemption. Preemption receives direct attention from Balanced Federalism under the Tenth Amendment balancing test, though complexities warrant additional attention. New Federalism constraints on Congress's power to interpret Section Five and its relationship to state sovereign immunity seem ripe for adjustment under Balanced Federalism, which leans toward a greater interpretive role for Congress. New Federalism limits on federal authority under the Commerce Clause might adjust toward the Balanced Federalism Tenth Amendment limits, replacing inalienability-rule protection for state entitlements beyond those limits with something approximating property-rule protection. The Court might clarify the point at which state-perceived coercion in spending power bargaining does or does not undermine the foundations of mutual consent that enable interpretive deference under the procedural test. These suggestions are cursory, and the book provides a mere a starting point for elaboration; further development of Balanced Federalism will require more detailed visits to these other doctrinal areas.

However we accomplish it, moving toward a more Balanced Federalism will advance the discourse at a critical time for both federalism and regulatory law. At stake is the ability of state and federal government to take on confounding societal problems by harnessing local innovation and interjurisdictional synergy in governance without compromising individual rights or democratic participation. Balanced Federalism insights will help public actors maintain a healthy balance between local and national power without catapulting any one value over all competing considerations, and without foreclosing the unique interpretive capacity that any of the three branches or various levels of government offers. Whether by legislative initiative, intergovernmental bargaining, or judicial oversight, governance that safeguards rights, participation, innovation, and synergy accomplishes what it is that federalism is designed to do. In the end, the move toward a more Balanced Federalism will foster a more thoughtful and dynamic equipoise between the federalism values and institutional capacities that—by very virtue of their internal tensions—have made our system of government so effective and enduring.

---

[1] *See supra* Introduction, notes 25–66 and accompanying text (explaining the Tenth Amendment focus).

Table of Cases

Table of Authorities

U.S. CODE

STATUTES

CODE OF FEDERAL REGULATION

Index